SEARCHING FOR PLACE:
UKRAINIAN DISPLACED PERSONS,
CANADA, AND THE MIGRATION OF MEMORY

Canada was not in a welcoming mood when Ukrainian Displaced Persons and other refugees began immigrating after the Second World War. In this compelling and richly documented account, Lubomyr Y. Luciuk maps the established Ukrainian Canadian community's efforts to rescue and resettle refugees, despite public indifference and the hostility of political opponents in Canada and abroad. He explores the often divisive impact that this 'third wave' of nationalistic refugees had on organized Ukrainian Canadian society, and traces how this diaspora's experiences of persecution under the Soviet and Nazi regimes in occupied Ukraine, and their subsequent hiving together in the cauldrons of the postwar DP camps, underlay the shaping of a shared political world-view that would not abate, despite decades in exile. Drawing on personal diaries, in-depth interviews, and previously unmined government archives, the author provides an interpretation of the Ukrainian experience in Canada that is both illuminating and controversial, scholarly and intimate. Skilfully, Luciuk reveals how a distinct Ukrainian Canadian identity emerged and has been manipulated, negotiated, and recast from the beginnings of Ukrainian pioneer settlement at the turn of the last century to the present. Written with journalistic skill and a clear interpretive vision, *Searching for Place* represents a meticulous, original, and provocative contribution to the study of modern Canada and one of its most important communities.

LUBOMYR Y. LUCIUK is a professor in the Department of Politics and Economics at the Royal Military College of Canada.

SEARCHING FOR PLACE

Ukrainian Displaced Persons, Canada, and the Migration of Memory

Lubomyr Y. Luciuk

With a foreword by Norman Davies

UNIVERSITY OF TORONTO PRESS
Toronto Buffalo London

© University of Toronto Press Incorporated 2000
Toronto Buffalo London
Printed in Canada

Reprinted 2001

ISBN 0-8020-4245-7 (cloth)
ISBN 0-8020-8088-X (paper)

Printed on acid-free paper

Canadian Cataloguing in Publication Data

Luciuk, Lubomyr Y., 1953–
  Searching for place : Ukrainian displaced persons, Canada, and
  the migration of memory

  Includes bibliographical references and index.
  ISBN 0-8020-4245-7 (bound)   ISBN 0-8020-8088-X (pbk.)

  1. Ukrainians – Canada – History.   2. Refugees – Ukraine.
  3. Ukrainian Canadians – History.*   4. Ukrainian Canadians –
  Attitudes.*   5. Refugees – Government policy – Canada.   I. Title.

  FC106.U5L82 2000   971'.00491791   C00-930887-3
  F1035.U5L84 2000

This book has been published with the financial assistance of the Canadian
Foundation for Ukrainian Studies, the Chair of Ukrainian Studies Founda-
tion, the Ukrainian Canadian Foundation of Taras Schevchenko, the Evhen,
Roman, and Paulina Kmit Foundation, the Ukrainian Studies Foundation of
British Columbia, and the John Stashuk Estate.

University of Toronto Press acknowledges the financial assistance to its
publishing program of the Canada Council for the Arts and the Ontario
Arts Council.

University of Toronto Press acknowledges the financial support for its publishing activities of the Government of Canada through the Book Publishing
Industry Development Program (BPIDP).

Contents

Foreword

History and Geography are siblings. Indeed, in some countries such as France, they have traditionally been taught together, as one subject. Time and place are essential constitutents of all events. Good historians need a sound grasp of geography; and good geographers need a sharp sense of history. For this reason, Lubomyr Luciuk, who is a professional geographer, makes an excellent candidate for analysing the complicated story of Ukrainian migration to Canada.

Ukrainian history is often misunderstood simply because Western readers have never learned the basic 'where' and 'when' of the context. Few people know, for example, that Ukraine first gained its modern independence in 1918, or that, at earlier stages, important parts of it had variously belonged to Poland, to Austria, to Romania, or to Czechoslovakia. Thanks to the preponderance of Russian-sourced information about Eastern Europe, it is often assumed quite inaccurately that Ukraine is basically a province of Russia, that its capital Kiev (Kyiv) has always been Russian, and that Ukrainians are just a rather peculiar sort of Russians. The ten years that have passed since the USSR collapsed and Ukraine recovered its independence have been all too short to counteract the preceding decades, not to say centuries, of propaganda and misinformation.

Nor does the ideology of Ukrainian nationalism necessarily help to clarify matters. While Ukrainians, like members of any nation, profess a wide variety of political views, the more enthusiastic nationalists among them have tended to contest propaganda with propaganda, opening up further sources of confusion. They often ignore or even deny the multi-ethnic, multireligious, and multicultural character of

Ukraine's population, thereby blurring the important distinctions among citizenship, nationality, and ethnicity.

The history of migration from Ukraine, therefore, is readily open to misrepresentations and misunderstandings. For one thing, it is necessary to recognize that important groups of Poles, Jews, and Russians, as well as ethnic Ukrainians, emigrated from various parts of Ukraine and for a similar variety of political, social, and economic reasons. For another, as regards ethnic Ukrainian migration – which is the main focus of the present study – it is extremely important to distinguish among the different waves of migrants who left Ukraine at different times and in different conditions. There is a very marked contrast, for instance, between the experiences of the late nineteenth-century generation, who principally fled the poverty and illiteracy of Austrian-ruled Western Ukraine, and those of the mid-twentieth-century generation, who under successive Stalinist and Nazi occupation had survived genocide, mass terror, political persecution, and slave labour.

Professor Luciuk's work centres on the fate of the large group of Ukrainian Displaced Persons who had found their way into Western Europe during the Second World War, and in particular on those who after numerous tribulations emigrated to Canada. It must be applauded for its thoroughness, its frankness, and its acute sense of location. The thoroughness can be observed in the large and fascinating section of notes, which take up almost half the total text. The frankness can be appreciated in the way the author discusses (in the Epilogue) his own particular connections within the Ukrainian Canadian community and his own road to an understanding of the subject. The sense of location can be felt at every turn. For this is no mere chronicle of events. *Searching for Place* painstakingly describes the interaction among the various generations of Ukrainian immigrants, among groups within the generations, and between all of them and Canadian officialdom. By so doing, it makes a major contribution both to Ukrainian studies and to migration studies; and it throws no small light on Canada itself.

NORMAN DAVIES

Acknowledgments

What a geographer does is explore place. Refugees are people who have been driven away from a place they try to replace, or return to. This book is fundamentally the work of a son of two persons who were displaced and, later, given shelter and protection in their new home, Canada. But, like anyone who has ever been forced to leave where he or she came from, my parents never abandoned the belief that they most truly belonged in Ukraine.

By this logic Canada should have been my place. I was born in Kingston, Ontario. And yet it was not quite that simple. In attempting to answer the most basic question any human must face – 'Who am I?' – I had to deal not only with the ancestry, religion, language, values, history, and customs bequeathed to me by my parents, but also with the undeniable fact that the place they were in, where I lived, was not the place where Ukrainians 'ought' to be. And I was raised to believe that my identity was inextricably linked to a purpose, that being the struggle for the liberation of enslaved Ukraine. Those coordinates of my identity distinguished me, separated me from most of my childhood friends, gave a meaning to my existence that others, my peers and my superiors, would often find troubling, inexplicable, conflicted. Often I could not fit in where I was, because, in essence, I had been dedicated to regaining another place. I learned who I was by coming to appreciate better who I was not. As often as not that also meant knowing whom I was against. These sometimes conflicting imperatives motivated and also complicated my personal search for place.

That journey began in 1976, when I began to wonder and write about the historical geography of the small Ukrainian community of Kingston. I wanted to know why there were Ukrainians there, who they had

Running Away to Home, Kassandra Luciuk

been. Between 1976 and 1978, in the microcosm of my own community, I was introduced to the study of the experience of the Ukrainians who began emigrating to Canada in 1891 for economic as well as political reasons. A few years later I began doctoral studies in the Department of Geography at the University of Alberta, in Edmonton. That was when I started to move beyond my previously somewhat limited inquiry to try to understand more about the so-called third wave of post–Second World War Ukrainian immigrants to Canada, how they impacted upon the previously settled Ukrainian population of Canada. This immigration was routinely described as being 'political.' Certainly the politics of these Ukrainians were unambiguously tied to one mission, namely, the re-placing of themselves in the place they had been driven out of, their Garden of Eden, their remembered Ukraine. Although I was not yet entirely aware of where I was heading with my studies, the path was certainly reconnected when I first visited Istanbul, in 1979. In that remarkably cosmopolitan place, known in Byzantine times as the 'city of the earth's desire,' and later by the Ottoman Turks as *alem penah*, or 'refuge of the world,' I could encounter the still vital remnants of the many dozens of different ethnic, religious, and racial communities who had made that great city their home over the centuries. Their continued existence and the emergent quality of their feeling about their places and identities within the modern secular society of Turkey inspired me. What is it that makes individuals and groups cling to, remember, and try to re-create something of the where of where they came from in the places they have gone to? Today's Istanbul, yesterday's Constantinople, became and remains my most favoured place on earth, for if you learn where to look it has all the answers.

Place must, eventually, be passed on. My life has been blessed with a daughter, Kassandra. In the pages that follow I have tried to chart out why Canada's Ukrainian community is as it is. I hope the map I leave behind will help Kassandra explore this terrain, if she should ever feel a need to. If she does, I have faith in her ability to leave her own profound inscriptions there. Although she is now only nine years old, she has grasped what it means to be a displaced person. Slightly adapted with her consent, a painting she created, entitled *Running Away to Home*, represents one theme in this book. In it a displaced family flees uncontrollable, terrifyingly elemental forces, seeking shelter in a disproportionately large home. Yet entrance can be gained only through a tiny doorway. Your place is where your home is, where you belong, and where you run to when there is danger. It is hearth, haven, perhaps even something approaching heaven. And yet, as Kassandra has shown, political refugees are people running away from their homes while also searching desperately for a place where they can perhaps, in time, begin anew. Such alternate places of shelter may not be easy to get into. Refugees carry whatever belongings they can manage and a memory of what they left behind, or think they did. Ideas, as another geographer, Ellen Churchill Semple, once wrote, are 'light baggage.' Searching for place is not only core to the nature of the refugee experience but essential to defining what makes each of us human. For being a person means having a place, remembering it, even moving a memory of it somewhere else, especially when your place has been taken away from you. I therefore dedicate this book to Kassandra. Canada is her place.

LUBOMYR Y. LUCIUK
Kingston, Ontario
9 July 2000

Good People and Their Places

Along this journey many people have taught me much about how good it is to have a place. Time and again, as I made my way through the winding channels of the research that went into this book and several others, these friends and supporters unreservedly shared their hearths with me and generously contributed to my education. I thank all of them, but a particularly great debt is owed to the several men and women who figure prominently in the chapters that follow, namely, Bohdan Panchuk, his wife Anne (*née* Cherniawsky), Stanley Frolick, Ann Smith (*née* Crapleve), Anne Wasylyshen, and Anthony Yaremovich. Without their help this book could never have been written. What I regret most is that it has come too late for several of them to read. I can only hope that their surviving friends and families will take some comfort in knowing that the remarkable achievements and great good done by them has now, finally, been set down for posterity, however imperfectly. What they accomplished in their youth, through a daring and dogged determination and a shared sense of purpose and faith, leaves me feeling humbled when I compare how little my own generation has done with its far greater resources and opportunities. I have written before and I repeat here that these once almost forgotten men and women were 'heroes of their day.' We will not, I think, see their kind in Canada's Ukrainian community ever again.

I owe another great debt to the hundreds of Ukrainian displaced persons, political refugees, victims of war, and Holocaust and Great Famine survivors, and to those who helped them through their displacement, whom I interviewed. The names of most of them appear in the list of oral history interviews. They shared memories of their Ukraine with me and reconfirmed just how important the cultivation of memory is for group cohesion, especially for maintaining a shared purpose through the generations. The migration of refugees who cultivate this species of memory and intertwine it with a political cause can preserve identity and their shared mission not only in new lands but also into the next generation, and likely beyond.

Others who counselled me well over the years in which this book took shape are now also gone. They will not be forgotten. I mourn the loss of Andriy Bandera, Christina Bardyn, Professor Robert F. Harney, Wolodymyr Klish, John Kolasky, Harold Marans, Bohdan Mykytiuk, Doris and Neil O'Brien, Steven Pawluk, Wilfred Pluard, the Reverend Mitrat Dr J.C.E. Riotte, who was my mentor early in life, Professor Ivan

L. Rudnytsky, the Honourable Mr Justice John Sopinka, and Senator Paul Yuzyk. They all helped along the way.

My parents, Danylo and Maria Luciuk, my sister, Nadia, and my uncle, Jaroslav Opyriuk, have always provided me with unflagging support, although I have not always been as demonstrably appreciative of that boon as I should be. Many others likewise furthered my work at various times by letting me know that with them I could find shelter, sage advice, and sanction, always mixed with good cheer. They might not all share my views or findings, but they know the importance of being able to tolerate differences without sacrificing friendship. And so my thanks again to Jim Adams, Marika Bandera, Ihor Bardyn, Professor René Barendregt, John Boxtel, Stefan and Sophia Boyechko, Marco and Marta Carynnyk, Eugene Cholkan, Alexandra Chyczij, Dacre Cole, Eugene Cornacchia, Bill and Nancy Daly, Linda Daniels, Wasyl Didiuk, Peter Dorn, Professor N. Fred Dreisziger, Marg Eckenfelder, Mike Fagan, Neil and Joan Fiertel, Reverend Dr Petro Galadza, Professor Anne Godlewska, Professor Peter Goheen, J.B. and Lizzie Gregorovich, Jerry and Olya Grod, Paula Groenburg, Lydia Hawryshkiw, Barry Hill-Tout, Andrij and Oksana Hluchowecky, Dr Stella Hryniuk, Professor Yarema Kelebay, Professor Martin Kenzer, Gerry Kokodyniak, Professor Bohdan and Danya Kordan, Professors Leszek and Marytka Kosinski, Dr Myron and Lesia Kuropas, Stefan Kuzmyn, Professor Michael Lanphier, Hedy Later, Martin LaVoie, Stefan Lemieszewski, Professor Giuseppe Lepore, Dr Leonard Leshuk, Marco Levytsky, André and Jacques Litalien and Debbie Collard, Gerry Locklin, Professor George Lovell, Zoriana Hrycenko-Luhova and Yuriy Luhovy, Reverend Bohdan Lukie, Olga and Volodymyr Lyczmanenko, Professor Hugh Macdonald, Professor Paul R. Magocsi, Victor Malarek, Dr M. Marunchak, Megan and David Mason, Geoffrey Matthews, Myron Momryk, Fernando Monte, Ann O'Brien, Stefan Petelycky, Paulanne Peters, Dr Lillian Petroff, Professor Roman Petryshyn, Walter Petryshyn, Professor Richard Pierce, Steve and Jan Rivers, Professor John Rogge, Professor Chris and Jayne Rogerson, Dr Oleh and Anna Romanyshyn, Cecilia and Professor Andrew Rossos, Dr Orest Rudzik, Professor Richard Ruggles, Hasan Selamet, Borys and Marika Sirskyj, Marsha Skrypuch, Slava Stetsko, Ron Sorobey, Professor Ihor Stebelsky, Rusty Surowy, Borys and Donna Sydoruk, Dr Robert and Julia Starling, Julia Stashuk, Professor Alastair Taylor, Professor Paul Thomas, Count Nikolai Tolstoy, Ann and Eddie Topper, Metin Tosun, Myroslav and Luba Trutiak, Professor Ron and Ona Vastokas,

Michael and Anna Walsh, Jane Watson, Jerry and Elaine Woloschuk, Professor Roger and Margaret Wright, Eugene Zalucky, Dr Vitaliy Zhuravsky, Irka Zubryckyj, Nykola and Maria Zubryckyj, Paul Zumbakis, Zenko Zwarycz, and, especially, Katharine Wowk.

My research was primarily supported by M.A. and doctoral fellowships from the Social Sciences and Humanities Research Council of Canada and the Canadian Institute of Ukrainian Studies at the University of Alberta. I was also privileged to receive one of the SSHRCC's prestigious Canada Research Fellow postdoctoral grants, which I took with me to the Department of Geography at Queen's University. Similarly, I enjoyed the support provided by a Neporany Postdoctoral Fellowship and the John Sopinka Award for Excellence in Ukrainian Studies, administered by the CIUS and Chair of Ukrainian Studies Foundation respectively. Over the years various other granting bodies supported my efforts, including the British Council, the Brotherhood of Veterans of the 1st Ukrainian Division of the Ukrainian National Army, the Canadian League for the Liberation of Ukraine (now the League of Ukrainian Canadians), the Canadian Foundation for Ukrainian Studies, the Canadian Institute of Ukrainian Studies, the Central and East European Studies Society of Alberta, the Chair of Ukrainian Studies Foundation, the Multicultural History Society of Ontario, the Petro Mohyla Institute, the Prometheus Foundation, the Royal Canadian Legion Branch #360, the Secretary of State–Multiculturalism Directorate (Ministry of Canadian Heritage), the St John's Institute (Edmonton), the UBA Trading Foundation, the Ucrainica Research Institute, the Ukrainian Canadian Centennial Committee, the Ukrainian Canadian Civil Liberties Association, the Ukrainian Canadian Congress–National Executive, the Ukrainian Canadian Foundation of Taras Shevchenko, the Ukrainian Canadian Research Foundation, the Ukrainian Free University (Munich), and the Ukrainian Studies Foundation of British Columbia. Research grants were also provided by the University of Alberta, Queen's University, and the Worobetz Foundation, and through the Academic Research Program and Principal's Discretionary Fund of the Royal Military College of Canada. Most of the documentation upon which this book is based can be found in the Archives of Ontario, the Association of Ukrainians in Great Britain archives, the Canadian Department of Foreign Affairs and International Trade, the Harvard Ukrainian Research Institute, the Hoover Institute on War, Revolution and Peace (Stanford University), the League of Ukrainian Canadians archives, the Multicultural History Society of Ontario, the National Archives of Canada, the Public Records

Office, the Ukrainian Cultural and Educational Center 'Oseredok,' the National Executive of the Ukrainian Canadian Congress archives, the Ukrainian Canadian Civil Liberties Association archives, and private collections identified in the notes.

After I became a tenured member of the Department of Politics and Economics at the Royal Military College of Canada, an institution where collegiality and broad-mindedness are a norm, I was able to revise this study for publication with the full encouragement and support of the administration and my colleagues at this 'university with a difference.' I am obliged to Professors Yvan Gagnon and Joel Sokolsky for their understanding and support of my work, and to RMC's Principals, Dr John Plant and Dr John Cowan, and the Dean of Arts, Dr Ron Haycock, for their many positive interventions on my behalf. I also enjoyed my years of association with the Department of Geography at Queen's University and the Department of Geography at the University of Toronto, and a brief sojourn in the Department of History at the University of British Columbia. Teaching students and interacting with colleagues at each of these fine universities has been one of my great pleasures.

I am particularly grateful to Dr Ron Schoeffel, editor-in-chief of the University of Toronto Press, to Frances Mundy, and to Tessie Griffin, my copy-editor. Their dedication and labour behind the scenes helped create a book from the hundreds of pages of manuscript text and notes that I felt obliged to place before them. Finally, I thank Professor Norman Davies for taking an interest in my work, and for writing the foreword that complements it. He has never failed to make himself available to help others when asked, the mark of the truly great scholar that he is.

Generous financial support for the publication of this book was provided by the Canadian Foundation for Ukrainian Studies; a Neporany postdoctoral fellowship from the Canadian Institute of Ukrainian Studies; the Chair of Ukrainian Studies Foundation; the Evhen, Roman and Paulina Kmit Foundation; the John Stashuk Estate; the Ukrainian Canadian Foundation of Taras Shevchenko; and the Ukrainian Studies Foundation of British Columbia.

Introduction

People are attached to place. Humans either are territorial or, at least, tend to behave territorially. It may be in our nature or it may be in our nurture. Certainly, whether as an individual or as a member of a family, clan, tribe, nation, or state, each person has, and needs, a place, a niche, a hearth, a home, a homeland. Most of us identify with some *place*, with some *where*, and with others from *there*. And we can usually identify others as being from somewhere else.

People have explored and made maps of many kinds and varying quality in order to explain why the world is divided up into places, said to be the most fundamental question studied by geographers. They have examined these different places in order to know better where they are – *geographical location* – and to help explain where they and others have been, or might be going. Human communities give character to places. In turn the *geographic personality* of every place shapes or influences the character of peoples. When people are forced to abandon their place, when they become *dis-placed* – refugees, exiles, expatriates – then their most natural reaction, assuming they survive, is to struggle to *re-place* themselves. The involuntarily displaced want to return to the place they came from, or think they came from, and fervently believe they must belong. The Bible's account of the banishment of Adam and Eve from the Garden of Eden reminds us of just how central and ancient the searching for place is. Paradise Lost = place loss.

What I have written is an account of how and why some people left a place they called Ukraine, a land at the edge of Europe which has been occupied and savaged by neighbouring states again and again over the centuries. Until quite recently some said Ukraine had never existed, did not exist, and never would exist.[1] And some of those opponents laboured mightily to secure just such an outcome. They tried to erase Ukraine from the maps of the world, to eliminate the Ukrainian tongue, to expunge the Ukrainian nation. Ukraine became a Golgotha, a place of skulls, as millions were murdered there. The lucky ones were just assimilated, or dispersed. Yet those who plotted Ukraine's extinction failed. As tragic as Ukraine's history has been, Ukraine is a success story. Despite the Ukrainians' many travails, their nation has re-emerged on the map of the world. It is a recognized place, again.[2]

The modern failure to eradicate Ukraine traces its roots to events which took place during the Second World War. Not only did an armed resistance movement, the Ukrainian Insurgent Army, emerge to struggle against both the Nazis and, later, the Soviet reoccupation of Ukraine, but several million Ukrainians moved west, involuntarily or otherwise, during the war years. These refugees and victims of war, officially known as the Displaced Persons (DPs), began coming into ever more frequent contact with the soldiers of the Allied armies as the latter advanced into the Third Reich. Many of these DPs insisted upon identifying themselves as Ukrainians. Those unfortunate enough to fall into the clutches of the advancing Red Army were, unceremoniously and often brutally, repatriated into the bowels of the Soviet Union, their immediate fate precarious, the survivors' long-term prospects bleak. Those who came under the control of the British, American, Canadian, and French armies originally thought they had a better chance of survival. They could not, however, have foreseen just how blinkered and biased were the attitudes of foreign policy establishments throughout the West towards Ukrainian independence.[3] Soon many of them, perhaps even a majority, would become victims again, this time of the Yalta Agreement, which provided for the repatriation of all persons deemed to be Soviet citizens, regardless of their wishes or of the miserable fate known to be awaiting them. To be labelled a Soviet citizen was to be branded for expulsion, perhaps worse.[4]

The governments of the West certainly faced a problem, and a serious one, when they came into contact with DPs who called themselves Ukrainians. To accept as legitimate these persons' claims to being Ukrainian would mean extending, at least implicitly, official recognition to a place called Ukraine, from which these refugees and victims of war said they had come. Doing so was impossible. Many Western statesmen insisted that there was no *real* Ukraine. As they well appreciated, any official acknowledgment of the existence of such a place, and of people called Ukrainians, would immediately embroil them in the tendentious issue of whether or not these people (if they even existed) should enjoy the right of national self-determination. Did the West really want a free Ukraine, knowing that admitting it would give serious affront to various other foreign governments, those of Poland and the Soviet Union in particular? The answer is no.

Even before the war, accepting Ukraine as a legitimate entity had been unthinkable, for Britain and its allies were committed to countering Nazi Germany's machinations on the Continent. If that meant siding with Stalin, even to the extent of covering up the Red dictator's genocidal policies in Ukraine and elsewhere, or tolerating Poland's repressive policies in occupied Western Ukraine, so be it. Betraying the liberal-democratic principles said to underpin Western society in the name of political expediency was not beneath them. London, Washington, and Ottawa all willingly collaborated in keeping Ukraine off the map, knowingly condemning tens if not hundreds of thousands of people to tyranny and death. How the Anglo-American powers rather inelegantly and sometimes inhumanely coped with what they labelled 'the Ukrainian problem' constitutes one of the more sordid parts of this story, certainly not an attractive heritage.

Acknowledging Ukraine and Ukrainians also had domestic implications, especially in North America, where many tens of thousands of persons from Ukrainian lands in eastern Europe had been lured before the turn of the century with promises of freedom and free land. Governments in the New World had expected that the immigrants to whom they had allowed entry would abandon Old World attachments and prejudices, anticipating that, over time, these settlers and their progeny would meld into the host societies, becoming loyal citizens of the Crown, or good Americans. Although not even a simple majority of those who came from Ukraine were necessarily conscious of the existence of such a country (which explains why they were often identified by themselves or others as Ruthenians, Galicians, Bukovynians, Rusyns, and so on), most of them, intending to settle permanently in North America, accepted this prescription and did exactly as was expected. They assimilated as best they could or were allowed to. But not everyone could, wanted to, or did meld with the majority. The North America in which these immigrants found themselves was dominated – politically, economically, and culturally – by others, people quite unlike themselves. Predominantly English-speaking and Protestant, the governors of this North American world were largely ignorant of, indifferent to, and sometimes even hostile towards those among them who were referred to disparagingly as the foreign-born. That term, in Canada at least, referred not only to the immigrants, those allowed into the Dominion, but also to the next generation, the progeny of those who had come from someplace else, even if the latter had been born in this New World. It was widely presumed that members of this second generation would not completely have divested themselves of their parents' ties to the old country. And so, in times of domestic and international crisis, many of the foreign-born might, and often did, find themselves suddenly transformed into victims of the prejudices and paranoia of the state and the public, not so much by virtue of anything they did or did not do, as by virtue of *where* they, their parents, or even their grandparents had been born. During the First World War, and for several years after the war's end, tens of thousands of Ukrainian Canadians would find themselves categorized officially as 'enemy aliens,' interned in concentration camps, forced to do heavy labour, disenfranchised, and subjected to state-sanctioned censure, all because of *where* they had come from. For *where* they came from was presumed to be indicative of who they might be and where their true loyalties lay, even though no credible evidence of their disloyalty was ever produced. During the Second World War an ever vigilant and quite intrusive Canadian state took less drastic, somewhat subtler measures to monitor, control, and shape Ukrainian Canadian society.

Under such conditions before, during, and after the First World War, and given that most of these people had no other viable place to go, many, probably the majority, of the Ukrainian immigrants to North America did the only thing they could do: their level best to conform and assimilate to North American society. Comparatively few – those already committed to Ukrainian causes before they emigrated, those alienated and radicalized by the mistreatment and injustice they had endured in Canada, those encouraged by the emergence of several ill-fated independent Ukrainian states between 1917 and 1920, and those roused by the formation of a Soviet Ukraine which promised to be a bastion of the rights of workers and peasants – took up positions on the Left, Centre, and Right of the Ukrainian political spectrum in North America. While this minority would, ever after, expend enormous amounts of emotional and financial capital in quarrelling about which Ukraine – the communist or the nationalist one – was legitimate, these factions all drew varying amounts of sustenance and political purpose from the fact that, in a land called Ukraine, there was a state referring to itself as Ukrainian, one that had appeared, disappeared, then reappeared – all duly sketched on, then deleted from, then inscribed again on the world's map. Although that state's political hue was a source of deep friction within Canada's Ukrainian population, everyone could and did, if to varying degrees, benefit from the existence of a *place* called Ukraine. After all, if Ukraine existed so did they. All of them knew that it would be near impossible to convince others of who they were, Ukrainians, if those others did not recognize that there was a place called Ukraine.

And so it came to be that a minority of the tens of thousands of immigrants who had left Ukrainian lands in eastern Europe to settle in North America maintained an abiding interest in the fate of a faraway place called Ukraine. They would often suffer for that choice. By continuing publicly to identify themselves as Ukrainians in North America they exposed themselves to the sometimes indelicate attentions of governments suspicious of the motives and intentions of all those who persisted in being attached to old country affairs rather than pursuing the more acceptable and desirable route of assimilating into Canadian or American society. Allegations of divided loyalties would dog the organized Ukrainian communities of North America from the pioneer period to the present. And as a result, particularly during the Second World War period, many of North America's Ukrainians would find themselves subjected to close surveillance, imprisonment, and censure, less because of what they actually did (although a few *were* guilty of having acted in ways inimical to the interests of Canada and the United States) than because of the well-entrenched prejudices of their host societies' bureaucracies and public opinion. Everywhere, most of the host society's mandarins presumed that those who continued to identify themselves and act as Ukrainians, even though they were living in North America, must be duplicitous and had to be screening disloyal activities.

The Ukrainian community in Canada after the Second World War differed significantly from that which emerged during the pre–First World War period. Like it or not, an enlarged state, a real country, known as Ukraine, or, more correctly, as the Ukrainian Soviet Socialist Republic, existed in the postwar world. However unpalatable the regime there might be and indeed was, the existence of such a place, encompassing most Ukrainian ethnographic territories in eastern Europe, could not be denied. And, by the 1930s, a North American–born generation of Ukrainians was coming into its own. Raised and schooled in Canada and the United States, many of these young men and women felt they had every right to expect and enjoy the same treatment accorded to all other citizens in their societies. Although not unaware of or unaffected by the prejudice sometimes directed against Ukrainians in interwar North America, the sons and daughters of the pioneer settlers had heard and, to a remarkable degree, believed Lord Tweedsmuir, the governor-general of Canada. In 1936 he had proclaimed on behalf of His Majesty the King that Ukrainians 'had become good Canadians' who had made 'a very valuable contribution to our new Canada.' He had also said to Canada's Ukrainians, 'You will all be better Canadians for being also good Ukrainians.' Precisely what His Excellency had meant by the term 'a *good* Canadian,' and how this related to his audience's notions about what being 'a *good* Ukrainian' in Canada might mean, is likely the most important question all those calling themselves Ukrainian Canadians have had to wrestle with then and since then.

There was another reason why some Ukrainians in North America felt they had a right to speak out on the 'Ukrainian Question' in Europe and about Ukrainian community affairs at home. Many of them, a number disproportionate to the size of their populations in Canada and the United States, had volunteered for the Allied armed forces during the Second World War. Their honourable service demonstrated unequivocally where their loyalties lay. This gave them the licence, they felt, to pursue their interest in the fate of their parents' and grandparents' homeland without any need for apology or subterfuge. And so, despite the domination of Canadian and American society by elites who were often indisposed to these Ukrainian Canadians and Ukrainian Americans, and even to the idea of an independent Ukraine, these veterans had earned, undeniably, the right to act. And they did. This proved to be a difficult obstacle for the naysayers, the appeasers, the fellow travellers, and the bigots who had tried to blot Ukraine and Ukrainians from the map. The Ukrainians who so acted may have been few, but they had dared to act. They became, as one contemporary described them and as I describe them myself, the 'heroes of their day.'

Of course even these Ukrainians had only guardedly asserted their right to maintain an ongoing interest in the fate of Ukraine, at least at first. Instead of being conspicuously political, they organized humanitarian, social, and cultural efforts – like providing canteen facilities for soldiers serving overseas or channelling relief supplies to Ukrainian refugees – activities they hoped would not be deemed objectionable by most outside observers, even governments morbidly sensitive to even the faintest whiff of political activity on the part of Ukrainians. Fundamentally, of course, what these Ukrainian Canadians were doing was most certainly political, as they well understood. Any action they took publicly as Ukrainians not only reconfirmed the existence of a place called Ukraine but, they hoped, reminded others that there were people living among them for whom the emergence of an independent Ukrainian state remained a priority. Decision-makers and security services, East and West, appreciated that. However loath they may have been to consider it, they knew they had a 'Ukrainian Question' to deal with.

And so the efforts of the organized North American Ukrainians were by no means untroubled, uncomplicated, or unthwarted. Sometimes hindered by the subterfuges of adversaries, they were also often undermined by the organizers' own apprehensions, by inexperience, and, if the truth be told, by the indifference to their efforts of most of the public, including most of North America's Ukrainians. The activists had a lot of convincing and cajoling to do, which they coupled with not a little frustrated complaining, for time and again their plans were fouled up or foiled.

They faced another difficulty. As they mustered and struggled to help the Ukrainian DPs, they did so in large measure because they sincerely believed that a transfusion of these Ukrainian refugees into North America would reinvigorate Ukrainian communities there. Only partially would that expectation be satisfied. For the DPs, involuntary migrants whose own notions of what it meant to be Ukrainian had been shaped in an occupied homeland, in the cataclysm of world war, and within the cauldrons of the refugee camps, did not always understand or appreciate the more cautious and pragmatic nature of the Ukrainian identity that had evolved in North America. For them Ukraine was enslaved and must be freed. So their cause – the national liberation struggle – was all that mattered or should matter. They did not always understand that things might seem different in a North American Ukrainian's eyes, or why. They were, after all, not from North America. They were from *elsewhere*, from another place.

So, as two different versions of how to be a Ukrainian in the emigration inevitably collided – as those favouring pragmatism, caution, and patriotism encountered those who were decided, uncompromising, militant, and nationalistic – frustration and alienation were the spawn. As a Ukrainian Canadian put it at the time, 'All we have now is trouble all around.'

But that much-lamented and unhappy consequence of the encounter between the Ukrainian DPs and their North American Ukrainian rescuers did not, in the long run, matter. What did matter was that some of North America's Ukrainians, and perhaps most of the Ukrainian refugees who were resettled among them, remained grouped around the notion that there *was* a place called Ukraine, and that, whether they had left that place voluntarily near the turn of the century or been forced to flee it during the war, they shared an obligation and had a right to remember embattled Ukraine, even to help free it. Liberating Ukraine became their shared cause, their crusade. And they came to regard and describe that mission as being as legitimate and honourable and principled as the attachment which other Canadians and Americans might have to their own ancestral homelands in Europe. What was allowable and deemed good for a Canadian of British or French heritage should be no less acceptable, no less good, for a Canadian of Ukrainian roots. So they reckoned.

Of course even if, by the late 1950s, Ukrainian Canadians and Ukrainian Americans had generally secured a comfortable niche for themselves in their host societies, asserting that they had earned that status by proving themselves on the battlefields of Europe and Asia, their struggle for equality and recognition was far from over. In the years which followed, their group would be tried time and again, not only challenged to prove that a place called Ukraine existed but questioned repeatedly, and sceptically, about their behaviour during the war.[5] Almost simultaneously they were exploited as needed in the Cold War. This often left the Ukrainian communities of the diaspora belittled, outmanoeuvred, and duped, by their own governments.[6] For all that time and to this day they would have to continue to endure insults and innuendoes as others tried to convince the world that Ukrainians had done much evil to others in Ukraine during the Second World War, that Ukrainians were in fact primarily victimizers, rather than victims.[7]

Even so, many of the DPs held on to their belief that someday, somehow Ukraine would be free. Emotionally pledged to freeing the place they had fled from or been forced out of, they taught their children to believe in what was for them the sacred cause of freeing Ukraine. Some would believe. And so more than one generation came to remember that there was a Ukraine, even if they had never seen it, and to believe that they should dedicate their time, energy, and resources to helping free that unhappy land. *The cause* came to be shared, and the memory of a place lost or of a lost place thus migrated through space, from

Europe to North America, and was passed on through time, from the refugees who came here to their children born here, among them the author of this book.

In the end, in a way, the supporters of this cause of national independence won. Ukraine is now an internationally recognized state, a country, a place, a *where* – found in every serious atlas published since 1991. Ukraine was not, of course, liberated by the Ukrainian emigration, by the postwar DPs or their children or children's children. It could not have been. Ukraine is free because the people who live *there* wanted it to be. But what the Ukrainian emigration did do was help keep the ideal of the struggle for an independent Ukraine alive over space and time. After being healed of the traumas of the war and the refugee experience, these Ukrainian DPs told and continued to tell and retell their stories about their Ukrainian homeland. And they persisted in styling themselves as Ukrainians even though they lived in western Europe, Australia, South and North America and had done so for decades. They did not forget about Ukraine. And many lived long enough to witness the emergence of an independent, sovereign, and internationally recognized state called Ukraine, in December 1991.

Today's Ukraine is certainly not the Ukraine the DPs had hoped for, or remembered, or wanted for their children. It is not now, nor was it necessarily ever, the place these displaced Ukrainians so often recalled and pined for, dreamt about, or described. It is also no longer their place, no matter what it might once have been. Most will never return. They will live out the remainder of their lives where they are. People rarely if ever can return to the place they were torn from and then kept from for many decades. Paradoxically, and no matter how many years they may have expended in searching for the place they lost, most refugees will never find it again, even if the very determined nature of their collective quest helped save something of that place. The tragedy and the greatest irony of the refugee experience is that very few if any of the displaced ever do get to *re-place* themselves. The place they once knew becomes irreplaceable. But at least they can take some comfort in knowing that Ukraine is again on the maps, shown not as a region or a territory or a part of someplace else, but as a sovereign state. Even if it is not their Ukraine, it is a recognized Ukraine, which others deem legitimate. Ukraine *is*, yet again. And so the refugees' long enduring, their searching for place, is finally over. And yet never will be.

Abbreviations

ABN	Anti-Bolshevik Bloc of Nations
AUGB	Association of Ukrainians in Great Britain
AUUC	Association of United Ukrainian Canadians
BAOR	British Army of Occupation on the Rhine
BUC	Brotherhood of Ukrainian Catholics
CCG	Allied Control Commission for Germany
CCUC	Central Committee of Ukrainians in Canada
CLLU	Canadian League for the Liberation of Ukraine
CPC	Communist Party of Canada
CRM	Canadian Relief Mission for Ukrainian Refugees and Victims of War
CUC	Co-ordinating Ukrainian Committee
CURB	Central Ukrainian Relief Bureau
CYM	Ukrainian Youth Association
DEA	Department of External Affairs (Canada)
DP/PW Section	Displaced Persons / Prisoner of War Section, CCG
EVWs	European Voluntary Workers
FO	Foreign Office (Britain)
FUGB	Federation of Ukrainians in Great Britain
IGCR	Intergovernmental Committee on Refugees
IRO	International Refugee Organization
KYK	Ukrainian Canadian Committee (UCC), now the Ukrainian Canadian Congress
KYK	Co-ordinating Ukrainian Committee (CUC)
LUO	Lobay group, or League of Ukrainian Organizations
NAC	National Archives of Canada

ODUM	Organization of Democratic Ukrainian Youth
OSS	Office of Strategic Services (United States)
OUN	Organization of Ukrainian Nationalists
OUNb	Banderivtsi, or Bandera faction of the OUN
OUNm	Melnykivtsi, or Melnyk faction of the OUN
PCIRO	Preparatory Commission of the IRO
PUN	Leadership Council of the OUNm
RCUC	Representative Committee of Ukrainians in Canada
SEP	Surrendered Enemy Personnel
SHAEF	Supreme Headquarters Allied Expeditionary Force
SUMK	Association of Ukrainian Canadian Youth
UCC	Ukrainian Canadian Committee, now the Ukrainian Canadian Congress
UCCLA	Ukrainian Canadian Civil Liberties Association
UCRF	Ukrainian Canadian Relief Fund
UCSA	Ukrainian Canadian Servicemen's Association
UCVA	Ukrainian Canadian Veterans' Association
UHO	Hetmantsi, or United Hetman Organization
UHVR	Supreme Ukrainian Liberation Council
UIS	Ukrainian Information Service
ULFTA	Ukrainian Labour Farmer Temple Association
UNDO	Ukrainian National Democratic Alliance
UNF	Ukrainian National Federation
UNRada	Ukrainian National Council
UNRRA	United Nations Relief and Rehabilitation Administration
UPA	Ukrainian Insurgent Army
URDP	Ukrainian Revolutionary Democratic Party
USRL	Ukrainian Self-Reliance League
UUARC	United Ukrainian American Relief Committee
UVO	Ukrainian Military Organization
UWVA	Ukrainian War Veterans' Association
WBA	Workers Benevolent Association
WO	War Office (Britain)

Note: Map courtesy Ihor Stebelsky. First published in Ihor Stebelsky, 'Ukrainians in the Displaced Persons Camps of Austria and Germany after World War II,' *The Ukrainian Historian* 23:3–4 (1986) 57.

SEARCHING FOR PLACE

1 The Plan

According to plan they gathered together in Toronto in the spring of 1949. No written record of their meeting was preserved. No photographs were taken. Their deliberations were covert. The participants believed in secrecy. Yet the talks held by this carefully picked group profoundly affected the nature and development of Ukrainian Canadian society. For on May Day, 1949, they created the League for the Liberation of Ukraine.[1]

Very little was known at the time of their meeting about the League's founders. Today we have their names; most of them were recently resettled refugee immigrants to Canada.[2] Since the time of their arrival, and following the emergence of a sovereign Ukraine in December 1991, there has been a partial relaxation of the conspiratorial mentality to which they had been inured by survival under several hostile foreign occupations in Ukraine. This loosening has provided opportunities for collecting some information about the experiences of these men.[3] Nevertheless, many details of their biographies and of their collective endeavours remain elusive. The inevitable passing of their generation has made it impossible to reconstruct a full account of what they set about to do. Unlike the bureaucrats, policemen, and government mandarins who challenged and tried to maintain close supervision over the activities of these Ukrainians and their political movement, the participants kept scarcely any written records, or at least none that are accessible.

What is certain is that these men considered themselves – to employ the argot of the Orhanizatsiia ukrainskykh natsionalistiv-banderivtsi (Bandera wing of the Organization of Ukrainian Nationalists, or OUNb, or Banderivtsi) – a 'second line' in a worldwide struggle being waged by a revolutionary nationalist movement whose principal aim was the freeing of Ukraine from Soviet domination.[4] They saw themselves as constituting a specially chosen unit, composed of highly disciplined and experienced operatives, sent into Canada to achieve specific organizational objectives within the Ukrainian refugee population being resettled there. In Canada – though in 1949 few of these men realized that they would spend the remainder of their lives there – they also had a secondary purpose, namely, the rallying of Ukrainian Canadians in support of the Ukrainian independence movement. To carry out this purpose they laid down the claim that *only* they could be considered the true representatives of the national liberation movement in the emigration. Of course, this did not endear them to other pretenders, of whom there were, until recently, more than a few.

That OUNb teams were dispatched to Canada and elsewhere has been confirmed by some of those involved in sending them out, particularly by the paramount leader of the nationalist movement, a member of that inner circle responsible for approving the selection, mandate, and dispatch of these cadres, the late Yaroslav Stetsko.[5] How successfully these teams carried out their missions remains contentious.

What these men assuredly were, however, were members of a group well qualified to form, train, and lead an expanded version of their nationalist organization in the 'New World.' Although it would hardly be appropriate to characterize any of them as average, given what is known of their life histories, they did have some life experiences and qualities in common. Each was a man in his early thirties; all had been born in Western Ukraine; and most were of the Ukrainian (Greek) Catholic denomination, with lower- to middle-class socioeconomic backgrounds. Most had been educated in a *gymnasium*, or high school, and perhaps had attended vocational school or a seminary after that; a few had taken university-level instruction in the underground Ukrainian University of Lviv (Lwow, Lemberg) or abroad. Even if formally of Polish citizenship, a typical member of this band would emphatically have affirmed his Ukrainian identity; indeed, he had done so many times before, even in the face of repression.

By 1949 such a man would repeatedly have proved his resourcefulness, personal loyalty to the nationalist movement, and courage, all qualities necessary for anyone hoping to survive active involvement in nearly two decades of underground Ukrainian resistance – the struggle against the Polish or Hungarian authorities and later against the Nazis, then against the first Soviet occupation of Western Ukraine in 1939–41, and finally against the Soviet reoccupation of all of Ukraine after 1944. While he would have served 'the cause' primarily in Western Ukraine, he may also have been part of one of the nationalist cadres sent to Carpatho-Ukraine (Transcarpathia) in 1938–9 to bolster that short-lived state's resistance to Hungarian domination, or, in the wake of the German Wehrmacht's 22 June 1941 invasion of the Soviet Union, have belonged to one of the OUN task groups, several of which advanced deep into the Ukrainian Soviet Socialist Republic, attempting to rouse Eastern Ukrainians in support of Ukrainian independence.

The OUN's members were also survivors. While many of their comrades had perished, those who made it to Toronto had somehow avoided capture or, if imprisoned, had suffered and survived brutalities in interwar Poland's jails, in Soviet captivity, or even in the genocidal fury of the Nazi concentration camps. Several decades later no small number of the leading Banderivtsi in the emigration would point, with an admixture of sorrow for those who had fallen but pride in their own endurance, to the tattoos which their Nazi jailers had imprinted on their forearms at infamous Nazi death camps like Auschwitz.[6]

For the Ukrainian revolutionary nationalist, the OUN was like a mother for the nation, a guiding force whose main task, in Stetsko's words, was to prepare the masses 'for a wider, armed liberation struggle, to show the nation the way, to create a revolutionary atmosphere conducive to securing an independent Ukrainian state, and to do so through our own strength, relying on no one else to liberate Ukraine for us.'[7] There were few such men, and even fewer women. What restored their hope and fortitude after all their travails, even as they found themselves sheltering in the war-ravaged ruins of the Third Reich, was their strong belief in the justice and continuity of their struggle. All around them were hundreds of thousands of other Ukrainian displaced persons – the so-called DPs – most of whom had fled homes in Ukraine as the battle lines of the Eastern Front had swayed back and forth. Many were victims of war or had been press-ganged into German service, becoming the Third Reich's slave labourers known as *Ostarbeiter*, or east workers.[8] All these Ukrainians had to be rallied to carry on with the good fight for a free Ukraine.

But this enormous Ukrainian refugee population – there may have been as many as 4.5 million Ukrainian DPs scattered throughout western Europe at the war's end, although an estimate of 2.5 to 3 million seems more probable – was quite heterogeneous.[9] How could they be

encouraged to form a common front? The Ukrainian refugee population represented every region, class, religious faith, and political tendency found in prewar Ukraine. The vast majority of these people
were not, of course, members of the OUN, or, for that matter, affiliated
with or sympathetic to any organized Ukrainian political party or
movement. Some – the socialists, the monarchists, the democrats –
were even actively hostile to the Ukrainian nationalist movement. The
DP camps became the cauldrons into which these disparate human
ingredients were dropped, by war, by fate, or by chance. What kind of
Ukrainian should emerge from these melting pots of the DP camps
was to become a fiercely contested point.

So among the first of the chores assigned by their high command to
the nationalists living in or near the displaced persons' camps, and
particularly to the Banderivtsi, was the shaping of this diverse
Ukrainian refugee population into a constituency willing to support
'the Organization.' By sustaining its work in the emigration, the DPs
were told, they would be contributing to the ongoing insurgency in
Ukraine. To a very marked degree conditions within the refugee camps
were conducive to the nationalists' efforts. The politicization of many
previously non-political Ukrainian DPs in these enclaves was to be one
of the most important consequences of the Ukrainian refugee experience in the post–Second World War period. At the time few outside
observers seem to have noticed.

Quite an opposite development would take place in Canada. When
the Banderivtsi eventually arrived there, many having spent three to
four years living in or near one of the DP camps, the reaction from
established Ukrainian Canadian organizations, whether politically to
the Left, the Centre, or the Right, was almost uniformly negative, even
if their respective complaints differed widely in content and timing.
For example, the leaders of the rather loose association of secular and
religious groups brought together under the aegis of the Komitet
ukraintsiv kanady, or KYK (Ukrainian Canadian Committee or UCC,
now known as the Ukrainian Canadian Congress), which portrayed
itself as the only legitimate representative of Ukrainian Canadian (and
sometimes even of the Ukrainian homeland's) interests, were anxious
lest new organizations like the one which became the OUNb-domi-
nated Canadian League for the Liberation of Ukraine (CLLU) undermine its own, largely self-appointed authority.[10] The anxiety of many
Ukrainian Canadians, furthermore, was intensified because the little
information they got about the Banderivtsi tended to be hostile propa-

ganda, circulated by competing political groups, some of which had established allies among Ukrainian Canadian organizations before the war. What many Ukrainian Canadians heard from friends and neighbours in their own communities, or read in major Ukrainian-language newspapers published in Canada and the United States, was crafted to paint the revolutionary nationalists in the most unflattering of terms.[11]

The attack against these postwar refugee nationalists came especially from within the ranks of the Ukrainian Canadian Left. The Tovarystvo obiednannia ukrainskykh kanadtsiv (Association of United Ukrainian Canadians or AUUC), which had formerly been known as the Tovarystvo ukrainskyi robitnycho-farmerskyi dim (Ukrainian Labour Farmer Temple Association, or ULFTA), was openly opposed to the immigration to Canada of anti-communist and anti-Soviet Ukrainian DPs, and began its negative campaign even before the coming large-scale immigration of such Ukrainians was apparent. Their reason for protest was obvious. They, and fellow travellers sympathetic to Soviet communism, had by far the most to lose if living witnesses to the reality of Soviet rule were admitted to Canada. As a result, the pro-communists spent many years and considerable wealth protesting, lobbying, and lying about who the DPs were and why they wanted to get to Canada. We now know that in doing so they were only following orders from Moscow.

But there was a more fundamental reason for the uneasiness about these in-migrating political refugees, a real concern over what impact their attitudes and behaviour might have on Ukrainian Canadian society as a whole. Principally – although this was not always as evident as it may appear in hindsight – the question was whether the DPs, the 'newcomers,' would introduce dissonance into the organized community over such basic issues as what constitutes membership in the Ukrainian minority in Canada and what affiliating oneself with this group entails. Such concerns were far from being as prosaic as they might seem today. Whereas language, folk arts, foodstuffs, and even architecture may be the *objective signals* of an individual's ethnic affiliation, these otherwise useful indicators of group membership often change over time and with place. Merely cataloguing what one social anthropologist has described as 'the cultural stuff,' the externals with which members of an ethnic group surround themselves in a particular place and time, is unsatisfactory for anyone attempting to understand the dynamics of ethnic affiliation. More important is an appreciation of the 'basic value' or 'orientation' around which members of a group unite. Their loyalty to that value and their ability to maintain it as a boundary between themselves and outsiders is what allows them to identify themselves and function as a distinct community, to measure one another's commitment to the group while also allowing others – the outsiders – to judge them as members of the group. Even if an ethnic group's boundary is not a visible element of the cultural landscape, its maintenance is crucial to the group's survival, far more so than the 'cultural stuff' it contains, for if the boundary between 'them' and 'us' is not maintained, the group's members become exposed to assimilatory pressures which eventually can overwhelm them and bring about the group's disappearance. From this perspective, *remaining* in the ethnic group, into which one must first be born, becomes a dynamic, lifelong process of maintaining the boundary that marks the group off from some other constituency, rather than surrendering it and becoming assimilated into that other constituency; this process can be voluntary or impelled.[12]

The view taken here is that being a Ukrainian Canadian meant (and still means), first, being born within the group, and thereafter maintaining an abiding interest in the fate of Ukraine. Staying or leaving the group is a matter of choice. And although it is quite apparent that a Ukrainian Canadian identity is still being forged (a process which may well be expedited now that there is an independent Ukraine), Ukrainians have simply not been in Canada long enough, nor – despite the undeniable imprint of the group, especially on the Prairies – have they developed a sufficient memorial culture in Canada, for anyone to speak of a distinctly Ukrainian Canadian entity as yet. So, at least until the very recent past, being a Ukrainian Canadian meant taking an abiding interest in the Ukrainian homeland – the place *over there* – rather than worrying much about the group's place in Canada, except in so far as the group's status in Canada helped or hindered its efforts with respect to what was going on 'over there.' While such an involvement did not, and did not need to, preclude participation in the day-to-day chores connected with living in Canada, the cause of Ukraine's independence would, in a Ukrainian Canadian activist's perception, generally take precedence over most other normal involvements. That often meant having to *negotiate* what the group's place in Canada was – with the host society and, more fundamentally, with a Canadian state whose primary and somewhat contrary purpose was to build a Canadian nation by fusing into one the disparate ethnic, religious, and cultural heritages of the many different peoples who have come to Canada.

Of course, only a minority of those who came to Canada from Ukraine, or were born into the Ukrainian Canadian population and later opted for remaining within it, fit the definition given here of what being a Ukrainian Canadian might entail. My object is not to exclude those for whom only one or another of the cultural or religious qualities normally associated with 'being Ukrainian in Canada' is, or was, meaningful. There have always been large numbers of people grouped loosely around the committed core of the Ukrainian Canadian minority, persons who, signalling an interest in some of the 'cultural stuff' often taken to constitute essential aspects of Ukrainian Canadian ethnicity, are, for the most part, much more thoroughly integrated into the larger society, often (from the perspective of the committed vanguard) nearly lost to the group. Hundreds of thousands of people are today classified by outsiders, or even by themselves, as belonging to a Ukrainian Canadian minority. Many of them do indeed exhibit an allegiance to the traditional Ukrainian churches and may speak some Ukrainian or admire Ukrainian cultural traditions. But even if these people have been and continue to be taken into account by politicians and census takers, they constitute only a backdrop to the tale told here. For in any analysis of the relationship between the Canadian state and the organized Ukrainian Canadian ethnic minority, only the relatively few men and women who publicly and persistently campaigned for Ukraine's right to exist were considered relevant enough to attract the not always kind attention of government, of the media, and of those who tried but failed to thwart their cause.

The way in which this interest in the homeland was expressed by Ukrainian Canadians varied considerably. Some, aligned on the political Right, were militant in protesting against what they viewed as foreign – that is, Soviet Russian or Polish or German or Hungarian – occupation of Ukrainian soil. Other Ukrainian Canadians, on the Left, were equally certain that the political system prevailing in Soviet Ukraine was desirable and was supported by the majority living there. Rather uncritically, they backed the Soviet Union. What is crucial is not whether the one group or the other was right or wrong, but that, whether of the Left, the Centre, or the Right, the members of each of these constituencies consciously or unconsciously defined and organized themselves in reaction to conditions in the Ukrainian homeland, even as they asserted that they were acting out of loyalty to their new homeland of Canada – either to free Ukraine so that it could be an ally of the West against Bolshevism, or to protect Soviet Ukraine because it was a bastion of the rights of workers and peasants, a model society which Canada would do well to emulate. These were both rationalizations. In truth, neither side cared as much about Canada as they did about Ukraine. Whatever their political stripe their focus was more on the 'old country' than on the 'New World.' They shared that value; it was their most fundamental orientation, it was what set them apart from other Canadians and made them all, no matter how outwardly dissimilar they might appear politically, members of an organized Ukrainian Canadian element. They would be so judged by others. And they would find that identifying oneself as a Ukrainian while living in Canada could sometimes prove to be an unfortunate pairing of choices.

2 'From a Police Point of View': The Origins of the Ukrainian Canadian Community, 1891–1920

'Stalwart Peasants in a Promised Land'

Few of the peasants lured from Ukrainian lands in eastern Europe who came to Canada's prairie frontier at the turn of the century were *svidomi ukraintsi*, or nationally conscious Ukrainians. Most came from the illiterate and downtrodden masses which had been exploited in the Austrian-ruled crownlands of Galicia and Bukovyna. So unpromising were conditions there that many Ukrainian peasants welcomed the chance of building a better life for themselves and their families by emigrating to America: 'When the Ukrainian peasant looked up, he could see above him, riding on his back, the Polish noble, the Romanian boyar, the Jewish innkeeper-lender, and a few of his own people as well; but when he looked down, all he could see was earth, and precious little of that.'[1]

Pulled to Canada by officially sponsored advertising which promised each pioneer the freedom to work a 160-acre section of fertile soil, approximately 171,000 immigrants from Ukraine had arrived in Canada by August 1914, before the outbreak of the First World War cut off international migration.[2] The pro-immigration policies of the day were the creation largely of the Laurier government's minister of the interior, Clifford Sifton; these policies were furthered by his successor, Frank Oliver.[3]

Almost from the outset of Ukrainian settlement in Canada, which began, officially, with the arrival of Ivan Pillipiw and Wasyl Eleniak on 7 September 1891, the immigrants hived together in colonies, clustering on the bases of family, kinship, village, and regional ties.[4] By June 1892 twelve families from Pillipiw's village had followed the first two pioneers to Canada, hoping to settle near Gretna, Manitoba, where Ele-niak had found work as a farm hand among German colonists. But the area had been closed by a smallpox quarantine, so they moved farther inland to the Beaver Lake area of today's Alberta, some sixty miles east of Edmonton. The following year another twenty families arrived; Pillipiw himself later settled among them.

What began as a trickle – immigrants from Western Ukrainian lands constituted only one-hundredth of 1 per cent of the total immigration to Canada in 1891 – soon burgeoned into a voluntary and large-scale movement of people. And no wonder. Prospective migrants were encouraged to emigrate to Canada by a variety of immigration boost-ers. Enticing stories about the good life to be found in North America were published in Ukrainian-language newspapers like *Svoboda* (*Liberty*), which began publishing out of Jersey City, New Jersey, in 1893. Other positive inducements were two Ukrainian-language pamphlets dealing with emigration to Canada published by the respected Pros-vita (Enlightenment) Society of Lviv, whose descriptions of life in the 'New World' influenced readers to think of Canada as a preferred des-tination, especially in contrast to South American climes.[5] And then there were the various immigration agents and boosters, like the North Atlantic Trading Company. This syndicate, made up of booking agents and steamship company officials, worked surreptitiously at the behest of the Canadian government, promoting emigration out of Galicia and Bukovyna even in direct contravention of Austro-Hungarian laws.[6]

But one of the main spurs to emigration was that the people them-selves appreciated the obvious. Those who had earlier left their vil-lages were not returning. It was therefore reasonable to assume that life must indeed be better in America than it was in the old country.[7] And so they began leaving, in their tens of thousands.

'These Strange People'

Ukrainian emigration to Canada grew steadily until it peaked in 1897. In that year just over 18 per cent – nearly 4000 souls – of the total immi-gration to Canada had come from Ukraine. The greatest number to enter Canada in a single year came in 1913, when nearly 22,500 people, constituting almost 6 per cent of the total immigration for that year, arrived at the entry ports of Halifax and Quebec City.[8]

In some circles this inflow provoked alarm. While Sifton would go on record generously, if rather patronizingly, explaining that the preferred immigrant was a 'stalwart peasant in a sheepskin coat born on the soil, whose forefathers have been farmers for ten generations, with a stout wife and a half-dozen children,' others, like Frank Oliver, then a Conservative MP from Edmonton, expressed disgust over Slavic immigration, and did so in a less than subtle fashion: 'We do not live to produce wheat. We live to produce people ... and to build up a country, and if you give us only those who can produce wheat, and who cannot take their places as citizens, you do us an injury ... You place an obstacle in the way of our progress.'[9]

Oliver complained that those who argued that assimilation would eventually integrate 'these strange people' were terribly naïve, for they were ignoring 'the harsh reality' of what that 'nice-sounding word' meant. Assimilation, he warned, was repugnant to any good Canadian, for what it referred to was nothing less than miscegenation, 'the intermarriage of your sons or daughters with those who are of an alien race and of alien ideas.'[10] In Oliver's view, and in that of many others in his day, it was manifestly impossible to build a Canadian nation, much less a social system or a civilization, on the basis of racial interbreeding. It would be better, he advised, to avoid the burden created by 'the millstone of this Slav population.' Active measures to curtail any further Slavic immigration to Canada should, he argued, be taken.

Others had sung a similar tune earlier. On 6 May 1899 the Montreal *Daily Star* published an article, 'British Institutions in Danger,' which expressed fears about Canada losing its British character should the immigration of 'Galicians and other foreigners,' presumably peoples 'opposed to British customs, lazy and vicious,' be allowed to continue unchecked. On 9 June 1899 a Mr C.P. Wolley criticized Sifton's pro-immigration policies in the *Ottawa Anglo-Saxon*, insisting that 'you cannot make Anglo-Saxondom of Doukhobors, Galicians, and Finns,' and that it was the 'principal object of all good Canadians ... to build up a race which shall hold and develop Canada for the Empire.' The 'Anglo-Saxon type' of man, Wolley continued, had reached the 'highest point of excellence,' and it was the Anglo-Saxon man's further duty to do whatever was necessary to 'bring mankind as a whole up to our level.' But that could not be accomplished by spoiling *the best* by reckless admixture of the *scum.'* Pouring Mennonites, Doukhobors, Galicians, Finns, 'and heaven knows what besides' into Manitoba could only imperil the racial purity of the country: 'The dogs may pick up the crumbs which fall from the children's table, [but] there is no reason why they should be asked to sit at that table, mix blood with and share the heritage of the children. And that is just what is being done today.'

Indeed newspaper editorialists, letter writers, and columnists across the country often expressed similarly disconcerting prejudices. The editor of the small Belleville, Ontario, newspaper *The Intelligencer* noted that Galicians, 'they of the sheepskin coats, the filth and the vermin,' did not make 'splendid material for the building of a great nation.' One look at these 'disgusting creatures' as they had passed through on the CPR, headed west, 'caused many to marvel that beings bearing the human form could have sunk to such a bestial level.' Citing these comments in its 18 March 1899 edition, the *Halifax Herald* concluded that the presence of these undesirable settlers 'tends to disgust and keep away, or drive away, persons who are really desirable.' Three days later the same paper repeated a hateful message: 'Every batch of Galicians put into the Northwest reduces the value of the country and tends to deter useful immigrants from going there.' Later, racial prejudice would turn into apprehension about the possible political implications of immigrant Ukrainians' being able to mobilize a bloc vote, somehow undermining the Canadian political system by becoming involved in it. Enfranchisement of these 'foreigners,' it was argued, should be allowed only *after* they had been completely indoctrinated into the British-Canadian way of life, for otherwise how would it be possible to ensure that their political demands did not run counter to Anglo-Canadian designs for the country's future?

Oliver's anti-Slavic tune changed, not surprisingly, when the practical responsibility for populating the Prairies fell on his shoulders, following the defeat of the Laurier government. Ironically, when he became overseer of Canadian immigration policy more Ukrainians and other Slavic immigrants were allowed into the country than had entered during Sifton's watch. And some Canadian commentators began pointing out that these Ukrainians had a real economic utility for the country. Even so, xenophobia and racial prejudice against Ukrainians remained by no means uncommon. Similarly disturbing sentiments would find an unwholesome echo in later decades.

What stopped the first wave of Ukrainian immigration into Canada was not, of course, racial prejudice but the outbreak of the First World War. Still, Canada's gatekeepers never adopted the sentiments put forward by a more enlightened parliamentarian, D.C. Fraser, who had urged his fellow citizens to be 'broad in this matter,' by providing immigrants with 'the liberty to expand their energies' free from the 'barbarism and oppression [and] despotism' known in Europe.[11] Ukrainians and other Slavic immigrants were allowed in only because they were deemed essential for populating Canada's Northwest, to keep it from remaining 'sterile and unproductive for centuries to come.' In short, Ukrainian pioneers were brought into Canada not out of kindness but to do hard work.

'A Virtual Canadian Ukraine'

Sifton's policies, in fact, dealt what has been described as a 'fatal blow to the imperialist notion of a British-Canadian west.'[12] When this realization dawned upon Ottawa's decision-makers they grew uneasy, particularly since they could observe that this mass immigration was pooling up around the original Ukrainian colony near Edna-Star, Alberta, creating what amounted to a vast, geographically contiguous territory, an ethnic bloc settlement populated and increasingly dominated by east Europeans – a region which has been described as a 'virtual Canadian Ukraine.'[13] This unforeseen development, perceived as antithetical to the assimilatory and nation-building plans of the government of the day, was countered finally between 1896 and 1905, with other settlement nodes for Ukrainian immigrants being chosen by government officials and incoming settlers channelled to them. In this manner the basic spatial pattern of Ukrainian settlement in Canada, a belt of Ukrainian ethnic enclaves anchored in the east by Winnipeg and in the west by Edmonton, closely paralleling the aspen-poplar woodland belt around which Ukrainian settlers had demonstrated a marked proclivity for settling, was established by government design.[14] By 1914, major concentrations of Ukrainian settlers could be found around Edna-Star in Alberta, Prince Albert, Fish Creek, and Yorkton in Saskatchewan, and Dauphin, Shoal Lake, Interlake, Stuartburn, and Whitemouth in Manitoba. The relics of this pattern are still evident to this day, a distinctly Ukrainian Canadian component of the Prairie region's cultural landscape.

Having been brought to Canada to meet prairie development imperatives, Ukrainians would remain essentially a rural folk for years to come. In 1901 nearly 97 per cent of Canada's Ukrainians could be found in rural settings, a figure which had decreased to just over 70 per cent by 1931, 66 per cent by 1941, and just under 50 per cent by 1951. In contrast, the Canadian population as a whole was 63 per cent rural in 1901, 46 per cent rural in 1931, 45.7 per cent rural in 1941, and 38 per cent rural in 1951.[15] Originally, therefore, Ukrainian Canadian group consciousness was consolidated within an agrarian setting. Certainly, it was from this rural, western Canadian environment that there emerged many of the leading community figures and organizations active within this population from the interwar period until well after the Second World War.[16]

'Controlling the Foreign Element'

Just as the large-scale immigration of Ukrainians had inflamed nativist sentiment, so too the increasingly visible presence of 'Mr Sifton's Galician pets,' living in group settlements, provoked widespread consternation. In 1899 the conservative *Winnipeg Telegram* not only took up the cry of alarm at what was described as an 'invasion' of the West by Galicians, but even hysterically predicted that Canada's English-speaking peoples would end up becoming aliens in their own country.[17] The following month an editorial in the same newspaper, entitled 'More Moral Lepers,' discussed the political implications of 'the Galician peril,' following which the paper carried another story giving voice to the harsh opinion that the right to vote should not be accorded to 'the most unfit of the scum of the lowest civilizations of Europe who are being dumped down among us.'[18]

By exploiting anti-foreigner and anti-Ukrainian xenophobia, Hugh J. Macdonald, a lawyer and the son of Sir John A. Macdonald, Canada's first prime minister, helped catapult his Conservative party into power in the December 1899 Manitoba elections, forestalling any likelihood of a 'Galician Government' of the sort the conservative press had rallied against.[19] Indicative of the bigotry directed against Ukrainians at that time was a 25 November editorial in *The Winnipeg Tribune*, entitled 'Galicians vs. White People,' which alleged that Ukrainians had been deliberately 'hived' together on the Prairies, set up in colonies so that these ignorant immigrants could be more easily manipulated for political purposes, by the Liberals. Simultaneously, it was claimed, their communal way of life kept them impervious to the civilizing influences which anglicization offered.[20] That Macdonald would cling to such racist assessments of Slavs in general, and of the 'Ruthenian, Russian ... Polish [and] Russian and German Jews' in particular, is evident from his subsequent correspondence with Arthur Meighen, minister of the interior in Sir Robert Borden's Unionist government. Writing to Ottawa in the summer of 1919, Macdonald expressed the sharp view that the 'undesirable aliens ... in our midst' had to be gotten rid of and that 'fear is the only agency that can be successfully employed to keep them within the law.' If that course was followed, he asserted, 'the foreign element here will soon be as gentle and as easily controlled as a lot of sheep.'[21]

But the most unmitigatedly injurious and unwarranted intervention ever made by the Canadian state into Ukrainian Canadian affairs had, by the time Macdonald penned his unkind suggestions to Meighen, already done much to intimidate this ethnic minority, reminding it of its perilous status in Canada. Sanctioned by passage of the now notorious War Measures Act (1914), along with various orders-in-council and proclamations, the Canadian government had already interned and registered thousands of Ukrainians who had been peremptorily classified as 'enemy aliens.' During Canada's first national internment operations of 1914–20, a total of 8759 men, accompanied by some women and children, were confined in twenty-four 'concentration camps' spread across the Dominion. Among the internees, some 6000 were civilians, officially described as 'Austro-Hungarians,' of whom the majority, approximately 5000 men, women, and children, were probably Ukrainians by nationality, most of them recent immigrants, although some were naturalized British subjects, Canadian-born. Interned alongside them were genuine German and Austrian POWs but also others of 'Austro-Hungarian nationality,' including Poles, Italians, Bulgarians, Rumanians, Turks, Jews, Croatians, and Serbians. Over 88,000 others, also declared 'enemy aliens' by the federal government, were obliged to register, to carry special identification papers, and regularly to report their whereabouts and movements to local police authorities, civilian registrars, or the chief commissioner of the Dominion Police. Being found without approved identification and travel documents exposed a person to fine, arrest, possibly even internment, and to intimidation and the prospect of having to pay bribes in order to escape imprisonment. Property and other valuables were confiscated from those interned; not all that wealth was returned at the end of these internment operations.

To oversee Canada's first national internment operations the special Internment Operations Branch was created within the Department of Justice, headed up by a retired major-general of the militia, Sir William Dillon Otter.[22] The Department of Militia and Defence supplied the military forces Sir William required, supplemented by Royal North West Mounted Police and Dominion Police officials, who provided internal security and related police services, as required.[23]

The hostility and suspicion Ukrainian Canadians were subjected to was, in part, the result of a heightening of prewar prejudice among Anglo-Canadians over the supposed genesis of a homogeneous Ukrainian territory on the Prairies, one allegedly under the control of a disloyal and demagogic ethnic elite. Later such fears would be exacerbated by the Red Scare, with its accompanying stories about Bolshevik intrigues among the foreign-born.[24] For the interned such subtleties were probably irrelevant. Many had been jailed for very dubious reasons. The remaining files of the Internment Operations Branch reveal that some Ukrainians were arrested simply for acting in what was described as a very suspicious manner, or for using seditious language, for being intemperate, for being found destitute, for hiding in a railway car, or even for being unreliable, of a shiftless character, or simply undesirable.[25] Ironically, some Ukrainian Canadians were interned even while attempting to enlist in the Canadian Expeditionary Force or even after having served in its ranks. The absurdity of these internment measures, and an indication of the traumatic impact they had at the individual and family level, is suggested by the case of Nick Chonomod, a Ukrainian Canadian who wrote to the authorities to press his case for release. He testified not only that he had lived in Canada for several years before the war, but that he owned a homestead, had married a Canadian-born woman, and had become naturalized. He had even wanted to enlist in a battalion being raised in Edmonton. Despite all these indications of his loyalty, he was interned near Halifax, without any evidence ever having been produced to prove disloyalty on his part.[26] Ukrainians were interned because of where they had come from, not who or what they were.

The threat of internment was employed to cow Canadian citizens of Ukrainian origin, even over such purely domestic issues as the fate of the bilingual (English-Ukrainian) educational system. When this became a hotly contested matter in Manitoba, one anonymous Liberal politician was quoted, in a February 1916 issue of the *Winnipeg Telegram*, as being in favour of the internment of 'all Ukrainians' as a means of resolving the issue. On being invited to attend a public, pro-bilingual meeting, he refused, snarling, 'If you Ukrainians don't stop this, I'll have you all rounded up and interned at Brandon.'[27] Meanwhile, ethnic newspaper editors, like Orest Zerebko, himself a naturalized Canadian citizen, were informed not only that their continued agitation in favour of bilingual schools was inimical to Canada's national interests, but that such behaviour might lead to the complete suppression of the non-English-language press by the Dominion censorship authorities.[28]

In the internment camp system itself German POWs and German-speaking Austrians were segregated into a 'first class' category and separated from those 'Austrians' who, falling into the 'second class,' were often transported to primitive work sites in desolate areas of the country's hinterland, as far away from major Canadian population centres as possible. There they were compelled to work, their labour sometimes exploited for the personal gain of unscrupulous jailers. Not infrequently they were also mistreated by the guards, a fact which even Sir William was forced to admit. In December 1915, in an official reprimand with respect to one such incident, Otter wrote to the officer commanding the 13th District, in Calgary, 'The various complaints made to you by prisoners as to the rough conduct of the guards I fear is not altogether without reason, a fact much to be regretted, and, I am sorry to say, by no means an uncommon occurrence at other Stations.'[29]

Not surprisingly, many internees suffered mental and physical hardship or were permanently disabled as a result of their internment experiences. Interned children died of illness contracted in the camps, the tragic fate of three-year-old Canadian-born Nellie Manko in the Spirit Lake (La Ferme), Quebec, camp being a case in point.[30] Some, unable to bear up, committed suicide. According to testimony heard before a tribunal investigating the death of William Perchaluk, the man 'came to his death at the Police holdover by strangulation, owing to having suspended himself by the neck from the top bars of a cell with one of his military puttees, while being detained there pending enquiries being made by the military authorities as to his nationality; his rash act would appear to have been committed during a fit of despondency.'[31]

Others resisted, either passively by working slowly or actively by staging work stoppages or protest strikes. Some escaped. Alberta's Castle Mountain internment camp, in what became Banff National Park, was particularly notorious for the number of successful escapes that took place there. Not all such attempts were successful. Andrew Grapko, interned at Brandon, Manitoba, was killed while attempting to escape, as was Ivan Hryhoryschuk, fleeing the Spirit Lake concentration camp. Dissatisfied with working conditions, abuse, and the injustice of their internment, a large group of prisoners even staged a full-scale riot at the Kapuskasing, Ontario, internment camp in 1916, a revolt which had to be put down by a large militia force. Some measure of the ferocity of that clash is suggested by newspaper stories which describe how subduing the prisoners took several hours and a contingent of over three hundred soldiers.[32]

Government action against Ukrainian Canadians was not limited to the internment of several thousands or the enforced registration of tens of thousands more as 'enemy aliens.' The War Time Elections Act, assented to on 20 September 1917, disenfranchised all 'enemy alien' immigrants who had been naturalized since 31 March 1902.[33] Since some 60 per cent of the Ukrainians living in the three Prairie provinces in 1911 were foreign-born, this act effectively sapped any electoral strength which Ukrainian Canadians might have been able to wield, cutting off one of the few forms of democratic protest they could have exercised against the injustices being done them.[34] Ukrainians in Canada were apparently considered fit enough to be worked but not worthy enough to vote.

Ukrainian Canadians protested against this act, and the other injustices, but their pleas for understanding were ineffective. They had few friends and, it seemed, many enemies. There was, for example, a very real danger of violence against them by some members of veterans' groups and other self-styled patriots. Although some labour newspapers did take up their case, editorializing against this particular legislation, these protests had little impact. A commentary in the *British Columbia Federationist*, which described the War Time Elections Act as 'so repugnant to every principle and concept of common decency as to preclude the possibility of meeting with the approval of any decent, clean-thinking person in the land,' had no effect. And even if the Kingston, Ontario, *Daily British Whig*, Canada's oldest daily newspaper, was equally condemnatory, its plea for tolerance, however prescient, was likewise without consequence:

> It is quite probable that if this proposal becomes law the alleged 'foreigners' and hitherto 'naturalized Canadians' will bear their reproach meekly, but they will have sown in their hearts the seeds of a bitterness that can never be extirpated. The man whose honor has been mistrusted and who has been singled out for national humiliation, will remember it and sooner or later it will have to be atoned for.[35]

Scarcely a month before the armistice ending the Great War was signed, another order-in-council was passed under the powers conferred on the government by the War Measures Act. Censorship was imposed on the publication of newspapers, books, and other printed matter in any 'enemy language,' including German, Russian, Finnish, Esthonian (sic), Livonian, and Syrian. Apparently uncertain about the difference between the two, if any, this legislation also prohibited the publication of material in both the Ukrainian and the Ruthenian languages.[36] On the same day the governor-general of Canada, on the recommendation of the minister of justice, declared fourteen left-wing organizations unlawful, including the Ukrainian Social Democratic Party.[37] Even after the end of hostilities, greater understanding of and a more conciliatory attitude towards dissent failed to emerge. Various officials continued to remain vigilant about the menace to order and good government in Canada that they believed was represented by radical foreigners. The western Canadian press censor, Fred Livesay, in trying to suppress publication of the leftist newspaper *Ukrainskyi robitnychi visti* (*Ukrainian Labour News*) in April 1919, voiced bluntly his opinion that this case was one which called not for 'supervision but for ruthless suppression.'[38]

The war's end on 11 November 1918 brought no prompt conclusion to the internment operations. In December of that year, 2222 persons remained incarcerated. It was not until February 1920 that the last inmates were released or deported and the remaining camps closed down.[39] The Internment Operations office in Ottawa remained at work until 20 June 1920.[40] Indeed, during the immediate post–First World War period the camps not only would continue to house a residue of wartime 'enemy aliens' but also would provide room for a fresh influx of 'radical aliens' – Ukrainians, Russians, Jews, and others – many of whom were destined for deportation.

The imprisoning of dissident immigrants and the monitoring of their organizational and social life were not the only steps taken by the authorities to cope with what was perceived as an internal security threat. In the early months of 1919 the government was inundated with appeals from veterans' groups, boards of trade, and provincial and municipal governments for the mass and forcible repatriation of 'enemy aliens.'[41] These appeals were rejected, probably owing to uncertainty as to the international repercussions of such mass expulsions. Then, too, there were serious concerns about overburdening the country's transportation network just as veterans were being brought home from Europe. But selective deportations did take place. After the Winnipeg General Strike, in May 1919, several Ukrainians were arrested, transported to the Kapuskasing concentration camp, and then shipped briskly out of the country.[42] Others, rounded up after the 21 June riots in Winnipeg, were treated similarly, without even the pretence of a formal hearing. It is worth noting as evidence of the double standard then in force that whereas British 'radicals' were processed through normal, comparatively lenient judicial channels, their foreign-born comrades were dealt with expeditiously by less fussy immigration tribunals. Justice for Ukrainian immigrants in Canada was not only selective, but rough and hasty.

Well before the war's end, many Austrian internees had been released on parole, to work as contract labourers with the national railway companies and for private businesses, farmers, and corporations. By the summer of 1916 serious labour shortages, brought on by the large-scale movement of Canadian manpower into the armed forces and overseas and the great slaughter on the Western Front, had forced the government to review its policy of keeping thousands of other men, whom it had by then come to regard as 'harmless Austrians,' forcibly idle.[43] Life in the workplaces to which these paroled workers were sent, in north-central Ontario for example, was often arduous, although, as one internee would recall years later, at least he was 'a free man again.'[44] But the parole system reflected no liberalization of government policy towards Ukrainians and other 'enemy aliens.' Instead, it only demonstrated Ottawa's realization that these 'aliens' had value as workers. No steps were taken to undo the injustice which had been done them. Their conditional discharges were as rooted in the labour needs and economic requirements of the nation at war as their initial admission into Canada had been tied up with the Dominion government's need to people and develop the Prairies and, later, the nation's mining and industrial frontiers. Those released, either during the war or just after, were never compensated for the indignities they had suffered as internees, for the injustice of their incarceration, for the lost years of their lives, or for their labour, nor were they refunded what had been taken from them upon their arrest, wealth administered by the Custodian of Enemy Alien Properties, some of which remains in Ottawa's coffers to this day.[45]

A number of contemporary observers tried to divine the impact of the internment operations and related repressive measures on the victims. H.A. Mackie, MP for Edmonton East, wrote to Prime Minister Robert L. Borden in mid-October 1918 seeking to explain the history of the Ruthenian people and of their newly formed, independent Ukrainian state, hoping his words would ameliorate the plight of

Ukrainians in Canada. According to him, 'Canadian public opinion, created by the action of the Government since the war, has made for oppression,' which was alienating those Ukrainian settlers who,' Mackie reminded the prime minister, had come to Canada at the invitation of the Canadian government.[46] Having been induced to leave their homeland by the promise of freedom, they were discovering, as Mackie put it, that 'the propaganda of freedom and liberty under British rule' was untrustworthy. Instead of being treated as free men in Canada, they were being dealt with as enemies. Worse, for some their freedom was being restricted even after they had been granted British citizenship. In Mackie's view, the unfair treatment meted out to these homesteaders and workers was alienating them. Some might even return to their now independent homeland. And that would be bad for Canada, since the very presence of these settlers on the Prairies had prevented the americanization of the region. As well, the existence of a sovereign Ukraine at the geopolitical focal point he called the 'Gate of Eastern Nations' was a key to the maintenance of international stability, a factor of considerable importance to the British Empire. Government actions disaffecting Ukrainians could therefore have negative international consequences for Canada and the British Empire as a whole.

To prove Ukrainian Canadians had been loyal to the Empire during the war, Mackie commented on how many of them had, despite the wrongs being done to their compatriots, enlisted in the Canadian Expeditionary Force, giving false birthplace information and even changing their names – he wrote that some had told the army's registrars their surname was 'Smith' – in order to join up. Mackie went on that 'these people, per population, gave a larger percentage of men to the war than certain races in Canada have, after having enjoyed the privileges of British citizenship for a period of a century or more.'[47]

Perhaps the greatest irony related to Canada's first national internment operations was that Ottawa had been informed by the British Foreign Office as early as January 1915, and again in February of that year, that Ukrainians, then still sometimes referred to as 'Ruthenes' or 'Ruthenians,' were among the national minorities of the Austro-Hungarian Empire who were hostile to Habsburg rule and who should accordingly be given preferential treatment as 'friendly aliens.' Ottawa's continued use of repressive measures against this minority cannot today be dismissed with the apology that it was the result of a misunderstanding about who the Ukrainians settled in Canada were, or where their true loyalties lay.[48]

Some Anglo-Canadians had other concerns about the impact of the internment operations. A Presbyterian missionary working among the Ukrainians observed that, as a result of 'real and imagined grievances,' they were becoming 'sullen towards Canadian institutions and ... towards Canadian people.' This was leading, he noted, to an increase in the influence of an (unidentified) 'Ruthenian nationalist organization' whose slogan, he reported, was 'No Assimilation by the English.'[49] For his part, the principal of Saskatchewan's Regina Collegiate confirmed that whereas many parents of his Ukrainian students had 'five years ago [thought] that they were really becoming Canadians,' as a result of various 'questionable actions' taken against them by the government they had become 'hurt, bewildered, shy' and were drawing back into 'their half-discarded alien shells.' Principal Black lamented over the 'pestilential mist of mutual suspicion and dislike' which had arisen between 'us and them,' a development he feared could only be 'ominous for the future' of the Canadian nation.[50]

By the start of the First World War, Ukrainians organizing themselves in Canada were beginning to realize that the largely Anglo-Canadian and Protestant society in which they lived was, if not actively hostile to them, certainly not interested in the perpetuation or growth of any Ukrainian constituency in Canada. They could read editorials like one published in the Edmonton Bulletin, which pointedly warned: 'Canada is Canada, and those who become Canadian citizens are expected to limit their activities to Canada and to Canada's place and duty in the British Empire. Whether Ukraine is to become a republic, or a province of Russia or Austria is none of Canada's business, and whoever tries to carry on in Canada a propaganda for settling the political status of the Ukraine is making trouble for Canada and therefore for himself.'[51]

The effect of the national humiliation Ukrainian Canadians were subjected to between 1914 and 1920 was, of course, by no means uniform in its impact. Not every Ukrainian Canadian grew suspicious of, or sullen towards, his Anglo-Canadian or other neighbours, nor were most Ukrainian Canadians necessarily any more attracted to the anti-assimilatory platforms of 'Ruthenian nationalist' organizations. Quite probably, in contrast, many abandoned or publicly played down their ethnic affiliation, rightly seeing a danger in too openly defining themselves as members of a Ukrainian minority.[52] Such a reaction was certainly evident during the war. A police constable in the Kootenay mining region of British Columbia reported to the superintendent of provincial police that the internment of several leaders of previously militant groups 'seems to have [had] a good effect on the remainder.' What did he mean? Well, 'from a police point of view' these Ukrainians were no longer giving any trouble.[53] A desirable result indeed.

3 'The Man Who Knew':
Organizing the Ukrainian Canadian
Community, from the 1920s to the 1940s

Divided Loyalties?

Self-imposed quiescence did not appeal to everyone in the Ukrainian Canadian community. Aroused by the struggle for independence waged in their homeland between 1917 and 1921, some Ukrainians in Canada attached themselves to the cause of self-determination for Ukraine. Others, entranced by the reputed achievements of the Bolshevik Revolution and the formation of a Ukrainian Soviet Socialist Republic, gave their personal allegiance to and entwined their ethnic identity with support for socialist and pro-Soviet groups.[1] Though a number of organizations were to emerge among Ukrainians in Canada during the interwar period, only three secular groups, each exceeding several thousand dues-paying adherents, achieved a truly national, mass appeal which allowed for the development of affiliated newspapers, women's, and youth sections. Two of these, the Ukrainian Labour Farmer Temple Association (ULFTA) and the Ukrainian Self-Reliance League (USRL), originated in the late pioneer period, although the latter was not formally set up until the interwar period. The third, known as the Ukrainian National Federation (UNF), constituted in 1932, was from its outset essentially a product of first- and second-immigration activists and Canadian-born Ukrainians, an organizational effort given added momentum through the eventual amalgamation into the Federation of a veterans' group known as the Ukrainska striletska hromada, (Ukrainian War Veterans' Association, or UWVA).[2]

Well before any of these major Ukrainian Canadian ethnic organizations was set up, however, smaller, local associations had taken hold. These were often patterned after the populist Prosvita Society, branches of which could be found in most Galician and Bukovynian villages by the eve of the First World War. Others took their inspiration from the socialistic, anti-clerical, and pro-independence political platform of the Ukrainian radical leader Mykhailo Drahomanov. Both movements, populist and radical, strove to raise the educational and cultural level of the Western Ukrainian peasantry, eradicating illiteracy and developing a distinctly national Ukrainian consciousness among the masses. Even though they warred among themselves, these groups contributed to the development of a national sentiment among a population which had often been fragmented on regional, linguistic, and religious lines. That sense of a common Ukrainian nationality would be transferred to Canada and further nurtured there, particularly within the ethnic bloc settlements of the West.

Since only a handful of Ukrainian clergymen settled in Canada during the late pioneer period, the task of organizing the immigrant community at first fell to lay persons. For the most part, they began their work by setting up *chytalni*, reading clubs, and *narodni domy*, national homes or community centres. The first Ukrainian organization in Canada to attract a broad range of adherents seems to have been the St Nicholas Brotherhood, formed in Edna-Star, Alberta, in 1897. In the years following, reading halls with names such as Borotba (Struggle) and Voila (Freedom) sprang up, the names reflecting initiatives taken not by priests but by activist supporters of populist, socialist, or radical ideas imbibed in Ukraine and then transported to the new homeland.

At first, these centres attracted immigrants of nearly every political or religious persuasion. There was simply no place else to go. However, by the early 1900s those who chose to get involved in organized community life had a little more choice and generally gravitated to one or another political or religious faction. Few would be able to preserve neutrality in the face of the often bitter and divisive infighting which plagued the Ukrainian Canadian community in its fledgling years. Most reading halls, national homes, and Prosvita societies gradually became focuses of intense intra-community strife, as competing factions attempted to wrest control over these centres, a process which radicalized some as it repelled others, perhaps even most of those who might otherwise have been drawn into these community institutions. Certainly, many Ukrainian immigrants retreated from active participation in the life of their ethnic group as a result of this internecine political strife. And this pattern would be repeated many times over as the immigration of each succeeding 'wave' of Ukrainians witnessed the formation of new Ukrainian groups which attracted supporters but also alienated those who resented having the organizations they had set up earlier supplanted or replaced.

Socialist sympathizers were the first to form their own distinct national societies. In 1906 a Taras Shevchenko Educational Association was established in Winnipeg. From it, there arose a Ukrainian Free Thought Association and, in 1907, a Ukrainian branch of the Socialist Party of Canada. By 1909 ten of its branches were active around the country. In 1914 they established the Ukrainian Social Democratic Party of Canada, an organization which existed until September 1918, when, along with other left-wing political groups, it was declared illegal by the federal authorities.[3]

Almost simultaneously groups with a populist orientation emerged. These were more concerned with cultivating national feeling than class consciousness; the efforts of these community activists were particularly noticeable in educational circles. In 1907 they formed a Ukrainian Teachers' Association in Manitoba, a body which championed bilingual (English-Ukrainian) public school education, helped organize school districts, and established several *bursy,* or Ukrainian student hostels, across the Prairies.[4] These *bursy,* providing accommodation for Ukrainian students moving from rural areas into the cities to enrol in vocational and secondary schools, also played a crucial role in husbanding the first Canadian-born generations of Ukrainians for community work. Years later a British Foreign Office official described what was probably the most important *bursa* of them all, the Petro Mohyla Institute in Saskatoon, as a 'training ground for most of the Ukrainian intellectuals in Canada.'[5] While the *bursy* were originally intended to be non-denominational and non-partisan institutions open to all students of Ukrainian background, most came under the influence of one or another competing subgroup, adherents of the independent Ukrainian Greek Orthodox Church of Canada being particularly successful in this respect. Whether allied to Orthodox or Catholic Ukrainian Canadian groups, the *bursy* were indisputably patriotic in a national Ukrainian sense. Thus the first centre, opened in 1915 by the Ukrainian Teachers' Association in Winnipeg, was named after Adam Kotsko, a young activist killed by rival Polish students during a demonstration at Lviv University in July 1910.

Denominational quarrels came to plague the *bursa* movement. Even before the Mohyla Institute opened its doors in the summer of 1916, the Ukrainian Catholic hierarchy had begun denigrating its organizers and questioning the nature of the Institute's mandate, the quality of its educational programs, and the personal characters of its founders. The Ukrainian Catholic newspaper *Kanadiiskyi rusyn* (*Canadian Ruthenian*) asked 'whether the *bursa* [Kotsko and Mohyla] are in accord with the views of Greek Catholic Ukrainians or against them?'[6] Replying on 1 November, Orest Zerebko, the editor of *Ukrainskyi holos* (*Ukrainian Voice*), not only touched on the religious issues involved in this debate but also indicated what the centre's founders perceived to be their primary task: 'Ukrainianism we place first and religious upbringing second, because all Ukrainians are members of one nationality, but not all are members of the Greek Catholic or Orthodox churches.'[7]

It was not a response calculated to be conciliatory or to appeal to Bishop Nykyta Budka, his priests, or many of his Catholic flock. Indeed, the profound differences in world-view between the national populists grouped around the Mohyla Institute and those who favoured the Ukrainian Catholic hierarchy would so exacerbate the schism developing among the Ukrainians of Canada that eventually a minority broke away. On 18–19 July 1918 they formed the independent Ukrainian Greek Orthodox Church of Canada.[8] Out of the ensuing religious, social, and political maelstrom there would eventually arise a secular organization, closely tied to this new Orthodox church, the group known as the Ukrainian Self-Reliance League.

But before any of what would come to be the other leading Ukrainian Canadian organizations was able to coalesce, a left-wing group, the Ukrainian Labour Farmer Temple Association, had been formed, essentially taking over where the banned Ukrainian Social Democratic Party had left off. From headquarters in Winnipeg, the ULFTA's leaders expanded their activities, particularly in the mining, industrial, lumbering, and railway centres of the country, first in the West and later in central Canada, concentrating on Ontario's mining, industrial, and manufacturing centres like Port Arthur, Sudbury, Toronto, and Timmins. By 1939 the ULFTA reportedly supported 113 temples, with 201 branches, and some 10,000 members.[9] Two satellite organizations, the Workers Benevolent Association (WBA) and the Association to Aid the Liberation Movement in Western Ukraine, were also established, in 1922 and 1931 respectively. The former served as a fraternal, mutual-aid insurance society, which, in fact, secretly siphoned financial support into the ULFTA's accounts and likely those of the Communist Party of Canada. The second group was designed to appeal to veterans of the unsuccessful liberation struggle in Western Ukraine, drawing them into the pro-Soviet movement and away from the nationalist fold.[10] These three groups had at their disposition a weekly newspaper, *Ukrainian Labour News*, founded in Winnipeg in 1919, which became the first and only Ukrainian Canadian daily in January 1935; it changed its masthead to *Nardona hazetta* (*People's Gazette*) in September 1937. The influence of this newspaper is reflected in its circulation, which rose from 6800 in 1925 to 10,000 in 1929.[11] After this pro-communist press was banned in June 1940, the ULFTA's leaders (who, after June 1941, had reorganized themselves into the Association to Aid the Fatherland) founded two new newspapers, the weekly *Ukrainske zhyttia* (*Ukrainian Life*), published in Toronto from August 1941, and another weekly published out of Winnipeg, *Ukrainske slovo* (*Ukrainian Word*), which began publishing on 20 January 1943.

Ideologically, the ULFTA was a pro-Soviet, Marxist-Leninist organization; if this characterization did not exactly fit the group's average member, it certainly applied to the majority of the ULFTA's leaders, several of whom were also highly placed members of the Communist Party of Canada (CPC). From the group's inception, its political orientation was closely tied to the Canadian communist movement. That this connection alarmed official circles is not surprising. A secret memorandum sent by the commissioner of the RCMP, Cortlandt Starnes, to O.D. Skelton, Canada's under-secretary of state for external affairs, in March 1929, expressed the commissioner's concerns about the ULFTA's plans to 'send a number of young Ukrainians of revolutionary views to the Ukraine, to be trained there to be agitators, and to return to Canada to "organize" for sundry revolutionary societies, including the Communist Party of Canada.'[12] Further evidence of the close ties between the CPC and the ULFTA is the fact that the latter's newspaper, *Ukrainian Labour News*, became an official organ of the Party; of 2500 to 3000 Communist party members in the early 1930s, some 900 to 1000 were Ukrainians.[13] Since the entire adult membership of the ULFTA in 1919 was only about 4000 people, it is apparent that the well-organized and disciplined CPC members active within this Ukrainian Canadian organization were able to play a major role in steering the ULFTA, and they did. Their role was made easier by the fact that many were also senior comrades in the Party.[14] That Party control over this mass organization was maintained through what were known as 'fractions' – secret caucuses of Party members – is further attested by a former member of both the ULFTA and the CPC, John Kolasky, whose eventual disenchantment with the Ukrainian

Canadian Left and the Soviet Union led him to expose these machinations.[15]

So slavishly aligned was the leadership of the ULFTA with the Communist Party of Canada that, at its Twelfth Convention, held 15–20 July 1931, both Stalin (in absentia) and Tim Buck, the Party's leader, were elected to the ULFTA's honorary presidium. And even after increasingly disturbing reports about the liquidation of the kulaks, about a politically engineered genocidal famine in Ukraine, and about the Great Terror began filtering into Canada, the ULFTA's national secretary would declare Soviet policies 'correct' and avow that he and his fellow communists continued to have 'full faith' in the Soviet government.[16] Even the manifest failures of communism were shrugged off as temporary, just as the alleged atrocities were decried as bogus anti-Soviet propaganda. The Stalinist line was swallowed, uncritically and whole.

Ironically, what the ULFTA's leadership failed to appreciate was that non-Ukrainian members of the CPC's Politburo did not entirely trust their foreign-born comrades. Even though the Party's leaders recognized the ULFTA as a 'powerful institution' among Ukrainians, and knew that it occupied 'an extremely important and strategical position' for the purpose of reaching foreign-born workers 'with revolutionary propaganda and agitation,' the ULFTA was criticized for having systematically retreated in the face of attacks by Canadian politicians, the 'bourgeois press,' and 'reactionary Ukrainian organizations.' Instead of launching the 'obviously correct' political counter-offensive called for, the ULFTA's leadership – 'all Party members' – had allowed articles to run in their own newspapers which denied any connection between the ULFTA and the CPC, and which contained statements emphasizing that their group had a 'purely educational and cultural nature.' Things had gotten to such a sorry state of affairs, the Party's policy-makers bemoaned, that not only had the Canadian national anthem been sung at some ULFTA 'entertainments,' but the ULFTA's national headquarters had been decorated with Canada's national colours during the 'capitalist celebration' marking the 'Confederation of the Canadian Provinces.'[17] Even worse, from the Party's perspective, was that this 'right danger,' as they labelled such political back-sliding in the ULFTA, was being encouraged by some of that organization's leaders, men who were paying more attention to Ukrainian affairs – giving them first consideration – than they were to the Party's directives and needs. Obviously, when 'leading Ukrainian comrades' spent so much time attending to peculiar 'Ukrainian problems' they had less time for Party work. This, the CPC's Politburo decided, 'must all be changed.' To the Canadian communists' surprise, however, they found that when they attempted to impose Party discipline upon the ULFTA, it was the Party 'fraction' which was defeated, the motion that the ULFTA accept a statement of censure being rejected by a vote of eighty to six. The Party's consternation over this rebuke was reflected in the statement it issued in response. The statement called for 'a whole series of measures' including 'agitprop' and 'an intensive enlightenment campaign' to combat what were described as the erroneous views held by the Ukrainian membership of the Party, people who, it was claimed, constituted a 'firmly knit federation' which had erred in setting 'its loyalty and its discipline' with respect to fellow Ukrainians higher than loyalty to the Party.[18]

Perhaps most intriguing about this exchange between pro-communist Ukrainian Canadians and their Party comrades is how it underscores that, even if the ULFTA and affiliated groups did not challenge the ideological tenets of the Canadian communist movement, they were equally unprepared to abandon what was derided as their 'Ukrainian peculiarity,' even in the face of the Party's obvious and concerted displeasure. Whatever contortions were necessary to allow them to remain in tandem with the Party on various political questions, some ULFTA leaders, and certainly much of the rank and file, insisted on their right to preserve their Ukrainian identity and national consciousness in Canada, regardless of what the Party might think about their 'peculiar' attachment. They would continue signalling this fact to outsiders through an extensive and varied program of cultural, social, and educational activities, which were, for the most part, demonstrably Ukrainian in content, if not always free of russification or pro-Soviet symbolism.[19] And many in the ULFTA, even as they took a political stand on the Left, did so while insisting that they would remain Ukrainian, a stance upsetting for the Party's avowed internationalists. It confounded them all the more when specifically Ukrainian issues arose, either in the homeland or in Canada, because even if these left-wing Ukrainians were expected to give up being Ukrainian and instead become good communists of a pro-Soviet, Stalinist persuasion, they did not.

The second Canada-wide organization to emerge was the Ukrainian Self-Reliance League, which, although not formally incorporated until December 1927, originated in the late pioneer period. Among its earliest leaders were the schoolteachers and activists who had founded *bursy* in Winnipeg, Edmonton, and Saskatoon, men who helped set up the newspaper *Ukrainian Voice*, most of them supporters of the Ukrainian Greek Orthodox Church of Canada. Not unimportant in the evolution of the USRL's ideological platform was the wartime experience of several of its founding fathers, such as Julian Stechishin, who either had been imprisoned or else had met with other indignities during the internment operations.[20] Having suffered odium because of their allegedly 'divided loyalties' – their foreign ties – these Ukrainian Canadians were quick to cast their group's official program in terms calculated to calm outsiders. The USRL's program stressed that Canada was the 'newly adopted homeland of Ukrainians' who were 'permanently settled' there. While Ukrainians should strive to perpetuate and cultivate their specific cultural attributes 'within the framework of Canadian citizenship,' they 'must not affiliate formally with any of the political factions in the homeland or in exile.'[21] And so the Ukrainian Canadian editor of *Ukrainian Voice*, Myroslav Stechishin, who had participated in the 1917 Saskatoon conference which propelled into being an Orthodox Ukrainian 'national church' in Canada, criticized not only the Ukrainian Catholic prelate, Bishop Budka, for having 'often conducted himself in a manner as to compromise Ukrainians in Canada' – a reference to the still controversial pastoral letter Budka penned in late July 1914 urging all Austrian subjects 'to defend the threatened Fatherland' – but also insisted on the fundamental importance of separating the USRL's supporters from those who still advocated 'living ties' with political movements overseas. Writing in October 1928, Stechishin emphasized that Ukrainian Canadians would dutifully assist Canada and Great Britain as loyal citizens in the event of any future war, claiming that by doing so they would give greater assistance to 'the Ukrainian cause' than through 'disloyalty, opposition and treason.' No doubt recalling his own troubles during the First World War, Stechishin warned Ukrainian Canadians that if they were even suspected of being disloyal no one, least of all themselves, would benefit, and they would only end up 'filling internment camps and prisons and encouraging all types of surveillance against their loved ones who did not even involve themselves.'[22] He added that Ukrainian Canadians had learned this lesson in the previous war. As for the Left, USRL spokesmen made it clear that their group's ideological outlook was one which favoured a 'harmonizing of class differences' as opposed to class struggle, for the former offered the only proper means of achiev-

ing the 'economic good and progress of humanity.' In so far as the
Canadian political scene was concerned, USRL supporters tended to
be ideologically liberal.

As with most groups of this kind, political principles sometimes
gave way to practical necessities. Despite the USRL's purported refusal
to ally itself in any way with specific Ukrainian movements outside
Canada, some of its creators, who included in their number a large
portion of the Ukrainian Canadian intelligentsia of the day, were not
entirely willing to abandon an umbilical attachment to the Ukrainian
nation in Europe. Their official program stressed opposition to the
'occupation' of Ukrainian territory by Soviet Russia, Poland, Rumania,
and Czechoslovakia; condemned the 'incursion' of the 'Russian Bolshevik Party' into Ukraine; and made clear that the USRL considered it
a 'holy duty' to work towards 'the total liberation' of Ukrainian lands
from their 'occupiers.' Careful to avoid being reproved for appearing
of dubious loyalty, USRL spokesmen also often declared their organization's unencumbered allegiance to the British Empire and Canada.
They insisted not only that Ukrainians in Canada and Ukraine had a
'common interest' in siding with the Empire, but that the emergence of
an independent Ukrainian state would be decidedly to Great Britain's
advantage.[23] But however politically antagonistic they were towards
the Ukrainian Canadian Left, these liberal-minded USRL activists were
no more prepared to abandon a definition of themselves as Ukrainians,
even after having experienced state and public disdain, than were
those 'Ukrainian comrades' who had similarly faced the displeasure of
the Canadian government as allies of the Communist Party of Canada.
While much distinguished these two constituencies, and indeed
divided them politically, both insisted on their right to be Ukrainian in
Canada, and in that sense both remained foreign to the place in which
they found themselves. This shared characteristic would make them
targets of government surveillance and intervention in the years
ahead, no matter how much they respectively denounced each other
while proclaiming their total loyalty to Canada. In Ottawa's eyes, they
were more alike than they knew.

A small group of Ukrainian monarchists known as the United Hetman Organization (the Hetmantsi, or UHO), whose conservative ideology, uniformed members, and strong ties to the Ukrainian Catholic
hierarchy set them apart; the even smaller Ukrainian Workers' League,
which represented a break-away faction of former ULFTA supporters
(the so-called Lobay movement); and the Brotherhood of Ukrainian

Catholics (BUC) – whose motto, Catholic Religion, Ukrainian Culture, and Canadian Citizenship, is a clear indicator of its world-view – were other important groups organized in the interwar period, although each had a rather more limited membership or impact. Far more relevant on the national Ukrainian Canadian scene was the militantly nationalistic association known as the Ukrainian National Federation, which would come closest to rivalling the ULFTA and the USRL in its organizational zeal, number of adherents and halls, and influence in Ukrainian Canadian society.

Although it eventually came to be dominated by Western Ukrainian, predominantly Ukrainian Catholic, interwar immigrants, the Federation had as its first national president Alexander Gregorovich, who had come to Canada before the First World War, worked as a railwayman, and later served as a schoolteacher in rural Alberta's Smoky Lake district. Later the Ukrainian War Veterans' Association, a body organized in 1928 by soldiers of the Ukrainian Sich Riflemen and Ukrainian Galician Army, strengthened the Federation's ranks. From its inception, the UNF was intended to be a secular body uniting all nationally conscious Ukrainian Canadians regardless of their personal religious affiliation or date of immigration. It set up its own newspaper, *Novyi shliakh* (hereafter *New Pathway*), in Edmonton in 1930, and the paper remains its official organ. Its headquarters were moved several times, in a process that not only reflected the shifting of the 'centre of gravity' for this group, but mirrored larger changes taking place in Ukrainian Canadian society. First located in Edmonton, the Federation's editorial office and press were later moved to Saskatoon, then to Winnipeg, and finally, in the post–Second World War period, to Toronto, where they remain.

The Federation's ideological foundations reflected Gregorovich's growing anxiety over the fractious confessional bickering that had so polarized the nationally conscious Ukrainian population of Canada. A real need existed, he and his fellow activists felt, for a new organization which would appeal to all nationally conscious Ukrainians who relished the dream of an independent Ukraine regardless of their religious persuasion, regional background, or date of immigration to Canada. What Gregorovich saw was that, as supporters of the Ukrainian Orthodox movement contested the authority of the Ukrainian Catholic hierarchy, and the latter retorted with allegations about the illegitimacy of this new Ukrainian Canadian church, both sides expended considerable, and scarce, resources in a fight which did considerable harm to Ukrainian Canadian society, and certainly no good. In his view only the pro-Soviet Ukrainians benefited from the national camp's divisiveness. The creation of a new body which could somehow unite the discordant elements within Ukrainian Canadian society – hence the word 'federation' in the name of this organization – became his principal aim. Although he was himself a Ukrainian Catholic, he had married a Bukovynian woman of the Orthodox faith. Their children were all baptized by Ukrainian Orthodox priests since no Ukrainian Catholic parish existed nearby, and Gregorovich, intent on preserving the Ukrainian dimension of the children's religious ties, had refused to allow their baptism in a Roman Catholic church.

Genuinely appreciative of the religious convictions of those Ukrainians who, finding themselves in Canada with a Catholic hierarchy which often seemed unsympathetic to or uninterested in Ukrainian national aspirations, had felt compelled to form their own independent Ukrainian Greek Orthodox Church, Gregorovich worked hard to pull Ukrainian Canadians of both faiths into a common organization. True, these Canadian Orthodox believers represented a minority, however well populated their ranks have been with some of the leading members of the Ukrainian Canadian intelligentsia. And certainly most new immigrants, mostly from Western Ukrainian regions, were of Greek Catholic faith. But if everyone, pioneer and interwar immigrants and their children likewise, could be united in a non-denominational, nationalistic organization, a Ukrainian presence in Canada would be assured. What seemed necessary and workable, therefore, was the creation of a new body without ties to a particular church and open to all *svidomi ukraintsi*, or nationally-conscious Ukrainians, in Canada, one which would actively promote the cause of Ukrainian independence. And so the Ukrainian National Federation was born.

At first, the UNF generally, and genuinely, tried to be non-sectarian, open to all patriotic Ukrainians, successfully including in its leadership Ukrainian Orthodox and Catholic believers, pioneer immigrants and those who had come during the interwar period. Gradually, however, it came to be increasingly controlled by interwar immigrants, particularly by the veterans and political activists whose own association had provided a critical mass around which the Federation had grown. Because of the personal involvement of several of the more active of these veterans with the Ukrainian liberation movement, the Federation's affairs became intertwined with those of the Ukrainian Military Organization (Ukrainska viiskova orhanizatsiia, or UVO) and, later, with those of its successor, the Organization of Ukrainian Nationalists (OUN), both European-based groups, both headed by Colonel Evhen Konovalets until his assassination by a Soviet agent in Rotterdam in 1938.

For the patriotic Ukrainians grouped into the UNF, most other Ukrainian Canadian organizations were either too parochial or too narrowly focused on Canadian affairs to be of much use to the cause of Ukraine's liberation, a goal on which the Federation's members felt the Ukrainian emigration should focus its attention and resources. Anything which distracted from that commitment, such as a preoccupation with church affairs or denominational quarrels of the type so evident among Ukrainians in Canada, was to the detriment of the ongoing national liberation movement and was deemed irrelevant or contrary. And so the Federation's platform unhesitatingly chastised those 'Canadian Ukrainians [who] waste much time, energy, money and paper' on tasks of 'lesser importance' while ignoring their 'greatest responsibility,' which was to support with all available strength the 'Ukrainian national fighting units ... waging a battle for liberation with the enemies of the Ukrainian nation.'[24] It was, in the words of the first *New Pathway* editorial, the unequivocal obligation 'of every Ukrainian who finds himself beyond the borders of his homeland' to remember this advice: 'When misfortune befalls the native land, forget your father, forget even your mother, go and fulfil your obligation.'[25]

Wedded to this belief, many key UWVA members and UNF supporters, men like Wolodymyr Kossar, Eustace Wasylyshen, Professor Toma Pavlychenko, Bohdan Zeleny, Pavlo Shteppa, and Dmytro Gerych, covertly became involved with the Ukrainian nationalist underground in Europe.[26] In order to be of use, they worked with great dedication in building up the UNF in Canada, for they saw in it a source of both moral and financial support for the liberation movement. In their fund-raising and organizational tasks they were aided considerably by the visits to Canada of leading nationalists, including Colonel Konovalets himself in 1928, Omelyan Senyk-Hrybivsky in 1931, and Colonel Roman Sushko in 1932. In their turn, the nationalists in Europe were able to develop within Canada a social, cultural, educational, and political network of supporters and sympathizers that was to prove very useful in mobilizing interest in the Ukrainian independence movement and collecting funds for the support of their ongoing armed struggle.[27] By 1934 there were forty-five UNF branches across the country, not including affiliated women's and youth sections, the latter known as the Young Ukrainian Nationalists. Although the first UNF branch was formed in Edmonton, by 1933 the offices of *New Pathway* and the UNF's headquarters had been moved to Saskatoon, where the first UNF convention was held in 1934. Saskatoon remained the main centre of the Federation for some time thereafter, largely because of the presence in that city of Professor Pavlychenko who worked as a plant ecologist at the University of Saskatchewan. Just prior to the outbreak of the Second World War, the Federation had grown to 50 branches nationwide, with 15 affiliated veterans' branches, 38 youth sections, and 33 women's sections.[28] As within the ULFTA and USRL, a few activists in the Federation essentially gave it a distinct political orientation by focusing their attention on the homeland's affairs. And no matter how much they might protest their primary allegiance to Canada, there can be little serious doubt that, at least for the leading members of the Federation, their primary loyalty was to the liberation movement in the old country. This characteristic would expose the UNF to official reprimand not much different in kind, if not always similar in measure, to that meted out to the Left's supporters, to the Hetmantsi, and even to some of those very same USRL supporters who had considered their program above reproach.

Official censure took many forms. Despite their claims to the contrary, not only the Ukrainian Left but also the Ukrainian Centre and the Ukrainian Right were affected, at the individual and organizational levels. The unmuted applause with which pro-Soviet Ukrainian Canadian groups had welcomed the Soviet–Nazi non-aggression pact of 23 August 1939, followed by the antiwar agitation of the pro-communist press and their cadres, was interpreted by Ottawa to be the equivalent of 'disseminating subversive propaganda.' Accordingly, on 4 June 1940 the Communist Party of Canada was declared illegal. Along with it the ULFTA was banned. The Workers Benevolent Association, investigated by a government-appointed accountant, was found to have been operating illegally by making numerous financial donations to the CPC's newspaper, *The Clarion*, and to the ULFTA. Accordingly, the WBA was forbidden to accept new members until further notice and would be placed under surveillance.

But it was the ULFTA that suffered the heaviest blow. Some of its leaders were interned,[29] its newspapers were shut down and their editors arrested, and sixteen ULFTA 'labour temples' were confiscated by the Custodian of Enemy Alien Properties and, in some cases, sold to rival Ukrainian Canadian organizations, mainly local branches of the

UNF or Ukrainian Catholic and Ukrainian Orthodox parishes. The ULFTA's impressive Winnipeg headquarters building was sold to the UNF.[30] Even after Nazi Germany's invasion of the Soviet Union on 22 June 1941, which overnight transformed the USSR into an Allied power, the federal authorities remained understandably suspicious of the Ukrainian Canadian Left. The latter responded to this changed political climate by forming the Ukrainian Association to Aid the Fatherland, which, in turn, sponsored publication of two pro-Soviet Ukrainian-language newspapers.[31] Indicative of the prevailing sentiments respecting the Ukrainian Canadian Left were Lester B. Pearson's comments included in a letter to Norman A. Robertson, then under-secretary of state for external affairs. Pearson, a future prime minister of Canada, observed that 'the sudden discovery by communists in Canada that the war is not imperialistic, but holy, is somewhat nauseating.'[32]

Still, Pearson admitted, 'whatever the reasons may be' the Russians were now 'fighting on our side,' and 'the communists have become ardent protagonists for an all-out war effort,' which meant that past transgressions had best be forgotten, at least for the time being. As a result, most of the pro-Soviet Ukrainian Canadians who had been interned were released by the late fall of 1942. Eventually, their confiscated properties and assets were returned – not always an easy chore, given how many of the ULFTA halls' new occupants were nationalistic, anti-Soviet groups like the Ukrainian National Federation.[33] Once these reparations were complete, however, often to the great discomfiture of the other Ukrainian Canadian groups, the pro-Soviet movement, basking in the uncritical atmosphere of admiration many Canadians had for their country's new-found Soviet ally, and for 'Uncle Joe' Stalin in particular, thrived. The Left's leaders and membership, previously frightened by the determination shown by Ottawa's repression of the ULFTA, renewed many of the social, cultural, and political activities for which their organizations had been known from before the war, and did so with great enthusiasm. Spectacular organizational growth was recorded as these left-wing organizers attracted new members in the urban-industrial centres and from within the trade unions. By playing on the sympathies of various often gullible civil libertarians, church leaders, and trade unionists, and by making a concerted effort at lobbying the Canadian public in general, the Ukrainian Canadian Left was actually able to convince many fellow citizens that grave and unwarranted measures had been taken against them by the federal authorities, and that an apology and redress were now appropriate. As well, through pamphlets like *Ukrainian Canadians Appeal for Justice*, William Kardash's *Ukrainian Canadians against Hitler*, and Raymond Arthur Davies's polemic *This Is Our Land*, they stressed the contributions that ULFTA members had made to the war effort and their many cultural works, and branded those critical of the Soviet system or of its policies as 'quislings' and 'fascists.'[34] In late July 1941, for example, the founders of the Association to Aid the Fatherland proclaimed, in their organization's newly crafted constitution, that one of their avowed duties was to defend 'the democratic cause against all ... internal enemies' and to organize and conduct 'irrevocable opposition to all enemies of Canada and ... of the Ukraine and particularly against any Ukrainians in Canada' who were 'fascist Hitler agents and fifth columnists who are now busily engaged in activities detrimental to Canada.'[35]

By 'agents' and 'fifth columnists' these Leftists meant Ukrainian Canadian supporters of the UNF and of the Hetman group, although essentially all those whose support was not unequivocally behind the Soviet system in Ukraine were also targeted. As for the dizzying reversal of the Left's attitude towards the war, that embarrassing detail was conveniently forgotten by most.

Nationalist circles fared little better than the Left, although they ran into trouble at different stages during the war years. For example, the UNF's eighth national congress, held in Winnipeg between 28 and 30 August 1941, was an event very closely monitored by RCMP undercover agents. Special constables were employed, including Ukrainian Canadians like Michael Petrowsky. Petrowsky compiled a lengthy report on what these Ukrainian Canadians were up to.[36] RCMP commissioner S.T. Wood, in forwarding this secret document to Mr Justice T.C. Davis, a deputy minister at the Department of National War Services in Ottawa, pointed out that while congress resolutions expressing loyalty to Canada and the British Empire were passed, 'there is no guarantee that the sentiments have the unanimous approval of the rank and file.'[37]

Petrowsky, who, given the breadth of his reportage, seems to have enjoyed access to a number of Ukrainian Canadian leaders, provided a much more detailed analysis. He suggested that many Ukrainian Canadians were uncertain about how serious Prime Minister Churchill and President Roosevelt were when, after their first face-to-face meeting at Placentia Bay, Newfoundland, between 9 and 12 August 1941, they had enunciated the eight points of the Atlantic Charter. Since there had been no 'clear cut declaration' on the 'Ukrainian Question' by the Anglo-American powers, many Ukrainian Canadians were confused about whether this document, which created expectations about Wilsonian standards guiding postwar international relations, provided any real solution to the issue of Ukrainian independence. Certainly points 2 and 3 confirmed that Britain and the United States of America desired 'to see no territorial changes that do not accord with the freely expressed wishes of the peoples concerned; they respect the right of all peoples to choose the form of government under which they will live; and they wish to see sovereign rights and self-government restored to those who have been forcibly deprived of them'; and these points were tantalizing. But would these principles be implemented? Would they be binding on the Soviet Union? Would they be applied to Ukraine? No one knew.

Petrowsky pointed out just how important this issue was to the Ukrainian Canadian community. After speaking with Teodor Datzkiw, the nominal leader of the Hetmantsi, he reported that Dr Datzkiw felt that since 'the idea of Ukrainian independence was dear to every Ukrainian, no matter under what conditions it existed,' it was likely that 'a certain segment of the UNF members' would not really support their leadership's publicly enunciated loyalty to Canada if they came to believe that other powers, including those of the Axis, might guarantee independence for Ukraine. Dr Mykyta Mandryka, a social democrat, was even more frank in his assessment of the Federation's sympathizers. For him, Wasyl Swystun, who had by this time left the USRL which he had helped create, had become nothing more than the UNF's 'hired Negro.' Even though Mandryka acknowledged that he had not personally attended the UNF congress, he confidently asserted that

> the majority of the UNF members and leaders are at heart enemies of democracy. They pay lip service to democracy for official consumption but privately they tactfully refute what the organ of the UNF, the 'New Pathway,' has said editorially about democracy. This is the tactic they use in order to spare themselves the consequences during war-time. Their organization is based on totalitarian ideology, despite claims to the contrary and the evident display of Canadian loyalty and the support given to Canada's war effort.[38]

Petrowsky concluded, after having listened to various contradictory opinions about the loyalty of Ukrainian Canadian organizations to

Canada, that the great majority of the UNF's members were hoping for a defeat of Soviet Russia, believing that if this happened 'Ukraine would emerge an independent country.' However, in order to demonstrate their loyalty to Canada and, they hoped, to court recognition and favour in any postwar peace settlement that might include the 'Ukrainian Question' on its agenda, they would probably support Canada's war effort loyally enough. As well, Nazi Germany's policy of enslavement for Ukrainians in Europe was already disaffecting those who had once been optimistic regarding the nature of German designs for eastern Europe. In short, these Ukrainian Canadian nationalists might not be absolutely happy about British war aims or the British Empire's support for Poland and the USSR, but they did not constitute any discernible internal security threat to the country. Their loyalty and assistance to the national war effort should simply be accepted at 'face value,' and the 'only logical attitude' towards the Federation's membership would be one of 'cautious watchfulness' to ensure that no genuine security threat emerged from within its ranks.[39] The government concurred.

Some members of the Canadian public were less sure about Ukrainian Canadian loyalty. For example, a Mr J.M. Gilroy of Northville, Alberta, writing to the editor of the *Edmonton Bulletin* on 6 March 1942, questioned the fidelity not only of the German, Italian, and Japanese minorities in Canada but also of the Ukrainian, alleging that while Canada's Anglo-Saxons had gone off to fight, members of these minorities had, for the most part, come 'to a ready-made British freedom which gave them legal protection to vilify us and to sneer at the country which gave them land, food, work, shelter, aid in sickness and in unemployment – how quick they were to rush for relief! – and how slow they are to rally to the colours.'[40] Echoing sentiments about Ukrainian Canadian loyalty that had been heard only a few decades before, he added that in his 'alien district' not one single man of the Ukrainian race had volunteered for active service. Perhaps the time had come to round up these aliens and make them fight, not 'for the dear old Ukraine' but for Canada? If necessary, a 'Loyal Legion' composed 'of the same sort of people who saved this country in other dark hours' should be organized to do what was necessary about the 'aliens.' There were 'only two sides,' Gilroy concluded, 'us' and them. He left no doubt about which side he felt the Ukrainians and the other ethnic minorities he had listed stood on.[41] They were the enemy, to be watched and, if necessary, interned.

However 'vile and pernicious' Gilroy's accusations were to a USRL activist like Peter Lazarowich, the latter had little choice but that of responding promptly to what he decried as Gilroy's 'morbid flights of the imagination,' 'prejudice,' and 'inaccuracy.' Still, even Lazarowich could not deny that some Ukrainian Canadians were uneasy and hesitant about enlisting. There was a reason for their reticence, Lazarowich riposted: 'No man with any self-respect will wish to risk his life for a country in which he is being continuously treated and looked down upon as an enemy alien, in spite of everything he might do to prove his loyalty.'[42]

If leading members of the USRL, perhaps the most avowedly pro-Canadian and pro-Empire of all the Ukrainian Canadian groups, felt uneasy at this time, how did the others feel? It is difficult to say. But certainly men like Lazarowich seem to have believed genuinely that, if only they kept reasserting their unflinching loyalty to Canada, then someday everyone would believe in it. Constant repetition of this theme did not, however, prove as convincing as Lazarowich and his associates would have liked.

Concerns over the loyalty of Ukrainian Canadians were not confined to the letter-to-the-editor pages of provincial newspapers. Officials in Ottawa found, to their dismay and probably to their persistent annoyance, that the activities of some Ukrainian Canadians had troubling implications for Canadian foreign policy. In the spring of 1940 there had been protests from the Polish embassy about Ukrainian Canadians and their ties with Ukrainian nationalists in Europe.[43] And even before the war, Polish authorities had provided the British government with detailed studies attempting to prove that Ukrainian 'spies and provocateurs' belonging to the Ukrainian Military Organization were maintaining close ties to Ukrainian groups in Canada.[44] While Norman Robertson of the Department of External Affairs would agree with the Polish consul general in Montreal that Canada's Ukrainians were indeed becoming 'very troublesome,' he did advise the Poles to adopt a more conciliatory approach to the Ukrainians in Western Ukraine, believing that a moderate policy there might quell the persistent lobbying of Ukrainian Canadians on behalf of their compatriots.[45]

Polish protests were not the only official complaints lodged with Ottawa over the behaviour of Ukrainian Canadians. In May 1943 Prime Minister Mackenzie King, who would reserve the role of secretary of state for external affairs for himself until September 1946, received a memorandum from Robertson which described an interview he had had with the first Soviet ambassador to Canada, Feodor Gosuev. The Soviet diplomat had insisted that 'Canadian Ukrainian Nationalists' be censured, for their newspapers were editorializing about the creation of an independent Ukrainian state. That, in Gosuev's view, could only be described as taking a 'pro-Fascist stand,' for advocating the 'breaking up of the territories of [Canada's] ally, the Soviet Union' amounted to nothing less than a species of aiding the enemy.

Robertson's reply was indicative of Canadian government thinking on such matters. He pointed out that while Ukrainians did indeed constitute 'a very large bloc' in Canada, they were absolutely not 'a factor in influencing Canadian government policy.' He went on to explain to the Soviet ambassador that while Ottawa would 'be much happier if [Ukrainians] would look at the world through Canadian eyes and think of themselves solely as Canadian citizens,' the process of assimilation 'takes time.' It would be more tactically sound, he counselled, for the Soviets simply to ignore Ukrainian Canadians than to try to get the Canadian government to suppress 'offending articles' in the ethnic press. After all, he added, these articles were 'not really important.'[46]

Just three weeks later, Robertson addressed a long, secret memorandum to the Canadian ambassador to the USSR, Dana Wilgress, who was at that time stationed in Kuibyshev. In this cable Robertson took up the issue of Ukrainian Canadian nationalism. While pointing out that Ukrainian nationalists in Canada were 'quite genuinely' supporting the war effort, he recognized that they had certainly not abandoned their objective of independence for Ukraine, although they were being 'very discreet' in their public statements on the 'Ukrainian Question.' RCMP surveillance of the major Ukrainian Canadian groups had so far revealed no serious internal security problem 'in spite of their interest in Ukrainian independence.' Robertson then pointed out that the situation was being 'watched' to ensure that 'extreme statements' were avoided. But, concerned over the Soviet response to such minor activities on the part of 'Ukrainian Canadian nationalists,' Robertson asked Wilgress to advise him if any further references to these Ukrainian Canadian activities were made in the USSR.[47] Meanwhile, he assured Wilgress, Canadian officials would continue to monitor this ethnic minority, a task made easier by the coming into being of a group known as the Ukrainian Canadian Committee in November 1940. Since the laboured formation of this group represents a notably artful intervention into Ukrainian Canadian affairs by the Canadian government, its genesis deserves a more detailed description.

'A Surgical Intervention'

There can be little doubt that the overwhelming majority of Ukrainian Canadians were loyal to Canada during the Second World War. Even if the wildly exuberant manner in which their spokesmen reacted to the declaration of war suggests that they were deliberately attempting emphatically and publicly to prove how unreservedly Ukrainian Canadians were for 'the King, for Canada, and for the whole British Empire!' there is no reason to doubt their sincerity in general terms.[48] But even such expressions of fealty were apparently not convincing enough for Ottawa's men. The loyalty of Ukrainian Canadians remained questionable in the eyes of some high government officials and a significant portion of the general public. Why? Because their various lobbying efforts, particularly on behalf of Ukrainian independence, though they had little if any discernible impact on Canadian foreign policy-making (indeed, these memoranda and petitions were almost routinely disparaged and rarely replied to), had been so voluminous that they had developed a significant public profile, one which reminded government decision-makers and the Anglo-Canadian majority of the presence of a large population of unassimilated Ukrainians in their midst. In peacetime the antics of such a minority were most often perceived as being of little concern. But in wartime, when the question of the citizenry's loyalty becomes paramount, the allegiance of this large Ukrainian constituency could not so easily be overlooked. And it was not.

Having moved swiftly to enervate the relatively homogeneous Ukrainian Canadian Left, Canadian officials pondered how they could best deal with the majority of Ukrainian Canadians, a population known to be organized into several major competing organizations. That they were being watched did not escape the attention of at least some Ukrainian Canadians. As Dr Vladimir J. Kaye-Kysilewsky, who had been serving since 1942 with the Department of National War Service's Committee on Co-operation in Canadian Citizenship, wrote, the 'Ottawa government seems to be very interested in Ukrainian affairs.'[49] At first it was thought that, as long as one or two 'reliable Ukrainian Canadians' could be brought to Ottawa, the government could utilize their knowledge of the community to ensure adequate communication between itself and this ethnic minority, by establishing 'some kind of centre of information.'[50]

In response to these official rumblings – of which Dr Kaye, and perhaps others, informed them – a voluntary merger of two of the leading Ukrainian Canadian organizations, the Ukrainian National Federation and the Brotherhood of Ukrainian Catholics, took place on 3 February 1940. The new body, known as the Representative Committee of Ukrainians in Canada (RCUC), quickly distributed literature proclaiming that its purpose was to cooperate with Canada and the British Empire in order to help win the war. The authors added parenthetically that they also hoped an independent Ukraine would emerge as a result of a geopolitical restructuring of Europe in the postwar period. Anxious not to be perceived as lacking in loyalty to Canada, adherents of the Ukrainian Self-Reliance League, the Hetman movement, and the Ukrainian Workers' League – an odd assemblage, when one recalls the antipathy of the USRL to the Hetmantsi in earlier years – united on 7 February 1940 to form the Central Committee of Ukrainians in Canada (CCUC), with aims not far different from those of the Representative Committee.[51] Beyond these two consolidations, however, there seemed to be little further hope of progress towards Ukrainian Canadian unity. As Kaye lamented in August 1940, 'these two Committees have not been able to find common ground and to unite their forces,' even though they had 'almost *identical* aims.'[52] After he had toured western Canada and met, in his own words, 'everybody who counts in Ukrainian Canadian life,' he wrote how imperative it was for Ukrainian Canadians to realize that it was in their own best interests to unite and dedicate all their resources to helping Canada and the United Kingdom win the war. If they did so, he said, they could then confidently expect support for the Ukrainian cause during future peace negotiations.[53] This was a theme Kaye had used before and one he would repeat many times, always appealing to Ukrainian Canadians' sentiments respecting the homeland while playing on their fears of what might await them in Canada should they be suspected of having 'divided loyalties' during wartime.[54] Undoubtedly, his line of reasoning reached a sympathetic audience in Ukrainian Canadian circles. At the time it was made, in mid-1940, the Soviet Union was still an ally of Nazi Germany and, at least theoretically, aligned against the British Empire. Poland and Czechoslovakia, both of which had been destroyed, were no longer players in the Ukrainian situation. These circumstances held out some promise for Ukrainian independence, as Kaye vigorously pointed out to his many correspondents and listeners, thereby diligently fulfilling his role as one of several government bureaucrats charged with managing the Ukrainian Canadian community.

Whether such considerations would have resulted in a voluntary union of the Representative and Central Committees will never be known. The pressures of wartime did not allow for any gentle manoeuvring on the part of Ottawa. Instead, in circumstances which still remain somewhat unclear, a handful of Ukrainian Canadians representing the leading secular and religious organizations were brought together in Winnipeg's Fort Garry Hotel between 6 and 8 November 1940, and from within that conclave the Ukrainian Canadian Committee was somehow negotiated, or impelled, into existence.[55] This new committee began its existence as an ad hoc structure composed of five organizations, The Brotherhood of Ukrainian Catholics, the Ukrainian Self-Reliance League, the Ukrainian National Federation, the United Hetman Organization, and the Ukrainian Workers' League. Its motto conveyed its motivating principle: In Unity Our Strength. Delicate deliberations within this new umbrella group resulted in the presidency of a Ukrainian Catholic, Monsignor Vasyl Kushnir, with the first vice-presidency going to a Ukrainian Orthodox priest who also represented the USRL, Honorary Captain Reverend Semen Sawchuck. The following were also elected: the Federation's Volodymyr Kossar as second vice-president; the Self-Reliance League's Jaroslaw Arsenych, Canada's first Ukrainian lawyer, as secretary general; the Hetman supporter Dr Teodor Datzkiw as treasurer; and the Ukrainian Workers' League's T. Chxwaliboga as financial secretary. No provisions were made for converting this Ukrainian Canadian Committee into a permanent representative or coordinating body for Ukrainians in Canada. Everyone apparently agreed that the UCC was to be only a temporary construct, a means for rallying Ukrainian Canadians behind the war effort, a body that would continue no longer than the duration of the war.[56] Significantly, clergymen rather than secular political leaders were entrusted with the highest positions in the Committee, even if an attempt was made to provide some measure of organizational balance by assigning other national executive posts to members of the smaller groups, and thereby ensure that every group had some members in the Committee's guiding executive.

A commentary offered by RCMP special constable Michael Petrowsky, who had been engaged in undercover work among Ukrainian

Canadians previously, explains why representatives of Ukrainian Canadian organizations which had up to that date railed against one another rather suddenly found it expedient to unite. Petrowsky summed up his explanation by noting that some leading Ukrainian Canadian activists were still in 'fear of the barbed wire fence.'[57] In other words, the prospect of internment and other repressive measures played a critical role in convincing the leaders of somewhat antagonistic Ukrainian Canadian organizations that they had little choice but to come together under the UCC umbrella. Among those who set it up were some who, like the USRL's Julian Stechishin, had personally experienced registration as an 'enemy alien' during the First World War. Most of the others could well recall those frightfully intimidating times. They also had before them the example of what had happened to their counterparts on the Ukrainian Canadian Left, men who, at just about the same time as the UCC was being constituted, were being watched, and in some cases hunted down and imprisoned. Whether any of the leaders within the UCC also knew that plans had already been laid within RCMP and Ministry of Justice circles to provide for the internment of 'enemy aliens' – not only German-Canadian members of the Bund but also Ukrainian nationalists – is not known. But there can be no denying that in wartime all of them well understood that Ukrainian Canadian activism of any sort might be perceived as inimical to the Canadian state's interests. And that could end up imperilling their own freedom.

Public reaction to the establishment of the UCC was generally favourable – a 27 November 1940 *Winnipeg Free Press* article endorsed this development with the headline 'All for One – One for All' – but few outside government circles realized the degree to which the Committee could be labelled Made in Ottawa.[58] Likely no one even considered whether the UCC might have any long-term impact on Ukrainian Canadian society, given the general feeling that it was intended to last only for the length of the war. As a result, the wartime organizational infrastructure that was accepted by, or imposed upon, the UCC at its inception, based on a formula which required the constituent groups to reach decisions by unanimous consensus rather than through a simple majority vote, bequeathed a crippling legacy to Ukrainian Canadian society. Time and again in the decades following the war, factional disputes impeded organizational flexibility, intelligent planning, and decision-making within the Committee, as one or another group vetoed various initiatives, imparting to the UCC a relentless and predictable orthodoxy. Even if the Committee would play an influential role in Ukrainian Canadian life after the war, its intrinsic limitations remained a debilitating source of numerous problems, precipitating a serious decline in its relevance. Today it is of far less consequence than it might have become.

Statements to the effect that the UCC was a superstructure erected principally by non-Ukrainians in order to manipulate Ukrainian Canadian affairs have not gone unchallenged. But this thesis seems more incontrovertible now that certain government documents, particularly those concerning the role played by an enigmatic and dapper Englishman, Tracy Erasmus Philipps, have become available.[59]

Philipps, who would describe himself as a 'soldier on special service,'[60] brought to his endeavours the idea that since 'citizens of recent European origin' constituted nearly one-quarter of the Canadian population at the outbreak of the war, this strategically placed, foreign-born population had to be instilled with a sense of allegiance to the Allied war effort and to Canada in particular.

> Since half the war has to be won in the shipyards and factories of North America, this Labour force ... is still regarded by the agents of the Russo-Germans, who are occupying their Old Countries, [as] a weak joint, in our harness ... I have now mixed in every foreign-born settlement and industrial center in Canada, well off the Anglo-Saxon track ... There are so many Canadas to understand and they understand each other so little ... The foreign-born from Eastern Europe have more reason than the British-born to appreciate what a good wicket they are on in North America. They are feeling rather neglected right now. But, with a little nursing, ninety per cent of them are likely to be more Canadian than the British and, in one way, 'more royalist than the King.' Meanwhile, in the background, they are the offshoots and complement to that (to us vital) human zone of the margin of Europe between the Russian and the Prussian empires from the Arctic Finns to the oilmen of the Caucasus. We shall need them, both here and there, not disunited but linked.[61]

However florid his prose, Philipps did appreciate that among the huge foreign-born populations in North America, and particularly in Canada, it was the Ukrainians who were 'the most difficult, the least known,' and, after the Germans, 'the most numerous' group.[62] He felt it regrettable that the 'English-speaking peoples' were only just discovering this 'unknown Nation,' and at that only because of their own fight for existence. He decried how the English-speaking world had previously 'refused to be interested' in Ukraine, 'which they still refuse to interest in our cause.'[63] For Ukrainians, on the other hand, this was 'the most momentous moment of their history,' which Hitler surely could not afford to fail to exploit, given the Ukrainian people's 'mystic dreams (just those visions for which men fight like mad men) for independence.'[64] In Canada, as elsewhere in North America, Ukrainians might be passively loyal, but this was 'not enough' for winning the war. Victory might well be an immediate aim, but more desirable was for Ukrainians to be consolidated slowly into the Canadian nation, a goal Philipps believed should be the long-term imperative of the government in Ottawa.[65] Ukrainians were, in his consideration, still thinking 'foreign' and 'almost every community is over-organized in a non-Canadian sense.'[66] How, Philipps wondered, using a mechanical analogy, could this 'foreign matter, like steel filings, [be attracted] from our outer edge to our centre?'[67] His answer was, through the process of 'Canadianism,'[68] which he said would involve a frank assessment by the Allies of the relationship between their publicly proclaimed commitment to the 'freedom of nations' as promulgated in the Atlantic Charter, and the question of Ukrainian independence – this assessment had to be made, if only to counter what 'the enemy offers.'[69] As well, the government must begin consciously to build up 'a dynamic and cohesive national mysticism for Canadianism and Canada,' through a delicate process of crafting increased confidence between foreign-born communities and the state.[70] Mutual trust, respect, and a genuine dialogue would, in time, become the agents through which the Ukrainians of Canada would be transformed into good and loyal citizens of the Dominion, or so Philipps argued.

He would find, to his dismay, that this was not what the government had in mind. Few in authority listened to his sage advice. For however sensitive Philipps's perceptions might have been, particularly his views about how the state could best foster a genuine loyalty to Canada among Ukrainians, the exigencies of war prompted the authorities to feel they must employ a more 'rapid, drastic and aggressive' method of achieving the twin goals of 'unification of new Canadians' and 'elimination of their discords.' To do so they used Philipps's services as a negotiator and expert, but they ignored the philosophical tenets upon which he had constructed his keen appreciation of the Ukrainian minority in Canada.

Being a good soldier, Philipps did what he was told to do by those he was sworn to obey. But, perhaps somewhat remorseful about what he had been forced to do, he candidly described the measures he had taken in dealing with the Ukrainian Canadians, whom he had united under the banner of the UCC, as a 'surgical intervention.' Certainly it was an intervention which had enabled him, 'in the time allowed,' to unite the 'half dozen discordant groups of Ukrainians in Canada.' But, he added, having to do things in this manner had been a 'regrettable wartime necessity.' He also cautioned that the 'permanence of the cure' – by which he meant the integration of Ukrainians into Canadian life rather than the manipulation of them in order to ensure their good behaviour – depended on the period and quality 'of subsequent nursing.'[71] He also described the method he would have preferred to employ, one which, while requiring patience and sympathy and no doubt 'slower,' was a 'sure' way of drawing the Ukrainian community 'towards the heart of Canada which is their only real and proper common ground.'[72] That method would, however, have demanded an input of time, common sense, and empathy that no one in Ottawa was willing to allow Philipps in his dealings with Ukrainians or any of Canada's other minorities. And so the Committee he cobbled together was, and would remain, little more than an improvisation, an unwieldy creature trapeezing between many blind spots and a few high wire moments, of which the Ukrainian Canadian refugee relief operations yet to be described would perhaps be the most daring.

Those in Ottawa who considered themselves hard-headed realists had rejected Philipps's masterful vision of immigrant Canadianism, preferring instead to monitor, and thereby control, the course of Ukrainian Canadian affairs through this newly minted Committee. But before they were able to do so, a radical transformation of the international situation, brought about by Nazi Germany's invasion of the Soviet Union, forced Ottawa's mandarins overnight to search for a discreet means of distancing themselves from the very Committee they had played such a pivotal role in fathering. For the UCC's patently obvious anti-Soviet orientation, which may have been welcome before 22 June 1941, could no longer be countenanced officially after the Soviet Union was forced into what became its wartime alliance with the Western powers. And so the UCC, created by Ottawa's men only a few months earlier, was all but abandoned. Simultaneously, it became imperative to the government to review its suppression of the Communist Party of Canada and affiliated groups like the Ukrainian Labour Farmer Temple Association. As could have been predicted, this task was made difficult by the fierce polemics that were quickly launched against the Committee by the resuscitated Ukrainian Canadian Left, attacks which singled out men like Philipps and Kaye for particular scorn. As early as December 1940, a left-wing American-Ukrainian newspaper published an editorial entitled 'Ukrainian Canadian Unity?' which criticized the UCC and Philipps's role in setting it up.[73] Philipps himself observed, in a report submitted on 13 January 1941, that by 21 December of that year 'Jewish-owned Newsletters' had begun attacking the UCC and his person, an effort furthered in Canada through a well-synchronized distribution of mimeographed literature spread largely by communists and their fellow travellers.[74] Echoing what he had written only a few days earlier, he observed that it was essential that the newly formed Committee be 'actively nursed and supported,' for otherwise it would 'not be able to weather the storms now raised against it.'[75] Even though the Committee had, by then, existed for nearly two months, nothing was being done by Ottawa to help get it established, nor would this indifference lift in the months ahead. By the early spring of 1941 the situation had grown so gloomy that even Dr Kaye started complaining, in a letter to Philipps, 'It would be a great pity if all our labour would be lost because Ottawa did not find it important enough to develop what you started.'[76]

The Ukrainian Canadian Left was quick to take advantage of the awkward situation the Committee found itself in after the Soviet Union became an Allied power. Mercilessly, its editorialists and speakers browbeat their adversary. By September 1941 the Left had regrouped sufficiently to set up the Ukrainian Association to Aid the Fatherland, many of whose leaders were members of the Communist Party of Canada, as police reports submitted to Robertson in External Affairs confirmed. These RCMP reports stressed that the new organization's activities were 'communist-inspired ... and subject to the policy of the Communist Party of Canada.'[77] In January 1942 one of the Left's newspapers, the Toronto-based *Ukrainian Life*, carried a sarcastic editorial captioned 'By Whom and Why Was the KUK Given Birth?' and a subsequent editorial was even fiercer in denouncing the Committee's leadership as little more than a 'handful of traitors' who were harmful to Canada and to Ukraine.[78] For some outsiders this squabbling was amusing. Norman Robertson, writing to a UCC sympathizer, Professor George Simpson of the University of Saskatchewan, pointed out that he had recently read a translation of the *Ukrainian Life* editorial that dealt with the Committee's 'birth' and found the tale, as presented, 'not without humour.' Given this attitude, and his apparent indifference to the editorial's explicit statement that the Committee had been created by the government, it is unlikely that Robertson, or anyone else in authority, took Philipps's secret report on the urgent need for protecting the Committee from 'attack by Communistic Ukrainians' very seriously.[79] Certainly no move was ever sanctioned, as Philipps had urged, 'definitely' to discourage and stop anti-UCC propaganda.

Understandably, given the government's apparent lack of interest in 'nursing' the Committee or even in shielding it from the pro-Soviet Ukrainian Canadians' attacks, many Committee supporters were left baffled. They had been brought together, or so they reckoned, by the very government which was now doing little or nothing to help them repel the verbal abuse they were being subjected to from the Left, or even to block the physical assaults launched against their supporters by the Left's thugs. Thus, when a former ULFTA temple located at 300 Bathurst Street in Toronto, which the UNF had acquired as a result of the government's confiscation of ULFTA properties in 1940, was raided by Ukrainian Leftists in mid-October 1942, nothing was done by the authorities to bring the culprits to justice. Similarly, when a Victory Loan parade held in St Catharines was disrupted, reportedly by 'former members and sympathizers of the now-illegal Communist Party of Canada,' the government also took no action.[80] The frustration of leading Committee members over this rather atypical government passivity is apparent in the correspondence of Wasyl Burianyk, a Ukrainian Canadian veteran of the First World War and one of the USRL's ideologues, publicists, and leading members. He complained to his colleague in the Department of National War Services, Professor Simpson: 'I'll be absolutely candid in telling you that the members of the Committee cannot figure out the millequetoast attitude of Ottawa towards the harmful activities of the Communists, especially in the case of Ukrainians ... This communist scum is being given all the latitude to besmirch, denounce and publicly cast vile aspersions against individuals and organizations which are opposed to communism. Our people resent this very much.'[81]

Such entreaties had no noticeable effect on government thinking or policies. Instead, covert surveillance of all Ukrainian Canadian activities was stepped up, the RCMP and External Affairs agreeing on the need to keep 'close checks' not only on the Left, to ensure that the new Association to Aid the Fatherland remained 'in conformity with its avowed aims and those of Canada in the war effort,'[82] but also on the Ukrainian Canadian Centre and Right, for exactly the same reasons. Whole new government agencies, such as the Wartime Information Board and the Committee on Co-operation in Canadian Citizenship, were formed and entrusted with developing policies for, among other things, coping with Ukrainian Canadian issues.[83] The RCMP's informants continued to monitor the community in general and to compile lengthy and detailed reports on events like the first national UCC congress, held in Winnipeg from 22 to 24 June 1943.[84]

Canada's officialdom had made it clear that no hint of disloyalty from Canada's Ukrainians would be tolerated. This was, of course, reasonable enough, especially in wartime. But this was not all that had been insisted upon. They also hoped to 'weave' all Ukrainians 'into the fabric of Canada,' in the process making them over into true Canadians, who would 'think [only] in terms of Canada and not [of] the land of their birth or origin.'[85] Of course, accepting of this 'wiser course,' which is how those bureaucrats who advocated assimilation described their goal, would have entailed a total abandonment of the Ukrainian Canadians' 'European hopes and ambitions.' That, in effect, would mean nothing less than the renunciation of the most basic value of the organized Ukrainian Canadian community, nothing less than its voluntary de-nationalization, a giving up of its abiding interest in the fate of Ukraine. This is a critical point. What was really being asked of the Ukrainian Canadians was that they stop being Ukrainian. What did that mean in practice? From Ottawa's view it was not the language these citizens used at home, or their religious affiliation, or their folk customs which mattered, but rather their ongoing political attachment to 'European hopes and ambitions.' That was the problem that had to be dealt with. So while immigrant culture posed no threat to Canada, any political attachment to the 'Old World' was disagreeable.[86] In contrast, this Ukrainian minority's persistent interest in a far-distant homeland not only complicated Canadian foreign policy but simultaneously 'retarded acculturation.' In Ottawa, this was unacceptable. Perhaps it is less unacceptable now; but it has always been unpalatable.

Ukrainian Canadian community leaders had seized quickly upon, and would often repeat, Governor-General Lord Tweedsmuir's 1936 remark 'You will all be better Canadians for being also good Ukrainians,' believing these words had somehow legitimized their commitment to maintaining a Ukrainian political and cultural identity in

Canada. In reality, identifying oneself as a Ukrainian while residing in Canada has often proved to have unfortunate consequences.[87] It is around this issue – what being, acting as, and remaining a Ukrainian in Canada entails – that much of the controversy over aid to Ukrainian political refugees overseas, and later over their integration into the existing Ukrainian Canadian community structures, would swirl. The argument would involve not only Ukrainians but government officials on both sides of the Atlantic. Out of the hurly-burly of that formative exchange many of the characteristics of Ukrainian Canadian society in the postwar period would be determined. By the time it was all over, the descendants of the stalwart pioneering peasants of yesteryear might well have paused to ask themselves if their forefathers had indeed reached the promised land. As for 'the man who knew,' Tracy Philipps, what came to pass would hardly have surprised him. Long before the war ended, Philipps had observed that if the Canadian government did not have the courage to be frank about its motives and principles in its dealings with the 'foreign-born,' Ottawa's mandarins would fail in one of their most important tasks, which was to 'consolidate the nation.' They would also end up believing that they had an internal security threat on their hands, one which required spending great resources on the preparation of 'voluminous reports about Ukrainians as potential enemies or at least as rather doubtful friends.' He was right.

4 'Saskatchewan's Son':
Ukrainian Canadian Soldiers Encounter
the Displaced Persons, 1941–1945

'Just Like a Bit of Home'

When the S.S. *Strathern* sailed for England in December 1941, carrying troops and war materiel across the Atlantic, it also ferried over the twenty-seven-year-old son of an early Ukrainian pioneer in Canada. This man was not in search of freedom or free land. He was headed to war. He believed it was the duty of every able-bodied Ukrainian Canadian to serve in this moment of great peril. Over a quarter of a century before, his father had travelled in the opposite direction, leaving behind the poverty and wars of his Western Ukrainian homeland, planning to homestead in a heavily Ukrainian-populated area of the Canadian Prairies, near Peterson, Saskatchewan. Neither the pioneer father nor the soldier son would really know the other. The settler, Mychajlo, died in 1915, shortly after his son, Bohdan, was born. But for the Yellow Creek schoolteacher-turned-soldier, a volunteer for overseas duty with the Royal Canadian Air Force, the image he cherished of his father was that of a man who had fought for the Ukrainian cause. A 1944 entry in Bohdan's personal diary observed that, just as his father before him, he intended to dedicate his life to serving his people, the Ukrainians.[1] And that is what Bohdan became, a servant of his people.

The young man's family name was Panchuk. There can be no doubt that it was Gordon Richard Bohdan Panchuk who played a pivotal, if not the singularly most important, role among that relatively small group of Ukrainian Canadians who set up, directed, and, in the end,

shut down Ukrainian Canadian refugee relief, rehabilitation, and resettlement operations among the Ukrainian displaced persons in postwar
Europe. As Panchuk's background played no small part in influencing
how he would interact with these political refugees, with the authorities overseeing them, and with other Ukrainian Canadian individuals
and organizations, it deserves consideration.

Although Bohdan Panchuk grew up in Canada, the setting in which
he was born had a peculiarly Ukrainian quality to it. A rural enclave,
part of that vast arc of Ukrainian bloc settlements which stretched
across the West, his birthplace retained its agrarian ethnic quality well
into the late 1920s. For all intents and purposes, Panchuk grew up in
more of a Ukrainian Canadian than an Anglo-Canadian Protestant
world. Years later he would recall that 'there was no outside world' for
him and for the other Ukrainian Canadians who lived in this bloc settlement.[2] Of course, that outside world did exist, and in 1928 Panchuk
first began living in an Anglo-Canadian, non-rural environment when
he moved to Saskatoon to continue his education. Subsequently, he
lived in both Meacham and Saskatoon, where he completed grades
nine through twelve and then took the one year of Normal School he
required to qualify as a schoolteacher. According to all reports he was a
diligent and intelligent pupil.

It was during the 1930s that his involvement with the Petro Mohyla
Institute came about, 'by accident.' He would also belong to the independent Ukrainian Greek Orthodox Church of Canada and the youth
wing of the Ukrainian Self-Reliance League, known as the Soiuz
ukrainskoi molodi kanady (Association of Ukrainian Canadian Youth,
or SUMK, established in 1931).[3] He remained committed to all four
organizations until his death in Montreal in 1987. Not surprisingly, the
attitudes he held about his personal identity as a Ukrainian Canadian,
and the obligations he felt he had both to the land where he was born
and to the land of his forefathers, were inculcated in him at this time.
His world-view was very much that of the liberal-democratic founders
of the Ukrainian Self-Reliance League, based on principles to which he
would remain true until the end of his life. For Panchuk, the question
of where his loyalties lay and of how his views might differ from those
of other Ukrainian Canadians could be given a straightforward
answer:

I think ... where we differed most from the other Ukrainian organizations here [was that] while we felt we should be devoted to helping solve the Ukrainian problem of lacking an independent homeland, we kept maintaining that the only way to serve it was, first of all, to be good Canadians. By being a loyal Canadian ... you could influence other Canadians and the Canadian government into policies supporting the liberation of Ukraine, which we all believed was necessary ... I think that this was what inspired our generation, at least my circle ... [We] didn't want to be seen as part of some European political organization, lest these ties appear suspect to the Canadian government ... Ukrainians in Canada had endured several years of internment operations in this country ... because many of them ... had been suspected of having dubious overseas sympathies and loyalties ... We accepted the British Empire ... that the flag was the Union Jack, that our mother country was Britain, and the Empire.[4]

While Panchuk, and many like him, often said that one could 'be a good Canadian [and] be a good Ukrainian, [because] both could be combined and worked out together,' whether they held to this belief more out of hope than real conviction is a question not easily answered.[5] What is certain is that Panchuk recognized that his willingness to get involved with Ukrainian issues, both overseas and in Canada, placed him in the ranks of a minority, even among those born of Ukrainian parents. As he remarked, 'the masses just wanted to be Canadian, to be left alone,'[6] and the 'average Ukrainian Canadian' of his generation 'just didn't care about what was happening in Europe that much.'[7]

Panchuk did, and he would energetically and impetuously dedicate his highly strung 'thruster's' temperament and nearly a decade of his life to working overseas with the Ukrainian displaced persons, dispensing aid and advice and helping resettle them in Canada and elsewhere. These labours reflected his dedication both to the Ukrainian and to the Canadian components of his identity. By saving nationally conscious Ukrainian refugees from repatriation to the USSR and assisting in their relocation to Canada, he nursed the dream that his efforts would infuse existing Ukrainian Canadian groups with new blood which, in turn, would ensure the maintenance of a viable Ukrainian Canadian corpus. He reasoned that a large-scale immigration of Ukrainian DPs would bring to the land of his birth benefits of exactly the same kind as previous Ukrainian immigrations had already bequeathed. In those years Panchuk never questioned the validity of these beliefs. Instead, he became so totally absorbed by his work and his vision that, by the end of his tenure overseas, he thought of himself as something of a father figure for the Ukrainian DPs, an authority to whom they should turn for counsel when they got around to organizing themselves and whose advice on how to behave in the diaspora they must never question. This well-intentioned if somewhat paternalistic attitude would, in time, disrupt his efforts among the refugees and prejudice his relations with others involved in the relief and resettlement operations, imparting an acridity to these endeavours which belies the undeniable and great good accomplished by him and his co-workers.

But that disillusionment was still far in the future. Shortly after disembarking in Great Britain, Panchuk sought out the tiny Ukrainian community of Manchester.[8] His joy at having found a familiar Ukrainian niche in a foreign land was unmistakable, as he promptly recorded in his diary: 'Who would have thought that it could be so, that far out in England we would find our own colony, just like a bit of home.'[9]

'A Very Unusual Set Up'

Finding the presence of this Ukrainian community consoling, Panchuk soon began canvassing to determine whether other Ukrainian Canadian soldiers felt a similar need for Ukrainian company in their overseas postings. Many did. When what he billed as a 'Get-Together' was held in Manchester, on 7 January 1943, Ukrainian Christmas Day, some forty Ukrainian Canadian soldiers participated. For the 'Second Get-Together,' held to co-celebrate Ukrainian Easter, 2 May 1943, and Mothers' Day, over seventy-five Ukrainian Canadian soldiers turned out.[10] Encouraged, Panchuk and some friends organized the Soiuz ukrainskykh kanadiiskykh voiakiv (Ukrainian Canadian Servicemen's Association, or UCSA, or Servicemen's Association).[11] This was the body around which the Central Ukrainian Relief Bureau (CURB, or the Bureau), and several related refugee aid groups, would later be structured.

One of the most notable characteristics of the Servicemen's Association was that its ranks included young men and women representing all the leading Ukrainian Canadian organizations and religious faiths. For several years, a reflection of wartime camaraderie, these Ukrainian Canadians of diverse backgrounds and political leanings intermingled, largely without the friction which undermined interwar Ukrainian Canadian society and had been overcome only with external prodding. As one UCSA member would record, 'it was a very unusual set up.'[12]

Shortly after UCSA was established, Panchuk, elected as its first president, wrote to the UCC asking to have his group formally admitted to membership. This request left the Committee's executive nonplussed, for they were themselves unsure of what it was they were supposed to be doing in Canada, much less overseas. Still, recognizing in the existence of this Servicemen's Association a justification for their own continued activities, the Committee did extend UCSA some modest financial support, enabling the Ukrainian Canadian soldiers to transfer their headquarters from the Ukrainian Social Club in Manchester to rented quarters at 218 Sussex Gardens, Paddington, London.[13] What became known as the 'London Club' would continue to serve as a canteen, hostel, and meeting place for the thousands of Ukrainian Canadian servicemen and servicewomen who would pass through London during the Second World War and for several months after the war's end.[14] Through its *UCSA News Letter* these young Ukrainian Canadians not only kept in touch with each other and with home, but preserved their ethnic identity while stationed overseas. The extent to which the 'Club' would come to have more than just a social or morale-building character is suggested by a report describing an UCSA 'Padre's Hour' presided over by a Ukrainian Catholic chaplain, the Honorary Captain Reverend Michael Horoshko. The purpose of his talk was to instruct returning servicemen about their 'duties' as Ukrainians once they returned to Canada. And so he did, for Horoshko's sermon not only addressed the need for all Ukrainian Canadians to stick together in the face of the racist and assimilationist pressures confronting Ukrainian Canadians, but urged them to reinforce their group distinctiveness – just as, in his view, English, Irish, and Scottish Canadians had done. They should make especially sure, Horoshko admonished them, that the 'Ukrainian Question' received far more attention than it was getting back home. Reverend Horoshko also advised that they do everything possible to help promote the immigration of Ukrainian refugees to Canada, for the greater the number of Ukrainians living in Canada the better it would be for the group as a whole. If the need arose, Horoshko concluded rather defiantly, 'the powers that be would have to be challenged.' And no one should feel awkward about doing any of this, or about speaking out as a Ukrainian in Canada, he ended, for the sacrifices Ukrainian Canadians had made during the war had certainly earned them the right, once and for all, to speak freely, to make their interests felt, and to do so without fear of reprimand.[15]

The unforeseen emergence of the Servicemen's Association had benefits no one could have predicted. Reeling from the attacks of the Left and uncertain of its mandate, the UCC found itself presented unexpectedly with a chance to demonstrate its full commitment to the war effort. What more demonstrably loyal act could there be than underwriting facilities for Ukrainian Canadian volunteers serving overseas with Canada's armed forces? The record shows that the Committee took full advantage of this godsend. At the first UCC national congress, held in Winnipeg from 22 to 25 June 1943, the most talked-about issue was Ukrainian Canadian allegiance to Canada and to the Empire's war effort.[16] With the emergence of UCSA, the Committee found itself with its first acceptable raison d'être, one that could easily be presented to the public as unequivocal proof of Ukrainian Canadian loyalty.

As for the Canadian government, it was pleased with this development, for not only was the entire subject of 'Ukrainian Nationalism' referred to only in a 'very general and guarded' manner at this UCC congress, but the organizers had also managed 'to avoid statements or discussions of a kind which would cause embarrassment to the Government or give ammunition to their Communist opponents.' In short, the Committee had proved that it could be safely categorized as 'wholly unobjectionable.'[17] American observers for the Office of Strategic Services (OSS) corroborated the RCMP's assessment, conveying to their political masters the welcome news that the UCC had 'abandoned the political campaign for Ukrainian independence, and in addition to efforts on behalf of Canadian war activities, restricted itself to cultural work.'[18] This 'evasion' of political questions, the OSS reporters wrote, was 'due to official advice from Ottawa,' which now intended to revert to its 'hands-off policy.' This meant, they hoped, that the Committee would, sooner rather than later, 'become dormant.'[19] Neither the federal government nor these external observers counted on the energy of a Panchuk or of his co-workers, or foresaw where their combined efforts would lead. Dormant was not a word Panchuk understood.

This did not mean that UCSA escaped official scrutiny. When UCSA applied for newsprint on which to publish its *UCSA News Letter*, the British authorities first consulted with their Canadian counterparts before issuing modest supplies of this rationed commodity. It was also made clear to the publishers that they were going to be watched to ensure that their behaviour was 'good,' which meant that they must not print anything that might irritate 'Soviet circles.' Panchuk, writing to several Ukrainian Canadian servicemen stationed in Canada, also hinted that UCSA had been permitted and approved of by the Canadian military authorities, noting that he too realized that the organization was kept under some kind of surveillance.[20] There can be no question but that governments on both sides of the Atlantic were very careful to make sure that these Ukrainian Canadians remained loyal, and, even more important, did nothing to prejudice Anglo-American relations with the Soviet Union or other Allied powers.

'Kicked About like a Football'·

Meanwhile Panchuk, who had been attached to RCAF Intelligence on 27 August 1942,[21] ended up as one of the first two Canadian air force officers to land with the invading troops of Montgomery's Second Army on the beaches of Normandy, on 6 June 1944.[22] And thus began a new episode in his career. For, as he wrote afterwards, from 'the day we first landed in Normandy'[23] he began to encounter Ukrainian refugees and to grasp the dimensions of the Ukrainian refugee problem. Appreciating that people in Canada were still 'largely unaware of what was ... happening in Europe [because] all our links to Ukrainians there had been cut off by the war,'[24] he and a few other Ukrainian Canadian soldiers became the first to realize the unparalleled human catastrophe the Second World War had represented for the Ukrainian nation. Suddenly aware of the scale of the Ukrainian refugee problem, Panchuk and a few of his fellow Ukrainian Canadian soldiers became the first conduits of information to Canada about the Ukrainian DPs. Later they would also help initiate the process of rebuilding links between Ukrainians in Europe and their counterparts in North America, forwarding uncensored mail and packages between the European mainland, the United Kingdom, and North America through the military post and with returning servicemen. These soldiers also served their new-found Ukrainian refugee compatriots in many other immediately useful ways, and served them well, given the circumstances. They provided direct counsel and sometimes intervened on behalf of the refugees with the military or civilian administrations, and they also helped provide medicine, shelter, and food.

All of this was accomplished only by those few soldiers who, like Panchuk, were interested enough in the Ukrainian refugees to want to help. These Ukrainian Canadians did not originally take an especially critical view of the DPs. They simply believed that these Ukrainian refugees needed help and that was all that mattered. They also felt that the displaced persons were not fundamentally different from Ukrainian Canadians – that they were Ukrainians was what counted. In taking this attitude the Ukrainian Canadians forgot to consider the particulars of where these Ukrainian political refugees, displaced persons, and victims of the war had come from and had been. Only years later, after the Ukrainian Canadians had come to know the Ukrainian refugees better and vice versa, did each side discover that the expectations of the other were not going to be met entirely, that the two groups were not as alike as they had once believed they might be. And when that happened they would experience a full measure of annoyance and disappointment. But that too was still far in the future.

Panchuk and other Ukrainian Canadian soldiers met ever greater numbers of Ukrainian refugees as they moved farther inland.[25] In May 1945, Panchuk came across a small group of Ukrainian women in Unterluss, near Hamburg. His diary entry for 12 June 1945 suggests that he was unhappy at their apathy, a condition he did his best to remedy. As he tersely described it, 'Really gave them the works! Got [them] organized.'[26] But such fleeting contacts would never be enough for Panchuk, who felt it was imperative that he take every opportunity to 'see my people,' something he did time and again.[27] And so it came to be that, on nearly 'a daily basis,'[28] he and a few other Ukrainian Canadian soldiers established contact with 'thousands and thousands of [the] slave labourers' who were 'making their tracks westwards,'[29] organizing relief committees among them wherever possible, and sending detailed reports about this Ukrainian refugee situation to Canada through the only open channel of communication between Europe and North America at the time, the military postal service.[30]

In an early report on the Ukrainian refugee situation, penned while he was in Hamburg and sent to Dr Walter Gallan (born Volodymyr Galan) of the United Ukrainian American Relief Committee, Inc. (UUARC), Panchuk attempted to give an estimate of the scale of this Ukrainian refugee problem. He came up with a total figure of approximately four and half million Ukrainian DPs.[31] This enormous population he subdivided into:

Old refugees (prior to 1939) 100,000
Refugees (mostly slave labourers) forcibly evacuated
  into Germany 1939–43) 1,650,000
Forcibly evacuated 1943–45 2,500,000
Political refugees (who *sought* refuge). 250,000

While it is more commonly estimated that there were between 2.5 and 3 million Ukrainian DPs sheltering in refugee assembly centres and DP camps in the months immediately following the end of the Second World War, Panchuk's early observations about the nature of the Ukrainian refugee experience have a deeper relevance than any attempt at numerical tabulation, for they contain several references which reveal a great deal about what he felt being a Ukrainian might mean.[32] For Panchuk, it was obvious that Ukrainian refugees were being 'kicked about like a football,' and were suffering this unhappy fate simply *because they were Ukrainian*. In his view, Ukrainians were always somebody's 'scapegoat.'[33] Not atypically, little was being done for this category of DPs – 'it is as if there were no such people' – even though, he maintained, the Ukrainians were 'the greatest majority of the forced slave labour that are not refugees.' Of even greater concern was that official indifference or even hostility towards Ukrainian refugees was becoming an assimilatory pressure; a very large percentage of these unfortunates, Panchuk insisted, had already lost, were in the process of losing, or would continue to abandon their Ukrainian affiliation because they found themselves in places where identifying oneself as a Ukrainian often had negative consequences. Lacking any kind of recognized representation, the Ukrainian DPs were therefore languishing, subjected to the pressure of those who were 'forever ... trying to make them into Poles or into Russians, or into Hungarians or Rumanians.' In effect, or so Panchuk believed, the Ukrainian DPs were being denationalized.[34] And that was enough to set him off, assimilation being an old foe against which he and his fellow Ukrainian Canadian community activists had struggled at home. Before, their fight had always ended up being something of a losing battle. But here, in just liberated Europe, Ukrainian Canadians were not as helpless as they had been in Canada. They were members of a victorious army, in whose ranks they had proved themselves. By helping to save Ukrainian DPs they would do something positive for the Ukrainian nation. And who could deny veterans of Canada's armed forces the right to help those who had been so unfortunate as to find themselves in the DP camps of western Europe? More important, Panchuk and his fellow servicemen reckoned that once these obviously patriotic Ukrainian DPs were rescued, provided they could be brought into Canada they would serve to infuse new vigour into Ukrainian Canadian constituencies. These constituencies, by the mid-1940s, were already showing signs of senility. And so the refugee situation came to represent a unique opportunity for reviving Ukrainian Canadian society, an opportunity of which Panchuk and his friends longed to take advantage.

'Get Cracking'

With the zealousness so characteristic of his temperament, Panchuk began actively lobbying Ukrainians in North America about their 'duty' to 'get cracking' and immediately dispatch 'missionaries' to Europe to save the human resource represented by the Ukrainian DPs. Now that hostilities were over he even offered UCSA's London facilities as a headquarters and staging area for the 'body of workers' he envisioned would be sent over to help. Panchuk was ready to organize this crusade and animate it with the physical and mental energy he brought to everything he did: 'If there is any way that my humble person can assist either now or when I am out of service, I am at the disposal of the Ukrainian people.'[35]

Mindful of how religious disagreements had disrupted Ukrainian Canadian society in the interwar years, Panchuk was careful to stress that this social welfare work among the DPs must be 'non-sectarian.' Even more anxious about how the authorities might respond, he also cautiously noted, at least twice, that this work would definitely 'not [be] of a political nature.'[36] The origins of what became the Central Ukrainian Relief Bureau can be traced to Panchuk's June 1945 summons to action. Significantly, even at this early date Panchuk wrote as if he more than suspected that dealing with as politically delicate an issue as the fate of Ukrainian refugees could place those involved at some risk. Certainly he appreciated that he and his co-workers, representatives of a minority which itself had many times previously suffered from the state's displeasure, would have to tread very carefully in order to avoid censure again.

Panchuk was not alone in this fear. Another USRL supporter, Peter Worobetz, writing to explain why some UCSA members were growing anxious about Panchuk's increasing involvement with the DPs, noted, 'After all, Gordon, you realize that we are being watched by people, not all of whom are sympathetic.'[37]

Restiveness among some UCSA members over whether or not to help the DPs was not new. Earlier that year, Panchuk had nearly resigned over a letter he received from members of the UCSA executive, a note which upbraided him for his efforts on behalf of what were euphemistically referred to as 'civilian personnel on the continent.'[38] The offending letter, dated 18 February 1945, does not appear to have survived, but later correspondence makes it clear that some of UCSA's leading members felt his activities 'were bordering on the precarious' because they touched on what was termed 'International Politics.' To protect themselves, or so Worobetz reported, UCSA's executive had drafted a letter to be kept on file so that if Panchuk's activities on the Continent were 'misunderstood,' the executive could plausibly disclaim all responsibility.[39] According to another veteran, Johnnie Yuzyk, these same members had begun to fear that 'being in UCSA [might] do them harm.'[40]

Panchuk's force of character – 'my gospel: Do Something' – took him past this brief and early challenge to his work with Ukrainian refugees, but he was in many respects a true innocent in those days, for the concerns of the UCSA executive were not entirely unwarranted.[41] Even before the war's end there were indications in Canada that groups there intended to protest vigorously against any influx of Ukrainian displaced persons into the country. A 12 February 1945 article in the *Edmonton Journal*, provocatively captioned 'Admission of Ukrainian Quislings to Canada,' chastised those lobbying the federal government in favour of such immigration: 'The admission of these Nazi zealots to Canada would be nothing less than a national disaster. They could no more be expected to be loyal citizens of this country than they were of their own.'[42]

'A Matter of Particular Political Importance'

Even more disturbing were the evident misgivings on the part of senior Canadian government officials about the Ukrainian Canadian Committee's application to set up a 'Canadian Ukrainian Refugee Fund.' Although the proposal was eventually accepted, albeit with important restrictions, on first review an attempt was made to veto it by Norman Robertson of External Affairs. Writing to the director of voluntary and auxiliary services of the Department of National War Services, George Pifher, Robertson argued that given the 'present political circumstances in Europe' any authorization of a 'Ukrainian Refugee Fund' would 'likely be misconstrued' by the Polish and Soviet governments. Although he was ready to agree that the Canadian government was 'absolutely certain of the loyalty of the Ukrainian Canadian Committee to Canada,' the proposed Fund might have 'international implications' and could prove to be a 'source of considerable embarrassment' to Canada. His counsel was that the Committee should 'be persuaded to abandon this project.' He concluded by asking Pifher to do whatever he could to have the Committee set aside its plans, without, however, letting any of the Ukrainian Canadians know the extent of the consternation generated by their proposal.[43] Robertson was, no doubt, further convinced of the wisdom of his advice after he received a letter from the Canadian ambassador to the USSR, Dana Wilgress. In Wilgress's view any official approval of a Ukrainian Canadian fund for refugees would prejudice Soviet–Canadian relations. As for the Ukrainian partisans still operating in what he termed 'liberated Poland,' these insurgents were, in his view, little more than 'enemy agents.' The Soviets, he reported, had already 'shot about 20,000 Ukrainian nationalists' and were 'probably biding their time before taking energetic steps to suppress these guerrillas.' He wanted Robertson to know that he was 'fully in accord' with the government's stand in not approving the formation of a 'Canadian Ukrainian Refugee Fund.'[44]

To its credit, the UCC's executive persisted in its efforts to have such a fund officially sanctioned. On 12 January 1945 the director of the Department of National War Services, General L.R. LaFleche, gave in to their entreaties, but only on the condition that their accounts be managed in a very particular, and circumscribed, way. The limitations imposed were as follows. First, the Fund was to be called the Canadian Ukrainian Relief Fund, rather than the Canadian Ukrainian Refugee Fund – the term *refugee* being considered too politically loaded. All moneys collected were to be made available to *anyone* of 'Ukrainian race' regardless of citizenship status; theoretically, non-refugees and even Soviet citizens could benefit from Ukrainian Canadian largesse. The total amount the Committee could raise was also fixed, and the Fund's accounts had to be kept in a Canadian bank (and not a Ukrainian Canadian credit union) so that expenditures could be monitored carefully. As a final control, the funds collected were to be administered by the Canadian Red Cross. As Robertson was duly informed, 'Upon this basis ... the Fund was authorized.'[45]

It is debatable whether any privately organized humanitarian relief operation in Canada has ever been so encumbered by restrictions imposed by the federal government. Yet, even so handicapped, what in the event was named the Ukrainian Canadian Relief Fund (the UCRF, or the Fund) met with considerable success. By the end of December 1945 its organizers had sent out forty thousand letters of appeal and collected nearly $70,000 in returns, $50,000 of which they duly turned over to the Canadian Red Cross.[46] Having made this geld, the UCRF continued with its own fund-raising efforts, siphoning moneys to

CURB and financing the latter's successors instead of making further payments to the Red Cross. Curiously, there seems to have been no official notice of this subterfuge. That a substantial amount was eventually gathered into the Fund's coffers is suggested by its June 1946 report, which noted that over $106,000 had been raised by the end of January that year.[47] Funds were solicited by mass mailings, through organizational collections such as a 'Carolling for Ukraine' campaign at Christmastime, and by bestowing merit certificates on particularly generous donors and inscribing their names in a 'Golden Book of Benefactors of the Ukrainian People,' which has long since been lost. That these various calls upon the charity of Ukrainian Canadians reached a wide and sympathetic audience is indicated by the fact that some ten thousand contributions came in after the first mass mailing, and that even smaller Ukrainian Canadian communities, such as the village of Krydor, Saskatchewan, Anthony Yaremovich's home town, were among the first to make generous contributions to the Fund.[48]

The Fund's appeal unambiguously targeted as prospective donors those Ukrainian Canadians who were anxious about what had happened in Ukraine during the war, those who still had family members, relatives, or friends there, and any persons sympathetic to the ongoing national liberation struggle in the homeland – the Fund's appeal was meant to mobilize all those who remained committed to the hope of independence for Ukraine. UCRF literature spoke to the need to 'save for us, for Ukraine, our brothers and sisters,' and referred to their 'martyr's mission to withstand and defend from perishing the most sacred ideals of our people.'[49] UCRF appeals also unblushingly exhorted Ukrainian Canadians to 'strive with all our hearts and resources' to 'aid what might easily be the last remnants of that gallant band of liberty-loving people who would prefer death rather than be deprived of freedom. Let not this vanguard be allowed to perish; let us do everything we can to save it; and by saving it, save ourselves and the rest of the world.'[50]

Not surprisingly, these Ukrainian Canadian endeavours did not go unnoticed by those of hostile or opposing viewpoints. In late April 1945 the Soviet ambassador to Canada, Zaroubin, called upon the acting under-secretary of state and noted that Moscow regarded the Canadian government's approval of a 'Canadian Ukrainian Refugee

Fund' as a matter of 'particular (political) importance.'[51] Possibly Zaroubin's admonition was what inspired J.E. Riddell of External Affairs to write to Robertson in mid-May, arguing that it might be appropriate for the government to reconsider its earlier decision to approve the formation of the UCRF. Indeed, he wrote, it would still be possible to 'block' the Fund's use of the moneys it had collected.[52]

In the end that was not done. By mid-September 1945, Panchuk and his colleagues had constituted the nucleus of a staff for CURB, a fact they communicated to UCSA's members by means of a circular letter.[53] Their Bureau's aims and mandate were formally stated:

1. To consolidate relief activities of the Ukrainian relief committees and institutions;
2. To act on behalf of these for the material and moral support of all Ukrainian refugees and displaced persons;
3. To co-operate with UNRRA. [United Nations Relief and Rehabilitation Administration];
4. To help reunite families;
5. To inform all interested and give advice.[54]

In Panchuk's personal opinion the Bureau was 'merely an extension of the UCSA,' for not only did it share the same premises, but its assets and staff were 'almost identical.' He observed that he himself bore 'common responsibility' for UCSA and CURB operations, being the elected president of the former and the appointed director of the latter.[55] As he would later also acknowledge, the transition from UCSA to CURB – a process somewhat complicated by the formation of the Soiuz ukrainskykh kanadiiskykh veteraniv (Ukrainian Canadian Veterans' Association, or UCVA) and the Association of Ukrainians in Great Britain (AUGB)[56] – 'was not very clear.'[57] Between the fall of 1945 and the late spring of 1946, Panchuk, who remained on the Continent except for several brief leaves in London, displayed the personal drive, organizing skills, infectious enthusiasm, and lively interest in detail that would inspire many of the Bureau's staff and supporters. Not only did he spend considerable time visiting various refugee camps, but, almost simultaneously, he attempted to mould UCVA into the kind of group he believed it should become in Canada; liaised with UUARC; helped the AUGB organize; ran CURB; and mobilized public opinion on both sides of the Atlantic in protest against the forcible repatriation of refugees to Soviet-controlled territories. Testifying to his energy is the fact that he somehow also found time to get married in February 1946, to Anne Cherniawsky, from Vegreville, a Ukrainian Canadian servicewoman whom he had first met at UCSA's 'London Club' and who would remain his faithful companion and helpmate to the end of his life.

Although Panchuk tried to control UCVA's development from abroad, doing so proved to be beyond even his organizational skills, and would remain so for as long as he remained overseas. He had hoped to keep Ukrainian Canadian veterans united in one group, aligned with, but otherwise independent of, the Royal Canadian Legion. This conception was not accepted or acted upon by most of his fellow veterans, certainly not to the degree he insisted was necessary. In Panchuk's opinion Ukrainian Canadian veterans had what he called 'interests and problems' that were 'often different' from those of the 'ordinary members' (non-Ukrainian Canadians) of the Legion.[58] His plans for creating a strong Ukrainian Canadian veterans' organization were foiled, however, not only because many veterans were content to join existing Legion branches, but also because, despite Panchuk's hopes, neither the USRL nor the UNF was eager to witness the emergence of yet another Ukrainian Canadian organization, particularly one which might siphon off the young men and women returning from overseas whom these existing organizations wanted to attract back into their own ranks.[59] While UCVA branches would be set up in several cities, and the organization would come to play a prominent role in the UCC until its demographic base disappeared, nothing could buffer it against the simple fact that UCVA did not attract even a simple majority of those who had been UCSA members overseas. Possibly, if Panchuk had dedicated his experience, talent, and enthusiasm into building up UCVA instead of devoting that same energy to CURB, this Ukrainian Canadian veterans' organization might have played a more crucial role in Ukrainian Canadian society during the postwar period. That remains one of the unresolved 'ifs' of Ukrainian Canadian history. Then again, it may be that UCSA's attractiveness overseas was due more to wartime camaraderie and the need many Ukrainian Canadian soldiers had for some familiar 'home away from home' – a sentiment which naturally enough dissipated after their return to their own communities – than to any deep-rooted desire on their part to create a new kind of Ukrainian Canadian group. Even if several of UCVA's members were to continue occupying important posts in Ukrainian Canadian organizations, working on behalf of the refugees and within Ukrainian Canadian society as a whole, the organization itself played, at best, only a very modest supporting role in refugee relief and resettlement efforts after 1946.

'Behave Carefully'

Panchuk was formally inducted as the salaried director of CURB by means of a telegram addressed by the Committee's president, Monsignor Vasyl Kushnir, on 17 November 1945.[60] Working with Panchuk were Captain Stanley Frolick, who became the Bureau's general secretary,[61] George Kluchevsky, a Ukrainian divinity student from Edinburgh who served as the bookkeeper and treasurer, and several UCSA officers who held advisory positions.[62] An annual budget of sixteen thousand dollars was proposed on 12 January 1946 and accepted by 8 February, this amount raised jointly by the Fund and by its American equivalent, the United Ukrainian American Relief Committee.[63] While Panchuk was to say that he was 'highly honoured' to be accredited by the Committee as CURB's director, he still made it clear that, in accepting, his 'primary ... wish' was to return to Saskatchewan, where he hoped to continue his war-interrupted studies.[64] Still, 'on the strength of the assurances' he had received from Winnipeg, he requested a year's leave of absence without pay from the RCAF,[65] presided over the 'official' closing of the 'London Club' on 10 November 1945,[66] and prepared himself for the visit to Europe by the president of both the Committee and the Fund, Monsignor Kushnir.

Kushnir's 'fact-finding' tour, which began in early January 1946 and lasted until mid-April, irked some Canadian officials even before it began. Permission had been sought for Kushnir to go overseas on 1 November 1945.[67] By 2 January 1946, Robertson of External Affairs was informing Canadian diplomatic representatives overseas, such as the Canadian ambassador to Belgium, W.R.A. Turgeon, that while Kushnir's journey was being billed as an 'entirely charitable' one with 'no political objectives,' there could be 'little doubt' that Kushnir would be 'watched with suspicion' by the Soviets and that he would indeed make contact with anti-Soviet elements among the refugees. So, even if Kushnir had 'assured' External Affairs that he would be careful to do nothing to embarrass the Canadian government, it was best to be prepared for just the opposite to happen, for his visit would almost certainly be interpreted by the DPs and the Soviets as having 'political significance.'[68]

That Soviet representatives, and their sympathizers among the Ukrainian Canadian population, would be opposed to the activities of the Bureau, and to visits like the one made by Monsignor Kushnir, is not surprising, nor were their protests long in coming. On 5 January 1946 the Workers Benevolent Association and members of the editorial board of *Ukrainian Word* sent a telegram to the Secretariat of the United Nations disputing the claim allegedly made by the Bureau to the effect that it represented all Ukrainian Canadians; in contrast, these protesters insisted, the Bureau's activities during wartime had been 'anti-Ukrainian and Fascist.'[69] Similarly, the Soviet Ukrainian delegation at the United Nations protested against the activities of CURB and the Ukrainian Canadian groups which supported it, an action which prompted a senior British Foreign Office official, Thomas Brimelow, himself a rather calm and reasoning person, to caution, 'This sort of accusation makes it essential that Dr. Kushnir should behave carefully.'[70]

And so Kushnir, before being allowed to proceed from London to the Continent, was shunted around from the rooms of the high commissioner for Canada in Great Britain to various other offices in Whitehall, asked to call on several senior officials whose responsibility it was to vet him and decide whether or not he should be furnished with the necessary travel papers. As these bureaucrats dissected CURB's plans they also assessed the character of the Ukrainian Canadian representatives whom they had been seeing 'a good deal of ... in recent weeks.'[71] Overall they seem to have been impressed. In a secret message, the high commissioner for Canada informed Ottawa that although Kushnir had been enjoined to 'be discreet' in his dealings with the Ukrainian refugees, Sir George Rendel of the Foreign Office's Refugee Department had formed 'on the whole [a] favourable impression' of

Kushnir.[72] A month earlier Robertson had likewise observed that both the Control Commission for Germany and the Foreign Office considered Panchuk 'a sensible and helpful person.'[73] But even such positive assessments were insufficient to persuade either the British or the Canadian authorities to accord CURB recognition of an official kind. As Brimelow minuted on the file dealing with this subject, Kushnir's attitude might well be 'one of correct neutrality,' and the Northern Department had no objection to 'non-political welfare work' among the Ukrainian displaced persons, but, 'We do not think that the Ukrainian Relief Bureau should be recognized as having any claim to represent Ukrainians in general or to advance political demands on their behalf.'[74] Even after the Bureau's efforts had been under way for over a year, and Foreign Office officials had, in their own words, come to 'take quite a good view' of it, no official sanction of its mandate, methods, or achievements would be forthcoming.[75] The reasons for this indisposition were common to both the British and the Canadian governments, neither of which wanted to see 'too many' visitors to the Ukrainians in Germany 'at one time,' largely because the British authorities were, as they themselves wrote, 'somewhat nervous' about such persons making 'indiscreet statements' which might encourage the DPs 'in their impracticable nationalism.'[76] As for the Canadian authorities, there was an additional concern that the arrival of Ukrainian Canadians in the DP camps would prove to be a source of 'endless, inaccurate, and misleading statements' about the prospects for Ukrainian DP resettlement in Canada. That was something which, Robertson wrote, should be discouraged actively: 'From our own point of view ... it is most desirable that DPs should not be given hopes of immigration to Canada which cannot be fulfilled. The unfortunate, homeless persons in Germany grasp at any straw for re-settlement abroad, and to the Ukrainians in particular Canada is heaven.'[77]

5 'A Subject Which We Cannot Ignore': Unexpected Problems with Ukrainian Canadian Relief Operations, 1945–1946

'A Subject Which We Cannot Ignore'

Ukrainian Canadians brought a different perspective to their work for the displaced persons, if only because they were becoming increasingly alarmed about the forcible repatriation of thousands of Ukrainian refugees to the Soviet Union. By late summer of 1945 the Bureau's staff were lobbying selected British parliamentarians, such as Rhys Davies, to protest not only against the 'shanghaiing' of Ukrainians deemed to be 'Soviet citizens' under the terms of the Yalta Agreement, but also against that of Western Ukrainians who, being of Polish citizenship, were not legally subject to compulsory repatriation.[1] Even the doughty Tracy Philipps, now back in London and working for UNRRA, was asked for help in influencing the British government, which he attempted to provide by writing to his own contacts in the Foreign Office[2] and by sending letters to the English press which criticized the 'man hunt' directed against Ukrainian DPs.[3]

Over the following several months a concerted dissent against forcible repatriation would, in large part, be orchestrated through CURB's good offices. In the process both Ottawa and London would be barraged with detailed descriptions about the injustices and brutality involved in these repatriation operations and about the tragic fate awaiting those sent to the Soviets. Robertson at External Affairs would receive a number of letters from the UCC on this theme,[4] and Prime Minister King would be similarly addressed by that friend of the Ukrainian Canadian Committee, Professor Watson Kirkconnell, writing on behalf of the Baptist Federation of Canada. Kirkconnell observed: 'To hand them over to the Red Army and the NKVD is to murder them ... It would be a moral calamity of the first order if our Canadian Government should share in the responsibility for these crimes ... Canada should try to prevent these crimes against humanity and bear its share in an offer of asylum to these fugitives from death.'[5]

In the United Kingdom a similar campaign was initiated. British notables, such as Lord Noel Baker, received petitions from Ukrainian DPs in the Regensburg camp,[6] and the British legation to the Holy See transmitted the concerns of the Apostolic Visitor to Ruthenian Catholics in Germany. In a similar vein, Bishop Ivan Buchko wrote to Foreign Secretary Bevin,[7] while CURB's Frolick continued to bring to Rhys Davies's attention new cases of the repatriation of non-Soviet citizens.[8] The Ukrainian Orthodox archbishop Polikarp raised this same issue with the Lord Archbishop of Canterbury.[9]

The Bureau was not, of course, the only body behind this outcry. Even if Ukrainian Canadians seem to have played an important role in bringing the issue to the attention of the public and the authorities on both sides of the Atlantic, Foreign Office records show that other independent observers, such as field workers of the Religious Society of Friends (the Quakers) were also aghast at what was happening.[10] Through the Bureau's secretariat a number of memoranda, such as one sent to London from the Ukrainian Central Relief Committee in Germany, which pleaded for the recognition of Ukrainians as a separate people entitled to their own national, cultural, and religious life and their right to freedom from 'physical or psychological compulsion to return' to the USSR, were also forwarded to Ukrainian groups in North America, as well as to many other interested parties. Likewise a letter described as having been written by 'a responsible Allied officer,' which referred to the 'anarchy' prevailing in the American Zone of Germany and the corrupting influence of 'Soviet secret agents' who were bribing Americans to abduct and even carry Ukrainians across the demarcation line 'with hands and feet bound,' received wide distribution. This officer's suggestion that what had happened in Nazi Germany during the war was no different from what was being done to the DPs – 'Belsen-Bergen are not ended' – could not help but strike a sensitive chord among the Anglo-American bureaucrats and statesmen of the time, who were well aware of the horrors that had befallen Europe's peoples during the war years, atrocities that many of them had known about but ignored.[11]

Precisely what impact these various entreaties had is rather more difficult to determine. In the immediate aftermath of the Second World

War, British, American, and French forces on occupation duty in Germany and Austria had become so proficient in returning refugees to the Soviets that, according to a British Foreign Office report, 'the Russians asked us to slow down as they could not cope with the flow,' estimated at eleven to twelve thousand refugees repatriated per day.[12] Despite the serious objections raised by British citizens such as Yvonne Marrack, a Quaker working with Ukrainian DPs near Goslar, who pointed out that some military personnel were deeply reluctant 'to carry out this policy' and that compelling Ukrainians, people of 'childlike faith' in British decency, to return to the USSR would strike an 'incalculable blow' against the image of Britain as an 'upholder of a way of life which respects the dignity and worth of human personality,' the trucks and trains kept moving, west to east.[13] By 1 September 1946, just over a half year after Marrack's appeal, a total of 5,115,709 persons had been repatriated, of whom 2,229,552 had been 'liberated' by the western Allies and then thrown back to the Soviets. Of these, 1,855,910 were handed over between 23 May and 1 September 1945 alone.[14] A large proportion, perhaps even a simple majority, of these unfortunates were Ukrainians.

Marrack explained why so many east European refugees, peasants and intellectuals alike, were afraid: 'For the simple people the fear is that they will be sent to Siberia, to work under conditions far worse than they now experience ... The fear of the educated people is far more definite ... [Their] conviction [is] that they will lose their lives as enemies of the Soviet regime.'[15] That repatriated 'Soviet citizens' were indeed being executed at dockside, in port cities as far apart as Murmansk in the Russian northwest and Odessa in Ukraine's south, had been reported to Whitehall by mid-1945,[16] yet it was not until mid-1946 that the British war cabinet's ruling of 4 September 1944, providing for the return of 'all Russians whom the Soviets wished to have back, irrespective of whether or not the men wished to return,' was cancelled.[17]

Although it might be impossible to determine the degree to which Ukrainian Canadian and other entreaties affected governmental decision-making on both sides of the Atlantic, it is apparent that the Canadian and British authorities did consult with each other on this issue, and that the Canadian government was vexed as to how it should respond to 'the large number of representations from Ukrainian organizations and their sympathizers protesting against the forcible return of Ukrainian refugees to the Soviet Union.'[18] As John

Holmes, then with the Office of the High Commissioner of Canada in London, would admit, in a letter sent to the Foreign Office's Brimelow, 'I am sorry to take up your time on this matter but it is a subject which we cannot ignore in Canada.'[19]

The problem was exacerbated after Prime Minister King received a telegram signed by twenty-four Canadian parliamentarians protesting against involuntary repatriation. The matter was afterwards taken up in the even more public forum of the House of Commons, on 18 December 1945, when King and a Ukrainian Canadian, the Social Credit MP for Vegreville, Anthony Hlynka, discussed the issue on the record. As External Affairs commentators subsequently observed, exhibiting an almost morbid sensitivity in hindsight, the prime minister had, on this occasion, 'said rather more than it would be wise for us to say.'[20] Yet all King had done was remark that, in so far as it was within Canada's power, the government would strive to protect the interests of Ukrainian refugees in the Allied zones of occupation, a comment immediately qualified with a caveat about how difficult it was to be sure of the accuracy of Ukrainian Canadian memoranda on the subject of forcible repatriation. Even such small cheese, however, was discomforting to some of the Canadian prime minister's advisers in External Affairs.

'Anti-Soviet Utterances'

As for the Soviets, who were closely monitoring Ukrainian Canadian affairs, they were quick to complain about the 'anti-Soviet agitation conducted by certain groups of Ukrainians in Canada,' arguing that such protests 'marred' Canadian–Soviet relations.[21] Even as exalted a figure as the commissar for Soviet Ukrainian foreign affairs, M. Manuilsky, lodged a complaint on this score with Leo Malania, the man in External Affairs' European and Commonwealth Division (Second Political Division) charged with supervising the Soviet Desk. A fortnight later, when Malania attended the preparatory conference leading up to the creation of the United Nations, Manuilsky raised the subject again, during the London sittings of a UN committee dealing specifically with the postwar refugee situation.[22]

What was significant about these two occasions was not so much the predictable Soviet disquiet over Ukrainian Canadian activities, which was routine, but the response made by certain high-ranking Canadian officials to these Soviet diplomatic protests. In the aforementioned instances both the confidential and the public remarks of senior Canadian bureaucrats show a decided irritation not with what could have been dismissed as Soviet meddling in Canada's internal affairs, but rather with those Canadians of Ukrainian origin who persisted in voicing their hopes about Ukrainian independence. Thus Malania, in a lengthy recorded conversation with Manuilsky, pointed out that 'from the Canadian point of view' the 'Ukrainian Question' had international and internal dimensions, both of which would gradually and naturally be resolved after this 'immigrant stock' was absorbed into 'one or the other of the two main ethnic groups in Canada.' The problem, Malania patiently explained to his listeners, was that this process would take some time. In the interim it was inevitable that the ideal of an independent Ukraine would continue to have sentimental value among these immigrants even if the 'remarkable growth of the Soviet Union had deprived this ideal of all practical meaning.' In Malania's view, or at least as he advised Manuilsky, Moscow would be wise simply to ignore Ukrainian Canadian affairs, in effect to wait out the Ukrainian Canadian nationalists. The nationalists, after all, would inevitably fade away. If, on the other hand, 'so powerful a country as the USSR took such vigorous notice' of the Ukrainian Canadian nationalists, then they would be doing themselves a disservice, for by continuing to react to Ukrainian Canadian agitation the Soviets were stirring up controversy and giving the nationalists an issue to cling to. Better, counselled Malania, studiously to ignore them. More tellingly, he added, this was the course of action that the Canadian government wanted Moscow to take, for by continuing to react to Ukrainian Canadian complaints the Soviet government was only going to 'retard the process of assimilation' which Canadian officials believed would ultimately eliminate this troublesome irritant to domestic tranquillity and good Soviet–Canadian relations.

In concluding, Malania suggested that the Soviet authorities should instead concentrate on their 'programme of improving the life of the Ukrainian people.' Measurable improvements in the standard of living in Ukraine would do much to undercut the authority and raison d'être of Ukrainian nationalists in Canada. In the meantime the two governments should also strive to develop 'good all around' relations, avoiding anything which might excite 'strong emotions.' In the end, Malania predicted, the Ukrainian Canadian nationalists were doomed to irrelevancy. Lest the under-secretary of state for external affairs, Hume Wrong, misinterpret the tone of his talk with Manuilsky, Malania concluded the official report on his chat by noting that this conversation with the Soviets had been 'conducted in an atmosphere of great cordiality and even intimacy.'[23]

Malania's Soviet-mollifying performance was not unique. In some respects it was surpassed by that of a socialist parliamentarian, Stanley Knowles. Responding to another critique of Ukrainian Canadians made by Manuilsky, Knowles pointed out that not only did he personally deplore the 'anti-Soviet utterances' of such people, but that, 'in this instance,' his criticism reflected the attitude of the Canadian government, on whose behalf he had risen in a United Nations forum to address this very issue. Indeed, he went on to say, 'not only the Government but all responsible parties in Canada, do deplore very much' the kind of Ukrainian Canadian behaviour which Manuilsky condemned. He added, echoing Malania's views, that he was glad to see that members of the press were not present at these evening UN deliberations, for that meant that what he and Manuilsky were talking over was unlikely even to be reported in the Canadian press. That was good, because any press reporting would only further incite 'the people who are doing the thing which my honourable friend and I both deplore.'[24] Keeping Ukrainian Canadian nationalists ignorant of what was going on was an effective means, Knowles suggested, of doing away with their unwelcome protests and challenges to the way in which the government of Canada wanted to conduct its internal and external policies towards and, in some respects, in concert with the Soviet Union.

Reporting on Knowles's remarks, Malania wrote to the prime minister to say that not only did he feel this MP had handled the situation admirably, but that he had done so with such 'sound and good humoured' commentary that all the Soviets present, including the Soviet Ukrainian delegates, had been 'greatly amused.' As a postscript Malania added, likely to the relief of many in External Affairs, that there had been no mention of the Manuilsky-Knowles tête-à-tête in the press.[25] No one in Ottawa need worry about Ukrainian Canadians getting wind of how Knowles, Canada's official representative, had described Canadian citizens of Ukrainian heritage. And so no protest would be launched by the Ukrainian Canadian community over what had been said, and there would be no political costs to pay. Even better, the Soviets had been shown that the Canadian government was hardly less critical of Ukrainian Canadian nationalist aspirations than was Moscow.

'Fomenting Canadian–Russian Friendship'

These internal communications between top members of the civil service and Prime Minister King, who at the time still wore the mantle of secretary of state for external affairs, reveal a persistent antipathy towards those advocating Ukrainian independence. Coupled with this was Ottawa's belief that all the 'problems' Ukrainian Canadian activism had generated would gradually disappear through the assimilation of the Ukrainian Canadian population into mainstream Anglo-Canadian society. But achieving such a disappearance, it was also understood, required more than a small measure of cooperation from the Soviets, for otherwise Ukrainian Canadians would keep rallying together on independence-related issues, furthering their group's solidarity. That was undesirable, for it would impede their integration and undermine what Malania called 'Canadian unity.' This desire on the part of Ottawa's men to further nation-building by quelling Ukrainian Canadian activism is understandable, given their vision of what Canada should become as a nation.[26] But their willingness to maintain, their recurring emphasis on maintaining, good relations with the Soviet Union even when that entailed dismissing the legitimate concerns of Ukrainian Canadians seems far less reasonable or defensible.

On 6 September 1945, Prime Minister King was secretly told about a 'vast espionage system' being run by the Soviets in Canada. This startling information came from the debriefing of a defector, a Ukrainian cypher clerk from the Soviet embassy in Ottawa, Igor Gouzenko. King must have been deeply shocked to discover, just as he and his colleagues were 'doing all we can to foment Canadian–Russian friendship,' that the Soviets had covertly set up and run an extensive spy ring in Canada.[27] Yet there is nothing to suggest that these revelations altered Canadian policies on the 'Ukrainian Question' in Europe, or that Ottawa thereafter adjusted its attitude towards Ukrainian Canadian advocates of Ukrainian independence. Instead of responding with outrage, the prime minister temporized, and even seems to have wanted to drop the matter altogether, fearing that it might occasion a complete break in relations between Canada and the USSR. That he deemed unconscionable.

As King fussed over what to do about the concrete evidence of Soviet untrustworthiness that had been placed before him, and consulted with the British and American governments over what they might do, External Affairs' Wilgress and Malania continued to submit reports which, if now devoid of the exuberant idealism of their earlier memoranda, nevertheless continued to explain events from what was essentially a pro-Soviet perspective. Neither man, as yet, knew anything about the Gouzenko revelations. The Canadian government took no action against members of the Soviet spy ring until 3 February 1946, and only then because a Washington-based journalist, Drew Pearson, revealed some of the Gouzenko details in an evening radio broadcast, thereby compelling King's government to act. But even after a formal protest was lodged with the Soviet government, and an order-in-council passed establishing a secret inquiry headed by two Supreme Court justices, Robert Taschereau and R.L. Kellock, the Canadian government moved cautiously. A press release issued on 15 February informed the public only that official secrets had been passed to unauthorized persons, including staff members of an unspecified foreign mission. The creation of a commission of inquiry was announced along with the detention of a number of suspects, including some civil servants. It was also stated that the government would lay charges in those cases where the evidence warranted. The Soviet Union was not named. Meanwhile, Wilgress continued his attempts to explain away the motivations behind Soviet behaviour, and did so well into the spring of 1946. By that time, however, a determination to hold the line against the USSR had taken root among the Anglo-American powers, making his interpretations seem rather anachronistic.[28] The 'Ukrainian Question' was about to be raised yet again by the senior practitioners of Anglo-American statecraft.

But the problem of what to do with the displaced persons remained. Rather than risk Soviet displeasure, the British, American, and Canadian governments had complied with Soviet demands for the forced return of hundreds of thousands of anti-communists and refugees in the wake of the war. Yet, as government archives show, and to the discredit of the Canadian state's servants, Ottawa's officials were not even aware that the Dominion was a signatory to the Yalta Agreement, which provided for the repatriation of 'Soviet citizens' to the USSR. Writing to Canada House in London, Hume Wrong observed, 'We have made a careful review of the documents on the Yalta Conference and have found no suggestion that the agreement on repatriation of Soviet nationals was signed specifically on behalf of Canada or other Commonwealth Governments.'[29]

Several months later, a 'personal and secret' letter to G. Riddell, Canada's consul general in New York, acknowledged that it was not until late March 1946 that External Affairs finally realized that the Yalta Agreement had been signed on behalf of Canada by Britain's foreign secretary, Anthony Eden. Until then – over a year after the Agreement came into force – the department had 'been blissfully unaware' of Canada's involvement.[30]

The degree to which Ottawa was impervious to the concerted and legitimate lobbying efforts of Ukrainian Canadians against this involuntary repatriation of tens of thousands of Ukrainian DPs is remarkable, particularly since the archival record demonstrates that these men were not 'unaware' of what was really going on. More likely, they simply felt they could discount Ukrainian Canadian protests as impolitic and unsubstantial. This disdainful attitude towards Ukrainian Canadian activism, which persisted from the late interwar into the postwar period, may seem extraordinary in retrospect, especially given the grandiloquent lip-service often paid to Ukrainian Canadian aspirations by politicians. But when one recalls that it was this same small group of men who, recruited to Ottawa to constitute the government's civil service elite, formed a more or less stable mandarinate for several decades, there seems less reason for surprise. These men 'personally, or the influence they exercised, continued well into the sixties.'[31] And for these men Ukraine as a viable polity did not exist, and Ukrainian Canadian aspirations did not matter.

It is highly unlikely that the UCC's executive had any lucid appreciation of just how truly indifferent towards them Ottawa's men were. As for Panchuk and his co-workers in Europe, they were faced with so many immediate and pressing problems that they had little time left over for ruminating about long-term plans, much less about the bureaucratic attitudes towards their work adopted by men in Ottawa, Washington, or London. Not untypical of the kinds of problems they were called upon to deal with, during late 1945 and early 1946, was the effort they had to dedicate to overcoming a British military order which not only stated that His Majesty's Government did not recognize Ukrainians as a nationality but ordered the disbandment 'forthwith' of all Ukrainian organizations inside and outside the refugee camps. Military personnel were instructed to be thorough to the extent that they were ordered to confiscate even the stationery of Ukrainian organizations located in their areas of command. The same order instructed military governors throughout the 30 Corps District of Germany to offer educational and welfare facilities to those styling themselves Ukrainian only in a language 'appropriate to their citizenship,' such as Polish; it was deemed 'impracticable' to publish books or other literature in Ukrainian.[32] That Foreign Office officials essentially concurred with this policy of non-recognition of Ukrainian nationality made CURB's exertions even more necessary, and arduous. Why Whitehall was against acknowledging the existence of Ukrainians as a distinct people was explained candidly by Brimelow: 'It is against the question for us to recognize the Ukrainians as a race apart, with a claim to asylum etc. I can think of nothing more certain to cause Anglo–Soviet friction.'[33]

'Political Differences Are Quite Alive'

Attempting to deal with such crises, as well as with the more common day-to-day needs of the DPs for welfare supplies and advice, Panchuk continued to visit refugee camps, to compile observations about conditions in these centres, to type numerous reports, and to forward copious amounts of documentation to London, Winnipeg, and the UUARC's headquarters in Philadelphia. He hoped his prolific reporting would keep CURB's benefactors appraised of the magnitude and complexity of the Ukrainian refugee problem, as well as arouse further support for the Bureau's work. By leaving these profuse accounts to posterity, the Bureau's staff, perhaps inadvertently, also made it possible for the chronology of CURB-initiated activities to be reconstructed. Also revealed in these documents are the changes in their expectations concerning the Ukrainian refugees as encounters between them and the DPs grew more frequent and more intense.

During the latter part of 1945, Panchuk travelled throughout western Europe visiting DP camps, even engaging in a little larceny, albeit of a humanitarian kind. In July–August 1945 he helped issue entirely unofficial 'Ukrainian Red Cross' ID cards (marked 'Geneva, Switzerland') to thousands of Ukrainian refugees who required a document establishing their citizenship, identity papers which they hoped would help them avoid forcible repatriation.[34] By early February 1946, Panchuk had returned to London to attend a conference that brought together CURB's workers and several representatives of the various Ukrainian relief committees active on the Continent.[35] Subsequently he went again to Utersen, near Hamburg, using that city as a centre from which he sallied forth to visit various Ukrainian-populated refugee camps. After each of his four major trips he prepared lengthy reports for the Bureau, the Fund, and their Ukrainian American associates.[36]

Peculiar to these four accounts is Panchuk's description of the Ukrainian DPs, for it differed significantly from his earlier portrayal of the refugees, after his first, mid-December 1945 trips into Belgium and northern Germany; that tour had included a visit to the Heidenau DP camp, which he had described as 'the best camp in the British Zone of Germany.'[37] At that time he had commented favourably that the camp was organized like 'a miniature state' by its 'disciplined' inhabitants, even if 'political differences [were] quite alive'; this less appealing fact of life was kept 'pretty well ... under the surface and ... not openly displayed.' Part of the strife, he had remarked, had emerged over religious issues, but there was also a 'marked division' between Eastern and Western Ukrainians because of 'the feeling of superiority ("Piedmont") which is a natural trait of the Western Ukrainians. Many of these also believe that the fact that they are hunted by the Soviet Repatriation Commissions is due to the presence of Eastern Ukrainians, and there is a belief amongst the masses that should the Easterners be repatriated or segregated they, themselves (the Westerners), as Polish citizens, would not be troubled by the Russians.'[38] More tellingly, Panchuk had written that the real struggle in the refugee camps was not so much over religious affiliation as among political groups struggling 'for the minds of the masses.' Each of these competing groups was trying to win for itself the support of the non-partisan DPs, hoping thereby to achieve ascendancy over camp life and over the diaspora as a whole. Displaying an attitude that would later trouble his relations with some refugees, Panchuk had recommended that the surest way of achieving political unity among these discordant groups – unity 'such as exists in Canada' – would be to have 'some authoritative person from Canada or the USA' come over and 'apply some pressure.'[39] It is unclear whether Panchuk knew at this time that exactly that kind of prescription had been used once before, when Ottawa created the Ukrainian Canadian Committee. Whether he did or not, it remains that his own remedy for curing disunity among the Ukrainian refugees was no less paternalistic and interventionist than the strategy employed by those who had imposed unity on the Ukrainians of Canada. The remedy was as flawed as its predecessor, and it would have equally unfortunate consequences in the years ahead.

'Not for Publication!'

At the 7 February 1946 CURB-sponsored London conference, political factionalism within the DP camps became a topic of lively debate – which is why the minutes of this meeting were marked 'Confidential – *Not* for publication!'[40] Participating were the Bureau's staff – Panchuk, Frolick, Kluchevsky, and Peter Smylski – as well as members of the Association of Ukrainians in the Polish Armed Forces, namely Mykyta (Nikita) Bura, Major S. Nahnybida, Captain W. Grenko, and George Salsky. Joining them were Danylo Skoropadsky, the suave son of the late Hetman Pavlo Skoropadsky, and envoys from both factions of the OUN, Dmytro Andrievsky of the Melnykivtsi[41] and a Dr Paul Shumowsky representing the Banderivtsi. Presiding was the president of the UCC and of the UCRF, Monsignor Kushnir. He opened the conference by suggesting that delegates candidly express their views about what the best method might be for fostering unity among the Ukrainian political parties now emerging within the DP emigration. That call was enough to set off an exchange, at times acerbic, between Andrievsky and Shumowsky on the nature of political life within this emigration, and particularly on the question of who should lead this postwar diaspora.

Andrievsky began by stating that the situation for Ukrainian DPs in Belgium was 'abnormal,' for refugee life there was relatively peaceful. Elsewhere, considerable strife existed. Furthermore, try as one might, the political problems fragmenting the Ukrainian refugee population could not be disentangled from relief work, for it was 'obvious ... that one cannot hope to fill the whole [of] Ukrainian life with relief.' As Andrievsky saw it, the Ukrainian problem must be solved in Europe, even if the material and moral support coming from the 'emigration beyond the seas' was both necessary and welcome. Even more important, he argued, was that Kushnir assume the role of conciliator, using his position of moral authority to gather the representatives of the various political parties together and 'effect a united front.'[42]

Shumowsky did not dispute the Ukrainian refugees' need for material aid, although he argued that the need to find a resolution to the legal status of the DPs was even greater. But he did caution Kushnir that it was critical for Ukrainian Canadians to review carefully all the facts concerning this refugee emigration before attempting to unite them: 'In dealing with the political factions [Kushnir] must first know who are active and who exist only theoretically, who constitute the majority and who are but an insignificant group, whose actions are motivated by our homeland and its present situation and needs, who has the support of the Ukrainian nation ... [as opposed to those] who exist only outside of the Ukraine who do not do anything except play around with politics.'[43]

An envoy of the Banderivtsi, of the Ukrainska povstanska armiia (Ukrainian Insurgent Army, or UPA), and of its political command, the Ukrainska holovna vyzvolna rada (Supreme Ukrainian Liberation Council, or UHVR),[44] Shumowsky alluded to the predominance of these groups in the political life of this postwar refugee population. He added an observation that was pregnant with significance for the future of relations between Ukrainian Canadians and the Ukrainian political refugees: 'Should the Ukrainian liberation struggle be unsuccessful [in Ukraine,] political activities on a grand scale must be transplanted to the North American continent. With this in view a principle of selection of new settlers to North America must be applied whereby only the most constructive and best people would migrate [there].'[45]

If Kushnir was alarmed by this declaration he kept his concerns private, stressing in response that he and his colleagues did not wish 'to create a mechanical unity' among the refugees but instead hoped the refugees would achieve an 'organical' solidarity. In the meantime he urged discretion upon them all, it being imperative, he had learned, that Ukrainians do nothing which might be perceived by the Anglo-American authorities as having a 'political colouring.' Indeed, as he pointed out, it was absolutely 'necessary to conceal even the least political activity under the cloak of relief work' so as to avoid official reprimand. Before the session ended, Kushnir added a further caveat, an oblique response to Shumowsky's remarks about a planned emigration of Ukrainian nationalists to Canada: 'Many of them will be coming ... and we do not want them to bring disunity and dissensions with them.'[46]

A few days afterwards, Panchuk and Kushnir set off for the Continent, where Panchuk for several weeks would guide his companion through the British Zone of Germany, before passing him over to others, who would take him, illegally, into the American and French zones.[47] Both had returned to London by mid-April, when they participated in another meeting that ratified the Bureau's structure, responsibilities, and staffing.[48] Subsequently, Kushnir returned to Winnipeg, leaving Panchuk behind until 7 May, when he and his wife boarded the *Queen Elizabeth* for passage to Canada.[49] The Panchuks were home on Saskatoon's Alexandra Avenue by late May 1946.[50] At the second national UCC congress, held shortly thereafter, Panchuk would hear Kushnir tell their fellow Ukrainian Canadians that it was up to the

Committee to provide 'some kind of leadership' for the Ukrainian DPs of Europe, of whom there were as many as there were Ukrainians in Canada. No public hint of any kind of factionalism among this refugee population was given.

'The Partisan Type Is Rare'

Before leaving for Canada, Panchuk had submitted four official reports about Ukrainian refugee-camp life in the British Zone of Germany, all rather different in kind from the descriptions he had penned before his first encounter with Kushnir and the stormy February conference in London. In none of these more recent descriptions did Panchuk mention political factionalism or any 'struggle for the minds of the masses' in the DP camps, as he had done in his 30 January 1946 report. This oversight is especially puzzling given that he wrote these four reports from quarters in Utersen, close to the very same Heidenau refugee camp where he had earlier observed so much political and religious factionalism. Indeed these latter reports, all written between late February and mid-March 1946 and forwarded from CURB to the UCRF and UUARC, suggest to a casual reader that Panchuk was encountering Ukrainian DPs for the first time. What did he tell his readers about Ukrainian refugees in this newer series of reports?

In his 'First Report' Panchuk noted that near Lübeck he had located a Ukrainian refugee within a half hour: 'It can safely be said here that there isn't a town in Germany where there aren't Ukrainians, and in the larger cities there are thousands. It is equally and by the same token safe to say that all estimates of Ukrainian DPs in Germany are under-estimates. It is humanly impossible to make any sort of count. Thousands are still in hiding under every nationality and every citizenship but Ukrainian.'[51]

Having established the scale of the Ukrainian refugee problem for his readers and commented on its geographical extent, Panchuk went on in his 'Second Report' to remark upon the impressive degree of order the DPs had brought to their lives. In this account he noted that 'every camp ... always had its own camp committee which consists of the DPs themselves.'[52] In his 'Third Report' he re-emphasized this order as a common characteristic of refugee camp life, and recorded further that each of the ethnic groups in the otherwise rather heterogeneous DP camps, like the one he visited at Wentorf, 'live in a cluster of

"a camp within a camp"' with their own committee and commandant.[53] Given his observations on the problems he had seen in Heidenau in January 1946, it is surprising to read his claim that, by late
February, the DPs there lived in the 'best organized' camp in the British
Zone and were all getting along nicely.[54] Indeed, Panchuk wrote
enthusiastically that a 'spirit of harmony had descended upon the refugee camps,' so much so that 'the partisan type is very rare and certainly the exception rather than the rule.'[55] What had happened to the
'struggle for the minds of the masses' among competing Ukrainian
political refugee factions? Panchuk did not say.

Another theme Panchuk introduced in his 'First Report,' and
brought to something of a crescendo in his fourth, concerned relations
between Ukrainian DPs and refugees of other nationalities. Gone were
references to religious and political tensions between Eastern and
Western Ukrainians, such problems being replaced by a discussion of
the friction between different nationalities within the refugee population.[56] Accordingly, Ukrainians were reported to be staying away from
Russian camps – 'there was never the freedom in a Russian camp that
there was in others'[57] – and experiencing discrimination in Polish-
dominated ones.[58] In one case, that of a small camp near Flensburg,
Russians and Poles had 'literally "broken up"' the Ukrainian camp,
exposing many of its DPs to Soviet repatriation missions. As a result,
the Soviets were able to remove forcibly about 140 of these unprotected
Ukrainians. Some of those who were rounded up by the Soviets, Panchuk added, had later managed to escape from transit camps located
near Stettin and Kolberg. Once safely in the West they had reported on
their traumatic experiences.[59] Concluding his fourth report for North
America's Ukrainians, Panchuk underlined a point he had raised earlier, namely, that the Ukrainian refugees' greatest need was not for
material supplies – 'the authorities see to it that the basic needs are
met'[60] – but for field representatives who could intervene to protect
them from the Soviets and from hostile representatives of other nationalities, and at the same time represent Ukrainian interests before the
occupation authorities.[61] He could not have been more subtly persuasive in penning a description of the hardships facing the Ukrainian
DPs and of the limitations of their own self-help efforts. All this,
of course, militated in favour of the energetic maintenance of the
Bureau's operations by Ukrainians in Canada and the United States,
presided over by Panchuk. It is hard to avoid the conclusion that

Panchuk had been instructed, perhaps by Monsignor Kushnir, to play down the factionalism that had become rife in the DP camps, at least in official reports for North America's Ukrainian audiences.

Panchuk had a surprise in mind, however, for at the same time as he completed his 'Fourth Report,' he let it be known that he was resigning as CURB's director.[62] As he wrote to Dr Kaye in Ottawa, he wanted to return home: 'I have been away for five years now.'[63] As his replacement Panchuk suggested Captain Stephen Davidovich, another Ukrainian Canadian veteran who, before the outbreak of the Second World War, had run a Ukrainian National Information Bureau in London financed by the Ukrainian nationalists of North America, on behalf of what was then still a united OUN.[64] He repeated this recommendation at the CURB meeting of 13–14 April, in the presence of Kushnir, Captains Frolick, Smylski and Romanow, Danylo Skoropadsky, George Kluchevsky, and Dmytro Andrievsky. It was also agreed at this meeting, as recorded in its minutes, that in the absence of a director, 'the General Secretary will act for and in his behalf with Director's powers and responsibilities.'[65] The general secretary at the time was Stanley Wasyl Frolick, although there is no indication in the surviving records that he was even considered for the soon-to-be-vacated post of CURB's director. That post, Panchuk hoped, would go to Davidovich.[66]

Certainly, personal reasons played a major role in Panchuk's recommendation that Davidovich succeed him. By early 1946 he had begun to show a dislike for Frolick despite their earlier friendship. Some of this antipathy seems to have been rooted in pique. In his personal diary he confided that Frolick was undeserving of a salary equal to his own. He, Panchuk, had almost single-handedly built up UCSA and CURB, while all Frolick had done was 'walk in, talk himself into a job, and then insist on an equal salary.'[67] He would also commit to his private notes his feeling that 'Stan' would 'spend all his time and our money gallivanting about the country and having a good time' since he was 'most irresponsible and undependable,' the 'playboy type.'[68] While such personal feelings soured relations between the two men, far more important were the fundamental political motives underpinning Panchuk's slighting of Frolick, considerations which would greatly disrupt CURB during the latter half of 1946 and eventually have a major impact on Ukrainian Canadian organizational affairs. Central, then, to the unfolding of this drama were the character and politics of Stanley Frolick.

'Relief Covers a Multitude of Sins, but Very Few Indiscretions'

Born in the small mining community of Hillcrest, Alberta, in July 1920, as the son of a twenty-two-year-old labourer, Yurko, who had emigrated to Canada from the village of Karliv in Western Ukraine in 1909, Stanley (Sviatoslav) Wasyl Frolick was to have an experience probably unique in the annals of Ukrainian Canadian history.[69] In 1932, in part because his father wanted to ensure that his son would grow up to be a Ukrainian, Frolick was sent to the Western Ukrainian village of Yablonitsa to live and study under the care of his uncle Vasyl, a Ukrainian Catholic priest entrusted with the spiritual care of the local parish. During the next nine years he would grow to manhood in an intensely patriotic Ukrainian setting, where he found himself, by reason of his nationality, pitted against the Polish state's rule over this part of Ukraine. After the fall of Poland and the Soviet occupation of the region in late September 1939, he was able to disguise his political sympathies from the occupation forces, in particular from the NKVD. His experiences made Frolick especially sympathetic to the Ukrainian independence movement. In time he became a full-fledged member of the underground OUN. This affiliation – once it became clear that he had sided with the revolutionary wing of the OUN headed by Stepan Bandera – would bring him into disfavour with several leading members of the UCC's national executive and eventually result in his ostracism from CURB. That, however, took place at the end of 1946. Before then Frolick's singular experience of having been born and raised in Canada and subsequently educated in Western Ukraine, and his close ties to the still unfragmented nationalist movement, made him something of a celebrity on his return to Toronto, via Siberia and Japan, in the summer of 1941. He quickly became president of the Toronto branch of the Ukrainian National Federation's youth group, the Young Ukrainian Nationalists, enrolled at the University of Toronto, and by 1943 had been elected the youth group's second national president, succeeding Paul Yuzyk.[70] As a spokesman for Ukrainian Canadian youth, Frolick was even selected to present a speech before the First All-Canadian Ukrainian Congress, held in Winnipeg in June 1943.[71] That he was given such responsibilities affirms that, prior to his departure for London in the fall of 1945, where he went to work for the Control Commission for Germany, Frolick had enjoyed the trust of the

UNF's national executive, particularly that of Wolodymyr Kossar, himself a former member of the Ukrainian Military Organization and of the *provid*, or leadership, of the OUN who had simultaneously served as the UNF's president.[72] Indeed, before he left for overseas, Frolick was provided with a note from Kossar introducing him to another *provid* member, Dmytro Andrievsky, requesting that the latter accord this young Ukrainian Canadian his *'full* trust' – a confidential document intended to alert Andrievsky to the fact that Frolick was a member of the covert OUN network and could be confided in absolutely.[73]

At first Frolick was extended every courtesy and confidence, being made the Bureau's general secretary shortly after his arrival in London in late June 1945, a position he retained until he took over as director in late May 1946. Throughout his stay he served essentially as an acting director of the Bureau by default, for more often than not Panchuk was on the Continent. It was also during this period that Frolick became not only more personally sympathetic to the Bandera faction of the nationalist movement but also involved in several endeavours which Ukrainians in North America would come to believe were directly inimical to their own interests. These entanglements would provide ammunition for Frolick's detractors, making it easier for them to bring about his precipitous dismissal from the Bureau in the late fall of 1946.

Frolick's granting of sanctuary to Dmytro Dontsov, the leading interwar ideologue of Ukrainian nationalism – assistance which included room and board at 218 Sussex Gardens along with gainful employment – was one of the earliest of Frolick's public acts to cause concern among those Ukrainian Canadians for whom any hint of political activity was anathema. But it was Frolick's close association with the Ukrainian Information Service (UIS) which more particularly alarmed some of the Bureau's most important patrons.[74] According to Frolick's own account, the UIS was set up after the 7–8 February 1946 London conference of CURB, a meeting at which Monsignor Kushnir was present.[75] Why the formation of the UIS subsequently troubled Winnipeg was a puzzle to Frolick because, as he accurately pointed out, Bureau staff had regularly sent out voluminous amounts of information about the Ukrainian DPs and the situation in the homeland. Indeed, they had done so 'from the moment we set up the Bureau.' According to a letter Frolick wrote at the time, UIS materials were intended to 'mobilize public opinion' and 'gain sympathy,' particularly among 'Englishmen who might not even know what a Ukrainian is.'[76] But in order to placate those who had raised objections to the UIS being identified with CURB, a decision was made to 'separate the Ukrainian Information Bureau from CURB because of the political nature of some of its activities,' and simultaneous provisions were made to expand the Bureau's efforts as a press agency. And so, it was thought, CURB would not suffer because of any work done by the UIS. Frolick also declared that the work he had done for the UIS had all been voluntary and after-hours, and that Bureau funds 'were never used' for the press agency's purposes. But this explanation did not seem to interest those in North America who objected to the UIS for partisan reasons.[77] What was really at issue, and Frolick realized it full well, was that even if the UIS sent out a variety of materials, much of it was undeniably political. This alarmed those who were, quite simply, afraid of official censure should they be perceived as playing a role which might complicate relations between the Anglo-American powers and various foreign governments. So however cogent Frolick's questioning of his detractors might be, particularly when he asked them rhetorically to explain how the UIS was supposed to avoid political matters when it was 'dealing with things like why are so many fleeing their homeland?' he never got a serious response.[78] His remonstrations proved futile, and at a joint UCRF and UUARC board of directors meeting, held in New York on 25 April 1946, it was decided that the UIS and CURB should be entirely dissociated. The joint meeting also decided that it would be inadvisable for CURB's secretary to be engaged in any activity other than channelling relief to the displaced persons. As for political activity, the UCC and the corresponding Ukrainian American Congress Committee insisted that such efforts were to be their exclusive responsibility, even if, in truth, they were themselves quite reluctant to do any such work.[79] A telegram, co-signed by Kushnir and Gallan, dated 4 June 1946, confirmed this decision and requested that Frolick acknowledge its receipt and his understanding of the message.[80] The point was further emphasized when the UUARC's Dr Gallan visited London in late June 1946 and repeated that the American Ukrainians had pressed for the termination of the UIS because its political undertakings were hurting the relief action.[81] Gallan, as Frolick may have known at the time, was a leading émigré supporter of the Melynk faction of the OUN.

That the authorities were becoming increasingly troubled by the circulation of what one British official described as 'Ukrainian propaganda' throughout their zone of occupation was indeed true. By mid-May 1946, officials of the British Army of Occupation on the Rhine

(BAOR) were complaining to the Foreign Office that anti-Soviet and anti-repatriation materials were being passed from Winnipeg, via CURB in London, to selected UNRRA teams in the zone, who then distributed them among the DPs, 'by-passing the censorship.' Although no BAOR officers could read these Ukrainian-language newspapers, 'the cartoons in them ... speak for themselves.'[82]

At about the same time other BAOR personnel were getting direct complaints from various UNRRA team members, especially those who were less than sympathetic to Ukrainian aspirations, about this 'Ukrainian propaganda.' For example, Marina Howson, attached to the Canadian Red Cross, wrote to Tracy Philipps explaining that she had received 'a furious telephone call' from a Miss Kerr of UNRRA. Miss Kerr insisted that Miss Howson stop 'spreading literature which contained anti-allied statements.' While Howson confided to Philipps that she wasn't sure whether this was just another example of UNRRA being 'troublesome' or whether someone in authority was 'clamping down,' she indicated that, unfortunately, she would have to drop the next lot of papers she received into the 'waste-paper basket.' Much as she felt sorry for the DPs, the Red Cross was supposed to be 'strictly noncombatant.'[83] Philipps, for his part, lost little time in alerting his confidants in Canada about the seriousness of the Bureau's apparently growing entanglement with political issues, writing that 'in matters of security, relief and education for refugees any national-naming or national bannering is not only a grave handicap but also *Une grosse gaffe.*'[84] He concluded his homily, addressed to Dr Kaye and Professor Kirkconnell, by observing that it was an error to send out 'national – (i.e. political) propaganda, however proper and true in itself' from the same address as that of the relief organization, for the 'label *relief* covers, like charity, a multitude of sins, *but very few indiscretions.*'[85]

'Hero of the Day'

Since Philipps's letter ended up in Panchuk's archives, it seems certain that Panchuk was briefed by one of Philipps's other Ukrainian Canadian friends about what they perceived to be the gradual politicization of CURB under Frolick and the problems this was likely to engender. By late May, Panchuk had been offered the position of full-time 'field representative' for the Fund overseas.[86] He was probably not surprised at this turn of events. He had himself expressed reservations about leaving the Bureau in Frolick's care in a letter he sent to Kaye even before he returned to Canada, earlier that same month.[87]

Whether Panchuk was as yet fully aware of the nature of Frolick's activities overseas, or informed himself only upon returning to London in October, remains unclear. But before his discharge from the RCAF, which took place in Winnipeg on 20 June, he was able to perform a sterling service on behalf of the Ukrainian Canadian Committee by appearing in uniform before the Senate's Standing Committee on Immigration and Labour, in Ottawa, on 29 May 1946. There, in the presence of such UCC luminaries as the Monsignor Kushnir and Reverend Sawchuk and community leaders such as Anthony Hlynka, MP, and John R. Solomon, MLA, he described what he had seen in Europe with such conviction that even some of the assembled Canadian senators, according to Dr Kaye, 'had tears in their eyes.'[88] This 'one big Victory' – scored over 'three communists' who had come to lobby against the immigration of 'war criminals, former collaborators, the beguiled and members of the Ukrainian Rebellion Army' on the ground that such an inflow would imperil 'the safety of Canada' – was achieved, wrote Kaye, largely because of Panchuk, 'the hero of the day.'[89] The extent of Panchuk's effectiveness that day was made clear by one of those senators, Mr Crerar, who, in responding to Stephen Macievich, the editor of *Ukrainian Life*, stated bluntly that he preferred the judgment of Flight Lieutenant Panchuk to that of a newspaperman. All Macievich could do was retort that he felt 'political considerations were at the root of the Senator's preference.'[90]

Panchuk's performance was indeed impressive, but the UCC's men had an additional advantage over their communist opponents even before they entered the Senate chambers on that late May morning in 1946. According to the testimony of John Solomon, members of the Standing Committee had been lobbied well in advance of the formal meeting by UCC-backers, with the result that several of them were already favourably disposed to the Committee's brief. A contrary reception for the spokesmen of the Ukrainian Canadian Left was thought to be almost a sure thing.[91] More important, it is debatable whether this exchange in the Senate chambers had any real influence on Canadian immigration policy, for on the very same day on which this Senate meeting was being held, the minister of mines and resources, J.A. Glen, announced in the House of Commons that, by order-in-council no. 2071, dated 28 May 1946, provision was being made under the 'Close Relatives Scheme' for the immigration of those

DPs who could demonstrate that they had family ties to residents of Canada, if those residents of Canada were willing to accept them and assume financial responsibility for them.[92] A door for the immigration of Ukrainians was now officially open; it had been opened even before the UCC's lobbyists knocked.

'Not without Its Influence'

Meanwhile, Frolick continued to work for CURB. He took on worthwhile projects like resettling Ukrainian Catholic orphans in Ireland. He attended conferences in Edinburgh and Paris which brought together Ukrainians who had served with the Polish armed forces. And he held a number of meetings with representatives of various Continental Ukrainian relief committees set up by the refugees themselves, sometimes with Bureau assistance. He also joined with the UUARC's Dr Gallan in protesting the forcible repatriation of Ukrainians to the USSR, taking the Ukrainian case right up to the level of the British foreign secretary, Ernest Bevin.[93] That the Bureau in London and the Committee in Winnipeg had some impact on British policy towards Ukrainian DPs in the British Zone of Germany was attested by Escott Reid, then Canada's acting under-secretary of state for external affairs. In writing to a Mr F. Foulds at the Canadian Citizenship Branch of the Department of the Secretary of State, Reid commented, 'You will observe that the pressure exerted by the KYK in Canada has not been without its influence on developments in UK policy towards Ukrainian refugees and displaced persons,'[94] an opinion lifted verbatim from a report he had received from Canada House in London a few weeks earlier, which had noted how the Ukrainian Canadian representatives were considered to be both 'understanding and sensible.'[95] The same confidential report to Ottawa from the acting high commissioner for Canada also pointed out, however, that the Foreign Office's men had advised their Canadian counterparts to explain to 'the influential Ukrainians in Canada that the best way in which to help those Ukrainians who were left in Germany was to behave reasonably and not force the British authorities into a position which would make it difficult for them to help.'[96]

'Mickey Mouse'

While Frolick stayed in London and took charge of the Bureau, Panchuk attended summer courses at the University of Saskatchewan and

kept in touch with overseas and Ukrainian Canadian issues by corresponding frequently with trusted advisers, among them Philipps in
London, Kirkconnell in Hamilton, and Kaye in Ottawa. At the same
time he was working hard to invigorate the Ukrainian Canadian Veterans' Association, a group he had high hopes for but had found more or
less moribund upon his return to Canada.[97] Two letters he wrote at this
time reveal something of his feelings about Ukrainian Canadian society
on the Prairies, upon seeing it again after five years of work in Europe
and life in metropolitan London. Writing to Frolick in a friendly tone
(circumstantial evidence which suggests that he had, as yet, no thought
of returning to London to take over CURB), Panchuk reported that he
had just finished touring much of western Canada. To his disgust, he
observed, the general state of affairs was 'most demoralizing, most
hopeless, most chaotic.'[98] 'If I could find enough adjectives preceded by
enough superlatives to emphasize the situation, I would still not do it
justice.'[99] The problem was that Ukrainian Canadians had arrived at a
condition similar to that described in *The Last of the Mohicans*:

> Our people don't read, don't study, don't listen, don't worship, don't
> attend anything higher than Mickey Mouse [movies] or drunken brawls.
> Our school teachers from coast to coast are a hopeless mob of stupid para-
> sites, with no spine or mind of their own ... The Refugees? The DPs? The
> Victims of War? Our people (generally speaking) don't know a thing
> about them and aren't interested. So long as they are alright the world
> doesn't concern them.[100]

As for the UCC, and its plans for settling Ukrainian DPs in new
'block settlements' scattered about the Prairies – or, according to one
unconfirmed account, concentrating the DPs in Manitoba to give
Ukrainian Canadians an enhanced political strength there – Panchuk
was smart enough to realize that any such scheme would 'hardly be
acceptable to *any* government,' much as it might appeal to Ukrainian
Canadians. 'Every government,' he wrote, 'is *afraid* of blocks. Canada
itself is more concerned what it will do to *liquidate or break up* definite
blocks of Ukrainians, Mennonites, etc. that already exist, and therefore
would be most reluctant if not completely opposed to any suggestion
of block settlement.'[101]

At best, Panchuk reasoned, such a settlement plan would be acceptable only if it were presented as a temporary measure. In such a case,
these 'colonies' should be described as nothing more than 'transient
camps' from which the resettled refugees would sooner rather than

later be dispersed to industrial and manufacturing centres throughout Canada, these centres being the only places capable of absorbing 'large numbers' of new immigrants. To cultivate sympathy for any large-scale immigration of Ukrainian refugees to Canada, Panchuk concluded, the Committee and its Fund must be very careful to avoid anything which hinted at 'block settlement.' Such schemes would only 'frighten' the nation's gatekeepers. It would be far better, he counselled, to concentrate on the 'humanitarian and Christian angle' in their pro-refugee immigration literature, rather than worry about where the new DP immigrants would go once they got into Canada.[102]

Although critical of some of the UCC's plans, Panchuk was, along with several other UCVA members, just as busy designing schemes others would find unrealistic. One such proposal, rather grandiloquently entitled 'Renaissance Plans,' was first presented to the UCC's national executive on 10 September 1946. Speaking on behalf of the Ukrainian Canadian veterans, Panchuk argued that there was a need for a 'roundtable conference' of Ukrainian Canadians to discuss how to bring about a 'rebirth of our life in Canada.'[103] Believing that UCVA's members constituted the few who treated Ukrainian Canadian affairs from a truly 'practical' point of view and 'objectively,' Panchuk suggested that the UCC focus on building Ukrainian Canadian 'community centres.' In these halls all Ukrainian Canadians could meet, regardless of their religious convictions or organizational affiliations. This proposal would make it possible to develop a workable infrastructure for the future development of a united and effective community. In many respects, of course, the 'Renaissance Plans' mirrored the 'London Club' experience which Panchuk and many of his fellow UCSA and UCVA members had so enjoyed. What UCVA offered the UCC in return for its acceptance, endorsement, and promotion of these community development plans were the services of Panchuk and several other UCVA colleagues, all of whom had agreed to lead a 'Relief Team' to Europe, and to stay there until 30 April 1947, if the UCC, in its turn, agreed to act on their proposal during this same time period.[104]

Rather naïvely, as he would admit more than once in later years, Panchuk had told his fellow veterans that, after this 'historical meeting,' at which he presented his 'strong and rather radical and revolutionary memorandum,' the 'honourable and venerable gentlemen' of the UCC had actually agreed to act along the lines called for in the 'Renaissance Plans.' Delighted, and keeping to their part of what was a rather informal bargain, the UCVA executive agreed to field a team of relief workers, headed by Panchuk, for work in western Europe.[105] This mission was composed of people who already had experience working among the refugees, namely Panchuk, his wife Anne, Tony Yaremovich, and Ann Crapleve. Utilizing people with direct relief operations experience was a wise decision, for they were ready to act almost immediately upon their return to Europe. Interestingly enough, no other UCVA members were willing, or able, to join this mission. Several others whose names had been suggested expressed no interest whatsoever in returning to Europe to work among the Ukrainian refugees. They were home again and content to remain there. Their indifference no doubt reminded Panchuk of the apathy of most Ukrainian Canadians regarding the Ukrainian refugee problem, even in the months immediately following the war. Nevertheless, he went; that was the kind of man Panchuk was.

The mandate of the group dispatched overseas was to bring material relief to Ukrainian refugees in Europe, to act in liaison with the Red Cross societies already operating there, and to coordinate activities with the UUARC's personnel after that body became established in the American zones of occupation in Germany and Austria. The Canadian Relief Mission for Ukrainian Refugees (CRM) was also supposed to work closely with CURB; that is, it was originally constituted without any formal instructions about having the mission supplant the Bureau, or replacing Frolick as the director of the Bureau.[106] The new mission, however, was to enjoy the same measure of support as CURB, being co-sponsored by the UCC and UCRF, with UCVA's assistance. And, just in case the government had any concerns over what they were up to, Panchuk addressed a letter to a non-existent 'Diplomatic Division' which he presumed existed within Canada's Department of External Affairs, repeating the now rather trite assurance that the team's work would be 'confined strictly to *relief*.'[107] It is not known whether anyone in Ottawa believed this assurance – most likely not.

'Conform to Orders'

The group Panchuk pulled together came to be known as the Canadian Relief Mission for Ukrainian Refugees and Victims of War, hereafter abbreviated to 'the Mission' or 'the Team.'[108] At about the time the group was assembled, the UCC's secretary, Andrew Zaharychuk, a member of the Hetman organization, wrote to Frolick insisting that he provide a detailed accounting of the Bureau's expenses to date.

Zaharychuk asserted that the financial records were 'not clear.' He added, almost as an afterthought, that a team composed of the Panchuks, Yaremovich, and Crapleve would be arriving in London during the next month and would move from there to the Continent.[109] The Team did indeed arrive just over three weeks later, on 13 October 1946.[110] Prior to that, Frolick was given no indication of any serious disquiet in Winnipeg about the way he was managing CURB's affairs. As for Zaharychuk's comments about Bureau finances, these were typical of the kind of complaints often made by Winnipeg to its overseas representatives. Minor bureaucratic problems had arisen regularly as the UCC tried to understand, manage, and, in some ways, control what was happening in London – obviously a difficult exercise given the distances involved and the frequent need for immediate decision-making by those overseas. And so the recent complaints provoked no alarm. Indeed, Frolick awaited the arrival of his fellow Ukrainian Canadians with pleasure, expecting that they would be a source of additional manpower, creativity, and resourcefulness, all of which would improve the Bureau's performance. He could not have been more wrong.

The tilting for leadership of the Bureau began almost immediately after the Mission's arrival in London. On 14 October Panchuk cabled Monsignor Kushnir to inform him that Frolick claimed he had received no 'official notifications' regarding the Team, and that, furthermore, he considered himself CURB's director, having been appointed to that position by the UUARC's Dr Gallan.[111] Panchuk asked for a clarification, suggesting that it would be wise to await the imminent arrival of Dr Gallan, who could resolve the issue on the spot. Gallan was expected in London on 17 October. But Kushnir would have none of it. On the next day he telegraphed Panchuk, stating bluntly that Gallan had made no such appointment and that Panchuk should tell Frolick to 'conform to his orders.' Frolick was also cabled a message to that effect.[112] With these clear instructions in hand, Panchuk called a meeting of CURB workers and his Mission, at which he stated that, as of 18 October 1946, he was taking over as CURB's director. He cabled this news to Winnipeg on the following day.[113] Nettled, Frolick responded that he did not wish to remain in the employ of the Bureau, nor would he accept Panchuk's offer that he join the Team, for that would mean employment at a rank below that of director.[114]

This by no means ended the matter. On 17 October, Frolick, still signing himself director of CURB – a title that someone in the Committee's headquarters inked over upon reading the relevant six-page statement when it arrived in Winnipeg on 24 October – offered a vigorous riposte to the charges of financial slovenliness raised by Zaharychuk the month before.[115] Offended by the tone of Zaharychuk's letter, which Frolick derided as being that of 'a feudal lord to his serf' and 'highly insulting,' he defended his record at CURB.[116] Tongue-in-cheek he congratulated Winnipeg's *apparatchiks* on their 'truly Ukrainian handling of business matters,' remarking that there 'was just nothing like' the 'tact, truthfulness, honesty and fairness' they had brought to their dealings with him. Bemoaning what he regarded as the UCC's mishandling of financial affairs, like the matter of his own partially unpaid salary, Frolick went on to observe that even more perfidious was the way he had been dealt with over the question of the directorship. He reminded his readers in Winnipeg and Philadelphia that Dr Gallan, acting in his capacity as 'Chairman of the Board of Directors' of the UUARC, had named him CURB's director because no one else had been willing to assume the position when Panchuk had left in May. This fact had even been publicized in *Visti* (*News*) a Ukrainian-language newspaper published in Belgium, in its 15 September 1946 issue, along with Frolick's photograph. There were also eyewitnesses to the fact of his appointment among those persons who had attended a conference of Ukrainian relief committee representatives held in Paris in late July 1946, among them Danylo Skoropadsky and CURB's treasurer, George Kluchevsky. Surely, he argued, all this prima facie evidence was convincing, even if Dr Gallan had, oddly enough, 'forgotten all about it.'[117]

Frolick ended his long and detailed rebuttal by admitting that there was really little he could do to fight against the 'injustice' being done him, but that he did reserve the right at least to try to set the historical record straight. He attempted to do just that at the third conference of representatives of the Ukrainian relief committees of Europe and America, held in Paris from 30 October to 3 November. Before those assembled in the UUARC-supported Paris 'Ukrainian Home,' a group which included Dr Gallan, Yaremovich, and Panchuk, Frolick openly questioned the Ukrainian American about whether or not he had been appointed CURB's director. Instead of goading Gallan into an argument, all Frolick managed to do was elicit the curt answer that he had never been so appointed. Following that, he was denied further access to the floor, a procedural move which made it impossible for him to continue his line of questioning.[118] Aghast but stymied, Frolick left the gathering, expelled from CURB. In the following weeks he would hold several private meetings in Europe with members of the OUN's Bandera faction. By late December 1946 he had returned to Canada. According to his own version of these events, recorded years later, he was never fully paid the salary owed him by the UCC and UCRF for the work he did abroad.[119] Instead, upon his return he was treated as a renegade and a pariah, ostracized and vilified by many of the same people and groups who had lionized him only five years before. His bitterness over this betrayal would never fully abate.

'A Lot of Conspiratorial Activity'

At face value this exchange, with its seemingly petty intrigues and gripes, might appear almost entirely personal and of little relevance to the history of Ukrainian Canadian refugee relief operations. But the principal reason behind Winnipeg's and Philadelphia's disquiet with Frolick had little to do with his management skills and much to do with the negative perceptions of his political sympathies and affiliations developed by the leaders of the UCC, the UCRF, and their Ukrainian American counterparts.

Zaharychuk explained this candidly in his letter to Panchuk of 18 October 1946. The Committee's executive secretary quite openly admitted that the UCC's *nomenklatura* had 'decided to let [Frolick] go' because he had 'too tightly cooperated with one political section amongst the Ukrainian refugees on the continent.'[120] Attached to this private note was a copy of the Committee's letter of the same date to Frolick, in which he was explicitly told to relinquish CURB operations to Panchuk as of 31 October 1946.[121] This letter of dismissal, although received by Panchuk in London before the late October conference in Paris mentioned above, was not actually handed to Frolick until 23 November, a day after he had returned to London from Germany.[122] Presented with this further and unequivocal evidence of his dismissal, Frolick left England for Canada shortly thereafter. He did not realize as yet that, while he had spent some six weeks on the Continent, Panchuk, aided by Dmytro Andrievsky, had uncovered additional evidence of his political ties and dutifully informed Winnipeg of these discoveries. Possibly the most damning proof was letterhead purloined from Frolick's locked desk, which Panchuk believed had been printed on 'English paper' and which bore the masthead 'General Secretary, Foreign Affairs, Supreme Ukrainian Liberation Council.'[123] In

Panchuk's view this and other clues proved that there was good reason 'for believing that there's a lot of conspiratorial activity hereabout which we know nothing about and possibly won't find out.' Although Panchuk urged that his reports should kept confidential – 'keep it all to ourselves, for the good of [the] Ukrainian cause'[124] – the damaging fusillades continued, as Frolick's political enemies in Canada made sure that rumours of what had happened overseas circulated well before he got home. Gentlemanly rules of engagement were not the order of the day; no quarter was given or expected. His political foes tried to do nothing less than hustle Frolick into a back alley of obscurity. In their cockiness, they did not foresee that their efforts might fail, nor the consequences of failure.

Panchuk faithfully, perhaps too faithfully, kept the Winnipeg empyrean well stocked with damning evidence. In a confidential letter to the Committee's executive on 7 December, he forwarded nine additional documents which, he claimed, provided further corroborating proof of the semi-clandestine intrigues Frolick had been involved in while in UCC employ. He followed this up two weeks later with another letter containing additional enclosures, all of which made obvious that Frolick had indeed played a major role in the operations of a covert Ukrainian nationalist network operating throughout the United Kingdom and on the Continent.[125]

For those privy to this intelligence, Frolick's political loyalties were, apparently, not much of a surprise. When Teodor Datzkiw confirmed the Committee's receipt of the evidence Panchuk had forwarded, he also bragged in reply that 'even before' Panchuk had first returned to Canada, in May 1945, there had been 'unclear news' reaching Winnipeg that Frolick was 'in some way' connected with the Banderivtsi.[126] Until they received what he termed the 'concrete proof' unearthed by Panchuk, the Committee had not felt able to act. Now that evidence was in hand, however, they had no compunction whatsoever about completely severing their links with Frolick.[127] It was quite impossible, Datzkiw pronounced, for the Committee's appointee as CURB's general secretary to have anything to do with any political movement, the two roles being, in his words, 'mutually exclusive.'[128]

Whether out of malice towards Frolick or simply because he was accustomed to keeping his confidants alert about developments overseas, Panchuk soon wrote Dr Kaye about some of the details of Frolick's fall from grace at the Bureau. 'Ever since Frolick came overseas last fall,' Panchuk recorded, 'we have never been too comfortable about his activities':

> He made the mistake of always mixing politics into everything ... Bad as that was for our services club and even worse for [the] Relief Bureau, such actions take on an even more detrimentally clear [sic] because his politics were very narrowly restricted to one party, namely [the] Banderivtsi (OUN). This we knew long ago although we kept it to ourselves hoping that in case of necessity he would be sincere and broadminded enough to take a more impartial attitude to his work. Unfortunately we were led astray in our beliefs. In spite of many warnings and the sincere advice that I tried to give him before I left for Canada this Spring, no sooner had we left when he offered himself into ... narrow party politics ... to the limit, using all the facilities of the relief bureau for his purpose ... The thing has reached such a state that it scares us to think what might have happened if we had not come when we did.[129]

Panchuk told Kaye that Frolick's code name as a representative of the Liberation Council was 'Sviatoslav Bojarsky' and that his activities had 'managed to alienate many good friends in England.'[130] Panchuk added, how sincerely we do not know, that he bore Frolick no ill will and wanted him to 'settle and get a good job.' Yet in the same sentence he cautioned Kaye against helping Frolick get any kind of government position, especially one having to do with immigration or which might bring him overseas again. He was convinced that if Frolick were to manage a return to Europe, 'our Ukrainian cause ... may suffer much more than it already has.'[131] He ended by warning Kaye that 'this same sort of thing has cropped into every relief committee on the Continent,' and noted that for that reason 'we must take a firm stand on where relief ends and where politics begin.'[132] As things would turn out, Panchuk seems not to have heeded his own counsel. Even if he was, by the first day of November 1946, the undisputed head of CURB, he was very soon to become as embroiled himself in the partisan politics of the refugee diaspora as his predecessor had been, and to suffer from them in his turn.

What came to involve Panchuk in controversy was the establishment of a group known as the Koordinatsiini ukrainskyi komitet (Co-ordinating Ukrainian Committee, KYK, or CUC). Interestingly enough, KYK is also the Ukrainian-language acronym for the Komitet ukraintsiv kanady (Ukrainian Canadian Committee, or UCC). Of course, this was no coincidence. When the Co-ordinating Ukrainian Committee was brought into being in March 1946, it was in part because Monsignor Kushnir insisted on the DPs forging their own 'umbrella' group in order to represent a united front before the West. Rather disingenuously given the Winnipeg Committee's own early history, Kushnir told his Ukrainian exile audience that the group he headed had come into being voluntarily, as a coalition of several different organizations which had agreed that unity among them was far more important than their political and religious differences. Kushnir knew better, of course, but he would say nothing about the true history of the Committee in front of the DPs. Ukrainian Canadians had a KYK; the Ukrainian DPs, Kushnir insisted, would also have a KYK.

At first, all appeared to go well for the new Committee. The Banderivtsi agreed to participate in the discussions which led up to its formation. Their willingness to participate would seem to ensure the involvement of what was arguably the largest and most dynamic of all the political movements active among this postwar Ukrainian political emigration. But they withdrew from the CUC shortly after its founding, when it became clear that a number of smaller, largely insignificant political parties which had grown up within the sump of the DP camps were to be given voting status equal to that of the OUNb. For the Banderivtsi this was unthinkable. It would effectively mean their subordination on a council where they could expect to be regularly outvoted by coalitions of smaller and less relevant groups, on the principle of 'one organization, one vote.'[133] They argued instead for voting strength based on 'representation by population.' Such an arrangement would have assured them of a large bloc of votes in the Co-ordinating Committee's executive, given the size of their constituency within the refugee camps. When this idea was rejected they quit and allied themselves with the Hetmantsi – who had refused from the start to participate in a body which included their sworn enemies, the republican Petliurivtsi who had deposed Hetman Pavlo Skoropadsky in 1918. Thus an opposition to the Co-ordinating Ukrainian Committee was born. In the future a measure of political collaboration between the revolutionary nationalist Banderivtsi and the conservative Hetmantsi would develop throughout the emigration, with effects felt as far afield as the United Kingdom and Canada. In the meantime, Panchuk, in keeping with instructions received from Winnipeg and probably because of his own predilections, became a forceful advocate of the CUC and of its successor, the Ukrainian National Council

(UNRada, or 'the Council'), not only among the DPs but in the Anglo-American world. For this he would eventually find himself expelled beyond the pale, and just as indecorously as Frolick had been. The only difference was that his foes would be the newly allied Banderivtsi and Hetmantsi; rather ironically, supporters of the Hetman movement, in concert with other Ukrainian Canadian groups like the UNF and USRL, had only a few months earlier joined forces to remove Frolick from his post with CURB. Neither director fared well once he ran afoul of the diaspora's competing political elites.

'Fatherly Advice'

But Panchuk's defeat was as yet in the future. Throughout November and most of December 1946 he had other pressing issues on his mind, for the Mission he headed found itself more or less stranded in England, denied permission to return to the Continent. Much of his time was therefore spent visiting various government ministries and officials, consulting with foreign embassies, and dealing with other groups connected with welfare and immigration work among the refugees. Everywhere he tried to cultivate friendship and support. For example, on 18 November 1946, Panchuk, Yaremovich, and Danylo Skoropadsky met with the Foreign Office's Brimelow to explain the purpose of the Mission. They soon found themselves once again reminded that they must confine their activities strictly to cultural and educational work, avoiding politics if they wished to escape official censure. 'Steer clear of anti-Soviet propaganda,' Brimelow bluntly told them.[134] They received a similar message at the British War Office on 22 November, where Panchuk and Danylo Skoropadsky's aide-de-camp, Volodymyr Korostovets, met Colonel Cooke of MI5's security office.[135] In the interim they had also briefed officials at the American embassy in London about the Team's purposes, repeating this description to the American Red Cross officials they met, to the Society of Friends (the Quakers) Relief Service in Great Britain, and to many others.[136] No one could say Panchuk and his comrades were less than energetic at this time, even if they felt they could have spent their time more usefully by working among the DPs on the Continent.

It was not until mid-December 1946 that Panchuk and his associates participated in what seems to have been the critical meeting between their group and senior representatives of the British government. As a result of that meeting they were allowed finally to move to the Continent. On 11 December, Panchuk and the Canadian parliamentarian Anthony Hlynka met with Sir Herbert Emerson, the director of the Intergovernmental Committee on Refugees (IGCR). They were told confidentially that Canada would admit a 'considerable number' of refugees over and above the announced categories. But as for those whom the International Refugee Organization (IRO) could not help – individuals who were 'leaders' of 'movements hostile to their countries of origin or those encouraging people not to return' – it would be up to the Vatican to care for them. Among those ineligible for IRO assistance under these terms – and Sir Herbert singled them out for special mention – were members of the Ukrainian Division 'Galicia,' most of whom were at that time confined as Surrendered Enemy Personnel (SEP) at Rimini in northeastern Italy; veterans of the Ukrainian Insurgent Army (UPA); and supporters of the Anti-Bolshevik Bloc of Nations (ABN), especially the Banderivtsi.[137] The 'concrete advice' Sir Herbert urged upon the Ukrainian Canadians was to focus their efforts on pressuring other governments to open their doors to refugee immigration, concurrently using all the 'influence at [their] disposal' to 'stop the militant and hostile propaganda that is so prevalent in some of the Camps – it is doing more harm than good and the people concerned are only cutting their own throats [and] the throats of their kinsmen who are eligible for assistance.'[138]

Either the minutes of the meeting were recorded poorly or Panchuk was introducing his own reflections, but Sir Herbert is also reported to have told the Ukrainian Canadians that they should counsel the political refugees to occupy themselves with 'more useful positive work' than what they were engaged in. The Englishman supposedly recommended that the political refugees concentrate on educational and cultural activities or spend their time engaged in handicraft work. That someone in authority would be naïve enough to suggest that political refugees take up folk arts and crafts, particularly given the ongoing insurgency in Ukraine, would be laughable if it had not came from such a presumably well informed and senior government source. Yet if Panchuk's minutes are to be believed, this seems to have been the advice Sir Herbert offered to people whose armed struggle for independence was still raging. Sir Herbert also recommended that the displaced persons could put their time to good use by organizing daily life in their refugee camps. As it turned out, that was precisely what they were doing, but not in any manner or for any purpose which Sir Herbert would have approved of.

On the day after their meeting with the IGCR's director, Panchuk transmitted a full report of Sir Herbert's 'fatherly advice' to Winnipeg, although he was careful not to identity this British statesman beyond referring to him as 'a person who held a responsible position on the international level connected with refugee work.'[139] Less than twenty-four hours later, Hlynka and Panchuk were again speaking with the British authorities, only this time in Canada House, in the presence of the Canadian diplomat John Holmes.[140]

Both CURB's 'confidential report' and Holmes's memorandum 'Ukrainian Refugees in Europe' have survived to provide us with an inside account of what took place. According to the Ukrainian Canadian version, one of the 'main points' discussed was the Soviet government's concern over Ukrainian separatism. According to Sir George Rendel, the Soviets were so troubled over the continuing pro-independence agitation of Ukrainians in the West that they were inclined to have a 'suspicious reaction' to any talk about relief for Ukrainian DPs. Consequently, Sir George warned his Ukrainian Canadian listeners that 'any talk of politics' would be 'most detrimental' to their efforts on behalf of the refugees. They were told, in no uncertain terms, that since this situation could prove to be 'most embarrassing' for the authorities, their activities would be closely scrutinized.[141] Holmes confirmed these points in his own memorandum, but added that Sir George had spoken of the 'danger' inherent in Ukrainians from North America 'encouraging' Ukrainians in Europe to work for the establishment of a sovereign Ukrainian state, something which was in his view 'quite impracticable' and would 'of course' be possible only if an 'armed intervention' were to be sanctioned by the Anglo-American powers – a course of action no Western government had any intention of following, whatever lip-service their spokesmen might have given to the principle of national self-determination as it was enunciated in the Atlantic Charter.[142] As for the Mission's report to Winnipeg, no mention was made of anything having been said by the Canadian or British participants about the Ukrainian nation's right to national self-determination. Holmes's remarks to Ottawa reflected the opinion prevalent among Canadian officials about what fundamentally motivated Ukrainian Canadian refugee relief and resettlement efforts, rather than being a direct response to something said by Panchuk or his co-workers. Canadian officials continued to be deeply concerned over what they thought of as Ukrainian Canadian nationalism and its potentially negative impact on Canada's foreign policies and nation-building plans.

'A High Regard for Mr. Panchuk'

This official concern is all the more curious given the behaviour of the Ukrainian Canadians at this meeting, and afterwards. Panchuk, having listened to Canadian and British officials on the dangers of Ukrainian nationalism in Canada and among the DPs, made a reply, but only concerning the issue among the DPs. He explained that he had personally tried to 'calm down the extreme nationalists among the Ukrainians,' attempting to persuade them why their behaviour was hindering their own cause. His listeners must have believed him, for after this meeting the Team was rewarded by the British and Canadian officials, being granted formal permission to 'reopen' their offices on the Continent. Holmes also observed, for the benefit of Ottawa, that the Foreign Office's Brimelow 'has a high regard for Mr. Panchuk.' This positive assessment seems to have penetrated into Canadian diplomatic circles at about the same time, early December 1946, largely as a result of Panchuk's seemingly tireless efforts on behalf of the DPs, his intensive lobbying of all and sundry, and his many discussions with various officials and relief workers around London.[143] Panchuk's blast at a Mr Moore, attached to the British element of the Control Commission for Germany (Displaced Persons / Prisoner of War Section), to the effect that the Team had not come back to England to '"view conditions," to "visit camps," or on a sightseeing tour [but] to deliver the goods (relief) as soon as possible (this winter),' and that unless they were allowed to go about their business soon they would just 'pack up,' go home, and turn the 'whole story' over to the British, Canadian, and American press, seems to have been unnecessary bluster.[144] As Sir George had promised after vetting Panchuk on 13 December, the Canadian Relief Mission was indeed allowed into western Europe and, by the end of that month, Panchuk had re-established numerous direct contacts with Ukrainian refugees.

This granting of permission for the Team to return to the DP camps was not motivated by disinterested humanitarian sentiment. By early 1946 officials on both sides of the Atlantic had realized that the refugees represented a good source of skilled and semi-skilled labour, a pool that could be drawn from to meet the needs of various industrial and manufacturing sectors in their own domestic economies.[145] There were advantages in having Ukrainian Canadians whom they could more or less trust or, perhaps more important, control, and in allowing the Mission to go about its work on the Continent among the DPs: the selection of prospective immigrants could be monitored, and the more politicized refugees could be at least partially pacified. A rather symbiotic, if uneven, relationship thus developed between the Mission's Ukrainian Canadians and the authorities, one that would ultimately help pave the way for Ukrainian refugee immigration to Canada. The Ukrainian Canadians wanted to get Ukrainian DPs resettled, and they recognized that doing so required the cooperation of the various governments involved. For their part, the authorities wanted to resolve the refugee situation as quickly as possible without prejudicing their relations with the Soviet Union, and at the same time take advantage of the skills, experience, and labour potential of this unexpected reservoir of people, most of whom were searching for the ways and means to rebuild their war-shattered lives.

Resettling the DPs outside Europe, or disposing of them by sending them to the Soviet east, emerged as the two most feasible solutions to the postwar refugee problem. Before either course was adopted, this mass of forcibly displaced people had been herded into dozens of refugee camps, where concerted efforts were made to keep them as docile as possible, and thereby both allow for the reconstruction of war-devastated Europe and minimize the international tensions provoked by the presence of these 'dangerous witnesses.' Unlike the Ukrainian Canadians who had stumbled across 'a bit of home' in the Ukrainian working-class district of Manchester or created UCSA's 'London Club,' the DPs found no welcoming niche in the West. And they faced an even greater threat, for the compulsory repatriation of tens of hundreds of thousands of their brethren into Soviet hands, orchestrated in collusion with the Anglo-American powers, was about to begin. Luckily, at first, for the Ukrainian displaced persons a few Ukrainian Canadians were there to 'get cracking' on their behalf.

6 'The Least Inspiring of Postwar Problems': The Anglo-American Powers, Ukrainian Independence, and the Refugees

'The Greatest Possible Offence'

Until recently, one of the most persistent beliefs held by members of the postwar Ukrainian diaspora was that the Anglo-American powers knew very little about Ukrainian aspirations or affairs prior to, during, and after the Second World War. Yoked to this belief was another, that none of these governments developed a consistent policy with respect to the 'Ukrainian Question,' that is, the issue of Ukrainian independence, or, more particularly, how to deal with its advocates in the West.

Nothing could be further from the truth. Throughout this period, with the possible exception of the wartime years – when access to reliable information was almost entirely cut off – the British, Canadian, and, later, American governments all, though with varying degrees of expertise and thoroughness and for somewhat different reasons, earnestly took note of what was happening among the Ukrainians of eastern Europe and their compatriots abroad. In part they did so in order to anticipate and, if need be, thwart the machinations of hostile Continental powers, notably the Third Reich and the Soviet Union. But they were also exercised over the effect of developments in Ukraine on the Ukrainian immigrant populations of western Europe and North and South America.[1] To forestall any internal security problems these populations might pose, particularly in the event of war, governments throughout the Western Hemisphere initiated policies of surveillance and superintendence directed against their domestic Ukrainian communities, and among themselves exchanged data on developments within the Ukrainian emigration whenever these seemed to be of common concern. The official repositories of all three Anglo-American governments, the 'ABC' powers (America, Britain, Canada), are crammed with copious reports that reveal an abiding interest in the 'Ukrainian Question' and an anxiety over the goings-on within their own Ukrainian immigrant populations.

Many of the attitudes which British, Canadian, and, later, American officials brought to bear in their dealings with the postwar Ukrainian refugee communities were carried forward from positions first articulated during the interwar years and elaborated upon thereafter. For the Ukrainians this proved particularly inauspicious. A variety of prewar misconceptions about critical matters such as the validity of Ukrainian nationality and the viability of the Ukrainian national movement were retained into the postwar period. So too were various racially prejudiced attitudes about Ukrainians, particularly within the British government's decision-making elites. As a result, the Ukrainian refugees, whether peasants or professors, often found themselves confronted by persons not only indisposed to Ukrainian independence but, in a few cases, unwilling to concede that there might legitimately be a people or a nation recognizable as Ukrainian.

Significantly, there are few traces of any real sympathy for the Ukrainian point of view in the British archives of this period. Instead, whenever their issues arose, Ukrainians seem to have been regarded as constituting no more than an irritation of one sort or another. In 1930, for example, a Foreign Office official minuted a file dealing with Ukrainian political movements in Eastern Galicia (Western Ukraine) thus: 'We are going to have some difficulties over all this business.'[2] British statesmen were never to abandon the view that when they dealt with Ukrainians they were dealing with a problem, and one brought by Ukrainians upon themselves. Rarely would they feel empathy for the Ukrainians. At the height of the Polish government's savage 1930 'pacification' operations in Western Ukraine, Sir W. Erskine described these brutalities to his colleagues as 'effective means' for achieving immediate objectives, and simultaneously derided Ukrainians for the 'mythopoeic faculty' they brought to their protests against these brutish measures. In his view, Ukrainian complaints could be rejected because their 'lyrical pathos' – to which he deemed the Ukrainian character was inclined – ensured that everything they said or wrote about the 'pacification' was probably grossly exaggerated.[3] The contrary reports of the Berlin correspondent of the *Manchester Guardian*, Mr Voight, who informed the British public that 'these atrocities are the most horrible thing I ever experienced and also the most senseless and inexcusable,'[4] and who complemented his written observations with photographic evidence, seem to have had little impact on the essentially pro-Polish bureaucrats in Whitehall. Indeed, throughout the 1930s they would, by and large, depend for their information and interpretation of Ukrainian–Polish relations on the reports of polonophiles like Frank Savery, then attached to the British consul in Warsaw. Savery was so markedly 'pro-Polish,' according to Voight, that he reported seeing 'nothing untoward' despite taking a tour in Eastern Galicia during the height of the 'pacification.' When pressed on this issue, Savery was also said to have defended the 'pacification' as 'an unfortunate necessity.'[5] Thus, while protest resolutions and even illustrated booklets like *Polish Atrocities in the West Ukraine* were accepted, collected, and noted by London, they were otherwise not acted upon.[6]

This inertia should not be taken as evidence that the British were uninterested in Ukrainian affairs. The Foreign Office continued to compile a substantial body of intelligence on such topics as 'political differentiation in Ukraine,'[7] and on the platform and activities of the electoral party known as the Ukrainian National Democratic Alliance (UNDO)[8] and materials such as 'Anti-Polish Activities of Ukrainian Nationalists Abroad.'[9] Ironically, given the attitude they would later take towards Ukrainian refugees from the Soviet Union, the prewar British government was unwilling to oblige when other governments demanded that Ukrainian nationalists active in the United Kingdom be deported. When, for example, the Polish authorities insisted that an alleged OUN representative in London, E. Lachowitch, be handed over, the file was minuted with a terse 'Surely not, if deportation can only be to Poland?' Such sensitivity to the fate of a supposed representative of a 'terrorist organization' in response to a request from a friendly government stands in sharp contrast to the way in which many British officials treated hundreds of thousands of Ukrainian political refugees and displaced persons less than a decade later, in favour of a Soviet regime which many of them realized or suspected was no true friend of the British Empire's interests, whatever lip-service Moscow paid to the notion of preserving the wartime alliance.[10]

What truly underlay British reactions to the political demands of Ukrainians was revealed perhaps most disingenuously in a file entitled 'Position of the Ukraine in the International Situation.' In response to a memorandum on this theme from Arnold Margolin, a Jewish-Ukrainian lawyer based in Washington, Laurence Collier and his colleagues in the Northern Department (the Foreign Office Department responsible for overseeing developments inside Poland and the USSR) penned a series of minutes, the contents of which expose the British point of view. Margolin argued that Germany's *Drang nach Osten* (drive to the east) was 'directed towards the Ukraine,' most particularly in order to secure that country's rich natural resources. In concert with the Italians and the Japanese, the Germans were using all means available to convince the Ukrainian people that the downfall of the Soviet regime would allow them a chance to create a truly independent Ukrainian state. What Margolin described as this 'skillful German propaganda' was also being used to point out to the Ukrainians that, since they had been abandoned by England and the other democracies, their only chance of establishing their own state was in allying themselves with Europe's revisionist powers, who promised a geopolitical restructuring of the Continental status quo. In short, the most basic 'hopes and aspirations' of the Ukrainians were being played upon by the Axis powers. Unless the British countered this propaganda campaign and held out some genuine promise of assistance, Margolin felt, they would forfeit any chance they might still have of harnessing the Ukrainians to their own side in the event of war.[11]

Whitehall was unwilling to accept Margolin's analysis. As a Mr Lasalles observed, 'Were we so misguided as to take Mr. Margolin's advice, we should give the greatest possible offence to the USSR, Poland, and one or two other countries, and would be encouraging a movement of national emancipation which we could in no circumstances support with anything but words, and which would almost certainly lead to wholesale massacres.'[12] Collier, in agreement, added that while it was evident that 'in theory there was much to be said for Margolin's contention that the Ukrainian national movement was bound to grow,' and that it 'should not be left to fall under Nazi-Fascist control,' it was equally clear that His Majesty's Government 'cannot encourage it.' Replying directly to Margolin in late November 1938, Collier glibly told him that if he felt the British public should be schooled in the importance of supporting the Ukrainians, then 'I can only say that it is open to anyone to try to persuade them to do so.'[13] Rather than give 'the greatest possible offence' to their Polish ally or to the Soviets, British policy, with a few notable exceptions, would not countenance any involvement or intervention on the side of those upholding the Ukrainian people's right to national self-determination until the postwar period. This was to become the persistent undersong of Anglo-American thinking on the 'Ukrainian Question.'

'Always Messed About'

British interest in the Ukrainian national movement was not thereby brought to an end, for even if the British had forsaken any obligation to support the Ukrainians, they would remain concerned about the designs of other European powers, particularly the Germans, on Ukraine. Throughout the latter part of 1938 and into early 1939, no doubt impelled by the crisis facing Czechoslovakia and the emergence of an independent if short-lived Carpatho-Ukraine, British diplomatic personnel prepared detailed studies for their foreign secretary, Lord Halifax, reports which indicated that 'the Ukrainian question seems likely to boil up before long.'[14] Other independent observers concurred. Walter Reiss, of the London-based Wool Trading Company Limited, wrote to Prime Minister Neville Chamberlain in the hope of alerting him to the danger Britain would face if Nazi Germany managed to align an independent Ukraine on its side, a state whose 'three million soldiers' would allow Germany to 'rule the world.'[15] Similarly, Finland's Marshal Mannerheim late in 1938 expressed it as his considered view that 'Ukrainian nationalism [would] become one of the chief factors in the political situation in Eastern Europe.'[16]

As Britain's statesmen well understood, finding a resolution to the Ukrainian problem agreeable to their own interests required not only checkmating German intrigues but also arranging for some form of reconciliation between the Polish authorities and the increasingly radicalized and nationalistic Ukrainians of Western Ukraine.[17] What complicated matters was that, while the Germans might have designs on Soviet Ukraine, they could establish what the British described as 'effective contact' between themselves and Soviet-controlled Ukrainian lands only by driving a wedge across Polish-held territory. The Poles were obviously unwilling to oblige, and were indeed urging Hungary to suppress the fledgling Carpatho-Ukrainian state (Transcarpathia) in order to block the formation of any such 'bridge' between German-dominated territories and what was widely understood to be the 'Piédmont' of Ukrainian nationalism in Eastern Galicia.[18] While, in mid-December 1938, there was concern about a possible alliance between the German and the Polish governments, directed against the USSR and predicated upon an exploitation of the Ukrainian national movement, British representatives in Warsaw recorded that such a joint German–Polish effort was unlikely, if only because Poland's foreign minister, Monsieur Beck, was 'an opportunist and the opportunity is not there.'[19] Equally important, the Poles did 'not intend' to grant autonomy to their Ukrainian population: 'There is ... a fundamental difficulty in Poland's championing a Ukrainian autonomist movement in Russia. In Ruthenia her policy is the direct opposite.'[20] Presciently, the British analysts concluded that since the Poles were unlikely to cooperate with German designs on Soviet Ukraine, 'it is difficult to see how an armed conflict between Germany and Poland can be avoided ... The outlook for Poland is a dark one.'[21]

Subsequent British investigations of Ukrainian nationalism, carried out in the summer months preceding the outbreak of the Second World War, confirmed the earlier view that 'the nationalist movement was growing stronger every day,' and that even moderate Ukrainian leaders, like UNDO's Wasyl Mudryj, were growing discouraged by official Poland's unwillingness to compromise.[22] What Mudryj and many of his colleagues hoped for, but lamented the Poles would not allow the Ukrainians, were rights at least similar to those 'which the French enjoy in Canada.' Since these were not being granted, 'the restlessness of the younger generation and of much of the peasantry and the visible success of the more radical groups has created a longing for a deus ex machina; and the melting-pot of war tends more and more to suggest itself.'[23]

By mid-summer of 1939 these same mandarins had come to realize that the Poles had 'always messed ... [the Ukrainians] about and missed all the psychological moments for conciliation.' It was now observed that the Ukrainians felt they had nothing to gain by cooperation with the Poles, and 'anyway nothing to lose and possibly something to gain by allying ... with someone else.' In short, the British came to appreciate that the Ukrainians were willing to take sides 'with anyone who offers them something.' Since the Poles had given them 'nothing' and German propagandists continued to be 'fairly active,' it was likely that, in the event of war, the Ukrainians would be friendly to the Germans and hostile to the Poles, even to the extent of breaking into 'open revolt.' Warsaw, complained the Foreign Office, 'greatly underestimates the danger of the Ukrainian movement' because the 'Poles are very stubborn when they want to be – and they want to be over Ukraine.'[24]

'The Atomized East'

During the interwar years, as they were compiling information on the

Ukrainian nationalists in Western Ukraine, the British also attempted to gather material about what was going on within Soviet Ukraine. While they were able to tap into some sources, and had been informed, for example, of the genocidal Great Famine of 1932–3, they were often unconvinced of the reliability of the evidence gathered. Still, several conclusions were inescapable. Not only was there 'no general feeling of Ukrainian nationalism in the Soviet Ukraine,' but the 'whole country' was so 'well controlled' by the authorities that the population, already 'atomized,' was unlikely to rally or establish any effective anti-Soviet movement 'unless the country is first conquered by a foreign army.'[25] Certainly there was 'widespread discontent,' but – as the OUN's task groups would discover in the latter part of 1941 – this resentment was unorganized and 'economic rather than political.' Furthermore, the Soviet Ukrainian population, or at least a 'vast majority' of it, had 'no inkling at all that the idea of an independent Ukrainian State [had] been raised outside' the boundaries of the Soviet Union. The Soviet Ukrainians were simply 'out of contact,' having 'lived in a vacuum for so long.'[26] And so, as Lord Halifax was advised by his experts, only a 'large scale invasion from abroad' could detach Ukraine from the Soviet Union. Since the Poles would not allow Hitler to strike out across their territory without a fight – and it was 'difficult to imagine the Poles voluntarily committing suicide by agreeing to the establishment of such a [Polish Ukrainian] state' – the Germans were, it was concluded, likely to 'expand West first,' there being 'no ripe plums in the Ukraine.'[27] That this represented the viewpoint of many senior British officials of the day is suggested by a 'most secret' cabinet paper, entitled 'Possible German Intentions,' which likewise concluded that Hitler's forces would deploy not to the east towards Ukraine but to the west, and would do so in the near future.[28] Paradoxically, these reports were both right and wrong.

Such an analysis, if it had been communicated to the Poles, might have comforted them, and it would possibly even been good news for the Soviets, but it proved to be partially wrong. Not long after this document was prepared and before Hitler's war machine swept west, German armies attacked to the east, dismembering the Polish state with a *blitzkrieg* (lightning) war, which began on 1 September 1939. In concert, Soviet forces, on 17 September 1939, began occupying Western Ukrainian and Belarussian territories previously administered by Poland. Why a Soviet communist government aligned itself with an ideologically inimical power like Nazi Germany, to effect the destruction of Poland and thereby secure the delimitation of 'spheres of influence' throughout eastern Europe, remains controversial. But by allying with Hitler the Stalin regime may have shrewdly forestalled a German attack on the USSR while acquiring additional buffer lands between the Soviet heartland and Nazi Germany's empire, 'space' which was later traded for the 'time' needed to meet and resist a foreseen Nazi onslaught. Or, more cynically, this division of eastern Europe may have been nothing less than a parcelling out of spoils between two fellow totalitarians – Hitler, the 'brown fascist' and Stalin, the 'red fascist.'[29] Whatever the truth, the 'Ukrainian Question' was once again about to move closer to the centre of the international political stage.

'The Collapse of the Walls of Jericho'

The decision-making process in Stalin's Politburo will likely never be fully understood. What is certain, however, is that by late 1938 and likely even earlier, the highest-ranking Soviet officials were very much aware of, and uneasy about, German interest in the 'Ukrainian Question.' And so, when on Christmas Eve of 1938 Gordon Vereker of the British embassy in Moscow had a chat with the Soviet foreign minister, Maxim Litvinov, the latter, without prompting, launched into a rather spirited discussion of the 'Ukrainian Question.' Litvinov informed the British diplomat that the Soviet government, 'conscious of its strength,' was not going to allow itself to be unduly alarmed by 'the latest German bogey – an independent Ukraine.'[30] Rhetorically, he questioned Vereker as to whether he believed the frontiers of the Soviet Union were likely to crumble just because of what he described as the 'horn blowings' of a handful of Ukrainians.

Litvinov must have been caught off guard by Vereker's piquant reply, laced as it was with Old Testament imagery, intended possibly as an oblique, if pointed, reference to this Soviet official's Jewish origins: 'I had always understood that it was something more than a mere blowing of horns, and that in fact it was nothing less than an earthquake that had caused the collapse of the walls of Jericho.'[31]

Vereker would later report that, in his opinion, the Soviet government, however much its foreign minister might profess calm over the 'Ukrainian Question,' was, 'naturally enough, seriously perturbed.'[32] A few weeks later he would note again that the 'Ukrainian question ... is no doubt seriously exercising the mind of the Soviet Government.'[33] At about this same time, early in 1939, British industrial and economic intelligence specialists presented a report on Ukraine which made clear that its loss 'would be fatal to the economy' of the USSR.[34] Presumably the Soviets were even more aware of this than far-distant British analysts. That may explain why their next foreign minister, Vyacheslav M. Molotov, signed the now infamous treaty of non-aggression with Nazi Germany's foreign minister, Joachim von Ribbentrop, on 29 August 1939, which led directly to the destruction of prewar Poland. For the Soviets, this treaty might well have represented their hope of being able to manoeuvre Hitler's legions away from the *lebensraum* (living space) the Nazis coveted in the east, in Ukraine, forcing the Wehrmacht to engage powerful enemies in western Europe.[35] Certainly, in the nearly two years which passed between the signing of this pact and Germany's invasion of the Soviet Union, Stalin's forces had time to begin making defence preparations, while initiating the liquidation of the Ukrainian nationalist underground movement in Western Ukraine. These territories were incorporated into the Ukrainian Soviet Socialist Republic after a supposedly democratic plebiscite confirmed the apparent ardour of the Ukrainian population there for reunion with their countrymen inside the USSR. A similarly bogus reunification took place between the western Belarussian territories, which had also been part of prewar Poland, and Soviet Belarussia, all in spite of the Polish government-in-exile's protests. Between the fall of 1939 and late June 1941, when Hitler's armies turned on their erstwhile Soviet ally, an estimated million, and probably over a million and a half, Ukrainians, Poles, Jews, Belarussians, and others were deported from the incorporated territories into exile inside the USSR. About one-quarter of them, perhaps more, would perish.[36]

Moscow would attempt to rationalize its attack on Poland by issuing a diplomatic communiqué on 17 September 1939 which spoke of the 'bankruptcy of the Polish State' and justified the Soviet move as necessary to stave off 'all manner of hazards and surprises which may constitute a threat to the USSR.' Given what the Soviets were soon to do to hundreds of thousands of Ukrainians and others in the lands they occupied, it is ironic that this communiqué also spoke of the Soviet government's 'generosity' in taking under its protection the life and property of the populations of Western Ukraine and western White Russia (Belarus).[37] Although the British ambassador in Moscow, Sir W. Seeds, cabled Whitehall to express his disgust at Soviet perfidiousness, there was nothing the British could or were prepared to do. 'I do not myself see what advantage war with the Soviet Union would be to us,

though it would please me personally to declare it on M. Molotov,'
Seeds remarked. But his diplomatic instincts also led him to comment
that there might now be an advantage 'to us' in the long run in the
existence of German–Soviet contact in an occupied country (Poland).
Such a situation would surely lead to 'a desirable friction' between Stalin and Hitler.[38]

The British war cabinet, meeting on 18 September, agreed, concluding that while the Anglo–Polish agreement provided for British aid to
Poland should the latter suffer aggression from 'a European power,' an
added but secret protocol recognized that this clause referred specifically to Germany, and not to any other power, including the Soviet
Union. And so there was no obligation to wage war against the USSR,
despite 'the Soviet invasion of Poland.'[39] The British, followed by Canada and the other Commonwealth nations, did at least stay true to
their formal obligations by declaring war on Nazi Germany, although
similar and no less aggressive Soviet behaviour escaped a punitive
response.

'If Ukraine Goes Off at Half Cock'

As for a role the British might have in these changed circumstances as
an intermediary effecting a rapprochement between the Poles and the
Ukrainians, the collapse of the Polish state and the unexpected emergence of the Soviet Union as an ally of Nazi Germany freed British
officials from their fixation with first and always considering the
'susceptibilities' of either the Polish or the Soviet government with
respect to the 'Ukrainian Question.' Not surprisingly, given their own
increasingly dire straits, the British mused over how they might attract
the Ukrainians into their own camp, hoping to use them to create troubles for both the Nazi and the Soviet regimes. A remarkable re-evalua-
tion of the 'Ukrainian Question' took place at this time, typified by an
observation by Collier: 'If the Poles will not play properly, and if the
attitude of the Soviet Government makes it desirable for us to raise up
Ukrainian trouble for them, I trust that we shall not be deterred by
undue regard for Polish susceptibilities from dealing directly with any
Ukrainian leaders we can get hold of.'[40]

Another Northern Department official, R.K. Leeper, echoed this sentiment, although he expressed a somewhat more delicate attitude
towards the defeated Poles: 'I am all in favour of embarrassing the
Russians over this Ukrainian question, but not through direct action by

us, only indirectly through the Poles. They will know how to play their cards in this part of the world better than we can, but we should make them do so. If Poles and Ukrainians came together they should be able together not only to embarrass Russia, but create as much trouble as possible between Russia and Germany where the two frontiers meet.'[41]

Faced with the disappearance of the Polish state, and knowing full well the role played by the Soviet Union in their ally's débâcle, the Foreign Office let Sir Howard Kennard know that, given that the Ukrainian areas of Poland were now occupied by Soviet armies, the 'Ukrainian problem' was hereafter to be considered entirely a Soviet one. But since the Soviet Union was no friend of Britain's, this also meant that it was now possible to 'relax' their previously rather negative attitude towards the Ukrainian national movement. In other words, it was no longer necessary to pay much attention to Soviet feelings. Looking ahead, J.H. Watson, an intelligence officer attached to the British embassy to Poland, observed that, once the Allied powers had finished with Nazism, they would not want to have 'to do more against Russia than is necessary.' Still, they would have a score to settle with the duplicitous Soviets. Doing so would be 'easier and cheaper' if they immediately began planning ways and means to allow the Poles and Ukrainians to work together to throw the Russians 'out of Eastern Poland.' That was certainly to be preferred to '[doing] it by force ourselves.'[42] Watson foresaw that, 'when the time was ripe,' Britain could supply small arms and other means of guerilla warfare to the Poles and Ukrainians, the combined effect of which would be the recovery of the territories now occupied by the Soviets. The key to the success of any such clandestine plan, however, was to get the Poles and Ukrainians to cooperate *before* the Germans moved against the Soviets, for a German occupation of 'Polish Ukraine' – now under Soviet rule – would allow the Germans to hold out again before the Ukrainians the hope of a 'Greater Ukraine,' independent of Poland. Naturally, Watson continued, the Ukrainians would be attracted by such a promise, and would certainly prefer it to the plan he was proposing. His scheme would, at best, bring some form of regional autonomy for Ukrainians only in a resurrected postwar Polish state.[43] And what the Ukrainians wanted, as every observer including Watson realized, was independence, not local self-government.

Responding to these ruminations, the Northern Department's Robert M.A. Hankey agreed with Watson's basic premises but added this caveat: 'If Ukraine goes off at half cock, before we are ready, the whole

thing may fizzle out, or if it succeeds, the Germans will just take over
the whole Ukraine. Unless I am wrong, we don't want a Ukrainian
revolt before 1941 summer; then we will use it to down the Russians
and the Germans together.'[44] Even so, Hankey, and presumably more
than a few of his Foreign Office colleagues, was unwilling to offer any
guarantees to the Ukrainians, for, as he put it, 'East Galicia is outside
our beat and always will be.'[45] And, like Watson, he also assumed that
all the stories put out by the Germans in previous years – propaganda
which suggested they would support Ukrainian independence – were
more or less a genuine expression of their intentions. As Watson had
earlier said, 'I do not think we can hope the Germans will treat the
Ukrainians badly.'[46]

The British, once again, could not have been more wrong. According
to a postwar report prepared by UNRRA, one based primarily on
Soviet sources, the devastation brought to Ukraine by the Nazis 'far
exceeded any comparable destruction in Western Europe.' The scale of
the ruin in Ukrainian lands is only partially evidenced by one report,
which records a total loss of 714 towns; 28,000 villages and hamlets; 2
million buildings; 540,000 outbuildings; 16,150 industrial enterprises
(which had employed 2 million workers); 127,000 electric motors;
81,600 metalworking lathes; 56,000 tractors; nearly 2 million pieces of
agricultural machinery; 7.5 million head of cattle; over 3 million
horses; over 9 million pigs; 59.4 million fowl; and 12 million tons of
produce. In other words, approximately 30 per cent of the national
wealth of Ukraine was lost. Some 10 million persons were also left destitute and homeless.[47] A more recently published analysis suggests
that between 5.5 and 7 million Ukrainians perished, with a total demographic loss to the country estimated at 14.5 million. In sheer numbers
alone no other European nation lost as many people as Ukraine.[48]

Soviet estimates do not, of course, even begin to tabulate the loss of
life and property which their reoccupation of Ukraine after 1945, and
their two earlier occupations of Western Ukrainian lands, in 1939 and
1944, had caused. Not surprisingly, given the horrors and devastation
they experienced under the Nazis and the Soviets, many Ukrainians
were, by the immediate postwar period, reduced to a 'dull apathy,' as
reports reaching London described them. While there might still be
'widespread discontent' in Soviet Ukraine, the population there had
been so downtrodden that it was unlikely, or so the British analysts
opined, that anyone or any group in Ukraine would be capable of taking independent political action, at least in the foreseeable future.[49]

'A Decidedly Oriental Kink in Their Brains'

The outbreak of the Second World War brought to a sudden close that period in British intelligence-gathering operations in eastern Europe during which the British authorities could rely on their allies and on friendly governments like Czechoslovakia and Poland to keep them informed about Ukrainian affairs. They had only limited opportunities for sending in their own diplomatic and other personnel for more direct and independent observation. Hereafter, what news they received from neutral countries, various governments-in-exile, their few remaining agents in eastern Europe, or the Soviets would inevitably be partial and, at times, tantalizingly vague. While they might continue to look for Ukrainians whom they would try to align on the British side, the occupation of Poland and its dismemberment between the Soviet Union and Nazi Germany had, in effect, removed any real chance of maintaining an effective link to the Ukrainian nationalists. Furthermore, once the Nazi invasion of Soviet-controlled territories transformed the USSR overnight into an ally of Britain, it became obvious that no concerted effort could be made to further ties with an independence movement whose basic platform called for the dismemberment of the Soviet Empire.[50] Perhaps this is why Frank Savery – of whom Collier had written, '[He] thinks, in these matters, more as a Pole than as an Englishman' – felt confident in continuing with his vilification of Ukrainians in dispatches. He peppered these communications with reminders that Foreign Office officials, whenever they met with Ukrainians, should 'bear in mind that most, even of the Ukrainian leaders, (a) are only just emerging from the status of 'semi-intellectual' and (b) have a decidedly oriental kink in their brains.'[51]

Whatever reservations Collier and a few others in Whitehall may have had concerning Savery's reports, Savery continued filing such bigoted appraisals of Ukrainians well into the postwar period. Although he noted in April 1940 that anti-Soviet feeling was rampant among Ukrainians, and that they would fight alongside the Poles 'when the rising comes in East Galicia in the spring,' he also immediately cautioned against thinking of the Ukrainians as trustworthy. In Savery's mind, any Ukrainian-Polish rapprochement was, for the former, 'a purely tactical move.' Not bothering to criticize his own government's indistinct attitudes towards the Ukrainian national movement, Savery claimed that even the 'vaguest promise' would be enough to induce the Ukrainians to turn in the direction of Berlin, implying that they had some real choice in the matter. He then proceeded to report at length that the Germans were launching various rumours about their intention of advancing as far as the Dnipro (Dnieper) River and then setting up an independent Ukrainian state. He added, as if this should surprise anyone, that this German stratagem was eliciting numerous signs of Ukrainian willingness to cooperate with German plans.[52]

It was at about this time that the British began receiving fitful accounts of refugee movements throughout Europe. In March 1940 a document prepared by the Information Department of the Polish government-in-exile, based in France, referred to the 'rigid measures' being adopted against Ukrainians and others in Soviet-occupied territories.[53] It was estimated that, as a result, some 120,000 Ukrainians had already fled to the German-occupied side of the former Poland. Some of these Ukrainians were being given preferential treatment by the Germans because, the Poles reported, 'it is understood that the Third Reich has no intention of letting the Ukrainian question slip entirely out of its hands.'[54]

While little concrete evidence was brought forward to confirm or contradict the charge of Ukrainian collaboration with the Germans, this theme, more than any other, would come to dominate British thinking during the war years, with echoes reverberating to the present day. Attention focused particularly on those Western Ukrainian lands where the nationalist movement was known to be firmly rooted, although it was also expected that, despite their 'general demoralization' after years of Soviet domination, Ukrainians in the east would probably support any movement promising to free them from the 'Soviet yoke.'[55] Accordingly, British specialists remained mindful of the supposedly better treatment which Ukrainians, in comparison to most other nationalities, were receiving in the Generalgouvernement. In the British War Office's view, 'doubtless the purpose of the above treatment ... is to foster anti-Polish and anti-Soviet feeling' – so that the Ukrainian movement could eventually be 'played' as a card against Soviet Russia.[56] Meanwhile, Whitehall's workers combed various émigré newspapers for further evidence that the Germans were 'secretly creating a Ukrainian *point d'appui* for a future movement eastwards.'[57] But all this raw intelligence, painstakingly collected, was just that – scattered titbits of news gleaned primarily, it seems, from secondary sources, some biased, some unreliable, some badly dated, like an article found in the Russian émigré newspaper *Narodne slovo* (*National Word,*) published in Pittsburgh, which the British apparently found somewhat credible.[58]

Even when such information lent support to British criticism of Ukrainian nationalist aspirations, Whitehall itself realized just how 'dangerous' it would be to make any wide deductions based on piecemeal and uncorroborated reports. Their only certainty was that the Germans were encouraging Ukrainian nationalists with talk about the creation of a sovereign 'Great Ukraine,' with a view to exploiting Ukrainians for Germany's ends, in particular for the war being planned against their totalitarian ally, the Soviet Union. Simultaneously, the Germans were earnestly engaged in the time-honoured game of divide and rule, playing off the Poles against the Ukrainians, in order better to control the population and dampen resistance to the conqueror.[59] Significantly, Polish government-in-exile sources more or less concurred with this analysis. They continued to provide London with scraps of information about a variety of developments in occupied Poland, such as rumours of the German-sponsored formation of a Ukrainian Technical and Economic Institute in Bohemia, the creation of a Ukrainian militia of eight thousand, and the return to the Ukrainian Catholics of their cathedral in Chelm. But at first even the Poles seem to have had only the vaguest sort of intelligence about precisely what was happening in occupied Poland, east or west of the Nazi–Soviet demarcation line, at least in so far as Ukrainian issues were involved.[60]

By early 1941, the situation had begun to clarify. The Ministry of Information of Poland's government-in-exile was able to release a detailed account regarding conditions in Soviet-occupied Eastern Galicia, which noted that while the Soviets had originally followed a policy of 'Ukrainianization,' they had abruptly switched to 'Russification and communism' and come to regard 'all Ukrainians as dangerous.'[61] Conditions were so difficult in this territory that, according to the *Polish Fortnightly Review*, even Jews were fleeing into German-occupied Poland.[62] Under those provisions of their agreement with the Soviets which dealt with minority population exchanges, German Repatriation Missions were also operating in the Soviet-controlled areas and issuing Ukrainians and Poles with documents permitting them to leave for their side of the lines. By doing so they were bringing thousands of Ukrainians under their control, many of whom ended up in refugee centres near Cracow, where it was said they were being organized into military legions by the Germans. The German Re-Evacuation Committee, based in Lviv, was rumoured to be especially active in this effort, so much so that by mid-June 1940 the 'Bolsheviks realized the purpose behind the Germans' transportation of Ukrainians and instituted strict control at the frontiers.'[63]

But as these reports were being filed and digested, time had nearly run out for Nazi–Soviet collaboration. By early May 1941, Polish sources were giving out that the Soviets were preparing for conflict along their entire western border.[64] Similar Czechoslovak government-in-exile reports spoke of the imminence of a breakdown in the 'tactical' collaboration which had hitherto characterized relations between the Nazis and the Soviets. The Germans, or so the Czechoslovak authorities reported, would soon attack the USSR, 'with the help of Russian, Ukrainian and Carpatho-Ruthenian emigrants who, on account of their hate for the Soviet regime, have become a willing instrument of Germany and are everywhere supported by her.'[65]

News that a split had ruptured the ranks of the Ukrainian nationalist movement was also logged, but apparently not otherwise given attention.[66] What had happened was that the younger, revolutionary cadres of the OUN, headed by Stepan Bandera and based for the most part in Western Ukraine, had rejected what they perceived as the more compromising position of Colonel Andrei Melnyk with respect to the Germans, had begun laying their own plans for demonstrating their independence of German designs.[67] When the German Wehrmacht launched its invasion of Soviet-controlled territories, on 22 June 1941, specially constituted 'task groups' of Ukrainian nationalists raced into Lviv. There, on 30 June 1941, the Banderivtsi and their sympathizers proclaimed 'An Act of Renewal of an Independent Ukrainian State.' Nazi reaction was swift and brutal. Both Bandera and the premier of this newly formed Ukrainian state, Yaroslav Stetsko, were arrested and imprisoned in the Saxsenhausen concentration camp. Thousands of their followers and other Ukrainians were imprisoned or executed.[68] Although badly mauled and partially exposed, the underground OUN network would, within weeks, reconstitute itself and eventually give rise to a major resistance movement that would later carry on a protracted guerilla war, first against the Nazi occupation and later against the Soviets. By the autumn of 1942 this force, which came to be known as the Ukrainian Insurgent Army or UPA, had initiated what amounted to a national armed struggle against the Nazis, a full and scholarly history of which remains to be written.[69]

'There Is No Free Ukraine'

Some Allied observers could scarcely contain their delight at the news that the Nazis, instead of mollycoddling the Ukrainians as had been predicted, were exploiting and brutalizing them. David V. Kelly, at the British legation in Berne, reported on a lengthy talk he had had with a Polish officer who had 'always been well informed on Eastern European affairs.' He had discovered that the Poles felt that the 'complete failure of the Germans to accompany their military effort in Russia by any sort of psychological front [was a surprise about which] he was himself very pleased ... The forcible suppression by the Germans of the attempted national movements in Lithuania and Ukrainian Poland [proves] that the German programme in fact just boils down to naked military conquest and exploitation of everyone.'[70]

While important differences of opinion existed among the Nazi leadership on how to treat the Ukrainians and other subjugated nationalities within the USSR, Hitler had spoken out against the creation of an independent Ukrainian state. The Fuehrer instead advocated direct Nazi control over this eastern European *lebensraum*. Ukraine, a land richly endowed with natural resources of exactly the type needed to build up the Third Reich, was slated to become a colony, not an independent state. To accomplish these goals Hitler appointed his loyal servitor, Erich Koch, as Reichskommissar of Ukraine.[71] Western Ukrainian lands, well known to be a hotbed of the Ukrainian nationalist movement, were kept separate from former Soviet Ukrainian territories instead being allocated to the Generalgouvernement. Completing Ukraine's territorial dismemberment, a belt of land running across the southern part of the country, incorporating the Odessa region, parts of Vinnytsia, Mykolaiv, and northern Bukovyna, was assigned to the Rumanians as war booty and came to be known as Transnistria.[72] The Nazis made it clear that they had no intention of allowing for the establishment of a united, sovereign, and independent Ukrainian state.

Koch, who stated that his mission was 'to suck from Ukraine all the goods we can get hold of, without consideration for the feeling or the property of Ukrainians,'[73] epitomized Nazi rule in Ukraine. Hitler's satrap, he spoke openly of the 'nigger people' he had been set to rule over, and blustered, 'If I find a Ukrainian who is worthy of sitting at the same table with me, I must have him shot.' In his inaugural speech, given at Rovno, the city he selected as his administrative capital, he boasted: 'Gentlemen, I am known as a brutal dog; for that reason I have been appointed Reichskommissar for the Ukraine. There is no free Ukraine. We must aim at making the Ukrainians work for Germany and not at making the people happy.'[74]

Given such an overseer, it is not surprising that between the summer of 1941 and the spring of 1944, when Nazi forces were finally pushed out of Ukraine by the advancing Red Army, Ukrainian national aspirations were ignored and the country pillaged. Ukrainian POWs from the Red Army, who had originally been segregated from other prisoners and who had gradually been paroled, were, after the OUNb's independence proclamation in Lviv, kept interned. Paltry food rations, gross and systematic maltreatment, mass executions, and exposure to the elements more than decimated their ranks. Of some 5.8 million Soviet POWs, many of whom voluntarily laid down their arms rather than fight for Stalin's regime, over 2 million perished. A further 1 million remain unaccounted for and presumably died along with their compatriots.[75]

A complex administrative network of German officials was brought into Ukraine to supervise agriculture, their mandate being to extract food supplies regardless of any negative effects on the Ukrainian population. Ukrainian cities, according to the Germans, were full of 'superfluous eaters' anyway. The death by starvation of such *Untermenschen* (subhumans) was of little serious concern to the occupation authorities. Urban populations plummeted. Kharkiv's population had dropped from 850,000 in 1939 to 450,000 by December 1941. One estimate suggests that between 70,000 and 80,000 residents of this Eastern Ukrainian city simply starved to death during the Nazi occupation.[76]

Ukraine was also drained of its population under the aegis of the Nazi plenipotentiary for labour recruitment, Fritz Sauckel, under whom a conscription of the civilian population for work inside the Third Reich was instituted. It was so relentlessly and remorselessly pursued that, of the 2.8 million *Ostarbeiter* carted off to Germany, some 2.3 million came from Ukraine.[77] Transported under horrid conditions, often mistreated as social pariahs in Germany, forced to wear degrading '*Ost*' badges, and generally overworked and underfed, as many as a hundred thousand of them perished in the prison-labour camps alone.[78] Tens of thousands more sooner or later were deported to the Nazi concentration camps, where they died alongside other Slavs, Gypsies, and Jews. Others, as a direct consequence of a secret agreement concluded between Heinrich Himmler and the Ministry of Justice on 18 September 1942, were worked to death.[79] But since Ukrainians were considered subhuman in the Nazi scheme of things, all their suffering and deaths mattered not a bit.[80] Those who survived the Nazis would eventually come to constitute the largest proportion of the refugee population with which the Western Allied powers found themselves coping in the immediate months after the capitulation of Europe's Axis powers.[81]

Made aware of these developments only by details gleaned from the German or neutral press, the Allies knew little as yet about the appalling nature of Nazi rule over Ukraine, even if their experts had been able to sort out a reasonably accurate picture of the infrastructure of the German occupation system both in the Generalgouvernement and in the Reichskommissariat Ukraine. They tended to cling to their unfounded, still critical ideas of what the Ukrainians might be up to under German rule. Generally, they found what confirmation they could for their preconceptions in a few unreliable sources. For example, after a purview of the Polish émigré newspaper *Nowy swiat* (*New World*) and the Russian-language paper *Novoye russkoye slovo* (*New Russian Word*), J.W. Russell suggested that the Ukrainians 'seem to be playing much the [same] game as they did in the last war' – both these newspapers had carried articles describing allegedly Ukrainian military units as constituting part of the Russian Liberation Army headed by General Andrei Vlasov.[82] While the Ukrainian nationalist movement never truly cooperated with these anti-Soviet Russians, the British continued to believe that Ukrainians represented nothing more than a collaborationist force, created and propped up by the Germans to a greater or lesser degree. This view proved to be quite incorrect, with respect not only to their jaundiced assessment of Vlasov's motives but also to their appraisal of the nature of the Ukrainian liberation movement.

'We Shall Be Sending Some of Them to Their Death'

During the early part of 1944 the situation came to be better appreciated, for that was when senior figures in the Foreign Office began pondering over what to do with the two hundred thousand or so 'Russian nationals' whom they had heard were collaborating with the Germans in occupied France.[83] Among them could be found nationalities as diverse as Ukrainians, Russians, Tatars, Kalmyks, and Turkmen, organized into 'Eastern Legions' and deployed not only as troops along the Atlantic Wall but also as labourers and anti-aircraft personnel. In the British estimate, these men were probably fully aware of the fact that they had 'burned their boats on both sides' and had little to hope for, no matter which side won the war. Their desperation would likely inspire them to fight well. The question, therefore, was how these

troops could be enticed to defect. Would some promise of good treatment and rehabilitation secure mass desertions? The British decided
not to try to resolve this tangled question alone. They contacted their
Soviet counterparts, doing so through their ambassador in Moscow,
Sir Archibald Clark Kerr. Instructed to discover the Soviet views of this
issue, Kerr wrote a 'personal and most secret' note to Soviet foreign
minister Molotov, in which he reported Allied concerns about the 'Russian' troops in German service and urged that a promise of amnesty be
issued shortly after the first day of Overlord, the code name for the
Allied invasion of Europe. Preferably, Kerr noted, the amnesty should
be signed by Generalissimo Stalin himself.[84]

Molotov replied promptly. He claimed that, according to Soviet
intelligence sources, 'the number of such persons in the German forces
[was] very insignificant,' and that a special appeal to them would 'not
be of political interest' to his government.[85] On 4 September 1944 the
British war cabinet therefore decided what it would do about any such
prisoners who fell into British hands. The secretary of state for war was
hesitant: 'In view of the probability that if we do as the Soviets want
and return all these prisoners to the Soviet Union, whether they are
willing to return to the Soviet Union or no, we shall be sending some of
them to their death.'[86] Nevertheless the cabinet ruled that all so-called
Soviet citizens, defined as those who had lived inside the USSR's
boundaries – meaning those which had existed on 1 September 1939 –
were subject to repatriation, whether or not they wanted to go.[87] This
ruling decided the fate of hundreds of thousands of men, women, and
children who, over the next few years, would be given no choice but
'voluntarily' to return to Soviet-dominated eastern Europe or the
USSR. The majority of those unfortunates were Ukrainians. What one
Whitehall observer would describe as 'the least inspiring of post-war
problems' – that of the DPs – had begun troubling the British even
before the war's end.[88]

Before any of the Western Allies even began to appreciate the scale
and complexity of the refugee problem, they were forced to concern
themselves with more mundane if nevertheless important matters,
particularly the question of how they should go about controlling the
extent and direction of the unauthorized 'mass trekking' of refugees,
just then scattering in all directions in the wake of Allied forces
advancing into the Third Reich. To avoid having their military operations complicated, to prevent the spread of epidemic diseases, and to
provide for the eventual 'orderly repatriation' of these refugees, first

the military and later the civilian authorities stepped in.[89] Within two months of the invasion at Normandy it was recognized that there might be well over nine million refugees, representing some twenty or more different nationalities, spread across western Europe. A Supreme Headquarters Allied Expeditionary Force (SHAEF) directive, stamped 'top secret,' was issued to instruct the armed forces about what they should do. First, key points should be set up, to which DPs could be directed. In these centres the refugees would be safe from the fighting, and relief supplies could be distributed to them in an efficient manner. At all costs, the memorandum cautioned, the refugees were to be kept from dispersing at will, for mass population movements would definitely hinder military operations and, quite possibly, incite unrest.[90] As soon became apparent, however, and as a report prepared by the British element of the Allied Commission for Austria later described, these assembly camps, originally organized to be nothing more than transit facilities, 'had rapidly instead become semi-permanent homes for those displaced persons who, for various reasons, mainly political, did not want to or were unable to return to their countries.'[91]

Over the next few years a number of schemes for coping with the DP problem would be proposed by well-intentioned observers. In early October 1945, Mr C.E. Heathcote-Smith wrote a paper entitled 'The Irrepatriates of Europe,' in which he argued for the establishment, under SHAEF control, of selected areas in Germany into which refugees of each nationality would move (the former German residents of these areas would be sent to live in the vacated DP camps).[92] In what were to become self-administering regional units the DPs would be able, Heathcote-Smith claimed, to recover their 'mental and moral health.' An added advantage, he thought, was that keeping the refugees together in Europe would demonstrate to the 'Autocratic Regimes' of the Continent the Anglo-American commitment to 'a world of free Democracies.' As for the alternative – an immediate 'expatriation' of these refugees to countries outside Europe – such a plan was based on a 'counsel of despair' and would only cause jubilation among the enemies of democracy. Far better, he felt, to let the DPs have a 'breathing space' where they were before resettling them all over the globe. After all, there might be some prescience in the hope of many of the DPs for a near-future collapse of the regimes ruling their homelands. If there was any chance of that, Heathcote-Smith argued, resettling the displaced persons too quickly would best be avoided. Once they were gone from Europe, they would naturally regard their chances of 're-incorporation with the Motherland as having reached vanishing-point.'[93] A delay in their relocation was therefore the route recommended.

Other, rather contrary plans were also proposed. In March 1946 one such scheme suggested that empty military training establishments in Canada could be used as temporary camps for the DPs – 'in effect this would transfer a number of European camps to Canada' – bringing them closer to supplies of food and other necessities and increasing their opportunities for becoming familiar with Canadian conditions.[94] Their 'absorption' could then proceed gradually and effectively, 'taking place as they became ready,' while 'they could feel that they were in a bridge head where, while still among old friends, they would continue to perfect their advance ... Discouragement and stagnation would vanish in an atmosphere of hope and greater encouragement than can be provided here.'[95]

A more cynical approach, suggested at the end of 1946, began with the premise that because 'there is plenty of dynamite in Europe as it is,' the DPs should be 'scattered far and wide,' this being the only sure way to remove the kind of 'inflammable materials' which 'rightly or wrongly irritate Russia.'[96] If this step was not taken, many refugees might grow disenchanted with the West and return willingly to their countries of origin in eastern Europe or the Soviet Union. That had to be avoided, for it would represent 'a priceless asset for the Soviets in their propaganda against the Western Democracies.'[97]

None of these proposals was accepted since, under the terms of the Yalta Agreement, persons who could be identified as 'Soviet citizens' – and this group made up the majority of the irrepatriates – were to be returned to the USSR, whether or not they were willing to go. By 1 September 1945 a total of 5,115,709 people had been repatriated, in return for which the Soviets sent some 21,000 Americans, 24,000 British citizens, 292,000 French citizens, 33,000 Belgians, 31 Dutch, 1,300 Luxembergers, and 1000 Norwegians west.[98] In mid-1945 the daily round-up and return of people into the Soviet zones often averaged between 11,000 and 12,000 people.[99] At the same time it was becoming obvious that there were many who refused to return and were prepared to resist repatriation, even at the cost of their lives. One report filed with the IGCR in August 1945, for example, related that a Soviet official had persuaded the British authorities that all Ukrainian DPs in a camp near Kiel were actually Russians and so must be repatriated. When one of them refused repatriation, he had his case resolved summarily: the dissident was simply 'shot dead by a Russian officer.'[100] Throughout this period, from the end of the war and well into 1947, reports also filtered into Whitehall describing the 'body-snatching' of DPs from the British and American zones,[101] the executions of those returned to the Soviets,[102] the 'kidnapping' and 'shanghaiing' of Ukrainians whose Polish citizenship should legally have exempted them from involuntary return,[103] and mass executions by guillotine, widespread murder, and rape and pillaging, all taking place under Red Army auspices in Soviet-occupied eastern Germany and elsewhere.[104] All the while the Anglo-American authorities were also subjected to a hail of Soviet government memoranda and protests, the common theme of which was that *all* persons who lived in 'the Baltic Soviet Republics, the Western Districts of the Soviet Ukraine, in Soviet White Russia, Carpatho-Ukraine and Soviet Bessarabia' prior to the attack of 'Fascist Germany' must 'indisputably' be considered 'Soviet citizens,' which meant they *must* be handed over 'without delay' to those to whom 'they owe their allegiance.'[105] It was also made clear that not only did all 'Soviet citizens,' by the Kremlin's definition, have to be returned, but that this must take place 'irrespective of their wishes and with the use of force if necessary.'[106]

While some British officials would express reservations about the degree of force being employed 'in deporting recalcitrants to Russia,' the consensus remained that the legal interpretation of the Yalta Agreement did indeed provide for a repatriation of all 'Soviet citizens.'[107] An attempt was even made at this time to discard the characterization of displaced persons as political refugees. 'It is rather misleading,' wrote a British legal expert, 'to describe these people as political refugees. They are not, for the most part, people who have fled from the Soviet Union in order to escape from the Soviet regime, but persons who were moved, either willingly or unwillingly, by the Germans and have now decided that they would rather not return to the Soviet Union in view of their association with the Germans.'[108] Unwavering, the British refused to countenance any attempt to sort out actual refugees and victims of war from alleged collaborators, arguing that any distinction between various categories of 'Soviet citizens' would constitute 'a clear breach' of the official interpretation of the Yalta Agreement.[109] Moreover, British officials maintained, not only would it be difficult in practice to draw a line between political refugees and 'traitors,' but attempting to do so would 'aggravate existing difficulties' and lead to 'interminable wrangles' with the Soviet authorities.[110] Better, some reasoned, just to send everyone back and be done with it.

By late May 1946, British policy had come into line with the some-what more lenient and discerning position adopted by the Ameri-cans.[111] The Americans had decided that only those 'Soviet citizens' who were actually captured in German uniform, those who were members of the Soviet armed forces on or after 22 June 1941 who had not subsequently been discharged from duty, and those who could be shown to have rendered comfort and aid to the enemy would be sub-jected to forcible repatriation.[112] Unfortunately, by this point in time the issue was largely academic. As a secret memorandum circulated to the British cabinet made clear, 'the vast majority of the Soviet citizens coming under the Agreement' had already been repatriated without disturbance.[113] While homesickness, increasing boredom with camp life, and 'DP apathy' may have convinced many refugees that they had no choice but to return home voluntarily, the forcible repatriation of hundreds of thousands of Ukrainians, Cossacks, Russians, and other east Europeans to the Soviet Union stands as perhaps the single most disgraceful episode in the history of Anglo-American diplomacy in the twentieth century, and it has rightly been condemned as such.[114]

The refugees themselves best described what was happening. A witness from Kyiv, Leo Dudin, wrote to British foreign secretary Bevin in early 1946, observing that it was only because he and his fel-low refugees had 'lived under the power of the Soviet Government' and 'know the secrets of the Soviet system' that they were being stalked, 'every day as the hare is pursued by the hunting dogs.'[115] He and the other refugees had done no wrong, Dudin protested. But since they knew what the Soviet system was really like they were considered 'dangerous witnesses.' To discredit them the men in the Kremlin were instigating active disinformation measures, trying to get the world to believe that they were 'war criminals' or 'politically suspicious elements,' hypocritically covering their real intentions 'under the mask of repatriation of ... beloved citizens.'[116] Like so many other thousands, Dudin begged for sanctuary. His personal fate is unknown, but similar appeals certainly fell on deaf ears, the peti-tioners being forced back to their deaths or long imprisonment in the metastasizing gulag.[117]

In the late spring of 1946, Tracy Philipps reported that perhaps as many as 1.5 million DPs were sheltering in the refugee camps of Europe and the Middle East, awaiting repatriation or resettlement.[118] Most of these homeless people were Ukrainians, Lithuanians, Latvi-ans, Estonians, Hungarians, and Germans; at least half a million of them would not be repatriable.[119] These were the very same men, women, and children described by the British cabinet as 'recalcitrants' – people whose repatriation could not be effected 'without resort to coercion.'[120] What to do with them would come to be a much canvassed subject not only in Whitehall, but in the General Assembly of the United Nations and the public domain.

From the outset two schools of thought emerged. The Soviets, supported by their communist allies in eastern Europe and sympathizers in the West, insistently demanded that these persons be returned, and pointed out that they would not ignore 'the numerous cases of infringement' by the British of their mutual agreement on repatriation.[121] In mid-September 1946, complaining Soviet officials noted that, even if their data were incomplete, nearly 150,000 'Soviet citizens' still remained in territories under British control.[122] Furthermore, they protested, some British camp commandants, like a Major Simmons in charge of a DP camp in Pegitz, Austria, were proving to be unhelpful when it came to locating 'Soviet citizens.' Indeed, Soviet spokesmen alleged, many refugees were even altering their citizenship documents in order to avoid repatriation, a fact which even the good major had willingly conceded. Moreover, the Soviets claimed, access to 'Soviet citizens' in the two hundred or so refugee camps found in the British occupation zones of Germany and Austria was being deliberately made 'extremely difficult,' with the result that their repatriation missions could not do their work effectively. Worse, in those cases where Soviet teams were able to get into the DP camps, they were often confronted by 'elements hostile to the Soviet Union.' Soviet representatives had even been beaten up, a case in point being a recent incident in the Burdoff refugee camp. This attack, the Soviets maintained, had taken place 'without hindrance from the British authorities.'[123] Also disturbing was the increasingly obvious growth of various anti-Soviet Ukrainian groups within the refugee centres. Singled out for particular scurrility was the 'Ukrainian Nationalist Centre' based in Hannover, for this body was not only issuing 'Soviet citizens' with documents that made it possible for them to claim that they were stateless, but also conducting 'bitter anti-Soviet agitation with the aim of disorienting Soviet citizens and preventing their return to the Soviet Union.'[124] Moscow demanded improved access to the refugee camps, active cooperation from the British in the repatriation of all 'Soviet citizens,' and the suppression of all anti-Soviet and anti-repatriation activities by persons or groups hostile to the Soviet Union.[125]

'No Obligation'

While there were those in London, like the thoughtful Thomas Brimelow, who realized the Soviet Union wanted to 'get back all its DPs lest they do harm abroad,' he and his colleagues were also growing rather tired and testy with the large number of Soviet complaints they received, many of which proved to be erroneous or based on such flimsy detail that investigation was impossible.[126] Since by the late fall of 1946 'all or almost all' of the 'Soviet citizens' who wanted to return to the USSR had already gone, the British were reluctant to take further action simply because the Soviets wanted them to.[127] Still, it was also obvious, as the Foreign Office's Hankey wrote to Sir Maurice Peterson, then in Moscow, that the Soviets were unwilling to accept the British refusal to use force in repatriating the remaining DPs. Since it was now 'unthinkable' that British troops should use force to return 'innocent men and women against their will,' it would be better 'to reduce the correspondence [with the Soviets on this subject] to a minimum,' for further notes would only inflame the controversy. It was decided finally that it would be best 'so far as possible' to avoid being drawn into a 'prolonged wrangle' over the repatriation issue. That meant that future Soviet complaints would be ignored to the greatest extent possible.[128] Should Sir Maurice feel, however, that it was essential to make some reply to the most recent Soviet message, included were some specific points to incorporate in his answer. These instructions reiterated the British government's position on the use of force and explained, yet again, why Britain's policy had been brought into line with that of the Americans; it was also noted that the repatriation agreement which the United States had entered into with the Soviets was phrased 'in similar terms' to those of the agreement between the USSR and the United Kingdom.[129]

Of course, being generally unwilling to turn 'Balts and Poles from eastern Poland' over to the Soviets was not the same thing as having any concrete plan for dealing with these 'irrepatriates' or 'disputed persons.'[130] Housing and feeding hundreds of thousands of destitute people was no simple task, and so far the prospect of their mass resettlement overseas was 'slight, not to say chimerical.'[131] How to dispose of the refugee problem quickly became a matter of pressing concern.

A new tactic had to be devised. In concurrence with UNRRA, of which the Soviet Union was a founding member, the British adopted a policy which, although it did not involve the use of force to return DPs to their homelands, did not, as Hankey put it delicately, 'preclude persuasion.'[132] While his colleague, a Mr MacKillop, bemoaned the fact that Britain had 'for good or evil' committed itself to a declaration that no persons were to be repatriated against their wishes – 'a bold statement of that kind should never be made' – he also pointed out that this declaration was now being interpreted to mean that 'we have a duty to resettle them elsewhere at our own expense and in effect to make them our pensioners and dependents for the whole of their lives. My view has always been that this is pure nonsense. There is no such obligation and if there were, we are totally unable to discharge it.'[133]

What then to do with that large number of refugees who had declared themselves unwilling to return to territories under Soviet control? MacKillop argued that those who did not return should not have their recalcitrance rewarded by being given the premium of sitting idly by in a camp – he added, tellingly, 'in all cases in conditions superior to those facing repatriates on their return.'[134] He argued that an effort should be made to segregate from the general DP population all persons 'having an interest in their refusing repatriation,' and that, simultaneously, propaganda supporting voluntary repatriation should be widely distributed. Contrary newspapers had to be shut down. Soviet Repatriation Missions should be allowed full access to all DPs. And daily life should get a lot tougher inside the camps.[135] In other words, if the DP camps were made little short of unbearable, the refugees would themselves 'voluntarily' opt to return to their homelands, thereby removing any need for the British to sully their hands by forcing refugee repatriation. It was an illiberal solution to what many Anglo-American officials saw as the burden of the DPs.[136] From MacKillop's vantage, his solution had one other fine consequence. Its implementation would clean up the displaced persons' camps and thus 'improve relations with Eastern European Powers.' He argued: 'At present we are in the quite ridiculous position of imposing utterly unnecessary and unjustified burdens upon ourselves and at the same time actually promoting serious friction with the Eastern European Governments. Surely it is a major Foreign Office interest that this absurd position should be reversed.'[137]

Certainly UNRRA, whose obligations in the months following the end of the war were confined to finding shelter and providing food, clothing, and other relief supplies for the refugees, did shift its emphasis away from caring for the refugees to their repatriation, as was widely remarked upon at the time.[138] In this, UNRRA, not surprisingly, enjoyed the USSR's enthusiastic support. And so throughout UNRRA's period of operations, from 1944 to 1947, there were repeated charges of sovietophilism against some UNRRA team members, who allegedly discriminated against anti-Soviet political refugees. This difficult situation changed, but only partially so, after the IRO came into being, for the Soviet Union did not join UNRRA's successor, which tended to focus organizational attention on resettlement rather than repatriation programs. Commenting on the former issue, Brimelow observed: '[Ukrainian] agents amongst the Ukrainian DPs [are] stirring up hatred of the USSR thus thwarting UNRRA's wish to send the DPs home ... On this question the interests of UNRRA are at one with those of the USSR, which wants no propaganda to be conducted against itself.'[139]

A more humane attitude about the DPs surfaced among some of the Allied military and civilian personnel who actually came into contact with them. For example, Lieutenant General Sir Frederick Morgan wrote to Foreign Secretary Bevin, in early March 1946, remarking on the folly of having gone to the trouble and expense of inflicting a military defeat on the Germans, 'of which almost the worst consequence [was] the loss of manpower,' only to contemplate 'making them a present' now in terms of both the quality and the quantity of DPs. Sir Frederick observed that a very large number of the refugees were people 'whom any ambitious nation would be glad to own,' a fact he did not feel was sufficiently absorbed in London.[140] Advocates of this view, which obviously never had any supporters in the Soviet camp, argued not only that the DPs should have their most immediate physical needs met – for shelter, food, medical supplies, and clothing – but that they should also be given asylum. Unfortunately for many refugees, the champions of this point of view had little influence in the late months of the war or even in the immediate postwar period. So indifferent were most decision-makers in Britain to the plight of the DPs that even firsthand accounts from their own officers, like Major S.J. Cregeen, who described the brutal mistreatment meted out to repatriated 'Soviet citizens' in Murmansk, saved no one. In fact some in Whitehall were even annoyed by the fact that Cregeen's appeal had reached them: C.F.A. Warner ominously minuted the file, 'I should like to know more about Major Cregeen.'[141] Aside from the Ukrainian Canadians connected with CURB and the UCRF, and a few other private religious and secular groups who saw their tasks as being humanitarian aid and the promotion of the refugees' interests, more than two years would pass before the British and Canadian governments grew disposed to thinking of the refugees not as a problem but as a godsend. Even then their attitude would be dominated not by goodwill but by self-interest: 'The problem is how to make the best use of this opportunity.'[142]

One way of making use of the 'opportunity' was to comb the refugee camps and draw out of them the kinds of persons who, as immigrants, would best contribute to any host country willing to accept them. A number of countries, by mid-1946, had already begun picking out DPs deemed suitable for resettlement. This selective process in turn created a 'hard core' – the ill, the infirm, the old, and those who stayed to care for them – most of whom would be left to fend for themselves, more or less destitute in the camps or surviving as best they could on the West German and Austrian economies. This 'hard core' would come to constitute the most truly forgotten human flotsam of the war.

Not unexpectedly, the Soviets promptly protested, repeatedly so, against any schemes which involved the out-migration from Europe of persons they considered 'Soviet citizens.' Thus, in mid-May 1946, Moscow lodged a formal grievance with the Foreign Office about an alleged transfer of six thousand 'Soviet citizens, inhabitants of the province of Western Ukraine,' to Canada, demanding that these refugees instead be shipped from the Dorsen DP camp back 'to their motherland.'[143] Nothing came of this protest because, in this instance, the story proved completely false, no such resettlement ever having been planned. Nevertheless, such protests made it clear to all involved that any resettlement of DPs would provoke Soviet ire.[144] And by now it was also obvious that the Ukrainian refugees had organized themselves inside and outside the displaced persons' camps in order to resist repatriation efforts, psychologically and, if necessary, physically. Fairly typical of the anti-repatriation resolutions adopted by Ukrainian refugees and sent to Whitehall was one written on 10 October 1946 by Ukrainian residents of DP camp #751, at 'Ludendorf Kasserne,' near Düsseldorf in the British Zone of Germany. It declared that the 650 persons present had unanimously agreed with the following statement:

Although the brown and black fashism [sic] was overthrown more than a year ago, we thousands of political refugees, banished, unhappy victims of the second world war, continue to live in an atmosphere of uncertainty, always afraid of tomorrow, always awaiting a new commission, fearing to be repatriated by force. We are living in the unbearable nightmare of the bolshevist N.K.W.D., of political persecutions, suspicions of being 'collaborators,' 'deserters of the red army,' 'war criminals' in order to have a pretext to give us over by force to the soviets and be killed by same. Such state of things causes depression among the D.P. and even leads some of them to suicide. We are all homesick, but cannot return to our country, where there is no shade even of democratic liberty owing to the regime of red totalitarism [sic] and physical and moral oppression. That same regime of terror stretches his hands even here to reach us. As real anti-fashists and democrats we protest before the whole civilized world against these effort of the red terror. Referring to the Atlantic Chart [sic], the statement of the UNO, Mr. Roosevelt's and Mr. Truman's declarations, in the name of high ideals of Christianity, humanity and democracy we call upon the whole Christian world to assure us human rights and democratic liberties. We ask unanimously: 1) to recognize for us the right of asylum, 2) to assign for us a safe place where we can live freely, 3) to give us the possibility to work according to our capacities, 4) to assure us the liberty of religion. We call upon the moral consciousness of the whole civilized world and the representatives of Christianity to free us from the everlasting nightmare and fear and assure us democratic liberties. We long to return to our country, but cannot do it so long as no democratic liberties are available there. We, Ukrainians of greek-catholic faith, assembled at this meeting, avail ourselves of this opportunity to express our deep gratitude to the British Military Government in Düsseldorf for their kindness and generosity, which they show to us, and hope that they will take further care of us and help us to become people, who have common human rights.[145]

Faced with many such petitions and with the obvious unwillingness of tens of thousands of DPs to return to communist-dominated eastern Europe or the USSR, Western governments recognized that resettlement would likely prove to be the only viable option, at least in so far as the DP 'recalcitrants' and 'irrepatriates' were concerned. Thus, while the IRO might formally continue to insist that its mandate was to return refugees to their homelands, its personnel, in effect, expended most of this international organization's resources on resettling DPs. The new reality was not lost on the Soviets. As A.W. Wilkinson observed, 'the sudden spate of Soviet propaganda' about refugees was 'due to the fact that they have finally realized that there is no longer any chance of repatriation and that we are concentrating on resettlement. This latter measure is, of course, fraught with danger for them, since the dispersal of anti-Soviet refugees over the whole of Western Europe will make the task of Soviet apologists and propagandists doubly difficult.'[146]

'A Compulsive Need to Return Home'

While diplomats wrestled with the particulars of who should or should not be repatriated and, if so, how, when, and where, other Allied specialists grappled with what they acknowledged was the 'extremely difficult' exercise of trying to understand the effects of physical, mental, and moral displacement – what would today be termed 'the refugee experience' – on 'its victims.'[147] This effort began soon after the Allied landings in Normandy, when a special team from SHAEF's Psychological Warfare Division spent several days in Verdun, France, gathering information with which to prepare a report they hoped would provide useful insights into how their armies should deal with the 'hundreds of thousands of persons who [would] be liberated as armies move into the industrial areas of Lorraine and Germany.' These four representatives of the Psychological Warfare Division's intelligence section concluded that the group of refugees they had found and interviewed at Verdun was 'fairly typical' of those likely to be encountered later.[148] That conclusion imparts particular significance to their observations.

They had found a camp in disrepair, into which approximately eighteen thousand Russians, Poles, Serbians, Ukrainians, and members of other national groups were crowded, and among whom 'the wildest melodrama is commonplace.'[149] One of the 'dominating attitudes' encountered was acute hostility among the various nationalities, which degenerated into backbiting so intense that some groups denounced others as people who were 'deceitful, dirty and can't be trusted.' Hatred for the Germans was strong, but so was dislike for the Russians. Some of the refugees, like the Poles, refused to believe that the Americans and the English were 'completely allied and fighting for the same purpose' as the Russians.[150] The number of real collaborators was 'rather small,' although here too antagonistic national groups readily accused each other of much treachery during the war. Morale among the camp inhabitants was extremely low; most spent their time 'thinking and brooding,' a malaise relieved sporadically by 'outbursts of animal vitality.' As yet there appeared to be no political leadership in the camp, but, it was concluded, that would emerge 'when everyone is settled down ... and the business of getting adjusted as to sleeping and eating conditions is over.'[151]

Once the war ended, other observers confirmed many of these early impressions. Lady Monkswell noted that the refugee camps she visited were in a 'seething state of unrest,' with refugees scurrying about packing or unpacking their few belongings in response to 'any and every political rumour' reaching them.[152] Under such conditions they could neither do useful work nor settle down. Inter-ethnic group troubles were also sharp, she reported, especially between Ukrainians and Poles; she added that difficulties of that sort seemed 'unending.'[153] Criminal behaviour was also widespread. As one officer marked, delinquency had from the start been 'one of the most difficult problems facing our authorities in Germany.'[154] Such problems would continue to try the occupation administrators' patience and resources for several years.[155]

What made things worse was that there were few outsiders who, like Sir Frederick Morgan, were empathetic enough to realize that the refugees' problems were rooted in a 'psychology quite unknown in the more fortunate countries of the British Empire and of America,' one wrought by their forcible displacement.[156] In Sir Frederick's view most refugees had come to be in a 'very highly neurotic state,' quite understandable when 'thought is given to the fact that many of them are highly uncertain as to their very existence.'[157] He also reported that if any attempt were made to force their repatriation, many Balts, Ukrainians, 'and such like' would probably 'indulge in suicide.'

Matters were further complicated by unremitting Soviet accusations that the Anglo-Americans were condoning anti-Soviet activism among the Ukrainian DPs. Anti-Soviet groups had as their purpose 'no more and no less than [the] tearing away [of] the Ukraine from the Soviet Union and [the] spreading [of] rumours about the inevitability of a war in the near future between the Western Powers and the Soviet Union.'[158] It was further asserted that these same formations were taking over the DP camps from the inside, a process made easier by the authorities, who had obligingly organized many refugee camps on ethnic lines.[159] Upon investigation this claim was found to have some merit: certain refugee camps were indeed bases for various 'politico-military formations,' and some of those groups were involved in clandestine cross-border operations.[160] But the Control Commission for Germany was equally alarmed by earlier evidence of Soviet duplicity on this score, for 'unauthorized penetrations of [the] Russian demarcation line' – from east to west – were being made by Soviet agents and provocateurs.[161] And many refugee camp populations were organized along national lines primarily because the inmates themselves had reclustered voluntarily into national groupings, preferring that to the more heterogeneous arrangement which had prevailed in the camps in the weeks immediately following the war's end.

Plainly, the DP camps – once everyone had settled in and basic needs had been attended to – did quickly become hotbeds of intrigue, arenas within which competing political movements sought to assert themselves and gain control. In the process, the groups involved not only struggled against one another and against Soviet agents and sympathizers, but also collided with the occupation authorities, with UNRRA's teams and later those of the IRO, and almost incessantly with members of those nationalities they perceived as inherently hostile. The refugee camps were real sociological and psychological cauldrons; few if any of those who went into a camp would leave unaffected.

How and why such a troubled situation might emerge within the refugee camps was actually foreseen by an Inter-Allied Psychological Study Group, attached to UNRRA's Welfare Division, which submitted a report based on its examination of refugee camps just after the war's end. The Study Group's final report, entitled simply 'Psychological Problems of Displaced Persons,' remains an insightful and cogent analysis of the refugee experience.[162]

The Study Group tried to assess not only the physical impact of forcible displacement but the moral and mental consequences as well. Acknowledging the difficulty of their assignment, the group's members nevertheless concluded that all the DPs had been through an experience characterized by several major features. First, each person had been more or less abruptly cut off from family, community, and national ties, connections which normally provide an individual with the basic stability, affection, and support all people require. The loss of these ties often left an individual lonely, homesick, depressed, disbelieving, and cynical. These effects, moreover, were magnified by the tremendous menace to life itself which most of the refugees had faced during a war in which their enemy had waged nothing less than a 'biological war on population trends.' In the Study Group's judgment, 'the moral and psychological disturbance caused by Germany [was] probably greater than the physical devastation.'[163] As a consequence the average DP had been left 'certain about almost nothing' – insecure about the duration and nature of the exile, about the fate of family and homeland, about whether basic needs would continue to be met, about whether there would ever again be an opportunity to realize personal ambitions, rebuild a career, or even start leading a normal existence. Troubling as such problems would be in normal circumstances, they were made all the more enervating by the near-total loss of privacy and lack of reliable information which characterized refugee camp existence. Not surprisingly, then, the refugee was left to become the 'victim' of mass emotions and rumours with his or her personal need for individuality being smothered by the group, while boredom, dullness, and feelings of monotony came to rule over daily existence.

At the psychological level all these factors had definite and adverse effects, although gradations in the negative impact of the refugee experience were certainly recognizable. At an early stage of 'repression,' a refugee would become irritable. Next, standards of personal hygiene would falter. Finally, most 'acquired forms of civilization' would break down. The ensuing 'restlessness' would undercut feelings of allegiance to a wider community, which reaction in turn would bring about 'social splitting,' clique and gang formation. Once that happened and the gangs began terrorizing fellow DPs, refugee camp life became even more unbearable. Ultimately, there was an even more 'difficult and dangerous' form of reaction, one the Study Group labelled 'complete apathy.' In such condition the refugee would become suspicious of authority and quite aggressive. 'Apathetic' DPs became like 'hurt children whose world has let them down, adults whose sense of security and confidence has been shattered, who regard all authority as tainted with ill will, and who may try to restore themselves by excessive egotism.'[164] The refugees themselves understood this and even had a name for it – 'DP apathy.'

And so, for the refugees, forced to live in groups 'bound mainly by the common difficulties of their situation and widely separated from their home community,' sheltering among other nationalities, some of whom they perceived as 'the enemy,' resort to a dream world was almost inevitable. According to the report of the study group: 'The sense of reality has become enfeebled and there is a tendency to revel in fantasies about the return home, and about the well-remembered family festivities, which are idealized to an extraordinary extent. Such thoughts tend to lead into a dream world. Thus those who are full of fear escape reality. More and more the mechanism of thinking is dominated by fantasies. Nothing must get into the way of the world of dreams.'[165]

Among the most powerful of the emotions dominating refugee existence, the Study Group concluded, was the 'compulsive need to return
home' – a desire on the part of the refugees not so much for geographical relocation as for a return to the emotional security they may have
had, or had come to believe they once had, in the place they had been
driven from, the lost homeland. On the issue of 'going home' the Study
Group observed, 'It requires no deep insight into human nature to realize that during the whole of their stay in the assembly centre the feelings, thoughts and actions of displaced persons are likely to revolve
very steadily round the central theme of when and how they will find
their way back to their old ... community and of what it be like when
they get there.'[166]

Significantly, this compelling need to return home did not abate with
the passing of time. Indeed, for people prey to rumours about a possible return home in the near future, psychological anxieties would actually increase, as they speculated not only about what 'home' would be
like when they got there, but about how long they would have to wait
before their return. This caused 'acute mental pain.' The Study Group
also noted that their assessment was particularly true for those refugees from rural regions, who had a strong attachment to the land. The
largest contingent among the Ukrainian DPs were precisely from that
category, having been country dwellers and farmers.[167]

These Allied psychologists did not stop at merely cataloguing and
commenting on the many adverse psychic consequences of forcible
migration. They also considered themselves as having a prescriptive
function. So they counselled their respective governments about how
to ameliorate the problems precipitated by the refugee experience.
Their essential recommendation was that, once the material wants of
the DPs had been met, every effort should be made to provide for the
growth of human relationships and 'the highest possible degree of satisfaction of emotional needs' within the displaced persons' camps. As
this was achieved, gradually, the refugees should also be allowed
increasing self-government. That would increase their sense of self-
worth and emphasize their understanding that they now belonged to a
new community. As this happened, a corresponding decline in the
responsibilities of the 'relatively ... benevolent control authority'
should take place. In short, the refugees would, at first, have to be
treated like infants, and only slowly, as they gained in confidence, self-
respect, and self-reliance, should they be weaned from their depen-
dence on the occupation authorities.

The refugees must also be provided with information about current events, with entertainment, and with cultural facilities, all of it geared towards minimizing their boredom. In other words, the best remedy for psychological dysfunctions was to be found in allowing the refugees to re-create within their own DP camps what amounted to new and functional communities that would, in effect, replace the ones they had lost, the homelands they were still searching for.[168]

'Little Ukraines'

To a perhaps surprising extent, many Ukrainian and other DP camps did indeed become cultural communities, and much more. In the Ukrainian case, the camps came to be referred to by their inhabitants as 'little Ukraines' or as 'our village.' In these refugee enclaves something of a national revival took place, as people from the various regions of Ukraine, representing different socio-economic, political, and religious affiliations, hived and, voluntarily or otherwise, learned to cooperate and live together. Indeed when the 'famous Ukrainian camp' at Heidenau was finally scheduled for closure, in August 1949, the people living there were reportedly very upset, 'for they have come to feel that this is a Ukrainian village, with its own church, dramatic society, and *Gymnasium.*' Another contemporary observer described other DP camps as having been transformed into Ukrainian cultural centres, and remarked on the high circulation numbers of various Ukrainian-language refugee newspapers, the large number of Ukrainian-language books published in the camps, and the reawakening of Ukrainian religious life therein.[169] By the late 1940s there were over 100 elementary schools, over 70 kindergartens, nearly 30 technical schools, and almost 40 high schools active in the Ukrainian DP camps of Germany, with a complement of about 1400 teachers servicing some 15,000 students. For religious guidance there were at least 186 Ukrainian Catholic and 86 Ukrainian Orthodox clergymen, administering 120 Catholic and 80 Orthodox parishes respectively.[170]

The Study Group's specialists appreciated that these DP assembly centres were transitional. And the DPs themselves understood this, at least intuitively. But the outside observers ignored an even more relevant fact. While most refugees were indeed strongly motivated by a 'compulsive need to go home,' the reality was that they actually had no place to go. For what the British and American specialists had not realized – not yet – was that for many DPs the enemy was not only the defeated Nazi regime but also the Soviet system dominating most of eastern and central Europe. Certainly, the refugees' deep emotional need to return to their native lands and the psychological afflictions suffered by those forced into exile were apparent to outsiders. But no one had given much thought to how these political refugees and displaced persons would react once they realized that they might *never* be able to go 'home.'

And the refugees were not exactly passive bystanders to their fate. Among them were many men and women who would take energetic steps to rebuild their own lives, their communities, and their organizations. Within many camps, cultural, political, religious, and social groups – exactly of the sort which the Study Group felt would cushion the individual psyche and reduce trauma among refugee populations – did indeed spring up. Some of the associations which germinated in the refugee camps were to prove so resilient that over five decades later their members still fraternize and commemorate their shared refugee camp experiences.[171] There were some genuinely positive consequences of the Ukrainian refugee experience. Another, quite different reaction was the banding together of many DPs around leaders and political movements, acting within and outside the camps, who seemed able to provide, in a phrase used by the Study Group, what amounted to 'strong parental authority.'[172] These organizations promised those refugees who would join them not only a purpose, but action and security. They served as focuses around which many of the refugees and DPs gravitated. There was nothing false-hearted about these movements. Their leaders believed sincerely that, once properly mobilized and disciplined, Ukrainians who had found themselves in exile could still contribute effectively to the ongoing insurgency in their Ukrainian homeland. Once victory was achieved, it would be possible for everyone who wanted to go home to do so, without fear. And these nationalists effectively communicated their zealous belief in the imminence of such a victorious return to everyone who would listen, insisting that the only real way to get home was by following them. For those hearing this clarion call – and few were not exposed to it on a daily basis in the DP camps – the message was virtually irresistible at the psychological level. In the main the summons was issued by proselytizers acting for one or the other of the two factions of the Organization of Ukrainian Nationalists, which emerged as the best organized and most widespread of the Ukrainian political movements reasserting themselves throughout the postwar emigration.[173] It was largely their activism inside the relatively safe havens of the refugee camps, and their attempts at rebuilding their war-shattered networks, which would precipitate friction among them, the authorities overseeing the refugee centres, and those responsible for Ukrainian Canadian refugee relief and resettlement operations. The greatest possible offence ended up being given, all round.

7 'Ironing Out the Differences':
Changing Ukrainian Canadian Attitudes towards the DPs, 1946–1950

'A Noticeable Deterioration'

They were gone. Many had been 'shanghaied, literally kidnapped by the Russians.'[1] Whereas, in the early months of 1946, Ukrainian Canadian observers had noted quite routinely that the 'number of Ukrainians from Eastern (Greater) Ukraine is equal to if not larger than that from Western Ukraine,' by the end of that year the forcible round-up and repatriation of tens of thousands of Eastern Ukrainian DPs had tellingly altered the nature of the refugee population.[2] A CURB memorandum written in early 1947, which dealt with the Ukrainian refugee population in Austria, took notice of how overwhelmingly Western Ukrainian in composition that population had become. Approximately 72 per cent of those left in these camps had originated in Galicia and Volhynia, 3 per cent had come from Bukovyna, and the remaining 25 per cent had come from Eastern Ukrainian lands.[3] What impact the outflow of this last subgroup had on the quality of DP camp life is contentious. Assuming that these Ukrainian Canadian observations are credible, we must conclude that camp life became even less palatable, for the Eastern Ukrainians were routinely described as being among the 'most skilled' of the displaced persons, 'professors and teachers ... artists, the chief technical men.' Many were also Ukrainian Orthodox believers[4] and survivors of the Great Famine and the Terror.

In early 1946, Panchuk had written that the Ukrainian DPs were all getting along, that this was one of the 'outstanding features' of Ukrainian refugee camp life. He claimed that religious tolerance and 'broad-minded understanding' existed among the Ukrainians, regardless of origin.[5] This had certainly not remained true. By the end of that year a transformation had taken place within the DP camps, one recorded by several contemporary Ukrainian Canadian commentators. They were alike in insisting on the importance of remembering that 'by far the largest majority' of the refugees represented 'an absolutely political emigration.'[6] And among these DPs most of the Canadians had always regarded the Eastern Ukrainians as 'much more reliable, dependable and positive.' But this group now represented a minority, most of their compatriots having been repatriated to the USSR as 'Soviet citizens.' Western Ukrainians now dominated refugee camp life, and they, by all accounts, were a rather different bunch, described as 'much more politically minded and talkative.'[7] Rising anxieties over the changed complexion of the Ukrainian displaced population were most strikingly captured in a letter Panchuk addressed, in late December 1946, to UCVA's president, John Karasevich. Conditions on the Continent, Panchuk wrote, 'were not what they were when the war ended' and 'certainly not what Dr. Kushnir saw or remembers.' Panchuk maintained that 'a noticeable *deterioration*' of 'type and character' had taken place among the Ukrainian DPs.[8] The camps now seemed 'full of politicians who are forever playing politics and games of God knows what instead of getting down to earth and realizing their true position.' Something had to be done about all this feuding and bickering. In Panchuk's view the first task was to teach these Ukrainian refugees to appreciate the stark reality of their position: '*They are displaced persons and not wanted by any country except perhaps the USSR.* Instead of rolling up their sleeves and getting down to work and learning something and making something of themselves, they find politics, black marketeering and even banditry and looting, stealing, beating up those they don't like etc. etc. etc. more "entertaining."'

Not surprisingly, Panchuk cautioned his fellow veterans not to publicize these findings. Indeed he was adamant that his observations 'never be spoken of or quoted publicly,' for all Ukrainian Canadians 'must defend' the 'principle of helping the Ukrainian DPs and victims of war.' But in his personal correspondence he was ready to admit that 'in actual fact God forbid and protect us if some of these parasitic bandits ever get into Canada.'[9]

Undeniably, 'it wasn't all black,' but the state of affairs overseas and in the refugee camps was definitely 'chaotic,' a situation which called for forceful measures on the part of the CURB team. It would be up to them 'to undo and liquidate a nest of political intrigue and an underground movement which even yet isn't eradicated. That is in itself a full-time job for almost all of us.'[10]

Privately, Panchuk also warned friends in Canada that they too had their work to do. Unless the existing Ukrainian Canadian organizations learned to act together and put bickering of the sort which had so characterized internal Ukrainian Canadian community relations in the interwar period behind them – 'unless we all find a common and solid foundation' – the 'goose in Canada [would be] cooked' once the DPs arrived.[11] Even more ominous was Panchuk's view that if the Ukrainian Canadian community were debilitated by the refugee 'newcomers,' then the Ukrainian diaspora as a whole would be enervated. In his estimation, Canada was 'the only country that can produce and that possesses *some quality*' in terms of its Ukrainian population.[12] The refugees must not be allowed to undermine that.

'An Agreeable Description'

Though beset with serious misgivings about the evolving nature and attitudes of the now well organized Ukrainian DP population, Panchuk did not, as yet, communicate his fears to the UCC's presidium or to the executive of the UCRF. Possibly this was because he, the man in the field, knew that the home office in Winnipeg did not really understand what was going on thousands of miles away. He worried that alerting them to the myriad problems he faced daily would only increase their level of meddling in his efforts, thereby complicating instead of aiding him in the performance of his many tasks. Certainly, the over-energized Panchuk often lamented on how stymied and frequently misunderstood he was by his rather pusillanimous Manitoba bosses. In the same letter in which he reported on the changing nature of the DP camps, he bemoaned the fact that during his time overseas, nearly two months by that date, he had sent 12 long letters, 35 enclosures, 35 short notes, 10 cables, and 10 air mail letters to Winnipeg, but had received only 5 letters in reply. He came to see the Winnipeg end of Ukrainian Canadian relief operations as heavy-handed, often unimaginative, and certainly inefficient: 'I can swear that there isn't *one man in KYK who will even read all we have sent*. Is there any hope of anyone understanding everything being sent? ... of any *actioning all that we have sent*?'[13]

Lacking precise directions from the Committee's or the Fund's executives, committed to rescuing Ukrainian DPs, and as yet resigned to keeping any hint of the changed circumstances in the refugee camps away from the general knowledge of the Ukrainian Canadian public, CURB personnel continued to circulate a very positive characterization of the Ukrainian refugees to anyone who was interested, and to many who were probably not. This agreeable description was routinely used in lobbying on behalf of the DPs, not only with Canadian officials but with other governments, and was certainly made part of the numerous packages of fund-raising materials sent out to thousands of Ukrainians in Canada, the United States, and elsewhere. This positive characterization of the Ukrainian DPs is worth describing in some detail. It constituted virtually the only common information which most Ukrainians in North America had about the Ukrainian refugees before their own encounters with those resettled among them prompted the emergence of more personal, and partial, evaluations. That would, of course, not happen for several more years.

In a CURB circular entitled 'Notes on Immigration of Ukrainian DPs and Refugees to Canada,' the immigrants were flatteringly described as being 'Western-minded' individualists, physically and morally fit survivors. They were 'deeply religious,' resourceful, and hardworking. They 'craved' a chance to rebuild their lives and so hoped to resettle in countries where they could make contributions to national development. And they would work not only with their muscles but also with their minds. CURB flyers assured their many readers that among the refugee population one could find farmers, manual workers, semi-skilled and skilled labourers, experts in various trades, 'many graduated and qualified professionals,' and 'statesmen' – people, furthermore, who having experienced 'the Eastern System,' were all the more strongly opposed to 'Totalitarian Government.'[14] This appeal, taken at face value, presented Ukrainian refugees in the most complimentary terms. They were both workers and anti-communists, a combination which could not help but prove attractive in these beginning years of the Cold War.

This CURB portrayal was, in many details, quite fair and factually accurate. The subsequent record of accomplishments of these Ukrainian refugee immigrants in various countries of resettlement throughout the Western Hemisphere has proved the truth of the description many times over in the decades since the end of the war. But obviously CURB's men were also telling government decision-makers and their own communities what they knew their audiences wanted to hear. They understood those markets well and tailored their promotional literature accordingly.

CURB's memoranda contained another message, a prophylactic one. The Ukrainian Canadians asserted that among the Ukrainian DPs there were few, if any, persons who could be described as 'collaborators' or 'war criminals.' As Panchuk declared: 'Even such groups as the Hetmantsi and the Melnyk National group which at one time were accused of "collaboration" refused to work for or with the Germans ... The Bandera group were the sworn enemies of both the Germans and the Russians and the first aim of either occupation power was to search out every possible hiding place for "banderovtsi."'[15]

This assessment would be all but forgotten in later years, as the Soviets and fellow travellers in the West attempted repeatedly to blacken the Ukrainian nationalist movement with charges of war criminality, a disinformation and defamation effort which faltered only somewhat after Soviet hegemony dissolved and an independent Ukraine emerged in 1991. Although a definitive history of Ukraine's wartime experience remains to be written, Panchuk's acute, if brief, appraisal of the Ukrainian nationalist movement is more accurate than the calumnious and politically biased 'evidence' contained in many tracts of Soviet authorship or inspiration.

'Not a Sight-Seeing Tour'

At the same time as its members were promoting their laudatory description of the refugees, the CRM, the Canadian Relief Mission for Ukrainian Victims of War, was struggling with a British bureaucracy markedly reluctant, at least at first, to permit visits to Ukrainian DPs on the Continent. Getting there would, in fact, prove far more difficult to arrange than Panchuk, Yaremovich, or Crapleve had anticipated when they arrived in London on 13 October 1946. By late December, their collective frustration overcame any hesitations they may have had about directly confronting British officialdom. Panchuk wrote several letters to friends in Canada, and to British officials, expressing anger at the impediments to the Mission's plans. Writing to Karasevich, and attempting to explain why they were experiencing such delays, Panchuk suggested that the authorities were trying to repatriate as many DPs as possible, this being 'the line of least trouble and inconvenience,' and so obviously did not want private relief organizations in Europe as witnesses to what was going on, for that would only complicate matters.[16]

For their part, British officials responded to Panchuk's initially quite cordial inquiries about when the Team would be allowed to move to the European mainland by replying that Messrs Craswell, Hlynka, and Klassen were already working among the Ukrainian refugees. There was therefore no pressing need for additional personnel on the Continent. Panchuk dismissed this reply as ridiculous, given that Klassen was dealing only with Mennonites, while Carswell, a Canadian Pacific Railway representative, had no specific mandate to help Ukrainian DPs. As for Anthony Hlynka, Panchuk reminded the British, accurately enough, that this parliamentarian's trip had not even taken place at the time British officials were insisting that Hlynka was already out and about visiting Ukrainian refugees.[17]

Panchuk's irritation peaked in early December 1946. He made that unambiguously clear to Mr. J.H. Moore of the German Refugee Department in London. Pointing out that he wanted permission for the Team to travel into the British Zone of Germany, with possible visits to the French and American zones, Panchuk threatened Moore with a public relations scandal if this request were denied.[18] Having spent months of enforced politeness in England, involved in seemingly interminable discussions with various British and Canadian officials in the hope of securing the necessary authority to move onto the Continent, the Mission's members had agreed that if they were further denied travel permits they would pack up and return to Canada. There, Panchuk made clear, they intended to do everything possible to arouse public opinion over what seemed to be a deliberate thwarting of their humanitarian relief effort. He went on:

> We have not come or been sent to 'view conditions,' to 'visit camps,' or on a sight-seeing tour. Each member of our relief team has been over here during the war and had no particular desire to leave home again ... I have had my fill of Europe ... It's not the love of travelling that persuaded me to interrupt my university studies a *second time* ... to come over ... Nor was it because I wasn't acquainted with conditions of the Refugees ... of whom I saw enough from Normandy to Hamburg, Lembeck to Kiel.[19]

The CRM's 'job' was to 'deliver the goods,' meaning relief supplies and counsel, and to do so that winter. Yet they had sat for nearly two months in London doing precious little of value other than working the embassy circuit, or so Panchuk fumed. The relief mission found itself in a ludicrous situation. Unless matters were rectified forthwith, he would ensure that the British had a public controversy on their

hands. As things turned out, Hlynka and Reverend Sawchuk, a leading prelate within the independent Ukrainian Greek Orthodox Church
of Canada, were able to visit Ukrainian DP camps briefly in the opening weeks of 1947, whereas Panchuk and Yaremovich were not destined to leave London until mid-February. Those intervening weeks
were taken up with yet more lobbying of various officials, representing
several different possible countries of DP resettlement, and in conferences with their Ukrainian American counterparts, like the UUARC's
Dr Walter Gallan.[20] Stamina was never much of a problem for Panchuk
and his co-workers, however frustrated they may have become with
the British bureaucracy.

At about the same time Panchuk received word that the UCRF and
UCC executives were receiving complaints about his stewardship, not
only with respect to the efforts he was making to mobilize Ukrainians
already relocated in the United Kingdom, but also about the state of
CURB's finances. Exacerbating his annoyance was an ill-informed reprimand he received from Winnipeg headquarters, questioning why the
Mission was tarrying in London when there was work to be done on
the mainland. These murmurs were harbingers of many of the troubles
that lay ahead for the Mission, and for Panchuk in particular, although
no one as yet realized just how troubled this venture would become.[21]

Once they finally arrived in western Europe, the CRM's personnel
deployed in order to work more effectively. Tony Yaremovich took up
responsibility for being the Mission's field representative in the British
Zone of Germany, with the added title of assistant director. Ann Crapleve, listed as the Mission's treasurer, also became a field representative, but in the American Zone of Germany. Their combined task was
to distribute Ukrainian Canadian relief supplies to the refugees, provide aid and advice to individuals, and liaise with Ukrainian DP committees and the officials overseeing them. The hard-working Panchuk,
as the Mission's director, travelled to the various DP camps, acting, in
effect, as an unofficial roving UCC ambassador, while also performing
a valuable role in advising Peter Molson, Dr Waddams, and other
Canadian representatives to the Preparatory Committee of the International Refugee Organization (PCIRO) in Geneva.[22] The Mission's personnel also attempted a limited amount of relief and welfare work
among the Ukrainian DPs in Austria. The only zone in which their
efforts were blocked was the French one, where, it was admitted, their
contacts were quite 'inadequate.'[23] Throughout this period, when the
Mission's members confined themselves essentially to humanitarian

work among the refugees, more or less scrupulously avoiding any openly anti-Soviet or political activities which might cause problems for them with the authorities, and counselling the DPs to do likewise, their efforts received favourable comment. As a Foreign Office official observed in May 1947: 'We take quite a good view of CURB ... Although it is anti-Soviet, it is not blatantly so, and so far as we are aware, it confines its activities to relief and resettlement.'[24]

Canadian officials in western Europe were likewise relieved to learn from their British counterparts that the Ukrainian Canadians were behaving themselves. Some positive assessments were, of course, generated by individuals who had long been sympathetic to the Ukrainian Canadians. Thus, Tracy Philipps did further service on behalf of his Ukrainian Canadian friends when he wrote to Canada's ambassador in Belgium, the Honourable Victor Dire, describing Panchuk as an individual for whom he had 'an exceptionally high regard,' the reason for praise being that this Ukrainian Canadian was 'not a politically minded person.'[25]

'Absurd, Almost Comic'

While they had originally contracted to stay together as a team until April 1947, the magnitude of the Ukrainian refugee problem, the need to concern themselves with the formation and workings of the International Refugee Organization, the particular issue of Ukrainian Surrendered Enemy Personnel interned near Rimini, in northeastern Italy, and other similar concerns kept all three of the Mission's members overseas well into the early fall of that year, when both Yaremovich and Crapleve returned to Canada. Only Panchuk agreed to remain longer – until April 1948 – after additional negotiations with the UCC and UCRF.[26] No replacements for his co-workers were immediately available. Not surprisingly, it was at about this time that Panchuk began to feel considerable pressure to come to at least some working arrangement with those Ukrainian Americans who, under the United Ukrainian American Relief Committee's auspices, were finally starting to establish a presence in the American zones of occupation. Writing to the UCRF's Anna Mandryka, Panchuk cajoled her about how 'vital' it was for the two North American committees to coordinate activities, and thereby both avoid any duplication of effort and keep up appearances before the British and American authorities. The latter, he reported, had hitherto been cooperating with the Bureau because they had assumed it enjoyed the joint support of the American and Canadian Ukrainian communities, even if, as he reminded Winnipeg, CURB had in reality been 'entirely and solely a Canadian effort.'[27] But, insisted Panchuk, that should not undercut any possibility of joint efforts. There was a real need for finding some common ground with the Ukrainian Americans. The main reason for doing so was purely geographical: most of the Ukrainian DPs were now found in the American Zone and not in the British one. It was imperative that Winnipeg take note of this reality and arrange a completely united effort by undertaking negotiations with their Ukrainian American counterparts in Philadelphia. At minimum, 'a very closely co-ordinated' effort was now required.[28] Panchuk concluded by reporting that he would be returning to Canada for a brief visit later that September.

There was actually little that was new in Panchuk's entreaties regarding the need for solidarity between American and Canadian Ukrainians involved with the management of relief efforts among the displaced persons. He had communicated with the UUARC's John Panchuk (no relation) in early 1947 on exactly this subject, pointing out that both groups had wasted considerable time, effort, and money in a duplication of services.[29] Outlining in some detail how he envisioned the structure of a cooperative effort, Panchuk emphasized that since 'the people for whom we must work are one people regardless of whether they are in the British, French or American Zone,' there was really a need for only 'one agency,' rather than a series of them, to meet the needs of the DPs.[30]

The difference between the situation in the spring of 1947, when he first wrote, and the fall of that same year, when he repeated his views, was that the intervening months had witnessed an outburst of antagonism between the Canadian and American Ukrainian committees, which made it unlikely that a truly joint effort would be possible. In the past, and yet again, such tensions were the result of internal political clashes, exacerbated by personality conflicts between members of the two committees and their communities. But there was a more fundamental rift between these two constituencies, one which reflected differences between how the Ukrainian Canadians viewed their duties towards the Ukrainian DPs and how their Ukrainian American counterparts viewed theirs. The Ukrainian Canadians had started CURB, and before that the 'London Club.' With the exception of an eight-thousand-dollar grant from the UUARC, Canada's Ukrainians had basically financed both operations. They continued to believe in an undivided approach to resolving the Ukrainian DP problem. As suggested in several of their lengthy memoranda, the Mission's members, and those of CURB before them (essentially, as we have seen, the same people), were willing to work wherever a need existed for their services. All through 1946 and into the early months of 1947, Ukrainian Canadians, like Yaremovich and Crapleve, could be found not only in the British but also in the American and French zones, going to work wherever possible wherever their help was required. Throughout this period they were virtually the only full-time advocates available to help the Ukrainian DPs. Living in close proximity to the camps, visiting them frequently, they had managed to become quite effective lobbyists in the offices of the occupation and refugee camp authorities, and had been of great use when it came to solving the many and various problems faced by hundreds of thousands of refugees. Panchuk would repeatedly, and rather undiplomatically, allude to the fact that, although the Mission's personnel gave out a story for official consumption which suggested that they had always worked for both the UCRF and the UUARC, the American Ukrainians had not stationed anyone overseas until late 1947. Until then Miss Crapleve, based out of Frankfurt, had been responsible for doing whatever was possible to help Ukrainian refugees in the American zones, while Yaremovich's responsibilities had included liaising with the British occupation authorities and Ukrainian DPs out of a UCRF office in Lemgo.[31]

For their part, the American Ukrainians, who finally established a UUARC representative in Munich, Roman Smook, accorded priority to providing material relief supplies to the Ukrainian refugees. They also preferred a piecemeal approach to dealing with the Ukrainian refugee situation, focusing their financial and human resources on helping only those Ukrainian refugees found in the American Zones, with only a secondary effort being mounted among resettled Ukrainians in France or elsewhere. They also sought only a loose affiliation of their efforts with those of the Canadian Ukrainians, regardless of what formal ties might exist between the UCRF and UUARC committees in North America.

For the Ukrainian Canadians overseas this was a dismal situation, one they greeted with disapproval. In a letter, dated 14 April 1947, sent directly to UUARC headquarters with a carbon copy forward to the UCRF in Winnipeg, they protested. Noting that the shared conviction of the Team's members was that the UUARC's modus operandi was 'unsound and impractical,' Panchuk, as mission director, underscored his belief that since the Ukrainian refugee situation constituted 'a single problem covering many areas' and not a series of unrelated problems, it was 'absurd, almost comic,' and certainly '*unwise*' to attempt to separate the efforts of the UUARC from those of the Mission.[32] Instead, all work should be united and coordinated under a joint board of directors, with expenses split equally, with whatever resources were available being devoted exclusively to the '*teams, missions or representatives*,' already in Europe, rather than on sending anyone else over 'to tour or visit.'[33] Before proposing four alternate plans for coordinating the efforts of the Ukrainian Canadians and the Ukrainian Americans, Panchuk reminded his Ukrainian American readers that, 'from the days during the war' until the present, 'the only field work of any concrete nature that has been done, including the organization of the London Bureau and the present Field Work, has been done exclusively and only by Canadians.'[34]

While he tried to soften this prickly criticism by adding that 'citizenship doesn't matter,' this ungenerous letter, probably more than anything else he ever wrote on the subject, soured relations between the UUARC's men and the Team, making it virtually impossible for any united effort on behalf of the DPs to be mounted by the Ukrainians of North America. As Dr Gallan retorted scarcely a fortnight after Panchuk's letter was mailed, the Ukrainian Canadian chief should spend less time involved in ungentlemanly criticism, write shorter letters, do more concrete work, and, instead of carping all the time, try to emulate the fine example represented by the Ukrainian American relief workers. If Panchuk did so, then, and only then, could it be said that Ukrainian Canadian efforts were not being wasted. In a further riposte, and in a manner obviously intended to goad Panchuk, Gallan added scathingly, 'If you accomplish in your time as much as I did during my short stay in Austria and Germany, then after our mission is completed, and our refugees are well taken care of and we have more leisure time, the Committees can get together and criticize and slander to their hearts content.'[35] Concluding in form, Gallan added sardonically that he wished Panchuk 'lots of luck.'

Panchuk, infuriated and disconcerted by what had turned into an exhaustive and bruising debate laced with personal innuendo, was well aware that Gallan had also attempted to damage his standing by forwarding copies of all their correspondence on to Kushnir and others. To counter the damage being done, Panchuk wrote directly to the Fund's executive. He enclosed a copy of Gallan's reproof, stating for the record that the CRM's members felt collectively insulted by Gallan's screed. They were now united in not wanting to have anything further to do with the American Ukrainians.[36] A week later, he wrote a more contrite and less confrontational letter to the UUARC, regretting that the tone of his mid-April letter had, apparently, been 'taken to heart so seriously.' But, he added, the Ukrainian Canadian mission should henceforth be regarded as a 'strictly Canadian venture.' If the American Ukrainians wanted anything from them, Philadelphia would first have to forward a request directly to Winnipeg, which would then instruct the Mission about whether or not to comply, and under what terms.[37]

Still, not willing to be outdone by Gallan in exchanging insults, an exasperated Panchuk did not resist the temptation of sending one more personal letter, in which he assailed the doctor for being unable to 'see the entire picture of the work before us,' despite having visited postwar Europe twice.[38] As for Gallan's claims about having accomplished something during his visits, Panchuk spared him nothing: 'You came with nothing, did nothing, accomplished very little or nothing, and went home with nothing, without leaving anything definite or concrete behind, *anywhere*.'[39]

Adding injury to insult, Panchuk insisted that both Gallan's trips, instead of paving the way for the Ukrainian Canadians (an accomplishment Gallan had claimed to his credit), had only placed more difficulties in their way. Not only had Gallan failed to consult with anyone – 'not on your life,' wrote Panchuk – but, whether in Belgium, France, Austria, or Germany, he had done little of value, or, even worse, had engineered calamities: 'You did accomplish one thing, once and for all you set UNRRA against Ukrainians and work for Ukrainians for good. The results are still being felt ... In Austria ... UNRRA issued a special order forbidding your entry to all camps ... How you managed to accomplish all this in such a short time is beyond me ... Anywhere we go in Austria or Germany (we) *deny any relations or connections with you or your committee*.'[40] This letter, which carried on in a similar vein for several pages, critiquing Gallan's 'sightseeing tour,' his empty phrases about the need for unity, and other claims, concluded somewhat less censoriously with the request that both men should now let the matter drop and, at least publicly, uphold each other's efforts, for the good of all concerned.

Not surprisingly, Gallan was unwilling to maintain this charade. Replying to Panchuk in late June, he indignantly pointed out that Panchuk's letter of 12 May, even though marked 'personal,' had apparently been copied to Winnipeg (Gallan claimed Kushnir had told him so). Accordingly, he felt honour and duty bound to write, yet again. His letter brusquely urged Panchuk 'to try and be a soldier and not a cheap politician,' and rebuked him and Reverend Sawchuk for 'mixing religion and relief' – an accusation both men would deny.[41] It was a mordant letter and no doubt vexed Panchuk even further. But, apparently not wanting to inflame this explosive situation further, Panchuk resisted the urge to counter-attack. Instead he sent a short note to Gallan, letting him know that copies of their correspondence had been forwarded to Kushnir and the UUARC's John Panchuk – on 24 July – and that he otherwise intended to conclude their fruitless correspondence.[42]

'Your Are Our Agent, Subject to Our Instructions'

These heated exchanges reverberated in North America. While Gallan and Panchuk raged on at each other, UCRF representatives were meeting with their UUARC counterparts to discuss how the two committees might work together in the future. At about the same time as Panchuk mailed his final note to Gallan, he received a letter from Winnipeg, sent by the UCC's executive secretary, Andrew Zaharychuk, which set forth the general policy and principles the two organizations had adopted for joint action. As Panchuk discovered to his dismay, the Ukrainian American viewpoint had prevailed. The two committees had agreed to maintain separate field representatives, paid for out of their own funds, with only the London Bureau functioning as a united venture, although a codicil to their agreement made it clear that the UCC was willing to carry the entire cost of that office if required. While cooperation between the American and Canadian Ukrainians was called for, the former clearly intended to operate only in the American zones of Germany and Austria, and expected the Ukrainian Canadians to stay out of those areas.[43] Most unacceptable from Panchuk's perspective was that he was clearly being instructed by Zaharychuk (in point #4 of the letter) not to disburse any Ukrainian Canadian moneys in support of Ukrainians already resettled in the United Kingdom, France, Belgium, or Canada.

This last directive, which undercut Panchuk's ongoing and determined efforts to build up a united, active, and patriotic Ukrainian community in Great Britain based on the postwar refugee immigration there, was totally unpalatable. Panchuk had grown convinced that the large-scale influx of European Voluntary Workers and veterans of the Ukrainian Division 'Galicia' to the United Kingdom could be shaped into a powerful community. Within the Ukrainian diaspora he foresaw a time when Great Britain would become a centre, if not the focal point, of the worldwide Ukrainian emigration. Such a high status for the emerging British Ukrainian community was almost assured, he believed, because London had been the world's principal metropolis before the war, and would, or so Panchuk incorrectly thought, remain so in the postwar world. And having a viable Ukrainian community there would give the Ukrainian people, Panchuk believed, a really good chance of influencing Anglo-American policy on the 'Ukrainian Question.' Yet this fledgling community would have no chance of reaching such a level if it was not financially supported, at least for a few years, by richer and better-established Ukrainian communities, like those of Canada and the United States. Convinced that the UCC was making a grave mistake by cutting off financial support for his efforts in the United Kingdom, Panchuk booked passage on the *Queen Elizabeth*. By 23 September 1947 he was in Montreal, and from there he went on to Winnipeg. He hoped a personal intervention would result in some modification of at least part of the UCC's plan.[44]

Panchuk brought a rich store of ideas and experience to Winnipeg, and not only about how the Ukrainian Canadian community should be helping the Ukrainian refugees. He also had rather imaginative notions about how the Ukrainian emigration as a whole might restructure itself – geographically, politically, and organizationally – in order to become a more effective lobbying group promoting the diaspora's interests and those of the Ukrainian cause in general. First of all, it was essential that there be 'something like a KYK in every country.' Wherever displaced persons were being resettled, Panchuk felt, there had to be an 'umbrella' organization uniting all Ukrainians, a body which would be 'above party and above sect.' The unifying principle should be 'the general Ukrainian cause from its social welfare, from its cultural and from its historical point of view.'[45] Once this goal was attained these various national organizations would be brought into some sort of central coordinating agency, which would become, de facto, an 'International Superstructure' presiding over all the constituent organizations of the Ukrainian diaspora. Of course, Panchuk insisted, the Ukrainian Canadian community would have a 'most important' role to play in the creation of this international superstructure.

Ivan Pillipiw, the first 'man in a sheepskin coat.' From V. Lysenko, *Men in Sheepskin Coats: A Study in Assimilation* (Toronto: Ryerson, 1947).

Women and children interned at Spirit Lake, Quebec. NAC PA 170620.

In the enclosure: Ukrainian internees at Castle Mountain, Alberta. G.W.H. Millican Collection, Glenbow Museum, Calgary.

The consecration of the Ukrainian Greek Catholic church of St Nicholas at Kenora, Ontario, in 1917 by Bishop Nykyta Budka. Multicultural History Society of Ontario.

Ukrainian emigrants at the CPR office in Ternopil arranging for passage aboard the SS *Melita*, September 1923. Ukrainian Cultural and Educational Centre 'Oseredok.'

The 'Man Who Knew': Tracy Erasmus Philipps, date unknown. Courtesy of L. Kolessa, Toronto.

Reverend Monsignor Dr Wasyl Kushnir, Sts Vladimir and Olga Ukrainian Greek Catholic Cathedral, Winnipeg, date unknown. Photo by Charles Photo Studio. Ukrainian Cultural and Educational Centre 'Oseredok.'

Flight Lieutenant G.R. Bohdan Panchuk, MBE. G.R.B. Panchuk Collection, Archives of Ontario.

The official opening of UCSA's Services Club, at the fifth UCSA 'Get-Together,' London, 15 April 1944. From left to right: Major Campbell Smith (CMHQ); Flying Officer Nick Bodnar (Edmonton); Captain 'Bunny' Mychalyshyn (Edmonton); Lieutenant Ivan Nokony (Regina): Lance Corporal Helen Kozicky (Calgary); Flying Officer Bohdan Panchuk (Saskatoon), president of UCSA; Reverend G.T. Chappell, vicar; Flight Lieutenant McDonald (RCAF-HQ); Leading Aircraftwoman Anne Cherniawsky (Vegreville); and Flight Lieutenant Belfry (RCAF-HQ). G.R.B. Panchuk Collection, Archives of Ontario.

UCSA at work, April 1944. From left to right: Leading Aircraftman John Yuzyk; Leading Aircraftwoman Anne Cherniawsky, club director; Pilot Officer Bohdan Panchuk, UCSA president; Lance Corporal Helen Kozicky, UCSA secretary. G.R.B. Panchuk Collection, Archives of Ontario.

Anthony 'Tony' J. Yaremovich, March 1946. A.J. Yaremovich private papers.

The sixth UCSA 'Get-Together,' Ukrainian Christmas, 6–7 January 1945. The banquet was held at the Knights of Columbus Services Club, Sunday, 7 January 1945. At the head table (2nd sitting), standing left to right: Captain Peter J. Worobetz, MC; Flight Lieutenant G.R.B. Panchuk; Major M. Syrotiuk; Honorary Captain S.W. Sawchuk; Lieutenant Ann Crapleve; Captain M. Cannon (Kalyniuk); Captain William Usick. G.R.B. Panchuk Collection, Archives of Ontario.

'Church parade,' outside 218 Sussex Gardens, London, 10–11 November 1945. From left to right: ?; Lieutenant J. Sawchuk; Flight Lieutenant J.R. Romanow; Flight Lieutenant Michael Oparenko; ?; Lieutenant Ivan Nokony; Lieutenant Wally Stechishin; Michael Checknita; Captain Wally Grenkow; Captain Stan Frolick; Captain Michael Lucyk; and Captain John Swystun. Photo by A. Louis Jarche. G.R.B. Panchuk Collection, Archives of Ontario.

Captain Stanley Frolick, en route to the Military Government detachment, Control Commission for Germany, near Oldenburg, Germany, December 1945. S.W. Frolick Collection, NAC.

Ann Crapleve, BEM, London, 1945. A. Smith private papers.

Dmytro Andrievsky, Danylo Skoropadsky, and G.R.B. Panchuk in London, 1945. G.R.B. Panchuk Collection, Archives of Ontario.

UCSA and CURB members, London, 1946. From left to right: Flight Lieutenant B. Panchuk; Captain Peter Smylski; Flight Lieutenant Joseph Romanow; George Kluchevsky; and S.W. Frolick. S.W. Frolick Collection, NAC.

The eleventh UCSA 'Get-Together,' London, 5–6 January 1946. At the head table, left to right: Captain S. Frolick (Control Commission for Germany); ?; Reverend Monsignor Dr W. Kushnir, president, UCC; Flight Lieutenant B. Panchuk, president, UCSA, and director of CURB; Sergeant Tony Yaremovich, secretary, UCSA; Captain B. Mychalyshyn. At the left front, the two women facing are Private Dorothy Tuskey and Lydia Pankiw. On the extreme right, looking at the camera, are Lady Hill and her escort, Prince Danylo Skoropadsky. G.R.B. Panchuk Collection, Archives of Ontario.

The wedding of Anne Cherniawsky and Bohdan Panchuk, London, 2 February 1946. From left to right: Captain S. Davidovich, Captain A.M. Homik, Captain S.W. Frolick, Captain D. Melnyk, Captain Walter Grenkow, and Captain Peter Smylski. The best man was Flight Lieutenant Romanow and the maid of honour was Leading Aircraftwoman E. Winarski. G.R.B. Panchuk Collection, Archives of Ontario.

The first Executive of the Ukrainian Canadian Committee, 1943. Front (left to right): S. Chwaliboga, J.W. Arsenych, Rev. S.W. Sawchuk, Rev. W. Kushnir, W. Kossar, A. Malofie, A.J. Yaremowich. Standing: M. Pohorecky, M. Stechishin, S. Skoblak, Rev. S. Semczuk, T.D. Ferley, P. Barycky, A. Zaharychuk. Third row: I. Gulay, W. Sarchuk, Dr B. Dyma, E. Wasylyshyn, Dr C. Andrusyshen, T. Melnychuk. Courtesy Ukrainian Canadian Congress.

Canadian Relief Mission for Ukrainian Refugees, London, 1946. From left to right, front row: Anne Cherniawsky, Bill Byblow, Ann Crapleve. Back row: Bohdan Panchuk, Michael Krysowaty, Anthony Yaremovich. G.R.B. Panchuk Collection, Archives of Ontario.

Visiting the Ukrainian Division 'Galicia' at Rimini, April 1947. Centre: Anne Panchuk, Flight Lieutenant B. Panchuk, and Ann Crapleve. G.R.B. Panchuk Collection, Archives of Ontario.

Cartoon of Bohdan Panchuk at Rimini, taken from *Wasp*, the mimeographed newsletter of the Ukrainian SEP at Rimini, 13 April 1947. G.R.B. Panchuk Collection, Archives of Ontario.

Members of a Ukrainian camp security detachment, 'Falkenburg' DP camp, ca 1946. From the collection of D. Luciuk, Kingston.

An anti-Communist protest march of Ukrainian DPs, Munich, 1949. From the collection of D. Luciuk, Kingston.

The Wasylyshens arrive at Bielefeld. Anne Crapleve, director of UCRF operations in Germany, greets Mr and Mrs Eustace Wasylyshen, 1 April 1949. E. and A. Wasylyshen private papers.

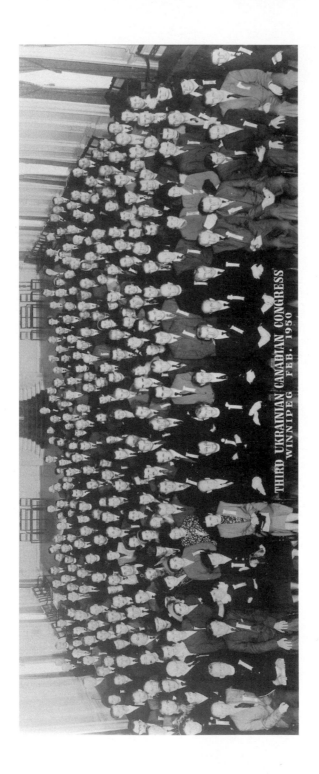

Delegates to the third UCC congress, Winnipeg, February 1950. Ukrainian Cultural and Educational Centre 'Oseredok.'

Negotiating an identity: Ukrainian Canadians greeting Her Majesty Queen Elizabeth II, Kingston, Ontario. Photo by D. Luciuk. From the collection of L. Luciuk, Kingston.

A 'good Canadian': presentation of the Order of Canada to Dr V.J. Kaye by His Excellency Governor General Jules Léger, Ottawa, 1975. NAC PA 202526.

An abiding interest: a 'Free Ukraine' placard at an anti-Soviet demonstration, Toronto. Photo by Lu Taskey. Multicultural History Society of Ontario.

Kassandra Luciuk: Canada is her place. From the collection of L. Luciuk, Kingston.

Several months later, writing to a Ukrainian veteran of the Polish armed forces, George Luckyj, Panchuk again articulated his belief in the importance of organizing the DPs then resettling throughout the Western Hemisphere on the basis of a 'solid foundation' akin to what he had earlier proposed. The only change he made to those original plans was that he no longer regarded the centre of gravity of the emigration as being in North America: 'Without doubt, England is an important "base," much more so than Canada (something I haven't quite been able to sell to our people in Canada) and our work there must be soundly and firmly established.'[46]

While he did not dispute that the 'men in Winnipeg' were truly devoted to the UCC and had 'good intentions,' Panchuk came to believe that most of them had fallen far short of accomplishing what might have been done, mainly because members of both the UCC and the UCRF executives tended to be big talkers but poor organizers, overburdened with work.[47] To cope with their ineptitude Panchuk evolved two stratagems. One was to 'flood Winnipeg with stacks' of reports, memoranda, enclosures, and the like to ensure that even if his superiors could not 'action' everything he sent them, he would at least be certain that a record of everything that he had attempted would be preserved. 'Some day in the future it may all prove of some interest,' he observed presciently. The other tactic was to strike out on his own initiative and do whatever he felt had to be done, as best he saw fit. Since 'KYK [was] not supplying' information or leadership, perhaps understandably given how far removed the executives were from the scene of operations, it was 'most important' for the field representatives to have 'almost complete freedom of action and decision.' In Panchuk's view it would be best if they were all simply accorded '*faith and confidence*' and told to do their best. Explaining how the ideal committee should treat its field representatives, and reflecting on his experience as he did so, Panchuk wrote: 'Sometimes it may appear in Winnipeg or Philadelphia that ... a decision is wrong or should be modified, but that cannot be helped. [The field representative] was sent out to do a job, he is doing it ... he is on the spot and knows the conditions ... his decision must be accepted ... If for any reason it cannot be, he should be recalled and replaced, but under no condition should a committee consistently hamper matters of detail ... that only undermines his ability and prestige.'[48]

Such a rational approach to dealing with the Ukrainian refugee problem did not, however, appeal to those in Winnipeg or Philadelphia, who often saw themselves as having a mandate to involve themselves in even the minutest details of the relief and resettlement operations – partly out of genuine interest, and partly out of an overdeveloped sense of their capabilities. Unfortunately, some rather intellectually and experientially ill equipped persons came to entangle themselves in trying to manage field operations from a distance of several thousand miles. Predictably, unhappy misunderstandings, with unfortunate consequences for the Ukrainian Canadian efforts, were the end result of their vanity and incompetence.

Coupled with the inability of most Ukrainians in North America to appreciate Panchuk's admittedly sometimes daunting plans was their scepticism about the appropriateness of many of the particular policies he put forward. Some Ukrainian Canadians were concerned over his apparently unflagging commitment to involving CURB and later the Mission in defending the Ukrainian Surrendered Enemy Personnel (SEP) at Rimini. Others wondered what he was doing on behalf of Ukrainians who had served in the Polish armed forces, and why. And his efforts aimed at imposing an organizational infrastructure on the DPs resettling in the United Kingdom were also questioned. Panchuk was certainly interested in moulding the future of this postwar emigration, based on his own perceptions of what was best for it. Many refugees also chafed at his efforts, particularly when they realized how informed many of his judgments were by understandings he had reached with the British and Canadian authorities, or, more fundamentally, how many were shaped by his own Ukrainian Canadian biases.[49]

And so, in the few hectic weeks Panchuk spent in Canada in late September through early October 1947, he held numerous meetings and private discussions with UCC and UCRF executive members, and with UUARC representatives who had travelled north to meet him, including both Dr Gallan and John Panchuk. Time and again he was asked to explain his actions, justify his expenditures, and report on conditions. Surprisingly, perhaps, things seemed to have gone well. As a result of all this chatter, Panchuk may even have thought that he had managed to get the principal players to accept his proposed plan of action, thereby reversing their summertime decision about keeping the American and Canadian field workers in Europe working independently of each other. In this he was mistaken, and his misjudgment brought him great difficulties.

Shortly after Panchuk returned to London, in mid-October 1947, and even while the UCC, UCRF, and UUARC executives were still deliberating over how best to apportion their resources and personnel, Panchuk took it upon himself to write to the UUARC's overseas representative, Roman Smook. After expressing his pleasure that a 'plan for joint action' had finally, albeit only 'in principle,' been adopted by the two committees in North America, Panchuk asked when and where they might meet to work out the necessary operational details.[50] About a week later, he sent another message to Smook, from Geneva, recording his thoughts on the importance of coordinating Canadian and American relief efforts. Panchuk even added a rather self-effacing remark to his letter, one he presumably felt would be ingratiating to the Americans. Quite in contrast to his earlier pronouncements, Panchuk claimed that the Ukrainian Canadians had only been 'pinch-hitting' as 'second rate deputies' while awaiting the arrival of the UUARC's personnel. Now that the American Ukrainians were in place, they should take charge.[51]

This was an alluring proposition, and certainly not one the American Ukrainians would have had any reason to reject out of hand. And so, after meeting together in Frankfurt on 7–8 November 1947, Smook and Panchuk reached a 'happy medium,' agreeing that there should be 'unity of action,' that a central 'European Operations HQ' would be set up to coordinate their efforts, that CURB should be moved to Germany and based in or near Munich, and that some kind of bureau should be maintained as a secondary headquarters in London. Additional representatives should be stationed in Lemgo, Frankfurt, Stuttgart, Vienna (and/or Innsbruck, Salzburg), Geneva, Brussels, and Paris.[52] All expenses would be shared. All personnel were to be either Canadian or American in origin, and interchangeable. The senior director was always to be whoever held the post of director of the UUARC's mission and would be responsible for all American Zone operations and for the running of the headquarters. The Canadian would be known as the deputy director, and would take charge of all joint actions and UCRF efforts. Any local personnel (mainly Ukrainian DPs) employed by the North Americans were to be persons of a 'non-political character and devoted solely and exclusively to relief.'[53] Panchuk forwarded this new agenda to the UCRF's Mrs Mandryka on 10 November 1947, writing John Panchuk on that same day about the 'marked success' of his negotiations with Smook. He stressed that what he most appreciated about Smook was that he was 'not a national or political fanatic.'[54]

Although Panchuk warmly endorsed Smook in this correspondence, other letters he sent were already expressing more personal anxieties

about his Ukrainian American colleague, probably sparked in part by
a disturbing report he had received from Tony Yaremovich, dated
15 October 1947. Yaremovich's letter from Canada had stressed that
while Ukrainian Canadians were interested in the immigration of
Ukrainian DPs to Canada, Ukrainian Americans seemed more inclined
to restrict their efforts to relief and welfare work. Yaremovich also
pointed out that Smook had written to Winnipeg and stated that the
American Ukrainians did 'not want any Canadians' in their zone. For
Yaremovich, the best way of coping with this Ukrainian American
arrogance – what he described as their habit of always 'running someone else down' while claiming they were the 'only ones accomplishing
anything' – was to compete openly with them by establishing independent Ukrainian Canadian operations. Then 'we will see who does what
along the lines of immigration.' He was cocky as to the outcome: immigration 'is what the people want to see happen. Relief is not wanted by
the people. They must have some but they feel that it is not solving the
problem [of the DPs].'[55]

Replying on 29 October, several days before he actually opened formal discussions with Smook in Frankfurt, Panchuk observed that he
was well aware of Smook's sense of his own self-importance. He
added dryly that, in his view, the agreement the American Ukrainians
had just signed with the IRO was nothing more than a copy of the one
which Ann Crapleve had drafted earlier, hardly the 'crowning achievement' it was being described as by Smook and his bragging colleagues.
As for Smook's boasts about having been able to do 'in four or five
days' what the Ukrainian Canadians had not been able to do in two
years, Panchuk waxed ironic about 'what a genius' Smook must be in
order to have accomplished so much in so little time.[56] Still, even if
Smook was 'vain,' Panchuk realized he would have to find some way
of cooperating with the American Ukrainians. He determined that the
best way to do so was to meet in Frankfurt with Smook and there to
draw up a new architecture for the refugee relief and resettlement
operations. So he got ready for these meetings, making no plans to
bring up the disquieting information Yaremovich and others had
shared with him about Ukrainian Americans' attitudes towards their
Ukrainian Canadian counterparts.

It was, in fact, perhaps rather proud of Panchuk to hope that his own
negotiations with Smook would receive unqualified approval from the
UCRF and UCC. These two bodies, apparently left with 'a sour taste'
as a result of Smook's agreement with the IRO, which made it seem the

Ukrainian Americans were far better organized and accepted by the authorities than their Ukrainian Canadian counterparts, were also confused over precisely what Panchuk was attempting to negotiate. And so, on 18 November 1947, they officially reprimanded Panchuk for overstepping the limits of his authority, reminding him that he was their representative in the field. By then, it is likely Panchuk knew that trouble was on its way, for John Karasevich, his long-standing friend and UCVA's president, had already written to say that the UCC presidium was quite upset over the disbursements Panchuk had been making to resettled Ukrainian DPs in England. Indeed, Karasevich warned, the UCC would soon insist that Panchuk account for all moneys spent by the Mission from July 31 and onward.[57] As well, one of Panchuk's most recent letters to Winnipeg, in which he had apparently insisted upon the Committee and Fund executives there taking immediate action instead of prevaricating as usual, had earned him no allies. Several of the UCRF's members were particularly antagonized for, as Karasevich noted, these leading members of the community felt that they had 'contributed immensely towards the general good cause of the Ukrainians.' They were not about to let their self-serving assessments get punctured by Panchuk.[58] Thin-skinned, they set out to teach him a lesson.

In the last week of November 1947 they did. Panchuk received a formal and quite caustic reproach for his words and deeds. His agreement with the UUARC's Smook, he was informed, was 'too fantastic' to be credible and was certainly not one which the Fund agreed to, since the Panchuk–Smook accord more or less alluded to a near-future 'fushion' (*sic*) of the two committees.[59] The Mission, he was instructed, was to remain 'an independent body.' And there were absolutely no funds (nor was there a need, in the view of the UCRF executive) for a permanent centre in Geneva, as Panchuk has proposed. As for whatever cooperation there might be with the Americans, it would extend only as far as was practical.

Winnipeg chastised Panchuk even more sternly for expressing a 'rather surprising' view. They inquired why he was 'asking now what your duties etc. are. You are our agent subject to our instructions and in duty bound to act within the scope of your agency. Keep in touch with all possible channels of immigration and assist in movement of Displaced Persons directly or indirectly.'[60] As for Panchuk's eager lobbying on behalf of the Ukrainian refugees resettled in England, the UCRF executive expressed further 'surprise': 'You are still harping at it. We have no funds for assistance of persons who have already settled in the process of immigration outside of the zones of occupation and camps and we put a stress on this.'[61]

The most exasperating part of the UCRF message was its confirmation of news which Panchuk had earlier received from Karasevich, namely, that he should expect the imminent return of Yaremovich and Crapleve.[62] This might seem welcome tidings, but it was not. As Jaroslav Arsenych and Anna Mandryka, the co-signers of the letter, 'bluntly' and 'with brevity and terseness' put it, Yaremovich and Crapleve were 'going to operate in the British and American zones. They will co-operate and keep in touch with you but they will make reports directly to the Committee. This was the condition demanded by them. You will co-operate with them and mutually co-ordinate your activities.'[63]

To remind Panchuk of who was boss, it was suggested that if any of the stated arrangements were unsatisfactory, or if he saw better opportunities elsewhere, the UCRF would not stand in his way should he wish to tender his resignation.

'With Deep Regret'

Not surprisingly, he did just that. Constrained by the policies emanating out of Winnipeg, whereby his plans for a united and cooperatively managed North American Ukrainian relief and resettlement program were fragmented and his own responsibilities and role curbed, Panchuk responded with bitterness. To make matters worse, he felt that even his fellow veterans, Yaremovich and Crapleve, had turned on him by striking out independently. It was all too demoralizing to cope with. Irked, he cabled Karasevich, 'My only desire to be given opportunity and facilities to produce results or to be left alone.'[64]

Even though he received repeated requests from fellow UCVA members to reconsider his resignation, their pleas fell on deaf ears. An overwrought Panchuk was changing sides. He would stay overseas, he wrote, but he was now willing to work only as an unpaid (expenses only) volunteer for the UUARC, and not for the Ukrainian Canadians.[65] That did it. On 5 December 1947, Monsignor Kushnir wrote formally to accept Panchuk's resignation on the Fund's behalf, effective from 31 December. In his letter Kushnir, 'with deep regret,' further admonished Panchuk for having 'refused to follow our plans,' as these plans had been elaborated during Panchuk's visit to Winnipeg earlier that year. He was asked to offer every assistance to Yaremovich, who was to take over the Bureau, and to 'liquidate all engagements that he made concerning the Bureau' without the UCRF's 'consent or instructions.'[66] Holding out one last chance for Panchuk to reconsider, Kushnir noted that if, after having thought it over, he would agree to 'follow strictly our plan and instruction,' there would still be a place for him 'on duty for the Committee and the Fund.'[67] Cabling Yaremovich on that same day, Kushnir added emphasis to the Committee's earlier instructions that all 'extra business' arranged by Panchuk without the Fund's approval was to be liquidated. First, however, Kushnir informed Yaremovich he had better get to the Continent, where Crapleve was already located, leaving the tidying up of the Bureau's affairs to a later date, when he could return to take charge formally.[68]

Panchuk seems to have floundered a little at this point. He wrote to Tracy Philipps to say that the 'main reason' for his resignation was a desire to return to Canada with his family. In the very same letter, however, he also claimed that a 'perhaps more important reason' for leaving was what he delicately termed a 'slight divergence in principle' between the UCRF and himself over how organizational efforts should be managed. The former had insisted, on several occasions, that its limited resources be directed to work among Ukrainian DPs, in the camps, on the Continent. In the Fund's view, those who were already resettled in the United Kingdom would have to 'fend for themselves.' Panchuk, to the contrary, believed that Ukrainian Canadians had a 'moral responsibility' to the British government and people to help look after even these resettled refugees, a liability they could not 'escape' by pleading a lack of resources.[69] In particular, they had to concern themselves with the Ukrainian POWs, European Voluntary Workers (EVWs), and Ukrainian members of the Polish armed forces who had begun arriving in England and whom Panchuk had been busily organizing into a new body, the AUGB, or Association of Ukrainians in Great Britain. As he explained in a letter to Dr Kaye, 'One thing I was and have not been prepared to do, and that is to sacrifice the future of our Ukrainian Division.'[70]

Keeping to his promise to assist Yaremovich in taking over as CURB's director, Panchuk issued a circular to 'all concerned' noting that, as of New Year, Yaremovich would be responsible for the Bureau, and self-servingly added that all responsibility for Ukrainians in Great Britain would be vested in the newly established AUGB.[71] This was duly noted in Whitehall, which, as might be expected, had been keeping a keen eye on the growth and nature of this new British Ukrainian group, mainly because they had begun receiving official complaints about anti-Soviet Ukrainian activity in the United Kingdom, even before the Association was formally incorporated, on 20 December 1947. In early June of that year, the USSR's diplomatic representatives first protested about the organization's existence. That prompted the Foreign Office to request that the War Office and the Home Office be advised not to provide any facilities to the AUGB for conducting anti-Soviet propaganda among the Ukrainians being brought over to the United Kingdom. Any such encouragement, Brimelow noted, would only lead to 'serious trouble.'[72] He did minute, however, that his department did not accept the grounds on which the Soviets had based their protest, for the Ukrainians brought to England were, from the day of their arrival, 'in our country,' and therefore no longer DPs. They could do whatever they liked.[73] British officials would keep abreast of the AUGB's activities, but they were far less censorious than they had been of similar Ukrainian groupings in the British Zone of Occupation. Presumably, they were also reassured by Panchuk's promise to keep 'all of the activities of the AUGB' subject to Ukrainian Canadian 'control and instructions.'[74] In effect the British government's experience of Panchuk gave them no reason to fear that this new association in any serious way would prove disruptive of good Anglo–Soviet relations. And so they tolerated it.

They could only have been further assuaged when, in March 1948, Panchuk was elected the second president of the AUGB, replacing N. Bura, a Ukrainian who had originally emigrated to England as a refugee along with the Polish government-in-exile.[75] When news about Panchuk's new responsibilities filtered back to Canada, reactions there were mixed. Dr Kaye, for example, wrote to Philipps that he did not envy Panchuk the arduous task of trying to get all Ukrainians in the United Kingdom organized and united within one group. He added that he hoped Panchuk would be able to avoid being used by those who would try to 'use PAN [Panchuk] for their political or personal purposes.'[76] While Kaye noted that he agreed with Panchuk's assessment about members of the Division constituting 'the best material' among this postwar emigration, since they were 'disciplined, devoted [and] would eagerly give their lives for principles defended by Great Britain which are the same they would like to apply to their own country of origin,'[77] he also recorded that in his opinion 'their greatest enemy is their own politics.' At that very moment, he observed, they

were being 'courted' by nationalists of both OUN factions, by Skoropadsky's monarchists, and by others. It would, Kaye concluded, be
necessary to give Panchuk 'adequate support' if he was to have any
chance of keeping these newly resettled Ukrainians 'out of politics,' by
which he meant out of trouble with the authorities.[78]

'Very Embarrassing and Unpleasant'

Although relations between Panchuk and Yaremovich would remain
more or less cordial, the camaraderie they had shared as UCSA members and veterans soured, at least briefly, after Yaremovich formally
accepted the mantle of director of CURB.[79] After a brief period in London, Yaremovich had followed Kushnir's orders and left to join Crapleve in the British Zone of Occupation in Germany, where he assisted
in administering UCRF operations and tried, with varying degrees of
success, to work with the UUARC's men.[80] During the time Yaremovich was on the Continent, Bill Byblow assumed the position of
CURB's deputy director. When Byblow, at Yaremovich's direction,
began to review CURB's financial status, and particularly to examine
its expenditures from late summer 1947 until Panchuk's departure at
the end of December, it became clear, to quote the UCRF's general secretary, Mrs Mandryka, that the former director of the Bureau had 'used
considerable amounts of Relief Fund monies, without the permission
of the Directors of the Fund, or without even informing them, for the
support of SUB [the AUGB].'[81]

What ensued was an exchange of correspondence involving, on the
one side, Panchuk and George Salsky, the president and executive
director of the AUGB respectively, and, on the other, CURB's director
and deputy director, Yaremovich and Byblow. This interchange moved
from the level of a few simple requests for clarification of certain
expenses to one of dyspeptic recrimination. In the end all that was
accomplished was the liquidation of CURB and the return of Yaremovich to Canada, in September 1948, a story which can now be told.

In replying to CURB's inquiries about various disbursements made
under his stewardship, Panchuk maintained that, while it was true
CURB had been made liable for some costs related to helping
Ukrainian POWs and EVWs in England –and that this had drained the
Bureau's budget – he felt the work done was part and parcel of CURB's
overall obligations. In his mind there was no contradiction between
helping Ukrainians in the refugee camps of western Europe and turn-

ing resources over to veterans of the Division and EVWs being relocated in England, whether from Italy or other Continental refugee camps. The costs involved, he argued, should be borne by the American and Canadian committees, and not by the AUGB, since the latter was still a fledgling group with limited financial resources.[82]

Panchuk's reply reflected his sincerely held viewpoint. But it was not the policy of the UCRF to provide financial support to individuals after they had been relocated out of the DP camps, and Panchuk had been reminded of this, unambiguously, in November 1947. His subsequent and deliberate failure to comply had been one of the main reasons for his parting with CURB and the UCRF in December of that year. Panchuk had knowingly ignored Winnipeg's instructions. The unfortunate consequence of his largesse, and one it is unlikely he foresaw, was that the Fund's executive now informed Byblow that CURB would have to be liquidated, a lack of money being given as the sole reason. As Byblow wrote to Panchuk, from what had become the Bureau's new, smaller office at 46 Seymour Street in London, 'A few weeks ago when our funds had completely depleted and we notified the UCR Fund accordingly, they replied to us that they are not sending more funds to the Bureau, but that we are to collect from SUB [the AUGB] the sum of over Six Hundred Pounds which was loaned to you by the Bureau.'[83]

Byblow went on to point out that the Bureau, without this infusion of funds, was faced with the 'very embarrassing and unpleasant' situation of not being able to meet its rent payments, or even to pay the landlord compensation for breaking their three-year lease. Asking Panchuk to reply quickly, Byblow also made it clear that he was forwarding copies of his letter to the UCRF in Winnipeg and to Miss Crapleve, who was then working out of an office in Lemgo.

Replying for the AUGB on 10 November, Salsky indicated that the Association would assume 'all reserves, assets and liabilities' of CURB. A week later Panchuk himself instructed Salsky, in a memorandum entitled 'Liquidation of and Commitments and Responsibilities of CURB,' that a special commission being appointed by the UCRF would soon be meeting to decide how to conclude CURB's operations. In the interval, the AUGB would 'alleviate the present difficult position in which [CURB] apparently find themselves.'[84] But Panchuk acknowledged no personal responsibility for CURB's situation, instead suggesting that the reason the Bureau was being shut down was an 'urgent need' to concentrate all available resources on the European mainland to meet the 'growing need' of the DPs there for direct relief.[85]

Three meetings of the committee struck to liquidate CURB were held. Involved were Ann Crapleve, serving in the role of executrix, assisted by Danylo Skoropadsky, Byblow, and Panchuk. No further mention of the moneys loaned or given to the AUGB by Panchuk was apparently made, at least none that was entered in the minutes.[86] Yaremovich, who had corresponded with Panchuk on this and related themes in August, made his dissatisfaction with this state of affairs plain, most explicitly by refusing to stay overseas longer than his original contract had provided for. By late September 1948 he had departed for Canada.[87] He would play no further role in this particular story, although in later years he honourably served the Ukrainian Canadian community as an executive director of the UCC and an active member of UCVA. He died in Winnipeg in 1993.

An attempt now had to be made to recruit new personnel to fill in the gaps appearing in the Ukrainian Canadian complement overseas. Before that, however, a final attempt was made by some veterans, among them Johnnie Yuzyk and John Karasevich, to affect a reconciliation between Yaremovich and Panchuk, in the hope that both men might be persuaded to remain overseas in service to the Ukrainian Canadian community. No such accommodation could be arranged. Panchuk refused to work either for the UCRF or for CURB.[88] For him it had, by then, become axiomatic that the best work he could do would have to be done outside the direct control of the UCC and UCRF. Thereafter his remarkable energies would be concentrated primarily on building up the AUGB. By mid-August 1948 he could report considerable success. His organizational efforts helped secure a membership of over nineteen thousand people for the AUGB, including, as he put it, 'every conscious and thinking Ukrainian regardless of his religion, political or other creeds or beliefs.'[89]

Panchuk was quite proud of this accomplishment. Although, as he confided to another veteran, Peter Smylski, the ideal of a central organization for Ukrainians in Canada had been a 'great one,' what had emerged, the Ukrainian Canadian Committee, was a great disappointment. He intended to do much better in Great Britain: 'I regret that what hope and faith I did have in those people had practically disappeared ... The ideal ... will never be realized with those people that are in Winnipeg and under the present system.'[90]

Better, he wrote, that he remain working where he was, since, 'having started something completely new and on a different basis,' he now felt he had an obligation to help the AUGB become a model for the entire emigration. Panchuk confidently stated that he had learned from experience how Ukrainian organizations should be constituted and run. The UCC was far from being the right model, so he set out to create a better one. Under his direction, he believed the AUGB would some day become a Ukrainian organization 'equalled by none.' And he would be present from its inception, a father to a new way of doing things. It was an irresistible opportunity for a teacher, a soldier, and a community activist – to serve as mentor, order-giver, and moulder of an entirely novel Ukrainian society and its most basic organizational infrastructure.

Now that Panchuk was out of the picture, at least as far as the Ukrainian Canadian establishment was concerned, it became obvious that there was a pressing need for new, but experienced, leadership. The clement Ann Crapleve was pressed into service, being appointed director of UCRF operations on the Continent effective 11 December 1948, the very same date on which CURB ceased formally to exist.[91]

While Panchuk would keep in touch with Crapleve, and continue dispensing advice to the UCRF and UCC, sometimes welcome, sometimes not, his preoccupation with the AUGB, with the 'civilianization' of Ukrainian POWs in the United Kingdom, and with the political crisis he would face in March 1949 – the after-effects of which would take him nearly two years to adjust to – all served to remove him from centre stage for a time.[92] Meanwhile, Ukrainian Canadian efforts on behalf of the Ukrainian refugees still left in the DP camps of western Europe continued.

April Fool's Day, 1949

Miss Crapleve had only just returned to the Continent after chairing the CURB's Liquidation Committee meeting when she received a letter from Winnipeg informing her that Mr Eustace (Stanley) and Mrs Anne Wasylyshen had agreed to come overseas for a year. Wasylyshen was appointed to serve as the director of UCRF operations, with his wife there to assist. Crapleve, whom Wasylyshen would accurately describe as 'a very capable and efficient young woman,' apparently was not distressed or put out by this information. Indeed she would record that this was 'the best news received for a long time.'[93] Unpretentious, hard-working, and realistic, she was less concerned with cosmetic issues, like who might hold the formal title of UCRF director, than with getting her job done. Having two Ukrainian Canadians to help with the work was, in her view, nothing but good tidings. As for Panchuk, who seems not to have been informed about the Wasylyshens or their mandate until a few months later, he too recognized how vital additional workers were to the Ukrainian Canadian effort. And so he likewise welcomed the report that the Wasylyshens had sailed for England, on 10 March 1949. Although his wife was ill at the time, and he was attempting to continue with his interrupted university studies, he promised Winnipeg that he would do everything he could to help the Wasylyshens during their stay in England, prior to their travel to Bielefeld in the British Zone of Occupation in Germany.[94]

In many respects, Eustace Wasylyshen was well qualified for the tasks now before him. An interwar immigrant to Canada, he later become involved with the St Raphael's Ukrainian Immigrant Aid Welfare Association of Canada (incorporated in 1925). He was a founding member of the Ukrainian War Veterans Association, and later a prominent member of the Ukrainian National Federation. Living in Winnipeg, and active in the Ukrainian community there, he knew personally all the leading members of the UCC and UCRF. In fact, when the Committee was first constituted, Wasylyshen took a seat on its national executive, filling in for the official Federation representative, Professor Toma Pavlychenko, since Pavlychenko, a native of Saskatoon, would have found it difficult to attend regularly the UCC executive meetings, which were always held in Winnipeg. Furthermore, Wasylyshen, being employed as an immigration agent for the Cunard White Star Line, already knew the rules and regulations of the immigration process and something about Canada's major gatekeepers, their personalities, and their politics. It is not surprising that with this background he was selected by the Fund to fill their most important overseas post.

What was less well known, being understood only by a few of the most trusted UNF members, was that Wasylyshen was also a member of the Provid ukrainskykh natsionalistiv (PUN), the Leadership Council of the Melnyk faction of the Organization of Ukrainian Nationalists-Solidarists (OUNm, or Melnykivtsi).[95] When Colonel Konovalets, the leader of what was then a still united OUN, visited Canada in 1929, Wasylyshen was at his side.[96] And when Wasylyshen went overseas in February 1949, one of the first men he contacted was Dmytro Andrievsky, a fellow PUN member. Andrievsky, then living in London, had – apparently at Kossar's insistence and with Kushnir's acquiescence – been attached to CURB as a salaried employee almost from the inception of the Bureau's work. Although Wasylyshen, in his work for the UCRF, seems to have handled his duties and responsibilities professionally, what evidence there is about his political affiliation does suggest that he was engaged simultaneously in covert work on behalf of the Melnykivtsi. Less than a half year would pass before his political foes would seize upon this fact to undermine his position as the UCRF's director. Like Frolick and Panchuk before him, Wasylyshen was to learn that no matter how competent his efforts, partisan politics permeated and complicated all aspects of these Ukrainian Canadian relief efforts. Even his enjoying the friendship of most of the members of the UCC and UCRF executives provided no shield against the barbs of those antagonists determined to uproot him. The primary concern of the Ukrainian Canadian leadership of the day was always over how the outside world perceived Ukrainian Canadian activities, and especially over what Ottawa thought. To avoid censure or worse, they were quite willing to sacrifice their own people, and they did so, repeatedly.

That realization, and the disappointment it would beget in Wasylyshen, was still months away. Having met with Panchuk in London – 'a terrifically energetic young man, with drive and initiative, idealistic, and devoted to his welfare work' – and toured through some of the Ukrainian hostels and POW camps in England, the Wasylyshens left for Bielefeld, Germany, arriving there on April Fools Day, 1949. 'Hope it's not an omen,' Wasylyshen scribbled in a note to his friend J.H. Patterson at the Cunard offices.[98]

The Wasylyshens got right down to work, and by all reports they were conscientious and capable once they learned the routines of UCRF operations. An indication of the psychological strains facing Ukrainian Canadians in the field – where, Wasylyshen reported, there were still over seventy-five thousand Ukrainian DPs in the spring of 1949 – is given in his wife's discerning observation about the differences between the two of them as Ukrainian Canadians and the Ukrainian refugees they had come to help: 'Our trouble is that we have a dual personality and can see both sides equally well. On one side you have a lack of understanding and human sympathy ... on the part of the "Haves," and on the other side you have what is called "DP Itis," which complains against everybody and everything, on the part of the "Have Nots." There are many, many faces to this problem.'[99]

'Big American Stuff'

The Wasylyshens soon arranged meetings with representatives of the British and American commands and, on 14 April 1949, consulted with the UUARC's Smook at his office in Hamburg.[100] A measure of cooperation was arranged between the UCRF team and the American authorities. Even prior to the arrival of the Wasylyshens in Bielefeld, the UCRF had received an official accreditation with the American Displaced Persons Commission operating in the British Zone of Germany, confirmed by executive order #36 of the Displaced Persons / Prisoners of War Section, dated 1 March 1949.[101] However, the Ukrainian Canadians and their Ukrainian American counterparts continued to have problems working together. In his Report #8, Wasylyshen alluded to these difficulties, noting that he had 'run into a good deal of unpleasantness' in dealing with Smook, largely because of Smook's methods of distributing the UUARC's 'Anonymous Assurance certificates.' These documents, which financially obliged the UUARC to the sponsorship of an individual or family of refugees, were apparently not being handed out by Smook to any Ukrainians in the British Zone, even though a group of them had been selected carefully by the UCRF and were described as 'honest, hardworking [with] farm experience, willing to complete contracts on farms.' While the UCRF team was careful to choose Ukrainians without any discrimination on the basis of political, religious, or regional background, Smook apparently employed a selection process that was far less fair, or so Wasylyshen suggested. Of 479 applications submitted by the UCRF as of 8 June 1949, only 214 were accepted, a winnowing which infuriated Wasylyshen. What made him angrier was that, in mid-June, Smook informed the UCRF that even those 214 supposedly successful applications were being cancelled.[102] The impact on the DPs so affected – who must have been told to prepare themselves for resettlement in the United States – can only be imagined. And the Wasylyshens were left to deal with the resulting grief as best they could.

Troubles between the Ukrainian Canadians and the Ukrainian Americans never really abated. Several months after the difficulties over these 'Anonymous Assurance certificates,' Anne Wasylyshen, writing to a friend in Canada, observed that while Smook was not autocratic in his demeanour towards the UCRF's team, another UUARC field representative, a Mr Rodyk, who was based out of Hannover, did consider himself 'Big American Stuff,' far superior in every way to the 'poor-white-trash-Canadians.'[103] Try as they might, none of the Ukrainian Canadians ever seem to have been able to develop comfortable or even simply efficient ties with their American counterparts overseas. No united North American Ukrainian effort to help the DPs would ever be sustained.

'The Sausage Machine'

After a few months of work, described by Mrs Wasylyshen as 'so absorbing and time consuming' that there was no time left over in an average day 'for sitting around and moping' about their lack of a social or recreational life, or even about the deficiency of decent rations, the Wasylyshens began to feel that they too were becoming displaced persons of a sort, cut off from their friends and community in Winnipeg.[104] Yet every day they would try to work not only in the large Bielefeld office but also in the UCRF's smaller Wentorf bureau. The scale of their efforts is suggested by their own description of how they wrote 'hundreds of letters, on as many different problems,' made 'thousands of telephone calls,' visited various refugee camps to interview perspective immigrants, and kept on doing so, week after week, with no apparent end in sight. All the while they made do with a largely untrained staff, composed primarily of Ukrainian refugees drawn from the DP camp populations. And there were too few even of these helpers who were experienced enough to be of much use.[105]

Making their life even harder were the conditions in which they laboured. Everywhere, according to Mrs Wasylyshen, there were 'nothing but tragedies' to be observed.[106] Disconcertingly, their hard work often seemed to have few obviously successful outcomes. When they did manage to have a real and positive impact on the lives of some refugees, as they did, for example, in the case of an eastern Ukrainian Orthodox priest and his family whom they saved from repatriation, they basked in well-earned satisfaction. Otherwise their work was an admixture of disappointments, frustrations, and setbacks, a blend they grew gradually accustomed to if never exactly comfortable with. From the remaining UCRF records it is clear that the Wasylyshens acquitted themselves well. Aware of the factionalism within the DP camps, and of the debilitating aspects of the refugee experience in general, they persevered, doing whatever they could to help. Showing great insight and compassion, Mrs Wasylyshen remarked in a personal letter that

she and her husband had both tried not to be too critical of the refugees' 'shortcomings': 'At the back of our minds we always try to keep
the questions – how would we act, and what would we be, if we had
lived under the same conditions for that length of time.'[107]

The Wasylyshens, like the other Ukrainian Canadians who had come
before them, were in Europe 'not to judge but to help.' And that is
what they did, or at least usually tried to do. Yet they could not avoid
the simple fact that all around them were 'dozens of the shiftless, stu-
pid, and sometimes depraved and vicious characters' whose shortcomings had 'been brought out by the unnatural and unhealthy conditions
of life' in the refugee camps.[108] For these two Ukrainian Canadians the
world in which they found themselves was a complex and too often a
depressing place. Few would want to be left there for any length of
time, although the Wasylyshens were certainly willing to stay as long
as they had to.

What troubled the UCRF's representatives, however, as they continued with their daily rounds of doing what they could to help
Ukrainian DPs emigrate – a process Mrs Wasylyshen described as 'the
sausage machine' – was their sense of being 'completely cut off from
Winnipeg.' 'Very seldom' did they receive any explicit instructions
from anyone in the UCRF or UCC executives.[109] It was as if, having
been assigned to their posts, they were now forgotten. This was not a
unique complaint, of course, similar murmurs having frequently been
made by Panchuk and the others.[110] And, just as for their predecessors,
for the Wasylyshens the lack of directives and information from headquarters was a portent of troubles to come.

'A Hetmanite-Banderite Bloc'

The first warning they received came in the latter half of November
1949. It was in the form of a letter penned by Dr Mykyta I. Mandryka, a
member of the Ukrainian Party of Socialist Revolutionaries, and later
of the Ukrainian Central Rada. Mandryka, who had emigrated to Canada from Prague in 1929, was affiliated with the Ukrainian National
Home in Winnipeg. As an active Ukrainian community worker, he had
helped set up an anti-Marxist Ukrainian labour association and participated in the UCC's first executive. Dr Mandryka took a particular
interest in the Ukrainian DPs. Under the aegis of the Canadian
Ukrainian Educational Association, which he had also helped set up,
he published an English-language booklet which described the plight

of these DPs sympathetically. Entitled simply *Ukrainian Refugees*, it had enjoyed wide circulation.[111] As well, his wife, Anna, who served as the first executive secretary of the UCC's women's council, took a similar posting with the Fund. Both husband and wife were thus fully committed to relieving the plight of their fellow Ukrainians.

Mandryka's letter to Eustace Wasylyshen, dated 14 November, presented his opinion about what was actually 'going on in Winnipeg' in the inner councils of the UCC and UCRF. His rather startling revelations cannot be dismissed, for both the Mandrykas were well placed to observe and reflect on what was happening in the Ukrainian community. None of the main actors in this drama remain alive, and two private archives which might shed some light on this episode remain closed. But Dr Mandryka was an informed, educated, and contemporary witness of Ukrainian Canadian community affairs,[112] and there is also a considerable amount of corroborative, if indirect, evidence to suggest that his allegations were not exaggerated.

Quite simply, Mandryka claimed, in his very first letter to Wasylyshen, that the first executive director of the UCC, Volodymyr Kochan, who had only recently arrived in Canada from Europe, was conniving with a group which Mandryka described as the 'Hetmanite-Banderite bloc.' This group, he asserted, 'now controlled' the UCC's national executive.[113] While Kochan might formally appear 'nonaligned,' Mandryka suggested, this appearance was only a public façade. As partial proof of his charges he pointed to the fact that Kochan had appointed as his personal secretary a man by the name of Wolodymyr Klish, a well-known member of the Banderivtsi. In the UCC's executive committee one could also find such prominent Hetmantsi as Andrew Zaharychuk, Dr Teodor Datzkiw, Major Osyp Nawrocky, and T. Mychaylywsky.[114] Surrounded by such 'friends,' Kochan and the 'Hetmanite-Banderite bloc' were doing everything possible to have Wasylyshen recalled and at the same time laying plans for expropriating the UCRF's moneys for their own partisan uses 'in Canada.' This 'clique,' which, Mandryka wrote, had 'all of KYK in its hands,' was employing a number of stratagems to bring about Wasylyshen's dismissal. For example, the conspirators had leaked a confidential letter from Panchuk to Wasylyshen, a copy of which had been privately made available to Monsignor Kushnir, the purpose of their action being to provoke trouble within the UCRF.[115] The negative report on the Wasylyshens which a Mrs Daria Yanda had earlier filed with the UCRF, after her visit to Bielefeld in July 1949, had also resurfaced as a topic for debate, most recently in front of a 'discussion club' of 'new-comers' set up and presided over by none other than Kochan.[116]

Anticipating that the Wasylyshens would want to know more about how all this could have taken place in the relatively short period of time between their departure for Europe and the date on which he was writing, Mandryka noted that the 'Hetmanite-Banderite clique' had been able to 'achieve supremacy' within the UCC executive by 'crushing ... all dissenting opinions' with its 'brutal aggressiveness.' Datzkiw himself was a major villain in this piece, for it was he, Mandryka alleged, who was now leading a 'drive to finish off' the rival UNF, whose own leader, Kossar, had fallen into a 'Tolstoy-like pacifism.'[117]

All these developments could have been prevented, wrote Mandryka, 'if only KYK had been reformed and kept up by the organizations who formed it.' Now, in his view, it was too late to do anything about saving the UCC, for it was, to the full extent of the proverbial lock, stock, and barrel, in the hands of members or 'sympathizers' of the Hetmantsi and Banderivtsi.[118] He predicted that these conspirators would next step up their 'campaign' to liquidate the UCRF mission overseas, so he warned Wasylyshen not to expect his UCRF mandate to be renewed beyond July 1950, when it was formally up for either extension or termination. Indeed, Mandryka even suggested that the Wasylyshens' tenure might be foreshortened by some kind of 'accident' in Winnipeg. What was certain, Mandryka claimed, was that everything possible was being done in Canada specifically for the purpose of removing Eustace Wasylyshen from his UCRF post overseas.

Why was the 'Hetmanite-Banderite bloc' so indisposed to Wasylyshen? It seems, Mandryka wrote, that they had somehow come to believe he was one of the leading Melnykivtsi in the prewar emigration.[119] Not knowing otherwise, Mandryka sneered at this notion. In fact it was true; Wasylyshen was indeed a high-ranking member of the OUNm. But in his ignorance Mandryka found the machinations of the 'Hetmanite-Banderite bloc' rather fantastic. His political naïveté, however, lends credence to the integrity of his report.

Whether Wasylyshen attempted to counteract the forces being raised against him, perhaps by calling on fellow Melnykivtsi like Kossar and asking to be shielded against these mounting attacks, is not known. Certainly, he manfully carried on with his duties for the UCRF, ignoring as much as possible the swelling tide of alarming reports he was receiving from Mandryka. By the end of January 1950, betraying none of the secrets Mandryka had imparted, he filed an annual report for the

UCRF, covering the activities of the 'European Mission of the Ukrainian Canadian Relief Fund,' which he had competently headed for the period from 1 December 1948 to 31 December 1949.[120] Pointing out that his group had three main duties – arranging for the resettlement of Ukrainian DPs, carrying out welfare work among them, and distributing amenity and relief supplies – he presented statistics on what had been accomplished during his watch. Among other items he noted that over 400 visits had been made to various refugee camps; documents for 2747 Ukrainian immigrants had been prepared; 422 contacts between sponsors and immigrants desiring to leave for Canada, the United States, the United Kingdom, Brazil, and Argentina had been set up; interventions had been made in 802 cases where delays were being experienced; and 7137 'souls' had been notified about permits for entry to Canada.[121] Reporting that there were still nearly 13,000 Ukrainian refugees left in the British Zone of Germany alone, he also alerted the UCRF's executive to the gloomy fact that nearly 3500 of them would not likely be accepted for resettlement anywhere, being maimed, aged, or chronically sick with diseases like tuberculosis, or being persons having to care for such aged, disabled, and sick refugees. Wasylyshen concluded by asking whether the UCRF's board of directors, faced with this real need, wished his Mission to continue operating overseas.[122]

Although Kushnir acknowledged receipt of this report, in a letter dated 16 March 1950, his reply provided no definite answers to most of the director's questions, not even to what was presumably the most important one, concerning the fate of the UCRF Mission. Wasylyshen, growing impatient, pointed this out in his own reply.[123] It must have been shortly afterward that he realized his tenure as director of the UCRF's operations in Europe was nearly over. As his wife wrote to a friend in Winnipeg in mid-April, there were rumours going around which suggested that they would have to be 'closing up the office after June 30.'[124]

Particularly disheartening were the opportunities wasted as a result of Winnipeg's decision. A great measure of professional cooperation had been established with the British authorities and the UCRF workers during the Wasylyshens' time overseas, which would likely be squandered if they left. Not only had the Wasylyshens been able to secure official Control Commission for Germany recognition for the UCRF's Mission, but they had been promised legal status and a stipend of approximately $2500 per month, allotments of rationed petrol, transport, and accreditation with the American Displaced Persons Commission – but only if their contract was renewed and their salaries covered by the UCRF. In other words, all the UCRF had to do was continue paying the Mission's administrative costs, including staff salaries, and the majority of their other expenses would be taken care of by the British.[125] Yet the Wasylyshens' entreaties about the need for maintaining UCRF representatives overseas, where they would be in the most advantageous position to help meet the continuing needs of the Ukrainian displaced persons, and their full report on the terms of the generous British offer, were ignored, or at least not acted upon. Instead, on 27 April 1950, they received telegraphic confirmation that their services were no longer required and that they should return to Canada, leaving the Mission in the hands of 'locally recruited DP personnel.'[126]

Doing so, Wasylyshen quickly replied, was totally 'out of the question,' for it would result in the loss of all the prestige and contacts that he and his co-workers had built up after months of hard work. Appealing the board's decision about his withdrawal, Wasylyshen pleaded that the moment 'Allied representatives of the UCRF leave the British Zone,' the Mission would cease to exist. He asked the UCRF executive, therefore, to reconsider and to authorize a continuation of the Mission's work.[127]

Reconsider they did, but not in the way he had hoped. His recall, and that of his wife, remained in force. And yet no one in Winnipeg was willing to take responsibility for shutting down the Mission entirely. Until then, with the exception of their efforts in promoting Victory Bond sales, maintaining Ukrainian Canadian relief operations for the refugees had been the UCC's most successful undertaking, possibly even its most notable accomplishment. And so even when, in August 1950, the Wasylyshens packed up and left, returning to Winnipeg on 12 September, the UCRF Mission was not terminated, nor was it turned over to 'locally recruited DP personnel' as Wasylyshen had feared it might be. Instead the directorship passed back to Ann Crapleve, a woman whose ability, thorough knowledge of the job at hand, and scrupulous honesty were well known and respected. Whatever his other feelings about leaving may have been, Wasylyshen remained the gracious gentleman when it came to writing about his successor. In his final report to the UCRF's board, written after he and his wife had returned to Winnipeg, he remarked that both of them felt that 'the Mission could not have been left in more capable hands.'[128]

Those who reportedly had political reasons for wanting Wasylyshen removed from the UCRF Mission had partially failed, if it was their intention to replace him with one of their own people. Crapleve would continue to represent Ukrainian Canadian interests well, working out of Hamburg, until nearly the end of 1951.[129] Scrupulously avoiding any obvious entanglements in the partisan politics of the DP camps, she seems to have been the only Ukrainian Canadian involved with UCSA, then CURB, then the Team, and finally the UCRF who never allowed herself the luxury of being drawn into the vortex of this frenetic emigration's politics – an achievement which is, in hindsight, truly remarkable. When she finally left Europe, all direct Ukrainian Canadian refugee relief and resettlement operations ended, once and for all. They had lasted a total of six years, during which time some thirty-five thousand Ukrainian DPs and political refugees had been resettled in Canada.[130] On the humanitarian level, most would agree, these efforts had accomplished a great deal. As for the impact of the resettling refugees on Ukrainian Canadian society, that was, and remains, a more controversial issue.

But what had blunted the complete success of the alleged plans of the 'Hetmanite-Banderite bloc' which the Wasylyshens had been warned about? Several letters received in Bielefeld, during December 1949 and January 1950, suggest that the cabal Mandryka described had been particularly active during this period. At a joint meeting of the UCC and UCRF executives, held in Winnipeg on 2 December 1949, an event which Mandryka described as being similar in tone to a 'street meeting,' his wife was censured severely by critics of the Mission. The meeting soon degenerated into a shouting match.[131] Two weeks later the good doctor informed the Wasylyshens that his wife had been so shaken by this episode that she had resigned as the UCRF's executive secretary, effective 20 December 1949.[132] Mandryka also reported that, during a UCRF meeting the day before, its chairmanship had been assumed by a Mr Tarnowecky, who was to be assisted by Tony Yaremovich. But 'within a day' Kushnir had personally intervened and turned UCRF operations over to the UCC's new and first executive director, none other than Volodymyr Kochan. Kochan was also being assisted by Wolodymyr Klish, a 'newcomer' whom Mandryka described as a 'leader of the Banderites.'[133] Having achieved as much as they had relatively quickly, Mandryka claimed, the plotters would now strike to finish off the Mission and use the remaining twenty-eight thousand or so dollars in the UCRF's coffers 'for purposes other than those for which they were collected.'[134] All this, he added, had precipitated an 'atmosphere of disintegration' within the Ukrainian Canadian community. As for what might happen next, no one could say. Certainly, Mandryka predicted, the next UCC national congress, the third such national assembly ever to be held, was going to witness a decisive confrontation between the 'oldtimers' and the 'newcomers.'[135]

'Two Onions in Your Borsch'

For the Wasylyshens, arriving in Winnipeg in mid-September 1950, there were no signs that their labours overseas had earned them much recognition, or even thanks – 'Nobody beat a fanfare or rolled out a red carpet,' Mrs Wasylyshen wrote to Crapleve – and they were to find that at least fourteen thousand dollars still remained on deposit with the UCRF, money which could have been used to sustain Mission operations for many more months, as the Wasylyshens well appreciated. At any rate, the amount left was certainly more than enough to disprove the pretext that insolvency had forced the UCRF executive to recall the Wasylyshens.[136] Ridiculing the UCRF's board of directors for their continuing insistence on 'economy' at a time when a not insignificant amount of money was still available in the Fund's accounts, Mrs Wasylyshen wrote to her friend Crapleve sarcastically advising her 'not to go in for riotous living,' and to remember that the UCRF executive expected her not to use 'two onions in your borsch when one will do!'[137]

'A Stampede, As Understood in Calgary'

As president of the Association of Ukrainians in Great Britain from March 1948, Panchuk and his helpers were able to accomplish a great deal in easing the process of resettlement and adjustment for thousands of Ukrainian EVWs and POWs coming to England.[138] Those efforts, distant now, should not be forgotten or slighted. Yet Panchuk's ascent to the presidency of the AUGB, and the work he did while occupying that post, would pale in significance when compared to the impact which his removal from that incumbency would have on diaspora affairs. All the associated backbiting and intrigue would affect not only the subsequent organizational history of the Ukrainian community in Great Britain but Ukrainian communities worldwide. For shocked Ukrainian Canadian observers of these events in England,

Panchuk's troubles were regarded as an omen of what they feared they would soon face in Canada, as increasingly large numbers of DPs resettled there.

As with the other internal upheavals which have so often debilitated Ukrainian organizational efforts throughout the diaspora, this 'coup-de-tête,' as Panchuk described an AUGB meeting held on the weekend of 12–13 March 1949, has become subject to several different interpretations. Contemporary spectators all agree that, as a result of this fractious annual meeting, an entirely new slate of AUGB executive council members came to power. Panchuk was replaced as president of the association by Dr Osyp Fundak, who would be assisted by Professor A. Mancibovich (vice-president), Teodor Danyliw (executive secretary), and Danylo Skoropadsky (honorary president).[139] Beyond these shared facts, opinions and recollections diverge as to why Panchuk was not given the vote of confidence he required to be re-elected. Panchuk's explanation, foreshadowing what Mandryka would write several months later about similar developments in Canada, was that the Hetmantsi had formed 'a very strong block' with the Banderivtsi in the AUGB, creating a powerful faction which had then 'unconstitutionally' helped engineer an illegitimate takeover of the Association and his own downfall.[140] This 'very unnatural,' but nevertheless united, political front, he complained bitterly, had brought together all who opposed UNRada, all who disliked him personally, and all who allegedly wanted to sow dissent between Ukrainian Catholic and Ukrainian Orthodox believers. These schismatics were, he insisted, 'inspired by foreign agents, both communist and other,' the other being 'devoted to the cause of keeping Ukrainians separated and disorganized so as to make them weak, and further devoted to the cause of creating doubt and suspicion among the British people with regard to the quality of the foreign workers.'[141]

To get rid of Panchuk and his allies, the Hetmantsi and Banderivtsi, he claimed, had 'resorted to every method, legal and illegal, under the sun,' and had turned the annual meeting into a near riot, complete with 'hooting, howling, whistling and stamping of feet etc. at the right moment and at a given signal [creating] a regular stampede in the true meaning of the word (as understood in Calgary) and the final result was that all the "solid" and dependable people who could not agree ... walked out.'[142]

Within a few days, Panchuk had sought the advice of a solicitor about the legality of the annual meeting's outcome. Shortly after, he and his wife returned their AUGB membership cards, letting the new executive know that he was informing the appropriate authorities that he was no longer responsible for the Association and would have nothing further to do with it. Somewhat spitefully, Panchuk insisted that any AUGB letterhead bearing his name be destroyed, or that, at a minimum, his name be obliterated from every single sheet. It was.[143]

The next Ukrainian Canadian to comment on what had taken place was Eustace Wasylyshen, who, as fate would have it, arrived in London with his wife just two days after this putsch. In a letter addressed to the UCC and UCRF executives, dated 23 March, Wasylyshen said that it was his duty to report on this subject. He claimed it was an issue of vital concern, for 'a similar pattern of events' was showing itself on the Continent, and, as he explained, 'we are afraid it may eventually show up in Canada.'[144]

Having opened with this dramatic flourish, Wasylyshen went on to allege that the 'whole action' taken against Panchuk had been planned 'months in advance,' and that the new AUGB council was now exclusively under the control of 'followers of the Bandera and Hetman Organizations,' although he added, revealingly, that he had yet to meet anyone who would 'openly admit' to a connection with the Banderivtsi.[145] But it is perhaps not surprising that members of the Banderivtsi would not come forward willingly and identify themselves as such to Wasylyshen, given that he was openly associating with Dmytro Andrievsky, a man whose political affiliations with the Melnykivtsi were well known.

When questioned about what had happened at the AUGB meeting, those who voted for the new executive maintained that, instead of having voted against Panchuk himself, they were in fact 'above politics' and entirely dedicated to the Ukrainian cause. Their claim was that the economic mismanagement of the Association had precipitated a financial crisis, and that voting Panchuk out was the only means available of resolving that problem. Significantly, Wasylyshen agreed that Panchuk had been 'careless' with AUGB funds, which shortcoming had left him open to criticism from the membership. Nevertheless, Wasylyshen was not entirely convinced by this 'very serious' allegation against Panchuk, mainly because its proponents had not produced 'any corroboration or proof' of specific incidences of financial incompetence or mismanagement.[146] Although he seems genuinely to have tried to reconcile the two parties, and reported to Winnipeg concerning the grievances of both sides to the dispute, it is clear Wasylyshen's sympathies lay more with the aggrieved Panchuk and the minority who had followed him out of the AUGB than with the majority who had remained in its ranks. In part this was probably no more than sympathy for a fellow Ukrainian Canadian who had already done so much for the DPs, particularly those resettling in Great Britain. But there can also be little doubt that Andrievsky had helped shape Wasylyshen's perception of events in London, warping his evaluations about who had done right and who had done wrong. Indeed, Wasylyshen reported quite candidly that Andrievsky had 'confirmed' his own assessment of the situation in the United Kingdom. Andrievsky went even further. For as Wasylyshen visited with the various adversaries, Andrievsky tagged along, tactfully absenting himself on only one occasion, when Wasylyshen held a conversation with the Banderivtsi. Otherwise he invariably introduced himself into the discussions, whether Wasylyshen was meeting with Ukrainian Catholic prelates like Father Josaphat Jean or with British officials.[147]

Responding to an inquiry from John F. Stewart, the chairman of the Scottish League for European Freedom, about the background to this dissent within the AUGB, and to Stewart's offer to serve as a mediator, Panchuk replied at length, giving a particularly detailed account of his own feelings on what had taken place.[148] In this account he claimed that he had been aware of 'forces of evil' working within the Ukrainian community in Great Britain for at least the previous six months. He claimed that he had received warnings about their nefarious intrigues from friends in Canada, France, and other countries in western Europe, and cautions from many British friends 'including some from Scotland Yard.'[149] Nevertheless a whole stable of foes had now emerged, all scheming relentlessly to break up the unity which had been one of the 'chief purposes' his Mission had been tasked with creating. Listing these adversaries, Panchuk asserted that not only were communists working against the AUGB, particularly Russian ones, but that they were being aided by 'the old "White" Russian émigrés,' Polish 'Imperialists,' a small group of Czecho-Slovaks, including some Carpatho-Ukrainians who felt they were 'Slavs first' and some Rumanians who refused to 'give up Bukovina and part of Bessarabia.' There were also disruptive internal Ukrainian political tendencies, including a pro-Polish faction headed by a Mr Solowyj and a federalist group headed up by de Korostovets ('who still claims to be a Russian') and Danylo Skoropadsky (whose father, Hetman Pavlo Skoropadsky, had 'sold Carpatho-Ukraine to Russians in 1927').[150]

Despite the fact that Panchuk and Kushnir, after touring the refugee camps early in 1946, had 'finally' gotten the various Ukrainian political leaders together 'and practically forced them to unite' into the Co-ordinating Ukrainian Committee, their original optimism about what that organization might accomplish had been misplaced.[151] The first group that broke away were the Banderivtsi; the Hetmantsi never even joined. Although the former eventually returned, they did so only as a self-styled 'passive' member group. When an attempt was made to overcome these problems, a process which led directly to the formation of UNRada, the Ukrainian National Council, on 16 July 1948, this new body included the OUNb, but only in the role of an opposition, and none of the monarchists of the conservative Hetman movement joined. Despite this, the AUGB, under Panchuk's leadership, had formally welcomed the formation of UNRada and extended it full recognition.[152] Shortly after, as Panchuk put it, the 'saddest part of the whole story' began, as both the Banderivtsi and the Hetmantsi began 'unofficially' to agitate against the Council. By doing so, Panchuk wrote, they had only 'played into the hands of the communists and other enemy forces opposed to Ukrainian unity.'[153] He even suggested that there was 'concrete evidence, in black and white, that the Cominform gave $500,000 to the communists and their fellow travellers' for the express purpose of breaking up 'national centres' of people from behind the Iron Curtain.[154]

Meanwhile, the revolutionary nationalists and monarchists had spent six months prior to the March 1949 annual AUGB meeting plotting to take over 'by any means *fair or foul.*' Two busloads of 'hooligans' were imported into London as insurance against the meeting going in any way other than against Panchuk and his allies. As a result, Panchuk recorded, the AUGB fell into the hands of the Banderivtsi and the Hetmantsi, whom he probably underestimated as comprising only 10 per cent of the entire emigration. In his view their 'illegal' seizure of the AUGB's executive and its assets left most Ukrainians then in Great Britain unrepresented. So he insisted that these usurpers had to be brought to their senses, and that steps be taken to rectify the unfortunate situation which their actions had caused.

Panchuk elaborated further on these themes in correspondence with his confidant, Dr Kaye, who seems to have been one of the very first Ukrainians in Canada to be fully appraised of what had happened to the AUGB.[155] Perhaps feeling surer of himself when writing to Kaye, who personally knew many of the main actors in this drama, Panchuk explained that it was only after Skoropadsky had returned from a visit to Germany, in November 1948 – from a trip during which he had met with Stepan Bandera and other nationalists – that the 'most unnatural "united front,"' which had ousted him from the AUGB, had been forged. He lamented that while these 'oppositionists' had been hard at work tunnelling within the AUGB, he and his friends had 'peacefully slept.' When it finally came to the meeting – packed as it was with 'extra hooters, whistlers and rioters' – it was simply too late for logic or reason to win the day, for 'youngsters, farm lads, with hearts of gold but no sense,' had been given clear orders to get rid of Panchuk, which they did, while Skoropadsky and 'his henchmen sat and gloated.'[156] Private animus seems to have been raised to the level of a political force within Britain's newly formed Ukrainian community. But of course it was much more than that; the voting at the March meeting had generally been political, not personal.

For official observers of the Ukrainian scene in Great Britain, what had taken place in the AUGB was little more than another 'typical "émigré quarrel,"' although one Foreign Office analyst revealed that he was not exactly sure what it all meant. All he could say was that, from now on, it would be up to the Home Office to cope with the 'tiresomeness' of having more than one Ukrainian organization active in Great Britain. But there was no point in pursuing an investigation into what had taken place.[157] A more astute, if cynical, appreciation was penned by Whitehall's A.W.H. Wilkinson, who commented that the real trouble lay in the resentment of the 'pure' Ukrainians at their 'domination' by 'foreigners' like Panchuk.[158] Now that they felt 'firmly established and not dependent on Canadian advice and support,' they had simply asserted their independence. Wilkinson added that, given British policies on avoiding recognition or support for 'break away organizations,' it would 'probably be just as well if we quietly dropped Mr. Panchuk,' a view seconded by his colleague, Mr Boothby. As for Panchuk's efforts to set up a rival body, the Federation of Ukrainians in Great Britain (the Federation, or the FUGB), the British commentators dismissed these as being due 'largely to personal *pique* on Panchuk's part.'[159]

'Anglo-Ukrainian Clubs'

The displeasure of the British authorities notwithstanding, Panchuk and a small group of supporters had, by 13 March 1949, announced the formation of a new Ukrainian Bureau, located at 64 Ridgmount Gardens, London, the prime function of which, they stated, was to serve as an advisory and information centre.[160] By mid-April Panchuk and his confederates had drafted a memorandum detailing the new Bureau's articles of association, making it clear that this new institution supported the Ukrainian National Council, even if he was quick to add that the Bureau would 'be non-political, ... cater to no particular political parties, sects or creeds and ... approach and handle all problems objectively, scientifically and scholastically.'[161]

This new Bureau's 'field of operations' was to be 'all of the United Kingdom,' wherever Ukrainian EVWs and POWs had resettled. Its principal mandate was to help the individuals concerned 'get acclimatized,' and also to 'introduce' British citizens to the Ukrainians now living among them. To promote this latter aim Panchuk envisioned the formation of what he termed 'Anglo-Ukrainian Clubs,' all of which would be registered at his central office. The EVWs were also to be actively encouraged to set up 'Ukrainian Self-Reliance Groups,' the prototype for which was Panchuk's own parent organization, the Canadian-based Ukrainian Self-Reliance League. As he grew increasingly frustrated with the factionalism and politics of this new emigration, Panchuk unselfconsciously returned to the organizational models he remembered from his early years in Canada, hoping to find in them structures that would provide solutions to the problems he was encountering in the present.

Whether conceived out of wounded pride or to meet real needs, these organizational proposals never blossomed as Panchuk hoped they might, even with the encouragement of such stalwart ukrainophiles as the cosmopolitan Tracy Philipps.[162] Instead, and despite his concerted efforts over the following year, Panchuk was never able to recruit more than a tiny fraction of the Ukrainians living in Great Britain to his cause. He did manage to have himself appointed director of the 'European Office of the Ukrainian Canadian Committee,' effective 1 September 1950, but this was but a small success, as was his reconciliation with the UUARC's Gallan. Apparently this reconciliation was founded on Panchuk's new appreciation that Gallan's group had itself suffered at the hands of the 'same people who used to go hunting' after him when he was in Europe and who had done 'their own work insofar as Mr. Smook' was concerned, although he did not explain precisely what he meant by this ambiguous statement.[163] By early April 1951, Panchuk's efforts had netted him the UUARC's formal recognition, as he was described by Philadelphia as its only 'proper representative' in England. Yet all these titles, and the very modest financial assistance they brought, did not make up for the fact that the AUGB remained by far the largest Ukrainian organization in the United Kingdom, and that there was no reversing the situation that had developed as a result of the March 1949 meeting.[164] Even Panchuk's support of the rival Federation, which brought together those who supported UNRada and those who were antagonistic to the Banderivtsi or Hetmantsi – many of them Eastern Ukrainian and Orthodox believers – could not restore the status he had once enjoyed.[165] Thus enfeebled, the best he was able to do was continue to snipe at the AUGB, in a largely ineffective attempt to diminish its authority within the emigration and its status before the British authorities.[166] Whatever the truth might be about the difference in quality between the supporters of the FUGB and those of the AUGB, the latter, everyone conceded, were a numerical majority. The AUGB's greater numbers provided a stronger material basis for this organization than was available to their opponents. And so their Association prevailed, while its rival limped along, and then pretty well faded.

Dispirited and simply tired out after having been away from their Canadian home and their families during many years of hard work, Panchuk and his wife returned to Canada in June 1952. They had been overseas more or less continuously for some eleven years. With their departure all Ukrainian Canadian refugee and resettlement efforts came to a complete stop, never to be resumed.[167]

'We in Canada Feel Bitterly about It'

While the Banderivtsi, allied for a while with the Hetmantsi, did prevail in the places where they were numerically superior and enjoyed a large measure of popular support, they had the benefit of neither advantage in Winnipeg, or anywhere else in Canada, where few Ukrainian DPs had as yet resettled, much less established themselves.[168] Still, those who had arrived, particularly the few who had managed to find positions within the UCC's secretariat, were able to play important roles in their own right. Although there had always been snags that disrupted the UCRF's fund-raising efforts, by the fall of 1948 these seemed to be getting worse, and there were ominous signs that the growing influx of DPs into Canada was itself provoking a new species of problem within Ukrainian Canadian society as a whole.[169] To Dmytro Gerych, who had written to him on this very subject, Panchuk responded with an excoriating jeremiad. 'True enough,' he observed, 'there are many good people among them,' but

unfortunately, there are also a lot of 'scum' who have forgotten what work means and who feel that somebody owes them a living. They are deeply disappointed that there is no UNRRA in Great Britain, as there are some in Canada who suffer from the same disappointment, and they are anxious to go anywhere wherever they can find milk and honey growing on trees. These people, unfortunately, not only cause a negative reflection on other refugees and DPs, but also on those organizations who have always been standing in their defence, and I am frequently forced to say things in their defence and on their behalf that in my heart I cannot fully justify. Still, that is one of the responsibilities we must face and carry.[170]

Panchuk seems to have been more long-suffering than most. Still, these bitter words were written even before the 'revolt' which toppled him from the AUGB's presidency, an experience that left him even more exasperated. For Ukrainian Canadians, or at least many occupying leadership roles in the organized community, the encounter they were about to have with Ukrainian refugees would come to represent a frustrating and upsetting experience, all the more so since they had not expected things to turn out as poorly as they did. The Ukrainian Canadians felt that the refugees owed them gratitude for all the help they had provided, and that their thanks should be translated into acceptable behaviour in all the countries they were resettling in. These Ukrainian Canadians ended up getting little of either. For their part, many DPs considered Ukrainian Canadians artless and unsophisticated, out of touch with contemporary Ukrainian realities, and so thoroughly assimilated that they were almost useless to the cause of Ukraine's liberation. This last was particularly galling, for as these political refugees continued vigorously to champion Ukraine's independence even as they themselves were being resettled in the 'New World,' they did not always discover much sympathy for their hopes or methods even in their 'fellow Ukrainians.'[171] Not surprisingly, as one Ukrainian Canadian observed early in 1949, the end result was that 'the fashion to help refugees' dissipated.[172] Certainly, when news reached Canada that Panchuk had been ousted from the AUGB, a number of Ukrainian Canadians were electrified, considering Panchuk's discomfiture nothing less than a direct insult to their community in general: 'We in Canada feel bitterly about it. It is a kick in the pants not only for you but also indirectly at us.'[173]

However, it was only after many more Ukrainian Canadians had begun to meet Ukrainian refugees face to face – as often as not coming away from the encounters rather nonplussed and discontented – that the degree of antipathy between these two populations became more evident, and more relevant. Of course, not all such early contacts had negative consequences. Many Ukrainian DPs fit easily into previously established Ukrainian Canadian communities and went on to contribute positively to their social, economic, intellectual, and religious growth. A few early encounters even had comical aspects. In one report sent to the Wasylyshens, for example, the somewhat humorous experience of a DP employed by the UCC is preserved. Spying a 'beautiful pair' of pyjamas in a Fort William, Ontario, shop window, the recent immigrant bought them without realizing precisely what kind of clothing he had acquired:

> The next day he came in them to Pulak's Restaurant for breakfast. The waitress refused to serve him. When the proprietor, Mr Pulak came, he found that the man was no other than a KYK organizer. He told him to go home and put on decent clothes. Is it any wonder that Soviet Russian officers had their wives appearing in pyjamas in Bolshoi Theatre when the Russians overran Poland and Austria? Some of the DPs pay attention to the Canadian way of life and try to adapt themselves. But others try to show up [off] and as a result make themselves look ridiculous.'[174]

'Troubles All Around'

The increasing visibility of Ukrainian refugees within Canada's Ukrainian communities, particularly those employed by the UCC as 'organizers,' provoked more anger than mirth, however. The same letter reported that these 'organizers,' who were 'all DPs,' were being met with 'quite a bit of hostility from the Ukrainian Canadians,' for not only did the Canadians want them to speak English, but they expected UCC activists to be helpful. Instead, organizers were too often unfamiliar with Ukrainian Canadian realities and virtually helpless in their new environment. Rather than providing leadership for the Ukrainians in Canada, the Ukrainian DPs had themselves to be led around, 'like a four year old child.'[175]

Troubles with the Ukrainian refugees resettling in Canada started being recorded more frequently within a few months of the 'revolution' in the AUGB. In part, this was a consequence of the arrival of increasing numbers of DPs. But it was also owing to concerted efforts on the part of the more politically inclined among them to exert their influence throughout the emigration. And Ukrainian Canadian observers knew it. Yaremovich wrote to the Wasylyshens to let them know that, while he was on a speaking tour of eastern Canada, he had observed that 'all one has around now is troubles,' mainly because the UCC headquarters' operations were not being competently managed. It would be far better if a Ukrainian Canadian took charge there, Yaremovich wrote, but what had instead happened was that the offices were under the control of a 'whole bunch of DP organizers.' These same people, in Yaremovich's view, were 'doing more to break up the Committee than keep it together.'[176] Charitably he acknowledged that this was mainly because the resettled DPs did not as yet 'know Canadian conditions.' Still, refugees and their peculiar attitudes constituted the root of the problem.

It was not only the social awkwardness and ignorance of some recently resettled DPs that troubled many Ukrainian Canadians. By late 1948 some of the 'newcomers' had exhibited considerable administrative skill and determination in getting their own kinds of organizations established and their message out, one of the clearest signals of which was the publication, beginning on 15 December 1948, of their own newspaper, *Homin ukrainy* (*Ukrainian Echo*), based in Toronto. Its first editorial, 'Preserve Our Ties with Ukraine,' set the newspaper's ideological tone and world-view. Furthermore, in the summer of that year, Dmytro Dontsov, the ideologue and polemicist who had exerted such an enormous influence on the interwar nationalist movement in Western Ukraine, went on a speaking tour of Ontario on behalf of the nationalists, provoking further negative reactions among Ukrainian Canadians.[177] And even when the UCC's 'DP organizers' went out, they too, as Yaremovich recorded, seemed all too willing to agree with anyone who 'came in with a complaint against KYK,' even though it was they who were the prime contributors to the problem, inclined as they were to make all sorts of unfulfillable promises to their audiences about what the UCC was going to do (but could never realistically be expected to do) for the community.[178] As two other contemporary onlookers, Dr Kaye and John Karasevich, wrote, in January and May 1949 respectively, there was a growing 'rift' between the 'newcomers' and 'oldtimers,' while the UCC was itself still 'so feebly established' that there was no telling what impact the newly arrived DPs might have on the infrastructure of Ukrainian Canadian organizational life.[179] When, on 1 May 1949, an entirely novel group emerged from within the ranks of these political refugees, the League for the Liberation of Ukraine, there were few Ukrainian Canadians who would disagree with Panchuk's trenchant characterization of the situation as 'scandalous,'[180] or quibble with Yaremovich, who wrote that 'the B group is dancing around quite freely.'[181] What, if anything, Ukrainian Canadians could do about such developments was quite another question. The UCC executive seemed paralysed – not surprisingly, if Mandryka's allegations about the infernal machinations of a 'Hetmanite-Banderite block' working surreptitiously inside the Committee are given credence.[182] What was needed, Yaremovich concluded, was for the UCC quickly to call another national congress, one in which the Ukrainian Canadians could rally and 'iron out' their differences with the refugees, and especially with the new groups forming among them.[183] Who would shape the future of organized Ukrainian Canadian society, the Canadian-born Ukrainians or the DPs? That was the question.

When Ukrainian Canadians had felt they needed to display their allegiance to Canada publicly, their first national congress had proved an ideal forum in which to do so. In 1946 they had organized a second such national assembly, their motive then being to prolong the UCC's mandate, rationalizing this step by pointing to the humanitarian responsibility of Ukrainian Canadians to help fellow Ukrainians in the refugee camps of western Europe. Thus the UCC, intended to last only 'for the duration' of the Second World War, had found a motive for carrying on. Now, a third congress was organized, and was held in Winnipeg on 7–9 February 1950. While its program may have suggested several different purposes, its principal aim was to determine how Ukrainian Canadians should react to the resettled Ukrainian refugees. Gone was much of the earlier goodwill towards the DPs. It had been replaced by a realization that these very same people represented a serious threat to the status quo within Ukrainian Canadian society. That rankled more than a few of the 'oldtimers,' particularly those who had the most to lose.

Panchuk returned to Winnipeg in order to attend this conclave. Subsequently he wrote that the congress had been a 'great success,' for it helped further unite the Ukrainians of Canada and 'strengthen their collective activities.'[184] More important, or so Panchuk claimed, the congress had dealt firmly with the 'dissident' element among the 'new-arrivals.'[185]

The third UCC congress was certainly far from a sedentary affair. Even the otherwise bland published proceedings cannot disguise that fact. What is perhaps more significant is that it was at this congress, held just over five decades ago, that the pattern for the relationship between established Ukrainian Canadian organizations and the communities they represented, and the most dynamic of the nationalistic elements within the in-migrating refugee population, was set. That troubled relationship would persist. But had the Ukrainian Canadians actually forged the 'common and solid foundation' which Panchuk had advised them to prepare if they did not want to have 'their goose cooked' by the politicized DPs? That was indeed the question.

8 'Locking Horns on Canadian Soil': The Impact of the DPs on Ukrainian Canadian Society, 1949–1959

'Doing More Harm Than Good'

Believing, as they did, that they had proved their loyalty to Canada during the war, few Ukrainian Canadians entertained any serious reservations about lobbying the country's gatekeepers to secure the postwar admission of Ukrainian refugees from Europe. To strengthen their case about the suitability of Ukrainian displaced persons as immigrants, these Ukrainian Canadians widely circulated a portrayal of the DPs as highly resourceful, religious, hard-working, educated, morally and psychologically fit individualists, whose recent experience under Soviet rule had confirmed them in their anti-communist and pro-Western ideological orientation.[1] Advocates of Ukrainian refugee immigration were sure that Canada's provincial and federal authorities already took a good view of Ukrainians, supposing they did so on the basis of their positive experiences of the prewar Ukrainian pioneer settlers. Yaremovich was quite explicit about this when he wrote to the premiers of Alberta and Ontario, and selected parliamentarians, emphasizing the historical record of Ukrainians in Canada and their having proved themselves good farmers and loyal citizens.[2] In retrospect, the belief on the part of these Ukrainian Canadians that their efforts met with some success because Canada's politicians were, for whatever reason, favourably disposed towards Ukrainians as immigrants and settlers, seems something of a delusion. Yet there can be little doubt that their efforts did help influence the federal government in favour of DP immigration.[3] What was decisive, however, was not the past record of Ukrainians in Canada. Indeed, if we recall the troubles the authorities had had not only with the organized Ukrainian

Canadian Left and Right but also with the Centre, it may seem odd that Ottawa would allow for any significant additional immigration of Ukrainians into the country. And yet they did.

Three factors seem to have inclined the nation's gatekeepers to take a relatively favourable stance on Ukrainian DP immigration. For one, there was a keen awareness on the part of a number of the politicians, including Prime Minister Mackenzie King, of the undesirability of alienating Ukrainian Canadian voters, who were then numerous enough in some federal ridings to have political strength. Second, it was appreciated that Canada needed another influx of semi-skilled and unskilled labourers in the industrial sector and in the mining and lumber camps, to take up various jobs which many Canadians were not willing to fill. Finally, and perhaps most important, there was a perception in Ottawa and elsewhere that these anti-communist Ukrainian political refugees would have considerable political utility inside the country in combating the influence of the Left, especially within their own ethnic constituency. Even before the outbreak of the war, the Office of the High Commissioner for the United Kingdom in Ottawa had reported to the British Foreign Office that the main reason one of the USRL's leaders, Wasyl Burianyk, had been able to speak to Prime Minister Mackenzie King was that the prime minister sat in the House of Commons for a Saskatchewan riding, one heavily populated by Ukrainians.[4] Similarly, when the UNF's president, Mr Kossar, visited London at the start of an eastern European tour which began in the summer of 1939, he was able to secure an audience with Whitehall officials in part because he was travelling 'with a recommendation of the Prime Minister of Saskatchewan.'[5]

What had helped dispose Canadian officials towards Ukrainian refugee immigration was the positive attitude most of their British counterparts had taken towards CURB and its personnel in the United Kingdom. Not only Panchuk but also Ukrainian Canadians like Monsignor Kushnir and Reverend Sawchuk and Ukrainian Canadian MPs like Anthony Hlynka had visited repeatedly with various bureaucrats and members of Parliament and the House of Lords on their visits to England. They had pleaded the refugees' case well and had also impressed on the British the notion that there existed a well-organized, mobilized, and apparently resourceful Ukrainian Canadian public, one which had to be dealt with sensibly. This constituency could not simply be ignored, as Canada's diplomats were quick to remind their counterparts in Whitehall.

Canadian diplomatic personnel in the United Kingdom were also impressed with the success of the Ukrainian Canadian efforts, as was noted at the time. For example, Panchuk wrote to the UCRF in early December 1946 observing that Norman Robertson of External Affairs had 'warmed considerably' to the principle of helping refugees and 'to our question in particular,' a development which Panchuk felt could be attributed to recent conversations between Robertson and Sir George Rendel, a senior British official involved with the postwar refugee situation and one of the very same bureaucrats whom the Ukrainian Canadians had made it a habit to 'visit formally and informally as often as possible.'[6]

At perhaps the most relevant of the many meetings between Ukrainian Canadians and the British authorities, which took place in London during December 1946 – before any of the UCRF people were actually allowed into western Europe – the Canadians were first unequivocally reminded about what kind of behaviour was expected of them on the Continent. They were also told what the Allied occupation and refugee relief authorities might do for the Ukrainian DPs if the Ukrainian Canadians cooperated. At this meeting, attended by Panchuk and Hlynka, the director of the IGCR privately told them that Canada would admit a considerable number of DPs, 'over and above' the categories already announced, although in no circumstances would assistance be extended to any 'citizens of the USSR.' The fate of such persons was left undecided, although it was pointed out that forcible repatriation would thereafter be used only in dealing with the cases of proved 'Quislings.' The IRO, they were also informed, was likewise not going to provide any kind of aid or support to any persons or groups 'trying to overthrow governments in their country of origin' or those 'encouraging people not to return' to their homelands. In the Ukrainian case, both the Ukrainian Insurgent Army and the Anti-Bolshevik Bloc of Nations were singled out for particular censure. Any individuals or groups considered ineligible for IRO assistance, the Ukrainian Canadians were told, might instead try looking to the Vatican for help.[7] As for what the Ukrainian Canadians should be doing, it was explained that it would be wiser if they concentrated their efforts on promoting emigration and resettlement, particularly of persons belonging to categories not provided for under IRO regulations. Thus, and to a very great extent, Ukrainian Canadian efforts, which originally had been intended to bring welfare supplies to the camps' inhabitants, came to be directed away from the former task and towards lobbying on behalf of the Ukrainian refugees' interests. And this had happened at the direct request of the British authorities. Indeed, as Panchuk paraphrased the British advice, 'our organizations' – instead of worrying about providing material aid to the DPs – should instead be bringing 'pressure to bear' on officials responsible for regulating immigrant intake in various countries of potential resettlement. In particular, immigration officials in South America, where considerable opportunities for resettlement were said to exist, should be approached by Ukrainian Canadian representatives. At the same time, the Vatican's aid had to be enlisted in disposing of particularly troublesome Ukrainian refugee issues like that of the Ukrainian Surrendered Enemy Personnel found in POW camps near Rimini, Italy.[8] Most important, or so Panchuk emphasized, was the fact that the Ukrainian Canadians had been instructed to 'use all influence at our disposal to stop the militant and hostile propaganda that is so prevalent in some of the Camps – it is doing more harm than good.'[9]

This point was re-emphasized a few days later in a meeting at Canada House in London, attended by Panchuk, Hlynka, John Holmes of External Affairs, and Sir George Rendel. A confidential memorandum prepared after that session confirms that among the 'main points' raised was the issue of what role Ukrainian Canadians might best play in helping to deal with this postwar refugee problem. It was stressed that, while the Canadian Ukrainians to date had been 'most discrete,' they must keep in mind the absolute necessity of giving the Soviet government no grounds for accusing the Anglo-American powers of encouraging Ukrainian separatism. While the British indicated how much they appreciated the voluntary aid Ukrainian Canadians had sent to the refugee camps, they made certain that the Canadians also realized they would be allowed to do nothing which 'might increase the misunderstandings' that apparently 'kept arising' between the British and their Soviet counterparts over the issue of Ukrainian political refugees. Convinced as they were that all Ukrainian Canadian visitors to the American and British zones of Germany and Austria were travelling there for conspiratorial purposes, the Soviets were acutely suspicious and critical of anything like an officially sanctioned relief effort for Ukrainian refugees. It was therefore crucial, the British told the Ukrainian Canadians, that they comport themselves in a manner which would give no offence to the Soviets or prove embarrassing to the British, Canadian, or American governments. Whenever speaking before refugee audiences, they should be careful to the extent of saying nothing even to suggest that things would soon be better for the refugees. Do nothing, the Ukrainian Canadians were firmly instructed, which might somehow buoy up the spirits of the DPs, nothing which might give them 'too much hope' on what were ambiguously termed the national and political points of view.[10]

'May They Never Step on Fair Canadian Soil'

Of course there were others, in Canada and abroad, who mounted a campaign of their own aimed at keeping Ukrainian and other refugees out of the country, or at getting them returned to the USSR, voluntarily or otherwise. Such persons were motivated by various emotions, most particularly by political and religious biases. For example, a Miss Zinaidi Timofeichuk, who may have been acting under duress, was one of many former refugees who wrote letters to Ukrainian DPs still living in the British Zone of Austria, urging them to reject anti-repatriation propaganda of the type which was then being circulated widely in the DP camps. Instead, she argued, they should return voluntarily to the USSR, as she had done:

> I wish, women, that I had returned earlier, but for a long time I listened in camp to the insolent lies about the Soviet Union. You surely were a witness of this, how camp leaders said ... that I, as a daughter of a priest could particularly expect a dire fate. They convinced me in this ... those lowly fascists! ... I think now how you women still believe these good for nothings ... Let me tell you about myself ... I immediately felt a friendly and warm attitude towards me on the part of the Soviet administration. Happily I rode up to my home ... My father is occupying the duty of a priest ... In the USSR there exists freedom of religion ... I work ... as a teacher ... By the example of my life you may convince yourselves that in the Soviet country of repatriates, no one is persecuted ... Therefore, my dear friends, be more decisive. Stop believing the enemy propaganda and return to your homeland in the Ukraine.'[11]

Such rosy descriptions of postwar Soviet reality may have persuaded some to accept voluntary repatriation to the USSR, but precisely how many may have been so influenced is not known. More likely, people returned simply because they were homesick or apathetic, or had no other apparent options. Others returned because of the prejudice they found directed against them by some of the UNRRA team members who had been given the responsibility of supervising Ukrainian and other east European refugees. Such discriminatory treatment was often motivated by ethnic and religious prejudices. One contemporary account, a CURB memorandum dated 8 October 1946, reported that UNRRA team #539, under the direction of a Mr Richardson, had deliberately set out to strip the predominantly Ukrainian, Polish, and Russian inhabitants of refugee camp 'Afbau,' near Pfakirchen, of their official refugee status. Individual refugees apparently were interrogated with hostile intent and in a biased manner. This UNRRA team's two Jewish interpreters even went so far as maliciously to introduce their own questions into the interviewing process. Reportedly, they also 'deliberately' gave false or misleading information to the presiding officer and otherwise prejudiced the proceedings against those being screened. The tragic consequence of their duplicity was that 64 per cent of the camp's inhabitants lost their official refugee status. That meant not only the loss of whatever protection UNRRA afforded them against Soviet repatriation teams or hostile Germans in the area, but, even more critically, the loss of daily rations, housing, and clothing. Incidents like this, and it was no isolated occurrence – fomented despair and panic, and exacerbated old hatreds.[12]

Other UNRRA employees were similarly ill disposed to east European DPs. A Canadian nurse, Miss Claire V. Tait, attached to UNRRA team #307, wrote to Prime Minister Mackenzie King to explain that while she had originally considered the refugees 'pitiful' and 'deserving of all possible help, physical and mental,' working among them for several months had changed her mind. She now felt strongly that

> practically all the Baltics and some of the others, notably Eukrainians [sic] came of their own free will, aided and abetted Germany in her fight ... worked in their factories for good wages ... helped to manufacture guns ... which helped to kill our own men and those of our allies ... These people merely bet on the wrong horse, and regret that it did not win. They now stand around demanding, yes, and getting the handout ... No good screening has been done ... almost always [they want to emigrate] to the U.S. or Canada. What I hope and pray for is that these Baltics especially be not allowed in our country. They are red hot Fascists ... may they never step on fair Canadian soil.[13]

Others protested against any DP immigration in similar terms, if for different reasons. Spokesmen for the pro-Soviet ULFTA made formal representations against refugee immigration before the Senate Standing Committee on Immigration and Labour in Ottawa on 29 May 1946.[14] While not suggesting that any immigration of Ukrainians was wrong in and of itself, the ULFTA asserted that Canada needed to develop an immigration policy which kept out those whom they described as 'Nazi collaborators' and instead attracted individuals from the 'laboring and farming classes,' without prejudice against anyone on the basis of religious background, creed, or nationality.[15] Later, the Toronto District Labour Council would recommend to the minister responsible for immigration, James A. Glen, that all immigration of 'alleged DPs' be suspended until Canadian officials had themselves travelled to Europe, where they could pick and choose from among potential immigrants. Should any tradesmen be among them, added the Council's secretary, Ford Brand, such individuals should be obliged first to pass certification tests if they wanted to continue with their professions in Canada.[16]

Also arguing against the admission of any large number of DPs was the Canadian Active Service Forces Association, whose president, Mr J. Hay, wrote to the prime minister in the summer of 1948, suggesting that refugee immigration be suspended or at least reduced on the ground that there was already too much unemployment in Canada and not enough housing, especially for veterans. As well, he cautioned the prime minister about the danger of admitting 'Nazi sympathizers' or 'Communists' into the country.[17]

Adding to this anti-immigration chorus were the prejudices of a number of officials involved in the development of Canada's foreign and immigration policies. Many in government circles undoubtedly shared the sentiments of Vincent Massey, who, ruminating over the possible admission of Polish refugees into Canada, observed that 'when three Poles get together there [is] always a political party and a newspaper [and] they do not easily assimilate ... One does not want too many of them about.'[18]

Of course, not all the impediments to Ukrainian DP immigration can be laid at the door of naysayers, bigots, or ideologically biased lobbyists. For one thing, both the UCC and the UCRF were far from being well enough equipped, financially or logistically, to handle the veritable flood of requests for advice, aid, and solace that poured into their offices from Ukrainian refugees, in Winnipeg and overseas. Many such entreaties had to be answered with stark replies dishearteningly pointing out that a lack of sponsors and funds prevented the Committee or its agencies from helping the particular supplicant get to Canada.[19] Then again, it must be remembered that the UCC and UCRF offices were staffed by unpaid volunteers, and that some of these well-intentioned people were occasionally inappropriately trained and intellectually ill equipped when it came to coping with the myriad issues and problems confronting them on a near-daily basis. However hard-working and motivated they undoubtedly were, their efforts were often circumscribed from the start by financial and other short-comings. Most, of course, had their own personal concerns and responsibilities to attend to, including earning their daily bread, which meant that they could not give as much of themselves to the refugee relief and resettlement campaign as they may have wished.[20] Lacking a professional staff and organizational infrastructure to deal with the Ukrainian refugee situation, or for that matter even with the needs of the Ukrainian Canadian community itself, the Committee and its various subgroups made do with what they had. Sometimes they were fortunate in finding gifted and committed individuals who came forward to work. Sometimes they were less lucky. It is surprising how much good they were able to do nonetheless.

Naturally, those Ukrainian Canadians and their friends who favoured the immigration of Ukrainian refugees, especially after they became aware of the anti-refugee efforts of others, redoubled their pro-admission campaign. They attacked those whom they denounced as 'cryptos' and 'Communists-under-Orders' who had 'crept' into the IRO and other immigration commissions, hoping to act against the refugees from within the system.[21] At the same time they deplored the scarcity of sympathetic persons in government positions. They claimed that crucial bureaucratic and advisory roles were often held by 'enemies of Ukraine,' a group more precisely defined on one occasion as being composed of 'Jews, Muscophites and even Poles.'[22] Panchuk himself would complain bitterly that 'somewhere in Ottawa' there had to be a 'nigger in the woodpile' who was undermining Ukrainian Canadian efforts, for how else could one explain the confusing vacillations of government immigration policies with respect to the Ukrainian refugees?[23]

'Energetic and Violently Anti-Communist Workers'

Ukrainian Canadian efforts were, of course, far more often prosaic and calmer than the aforementioned examples suggest. An enormous amount of letter writing and pro-refugee immigration lobbying was done by Ukrainian Canadians representing all walks of life, professions, and backgrounds, on both sides of the Atlantic, within the Ukrainian community itself and before the wider Canadian public. Thus Panchuk, hoping to get positive support in Ottawa, wrote from Geneva to the Ukrainian Canadian parliamentarian Fred Zaplitny, observing that 1947 was going to be 'one of the greatest immigration years in history,' and insisting that Canada should be one of the countries 'bold enough' to take immediate action and secure for itself 'some of the fittest and best' immigrants to be found anywhere in the world at that time.[24] As for those who he had heard were objecting to a DP immigration to Canada, all he could say about them was that they were 'doing Canada and Canadian nationhood' the

> greatest injustice that could be done at this time ... Among the million odd refugees ... there is some of the best and highest quality that could ever be hoped for. Providence has arranged, as never before in history, to have created this greatest number of refugees and displaced persons ever known of. Most countries are now waking up to the fact that the bulk of these people are not just ordinary average people but that among them there are very large numbers of skilled craftsmen, artisans, technicians, intellectuals, professionals.[25]

Canada, which in Panchuk's view ranked 'highest' among all of the countries these DPs wanted to emigrate to, would do well to take in at least fifty thousand of them, to the mutual advantage of the country and the refugees.[26]

A few months later a delegation composed of Panchuk, Crapleve, Yaremovich, Reverend Sawchuk, and the UNF's Mr Hultay travelled to Ottawa to meet with the deputy minister of mines and resources, Dr Hugh Keenleyside, the well-respected director of the Immigration Board of that ministry (and, later, special adviser on immigration in the Department of Citizenship and Immigration) A.L. Jolliffe, various officials from External Affairs, and the secretary of state, Colonel Colin Gibson. Everywhere they went these Ukrainian Canadians emphasized the positive qualities of the prospective Ukrainian DP immigrants. They did so in personal interviews, where they had a chance to describe their own overseas experiences, and by means of printed materials, which they circulated to the offices of the relevant ministries and the press.

These delegates found government officials rather favourably oriented to the prospect of allowing in Ukrainian DPs, even those who had SEP status, mainly former members of the Ukrainian Division 'Galicia.' Prominent among the reasons government officials gave for what seemed to be this new and welcoming attitude towards the DPs was the knowledge that the Ukrainian refugees were of a 'very strong and definite anti-communist character,' a trait said to belong especially to veterans of the Division.[27] This quality impressed more than one Canadian gatekeeper, as Dr Kaye remarked upon. At the provincial level, 'Ontario embarked on a most ambitious immigration programme which is not restricted to immigrants from the UK but is also from the DP camps. [Premier George] Drew is impressed by the type of energetic and violently anti-communist worker brought in from the DP camps.'[28]

While they were not privy to the deliberations of government councils at either the provincial or the federal level, those promoting Ukrainian refugee immigration to Canada had quickly come to recognize that it was not simply the country's need for semi-skilled and skilled workers which made the refugees an attractive commodity. Just as important, if not more so, was their militantly anti-communist orientation, a trait some Canadian officials felt might be of especial use both domestically and in the international arena, particularly one being shaped by Cold War politics.

By 1947 many, if not most, Ukrainian refugees had either voluntarily returned to Soviet Ukraine or been sent there. Those who remained had little choice but to begin considering emigration as their only viable alternative to languishing in the 'midway-to-nowhere' life of the refugee camps. 'The desire to emigrate,' wrote Yaremovich at the time, had become 'very strong.'[29] This observation was echoed a few months later by a British officer, Lieutenant Colonel R.L. Telfer, who reported that 70 per cent of those he labelled 'recalcitrants' in so far as returning to the USSR was concerned, were now eager to emigrate, just about anywhere.[30]

Well before 1947, of course, a limited emigration of Ukrainian DPs to North and South America and to various other western European countries such as Belgium and France had begun. Several governments, particularly in South America, had actively sought out potential immigrants from within the refugee camps, selecting individuals they felt could serve their countries' nation-building prerogatives. While many Ukrainian and other refugees would have preferred to resettle in the United States or Canada, circumstances often forced them to opt instead for South American destinations. So while Panchuk and his colleagues might have been accurate in estimating that 90 per cent of the DP camps' inhabitants wanted to go to Canada in preference to any other country, the 'Close Relatives Scheme' established by Ottawa provided for an immigration only of those with family members or relatives already living in the country.[31] Not having any foreseeable chance of getting to Canada, many Ukrainians therefore resettled in countries as diverse and far apart as Brazil, Australia, France, and England.[32] Others tried, by corresponding directly with the UCC and UCRF executives and with various other Ukrainian secular and religious groups in Canada, or even by advertising in various widely read Ukrainian-language newspapers published in Europe and North America, to find relatives who might sponsor them.[33] Sometimes that tactic worked, sometimes it did not. Not everyone, even a relative, was willing to accept the financial obligations and potential burden involved in helping DPs relocate to Canada.

'Not Stock for Market but Human Beings'

Canadian officials were of several different minds about the general issue of refugee immigration, and about the desirability of Ukrainians as immigrants in particular. Feeling a moral obligation to the Poles, who had fought courageously on the Allied side throughout the war only to be betrayed to the Soviets by the Anglo-American powers at its end, they first tended to favour Polish veterans as immigrants. The British did likewise, establishing a Polish Resettlement Corps to that end. They also made it clear that His Majesty's Government had no objection to Canadian recruitment officers drawing off what were termed their 'excess' Poles, provided only that Canadian officials confined their efforts to attracting 'agricultural and lumber workers,' Britain wishing to retain any 'industrial workers and miners' for its own needs.[34] Even though theoretically prohibited from doing so, Canadian officials ended up recruiting some Poles for work in the mines of north-central Ontario, because they knew full well that most Canadians showed 'little disposition' to seek employment in such a dangerous occupation.[35]

As for whom to admit, and why and when, opinions varied. H.H. Carter of External Affairs was quick to criticize a proposal by his colleague Mr Nair, who suggested that immigration quotas be set on a proportional basis, reflecting the percentage which each ethnic minority already in Canada represented of the country's total population as of 1941. In Carter's view, it would be 'inadequate' to base quotas on the basis of the 'present racial origins of Canadians,' without first 'giving consideration to our experience of the various peoples as settlers.'[36] Carter urged a 'frankly discriminatory' policy, one which candidly 'recognized' that British, Dutch, and Scandinavian immigrants, being 'similar to us in political outlook and mode of living,' should be given preference over other nationalities, such as the Italians or east Europeans. As for Ukrainians, Carter felt, in general they could be 'considered the next best group after the Baltic peoples,' since

> they are largely industrious, conscientious peasants, very religious and without much initiative. While these docile qualities have made the Ukrainians well liked by the occupation authorities, it seems doubtful that they would prove more valuable citizens to a country such as Canada than would the Jews or Poles, both of which groups are regarded as the 'problem children' of the camps, but who generally have much more initiative and intelligence than the Ukrainians.[37]

Canadian immigration policy, if the country can be said to have had one, ended up being designed, as Lester B. Pearson described it in a letter to Norman Robertson, so as to ensure that no 'major change in the racial, religious or social constitution of the country' took place. It was a policy intended to be 'scrupulously selective and very carefully adapted to Canadian needs,' and resistant to the 'pressures of racial, religious and political influences.'[38] In short, it was intended to preserve what amounted to Canada's Anglo-Protestant status quo.

For Canada's Ukrainians, Ottawa's 'vacillating and indefinite policy' regarding the admission of Ukrainian DPs was a source of 'deep dissatisfaction,' particularly given the government's apparent 'helplessness' in countering the work of the 'Bolshevik-propagandists' who were then vociferously protesting against any such DP immigration.[39] Panchuk, at the time based in Geneva, where he was assisting Canada's delegation to the PCIRO, submitted a memorandum on Canadian immigration policy in which he attempted to express the views of the Ukrainian refugees themselves on the subjects of emigration and resettlement. In this lengthy statement, he listed seventeen interrelated issues of particular concern to the refugees, making it clear that the DPs resented the approach taken towards them by immigration officers in the camps. As far as they could tell, immigration policy was motivated by nothing more than a utilitarian and economic 'selection of the fittest' mentality, which cast all refugees in the role of a 'labour commodity' to be picked over or discarded without the slightest compunction. The refugees argued that such an approach was neither 'Christian' nor 'Human.' They wanted officialdom to know that they were not 'stock for market' but human beings, something they felt many immigration officers too often forgot. The refugees protested that family groups were being split up, often because immigration agents focused their attention on the young, single, and healthy males within the refugee population and excluded the elderly, the infirm, and young children from the lists of those allowed to emigrate. To protect the young adults against 'unhealthy influences' in the countries of resettlement, it was essential, Panchuk maintained tenaciously, that some older people be sent with them as a 'steadying, controlling, conservative, balancing element.' Similarly, cultural workers, priests, choir leaders, and members of the intelligentsia should also be resettled with these younger workers. One must, the CURB memorandum analogized, transplant not only the roots of a plant but also 'much' of the soil in which the roots could take hold. If they behaved like 'good and wise gardeners,' Canadian immigration officials would help ensure a successful and untroubled adaptation of the DPs in their new homeland.

Other issues also bothered the DPs. Thousands of them were living outside the refugee camps, many because they had not qualified for UNRRA or IRO support, and others because they feared being deported by one of these international agencies or the occupation authorities to the USSR or some other communist-controlled state in eastern Europe. Better, these people felt, to forgo the foodstuffs and other supplies available within the DP camps and have the security of living in the larger society of their various countries of first asylum. Yet something also had to be done about these DPs, noted Panchuk, for not all of them would be able to continue indefinitely finding shelter and work among their German, Austrian, or other hosts. They might not be in the camps but they were still displaced persons.

There was also a real need to develop an improved system for circulating information about resettlement opportunities, since far too many DPs remained largely ignorant about where they might move for a chance of rebuilding their war-devastated lives. As well, there were the special groups within the overall DP population – students, intellectuals, voluntary agencies, and national committees – all of whom had specific needs which were barely being met by the occupation authorities and international relief agencies. Since these groups performed valuable functions within, between, and outside the refugee camps, surely, Panchuk argued, they also deserved consideration and some allotment of resources.

As for the problems that would ensue if these concerns were not given prompt and intelligent attention, Panchuk recalled the difficulties which had emerged after the first large-scale relocation of refugees into one country of resettlement, namely, in the case of the DPs sent to the coal fields of Belgium.[40] Many of the problems encountered in that resettlement experience could be avoided or overcome if a 'specialist consultant' for each of the national groups found in the refugee camps was appointed and given the facilities required to do whatever was necessary to ease their adaptation and resettlement.

Throughout the late 1940s a tug of war took place between Ukrainian Canadian activists boosting DP immigration and Canada's gatekeepers, as the latter waxed and waned over whether or not to allow for any large-scale immigration of the refugees, and the former kept up lobbying for just such an immigration. Both sides would find each other, at times, obdurate and bewildering, although everyone knew that the final decision and all the real political power rested on the government's side. As a result the Ukrainian Canadians found themselves having to be more flexible and accommodating than they might otherwise have liked. A case in point was a late February 1949 meeting in Ottawa between the UCRF's Wasylyshen, parliamentarian A. Hlynka, and Hugh Keenleyside, the minister responsible for immigration. During this gathering Keenleyside made it clear that the government wanted the UCC and UCRF to use all their influence with the DPs to get these 'newcomers' to remain in Canada's 'rural districts and on farms, and not to congregate in the cities.' Public opinion, the minister explained, was sure to swing further against any DP immigration if the refugees were perceived to be taking jobs away from Canadian-born workers, especially in the cities.[41] A few days later another official, James Colley, IRO's representative in Ottawa, pointedly criticized both the UCC and the UCRF during a talk he had with Wasylyshen. As Wasylyshen reported it, Colley had referred to the Committee specifically and 'expressed his dissatisfaction with the lack of co-operation' which Winnipeg had shown in terms of working with him on the refugee immigration issue. Colley claimed that despite his many efforts to keep in touch with the UCC he had never received a single satisfactory reply to any of the various letters he had addressed to it or to the Fund. While Wasylyshen went on to report that he had tried to explain to Colley that any misunderstandings were the result more of 'a lack of experience' than of 'bad intentions,' the IRO representative was apparently neither mollified nor convinced.

For their part, the Ukrainian Canadians had their own complaints about UNRRA, later IRO, and, almost always, about Canada's immigration officials, at home and abroad.[42] In the early summer of 1948, Yaremovich, writing to the MP, H.W. Herridge, thanked him on behalf of the Ukrainian Canadian community for the favourable remarks he had made in the House of Commons about the desirability of further refugee immigration, but went on to find fault with the immigration teams being sent to Europe, pointing out that they tended to seek only the 'physically fit' and to leave all others behind. Following that course would actually do little to help resolve the overall DP problem, Yaremovich noted. Unless a 'fair-share plan' was devised, by which every country would agree to 'take the good with the bad' and thereby ensure that the refugee camps were completely cleared of their inhabitants and not simply emptied of the physically fit, the refugee population might become smaller in absolute numerical terms but worse-off overall, as a 'hard core' of cases remained pooled together in these repositories, stuck without any hope. Surely, Yaremovich insisted, the ill, the elderly, the victims of war, all these people could not simply be abandoned. And in the meantime, he added, there was another problem, namely, the 'terrific nervous strain' associated with living in the DP camps, 'always' under a 'shadow of uncertainty.' This psychological pressure was having a markedly negative effect on the DPs.[43] Canada, in his opinion, could and should be doing far more to empty all the camps quickly, accepting its share of the international chore of resolving the refugee situation while making a fine humanitarian gesture.

By 1946 the 'Close Relatives Scheme' had already begun providing for a limited immigration of Ukrainian refugees into Canada. Eventually, labour needs within the country would more or less dictate the number of Ukrainian and other east European DPs admitted. Up to 31 December 1947, Panchuk noted, various groups and companies had filed 20,201 applications for workers, although by February 1948 only 5091 refugees had been processed. Atypically, when the Great Lakes Paper Company Limited requested 420 workers, it got them. More often, companies' requests were not met: Sigma Mines of Quebec, which asked for 35 men, was allocated only 5, and the Canadian Pacific Railway Company, having sent in 2055 applications, received only 175 workers.[44]

Even though Canadian businesses were not allocated the total number of workers they wanted from among the refugee population available, Canadian officials seem to have been impressed, overall, with the quality of those admitted and by their subsequent employment records. Most displaced persons were allowed in the country after agreeing to a one- or two-year period of contract labour, the length and place of the employment decided upon at the discretion of the government's immigration officials, and then accepted, or not, by the refugee applicant. Writing to Mr Jolliffe, the Department of Mines and Resources reported that the record of the DPs in completing these kinds of contracts had been 'remarkably good.' As of the winter of 1949, over 95 per cent of the original contracts had been completed and an estimated 50 per cent of the refugees were staying with their jobs, in the communities to which they had been channelled originally, either with their first employers or in similar occupations. Between April 1947 and the end of January 1952 the federal authorities would count 26,130 Ukrainian DP immigrants in Canada, compared to some 4000 Russians and 34,000 Poles.[45] Ukrainian Canadian estimates, significantly enough, were nearly double those produced by Canadian officials. Writing to Crapleve, then still in Bielefeld, Panchuk suggested in February 1951 that around 50,000 Ukrainian refugees had resettled in Canada, although not all were listed as Ukrainians in the official records. He categorized this DP population further by regional background: 50 per cent were from Western Ukraine (Eastern Galicia); 20 per cent were from Soviet Ukraine; 5 per cent were from Rumania (Bukovyna and part of Bessarabia); 5 per cent were from Czechoslovakia (primarily from Carpatho-Ukraine); 3 per cent were Nansen refugees; and 2 per cent were Ukrainians who had lived in western Europe before the outbreak of the war and then become displaced. The remainder were of unknown origin.[46] Of this total, he added, at least 80 per cent were 'official' DPs – persons sponsored by UNRRA, the IGCR, or IRO – while 10 per cent were Ukrainians who had served with the Polish armed forces, 7 per cent were 'old émigrés,' and 3 per cent were veterans of the Ukrainian Division 'Galicia.'[47]

Whatever the precise number of Ukrainian DPs who resettled in Canada between 1945 and 1952 – a figure of approximately thirty-five thousand seems credible – the size of this immigrating cohort was less important than its geographical clustering in the urban-industrial centres of central Canada's heartland and the nationalistic world-view which these Ukrainian 'newcomers' had brought with them, for, more than any other quality, it was their political fervour which would determine their profound impact on Ukrainian Canadian society.[48]

'A Struggle for the Minds of the Masses'

'The refugees are coming,' the Ukrainian Canadian wrote, and 'among them you can find anything you like,' including 'a mania that in Canada they won't have to work, that dollars can be picked up off the streets. But when they find out that it's not like that here, they get angry and a few even say that they'd return – but where to? They themselves don't know. I suppose they'd like to go where one can live easily, but there's no UNRRA here. True, there are only a few of this type in every hundred, but they're damaging opinion about the refugees.'[49]

When Dmytro Gerych shared these impressions in his letter to Panchuk, he had no way of knowing that only a few months later one of the 'newcomers' would come to the conclusion that the 'fashion' to help the DPs had passed. Nor could Gerych have known that Panchuk himself, the greatest booster of Ukrainian refugee immigration ever to work overseas, would, a scant year later, be forced to admit that Ukrainian Canadians had had enough of the DPs, who had managed, as he put it, 'to get under everybody's skin.'[50]

What happened so to estrange the Ukrainian Canadians? An answer can be found by studying the nature of daily life in the European DP camps. For it was within those enclaves that tens of thousands of Ukrainians, of all ages, political philosophies, religious beliefs, regional and socio-economic backgrounds, had been forced to cluster for several years or more. In these refugee camps they had gradually been transformed from a rather heterogeneous mass into something of a schooled cohort, united in its world-view, under the almost complete control of the militant nationalists active among them. Panchuk was probably the first Ukrainian Canadian to observe this metamorphosis. He was hardly the last. Visiting a DP camp at Heidenau, in the British Zone of Germany, early in 1946, he recorded that it already had the quality of being a 'small state,' whose population was 'disciplined' and of good morale, even though they lived 'in constant fear' of forcible repatriation.[51] Yet conditions were not completely settled. Political differences were 'quite alive,' even if there was some attempt to keep these internal disputes 'under the surface,' so as not to evoke official censure. Significantly, two years later Crapleve would pen an almost identical picture of another DP camp, a coincidence suggesting just how persistent and widespread this transformation was.[52] What Panchuk and others saw taking place in the refugee camps he had tellingly described as 'a struggle for the minds of the masses of the DPs.'[53] This contest between members of rival political groups was over which political vision would come to saturate and dominate the daily lives of the, as yet, largely non-partisan populations of the refugee camps. The nationalists won.

It all began with the increasing self-segregation of various nationalities within the originally rather mixed refugee population of the camps. As the various ethnic groups cloistered in these centres generally strove to establish their own 'camp within a camp,' presided over by their own committees and leaders, the ethnic clusters came under the influence or direct command of various competing political groups. It was relatively easy for nationalists to gain control over Ukrainian DP camps. Panchuk noted this voluntary regrouping in a number of displaced persons camps. For example, in Wentorf, some thirteen miles east of Hamburg, Poles, Ukrainians, Russians, and refugees from the Baltic countries of Estonia, Latvia, and Lithuania had voluntarily regrouped themselves in their own sectors, clearly preferring ethnic enclaves to the more mixed settlement that had existed originally.[54]

This regrouping facilitated the efforts of competing Ukrainian political movements. Yaremovich would be neither the first nor the last outsider to comment on the 'intense political activity' common within and between the various national groups found in most of the DP camps. The leaders of each group first rallied their countrymen into their own distinct area, within which whatever political faction happened to prevail (and generally Ukrainian nationalists ended up controlling the majority of the Ukrainian-inhabited refugee camps) then took control over many of the internal functions of the camp administration. These duties ranged in importance. But, obviously, those responsible for assigning living space and rations, running camp schools, publishing camp newspapers, serving in the DP camp police, and so on had the means to exert considerable influence over the daily comings and goings and the thoughts of most of the other refugees. For as long as opportunities for resettlement abroad were limited and the spectre of forcible repatriation hung over their heads, the DPs would remain hived together for mutual protection, aid, and comfort. Of course, this living together made life somewhat easier, for at least one could make oneself understood among one's own people. Segregation was also deemed desirable by many because of the historically antagonistic relations between many of these now displaced peoples in their countries of origin. Poles did not like Ukrainians or Russians, or Jews; Ukrainians did not like Poles, Russians or Jews; Latvians, Estonians, and Lithuanians hated Russians; Croatians detested Serbians; Jews hated all others, and vice versa; and so on. While there were exceptions, of course, most of these peoples, Poles and Jews, Russians and Ukrainians, Hungarians and Romanians, and many, many others, fundamentally did not want to live together for reasons good and bad and common to most of them. The prejudices, hatreds, and experiences in the prewar years of each of the nations concerned had certainly in no way been diminished or obliterated by the atrocities which some members of each had committed against members of all or most of the others during the cataclysm of the war.[55]

In time, as a British parliamentary commission sent to investigate conditions in the camps reported, many DPs came to share a common story about how they had come to be refugees and why they could no longer go home. The initial cause of their plight was usually given as either Nazi or Soviet aggression, sometimes as both. And the reason they could no longer return was that their countries had fallen under Soviet rule or were under the control of a communist regime subordinate to the USSR. Both these factors, the DPs would claim, had turned them into political refugees. This story – which the evidence available suggests had a strong element of truth – was also one in which the displaced population as a whole had been steeped so thoroughly, largely through constant repetition, that it was the rare inmate of a camp who thought or spoke otherwise, or so the British parliamentarians had recorded.[56]

Inculcating a shared world-view among the majority of the DPs was made easier by the fact that most schools, cultural centres, churches, and newspapers organized within the DP camps sooner or later came under the influence or control of one or another political faction. That this was the case with many camp newspapers was noted by both Yaremovich and Crapleve, in the summer and fall of 1947. Being able to control the news and information circulated to the refugees in their own language, and to determine how it was presented, made the proselytizing efforts of the various political groups all the easier. With few other sources of reliable information, the majority of DPs, immersed in the anti-Soviet, anti-repatriation propaganda of able and experienced polemicists, naturally enough absorbed much of the collective message of the militants. As Yaremovich remarked, 'The international news [is] reported in such a manner as to exaggerate the differences between the Eastern and Western powers. This keeps the DPs in a state of suspense as to how another war will be started.'[57]

Many displaced persons quite fervently came to believe exactly what their political leaders told them, namely, that the 'only resettlement scheme' they could truly count upon was the one embodied within the nationalist political agenda. It was assumed that by supporting the Ukrainian national liberation movement, in the not too distant future they could all return to a homeland freed from its foes. That was the promise. But such an outcome would be possible only if the DPs first gave sufficient material and moral support to the continuing insurgent struggle for political and military victory. That meant they must also remain where they were, in place, in or near the refugee camps. Emigrating overseas was discouraged, for it would involve a further geographical distancing from what they were told was their only proper place, their homeland Ukraine. Abroad they would also be too far removed from the political centres of western Europe which served as focal points for the resistance movement in the various centres of the diaspora, which nodes in turn were said to be the only locuses of reliable information about what the refugees should be doing to help the struggle. Many Ukrainian and other east European refugees were thus caught up in the unenviable situation of being unwilling to return to their Soviet-occupied homelands and simultaneously being told by the respected leaders of their exile communities that they must not opt for resettlement and the chance to rebuild their lives abroad. If they left western Europe, they were told repeatedly, they would in effect be deserting the struggle, breaking faith, weakening the movement's chances of success. And if their compatriots' struggle in the homeland failed, most refugees' chances of ever returning home would become non-existent.[58] Nearly everyone felt a 'compulsive need to return home,' and the nationalists succeeded in utilizing this need, which is highly characteristic of the refugee experience, both to mobilize and to preserve the strength of their movement in the landscape of exile in which all had found themselves.

An often violent struggle took place in the DP camps as competing

Ukrainian political groups, including some unique to the camps and others representing prewar movements, strove to establish their legitimacy and even impose hegemony over the refugee population. Different factions gradually came to dominate particular centres. While some camps remained unaligned, most others became partial to one political group or another, as was widely understood at the time. Most refugees, for example, knew that the OUNm controlled the refugee camp near Berchtesgarden, in Austria, while the Ukrainian Revolutionary Democratic Party, a group of Eastern Ukrainian vintage, was particularly active in Neu Ulm. Crapleve, writing in the fall of 1947, pointed out that the 'active propaganda' of these political parties was making many DPs feel not only that a war against the Soviet Union was likely but that such a war would come 'soon.' Emotional news of this type was obviously retarding resettlement plans, for few refugees would voluntarily leave western Europe, and thereby distance themselves from their Ukrainian homeland, while being told that dithering a while longer would give them the chance of returning to Ukraine. They had never wanted leave Ukraine; they had been forced to, and they wanted to return. So they were prepared to wait, at least a while longer, if there was still a chance of getting back to their families, homes, friends, and country. Replacement was what they wanted, not resettlement.

Crapleve also wrote that there was a 'definite effort' by each of the wrangling DP groups to ensure that refugee camp executives were dominated by members or supporters of their own organizations, 'the net result' of all these partisan electoral victories being that 'members of the party in power are favoured wherever possible.'[59] Graft, corruption, hooliganism, and influence-peddling became common features of camp life. Whom you sided with often determined how well you fared in the DP camps.

Throughout the immediate postwar period, émigré nationalist leaders confidently predicted the imminence of war between the Anglo-American powers and the Soviets. Such a war did break out, as they and others had prophesied, but it was a 'cold' war, not the 'hot' conflict they had expected. Yet, rather paradoxically, it was the Cold War which saved many nationalists, creating an international political climate in which the Western powers grew sympathetic to preserving at least a small pool of militant anti-communists against possible future needs. Expecting someday to use these men and women against the Soviets and their allies in eastern Europe – and they did use some of them, although the relevant intelligence files remain classified – the Anglo-American powers came to shield the nationalists. And so these political refugees were given an opportunity to accept asylum in the West, where they would be allowed to carry on with their struggle. Not surprisingly, most of them finally took what was, after all, their only way out.

'Obviously "Planted" Agents'

The rivalry for domination of refugee camp life – a contest for control of the camps' resources of food, shelter, and safety – was critical, for whichever group controlled these amenities would enjoy a distinct advantage in the struggle to win over the 'minds of the masses of the DPs.' So intense were these antagonisms that politics, according to a Roman Catholic adviser attached to the Control Commission for Germany, had 'permeated even the religious field.'[60] Denominational tensions and unrest, often exacerbated by political considerations, became so fierce that full-scale riots among competing confessions were reported in several DP camps. This, the usually clement Crapleve reported, was giving Ukrainians in general 'a bad name.'[61]

Panchuk had insisted, in the early spring of 1946, that 'the partisan type' of DP was still 'very rare.' By year's end he was of a different opinion. In addition to the 'normal and ordinary DPs' who had flocked to refugee centres like the 'Lysenko' camp, near Hannover, there were others among them who had been 'obviously "planted" there' by what he described as an external power.[62] He went on to say that the purpose of such agents was to sow 'seeds of discord' in the DP camps. The results of such subterfuge were becoming increasingly apparent, even to outside observers. Considerable discord was evident in most of the camps, between Eastern and Western Ukrainians, between Catholic and Orthodox believers, between labourers and the intelligentsia, and among persons of different citizenship, even though they all shared a common Ukrainian nationality. Panchuk also noted, 'Based on experience and first hand knowledge of conditions in the DP camps ... 75 per cent to 90 per cent of the "political movements" credited to the camps are deliverately [sic] inspired and often planted by the agents of the USSR ... in order to provide "ammunition" [for] creating conditions ... which will assist in the repatriation of as many DPs of Slavic origin as possible.'[63]

Since Ukrainians constituted the 'bulk' of the displaced population, and were 'the greatest danger' to the communist regime in the USSR, they bore the brunt of these nefarious disinformation and destabilization operations. Panchuk added that Soviet agents of influence had been introduced 'well before the cessation of hostilities' because the Soviets had understood even then that they would find themselves in competition with the Anglo-American powers, whom they had also outmanoeuvred at Yalta.[64] A few months later he would reaffirm these conclusions, writing about the 'scandalous state of affairs' prevailing in places like the 'Lysenko' camp.[65] The only way to resolve the situation was to 'remove the small group of *other* elements,' composed of 'non-Ukrainians,' thereby turning camps like 'Lysenko' into 'strictly Ukrainian' centres. In such all-Ukrainian camps, Panchuk confidently presumed, whatever small problems might still arise could be resolved 'easily' through 'ordinary democratic elections' and procedures. Ukrainian DPs, he implied, would never argue among themselves if left untroubled by outsiders.[66] This analysis was to prove remarkably naïve.

'The Ultra-Patriots'

By the end of 1947, Panchuk, a quick study, had realized just how misplaced his original optimism had been. Increasingly, it became clear to him that the internal strife reported among the Ukrainian DPs could not be blamed exclusively on the covert artifices of Soviet agents. Writing to his friend Tracy Philipps, in mid-November, he revealed how particularly upset he was with the behaviour of both factions of the OUN inside the camps, and he reserved especial scorn for the Banderivtsi, their Supreme Ukrainian Liberation Council, and the affiliated Anti-Bolshevik Bloc of Nations. Still, he was not quite willing to blame Ukrainians for all the problems brewing in the camps and in the emigration: 'There is some reason to feel that in this whole action of OUN(B), UHVR and ABN there may be some first class, Soviet agents and provocateurs,' though 'in all such things it is very difficult to tell.'[67] As to why these Ukrainian nationalists might not like him and other Ukrainian Canadians working in the refugee camps, Panchuk suggested the main problem was that his political world-view and working methods were considered 'too Canadianized' and 'pro-British.' Some critics were even going so far as to 'accuse us of endeavouring to make Ukraine a British Colony (which actually in my humble opinion might be a good idea).'[68]

Throughout 1948 and into early 1949, Panchuk would continue to receive sporadic reports underscoring that he was becoming a target of opprobrium among certain elements active within the DP camps, and even among those who had been fortunate enough to resettle in Canada.[69] Matters came to a head in March 1949, when Panchuk was forced out of the AUGB by the concerted efforts of the Hetmantsi and Banderivtsi. Ukrainian Canadians, at that time, expressed their shock and deep annoyance with what they regarded as this mutinous turn of events. Fort William's Dr Wenger had reported that many Ukrainian Canadians were bitter about the way things had turned out.[70] Panchuk reciprocated, writing letters to local community leaders like Wenger and others like Joseph Choma. In these missives he bemoaned the activities of those refugees, whom he would identify only as the 'ultra-patriots.' Sorrowfully, he reported that analogous developments were disrupting the postwar emigration in France and elsewhere on the Continent and predicted that a similar pattern might soon appear in Canada.[71]

By the end of 1949, Panchuk had all but forgotten his earlier idea that most of the troubles in the camps were inspired by outsiders. Increasingly, his anger focused on the nationalistic Ukrainian political movements, particularly the Banderivtsi. 'Circumstances,' he wrote to UCVA's Karasevich, 'have forced me to come out into the open against the Banderivtsi and Hetmantsi'; he wondered, however, if that would somehow adversely affect his position in Winnipeg within UCC and UCRF circles.[72] He need not have worried, for, by then the Banderivtsi certainly enjoyed little if any favour in Winnipeg. In the months to follow, Panchuk would be able to pursue his Banderivtsi foes with a passion, an anger not at all surprising given the drubbing he had received at their hands and those of their allies during the AUGB's annual meeting in 1949. He would do so with Winnipeg's tacit approval. In the course of this tenacious anti-OUNb campaign, not only would Panchuk denounce Yaroslav Stetsko to Philipps and the British Home Office, but, attempting to counter the influence of the UHVR, he would vigorously promote the Ukrainian National Council before all and sundry. In his view, the UHVR was neither legitimate nor representative of the Ukrainian nation.[73] He never did try to explain how UNRada could itself be representative without the participation of what everyone knew were the numerically dominant Banderivtsi and the conservative forces represented by the Hetmantsi.

What particularly alienated Ukrainian Canadians from the Ukrainian refugees resettling among them was the political world-view of the refugees, particularly its militantly nationalistic pitch, reflecting an ideology which had been further cultivated within the DP camps and subsequently exported as part of the cultural baggage the refugees brought with them to Canada. Panchuk, not unexpectedly given his years of personal work among the Ukrainian DPs, provided the most cogent description of what he and others had witnessed taking place within the confined space of the refugee camps:

> *All* refugees and displaced persons, whatever their nationality, consider themselves *political refugees* (although many of them are far from that) and therefore feel that their prime and most important duty and mission as 'émigrés' is to carry on political work and activities, for the liberation of, and their own ultimate return to, their native land.[74]

In actual fact, he claimed, 'the majority' of the DPs were nothing but 'economic refugees' who had 'always' been in search of a place to live where they would be better off. What had happened in the refugee camps was that this majority, closeted together with the revolutionary nationalists of both OUN factions – Panchuk candidly labelled these militants as the only real 'political refugees' – had been transformed, in part or in whole, by the nationalists, who had 'imposed and forced their influence' and 'thus "coloured" all refugees and displaced persons.'[75] In Panchuk's view, the immediate result was that trying 'to *eliminate politics*' from the lexicon of the Ukrainian DPs was going to be the 'hardest problem' facing Ukrainian Canadian refugee relief and resettlement workers overseas. By the time Panchuk came to promote this understanding publicly, however, it was much too late for his Team to do anything about what had taken place inside the DP camps, even assuming that the transformation of this refugee population could, somehow, have been countered.

'It's the Mentality That Counts'

What was more troubling for those at home was how very obvious it was becoming to them that the refugee immigrants were transplanting their political divisions 'to Canadian soil,' as Yaremovich put it, and that, for the most part, these refugees remained uninterested and uninvolved in existing Ukrainian Canadian community organizations. This was exactly the opposite of what the Ukrainian Canadians had anticipated. Needless to say, considerable friction arose between the 'newcomers' and the 'oldtimers' as a result.[76] Indeed, as Kaye would write to Panchuk at the end of January 1949, 'a definite rift' had emerged between what had become two rather distinct Ukrainian constituencies in Canada.[77]

Problems arose particularly after supporters of the national liberation movement, guided by Stanley Frolick, made it clear that they desired and had the ability to act independently of the Ukrainian Canadian establishment. The most unambiguous signal of this was the founding of a new Ukrainian-language newspaper, *Homin ukrainy*, or *Ukrainian Echo*, based in Toronto, catering to the needs of the 'newcomers.' First published on 15 December 1948, it would become the organ of the League for the Liberation of Ukraine and an unflagging advocate of revolutionary nationalist principles.

The reaction of men like Panchuk, who heard about this development from one of his regular correspondents, Dmytro Gerych, was anger and abhorrence. He explained that, as of mid-February 1949, he had still to see a copy of the newspaper. Even so, he felt sure that this newspaper's appearance boded ill for Ukrainian Canadian society, for *Ukrainian Echo* was obviously under the control of the very same nationalists whom he had grown so to dislike.[78] He was certainly right in asserting that the newspaper was the press organ of the movement headed by the Banderivtsi. And, at least at the start, *Ukrainian Echo* was even published on the same printing press which turned out the United Hetman Organization's newspaper – further evidence of the collusion between Banderivtsi and Hetmantsi at that time.

As for the DPs who had resettled in Canada, and the impact they were having on Ukrainian Canadian life, Panchuk agreed that while many of these immigrants were 'very excellent ... highly educated, refined, willing and capable' persons, there were also, most regrettably, a 'large amount' of 'rather useless and unworthy' types among them. Such people neither had lived up to Ukrainian Canadians' expectations of the political refugees, nor were making the expected contributions to organized Ukrainian Canadian society. This, he finally and candidly admitted, left him utterly scandalized, wondering whether his years of lobbying and working for these Ukrainian DPs had been worth all his blood, sweat, and tears. The bad types 'constantly bring us shame and disgrace and it is a problem which is most difficult if not impossible to remedy. You can be sure we have the same type and therefore the same difficulties here in England as you have in Canada and the same situations arise in every country to which these people immigrate.'[79]

Wishing, however, to be 'broad minded,' Panchuk insightfully pointed out that even if the large number of such unwelcome individuals was ample reason for regret, the 'blame' for their behaviour had to be placed 'not on the people themselves' but on the war, and on the 'conditions which made them' the way they were, particularly their experiences of exile and refugee camp life.[80]

Not everyone, as yet, was quite as pessimistic, nor as downcast about the chances of Ukrainian Canadian society being able to cope with the refugees. John Karasevich admitted that the UCC was 'still feebly established.' And he agreed that the growth of new refugee-based groups in Canada made matters even more complex. But he also wrote that he believed the Banderivtsi, and their affiliated Ukrainian Youth Association (CYM), might still end up having a salutary effect, for their very existence was forcing the prewar groups to rally together into 'a closer unity.'[81] Panchuk, replying a few weeks later, was not convinced, repeating that he felt there were many 'worthless and negative' elements among the postwar DP immigrants to Canada, and that their creation of new organizations was nothing short of 'scandalous.'[82] Of course, by the time he wrote those words, a large number of DPs had emigrated to Canada, the League for the Liberation of Ukraine was established, and its affiliated newspaper, *Ukrainian Echo*, had been published for nearly a year. Indeed the League, by the summer of 1949, had several active branches across the country, most in southern Ontario's urban-industrial centres, where the majority of the DP immigrants had resettled. In towns and cities where no branch of the League or CYM had formed, the Banderivtsi and their supporters often just joined local parish or secular groups, such as choir ensembles, theatre groups, and Prosvita reading clubs, or else took out memberships in exiting national, if largely apolitical, Ukrainian Canadian organizations, such as the Brotherhood of Ukrainian Catholics. When some of these local groups were eventually taken over by the 'newcomers,' the established Ukrainian Canadian community was further alienated, seeing in these 'takeovers' evidence of the disintegration of the Ukrainian Canadian community structures they had laboured so hard to erect and were unwilling to abandon without a fight.

As for the smaller numbers of Melnykivtsi among the 'newcomers,' they found their niche within the Ukrainian National Federation and its affiliated youth, veterans,' and women's groups, a development which would later precipitate serious internal difficulties for the Federation.[83] Some of the relatively small number of Eastern Ukrainians who came to Canada, generally Orthodox believers, also set up branches of organizations never seen before in Canada, groups like the Ukrainian Revolutionary Democratic Party (URDP), which had been established in the Neu Ulm refugee camp in 1948. They too had their own affiliated youth group, the Organization of Democratic Ukrainian Youth (ODUM). Other Eastern Ukrainians, formerly considered 'Soviet citizens,' joined groups like Suzero – the acronym for the Ukrainian Association of Victims of Russian Communist Terror – which represented survivors of the politically engineered Great Famine of 1932–3 and Stalinist oppression. A few of these 'newcomers,' perhaps striving to adapt themselves more completely to existing conditions, also joined existing Orthodox church parishes, the adults becoming members of the Ukrainian Self-Reliance League, while their children joined its youth wing, SUMK. In a few such parishes, a preponderance of incoming eastern Ukrainian Orthodox believers meant that the 'newcomers' quite naturally took over parish life even if they had not intended to do so, and this development provoked not a little friction. Few, if any, of the postwar Ukrainian refugee immigrants even considered joining the pro-Soviet Association of United Ukrainian Canadians. Indeed, during the late 1940s and early 1950s many of the political refugees would play a significant role in orchestrating the precipitous decline of the Left wing of the Ukrainian Canadian community.

Whether they formed new groups or joined existing ones, these refugee 'newcomers' often discovered that they were not able to adjust easily to the patterns of organized Ukrainian Canadian community life. Nor, for their part, were many Ukrainian Canadians particularly adept at accepting or even coping with the attitudes and associated behaviour of the political refugees. While it would be unfair to suggest that the sole outcome of the encounter between refugee immigrants and Ukrainian Canadian society was disillusionment and feuding, the evidence overwhelmingly suggests this as the major consequence.[84] Traces of those controversies can still be detected in Ukrainian Canadian affairs, and they continue to undermine the integrity of the worldwide Ukrainian diaspora, one of the long-term and largely unanticipated impacts of the dispersal and resettlement of this refugee population. What is even more remarkable is that even the presence of an already established population, one outwardly sharing cultural, regional, and religious traits with the immigrants, proved insufficient to ensure a relatively untroubled intermingling of the two groups. However much some Ukrainian Canadians may have wanted to help or understand the Ukrainian DPs, they had not themselves been exposed to the traumas of forcible migration or the refugee experience, nor were most of them able to appreciate the psychological consequences of such abuse. The result was not the anticipated and much-hoped-for strengthening of the Ukrainian Canadian community, but its further fragmentation.

As Yaremovich put it, in order to 'iron out the differences' between 'the "B" group' and Ukrainian Canadian supporters of the UCC a third national congress was called, in February 1950, in Winnipeg.[85] Since 'all one has around now is trouble,' and because certain 'DP organizers' were doing everything possible to 'break up the Committee' – Yaremovich figuratively proclaimed, 'the "B" group is dancing around quite freely' – it was time for Ukrainian Canadians to rally round their national organization and put matters right. After all, he noted, the 'newcomers' had no concept whatsoever of Canadian conditions or the proper rules and norms of behaviour for a Ukrainian in Canada, which explained why they ended up behaving in all kinds of odd and unrealistic ways, generally making all Ukrainians in Canada look bad.[86] The anxiety in Ukrainian Canadian minds was that the DPs resettling among them would somehow, in their nationalistic zeal, do something to call down the displeasure of the Canadian state on the community as a whole. They did not want to savour that displeasure again.

Even Ukrainian Canadians who had intimate contact with the DPs were disturbed by the 'newcomers.' A Canadian veteran and prominent USRL member, Dr Peter Smylski, at the time establishing a dental practice in Hamilton, wrote to Panchuk to remark on how much events in Canada seemed to be paralleling what had taken place earlier in the United Kingdom. More charitable than many other Ukrainian Canadians, Smylski suggested it would just take time for the 'newcomers' to become 'readjusted psychologically and acclimatized,' after which the Ukrainian Canadians would be able 'to train them' to appreciate how a Ukrainian must or must not act in Canada. There was reason to be hopeful, Smylski wrote, since even the USRL's arch-rival, the once nationalistic Ukrainian National Federation, had finally become 'a good Canadian organization.' What Smylski saw as 'good' about the UNF was that most members had given up their militant nationalism and pretences about returning to the homeland. He wrote, in a tone half mocking, half incredulous, that the Federation was even 'spending money on material things in Canada' instead of 'raving' against anything which might detract from maintaining 'living ties' with Ukraine.

'It's the mentality that counts,' Smylski concluded rightly. And so the cultivation of an acceptable sense of place, one which would help 'Canadianize' the DPs, was something which USRL members and those in affiliated organizations would now have to work on if they wanted to integrate the refugees. For only they could draw the DPs away from the 'warped and fantastic type of creatures and organizations' taking root among them, sadly diverting the energies of the refugee immigrants away from their proper business of adjusting to the host society. After all, Smylski reminded Panchuk, only the USRL had, from its inception, publicly declared itself a strictly Canadian organization, one which had no 'living ties' to political movements abroad, and wanted none. And it was particularly important, Smylski asserted, that the UCC be kept strictly independent of and unentangled with any foreign-based political groups or movements. Such 'connections' had brought nothing but trouble in the past, not only for organizations like the Federation, which had once insisted on building such links with the homeland, but for the organized Ukrainian community of Canada as a whole. Intermittently, but collectively and more than once, they had all run foul of accusations of 'divided loyalties,' and had suffered government-sponsored stricture as a result. They wanted no more of that.[87]

'Get Acquainted before Trying to Take Over'

As the date on which the third UCC congress was to be held drew nearer, fighting intensified between the two OUN nationalist factions relocated in Canada. Both groups had members who had piggybacked into Canada on the DP immigration. While the Banderivtsi were able to place some of their people in the UCC's Winnipeg office, and had set up the League and CYM branches across Canada, the Melnykivtsi, though fewer in number, had made full use of their initial advantage of a welcome niche within the Ukrainian National Federation, a group which already sported a well-established national network of halls, a newspaper, New Pathway, and affiliated youth, veterans', and women's groups. Both sides were thus well positioned in Canada for carrying on with their polemics against each other. They entered into these disputes with relish, while other Ukrainian Canadians watched with an admixture of disgust and amusement. As Yaremovich chronicled: 'The Banderivtsi-Melnykivtsi fight is finding itself locking horns on Canadian soil. They certainly are going at each other with typical Ukrainian vigour. No quarter is given by any side.'[88]

While he remarked, rather condescendingly, that Ukrainian Canadians were having 'quite a bit of fun' watching this squabbling from the sidelines, he did add that he was worried about the wider repercussions of this internecine quarrelling, which suggested to him that Ukrainians as a group had 'some years' to go before they would 'reach the age of maturity.' This, he ominously reminded his readers, was not being 'concealed from other people.' For Yaremovich and for many of his Canadian-born peers and contemporaries, the suspicion that their every move was being closely followed by those outside the Ukrainian Canadian world was seldom absent from their thoughts. Consequently, they wanted as little as possible to do with groups or causes that might expose them to censure, or worse. Anxiously, they worked to keep Ukrainian-oriented problems away from the purview of governments and the general public. For those who did not believe that the Ukrainian Canadian community was under surveillance, Yaremovich wrote, 'If Ukrainians are fooling anyone on this score they are fooling themselves and no one else.'[89]

The third UCC national assembly turned out to be an acrimonious affair, as pro-OUNb advocates, participating under the auspices of the Brotherhood of Ukrainian Catholics, were harried and jeered out of the meeting hall. Pandemonium prevailed. Their departure was accompanied by a stern reprimand from the podium by none other than Monsignor Kushnir, who denounced those whom he accused of trying to 'take over' Ukrainian Canadian organizational life. Traditional rivalries between several of the UCC's constituent groups seem to have been downgraded for a brief moment, as common cause was made against the revolutionary nationalists. Panchuk, who witnessed this rather ignominious checkmate of the Banderivtsi, would write gleefully to Tracy Philipps, observing that the sternness with which the nationalists had been treated ensured that this meeting would be forever remembered as 'a great success,' exhilarating and cathartic. In his words, the 'dissident' element had been 'plainly reminded' that 'Canada was *not* Galicia, and Winnipeg not *Lvow*, and [that] they must first of all settle down and get acquainted with things before trying to "take over."'[90]

'No Rhyme or Reason, Just Orders from Above'

Yet even after the 'marked success' of this national meeting, matters did not change drastically within the UCC's headquarters. Zaharychuk remained in charge of the executive staff, and he continued to work with 'an office full of DPs.' Mrs Mandryka was not reinstated as the UCRF's executive secretary. And the UCC's first executive director, Volodymyr Kochan, allegedly continued to seek an accommodation with the Hetmantsi and their allies, the Banderivtsi, or so Dr Mandryka's letters would assert.[91] But, as even Panchuk admitted, in almost the same breath as he complained that the DPs had managed to 'get under everybody's skin,' the situation in Winnipeg could not be blamed on the refugees alone, for 'after all, half a million Ukrainians should be able to find a Canadian to run the offices.' Apparently, they were unable to do so.[92] That most Ukrainian Canadians seemed untouched by the spirit of voluntarism which motivated Panchuk and his co-workers was discouraging. And, as many Ukrainian Canadians grew increasingly annoyed with what they decried as the antics of the DPs, an ever more obvious 'break-up' into 'two camps' took root throughout North America, one which pitted many DPs against members of the previously settled Ukrainian communities. Panchuk wrote that the split was 'deep and thorough ... I am afraid unless things change radically, final and irrevocable. The people don't want it but certain leaders act only on the instructions they receive from Munich and it's hopeless to do anything. There is no rhyme or reason to anything they do. It's orders from above.'[93]

The archival record is profoundly incomplete, but enough material survives to give insight into the nature and workings of the OUNb's reconstituted network in Canada during its initial years of existence. Complemented with the recorded minutes of various national executive and annual conference meetings of the League for the Liberation of Ukraine, these documents represent a paradox. They confirm some Ukrainian Canadian opinions about what the Banderivtsi were up to, yet also reveal a far more complex, dynamic, lithe, and even democratic organizational structure at work among these nationalists than public perceptions would suggest could be possible.

The story begins with Stanley Frolick's return to Canada, in early 1947. He was living in Toronto, bearing something of a grudge against the UCC. As Smylski would write, after meeting him at a community function in Hamilton in February 1948, Frolick's 'biggest kick was against KUK.'[94] If the only issue had been a personal dispute between Frolick and the UCC's directors, over nothing more substantive than his pay and perks, Frolick's actions would be of little further interest. The issue, however, was much more than that.

Frolick was not just a disgruntled employee. Even before he left the United Kingdom he had served as the *rezident* (or *terenovyi providnyk*) of the UHVR, the Supreme Ukrainian Liberation Council. In that capacity he had met with Mykola Lebed, the head of the OUNb's intelligence service, the Sluzhba bespeky, and the movement's leader, Stepan Bandera, in Munich during early November 1946. He had kept in touch. From them he accepted the commission of acting as the underground's control officer for Canada. This assignment obliged him to structure both a private and a public network of members and sympathizers for the nationalist movement, establish a newspaper to keep them informed no matter where they might resettle in Canada, and thereafter function as a channel of information and orders to the relocating Banderivtsi from their superiors in Europe, who were headquartered in Munich. It was an important and unique role for a Canadian-born Ukrainian to take up, and in embracing it Frolick probably became the only man in the Ukrainian nationalist underground's history to have served as a *rezident* in two countries, the United Kingdom and Canada. Still, he was ideally qualified for this role. He had lived and been educated in western Canada and Western Ukraine, and had belonged to a Ukrainian nationalist underground cell before the OUN split into its competing factions. While living in Western Ukraine, Frolick had travelled widely and become acquainted with Ukrainian life throughout the region. And he had personally come to know several key members of the nationalist movement. After his remarkable escape from the NKVD, through Siberia to Japan, Frolick had returned to Toronto, where by late 1941 he became active in the UNF's youth wing.

Before the outbreak of the war it was the Federation which represented the Ukrainian nationalist movement in Canada. Frolick was so trusted by the UNF leadership that he was elected second president of the Young Ukrainian Nationalists and given the mandate to deliver a speech entitled 'The Future of Ukrainian Youth in Canada' to delegates gathered at the first UCC congress in Winnipeg, on 24 June 1943. When an opportunity arose to return overseas, in 1945, to work with the Control Commission for Germany, Frolick was delighted. He travelled carrying a private note from Kossar which informed Kossar's Ukrainian nationalist comrades that Frolick was a young man in whom 'complete trust' could be placed. Frolick was already being groomed for a top position in the nationalist movement. His subsequent defection – from the UNF perspective – into the ranks of the Banderivtsi represented a unforgivable betrayal, an insult for which he was eventually purged from CURB and shamed by the UCC.

'You Decide, You're the Boss'

Private correspondence between Frolick, some of the resettling refugees, and a disaffected member of the UNF's leading council, Pavlo Shteppa, who had also transferred his loyalties to the OUNb, reveals how a clandestine network of Banderivtsi was established in Canada in the immediate postwar period.[95]

The correspondence between Shteppa and Frolick began even before Frolick left London, when the older, former UNF supporter wrote from his home in Amherstburg, Ontario (near Windsor), to inquire how Ukrainian Canadians might help Dmytro Dontsov get out of Europe to safe haven in North America.[96] Once Frolick returned to Canada, Shteppa, who had grown increasingly agitated over what he saw as the gradual atrophy of the nationalist movement in Canada and the scheming of local UCC activists to undercut the growth of popular sympathy for the Banderivtsi, began urging him to vigorous promotion and propagation of the new, revolutionary nationalist movement. The line Frolick must take when addressing Ukrainian Canadian audiences, Shteppa advised, was that the Banderivtsi, rather than harming the nationalist movement by having broken away from it (as the Melnykivtsi claimed), were instead rejuvenating and revitalizing Ukrainian nationalism. Accordingly, the Banderivtsi deserved public support rather than criticism.[97] Convinced that the Ukrainian community in Canada would 'sink to the dogs' if it was not infused with a modern, nationalistic immigration, Shteppa, naturally enough, was delighted by the postwar influx of dynamic and patriotic individuals who tended to represent the younger element among the DPs. And his experience of these early arrivals suggested that most refugees were 'definitely Bandera-oriented.' It was crucial, he argued, to make certain that this 'valuable new material' was not lost to groups like the UNF, which he considered moribund. The easiest way to prevent that was to infiltrate existing national organizations and take control of them from within. That, Shteppa insisted in his many letters to Frolick, was a much easier and surer technique than setting up entirely new groups in Canada, for the latter strategy was time-consuming and would exhaust the movement's limited resources.[98]

Frolick disagreed, but only mildly, not wanting to offend an older man whom he admired and who might well prove a useful ally. In Frolick's view, the essential first step was the creation of a nationalistic Ukrainian Canadian newspaper which would keep resettling refugees and members of the Organization aware of what was happening in Europe, and of what was expected of them even now that they had gone out into the emigration. Such a press organ, perhaps under the editorial supervision of an experienced polemicist like Dontsov, Frolick speculated, might end up of such high intellectual and political standards that it would be above the comprehension of the average Ukrainian Canadian 'oldtimer.' But even apart from that, exactly that kind of newspaper was essential as a cement for the new emigration.[99] As Frolick told Shteppa, 'Many of our members find themselves in the lumber camps' of north-central Ontario. The only sure way of keeping them informed and, more important, involved in the movement, was to get 'our own' newspaper delivered directly and regularly to them, wherever they might be temporarily resettled, taking advantage of Canada's efficient postal system as a distribution network.[100] And Frolick also confirmed that the infrastructure of the Organization was already in place in Canada and had a number of good people at its disposition along with the funds necessary to get a newspaper established. Although Shteppa remained less than sure of the merits of starting anew, he conceded; as he wrote to Frolick, 'You decide, you're the 'boss' in fact and formally.'[101]

More illuminating was how this correspondence reflected the sometimes complementary, sometimes contradictory beliefs and hopes of two Ukrainian nationalists, one an interwar immigrant, the other Canadian-born, as the latter wrestled with the problems involved in constituting a nationalist network in Canada, and the former sought to help by offering counsel based on his years of experience as an Ukrainian Canadian activist representing an earlier generation.

Explaining that he felt there were only two people in North America with whom he could honestly consult, namely Frolick and Dontsov, Shteppa wrote that he wanted a chance to join in the ongoing insurgency in eastern Europe, the liberation struggle being waged to remove 'the great stone weight' that was squeezing life out of the 'body of Ukraine.' Referring directly to the Ukrainian poet Ivan Franko's allegorical poem *The Stonecutters*, Shteppa asked if Frolick could arrange passage for him overseas, where he could join the armed struggle: 'I wish,' his petition continued, 'to find death there and not here,' for dying in battle against Ukraine's oppressors was honourable and purposeful. In contrast, life in the emigration was deadening, for once a patriot was trapped outside his native land he was of little value to the movement. For Shteppa, the standard by which all true Ukrainians should be judged was clear: all that mattered was what they were doing to help free Ukraine.[102]

Frolick tried to dissuade Shteppa, at least for the time being, from his dream of joining the insurgents. The Organization, he confided, was not undertaking any transfer of 'its people' to countries behind the Iron Curtain, or vice versa. Experience had shown that most such attempts were tragically foiled. Better, Frolick wrote, to keep the Organization's people alive, whether in Ukraine or abroad, than to have them end up as corpses 'on the cordon.'[103] But do not despair, he advised Shteppa, for while it might be too risky as yet to attempt a return to the homeland, 'in just a matter of time' people would be needed for 'important work' in Canada and in Ukraine.

What did Frolick and his followers hope for? Nothing less than another war, one in whose wake, 'just like in 1941,' fresh opportunities for the Ukrainian national movement to organize an independent state would arise. As soon as this armed conflict between the Anglo-American powers and the Soviets broke out, their movement would 'be sending "task groups" to the East, whether or not the Americans and British agree or not.'[104] When that happened, Frolick promised, Shteppa could join one of these 'task groups.' But until that day, Shteppa and like-minded comrades would have to sit tight in Canada, and wait. After receiving more or less the same advice from Dontsov, Shteppa had little choice but to agree. He ended up dying in Canada, his hope of becoming an active participant in an armed Ukrainian national liberation movement left unrealized, a fate not untypical of that of many an exile.[105]

'In a Planned Way'

Frolick, as the OUNb's *rezident* for Canada, had an organized if modest nationalist network in place by the fall of 1948, one which had sufficient resources to set up *Ukrainian Echo* by the end of that year. Throughout this period he was in regular communication with the nationalist *provid*, or leadership) in Europe. He was able, therefore, to reply authoritatively to Shteppa when, in correspondence, the latter queried him about whether or not the Organization had provided for a 'planned resettlement' of nationalists throughout Canada.[106] Frolick replied quite candidly that in a few days he would be sending out instructions to all the OUNb's clandestine cells in Canada, directives which dealt with just this issue. He promised to forward a copy to Shteppa. Although that document apparently did not survive, Frolick's subsequent correspondence revealed that everything possible was being done to ensure that nationalist cadres were spread out 'in a planned way' across Canada, to ensure that the Banderivtsi would have some of their people in every centre where they might be able to work on behalf of the liberation movement. Definitely, he assured Shteppa, at least some 'of our people' would end up in the Windsor area.[107] It was on the basis of this planned distribution of Ukrainian nationalists throughout Canada that *Ukrainian Echo* built up its subscription lists. Eventually, the League for the Liberation of Ukraine and its affiliated women's and youth groups were also founded as the public manifestations of this new revolutionary nationalist movement in Canada.

Of course, Frolick did more than correspond with Shteppa. His duties included pulling together the resources and personnel needed to get *Ukrainian Echo* established as a going concern while keeping in touch with his superiors overseas. Simultaneously, he also helped newly resettled Ukrainian DPs cope with the many problems they were encountering in adjusting to Canadian conditions. The DPs often found themselves placed by government immigration officials in various contract jobs, where they were obliged legally to remain for one or more years, in communities often far removed from any other Ukrainians or refugees like themselves. These refugee immigrants were often bewildered about what they should be doing, particularly in terms of staying in touch with their comrades in the nationalist movement. As well, more often than not they found themselves meeting Ukrainian Canadians who described a confusing set of secular and religious organizations, none of which were at all familiar to the DPs. Whom could they trust? What groups should they join? Which Ukrainian Canadian institutions could they turn to for advice or support? The many dizzying choices facing these DPs often overwhelmed them.

The case of a Mr Kulyk, sent to Minnipuka, Ontario, to work for the Abitibi Power and Paper Company Limited, was rather typical of the plight of recently arrived Ukrainian DPs. On 3 August 1947 he wrote to Frolick in Toronto, explaining that he had received his address 'from Munich' – a signal that he was a member of the OUNb, a person who could be trusted and helped.[108] Kulyk described life in lumber camp

#29, where he and another 116 Ukrainians found themselves. They all felt 'a little lonely,' for not only was there no town nearby, but they had no clear instructions about what they should be doing, how they were to behave, or even, as Kulyk admitted, what they should be thinking about. At least their religious needs were attended to, for a Ukrainian priest had emigrated with them, although he had been forced to conceal his vocation. Certainly they were all busy working as lumberjacks. But they had a problem. As they were being transported to the camp by Canadian National Railways, they had met Ukrainian Canadians who were full of praise for something called the Ukrainian Canadian Committee. Supposedly this Committee, Kulyk wrote, had sent a great quantity of relief supplies to the very same refugee camps from which he and a number of his fellow DPs had just come. That was puzzling. For while, he recorded, 'among us there are people who come from many different *lagers* [camps], no one ever got even a handkerchief to blow one's nose in from them. So what's the truth? ... None of us ever even heard of this relief or got any of it.'[109]

Kulyk also pointed out that their lumber camp was being visited, from time to time, by agitators full of praise for communism, although none of these visiting Soviet sympathizers had actually 'ever known' life under Soviet rule. One such fellow, he wrote, had recently come from a nearby factory, singing the praises of Stalin and the Soviet system. He had left singing a different tune, after having listened to what Kulyk and his fellow workers had told him about their personal experiences of Soviet rule. The man had departed exclaiming that, until he had met these living witnesses to Soviet reality, he had never guessed 'what a swine' Stalin was.[110] The DPs were indeed becoming powerful witnesses against Stalinism and Soviet rule, precisely as the British had predicted and the Kremlin's men had feared.

A few weeks later Kulyk wrote again, this time to explain that he and his friends had organized twice-daily meetings and prayers. What they really needed most now was a blue and yellow Ukrainian national flag, which they intended to fly from a tall evergreen near their camp. That way, Kulyk declared, whoever came to visit them would know, from a distance, who they were and 'how to speak to us.' Starved for news about Ukrainian affairs, Kulyk also asked for advice about which newspapers his group should subscribe to, and whether they should join the UNF, which had recently sent a recruiter around. He added that the Federation's man had not had much luck, for he had tried to explain that there was no such thing as an OUN, adding that

no one had ever even heard of such a group in Canada.[111] The ignorance was somewhat reciprocal, for few if any of Kulyk's fellow refugee workers had ever heard of the UNF.

Kulyk had another urgent matter to raise with his chief. Within a few
days another two hundred or so Ukrainian workers would be arriving
at his camp. Kulyk wanted to know 'what he had to do,' particularly
what he should tell 'our people' was expected of them now that they
had arrived in Canada.

Unfortunately for the Organization, Frolick's limited financial
resources did not allow him much latitude in terms of helping the displaced persons who were being scattered around Ontario, often in
such remote lumber camps and mining settlements, far removed from
his home base in Toronto. Still, he did try to help, answering the mail
that came in and coping as best he could with their more serious questions. Meanwhile, he devoted most of his energies to getting *Ukrainian
Echo* published and edited, believing that, more than anything else, a
regular newspaper would tie this widely dispersed population of refugee immigrants together and keep them united until some more formal
infrastructure could be set up. In accomplishing even this much,
Frolick performed a valuable, perhaps even a crucial, role for the Organization. Not only did he help the DP immigrants adjust to their new
surroundings, but he gave them some assurance that they were not
entirely alone or forgotten in the 'New World.' That knowledge helped
build their confidence, eased the process of their adjustment to unfamiliar Canadian conditions, and husbanded their psychic and material
resources for the movement. As one of them would write near the end
of 1948, he and his comrades had been faced with 'many obstacles,' but
having *Ukrainian Echo* to read had left them feeling better, for it preserved their links with their own kind and kept their morale high.[112]

'Ghettoizing and Our First Thoughts'

Unquestionably, the formation of the League for the Liberation of
Ukraine, a deed announced publicly in Toronto on 1 May 1949, was
one of the axial points of Ukrainian Canadian history, similar in importance to the formation of the other national organizations and certainly
critical in so far as any understanding of the postwar immigration is
concerned. No other group set up by Ukrainian DPs and political refugees would ever come to have as large a membership, or as national a
field of operations, as the League. From its inception, however, it was

no more monolithic than any previously established Ukrainian Canadian group, in spite of many public misconceptions to the contrary. While those who joined the League tended to be members or supporters of the OUNb, adherents of the UHVR, or veterans of the UPA, its constituency was far from homogeneous. The League's first president was actually an interwar immigrant from Eastern Ukraine, Yakiv Nesterenko, unlike the majority of the League's members, who were Western Ukrainians and postwar refugee immigrants. There were also, from almost the first day of its existence, at least two major orientations among the League's leaders about what the nature and aims of their association, as an entity operating in Canada, should be. This became quite evident by the time the second League congress was held, in Toronto, in late December 1950.

The fundamental issue addressed at this meeting was the relationship between the League and its individual members and the established Ukrainian Canadian community, particularly as it was represented by the Ukrainian Canadian Committee. On the one hand there were those who rejected anything having to do with the UCC, arguing that since the League's membership consisted of persons who had only one purpose, which was to 'exist for Ukraine,' there was no value to be had from trying to reach an understanding with other Ukrainians in Canada, who seemed content to remain here. Besides, most 'newcomers' shared in the conviction that they would return home to Ukraine before long, that their exile would be – must be – little more than a brief interlude. There was no need, or time, they argued, to try to educate Ukrainian Canadians about the contemporary Ukrainian national liberation movement.[113] For advocates of this viewpoint, it was more important that the League support the creation of 'military cadres' to draw in the younger people of the DP immigration and prepare them for a return on short notice to the homeland. There they could participate in the war of liberation which many League leaders felt certain was imminent. And that struggle was certainly a more important goal than worrying over what Ukrainian Canadians were up to, or might be thinking.

On the other hand, there were those attending the congress who, while a minority, insisted that the League would gain nothing from 'ghettoizing' itself. More could be achieved, they reasoned, if the League instead accommodated to the existence of the UCC and even joined that 'umbrella' group. If the League did so, its members would have a chance of convincing Ukrainian Canadians about the legitimacy of their aspirations, which could serve to strengthen the material and moral bases they drew upon to provide assistance for the ongoing insurgency. As well, by working from within the UCC, apparently an officially recognized body in Canada, they might also be able to influence government policy. It was indisputably in the League's interest to try to steer Canadian government support in the direction of the Ukrainian national liberation movement. Supporters of this line had, of course, no notion of how little influence the UCC really had within government circles or how indisposed were those in External Affairs to their goal of independence for Ukraine.

The viewpoint of the more conciliatory faction did not prevail. The idea of approaching the UCC's national executive to discuss a compromise or a merger was also rejected. Yet a limited objective was achieved by the moderates, for they were able to get the League's name changed. After this congress it came to be known as the Canadian League for the Liberation of Ukraine, or the CLLU, the prefix 'Canadian' being deliberately adopted to signal to a wider public that the League's membership was involved in legitimate political activity rather than émigré politics. This name change fooled few in the Ukrainian Canadian community, and no one in Ottawa.

As for the issue of how to deal with the UCC and its constituent groups, this proved to be a persistent problem, for it was no more possible for the League's members to ignore existing Ukrainian Canadian organizations than it was for those organizations to ignore the League. Ironically, just as the interwar immigrants and the organizations they had created had been forced to reach an understanding with the Ukrainian groups established before then, so too the DPs now wrestled with a Ukrainian Canadian establishment which regarded them as novel, disruptive, and unnecessary. And so the issue of the CLLU's relationship with the UCC kept coming up, particularly during meetings of its national executive. In the minutes of that body this matter was debated vigorously several times between the spring and the early summer of 1951, one result being that, in June 1951, 'informal' talks of 'an unofficial character' were held among League representatives, the UCC's Monsignor Kushnir, and his executive director, Kochan.[114]

Despite these quiet talks, when the subject of some form of accommodation was again raised openly at the third national congress of the League, held in Toronto in late December 1951, those who had counselled compromise fared even less well than before. For, by then, the third UCC congress had been held, and the memory of the unpleasant débâcle experienced by League supporters was still fresh and rankling. Some of the very same men who had been driven out of the Winnipeg congress hall were senior members of the CLLU. That made their opposition to the UCC all the more telling. And so the hardliners won the day. Even if many League members were, by 1951, prepared to agree that the UCC had relevance for Ukrainian Canadians, and that there was no point in trying to tear down a body which had proved its utility in Canada, they also agreed that the Winnipeg-based UCC was of little value to them. And while some boasted that they could easily penetrate the Committee and disrupt it from within, no such effort was deemed appropriate or necessary. Their 'first thoughts,' delegates to this League congress agreed, should instead be directed towards Ukraine. As for working out some kind of arrangement with the Ukrainian Canadians, there was little point in wasting time or effort on such negotiations. After all, these more conservative spokesmen added, all the UCC's men really wanted to do was preserve the prewar status quo of organized Ukrainian Canadian society, and that left no room whatsoever for the existence, much less the growth, of their League.

Having no apparent or at least immediate stake in helping the UCC prosper, the League's leaders chose to ignore it, responding only when they felt provoked. What helped clinch their argument against any reconciliation with the UCC was that the UCC's organizers were, reportedly, travelling around the country portraying the League's members as political 'extremists,' and not only within Ukrainian Canadian circles. As one delegate to the League's congress underscored, most Canadians 'look askance at the preoccupation [of immigrants] with European homelands.' The UCC's anti-League propaganda, therefore, was potentially very harmful to the revolutionary nationalists' immediate and long-term interests.[115] Better not to have anything to do with as inimical an organization as the UCC.

'All Attention to Freeing Ukraine'

Another phenomenon worried delegates at this third League congress. Already, their ranks were being decimated by what was described as an increasing 'Canadianization' of their membership, a development which was allegedly not only sapping the Organization's ranks but also retarding membership drives and alienating the youth, who were not joining CYM or the League in sufficient numbers. To combat this growing lack of interest in their work, particularly among the young, the League considered the suggestion that it begin publishing an English-language newspaper or magazine. A publication of that sort could serve two purposes: it would inform Canadian-born Ukrainians who could no longer read their native language about contemporary Ukraine, and it would do likewise for a wider Canadian audience. This suggestion, however, was not actually taken up until 1977, when an English-language version of *Ukrainian Echo* first began appearing as a supplement to the parent newspaper, under the editorial supervision of Andrij Bandera, the son of the OUNb's assassinated leader, Stepan Bandera.

Remarkably, those who had earlier argued for a more accomodating line with respect to the UCC were not easily put off. Throughout 1952 they tried, again, to advance the notion that the League would be better off as a constituent organization under the 'umbrella' of the Committee, certainly better positioned there than they would be as a group working outside that body. By remaining uninvolved in the UCC's affairs, they argued, the CLLU ended up unaccepted and unrecognized by the Canadian government and public alike. At a minimum, they pleaded, individual League members should be encouraged to join groups like the Brotherhood of Ukrainian Catholics, which was represented on the national executive of the UCC. By working from within such accepted groups the nationalists could at least hope to introduce League ideas and plans into the Ukrainian Canadian domain.[116]

Various leading UCC figures were aware of this debate in the League, although there seems to have been little desire on their part to pave the way for peaceful coexistence or compromise. Others seemed intent on goading the League. Thus, instead of staying formally neutral in terms of supporting one or another political movement outside Canada, the UCC's national executive officially announced that it recognized UNRada, the Ukrainian National Council, as the *only* authoritative body representing Ukraine in the international arena. This conscious slighting of the UHVR, the Supreme Ukrainian Liberation Council, supported by the Banderivtsi was nothing if not provocative. The UCC's decision was duly noted by the League's national executive in the minutes of a meeting held on 5–7 December 1952. Predictably incensed, the League subsequently broke off all discussion about becoming a member group of the UCC.[117] Belonging to the UCC was not 'the essence of our existence,' as the nationalist leadership proclaimed to delegates attending their fourth League congress. Supporting the UHVR, on the other hand, was an essential plank in the national liberation movement's platform, one that which could not be sacrificed simply to take up a seat in the UCC's executive. 'All attention' must be directed to 'freeing Ukraine,' even if that took another twenty to thirty years of concerted effort. And if this liberation struggle was not brought to a triumphant success within that time span, then the League's members would have to ensure that they raised their offspring in a spirit of self-sacrifice, so that the next generation would carry on with the fight their parents had begun.

A prominent member of the League, a former political prisoner and OUN member from the early 1930s who had been sent specifically to Canada in 1950 to work for the Organization, explained how his peers thought of the League and why they felt that reconstituting a nationalist organization was critical.

> Our movement was not directed against Canada in any way. It existed so that, at any moment, we would be ready to help liberate Ukraine, if the right situation arose ... Others capitulated, compromised, but we didn't, for if we had, all would be lost ... We had to keep the spark alive, husband it ... propagate it, and find allies among the nations of the world, particularly those threatened by Russian imperialism ... We did a great service to Canada by alerting its people to the Soviet threat ... Our people are of high moral standards, honest, hardworking, and we did, truthfully, stand on guard for Canada by carrying on with our fight against Moscow.[118]

As for the UCC, and the clique running it under Kochan's direction, delegates to the League congress were told this cabal was attempting to impose monopolistic control over Ukrainian life in Canada. That was simply unacceptable.[119]

Even when, by summertime 1954, there were indications from within the UCC that some of its executive members wanted to see the League brought into the Ukrainian Canadian fold, the notion of a merger was rejected decisively by the League's leadership: 'We are not trying to build Ukraine in Canada,' the League's president, Dr Roman Malaschuk, reminded his membership. 'We are trying to do everything possible to help liberate the homeland and thus make [our] own return there possible. Thoughts about Canada becoming like Switzerland are fantasies.'[120] There was really no need or particular value in being a part of Ukrainian Canadian society. These displaced persons wanted to relocate themselves in Ukraine, not root themsleves in Canadian soil.

'Out of Touch'

So matters would remain for nearly a decade. The CLLU did not formally join the UCC until the spring of 1959.[121] By then most of its members had spent over ten years in Canada, a decade during which they had been unhappy witnesses, albeit from a distance, of the suppression of the insurgency they had supported. Many had also been disabused of the notion that the supposedly anti-Soviet West was supportive of their struggle for freedom. Despite their efforts to publicize the Ukrainian independence movement and secure aid and sympathy for it from the Anglo-American powers, their struggle was, at best, exploited for Western intelligence and propaganda purposes, and otherwise abandoned, sometimes betrayed. The nationalists were left nonplussed and discouraged, fewer and fewer having the fortitude to persist when their hopes of freedom for Ukraine were treated with such overwhelming apathy and even antipathy on the part of some Ukrainian Canadians, the Canadian public in general, and the Anglo-American governments in particular. Since neither the UHVR nor UNRada retained much of its political relevance in the late 1950s, the former eliminated by force of arms, the latter fading into émigré pomposity and irrelevance, one of the principal issues which had kept the League and the UCC at loggerheads also disappeared. Although neither the League nor the UCC formally renounced its respective commitment, both, for reasons of tactics and tact, quietly let the issue drop.

This was duly noted by long-term observers of the Ukrainian Canadian scene. Dr Kaye summarized the two antagonistic camps by reporting that adherents of the League were 'nationalistically-minded young immigrants with fresh memories of happenings in Europe' who found it difficult to 'fit' into existing Ukrainian Canadian society. For them that society was 'too "Canadianized," out of touch with European affairs, not enough interested in the active fight for the independence of Ukraine.'[122] Supporters of the UCC, as Kaye had noted earlier, insisted that the League's people had to realize that their organization must first cease being 'an alien body' in Canada in order to gain acceptance from Ukrainian Canadians. The League, Ukrainian Canadians argued, was far too 'conspiratorial'; it had to adapt to the 'Canadian' and 'democratic' characteristics they claimed the UCC exemplified if

League members wanted to occupy a place in Ukrainian Canadian society.[123]

It may appear naïve in hindsight for Ukrainian Canadians to have asked recently resettled DPs to give up behaviour and attitudes they had been forced to adopt in order to survive the exigencies of wartime and the refugee experience. Doing so, for many of these political refugees, would have represented giving up their cause, abandoning those with whom they had associated from their days in the refugee camps or even before, breaking ties painstakingly rebuilt in Canada. Equally, however, it was unrealistic for those who supported the CLLU to expect that the Ukrainian Canadians among whom they now found themselves would, or could, break out of the mould into which their collective experience as Ukrainians in Canada had cast them. As an ethnic minority, they had learned the hard way that those who remained active in the organized Ukrainian Canadian community here would be wise to show caution in what they did or did not do as Ukrainians in Canada. For Ukrainian Canadians the assertive, and sometimes aggressive, nationalism of many DPs, particularly that of the Banderivtsi, was unacceptable, indeed unwelcome. For them being a Ukrainian in Canada carried with it an understanding that, should they appear to have 'divided loyalties' of any kind, they would risk calling down upon themselves the wrath of the state. Experience had taught them to avoid, scrupulously, the many bitter experiences of the past.

And so two distinctly Ukrainian yet different communities encountered each other. Very similar in terms of cultural, regional, and religious backgrounds, they never fully integrated. Indeed, as a result of their inability to arrive at a rapprochement, pre-existing cleavages within the Ukrainian population of Canada were exacerbated, and entirely novel ones appeared. The divisiveness which had so characterized Ukrainian Canadian society before the war remained. Any semblance of Ukrainians in Canada being united under the UCC 'umbrella' receded. Both the Committee and the League would compete within the forum of organized Ukrainian Canadian society, each striving to achieve predominance, all the while courting the general public and Ottawa in the vain hope that recognition would secure their status in Canada and perhaps prove useful to the Ukrainian cause as a whole. In the end, neither would succeed.

The Committee was quickest off the mark in trying to squelch its new-found opposition. On 11 September 1950 it forwarded a letter to

Lester B. Pearson of External Affairs, including an UNRada memorandum on the issue of Ukrainian independence. The covering letter described this Council as a 'parliament in exile,' and indicated that the UCC recognized it as the 'only authoritative and legal representative of the Ukrainian nation.' It was also the sole body which could expect to receive Ukrainian Canadian 'moral and material support.'[124] As for the Banderivtsi, their League, and the affiliated ABN, the UCC's executive made it plain to Pearson that it had nothing to do with them, a point further underscored in a letter to the editor of the *Winnipeg Free Press* published in February of that year. The ABN, according to the UCC's view of things, had 'no right to act for Ukrainians,' since it represented only a 'small extremist political organization.'[125]

This in-fighting did not go unnoticed, or unremarked, within government offices. Some civil servants saw in this factionalism an opportunity for dealing, once and for all, with this troublesome ethnic group's political demands, especially when it came to the issue of Ukrainian independence. These mandarins, and the bureaucrats who served them, plotted accordingly. Which Ukrainian faction in Canada ended up doing the most harm or good, and to what cause, remain open questions, even in the wake of Ukraine's reasserted independence.

9 'The Vexed Ukrainian Question': Curbing Ukrainian Nationalism in the Postwar World

'The Final Solution'

Well before the war's end British Foreign Office officials reviewed the 'minorities problem' in Europe and concluded that the continued existence of such separatist and irredentist elements was 'dangerous to peace.'[1] Contemplating their options for dealing with the predictable difficulties which would arise once a peace settlement was reached, the British decided that, no matter how 'drastic' the peace terms might be, minorities would remain who could not easily 'be gotten rid of.' They judged, therefore, that only large-scale population transfers would provide what was termed – rather ominously, to modern ears – as the 'final solution' to the 'minorities problem.'[2] At the very most, all the British were prepared to commit themselves to were vague assurances about protecting the human rights of such national minorities.[3] But it was decided that the British government would not pledge itself to the recognition or defence of the right to national self-determination of such minority groups, for that policy seemed always to end up entangling them in exceedingly complex and tendentious issues. Thus, commenting on an article on the postwar minorities issue written by the Czechoslovakian leader, Dr Edvard Benes, published in the January 1942 issue of *Foreign Affairs*, Whitehall's Philip Nichols noted that while it was acceptable for members of minorities to preserve their *personal* nationality' they should not be encouraged to retain their *political* nationality' given the difficulties this inevitably introduced into relations between nations.[4]

Turning to specific minority problems, and particularly to that of Ukrainians in Poland, Frank Savery, the polonophile who even before the war had exhibited a distinct dislike for the Ukrainian national movement, prepared a series of suggestions about how this issue might be resolved. His proposals boded ill for the Ukrainians. Reminding his readers that Stalin had once said to the Polish general Wladyslaw Sikorski that the Soviet Union and Poland would have to take 'common measures' to put a stop to the Ukrainian 'nuisance,' Savery observed that the Soviets now had 'a whole continent in which to execute, starve or exploit those who impede his policy.' Poland, of course, had no Siberia at its disposal and was, moreover, inhibited from taking brutal measures against its Ukrainian minority because, Savery argued, it was a state whose politics were underpinned by moral principles 'like our own.' While Stalin, if he so wished, could get rid of anyone or any minority, or could command settlers by the thousands to move into Ukraine and change its ethnic character, the Poles would somehow have to come to terms with their Ukrainians.[5] That, of course, left Poland with quite a problem for, in Savery's mind, the Ukrainians were unlikely suddenly to become 'reliable citizens.' The simple fact that they would 'certainly' continue to interest themselves in the fate of their fellow Ukrainians outside Poland would only lead to ongoing trouble between Poland and the USSR. Though Savery claimed to feel 'profoundly sorry' for the Ukrainians, he decided the only way to circumvent future regional tensions was by removing all Ukrainians from the Eastern Galician territory, which he assigned exclusively to the Poles. As for the Ukrainian inhabitants of those lands, they should be sent to the USSR: 'The Ukrainian population of Poland must be left so small that not even the morbidly sensitive Bolsheviks will regard it as a potential danger.'[6] Summarizing his prescription with a rather dramatic flourish, Savery observed that no viable solution to Poland's Ukrainian minority problem existed short of this proposed 'exchange of population on a large scale,' at least none which would be satisfactory for Poland. But, he conceded, sending Ukrainians off to 'the tender mercies' of the Soviets did pose a certain moral dilemma: 'If they do not want to go, shall we and the Poles be able to square it with our consciences to put compulsion on them and to drive them out of Europe and into Asia?'[7]

When Savery composed his memorandum, he probably did so thinking that the Polish government-in-exile, the 'London Government,' would be responsible for dealing with the postwar Ukrainian minority question. As matters turned out, it was the 'Lublin Government,' umbilically tied to the Soviets, which dealt with this Ukrainian minority. They resolved their problem much as Savery would have liked, and in a manner consistent with their own understanding of Polish and Soviet state interests. A large-scale, often forcible transfer of Ukrainians to Soviet-controlled territories was authorized, a process complemented by the return of Poles who had found themselves on the Soviet Ukrainian side of the Curzon line. This population transfer went hand in hand with counter-insurgency measures instituted by the Polish, Czechoslovak, and Soviet governments against the Ukrainian Insurgent Army, anti-guerilla operations which reached their crescendo with the initiation of 'Operation Vistula' in the fall of 1947. According to a British embassy report, some 484,000 Ukrainians had been expelled under some form of duress from Poland to the USSR by the early spring of that year.[8] A remaining Ukrainian community of some seventy-four thousand people was deported to the 'Western Territories' ceded to Poland at Germany's expense, land granted in compensation for the Ukrainian ethnographic territories Poland had previously ruled over in Eastern Galicia, which were reincorporated into Soviet Ukraine at the war's end. No one in the West seems to have paused to ponder the bitter irony of Stalin being rewarded with the same territory he had been given once before, by his previous ally, Adolf Hitler.

Polish families also suffered relocation, particularly those 'known for their political hostility to the Government.'[9] Undeniably, however, the Ukrainians were hardest done by, for, unlike their Polish fellow sufferers, the Ukrainian deportees were experiencing a systematic and deliberate attempt aimed at the utter eradication of their community structures and group cohesion. The deported Ukrainians were intentionally scattered throughout the 'Western Territories' of Poland in order to prevent their reconsolidation as a viable ethnic community. Subsequently, every attempt was made to assimilate them into the Polish population, willingly or not. At the same time Polish officials in western Europe made it clear they were not interested in helping Ukrainian refugees, even those who were bona fide Polish citizens, return to Poland. Ukrainians were not wanted. As R. Crawford of the Control Commission for Germany and Austria told C.J. Edmonds of the Refugee Department, the Polish Repatriation Missions had been instructed recently by Warsaw 'not to send back Polish Ukrainian DPs' since 'they do not want a Ukrainian Minority in Poland.'[10] This decision, perhaps more than any other except for the obvious determination of many DPs not to return to countries under communist domination, was responsible for leaving almost a quarter of a million Ukrainians stranded in the refugee camps of western Europe. Whereas the Anglo-American powers had clearly demonstrated their willingness to repatriate 'Soviet citizens' to the USSR, in accord with or against those refugees' wishes, Washington and London were forced by their own legalistic interpretation of citizenship into the quandary of being consistent. They had no legal grounds for the repatriation of Ukrainians bearing legitimate Polish citizenship papers to the Soviet Union. Such persons were, after all, legally Polish and not Soviet citizens. But after the Polish government had made it clear that it had no intention of accepting these Ukrainian refugees, there was nowhere left in the East for them to go. A large Ukrainian refugee population, one which could not be readily disposed of, was left in the DP camps of western Europe, awaiting resettlement somewhere else. But where?

'Too Hot to Touch'

Continuing Ukrainian resistance to population expulsions to the USSR and to forcible transfers within Poland were, not surprisingly, of interest to the Anglo-American governments. As the British Foreign Office's annual report on Poland for 1946 indicated, 'Ukrainian bands' were seriously harassing the authorities in the southeast. What made the situation especially grave was that these Ukrainian guerrillas 'frequently collaborated' with anti-communist 'Polish bands.'[11] In late May 1947 the British embassy in Warsaw noted that the Polish government's actions against these Ukrainian insurgents had not achieved much over the 'past two years,' even though large units of regular army troops and police and internal security forces, aided by Soviet and Czechoslovakian units, had been deployed.[12] While in its annual report for 1947 Whitehall suggested that, inside Poland, the 'Ukrainian Question' was 'at an end,' before the end of 1948 its observers had to rethink that conclusion, for there were new sightings which suggested an *increase* in the fighting between Ukrainian insurgents and East Bloc forces. Indeed, contradictory intelligence reports about the extent of the insurgency kept flowing into London until the fall of 1950. Most suggested that there was still 'heavy fighting' taking place.[13] Earlier analyses, which had claimed that by 1947 the UPA had been made extinct, were obviously and seriously flawed. And so, while there may have been British analysts who believed that mass deportations and military measures would shortly resolve the 'vexed Ukrainian Question' – one which they remembered had been so deeply troubling to international affairs in the interwar period – others realized that even if the Ukrainian problem became strictly 'an internal affair of the Soviet Union,' Ukrainian nationalism was far from being a spent force. They therefore determined it would be in Britain's national interests to continue monitoring Ukrainian affairs, not only in eastern Europe but in the Ukrainian emigration as well.[14]

Precisely when those responsible for formulating and guiding Anglo-American statecraft decided that the Ukrainian national liberation movement might be useful for their own purposes is hard to fix. Until the war's end they were certainly reluctant to appear too attentive, lest 'our interest be misunderstood' by the Soviets. Still, as the British embassy in Moscow made clear to the Foreign Office, its officers would 'keep [their] ears cocked' and let Whitehall know of any important developments.[15] And, in fact, a number of detailed reports concerning Ukrainian nationalism, in some cases based on captured German documents, were prepared and forwarded to the Foreign Office throughout the immediate postwar period.[16] American experts were likewise intrigued by the nature, scale, and persistence of the Ukrainian liberation movement's struggle.[17] While analysts with the U.S. Office of Strategic Services, the forerunner of the CIA, concluded, in the early spring of 1948, that the Ukrainian guerilla bands would probably be 'exterminated in the near future,' they also observed that these insurgents had remained active for a lot longer than anyone had predicted: 'Their continued survival suggests that the local population furnished them at least with food despite near-famine conditions in 1945 and it is evident that only people who strongly hate the Soviet way of life would have supported what many of them undoubtedly realize is a lost cause.'[18]

Official Anglo-American attitudes apparently changed, somewhat in favour of the Ukrainians, during the summer and fall of 1948, or perhaps even before then, as various foreign service and intelligence officers within the American, British, and, later, Canadian governments began ruminating over what their governments should do in the event that an independent Ukrainian state came into being in the aftermath of another European war. In a 'top secret' paper, circulated with a U.S. National Security Council report entitled 'Appraisal of the Degree and Character of Military Preparedness Required by the World Situation,' it was concluded that a policy of 'outward neutrality' was best, as long as American interests, military or otherwise, were not immediately affected. However, should an independent Ukraine somehow arise, 'we should be careful not to place ourselves in a position of open opposition ... which would cause us to lose permanently the sympathy of [the Ukrainians]. On the other hand, we should not commit ourselves in their support to a line of action which in the long run could probably be maintained only with our military assistance.'[19] Even though they were unwilling, politically or militarily, to commit themselves to the liberation of Ukraine, as this memorandum made explicit, discussions of precisely this subject were still kept very secret in Whitehall and Foggy Bottom.[20] At best all these Western governments were prepared to do, or so British analysts concluded, was direct just enough covert support to the Ukrainians to make them a useful source of intelligence.[21] In this reluctance to pledge themselves to aid for the Ukrainian national liberation movement the British were not markedly different from their American counterparts, who concluded, by the winter of 1949, that 'at this stage' they did not propose 'either to play up, or to discourage, Ukrainian separatist feeling.'[22] Use them, became the policy – just don't get caught. That, in effect, was the sum of Anglo-American acumen on this subject.

When Yaroslav Stetsko, the leader of the Anti-Bolshevik Bloc of Nations, presented information to the British about forced labour camps in the USSR in August 1949, the Foreign Office's C.R.A. Rae was quite willing to make use of it, since the British had determined that the 'Bandera group' was the only one which could realistically claim to be directing partisan activity behind the Iron Curtain. Presumably, this meant the Banderivtsi could also be a valuable source of information.[23] But, Rae minuted, only 'unofficial contacts' with ABN representatives were permissible, and only if these could be arranged 'with discretion.'[24] In being cautious he echoed the sentiments of his colleague R.M.A. Hankey, although Hankey added that, even if 'hitherto [we have] steered clear of ABN because it is a frankly subversive organization,' which made it 'too hot to touch,' the need to stay aloof was, frankly, 'a pity.'[25]

It seems that for the most part the Anglo-American powers kept their political distance and material aid away from the Ukrainian liberation movement, with the exception of extracting titbits of raw intelligence and, occasionally, using the movement for secret, para-military intelligence-gathering missions behind the Iron Curtain.[26] This period may have lasted into the early 1950s, although by mid-January 1951 the British view was that the strength of the resistance movement was finally waning. By that time doubts were also being raised within Whitehall about whether the 'disintegration of the Soviet Union on ethnic lines in the event of war' should even be considered a desirable or a 'proper objective' of British foreign policy.[27] It was decided finally that the ABN's pronouncements should not be taken too seriously – the counsel of the Foreign Office's Richard Faber – although, admittedly, the ABN did represent a potential force which 'should not be underrated; and it may one day assume a practical importance for us which at present it largely lacks.'[28]

'What the Devil?!'

When Canada's civil servants and gatekeepers somewhat reluctantly allowed for an immigration of Ukrainian and other east European displaced persons into the country, they did so more for economic and political reasons than as an expression of humanitarian goodwill. They also had certain expectations about the role these militantly anti-communist and anti-Soviet political refugees would play in undermining the influence of the Ukrainian Canadian Left.[29] Their presumption was well founded, and they were indeed well served, for shortly after the displaced persons began arriving in the cities and industrial centres of Canada, these 'newcomers' actively challenged pro-Soviet groups like the Association of United Ukrainian Canadians. In Toronto, for example, the *Globe and Mail* reported physical violence in Bathurst Street's Alexandra Park between DPs and unidentified 'citizens' – the latter in fact being members of the Ukrainian Labour Temple situated across the road, at 300 Bathurst Street.[30] Uninformed or perhaps biased as the coverage of this particular event was (and its 'spin' was protested by various Ukrainian Canadian organizations), what the article did was reveal the intensity of the hatred between Ukrainian nationalists and communists.[31]

Several months later, violence between DPs and the Ukrainian Canadian Left was again in the news, although this time it had erupted at the AUUC's temple in Winnipeg. Bill Kardash, a member of the Communist Party of Canada and a Ukrainian Canadian veteran of the Spanish Civil War, reported to the *Winnipeg Free Press* that a peaceful assembly had been disrupted violently by extremists from among the newly resettled refugees.[32] Retorting, another Ukrainian Canadian, S. Skolbak, reminded this newspaper's readers that in 1933 communists like Kardash had formed their own 'shock brigade,' which they had used to terrorize the non-communist Ukrainian community. By way of example, he recalled a raid mounted by the Left against the Ukrainian Reading Hall at Flora and Mackenzie Streets, on Sunday, July 16. He concluded that while the AUUC might claim to be nothing more than a cultural and educational association, it was actually a 'political front organization of the Communist Party.' Men like Kardash and his fellow travellers, Skolbak pointedly declared, were loyal not to Canada but only 'to the Kremlin.' It would be better, he chided, if they took heed of the old Ukrainian saying which advised people not to go out into the hot sun with their heads smeared in butter, for if they did so they would only find their lies melting in the glare of honest scrutiny.[33]

These fitful incidents of open warfare between the pro-Soviets and nationalists within the Ukrainian community in Canada – similar disturbances were reported in Sudbury, Kingston, Vancouver, and Timmins, to list but a few[34] – reached their culmination on 8 October 1950, with the bombing of the Ukrainian Labour Temple at 300 Bathurst Street in Toronto. At approximately 9:00 p.m. on that Sunday an explosion, which did considerable damage to an outside wall on the south side of the building, interrupted a children's concert taking place inside the hall. Although no one was hurt the detonation was of sufficient force to frighten badly those attending. And the apparent intention of this action, a poignant demonstration of what might happen to those affiliated with the Ukrainian Canadian Left, could not have been more intimidating.

Canadian public reaction was swift and condemnatory, and rightly so. But, as has so often happened when poorly informed reporters have taken to writing about Ukrainian Canadian affairs, the conclusions leapt to in the mainstream media were based more on innuendo and rumour than factual evidence. On 10 October, Allan McPhee, speaking on CBC radio, reported the story as if it were an established fact that the persons responsible for the bombing were 'members of an SS Division.' His colleague Gordon Sinclair was no less unrestrained, making use of his airtime on CFRB radio to denounce those who he claimed were bringing their foreign quarrels with them to Canada: 'Fascists, Leftwingers, Reds, Rightwingers ... What the devil?! Why don't you leave us alone in Canada?'[35]

Official action was taken on 13 October 1950, when the acting chief constable of the metropolitan police, M. Mulholland, announced a fifteen-hundred-dollar reward for information leading to the arrest of those responsible.[36] No one was ever charged, the reward money remained unclaimed, and no evidence ever emerged to expose the perpetrators. For the AUUC and its supporters, however, there was never any doubt who was responsible – namely, Ukrainian nationalists who had recently immigrated to Canada along with other displaced persons.[37]

Other Ukrainian Canadians had a different explanation. One observer of the Ukrainian Canadian Left suggested that they were themselves responsible for the blast – 'a large and stinking rat' from within the labour temple had planted the explosive, hoping that the inevitable public outcry would alienate Canadian public sympathy for the refugees. The bombing was, in this view, nothing more than a 'good way of preventing [the DPs'] admittance to Canada.'[38]

Whether this incident was a 'Communist conspiracy' aimed at discrediting the DPs, or the act of a particularly militant individual or group of nationalists, was never and cannot now be determined. What is clear, however, is that this dramatic and frightening event had a debilitating impact on the Ukrainian Canadian Left. Suddenly, members of the AUUC and Worker's Benevolent Association found themselves, in effect, under siege. Many came to believe they were the targets of determined and ruthless men, that their continued involvement in the groups of the Left might well endanger life and limb. They also grew increasingly worried about the RCMP, which, allegedly, was collaborating with the Ukrainian nationalists, sheltering them from exposure. Participating in AUUC-sponsored functions, even outwardly cultural or social events, rather abruptly became less attractive. This fear of falling prey to terrorism was coupled with a growing awareness of public hostility to individuals or groups in any way associated with communism – the Cold War had dawned. So it is little wonder that many former members of the AUUC began playing down their affiliation with that organization, or tried representing it as nothing more than a cultural group. Large numbers quit altogether, and the AUUC entered a period of protracted decline, one which was never arrested. Today its small membership represents an ever dwindling and aging relic of what was once a major Ukrainian Canadian organization of national scope and relevance, however misdirected.

If it was the government's intention to utilize the in-migrating Ukrainian DPs for 'countering communist influence among foreign-born Canadians,' then Ottawa's designs succeeded. Even if the vast majority of the Ukrainian and other east European refugee immigrants had nothing to do with such attacks or intimidation and could not be held responsible for them, their simple presence in the country and the emerging strength of their militantly nationalistic organizations and press brought genuine trepidation to the rank and file of the Ukrainian Canadian Left.[39] Curiously, the government did not, on this occasion, intervene in Ukrainian Canadian affairs, in effect allowing the nationalists a chance to emasculate their opponents. By doing so these 'newcomers' debilitated that element within Ukrainian Canadian society which had long represented nothing but trouble for the authorities. Ottawa may not have been directly involved in exploiting one Ukrainian faction against another, but the nation's managers and policemen could not have been displeased at the outcome.

'The Line We Shall Have to Hold'

Whether they planned for it or merely accepted as a given that this postwar DP immigration would have an enfeebling impact on the Left, Ottawa's men were not at all pleased with the other outcome of this new immigration – namely, the vitality with which the 'newcomers' set up their own organizations in Canada, groups which essentially traced their roots and purpose to an eastern European homeland. Just after the bombing of the AUUC labour temple, Dr Kaye wrote to Professor Kirkconnell: 'I personally do not consider the propagation in Canada of European group politics and hatreds a wholesome activity. It only diverts the attention of new-Canadians from Canadian problems [and] retards their acculturation.'[40]

Kaye would have let his colleagues in Ottawa know that this was his view. And he would have found that other bureaucrats concurred. For what Canadian government officials wanted, at least at first, was to get Ukrainian immigrants to enter into Canadian life rather than concern themselves with the formation of committees or groups intended 'to perpetuate ... the political life of the countries from which they come.'

By the early spring of 1951, if not before, they began to reconsider that notion, at least partially. So had their British counterparts. What spurred this rethinking was an American policy statement, copied to External Affairs from London on 16 March 1951, which suggested, rather floridly, that 'every effort' should be made 'to preserve' from among this Ukrainian political emigration its 'human resource of potential leadership against the days of liberation.'[41] Ukrainian nationalists had now become assets in the war planning of the West, for use behind and in front of the Iron Curtain. Canadian government circles therefore reconsidered their policy on émigré organizations in the early months of 1951. Since these deliberations, and the conclusions reached, would have more than a little influence on Ottawa's dealings with Ukrainians in Canada well into the postwar period, they deserve particular attention.

Although A.F. Broadbridge of the European Division at External Affairs expressed the view that, as of early 1951, émigré-based groups were still 'not very active' in Canada, he observed that various groups of this type were being formed and that some had even begun to approach External Affairs asking for an indication about how the Canadian government regarded them and their activities. Broadbridge added that 'in recent months' all the Western democracies had become 'increasingly aware' of such émigré organizations. Most could be characterized as having three basic purposes: '(1) to render assistance to refugees from Communist-dominated countries; (2) to condemn the present Communist regime in their homelands; and, in some cases, (3) to sponsor liberation movements in territories long consolidated under Russian rule.'[42]

What should be the Canadian government's policy towards such groups? Broadbridge registered three main considerations. First, it was already general government policy to avoid giving them 'any official encouragement' because 'the formation of European émigré organizations in this country' could 'and probably would run counter to our citizenship policy of attempting to assimilate immigrants into our democratic life.'[43] Broadbridge asserted that if these groups were given recognition, or any kind of sanction for their activities, then their leaders would likely 'direct the energies of their fellow-citizens into channels which [would] to some extent keep them apart from normal Canadian activities.'[44] Second, any such émigré groups, if granted official recognition, might insist on being considered bona fide governments-in-exile, a status which conferred far too much importance on them, especially at a time when they had yet to prove their utility to the West. Third, it would be most difficult to ensure that any émigré group, even if given official backing, would act in a 'responsible manner' – in other words, in a way which would not end up 'embarrassing the host government.'[45]

Broadbridge therefore advised that whenever the representatives of any émigré group approached the government, it would be better if the officials meeting with such petitioners told them that in Canada they were free to do whatever they liked, as long as they did not contravene the laws of the land. But 'no hint' of anything which might even 'in the slightest way be interpreted as official approval' should be construed.[46] Be polite, listen, but remain stolidly noncommittal, Broadbridge counselled – good advice, which was generally taken.

This did not mean that the government's men would not be interested in what these associations were up to, or in what intelligence information they might, from time to time, be able to provide. Any 'unofficial reports' émigré groups submitted should be accepted, said Broadbridge, and forwarded to the proper officials. This had the double advantage of keeping open a source of potentially useful intelligence and allowing the government to keep tabs on the comings and goings of the émigré groups. And, if an occasion should arise 'when their usefulness could be demonstrated,' then at that juncture they could 'be directed into the appropriate channels.' Two such purposes suggested themselves to Broadbridge. Emigré formations could be used for 'counteracting Communist influence among foreign-born Canadians or recent emigres,' and 'in rare cases, under the aegis of the Canadian Government, of conducting psychological warfare abroad.'[47]

These points were repeated more succinctly in another memorandum prepared by J.A. McCordick, of a special intelligence unit at External Affairs, known as the Defence Liaison group. Indicative of the serious attention being given to how the government should treat with émigré groups in Canada is the fact that this memorandum ended up on the desk of Jules Léger, then under-secretary of state for external affairs.[48] The guidelines proposed became an accepted credo within the highest circles of the Canadian government and apparently remained so for many decades thereafter.

While officials in External Affairs wrestled with the larger issues involved with granting or not granting recognition to the émigré political groups being formed within many of the east European communities established in Canada, they also had to cope with various memoranda being forwarded to their attention. These came from newly established groups like the League for the Liberation of Ukraine and also from better-known organizations like the UCC. They all clamoured for government recognition, claiming for themselves the exclusive right to represent Ukrainians in Canada and even their compatriots in Ukraine. In the early fall of 1950, for example, the UCC not only staked out a claim for the Ukrainian National Council as the sole and true voice of the Ukrainian nation in the diaspora, but implicitly asked for official recognition of itself as UNRada's proxy in Canada.[49]

Not wanting to recognize the Council as any more legitimate or representative than the Supreme Ukrainian Liberation Council championed by the Banderivtsi, and being particularly disinclined to give the UCC any grounds for false pretensions about its own status, Ottawa's decision-makers simply ignored this petition.

A few months later, another group of senior government and RCMP officials, meeting to discuss what steps should be taken to dispose of confiscated or sold ULFTA labour temples impounded during the war, went even further. This group concluded that, given the particular delicacy of the 'Ukrainian Question' at home and abroad, the Canadian government 'should not show favour towards either group,' meaning the UCC or its rival, the Association of United Ukrainian Canadians.[50] Whether of the Centre, Left, or Right, it seems, Ukrainian Canadian groups could not expect to find favour, much less official approval or recognition, in Ottawa. Having identified and organized themselves as Ukrainians in Canada, members of this minority were perceived as having opted – and the reasons for their doing so were never entirely appreciated by Anglo-Canadians – to be different and apart. Since these hyphenated Canadians therefore seemed unwilling to be fully integrated into Canadian society (the assumption being that they could have if they had wanted to), they were considered suspect. Faced with such an unassimilated minority, those in power – Canada's appointed nation-builders, its decision-makers and mandarins, policemen and bureaucrats – came, paradoxically, to treat Ukrainian Canadians, regardless of their political affiliation, more or less equally, that is, with suspicion bordering on aversion.

Strangely, senior Canadian officials, given the influential role that some of them had played in creating the UCC, proved quite unwilling to accord partiality to any segment of the Ukrainian Canadian community. For their part, British officials came to a similar conclusion after considering a related question, namely, whether to favour established groups like the UCC or deal with recently founded ones like the ABN. That question first arose when the secretary of state for the Commonwealth was invited formally to attend a UCC-sponsored celebration of the sixtieth anniversary of the arrival of Ukrainian pioneers in Canada. What might seem to be a minor issue precipitated a surprising flurry of notes in Whitehall. It was noted that a 'vociferous Communist minority' had recently held its own commemoration of this historic event, which had apparently 'inflamed' Canadian public opinion. This was deemed significant because, the British concluded, there was 'no distinction' in most peoples' minds between non-communist and communist Ukrainians. As a result, the entire Ukrainian Canadian community had been 'discredited.' For such reasons the Canadian government had decided that it was preferable to 'exercise caution' when dealing with its Ukrainian minority. Rather than take a stand, they would favour neither the AUUC nor the UCC.[51]

Comparably, His Majesty's Government was also anxious not to take any action which 'might appear to commit them to recognition of the émigrés' nationalist and other claims,' or which would suggest that any particular émigré organization enjoyed the patronage of the British government.[52] Two problems, in particular, concerned British policymakers. They clearly did not want to do anything which might commit them 'on the question of Ukrainian separatism.' And they also refused to be drawn into participating in any event which might leave the impression that they accorded 'special support' (let alone any official recognition) to the UCC, particularly in preference to more nationalistic groups like the Ukrainian-dominated Anti-Bolshevik Bloc of Nations. Even more telling is that the British did not really discern much in the way of a fundamental difference between these two seemingly opposed groups. Both, in their view, were composed of émigrés who, even if of different vintages, nevertheless all stood 'in favour of the emergence of a Ukrainian state, independent of any Russian government,' and were involved in political lobbying to that end. Even if it was admitted that the UCC in Winnipeg was little more than a 'welfare organization,' its London Bureau under Panchuk had been 'quite active politically.' All this meant that it was 'far from certain,' or so noted a Mr Uffen at Whitehall, whether it would be more desirable to deal with the constituency Mr Panchuk represented rather than 'some other émigré group.' Perhaps it would be best to ignore both, for the aspirations of the Ukrainian emigration in general, he cautioned, 'could have far-reaching repercussions in international affairs.' At any rate the matter would have to be considered very carefully, if indeed His Majesty's Government had any intention of lending even a small measure of support to the Ukrainian national movement in the first place.[53] As matters turned out, it really did not.

Whether they took their cue from the British or, as is more likely, developed their own policy based on their much greater experience with Ukrainians, Canadian officials would take a line with respect to Ukrainian aspirations not very different from the one formulated in Whitehall. When, for example, a UCC brief, which presented what was derisively labelled as 'the familiar Ukrainian nationalist case,' was submitted to the prime minister on 10 September 1952, his advisers in External Affairs remarked that the submission could be rejected out of hand, for 'it is not Canadian policy to support movements or organizations having as their aim the dissolution of the Soviet Union.'[54] Furthermore, they advised, since it 'would not be in character' for the UCC to refrain from further attempts to get the government to accept its 'line' or at least some part of it, they had decided to draft a basic reply, which was to be employed in response to any and all future submissions of this sort. Taking such a step would ensure that, no matter how often Ukrainian Canadians came to Ottawa with petitions and protests, the government would have, ready and waiting, a rejoinder which committed it to nothing but served to mollify the supplicants.[55] This standard Canadian government policy would not change until late 1991, when Ukraine re-emerged as an independent and internationally recognized state. Of course, concessions were sometimes made, at least in the form of acknowledging the receipt of Ukrainian Canadian submissions, which External Affairs officials then pretended they intended to consider. At other times even such minor courtesies were not observed. Most important, however, not even the slightest hint of official approval or support for the legitimacy of Ukrainian Canadian concerns about the 'Ukrainian Question' was ever shown. This was all orchestrated very politely, just enough cajolery being deployed to keep many Ukrainian Canadian community leaders fooled and pacified.

As for the UCC's request that the government should consult with it on matters pertaining to Ukraine, such a 'presumptuous proposal' was deemed 'quite unacceptable.' As C.S.A. Ritchie remarked, while agreeing with his colleagues about the nettlesome character of continuing Ukrainian Canadian lobbying, all such submissions should be countered by employing an agreed-upon formula mixing ambiguity and aloofness: 'The Ukrainian Canadian Committee is at it again. This is a good statement of the line we shall have to hold in resisting their pressure.'[56]

'It May Be Believed but It Should Not Be Preached'

Preparing a report for the under-secretary of state for external affairs entitled 'Canadian Policy Concerning the Ukraine,' a copy of which was forwarded to the Canadian embassy in Moscow, External Affairs analysts noted that because the Canadian government was 'subject to a certain amount of pressure' from members of the large Ukrainian Canadian community, it was necessary to examine the 'validity of the proposition that the Ukraine can be considered a national political entity.' Reviewing the history of Ukraine and of its liberation movement, one External Affairs official concluded that Ukrainian nationalism had only just begun to reach maturity in 1917 when it was 'nipped in the bud' by the Bolshevik Revolution.'[57] Since, in this rather skewed interpretation, it had never recovered, 'there would appear to be ... no justification under present circumstances for the Canadian Government to include the Ukraine among those nations under Soviet domination whose claims to national independence and freedom we endorse.'[58]

This analyst then noted that the 'liberation of Ukraine' should not directly, or even indirectly, be supported by the Canadian government 'as an objective of Canadian policy,' for any such movement had little prospect of success and would 'in any case, seriously offend all Great Russians.' The man penning these conclusions, Jules Léger, ended by offering some prophylactic advice about how the Ukrainian Canadian community should be treated. The goal was to make this constituency believe that Ottawa was really interested in its views, even sympathetic to them, without actually saying anything which might commit Canada to substantive action. Léger suggested that the best manner in which to do this would be for government spokesmen and politicians, whenever they were confronted by Ukrainian Canadians raising the issue of Ukrainian independence, to couch their replies in words expressing sympathy with Ukrainian 'cultural survival' and 'the hope that ... Ukraine will not be swamped in the communist tide,' but to go no further. As he well knew, the government had no intentions of doing anything whatsoever for Ukraine, aside from rhetoric.[59]

Not surprisingly, Ukrainian members of the Canadian League for the Liberation of Ukraine fared no better in front of Ottawa's decision-makers than did their UCC counterparts. Officials in External Affairs had originally even been hesitant about granting Yaroslav Stetsko – whom their colleague, the Canadian ambassador to Madrid, had described as 'the peripatetic president of the self-styled Anti-Bolshevik Bloc of Nations' – permission to enter Canada.[60] They had followed his activities before he arrived; they knew, for example, that he had tried to enter Canada in July 1949 under the pseudonym of Wasyl Dankiw.[61] And so, when he applied formally for a visa, McCordick of External

Affairs' Defence Liaison minuted, 'From available evidence I see no reason to hope for particularly useful or desirable results from Stetsko's visit, and some reason to be mildly apprehensive.'[62] McCordick's concerns focused on the fact that Stetsko and the ABN were 'preaching the inevitability' of war with the Soviet Union ('it may be believed but should not be preached') and the dissolution of the USSR into a galaxy of successor states. 'Western thinking,' added McCordick, 'was proceeding very cautiously on the subject of war aims and the future of a defeated Soviet Union,' so it would probably be 'premature, embarrassing and of adverse effect in psychological warfare' if too much attention were drawn to the ABN.[63]

Still, in the realization that it might be 'useful and valuable' to hear Stetsko's views directly, ultimately it was decided to grant him a non-immigrant visa, allowing him into Canada for up to three months. After arriving in March 1952, Stetsko toured Canada, visiting CLLU and CYM branches to give speeches, and travelling to Ottawa, on 24 April, for an interview with Messrs Watkins, McCordick, and Crowe at External Affairs. He left them unimpressed, both with his personality and with what they later termed the ABN's 'impractical plans.'[64] Much the same thing happened a year later, when a twelve-man delegation sponsored by the League went to Ottawa, headed by Stanley Frolick, bearing a memorandum entitled 'The Policy of Liberation as an Aspect of Canadian Foreign Policy.' As with previous delegations, these Ukrainian Canadian envoys were, in keeping with the agreed-upon methods established for coping with such representatives, received and politely heard by the minister responsible for external affairs. But, as J.B.C. Watkins later minuted, all the minister really did was 'make them all feel important, which as far as I could judge, was the main object of their visit.'[65] The delegation's members, as Frolick would swear years later when he finally learned of this official appraisal, would have been outraged if had they known then what had been written about them and their motives. He certainly was. But they had no way of knowing, and by the time these documents became public it was far too late for outrage. Many more Ukrainian Canadian delegations were duped in this way, for the men at External Affairs were nothing if not masterful at the art of duplicity.

The government's position on Ukrainian nationalism and the issue of Ukrainian independence did not change appreciably even with the passage of time. In 1962, Norman Robertson, preparing for his minister the memorandum 'Canadian Attitude to Ukrainian Nationalism,' counselled that it was impossible for the government to recognize Ukraine as a 'political individuality.' Just as Léger had before him, so Robertson offered his political masters a technique which would make them appear sympathetic in front of Ukrainian Canadian audiences without committing the government to anything – sensible advice, given that no politician would want to risk antagonizing such a large body of potential voters. Robertson cleverly suggested that, his strictures on the Ukrainian independence question notwithstanding, politicians were not otherwise prevented from commenting publicly on 'those aspects of the Ukrainian problem which might come under human rights provisions.'[66] Talking about individual human rights and civil liberties would, it was to be hoped, distract audiences' attentions from talk about a people's right to national self-determination. The fundamental truth, that the Canadian government was not supportive of Ukrainian independence, could thus be obfuscated, while good publicity would likely be given to selective official efforts on behalf of a few Ukrainian political prisoners and dissidents. No significant evolution beyond this very modest modification of the earlier government recipe for dealing with Ukrainian Canadians would be crafted until the early 1990s, if even then.[67]

Advocates of Ukrainian independence, whether landed immigrants or Canadian-born Ukrainians, could expect no satisfaction on the 'Ukrainian Question' from their elected representatives, advised as the latter were by bureaucrats and mandarins whose minds had long since been determined against the Ukrainian national independence movement. Official Ottawa was generally indifferent or even hostile to Ukrainian independence. At best, Ukrainian Canadians could expect expressions of sympathy about the 'cultural survival' of Ukraine, and sporadic efforts on behalf of the 'human rights' of individual Ukrainian dissidents imprisoned in the Soviet gulag. As for the essence of the 'Ukrainian Question' – namely, the right of the Ukrainian people to national self-determination – supporting that prospect was firmly excluded from Canada's political agenda. The persistent preoccupation which some Ukrainian Canadians exhibited over the fate of their homeland was seen by Ottawa as a disturbingly un-Canadian fixation. Ukrainians in Canada for whom Ukrainian independence was an abiding concern, either members of the League or supporters of the UCC, were, of course, never made privy to the workings of the bureaucracy, nor granted discourse with the predominantly Anglo-Canadian bureaucrats who had reviewed and pronounced a contrary judgment on the 'Ukrainian Question.' They never knew, or were even meant to learn, that the Anglo-American powers had never wanted, or felt they needed, a free Ukraine. Ignorant of their true situation, the organized Ukrainian Canadian community was rendered impotent, a condition in which it has remained to the present day. Ukrainian Canadian leaders thought otherwise and preached accordingly to their communities. It would have been better if they had not been believed, but unfortunately, they were.

10 'A Good Canadian':
The View from Ottawa

'Ukraine Is Not the Name of a Country'

The men who congregated in Toronto in the spring of 1949 and fash-
ioned the League for the Liberation of Ukraine believed that their
action would give succour to the ongoing liberation struggle in their
homeland, Ukraine. They also hoped to rally support among Ukrainian Canadians for this independence movement. They thought that
somehow, using what they believed were officially recognized Ukrainian Canadian institutions, they might even secure the patronage of the
Canadian government for their course. Seeing themselves as the *druha
liniia*, or second line, of the Ukrainian national liberation movement,
they expected that the Cold War would soon offer them a second
chance to return to Ukraine, either in the wake of a victorious war of
independence or to participate directly in such a contest. Few in the
late 1940s or early 1950s realized that they were fated to spend the
remainder of their lives in exile. So strongly did they hold to their émigré faith that some of them, even after the passage of five decades and
despite the more phlegmatic attitude taken by many other Ukrainian
resettled DPs, would still tell an inquirer in the late 1980s that they
expected to see the land of their birth freed. They were certainly not all
worn down by the corrosive cynicism which so often enervates émigré
life. By any reckoning, theirs was certainly a long enduring. What is
peculiar about their struggle is that, unlike those of many other exile
communities, they won. Today there is a free Ukraine.

These Ukrainian political refugees, and many other DPs, had been
allowed into Canada because they could fill semi-skilled positions in
industries which otherwise attracted few Canadian-born workers. No

less, their admission reflected Cold War realities. Militantly anti-Soviet and anti-communist as the majority of these Ukrainian refugees were or had become, they represented a desirable commodity in the eyes of the nation's gatekeepers. The DP immigrants, it was thought, could provide not only 'strong backs' but also the 'muscle' – physical and intellectual – required to help root out the Ukrainian Canadian Left, and do damage to the Left in Canada in general. The evidence remaining suggests that they accomplished just that task, set out for them by the bureaucrats who had allowed them into the country and who understood who they were, what they had gone through, and what they had become as a result.

Posing the question of whether postwar Canadian refugee policy reflected official indifference or official opportunism, a student of this subject concluded that both motivations had helped shape the nature of the government's response.[1] In the case of Ukrainian DPs, such an inference is not very convincing. Certainly, most Canadians, even in the civil service and at decision-making levels of the federal bureaucracy, always were, and remain, profoundly unconversant with Ukrainian affairs. Only the most dedicated advocates of Ukrainian causes would argue that things should be different. But it would be very wrong to assume that this general public lack of interest in matters Ukrainian was reflected at all levels of the Canadian state's apparatus. Ottawa's men, no matter how muddled a collection of mediocrities they generally seem to have been, did at several points in time purposefully intervene in Ukrainian Canadian affairs, doing so not in order to undermine one faction rather than another, but in a more profound attempt to do away with the abiding interest on the part of the organized Ukrainian Canadian minority, including both immigrants and the Canadian-born, in Ukrainian independence. The rationale behind these intrusions was that foreign ties were contrary to Canadian nation-building and complicated the country's foreign policies. These various manipulations of the Ukrainian Canadian population had a traumatic and long-term impact on the nature of Ukrainian Canadian life, for they influenced the organized group's collective understanding of what was and was not permissible when it came to identifying oneself publicly as a Ukrainian in Canada or acting together as a group known as the Ukrainian Canadians.

Those within the government who, from the pioneer years to the postwar period of Ukrainian immigration, had decided when and why people calling themselves Ukrainians would be allowed into the coun-

try, where each of the three major 'waves' of immigrants would be fun-
nelled, and what tasks would be set for them – whether opening up the
Canadian West or undermining the Left – played a definitive role in
the creation and consequent evolution of Ukrainian Canadian society.
The fateful and formative decisions these men made, and the policies
they put into place, directly and indirectly moulded this ethnic community's organizational infrastructures and shaped Ukrainian Canadian perceptions of their status as an ethnic minority in Canada.
Certainly, the vast majority of the Ukrainians who were admitted to
Canada, and their descendants, never questioned the motives of Canada's gatekeepers. Instead, and quite understandably, they tried to do
their best to conform to the norms and rules of behaviour of the dominant Anglo-Protestant society they found. Those who took a more critical view of their situation, or who articulated a durable political
interest in Ukrainian as opposed to Canadian affairs – again, no matter
how much they might try to link the two or camouflage the former by
invoking the latter – would experience state-sanctioned responses
ranging from repression to condescension. But never would the Canadian state cease watching them, nor would Ottawa's bureaucrats and
controllers stop wondering about where Ukrainian Canadian loyalties
might truly lie.

Curious anomalies exist in the historical record of the relationship
between members of this Ukrainian minority and the government officials charged with their supervision. Perhaps the most puzzling of
these is that even though some Canadian officials spent a great deal of
time and energy monitoring Ukrainian Canadian developments, they
had no very good grasp of exactly what a Ukrainian might be, at least
not until more recent times. Possibly this was because, as the doughty
Tracy Philipps once put it, the 'average Englishman' doesn't 'understand Volhynias or Podolias, which he probably thinks are exotic garden flowers or tropical diseases.'[2] With a few notable exceptions, most
of the Canadian bureaucrats involved in monitoring Ukrainian Canadian affairs seem to have been scarcely more knowledgeable, although
they often quite pompously thought otherwise.[3]

Matters of state prevented government officials on both sides of the
Atlantic from extending recognition and thereby some trace of political
legitimacy to the Ukrainians as a distinct people or nation. Ukrainians
for them, until the very recent past, were simply a 'nation without a
history.' Even when confronted with 'formidable lists' of refugees who
claimed to be Ukrainian and who manifestly did not want to be 'either

Poles or Russians,' the Foreign Office's Patrick Dean noted that 'Ukrainian nationality ... is not a nationality known to English law.'[4] His colleague Thomas Brimelow elaborated revealingly upon the reason for this policy of non-recognition: 'It is against the question for us to recognize the Ukrainians as a race apart ... I can think of nothing more certain to cause Anglo-Soviet friction.'[5]

The British, in concert with their American allies, tried to resolve this census problem by deciding that Ukrainians were to be treated, along with Croatians, Georgians, Kalmyks, and Armenians, as a 'national sub-division.' Not surprisingly, they remained unhappy with this categorization, given the undeniable fact that 'in the field' there were tens of thousands of people who insisted on describing themselves as Ukrainians, whatever the formal recording regulations.[6] For a time Anglo-American functionaries settled for the workable, if insensitive, expedient of simply refusing to recognize Ukrainian as a nationality.[7] When this failed to be practical, as tens of thousands of refugees kept claiming to be nothing more and nothing less than Ukrainian, the British selected as their key criteria for purposes of definition the language spoken by a refugee and the refugee's expressed nationality preference. The 'only criterion,' wrote A.E. Lambert in the spring of 1946, was that refugees claiming to be Ukrainians had to speak the language and indicate that they did not wish to be treated as Poles, Russians, or Czechs – a rather inelegant solution to the issue of determining a refugee's nationality, particularly since it was also stated that the acceptance of this 'working definition' was not meant to suggest any change in British views about Ukrainian nationality: 'Ukrainians are not considered to have a separate nationality,' minuted another complacent Whitehall bureaucrat, bequeathing a further precious example of English humbug to posterity.[8]

While British temporizing on the question of Ukrainian nationality can be explained away by invoking their desire not to prejudice relations with the Soviets, the similar treatment Canadian government officials accorded to this matter is less understandable, unless one insists that Canada's historical relationship with Great Britain determined domestic policy towards Ukrainians. But that is not entirely satisfying. By the early postwar period Ukrainians had been settled in Canada for over half a century and were well known to the authorities as a distinct group. The authorities, as we have seen, had carefull' monitored this Ukrainian Canadian minority's activities and, ever reluctantly, had allowed for the formation of UCSA and its 'Lor'

Club' and, later, of the UCRF. But when it came to the issue of determining the nationality of the DPs, Canadian policy seems to have been
in no way different from that of the British or the Americans. For
example, the HQ of the 3rd Canadian Division instructed its officers
that, with respect to the 'Disposal of Ukrainians,' Canadian policy
would follow guidelines set by SHAEF, namely: 'Ukrainians are *not*
considered as a nationality and will be dealt with according to their
nationality status as Soviet citizens, Polish citizens, Czechoslovak citizens, nationals of other countries of which they may be citizens or as
stateless persons. Persons styling themselves as Ukrainians who are
Soviet citizens displaced by reasons of war ... will be repatriated to the
USSR without regard to their personal wishes.'[9]

To escape what many DPs regarded as a dire fate, namely repatriation to Soviet-dominated eastern Europe or the USSR, large numbers
of these refugees deliberately misrepresented their national identities
and falsified birthplace information. As Panchuk noted in a memorandum entitled 'Ukrainian Refugees and Displaced Persons – Relief,
Social Welfare, Immigration, and Resettlement,' distributed to dozens
of government offices as well as to the PCIRO in mid-September 1947,
'thousands' of people were hiding under false papers. The result of all
this was that more than a few Ukrainians could be found among those
claiming to be Poles or in the category of 'undetermined nationalities.'[10] For the British authorities, Panchuk's report was not news.
Earlier that year the Church of England's Council on Foreign Relations had reported that among the refugees in Germany 'this word
"Ukrainian" is used throughout the Western Zones to denote not only
Ukrainians but in fact all of Russian origin whether they are Great
Russians, Little Russians or Byelo Russians. Use of the word Russian
seems to have been deliberately dropped in order to avoid any suggestion of connection with the Soviets.'[11]

'A Foolish and Dangerous Fallacy'

This still does not explain why the Canadian authorities, who had so
often been anxious about Ukrainians in Canada, were unwilling to
agree that there might be Ukrainians among the refugees of Europe.
The only reasonable conclusion seems to be that it was not a question
of information – the British, Americans, and Canadians knew full well
that there were Ukrainian DPs, and who these people were. Instead,
the Anglo-American powers' unwillingness to accord any political recognition or legitimacy to Ukrainian aspirations for an independent

homeland militated against official acceptance of Ukrainian as a legitimate category of identification. Ukrainians could not exist because
Ukraine was, at best, 'a nation without a history.' This charade was
kept up for a number of years. In the late summer of 1948, C.R.A. Rae,
commenting on another submission by Panchuk entitled 'Memorandum on Ukraine and Ukrainians,' acknowledged frankly that although
'we shall have to keep Ukrainians in this country happy,' it was 'clearly
impossible' to call them Ukrainians 'pure and simple'; and Rae had no
idea of how to resolve the ensuing definitional conundrum.[12] The British Home Office suffered a similar dilemma when it came to completing resident alien registration certificates in the early part of 1949.
'Under no circumstances,' prescribed Home Office Circular no. 5, 'will
the word "Ukrainian" be entered' on such documents.[13] Canadian officials conformed. Mrs A. Freeman of the Department of Citizenship and
Immigration, replying to a letter from a Mrs A. Goralezuk in the spring
of 1955, expressed her regrets but nevertheless informed the applicant
that since 'Ukraine is not the name of a country,' she could not have
been born there, no matter what Mrs Goralezuk might say.[14]

So when it came to dealing with the Ukrainians, a people who on
one level did not officially exist but who on another were the cause of a
considerable expenditure of resources and intellectual effort on the
part of senior members of the Canadian, British, and American security, intelligence, and foreign policy establishments, these extablish-
ments were unwilling to relax or drop their guard. If Ukrainians did
not exist, then there would of course have been no need for a Canadian
MP, R.B. Homer, to question the incorporation of the Ukrainian
National Federation in Canada in March 1950, or for him to ask the
UNF's representatives, 'Why do you build separate halls?'[15] Nor was
there any need for confidential studies like that by the federal government's Citizenship Branch describing in some detail the weaknesses of
the UCC.[16] But since there were those in Canada who persisted in
describing themselves as Ukrainians, and who were willing to be
judged by outsiders on the basis of that self-description, the government had to handle many complex issues resulting from the continued
existence of these persons. It seems these Ukrainian Canadians had
taken to heart the oft-repeated words of the British statesman John
Buchan, Lord Tweedsmuir. As the governor-general of Canada, Lord
Tweedsmuir had visited a Ukrainian colony near Fraserwood, Manitoba, in September 1936, and there not only had told his Ukrainian
Canadian audience that the 'Ukrainian element' had made a 'very
valuable contribution to our new Canada' (a standard accolade, then

and since), but had said, 'You will all be better Canadians for being also good Ukrainians.'[17]

For Ukrainians in Canada the governor-general's words were heady stuff indeed. They represented not only an acknowledgment of the Ukrainian contribution to Canada's development but, far more important, an official affirmation of the acceptability and legitimacy of Ukrainian Canadian organizational activities, rooted as these often were in an abiding interest in their Ukrainian homeland's affairs. Lord Tweedsmuir's brief and probably unwitting remark would be widely circulated among Ukrainian Canadians of various political stripes and religious beliefs in the years that followed, always presented as if some authoritative and official seal of approval for Ukrainian Canadian endeavours and activism had thereby been granted.[18] To this day, this sentiment remains entrenched among Ukrainian Canadians, although few now bother to attribute it to Lord Tweedsmuir. That, time and again, the hope it reflects has proved chimerical is oddly forgotten. For the Ukrainian Canadians who had placed so much stock in the governor-general's remarks were misguided. His words carried no magisterial sanction, nor did they represent a formal statement of government policy. For that matter, they probably did not even reflect the sentiments of the Canadian public. What the governor-general had done was make a soothing off-the-cuff comment. But his words were seized upon with a passion by the leaders of an ethnic constituency that was constantly searching for approval rather than the usual opprobrium or paternalism they encountered.

Ukrainian Canadians would have been better advised to remember, if not necessarily take to heart, the words of a 1929 editorial in Toronto's *Globe* in which they were told bluntly that they had an obligation to conform and to become as British in character and worldview as possible rather than to cling to their Ukrainian behaviour and attitudes. Canada, they were advised, 'is a British country and must remain British and the European immigrants have no moral right to protest against a policy designed to this end.' As for those Ukrainians in Canada who were protesting at the time against a ruling limiting the immigration of additional Ukrainians into the country, the *Globe* cautioned its readership about the 'threat' to the country represented by these Ukrainian petitioners. By publicly manifesting their 'racial consciousness,' these people made it obvious that they were 'Ukrainians still,' which proved that despite the fact that they had taken an oath as Canadians and Britishers, their 'first sympathies' had remained 'with their own people.' Obviously, Canada was for them 'secondary.' That Ukrainians now claimed to be 'the third largest race in Canada' and were demanding that no restrictions be placed on their numbers was even more alarming, because, as the editorialist asked rhetorically, 'What [would] they demand if their present strength were multiplied several times?' He answered by claiming that they would want to make 'the whole of Western Canada into a replica of Europe.' Allegations of this sort were cobbled together to substantiate a claim that the Ukrainians preferred 'to act together as Ukrainians rather than to serve the country as true Canadians.'[19]

Accusations of 'divided loyalties' would continue to haunt the organized Ukrainian Canadian community for years thereafter. Even if the rebuke published in the Globe had long since faded from their collective memory, Ukrainian Canadians of the postwar era could have disabused themselves of their infatuation with Lord Tweedsmuir's remarks by reading an April 1948 editorial in the Windsor Daily Star entitled 'Divided Loyalties Refutation of Good Canadian Citizenship.' It directly refuted the governor-general's remarks by proclaiming that it was a 'misconception' for anyone to believe that 'to be a good Canadian we must first be good Ukrainians.' No one 'can be a "good Canadian" who has divided loyalties ... Canada expects that these be merged into Canadianism, not retained as something apart ... It is a contradiction in terms; a strange, foolish and dangerous fallacy. The sooner it is dissipated the better – the better for Canada and for all persons of foreign origin.'[20]

'A Good Canadian'

Furthermore, in no circumstances was the Canadian government going to accept the liberation of Ukraine as 'an objective of Canadian policy.' Indeed, the less attention paid to Ukrainians and their distant, complex, and confusing east European problems the better, for such attention could only 'seriously offend all Great Russians,' presumably non-Soviets and Soviets alike, retarding Canadian nation-building plans in the process. People over-occupied with their European homeland were likely to be too distracted ever to integrate fully into Canadian society and become proper citizens. Certainly, as one Canadian bureaucrat advised, government 'expressions of sympathy' for Ukrainian cultural survival or on human rights issues were tolerable, for articulating commiseration of this sort in no way bound the government to support for Ukrainian claims about a right to national independence and sovereignty. But even so, the less said and done on Ukrainian matters the better. It was to be hoped that with the passage of time, and provided that no individual, group, or government inside or outside Canada stirred up the organized Ukrainian community, this irksome constituency would gradually erode away, having no issue around which to coalesce, no protagonists to face off against, no reason for the maintenance of group cohesion. What Ottawa hoped for, in effect, was that Ukrainian Canadians, if left undisturbed, would sooner rather than later 'forget about their European hopes and ambitions' and, by abandoning those attachments, become good Canadians.

Is this perhaps too harsh a judgment upon Ottawa? The answer can be discerned in what was written about Dr Vladimir J. Kaye, one of the few Ukrainians in Canada with whom government officials had more or less regular contact over the span of years with which this account is primarily concerned. Kaye had proved himself, many times, a man with whom officialdom could deal. Not only had he given good service to the government as a monitor of Ukrainian Canadian society just before, during, and after the war, but he had served Ottawa's purposes well whenever a need arose for an intervention into Ukrainian Canadian affairs. Yet Kaye was more than a tool of the state. He was also a willing participant in his own integration into its apparatus, desiring assimilation into the world of the governors. As the bureaucrats themselves observed, he had done all the right things as far as they were concerned. He had changed his unpronounceable and unspellable Ukrainian surname of Kysilewsky to Kaye. Even more indicative, he had married an Englishwoman. Kaye also made it clear, to anyone who would listen, that his idea of 'the good life' was settling down on a farm. But what endeared him most to those in Ottawa who found the Ukrainians of Canada such a politically troublesome bunch was that Kaye had told everyone he was not interested in what he termed 'parochial' Ukrainian issues, including in that sweeping repudiation the cause of Ukrainian independence. That was satisfying news indeed for Ottawa's men, a harbinger of what they planned for and hoped would happen to all those styling themselves Ukrainians in Canada. As one of them minuted frankly on a file about Kaye, he could be trusted and counted upon as a 'good Canadian' for he 'would never leave Canada for any Ukraine, however free.'[21] For Ottawa that was and has remained the definition of what being a good Ukrainian in Canada is.

Epilogue

I first went to Ukraine in 1989. There was no independent Ukraine then. But you could already sense that there would be, soon. The Soviet Empire was disintegrating. I welcomed that. I had been raised to believe that a free Ukraine would be a good thing, and that sooner or later there would be such a place. 'Freeing Ukraine' was, in essence, 'the cause.' Indeed, the *only* really important cause. Most of my generation, the sons and daughters of the DPs, had been pledged to that end by our parents and grandparents. We were to carry on, if necessary, what they had begun.

Most of us, myself included, did not honour the obligation. At least temporarily, from around the early 1960s and into the 1980s, many of us jettisoned our parents' struggle, one which we never fully understood. In doing so we also, if not entirely, abandoned their place, their Ukraine. Most of us had never seen Ukraine and, generally, never expected to. All we knew about that distant land was what our parents, and their parents, and their friends (almost all of whom were DPs themselves) had told us about it. Those accounts were often frightening, frighteningly unbelievable.

I remember how puzzled I always was about the fact that Ukraine wasn't even on the maps I studied at school. Not really, anyway. It might show up as a Soviet republic, it often was portrayed as a region, but it certainly never had the status accorded to, say, Italy or Ireland or Indonesia. It was part of someplace else. It was not a country, it was not a state. It was something lesser, something less relevant, something half hidden and all but forgotten.

And so, when our parents tried to pass on their mantle to us, most of us declined the offer. For us their generation was 'too political,' too fragmented against itself, too out of touch with North American realities, too right-wing. It was trendy to be Left then, at least in the North American world in which we had been born and raised. And then there were all those other distractions of the 1960s and 1970s and 1980s.

Our 'rebellion' against our parents was welcomed by many of those around us. We were schooled to think that their nationalism was an evil, responsible for some of the greatest crimes of the century, that nationalism was a dirty word. And 'The Ukraine,' we kept being told, was really not a real place, it was just 'Little Russia' or – and this was offered to us as almost a concession – at best, a region or part of the Soviet Union, happily so. As for what our parents had tried to tell us – about the Polish, Hungarian, German, and Russian occupations of their land, the genocidal Great Famine of 1932–3, the war years, their own escape to freedom, the millions massacred by the Nazis and the Soviets – we concluded that their stories were probably exaggerated, confused, certainly biased against Soviet reality, past and still present. Most of us just did not believe our parents. How could we, living in societies whose educational systems, media, and politicians, overwhelmingly, told us that what our foreign-born parents said was histrionic hyperbole? And so, in the main, if kindly and quietly, we discarded our parents' memories and accounts, dismissed them as the right-wing distortions of 'militant anti-communist nationalists' and 'extremist émigrés.'

Presented with the idea that it was the political Left which was a progressive, objective, humane, and liberating force for change in society, many of us drifted or were lured to that end of the political spectrum. Some of the 'radicals' among us began to champion the cause of anti-colonialism, anti-imperialism, anti-Americanism, cheering on every alleged 'national liberation movement' active in the Third World, attracted to various Trotskyite or Marxist movements. At the same time most of us ignored what was going on in Ukraine. Everything was basically okay there. We were taught to think that.

Most of us did not become political activists on the Left, of course. From what I could see, a majority simply strove to remain aloof from 'Ukrainian politics,' determined to avoid any involvements other than socially acceptable ones like promoting Ukrainian folk-dancing ensembles and language schools for our children, or occasionally going so far as to take part in those limited and sporadic protest efforts which others organized on behalf of Ukrainian dissidents – Moroz, Chornovil, Lukianenko, and others – who braved the Soviet system and suffered for it. Standing up for those courageous souls became a hallmark of our generation's activities on behalf of Ukraine in the seventies. Those who did so, and they came from all points on the political spectrum, did good work. In fact, it may have been because of their efforts that gradually, haltingly, our emigration was transformed. The North American supporters of the dissidents promoted the notion of universal human rights and civil liberties. It became obvious that in Ukraine and elsewhere in the Soviet Union there were many people who were suffering only because of their simple insistence on enjoying the same individual human rights and freedoms that we do. To say nothing of a nation's right to self-determination. Those of us who had protested against the suppression of the basic human rights of many peoples in the Third World, whether we were of the Centre or the Left, began to wonder why few if any of those with whom we had joined in righteous indignation over oppression in the Third World seemed unwilling to endorse our call for human rights and freedoms for Ukrainians. When we raised this issue we found ourselves being ignored, marginalized, separated from 'the movement,' as if anyone questioning Soviet rule, much less calling for the 'decolonization' of the 'Soviet Empire' and freedom for its 'captive nations,' was a counter-revolutionary, an American stooge, a fascist.

At about the same time many of us became increasingly curious about how and why Ukrainians were in North America, far from where our ancestors were. Tentatively, an exploration of the roots of Ukrainian life in North America began, particularly in Canada, where the study of the contributions made by the pioneer settlers came to be intimately bound up with community-based lobbying in support of the adoption of multiculturalism as official Canadian government policy. When this happened, in 1971, it became evident that Ukrainian Canadian activists (who certainly had emerged by then) were at the forefront of the campaign to enshrine multiculturalism as an official Canadian policy.

I began studying my own roots, those of a son of two Ukrainian DPs, in the late 1970s. Born in 1953, in the small eastern Ontario city of Kingston, I was not then past the first quarter century of my life. But I already wanted to know more about how and why Ukrainians had come to be in Kingston, why they had left Ukraine, what their experiences were as they were leaving the 'old country' and moving to the 'New World.' I began collecting oral histories from as many of the Ukrainians living in Kingston as would talk with me. I kept hearing tales similar to those my parents, and uncle, and their friends had told me as I grew to manhood in a Ukrainian nationalist milieu – stories about the Great Famine, about the Organization of Ukrainian Nationalists, and about the Ukrainian Insurgent Army. I had heard most of it before. But I couldn't help but think that these witnesses, from many different regions in Ukraine, of different social, economic, political, and religious backgrounds, couldn't all be making up what I was hearing. I began to gain a better sense of what a Golgotha twentieth-century Ukraine had been. But I also learned that it was not all death and destruction. For, no matter whom I spoke with, whether prewar or postwar immigrant, I sensed too just how strong an interest Ukrainian Canadians still had in their ancestral homeland, and how many of them, particularly those who had been forced to leave Ukraine, had a memory of a place that was in some unquantifiable way better than the place they had found themselves in, almost Edenic, a paradise lost. I wondered why anyone would think that Ukraine was better than Canada. This was an identifiable place, this was a good place; no one disagreed with that. So what was better about what they had left behind, four decades before, or ten?

As I continued studying the historical geography of *all* the Ukrainians in Kingston, recording the stories of people who had come to Canada before the war and after, I also heard testimony which surprised, then perplexed me. There had been a pro-Soviet hall in Kingston, organized from among the large number of Ukrainians who worked in the Davis Tannery and in the shipyards, grain elevators, and factories of the city. Ukrainians had even been interned as 'enemy aliens' in Fort Henry during Canada's first national internment operations of 1914–20. None of this was in the Canadian history books I had read, none of it had ever been taught me; it was all, slowly but surely, being forgotten. I could understand, intellectually, why the postwar immigrants might not wish to have anything to do with their pro-communist rivals, might prefer that those enemies be forgotten and their stories left out of even local histories, but why would those who had been interned, or who had worked so hard to set up their workers' hall and organize their own social and cultural life, be so willing to let it all slip away? I had no real understanding then of just how powerful the forces of the state were, of how the Ukrainians who had come to Kingston had first been selected and only then been allowed entry into Canada, how they had subsequently been deemed to have 'divided loyalties' and therefore were regarded as suspect, as persons to be watched and manipulated, as persons fit for internment. Many of them knew this, for they had lived through it all, whether they came before or after the war. Understandably, they were reluctant to focus on this aspect of their experience. Some, the internees, the politically suspect, were still afraid of the state. Others, especially the DPs, had found themselves willingly playing the part of handmaiden to the state; for them their role in enervating the Ukrainian Canadian Left was a matter of pride but secondary to their principal chore, which remained 'the cause' of liberating Ukraine.

I did what I could to record what could be preserved of the past of Kingston's Ukrainian community, and made that effort into a master's thesis, which later became the basis for my first book, *Ukrainians in the Making: Their Kingston Story*. In some ways, it remains my favourite.

Just as I was concluding my master's thesis, a book appeared in Canada which catapulted to national prominence a gifted writer's reflections on the experiences of Canada's Ukrainians. In *All of Baba's Children* Myrna Kostash eloquently gave voice to the sufferings, the aspirations, the triumphs, and the failures of those Ukrainians who had settled the prairies near the turn of the century. Yet this remarkable literary achievement was also disturbing. For, as much as I embraced her text, that attraction was partial. Kostash had sprinkled her prose with more than one unkind and, I thought, unwarranted comment about the Ukrainian nationalists. Her ignorance of their struggle and her indifference to their aims left me troubled. How could she, why had she so well captured the essence of the Ukrainian pioneers' experiences, but so badly misunderstood the experience of those who had followed them, those who would reshape the nature of Ukrainian Canadian society?

Of course, as Kostash has since recognized candidly, she was a rather typical example of the Left when she wrote *All of Baba's Children*. Talented as a writer, she was quite incapable of overcoming the prejudices of the Left about nationalism in general and Ukrainian nationalists in particular. Praising hard-working prairie peasants who allegedly were oppressed in their homeland and then were oppressed in Canada was acceptable. Saying anything positive about the nationalists who followed, however, was just not something one would or could do if one wanted to work and play with those of the Left. One wonders if *Baba's Children* would ever have achieved the success it did if she had taken a different line politically.

It probably does not matter. Once a book has been launched it has its own life and its many, varied interpreters. What I got out of *Baba's Children* was the sense that a history of the Ukrainian experience in Canada had yet to be written, objectively, that there was certainly a story out there which needed to be told. And I knew that what I had to know more about was the experience of the DPs – people like my parents, who had come to Canada after the war as political refugees, not people like Kostash's parents, born here, or her grandparents, who had settled the Canadian frontier decades earlier. I then thought that I had nothing in common, nor did my parents, with those prairie sod-busters. I was wrong.

There were already a few leads for me to follow. I had heard about a Ukrainian Canadian, Bohdan Panchuk, who had, I was told, done a great deal to help the DPs. When I finally located him, in Montreal, I found myself immersed in dealings with a man whose exploits and efforts had gone largely unnoticed by the Ukrainian Canadian community I had grown up in, and which certainly were being forgotten. Quite literally, I also found a man who was sitting on dozens of boxes of documentary material – the preserved records of the Ukrainian Canadian Servicemen's Association, the Central Ukrainian Relief Bureau, the Canadian Relief Mission for Ukrainian Victims of War, the Ukrainian Canadian Relief Fund, and the Association of Ukrainians in Great Britain, to mention only the most important. 'G.R.B.' had dedicated his life to what he understood to be 'the cause,' and here was I, a doctoral candidate, uncovering a graduate student's dream, thousands of pages of primary archival evidence, most of it unique.

From Panchuk, I learned about the others. About A.J. 'Tony' Yaremovich, Ann (Crapleve) Smith, Peter Smylski, and Stanley Frolick. Eventually, I got to speak to them all. And at about the same time (this was the early 1980s), I began seriously exploring official British and Canadian documents for what the Ukrainian Canadians had done overseas and at home throughout the 1940s and 1950s. Those records, somewhat surprisingly, also proved voluminous. The American, British, and Canadian states (the 'ABC' powers) watched and watched and watched, just about everything the Ukrainian Canadians did, at home and abroad. Obviously, these governments believed the Ukrainian Canadians were doing something that bore their intense scrutiny. The Anglo-American powers, I also learned, had intervened in Ukrainian Canadian affairs, repeatedly. Whenever they felt a need to ensure that, whether by virtue of their own inclinations or as a result of the machinations of foreign powers, this 'foreign-born' population would remain loyal, they acted, sometimes surreptitiously, at other times not. And so thousands of Ukrainian Canadians were interned in the First World War. Fewer suffered a similar fate during the Second World War – and probably with more just cause – for Ottawa more cleverly manipulated the community by creating the Ukrainian Canadian Committee 'for the duration,' succeeding in the creation of an organization that ensured Ukrainian Canadian loyalty during the war years, even though there was little likelihood they would have been anything but loyal. Remarked upon at the time, Ottawa's creation of the UCC has been rather conveniently forgotten since then by those who disapprove of, but have never disproved, this interpretation of what happened. Curiously, it is an episode in the Ukrainian Canadian experience which even Ottawa's interests dictate should be forgotten.

Ottawa's surveillance of and reporting about Ukrainian Canadian society did not end with the close of the Second World War. It continued into the 1960s, as documentary evidence proves, and probably continues to this day, although the evidence for that is much less complete. What is certain is that, for the most part, the government departments most likely to be interested in Ukraine and the internal affairs of Ukrainian Canadians – our ministries of foreign affairs and of justice, and stumps like multiculturalism (essentially a descendant of the body brought into being by the likes of Simpson, Philipps, Kirkconnell, and Kaye-Kysilevsky) – have remained wary of, sometimes annoyed by, and yet always interested in Ukrainian Canadian affairs. Curiously, these very same ministries have remained singularly underpopulated by Canadians of Ukrainian heritage, or at least those willing to articulate such a personal identity and commitment. To get ahead in mainstream Canadian society, to succeed in political life, to enter into government service or become part of the national media has generally carried with it a very significant cost – it has, all too often, meant the abandonment of that abiding interest in the fate of Ukraine which, as I have argued, is or once was so intrinsic to the quality of being a Ukrainian in Canada. There have been exceptions, I know, but very few.

Which brings me back, not to Panchuk or Frolick, both of whom I admired and will never forget, nor to those others who staffed UCSA and then CURB. Instead I wish to return to Dr Kaye, to Kaye-Kysilevsky. I was wrong about him. I always suspected that he was, by nature, a cautious man, perhaps even meek. I never met him. But I also know that the record shows that he tried to, and did, serve his people and his country. Others can judge how well. I was critical of Kaye not so much because of anything specific he did but because Ottawa's men thought his marriage to an Englishwoman, his name change, his predilection for farming, his unwillingness to leave Canada for Ukraine, however free, all together constituted the ideal prescription for being a 'good Ukrainian' in Canada. When I first wrote this manuscript there was no independent Ukraine on the maps of the world. The assimilatory formula Ottawa directed could not, not then, create a 'good Ukrainian.'

Not then. But now? What I find is that my distaste just a few years ago with what I perceived as Kaye's voluntary and therefore all the more disagreeable subservience to Ottawa's dictates has muted. I too would now never leave Canada for any Ukraine, even the one there is today, which, apparently, is free. Nor would most of my Ukrainian Canadian contemporaries. Canada, I have discovered, is my place; it is as much the place by birthright of over one million Canadians of Ukrainian heritage as it is that of any other Canadians, whether they, their parents, their grandparents, their great-grandparents, or their distant forefathers got off the proverbial boat. No matter where from or when, 'First Nation' or most recent arrival, Canada belongs to all these others, equally, and also to me. For Canada's Ukrainians, it is our place, and we will never leave it unless we are forced to, as my parents were forced to leave Ukraine, which used to be theirs but no longer is. We are all here, and probably always were, to stay.

Notes

Introduction

1 The most egregious example of an attempt to eradicate the Ukrainian language occurred in May 1876. Tsar Alexander II, while 'taking the cure' at a spa in Ems, Germany, accepted the recommendations of a commission he had appointed to report on the 'ukrainophile propaganda in the southern provinces of Russia.' The secret Ems Ukase, as this document came to be known, prohibited the printing in Ukrainian of any original works or translations and forbade the importing of Ukrainian-language publications, the staging of plays and public readings in Ukrainian, and the printing of Ukrainian lyrics to musical works, thereby dealing a severe blow to Ukrainian national aspirations. The ukase was never formally revoked. Even Prince Wolkonsky , author of *The Ukraine Question: The Historic Truth versus the Separatist Propaganda* (Rome, 1920), admitted that the 'only sin of the Tsarist power against the Little Russian population as such consisted in the restraint put upon Little Russian Literature and, thereby indirectly, on the Little Russian dialect.' While he went on to concede that this 'mistake must not be repeated' because, in 'literature, as in life, a free competition must be established between the Russian and Little Russian languages,' he was sanguine about the outcome: 'There can be no doubt that victory will remain with the Russian language, which, from the point of view of universal culture, is not to be regretted.' Wolkonsky denied the existence of a distinct nation known as the Ukrainians, scoffing that the very idea was nothing more than the stuff of legend. Certainly these 'Little Russians' had certainly never suffered under any 'Russian yoke.' Indeed, only the intervention of Russia had spared them from domination by Polish imperialists. Ukraine was, according to Wolkonsky, a construction 'torn from the living body of Russia'; it had

'never been independent,' and its separation from Russia was being carried out in violation of the Wilsonian principle of the right of national self-determination, a move orchestrated by Russia's 'enemies and the Allies.' Concluding his impassioned statement against Ukrainian separatism, Wolkonsky told the Allies: 'It is impossible to understand you. The Russian nation has given two million lives to secure you two years for war preparation; many times it has helped you when you were in a tight place; it has hurled back in disorder the forces of the enemy and prepared your triumph; while you – you have suspected us of traitorous designs against you. The real traitors appeared – Bronstein (*alias* Trotsky) and Co. – who betrayed Russia and you: you accused all Russia of treason and began to settle her destinies without referring to us, your Allies ... You divide Russia and tear into fragments the Russian people ... Divide Russia if you will. But remember that your decree is not law binding on us.'

Twenty years later, Pierre Bregy and Prince Serge Obolensky took up very similar themes in their tract *The Ukraine – A Russian Land* (London, 1940). They argued that it was impossible, geographically speaking, to fix the frontier of Ukraine as distinct from Russia. And there could be no independent Ukraine, for 'Ukrainian independence is not justified in itself and is contrary to the interests and aspirations of her people. It cannot be realized without the help of the Germans, an eventuality which ought never to be wished for by any Ukrainian who loves his country.' Instead, to ensure that Ukraine might 'live and may enjoy her riches, her culture, and her genius, and in order that she may not become a prey to German imperialism and that the Ukrainian problem ceases to be an international problem,' they proposed that Poland become a 'nationally homogeneous country' and Russia be 'endowed with a national regime, capable of assuring to all the Russian countries, including the Ukraine, economic well-being, and cultural and religious liberty, and that she should reunite these countries and thus resume her place of honour – to be a fortress against German expansion and the guarantee of equilibrium and peace in eastern Europe.'

Of course there were also advocates for Ukraine, like Bedwin Sands, who argued in *The Ukraine* (London, 1914) that Ukrainians 'offered the purest type of Slavs,' and that their movement was neither pro-Austrian nor pro-Russian but rather pro-Ukrainian – 'They want to be their own masters, instead of filling the pockets of Russians and Poles' – or Gustaf F. Steffen, in *Russia, Poland, and the Ukraine* (Jersey City, New Jersey, 1915), who noted that Ukrainians hoped for 'a time when a free and independent Ukraine [would] grow out of the ruins of the Russian empire, that burial-ground of many nations.' A contemporary geographer's viewpoint was provided by Stephen Rudnitsky, in *Ukraine: The Land and Its People* (New York, 1918). Rudnitsky noted that 'there are few lands upon the whole globe so imperfectly known to geographic science' as Ukraine, in part because the Russian government had been determined to 'erase the old name of the land and the nation from the map of Europe.' A similar theme was taken up by Lancelot Lawton in an address given to the Anglo-Ukrainian Committee on 29 May 1935, published as *The Ukrainian Question* (London, 1935). Lawton began his commentary by stating that 'the chief problem in Europe to-day is the Ukrainian problem ... To an extent unrealized by most people, it has been a root of European strife during the last quarter of a century. That so little has been heard of it is not surprising; for suppression of Ukrainian Nationality has been persistently accompanied by obliteration of the very word Ukraine and concealment of the very existence of Ukraine. So successfully was this erasure effected that over the greater part of the world, Ukraine only survived in poetry and legend, and invariably it was thought that if ever it existed, it had long been buried in the cemetery of dead and forgotten nations.'

In touching on why a British audience should be interested in the Ukrainian independence movement, Lawton echoed some of the points that had been raised during the First World War by pro-Ukrainian writers like George Raffalovich. In *The Ukraine and the Small Nations* (London, 1915), Raffalovich had railed against those who, like a Dr Dillon writing in *The Telegraph*, had tried to assure the British public that the Ruthenians were Russians at heart: 'I know that to be contrary to the truth.' He also took on Mr H.G. Wells, who, he claimed, 'would probably assert that there is a Ukraine, but that it is a Hapsburg babe, suckled by that ideal wet-nurse, Prussia.' Raffalovich went on to expose what he felt was the hypocrisy of those Englishmen who attempted to argue that the war was being fought on behalf of the small nationalities of Europe. That was 'utterly untrue,' he wrote: 'The truth is that you people of England do not believe in your hearts in the rights of small nationalities. Only the Irish and, perhaps, the Welsh do that. When it suits you, you take up the dear oppressed peoples. When it does not, you turn a deaf ear to their claims. The English love for the weak is a piece of arrant humbug *à la* Gladstone ... Our ears will be closed, our eyes will be shut. What the Ukrainians need is a friendly statesman with two million bayonets behind him. This they will never get from England until it suits England's book. Cease then to rave about chivalry. Do not insult our intelligence by prating about the sacred cause of smaller nationalities. Or else help them all alike!'

Taking up some of these themes twenty years later, Lawton reminded his listeners that even Voltaire had noted 'admiringly the persistence with which Ukrainians aspired to freedom and remarked that being surrounded by hostile lands, they were doomed to search for a Protector.' Until Ukrainians were assured of liberty, 'they will be faithless to whichever State they are bound [to] and will continue freely to shed their own blood and that of their conquerors. So long, too, as this situation continues other nations will be tempted to exploit it. What then is the use of pretending that there is peace when there is not peace? Nor will there be any until this Ukrainian question is satisfactorily disposed of.'

For a useful treatment of the conflicting interpretations of Ukrainian history as offered by Russian, Polish, Soviet, and Ukrainian historiographers, see chapter 2, 'Historical Perceptions,' in P.R. Magocsi's *A History of Ukraine* (Toronto, 1996). Magocsi has pointed out that scholars in the West essentially adopted the traditional Russian view of the history of eastern Europe, a situation that regrettably still prevails, as even a cursory review of textbooks published after the implosion of the Soviet Union reveals.

2 Interviewed by the staff of *Ukrainian Weekly* on 17 January 1995, Ukraine's first president, Leonid Kravchuk, was asked what he considered the most significant accomplishment of his presidency. He replied: 'Simply, the greatest achievement is that Ukraine appeared in the world. It appeared peacefully, without bloodshed, without major conflicts. The fact that Ukraine gained world recognition will suffice ... We achieved our freedom – in peace, calm, and harmony. That's enough. Just to get out from under that horrible empire.' See 'Interview: Leonid Kravchuk on Culture, Politics, and Society,' *Ukrainian Weekly,* 5 February 1995, 3, 16. Recognition of the changed status of Ukraine is certainly reflected in the growing body of important literature dealing with the country. For some recent examples, see J.E. Mroz and O. Pavliuk, 'Ukraine: Europe's Linchpin,' *Foreign Affairs* 75:3 (May–June 1996): 52–62; the intriguing discussion of the civilizational fault line in Ukraine discussed by S.P. Huntington, *The Clash of Civilizations and the Remaking of the World Order* (New York, 1996); A. Wilson, *Ukrainian Nationalism in the 1990s: A Minority Faith* (Cambridge, 1997); the essays in *Ukraine in the World: Studies in the International Relations and Security Structure of a Newly Independent State,* ed. L.A. Hajda, Harvard Papers in Ukrainian Studies (Cambridge, Mass., 1998); B. Nahaylo, *The Ukrainian Resurgence* (Toronto, 1999); and S.W. Garnett, *Keystone in the Arch: Ukraine in the Emerging Security Environment of Central and Eastern Europe* (1999).

3 In the compelling introduction to his book *Europe: A History* (Oxford, 1996) Norman Davies elaborates on how our understanding of Europe has been influenced by the emotions and experiences of the two world wars. Seen through what he has labelled the 'Allied Scheme of History,' Western civilization is presented as the pinnacle of human progress, opposition to fascism is seen as being the principal measure of merit, Germany is condemned as

being the source of malignant imperialism and war, and an indulgent view is always taken of tsarist Russia and the Soviet Union, whose many faults are never to be classed with those of the enemy. The implicit notion is that Russia has an understandable desire for domination in eastern Europe that should be accommodated, however conflicting the facts. In considering Western attitudes towards Ukraine's record during the Second World War, Davies caustically observes that, for the Allies, like the Poles the 'Ukrainians ... defied classification. Although they probably suffered absolutely the largest number of civilian casualties of any European nation, their main political aim was to escape from Soviet and Russian domination. The best thing to do with such an embarrassing nation was to pretend that it didn't exist, and to accept the old Tsarist fiction about their being "Little Russians." In reality they were neither little nor Russians.'

4 Even the fate of an infant born in Graz, after the war's end, could be uncertain. For example, on 9 March 1946, a young blue-eyed, blond-haired boy, Stepan, was born in DP camp 'Wagnar,' near Leibnitz, to Nadeshda Bilka, a single mother from Zaporizhzhia, whose nationality was listed originally as 'Ukrainian.' During the birth, this twenty-one-year-old mother became violent, reportedly tearing at the navel string, gnawing on the placenta, and behaving aggressively towards the infant. She was soon removed to a mental hospital, 'Feldhof,' where attending physicians diagnosed her as having 'always been a mental case,' currently incoherent, with 'very bad' prospects for any cure of her 'mental weakness.' Without consultation with her, this illegitimate son was certified to be a Soviet national. The fact that Nedeshda remained confined in the 'Feldhof' hospital, so that technically her boy was not an 'unaccompanied' minor in Austria, was ignored. On 6 May 1947 the Welfare Officer for UNRRA Team 327, Mrs M. Klok, reported that while Stepan had been suspected of having tuberculosis, he was getting better. Finally, on 29 September 1947, the infant was repatriated to the U.S.S.R., without his mother. UNRRA's decision was aided by a letter from Soviet colonel Starov: 'To your letter concerning Bilka, Nadeshda, and her child, Bilka, Stepan, who are located in the children's home in Leoben, I deem them absolutely liable for repatriation to U.S.S.R.' The chief of the Child Search Branch for UNNRA, Aleta Brownlee, concurred, and so the 'transfer of the child as stated above is hereby authorized.' The entry on the 'Separated – Child' form giving the boy's nationality as 'Ukrainian' was crossed out and replaced with the entry 'U.S.S.R.' The ultimate fate of both the boy and his mother are unknown. Copies of their documents are found in Box 2, A. Brownlee Collection, Hoover Institute on War, Revolution and Peace. For a recent commentary

on the issue of forcible repatriation, see P. Worthington, 'Britain's Dirty Little Secret,' *The Sunday Sun*, 11 July 1999, 6.

5 For example, the Nobel laureate Elie Wiesel penned an especially distasteful example of ukrainophobia in his book *The Jews of Silence: A Personal Report on Soviet Jewry* (New York, 1966). Writing about a visit to Babyn Yar (Babi Yar), near Kyiv, Wiesel describes how he spent three days in the Ukrainian capital 'without finding anyone who would take me to Babi Yar. Everyone had an excuse.' Finally he took a taxi. After following what he describes as a circuitous route, the driver brought him to a site, about which he wrote, 'There is nothing to see at Babi Yar.' Only later, in Moscow, did Wiesel, apparently reflecting on his experiences in Ukraine, conclude that the taxi driver had deliberately taken him to a wrong location and thus cheated him. But no matter, wrote Wiesel, for 'thanks to him and to his deceit, I was finally able to understand that Babi Yar *is* not in Kiev, no. Babi Yar *is* Kiev. It is the entire Ukraine. And that is all one needs to see there.' For a more measured commentary on commemorative efforts at Babyn Yar, see A. Chyczij, 'Cries from Beyond the Grave,' *Globe and Mail*, 12 October 1991. Unfortunately, some of the Israeli press still seems to ignore the Ukrainian government's concerted efforts since independence to properly hallow the tragedy at Babyn Yar. See, for example, E. Wohlgelernter, 'Remembrance at Babi Yar,' *Jerusalem Post*, 14 April 1999, which disingenuously implies that this mass gravesite is little more than a parking lot, marked only with a plain menorah. The denigration of Ukraine and of the Ukrainian national movement, fuelled by Soviet propagandists and fellow travellers in the West before 1991, has continued apace since independence. For example, on 23 October 1994 a segment of the CBS-TV program *60 Minutes*, hosted by Morley Safer, entitled 'The Ugly Face of Freedom,' described Ukrainians as 'genetically anti-Semitic' and attempted to portray contemporary Ukraine as an unstable and dangerous nation about to be taken over by 'nuclear-armed Nazis.' Despite the predictable outrage of North America's Ukrainian communities and some Jewish supporters, CBS-TV spokespersons continue to insist that their commentary was fair. See M.B. Kuropas, *Scourging of a Nation: CBS and the Defamation of Ukraine* (Kingston and Kyiv, 1995). Similar allegations were made in the immediate post–First World War period, requiring similar retorts by American Ukrainian activists and righteous Jews. See, for example, J. Batchinsky, A. Margolin, M. Vishnitzer, and I. Zangwill, *The Jewish Pogroms in Ukraine: Authoritative Statements on the Question of Responsibility for Recent Outbreaks against the Jews in Ukraine* (Washington, 1919). In today's Ukraine, Jews are constitutionally accorded the same rights and responsibilities as all other citizens and are no more likely to be discriminated against than anywhere else

in the world. When the Israeli prime minister, Benjamin Netanyahu, and foreign minister, Ariel Sharon, visited Kyiv in March 1999, local Jewish community leaders made no reports of anti-Semitism, and Ukrainian president Leonid Kuchma joined Prime Minister Netanyahu in laying a wreath at the Babyn Yar monument (see 'Israeli Leaders' Visit to Ukraine Underscores Cordial Relations,' *Ukrainian News*, 24 March–6 April 1999, 5).

6 That Western intelligence agencies exploited the Ukrainian resistance movement for their own ends has yet to be fully documented, but J. Ranelagh has noted, in *The Agency: The Rise and the Decline of the CIA from Wild Bill Donovan to William Casey* (New York, 1986), 137, 228, that 'the Office of Policy Coordination and the CIA's Office of Special Operations entered battle on this field. Agents were briefed and given false papers and sent on missions throughout the Eastern bloc, including into the USSR itself, where for several years after the war a Ukrainian resistance movement continued to fight the Red Army. This was a major and fascinating undertaking. The Ukraine was an acknowledged part of the USSR, so the operations were tantamount to war. It demonstrated a cold ruthlessness: the Ukrainian resistance had no hope of winning unless America was prepared to go to war on its behalf. Since America was not prepared to go to war, America was in effect encouraging Ukrainians to go to their deaths.' On 27 December 1952, at about the same time as the last radio messages were received from CIA-trained operatives in Ukraine, Polish radio publicly revealed that their security forces had penetrated the anti-communist Polish resistance movement as early as mid-1947. Although Ranelagh observes that CIA and National Security Council proponents of paramilitary operations behind the Iron Curtain kept lists of émigrés willing to fight the Soviets in the event of war, for some years thereafter the 'real lesson – that the United States was not prepared to launch a war to liberate eastern Europe – was not recognized by those who hoped to benefit from it. It would take uprisings in East Berlin and Hungary before European hopes of paramilitary action sponsored by the CIA or of straightforward military action by the United States were finally dashed.' One reason why Anglo-American efforts to aid the Ukrainian resistance floundered was revealed by the British traitor Kim Philby, whose *My Silent War* (New York, 1968) observes that the British and the Americans exchanged precise information about the timing and geographical coordinates of their spring 1951 operations into Ukraine, which Philby, as the British liaison officer with the CIA, was privy to. 'I do not know what happened to the parties concerned,' he wrote, 'but I can make an informed guess.' Philby, who was not above exaggerating his own importance, died an exile in Moscow in May 1998.

7 Since the end of the Second World War the issue of bringing alleged Nazi

war criminals and collaborators to justice has been a matter of some controversy in Canada and elsewhere, especially given repeated allegations that many such villains found shelter in the West. While it is not within the ambit of this work to dissect this issue thoroughly, a few comments are called for. I have served for several years as director of research for the Ukrainian Canadian Civil Liberties Association (previously known as the Civil Liberties Commission / Ukrainian Canadian Congress). My position is that those who collaborated with either the Soviet or the Nazi regime in Ukraine acted, first of all, as *individuals*. Whether out of fear or out of prejudice, in naïve hope or in ideological fervour, under duress or willingly, these criminals committed themselves to behaviour that ranged from the purblind and the cowardly to the purulent and unforgivable. It is essential, however, that we remember that such miscreants *never acted as representatives of any minority, or people, or nation*, even if some of them may have claimed otherwise. Yet, ever since the end of the war, their wrongdoings have been mis-described by the ignorant or the invidious in stereotypical language. The result has been that an entire nation, Ukraine, is often blamed unfairly for the evil deeds of a few during the Second and even the First World War. The same species of miasma has been generated about most of the other once captive nations of eastern Europe. Furthermore, the repeated use of these half-truths and sometimes utterly prejudiced allegations over several decades has bestowed upon them the patina of legitimacy. The ensuing struggle for memory, particularly between some Jews and some east Europeans, has ranged from the trite to the tragic. What is lost sight of in all these debates over who did what to whom, and when, why, and for what end, are the millions of victims themselves. Professor Davies's assessment of Ukraine's wartime losses in n3 above are worth reflecting on, as is the finding of another leading historian of the twentieth century, Alan Bullock. In *Hitler and Stalin: Parallel Lives* (New York, 1992), 974, Bullock reminds his readers that 'the Stalinist repression was responsible for a greater number of deaths – by some calculations up to double the number put to death by the Nazis.' Many of those millions of victims of Soviet crimes against humanity and war crimes died in Ukraine. I have come to the conclusion that no minority, people, nation, or state in Europe can claim absolute innocence or assert that all its people were *only* victims, whether under the Soviet or the Nazi tyranny. There were villains *and* heroes within every community, the Jewish one not excepted. For that reason I endorse plans for an *inclusive* Genocide Museum in Ottawa, a commemorative and educational centre that would recall the many episodes of genocide that have taken place not only in Europe but also in Africa, in Asia, in Latin America, and elsewhere during and before the twentieth century. My views on this theme are further developed in 'Museum of

Reconciliation: Appropriate for Canada,' *Ukrainian Weekly,* 29 August 1999,
6, an edited version of which was published as 'Museum Should Honour
All Victims,' *Toronto Star,* 31 August 1999, A15, and in 'Inclusive Memory,'
brief of UCCLA to House of Commons Standing Committee on Canadian
Heritage, 8 June 2000, available at http://www.infoukes.com/uccla/issues/
genocide.

As for the question of how to deal with war criminals, I have seen no compelling evidence that there are any Nazi war criminals in Canada, and certainly government officials have shied away from trying to make any such
case in a Canadian criminal court. Nevertheless, *if* the evidence is found, then
Canada *must* take measures to bring to justice, in Canada under Canadian
criminal law, *all* war criminals and persons involved in perpetrating crimes
against humanity. That should happen regardless of the accused's ethnic,
religious, or racial origin, the period or place where the crimes were committed, and the ideological orientation of those involved. I do not believe that
any statute of limitations should prevent prosecutions. All civilized nations
should be expected to follow a similar course. Regrettably, Canada's attempts
to bring alleged war criminals to justice have been selective and undermined
by the proclivities of the system. And the continuing and seemingly wilful
desire of Canadian officials to ignore Soviet and other communist atrocities is
near inexplicable. On this subject, see L. Luciuk, 'Where's the Justice for
Gulag Victims?' *Globe and Mail,* 10 September 1991; the editorial 'Holding
Communism to Account,' ibid., 30 August 1997; and R. Harris, 'The West Prefers Its Dictators Red,' *National Post,* 1 December 1998.

For a perspective on the impact of these denaturalization and deportation
hearings on one Canadian family, see O. Odynsky, 'Canada Intends to
Deport My Father without a Fair Trial,' *Globe and Mail,* 5 January 1998, and
the supportive editorial, 'Will Nazi Hunters Misfire?' ibid., 14 January 1998.
On 10 May 1996, a Ukrainian American, forced to abandon the United States
after unsubstantiated allegations tendered by the Office of Special Investigations, had portrayed him as a Nazi collaborator, wrote the author. This elderly man, who prefers to remain anonymous, described some of the angst he
has endured in exile: 'Unfortunately my difficulties have now gone on for
some 17 years ... What I have learned in that time is that those with great
political strength, influence and finances can do whatever they like, forget
the truth. Bitter personal experience has also taught me that nothing can be
gained by anyone taking up my case. Doing so would only anger those Jews
who profit by giving me no peace ... If I have any chance of clearing my good
name before I die it can only happen through the Procurator's office of
Ukraine, but I am not hopeful ... Try to imagine how my heart aches and my
tears flow when I think that while I, then only a student, took an active role

in the struggle for Ukrainian independence and was even wounded by the Germans, today an independent Ukraine won't give me even a small amount of help. I fought and prayed for that country's independence. I longed for Ukraine's freedom all my life. Yet today I can not even visit my native land to pray at the graves of my parents and friends. For the people who are in power there are the same as those who tried, on the basis of fabricated lies, to ruin me, an innocent man. Because of them I lost my son, the possessions we had accumulated over 30 years of hard work in America, my old age pension, my health and my citizenship ... The greatest wrongs done to me were done by the KGB from the *oblast* of Ivano Frankivsk ... The KGB there [were] the worst in all of western Ukraine, turncoats more vicious even than the enemy. For them I was a war criminal because I had been a young Ukrainian nationalist who loved and fought for the independence of Ukraine ... I am now old, and have no strength left to fight. In truth my entire situation was always, and remains, a political matter, not one of criminal justice.'

For an insightful overview of the vagaries of the government's case against a Mennonite from Ukraine, see K. Makin, 'Witch Hunt: For Crimes Not Committed,' *Globe and Mail*, 20 February 1999, and the editorial 'Pursuing Johann Dueck,' ibid., 23 February 1999. Mounting public unease with the nature of these proceedings is reflected in the letters column of *Globe and Mail*. See, for example, 'No Justice for Dueck,' by Dr D.A. McMillan, 22 January 1999; the four letters published under the title 'Inside the Johann Dueck File' in the 24 February 1999 edition; and John Martin's letter, 'Misplaced Revenge Is Not So Sweet,' 3 March 1999. While Canada has bumbled on this issue, Lithuania has dealt with it very sensibly, in part by establishing a government-funded Genocide and Resistance Center and associated museum. See L. Luciuk, 'A Man-Made Hell Preserved for All to See,' *National Post*, 15 April 1999. Ukraine, regrettably, has yet actively to investigate Soviet war crimes and bring to justice the communist collaborators who perpetrated atrocities, despite the efforts of Canada's Ukrainian community to alert members of the Ukrainian parliament, the Verkhovna Rada, to the international importance of this matter. See the booklet *War Crimes: A Submission to the Government of Ukraine on Crimes against Humanity and War Crimes* (Winnipeg, 1992). Ukraine's failure to deal with this issue is now being criticized within that country. See, for example, J. Koshiw 'When Will Soviet Killers Be Put on Trial?' *Kyiv Post*, 8 April 1998; Koshiw, is the deputy editor of that newspaper.

Regardless of the outcome of these denaturalization and deportation hearings, the inescapable truth is that all the regimes for whom the killers did their dirty work, whether fascist, Nazi, Soviet, or communist, have long since been discredited by history. We now understand that the many millions murdered in the twentieth century for the sake of achieving the utopia imagined by the communists or the fascists were sacrificed for nought. There is no excuse for those who, out of fear, ignorance, self-loathing, prejudice, or greed, helped butcher their neighbours. It would be best to bring *all* such murderers to justice. But there will never likely be a meeting of minds on who were victims and who were victimizers. For the spoils of this struggle over memory are the all-too-human hearts and minds of generations yet to be born. And no nation can lose its children and hope to survive.

Chapter 1: The Plan

1 See the 'Declaration of the Temporary Central Organizational Bureau of the League for the Liberation of Ukraine,' 1 May 1949, Toronto. It located the 'front line' of the national liberation movement in Ukraine, but proclaimed that a 'second line' also existed, encompassing the entire Ukrainian emigration. The universality of the battle against Bolshevism, described as 'an aspect of Russian imperialism,' meant that Ukrainians in Canada must also get involved in the struggle. This declaration, published in the *Ukrainian Echo*, listed Yakiv Nesterenko as the League's president, Sviatoslav (Stanley) Frolick as vice-president, Evhen Dudra as second vice-president, and M. Sosnowsky as secretary. At the League's first national congress in Toronto, 25 December 1949, a slightly different executive emerged. It included Nesterenko as president; Dr Roman Malaschuk as first vice-president; M. Kravchiv as second vice-president; and W. Beszchlibnyk, P. Bashuk, O. Kushnir, M. Sosnowksy, Iryna Demydchuk, S. Stepa, and I. Boyko as executive members. Citing other responsibilities, Nesterenko soon stepped down as the League's president and was replaced by Malaschuk. One of the guest speakers at this conference was Lieutenant B. Melodia-Kruk, an UPA veteran. The organization was renamed the Canadian League for the Liberation of Ukraine (CLLU) after its second national congress, held in Toronto on 24 December 1950. By the time of the fourth congress, held in Toronto on 18–19 July 1953, there were reportedly 1257 members, a figure participants admitted was far too small given their four years of organizational efforts. The group underwent another name change, in 1993, becoming the League of Ukrainian Canadians. The documentation cited is located in the national archives of the League, in Toronto, and was kindly made available by the late Andrij Bandera. For a sympathetic interpretation of this group's history, see *A Historical Outline of the Canadian League for the Liberation of Ukraine*, ed. W. Solonynka (Toronto, 1984). As a document released under the Access to Information

Act confirms, the RCMP was provided with a translation of the 25 December 1949 resolutions of the first conference of the League for the Liberation of Ukraine, held in Toronto. Attended by M. Sosnowsky, M. Lucky, J. Spolsky, D. Woinariwsky, S. Frolack, J. Bojkov, R. Rachmanny, W. Nahirny, J. Kolisnyk, and others, this meeting produced a document which underscored how the League hoped to create 'a truly Ukrainian national leadership in Canada,' one of whose goals would be to organize the Ukrainian emigration in Canada for the purpose of 'strengthening the Ukrainian revolutionary-liberation front and ... aiding the cause of political liberation of the Ukraine.' Resolution 3 added that 'this constitutes the basic task of all the Ukrainians living in this terrain.' Commenting on the UCC, Resolution 7 spoke about the need for organizational reconstruction, frankly stating that the UCC's existing structure did not offer any guarantee that the institution would be capable of 'fulfilling the tasks placed upon it by the exigencies of the Ukrainian liberation struggle in Ukraine and the situation of the Ukrainian group in Canada.'

2 According to the organizing committee's protocols, those present at the League's creation were Yakiv Nesterenko, Mychailo Sosnowsky, Sviatoslav Frolick, Evhen Dudra, Dr Shkurat, Stepan Bihun, Myroslav Velyhorsky, Lev Husyn, Olha Ivanchuk, Stepan Luikish, Semen Mackevych, Yuri Roussow, Yaroslav Spolsky, Roman Malaschuk, Ivan Boyko, and Volodymyr Lyzanivsky. See 'Declaration of the Temporary Central Organizational Bureau of the League for the Liberation of Ukraine,' 1 May 1949, Toronto.

3 On their involvement with the Ukrainian nationalist movement and the League, interviews were held with W. Bezchlibnyk, Toronto, 30 June and 1 July 1981 (MHSO); S.W. Frolick, Toronto, 1 July 1981, 10 January 1983, 16–24 December 1983, and 4–6 January 1984 (MHSO and CIUS); O. Kushnir, Toronto, 5 April 1982 (MHSO); and R. Malaschuk, Toronto, 25 March 1982 (MHSO). Useful background information can be found in interviews with I. Eliashevsky, Toronto, 11 February 1982 (MHSO); Reverend Semen Izyk, Winnipeg, 21 May 1982 (MHSO); V. Makar, Toronto, 23 March 1982 (MHSO); A. Matla, Toronto, 24 March 1982 (MHSO); Evhen Shtendera, Ottawa, 7 September 1982 (MHSO); Bohdan Stebelsky, Toronto, 17 March 1982 (MHSO); P. Bashuk, Winnipeg, 24 January 1983 (CIUS); and W. Klish, Toronto, 21 June 1983 (CIUS).

4 The term 'second line' or *druha liniia* was first mentioned during an interview with Petro Bashuk in Winnipeg, 24 January 1983 (CIUS). Bashuk, a member of the OUNb and a survivor of Auschwitz, was one of the early organizers of the League. The term is used in the 'Declaration of the Temporary Central Organizational Bureau.' The OUN split into two factions, known popularly after their respective leaders, Stepan Bandera and Andrii Melnyk,

as the Banderivtsi (OUNb) and the Melnykivtsi (OUNm). At the end of May 1941, during an OUN congress in Cracow, Colonel Melnyk was repudiated as the OUN's leader, and resolutions supporting him, which had been passed at the Second Grand Assembly of the OUN held in Rome, were declared null and void. Stepan Bandera was then affirmed as the OUN's new leader, an action which cemented the original OUN's split into two competing factions. A German-language version of the resolutions of the second OUN congress is reproduced in *Litopys UPA: The UPA in Light of German Documents*, Book 1 (Toronto, 1983), 33–43.

5 The existence of this 'second line' formation was confirmed by the late Yaroslav Stetsko, Bandera's successor, in an interview held in Munich, 14 July 1982 (MHSO).

6 Several leading members of the League and the OUNb spent the war years incarcerated in Nazi concentration camps. For example, Dr Roman Malaschuk bore Auschwitz tattoo #57349, and Wasyl Bezchlibnyk was imprisoned with Stepan Bandera and Yaroslav Stetsko in Saxsenhausen. The interviews with Malaschuk and Bezchlibnyk (n3 above) include reminiscences on the Nazi concentration camps. In his *From the Book of My Life: Memoirs, You'll Grow Up My Son, and Find Your Way* (Toronto, 1987), 266–8, Malaschuk lists the names and tattoo numbers of sixty-seven Banderivtsi he met in Auschwitz, seventeen of whom perished. Stepan Bandera's two brothers, Wasyl, #49721, and Oleksa, #51020, were among those murdered in Auschwitz. For two other Ukrainian nationalists' accounts of their experiences in the Nazi death camps, including Auschwitz, see P. Mirchuk, *In the German Mills of Death* (New York,1976) and S. Petylycky, 'No. 154922 remembers,' *Ottawa Citizen*, 31 March 1997, A12, also published as 'Bring War Traitors to Justice,' *Edmonton Journal*, 6 April 1997, A10. See also S. Petelycky, *Into Auschwitz, for Ukraine* (Kingston, 1999) for a personal account of one of the OUNb activists arrested by the Nazis.

7 Interview with Y. Stetsko, Munich, 14 July 1982, (MHSO). Born in Ternopil on 19 January 1912 as the son of a nationally conscious Ukrainian Catholic priest, Stetsko joined the UVO in 1927. After being imprisoned in 1929 by the Polish authorities, he became an early member of the OUN, eventually a supporter of the Bandera faction. On 30 June 1941, when Ukrainian nationalists proclaimed the renewal of an independent Ukrainian state in Lviv, Stetsko was named premier. On relations between the Ukrainian nationalist movement and the Germans, Stetsko stated: 'Only three nations stood against Bolshevism at that time – Germany, Italy, and Japan. We were not interested in the political systems prevailing in those countries, any more than Churchill was interested in what was going on in the Soviet Union when

he said he'd join the devil himself if the latter went against Hitler. Those
three states were against the international status quo ... When we proclaimed
Ukrainian independence we wanted to demonstrate to the Allies that there
was another conception, another force, at play in the world, that they should
be fighting against *both* the Nazis and the Soviets, allying themselves with the
nations and peoples oppressed by the Russian Empire and the German one
... yet no one helped us.' Stetsko was arrested by the Gestapo on 12 July 1941
and interned at Saxsenhausen. After the war he settled in Munich and came
to head the ABN and, after Bandera's assassination on 15 October 1959, the
OUNb or OUN-Revolutionaries, as the Banderivtsi were more formally
known. Now that Ukraine is independent, members and supporters of the
OUNb have formed a political party known as the Congress of Ukrainian
Nationalists. At its first general assembly, held in Kyiv on 2–4 July 1993, Slava
Stetsko was re-elected president of the Congress. She is also president of the
ABN and was elected a deputy member of the Verkhovna Rada of Ukraine.

8 For general works on Ukraine during the Second World War see G.
Reitlinger, *The House Built on Sand: The Conflicts of German Policy in Russia,
1939–1945* (New York, 1960), and A. Dallin, *German Rule in Russia, 1941–
1945* (1957; 2nd rev. ed. Boulder, Colo. 1981). The subject is also well treated
by B. Krawchenko, *Social Change and National Consciousness in Twentieth Century Ukraine* (London, 1985); I. Kamenetsky, *Hitler's Occupation of Ukraine,
1941–1944: A Study of Totalitarian Imperialism* (Milwaukee, 1956); and *Secret
Nazi Plans for Eastern Europe: A Study of Lebensraum Policies* (New York, 1961);
B. Wytwycky, *The Other Holocaust: Many Circles of Hell* (Washington, 1980);
Ukraine during World War II: History and its Aftermath, ed. Y. Boshyk (Edmonton, 1986); and L.Y. Luciuk, 'Ukraine,' in *The Oxford Companion to the Second
World War,* ed. I.C.B. Dear and M.R.D. Foot (Oxford, 1995), 1159–65.

9 The figure of 4.5 million displaced Ukrainians is an overestimate made by a
Ukrainian Canadian soldier, Bohdan Panchuk. Ihor Stebelsky cites a more
plausible figure of 2.5–3 million Ukrainian refugees in 'Ukrainians in the Displaced Persons Camps of Austria and Germany after World War II,' *Ukrainian
Historian* 23: 1–2 (1986). F.K. Hoehler, in *Europe's Homeless Millions* (New York,
1945) estimated that there were in excess of 2 million Polish refugees. Just as
Panchuk overestimated the number of Ukrainian DPs, Hoehler underestimated the number of Ukrainians classified as Poles on account of their prewar Polish citizenship. Panchuk's memorandum of 10 June 1945, entitled
'The Situation with Regards to Ukrainian Refugees,' is found in 'the G.R.B.
Panchuk Collection' (hereafter the Panchuk Collection), now located in
Toronto at the Archives of Ontario. A detailed description of this collection,
comprised of approximately 61 cubic feet of archival boxes covering a period

from the 1930s to the early 1970s, is available from the Archives of Ontario. Series A, B, C, D, E, F, and H contain materials on CURB, UCSA, UCVA, the UCC, the UCRF, and the AUGB, and some of Panchuk's personal papers. This is one of the most important archival collections for the study of this particular period in Ukrainian Canadian history. For an earlier description of these materials, see L.Y. Luciuk and Z. Zwarycz, 'The G.R.B. Panchuk Collection,' *Journal of Ukrainian Studies* 7:1 (1982): 79–81.

10 For sympathetic interpretations of the UCC's early history, see O. Gerus, 'The Ukrainian Canadian Committee,' chapter 9 in *A Heritage in Transition: Essays in the History of Ukrainians in Canada*, ed. M.R. Lupul (Toronto, 1982), and W. Veryha, 'The Ukrainian Canadian Committee: Its Origins and War Activity,' M.A. thesis, University of Ottawa, 1967. A more critical and persuasive view is presented in B.S. Kordan, 'Disunity and Duality: Ukrainian Canadians and the Second World War,' M.A. thesis, Carleton University, 1981. According to Tracy Philipps, who was very active in Ukrainian Canadian affairs during the war, he himself was responsible for creating the UCC at the behest of the Canadian government. See Document #28 in *A Delicate and Difficult Question: Documents in the History of Ukrainians in Canada, 1899–1962*, ed. B.S. Kordan and L.Y. Luciuk (Kingston, 1986), 74–6.

11 For example, the bi-monthly tabloid *The Ukrainian Canadian* editorialized on 15 January 1949 about how the DPs were involved in 'organized hooliganism,' and subsequent issues carried 'D.P. Gangsterism' (1 August 1949), 'Deport D.P. Thugs!' (1 November 1949), and other stories critical of the 'anti-Canadian' and 'terroristic' work of the League for the Liberation of Ukraine (1 March 1950). This critical commentary on the nationalists found some public support. For second-hand criticism of the Banderivtsi voiced by a Canadian-born Ukrainian, see the interview with Mr and Mrs J. Stratichuk, Sault Ste Marie, 15 May 1982 (MHSO). In dismissing the postwar DPs Mr Stratichuk stated: 'They thought they were all heroes. But they weren't the ones whom the police had beaten over their heads, as we were beaten when we rode the rails in the Depression, looking for work.'

12 Perhaps the most cogent essay on the nature of ethnic group boundaries is by F. Barth in *Ethnic Groups and Boundaries: The Social Organization of Culture*, ed. Barth (Boston, 1969). Barth's themes have been well expanded by W. Isajiw, 'Definitions of Ethnicity,' *Ethnicity* 1 (New York, 1974).

Chapter 2: 'From a Police Point of View'

1 See J.-P. Himka, 'Background to Emigration,' in *A Heritage in Transition: Essays in the History of Ukrainians in Canada*, ed. M. Lupul (Toronto, 1982),

14, and S. Hryniuk, *Peasants with Promise: Ukrainians in Southeastern Galicia, 1880–1900* (Edmonton, 1991). According to J. Petryshyn, *Peasants in the Promised Land: Canada and the Ukrainians, 1891–1914* (Toronto, 1985), nearly one million Ukrainians left Bukovyna and Galicia between the mid-1880s and 1914. The outbreak of the First World War disrupted an international exodus which had been prompted largely by rural overpopulation. Himka points out there were 84 persons per square kilometre in Galicia in 1890, a figure that grew to 102 persons per square kilometre in 1910, despite mass emigration. In 1900–2 most peasant families owned less than five hectares of land, the minimum amount required to sustain a family, whose average size was five people. A lack of industrial development in Western Ukraine, peasant familiarity with seasonal labour, and the short-term migration associated with working elsewhere in east central Europe were other factors which stimulated transatlantic emigration.

2 For population data on Ukrainians in Canada, see *A Statistical Compendium on the Ukrainians in Canada, 1891–1976*, ed. W. Darcovich and P. Yuzyk (Ottawa, 1980). Unless otherwise cited, all statistics are taken from this source. An update is provided by B.S. Kordan, *Ukrainians and the 1981 Canada Census: A Data Handbook* (Edmonton, 1985).

3 On Sifton's personality and career, see D.J. Hall, *Clifford Sifton: The Young Napoleon* (Vancouver, 1981).

4 On the nature of the Ukrainian Canadian settlement experience during the pioneer period, see J.C. Lehr, 'The Process and Pattern of Ukrainian Rural Settlement in Western Canada,' Ph.D. thesis, University of Manitoba, 1978. For a more specific account, see O.T. Martynowych, *The Ukrainian Bloc Settlement in East Central Alberta, 1890–1930: A History'* (Edmonton, 1985). Other useful books include *New Soil – Old Roots: The Ukrainian Experience in Canada*, ed. J. Rozumnyj (Winnipeg, 1983), and M. Kostash's popular account, *All of Baba's Children* (Edmonton, 1977). For an analysis of how various Anglo-Canadian writers interpreted the Ukrainian Canadian experience see F. Swyripa, *Ukrainian Canadians: A Survey of Their Portrayal in English-Language Works* (Edmonton, 1978).

5 See V.J. Kaye, *Early Ukrainian Settlements in Canada, 1895–1900: Dr Josef Oleskow's Role in the Settlement of the Canadian Northwest* (Toronto, 1964).

6 On the activities of the North Atlantic Trading Company, see Petryshyn, *Peasants in the Promised Land*, 22–6, and P. Berton, *The Promised Land: Settling the West, 1896–1914* (Toronto, 1984).

7 Petryshyn, *Peasants in the Promised Land*, 48.

8 See Series 50.62–77 in *A Statistical Compendium*, ed. Darcovich and Yuzyk, 514.

9 For Frank Oliver's remarks in the House of Commons, 12 April 1901, see Document #2 in *A Delicate and Difficult Question*, ed. Kordan and Luciuk, 20.
10 See Document #2, ibid.
11 For D.C. Fraser's remarks in the House of Commons, 12 April 1901, see Document #2, ibid., 21.
12 Petryshyn, *Peasants in the Promised Land*, 26.
13 This process is well described by Lehr, 'The Process and Pattern of Ukrainian Rural Settlement.'
14 Ibid.
15 See M.I. Marunchak, *The Ukrainian Canadians: A History* (Winnipeg, 1970), 351.
16 By allowing for this immigration of large numbers of unskilled labourers, Canada's gatekeepers unwittingly helped create a Ukrainian Canadian proletariat in the mining and industrial centres of north-central Ontario, Quebec, British Columbia, Alberta, and Nova Scotia, a population removed in space and working experience from the Prairie hearth of the Ukrainian pioneers. Of the approximately seventy-nine thousand Ukrainian males who arrived in Canada at the ports of Halifax and Quebec City between 1905 and 1914, just over forty-four thousand described themselves as general labourers rather than farmers. By 1914 nearly 54 per cent would characterize themselves as workers. In the same period, 58 per cent indicated that they intended to proceed to the Prairies, most of the remainder declaring that they intended to search for work in Ontario or Quebec in the urban-industrial centres, on the railroads, in the timber camps, or in the mines. Most of these immigrants were single, young males. (In contrast, most Ukrainian women arriving in this period went west.) Some of them later became leaders of the Ukrainian Canadian Left, among them Matthew Shatulsky, John Navis [Navizivsky], Matthew Popovich, and John Boychuk. Navis was one of the 'little band' who met secretly in a barn near Guelph, Ontario, at the end of May 1921 and set up the CPC. Popowich, a cosmopolitan intellectual, happily married to a Jewish woman, reportedly introduced the CPC's leader, Tim Buck, to the writings of Lenin. Boychuk played a leading role in the pro-communist movement in Toronto, while Shatulsky, one-time editor in chief of *Ukrainian Labour News*, gave the movement ideological direction while serving as the ULFTA's national secretary. All four men were pre–1918 immigrants. See Petryshyn, *Peasants in the Promised Land*, 141–53, and J. Kolasky, *The Shattered Illusion: The History of Ukrainian Pro-Communist Organizations in Canada* (Toronto, 1979), 7–8, for a listing of the other major figures in the ULFTA's leadership.
17 *Winnipeg Telegram*, 10 February 1899.

18 *Winnipeg Telegram*, 7 March 1899 and 24 March 1899.
19 *Winnipeg Telegram*, 24 November 1899.
20 *The Winnipeg Tribune*, 25 November 1899.
21 For MacDonald's remarks, 3 July 1919, see Document #12 in *A Delicate and Difficult Question*, ed. Kordan and Luciuk, 44. Another expression of anti-Galician sentiment is found in Reverend Captain W. Bridgeman's *Breaking Prairie Sod* (Toronto, 1920). Bridgeman contended that unless the 'Galicians' and 'Huns' were swept out, Canada would never know industrial stability.
22 See D. Morton, *The Canadian General: Sir William Otter* (Toronto, 1974).
23 For more information on Canada's First World War period internment operations, see J. Boudreau, *The Enemy Alien Problem in Canada, 1914–1920* (Los Angeles, 1965); P. Melnycky, 'The Internment of Ukrainians in Canada,' in *Loyalties in Conflict: Ukrainians in Canada during the Great War*, ed. F. Swyripa and J.H. Thompson (Edmonton, 1983), 1–24; L. Luciuk, *A Time for Atonement: Canada's First National Internment Operations and the Ukrainian Canadians, 1914–1920* (Kingston, 1988); and B. Waiser, *Park Prisoners: The Untold Story of Western Canada's National Parks, 1915–1946* (Saskatoon, 1995). Internees often protested about the injustice of their treatment. For example, G.C. Woodward, the American consul in Calgary, noted that all the prisoners he visited in two western Canadian camps had complained repeatedly about their imprisonment and told him they had done nothing to warrant internment as 'enemy aliens.' See Woodward's 'Reports on Camps at Lethbridge, Alberta-Morissey, British Columbia,' 19 August 1916, FO 383/240. Major-General Otter likewise noted, in his final report, that 'the tendency of municipalities to unload their indigent poor was the cause of the confinement of not a few.' In a file entitled 'Treatment of Enemy Subjects Interned in Canada,' M.B. Kirk, the American consul in Orillia, noted that a 'great number [of the prisoners] were men who are out of work and in need of charity.' None, he reported, had been attempting to return to Europe to serve in the Austro-Hungarian army. See his report of 27 March 1915 on the Kapuskasing camp, FO 383/240. Otter's *Report on Internment Operations, 1914–1920* is reprinted in *Ukrainian Canadians in Canada's Wars: Materials for Ukrainian Canada History*, vol. 1 ed. J.B. Gregorovich, (Toronto, 1983), 74–94. A general account dealing with western Canada during the war can be found in J.H. Thompson, *The Harvests of War: The Prairie West, 1914–1918* (Toronto, 1978), while D. Morton and G. Wright provide information about the attitudes of some Canadian veterans towards 'enemy aliens' in *Winning the Second Battle: Canadian Veterans and the Return to Civilian Life, 1915–1930* (Toronto, 1987). On contemporary attempts to secure acknowledgment and restitution, see B.S. Kordan, *Righting Historical Wrongs: Internment, Acknowledgement, and Redress* (Saskatoon, 1993); J.B. Gregorovich, *Commemorating an Injustice: Fort Henry and the Ukrainian Canadians as 'Enemy Aliens' during the*

First World War (Kingston, 1994); and *Righting an Injustice: The Debate over Redress for Canada's First National Internment Operations*, ed. L.Y. Luciuk (Toronto, 1994). On 27 September 1991, Peter Milliken, MP (Kingston and the Islands), moved in the House of Commons that the government of Canada should acknowledge that the internment and disenfranchisement of, and related repressive measures taken against, Canadians of Ukrainian origin between 1914 and 1920 were unwarranted and unjust and called for negotiations on redress. The complete text of his remarks and those of other MPs is reproduced in *Righting an Injustice*, ed. Luciuk, 203–11. As leader of the opposition, the Honourable Jean Chrétien wrote, on 8 June 1993: 'The Liberal Party understands your concern. As you know, we support your efforts to secure the redress of Ukrainian-Canadians' claims arising from their internment and loss of freedoms during the First World War and interwar period. You can be assured that we will continue to monitor the situation closely and seek to ensure that the government honours its promise.' Inexplicably, this pledge has not been honoured by Mr Chrétien or the Liberal Party of Canada even since the former became prime minister of Canada. More recently, on 10 October 1997, Inky Mark, MP (Dauphin–Swan River), of the Reform Party of Canada, rose in the House of Commons and spoke of the injustice that had been done to thousands of Ukrainian Canadians during Canada's first national internment operations, and asked the government of Canada to acknowledge this wrong and provide for the restitution of the wealth confiscated from the internees that still remains in federal coffers. See Canada, House of Commons, *Debates (Hansard)*, 10 October 1997. A favourable commentary on Mr Mark's efforts, 'Ottawa Must Keep Promise to Ukrainians,' by Marsha Skrypuch, was published in the letters section of *The Expositor*, 15 October 1997. Other recent commentaries in support of the Ukrainian Canadian community's claims include J.B. Gregorovich, 'Ottawa Must Redress Injustice to Internees,' *Toronto Star*, 31 March 1998, Katharine Wowk, 'Canada's Cemetery of Shame,' *Ottawa Citizen*, 16 September 1999, and Ian Hunter, 'An Apology Long Overdue,' *National Post*, 16 March 2000. For more see http://www.infoukes.com/history/internment/. And on 4 August 2000, Governor General Adrienne Clarkson described Canada's first national internment operations as one of the 'nation's sadder stories.' See Helen Fallding, 'Clarkson Recognizes Ukrainians' Grievance,' *Winnipeg Free Press*, 5 August 2000, A3.

24 On 21 December 1918 the Toronto *Globe* defined 'Bolshevism' as 'a label for any act or tendency which happens to offend our beliefs and prejudices.'

25 See Melnycky, 'The Internment of Ukrainians in Canada,' 6.

26 See Luciuk, *A Time for Atonement*, 25.

27 *Winnipeg Telegram*, 3 February 1916.

28 See D. Avery, 'The Radical Alien and the Winnipeg General Strike of 1919,'

in *The West and the Nation: Essays in Honour of W.L. Morton*, ed. C. Berger and R. Cook (Toronto, 1976), 214, 227. The bilingual school system of Manitoba, which offered English- and Ukrainian- (Ruthenian-) language instruction, was abolished by the Liberal government of T.C. Norris on 8 March 1916, despite protests from the Ukrainian Central Committee for the Defence of the Bilingual School System, headed by a member of the provincial legislature, Taras Ferley. On 3 February 1916 a petition signed by six thousand people, urging the retention of bilingual schools, was presented to the premier and his cabinet. It did not, however, prevent the official burning of Ukrainian-English textbooks on the grounds of the Manitoba legislative buildings. See Petryshyn, *Peasants in the Promised Land*, 189. The Canadian, American, and British authorities understood that they were imprisoning Ukrainians. See, for example, the report entitled 'Prisoner of War Camp at Banff,' by Harold D. Clum, the American consul in Calgary. He noted that of 429 prisoners only 2 were Germans. The rest included Ukrainians, Poles, Russians, Serbians, Croatians, Italians, Bulgarians, and Rumanians. See his report of 25 May 1916, FO 383/239. O. Martynowych and N. Kazymyra estimated that over 2000 Ukrainians were concentrated in the camps at Brandon, Spirit Lake, and Kapuskasing. See their 'Political Activity in Western Canada, 1896–1923,' *A Heritage in Transition*, ed. Lupul, 85–107. It is now estimated that as many as 5000 of the 'Austro-Hungarian' civilian internees were of Ukrainian nationality. See Luciuk, Yurieva, and Zakaluzny, *Roll Call* (Kingston, 1999).

29 See Luciuk, *A Time for Atonement*, 19–20.

30 In total, 107 internees died, 69 of them of 'Austrian' origin, including a few children. Watson Kirkconnell, eventually president of Acadia University but then a young militia officer serving first at Fort Henry (Kingston) and later at the Kapuskasing internment camp, wrote of his experiences in 'Kapuskasing – An Historical Sketch,' *Bulletin of the Departments of History and Political and Economic Science in Queen's University* 38 (January 1921): 1–15. He noted that 'among the camp inhabitants there were few on whom the long years of captivity had not left their mark ... Confinement in a strange land, inactivity and hopeless waiting were in themselves enough to shatter the nerves and undermine the health.' Dr G.E. Duncan, medical officer for the Vernon camp, wrote to the commandant, Major E.A. Nash, about the case of prisoner no. 635. This Ukrainian, Andrew Baychick, 'is still melancholy and broods constantly because of his internment.' Another contemporary observer, O. Gaylord Marsh, the American consul in Ottawa, noted that of 9 prisoners in the Kapuskasing hospital in mid-March 1916, 3 showed signs of 'dementia.' See 'Austro-Hungarian, Bulgarian, and Turkish Subjects Detained in Kapuskasing, Ontario,' 12–14 March 1916, FO 383/239.

31 See Luciuk, *A Time for Atonement*, 20.

32 See the *Globe and Mail* (Toronto), 16 May 1916 and 19 May 1916, and the *Telegram* (Toronto), 16 May 1916.

33 This act is reprinted in *Loyalties in Conflict*, ed. Sywripa and Thompson, 187–9. The conservative Ukrainian Catholic newspaper *Canadian Ruthenian* declared that there was 'no worse shame' than being disenfranchised.

34 See J.H. Thompson, 'The Enemy Alien and the Canadian General Election of 1917,' in *Loyalties in Conflict*, ed. Swyripa and Thompson, 33, 43–4.

35 *British Whig* (Kingston, Ont.), 7 September 1917.

36 This order-in-council is reprinted in *Loyalties in Conflict*, ed. Swyripa and Thompson, 190–2.

37 These regulations declaring certain organizations illegal are reproduced ibid., 193–6.

38 See D. Avery, 'Ethnic and Class Tensions in Canada, 1918–1920: Anglo-Canadians and the Alien Worker,' ibid., 83–4, 95. Livesay's wife was the writer Florence Randal Livesay. He was keenly interested in Ukrainian affairs and favoured the release of thousands of Ukrainian internees because, he wrote, they were 'ignorant and illiterate.' While he reported that there were many 'pro-Austrians' and 'noisy agitators' who deserved imprisonment, he hoped 'something could be devised for separating the sheep from the goats, the well-satisfied and right-intentioned Canadian peasant farmer from the Teutons.' Livesay quit advocacy on behalf of these Ukrainians – 'I [would] rather wash my hands of it' – when the issue of releasing innocent Ukrainian internees became intertwined with the escalating controversy over the future of Manitoba's bilingual school system. See Melnycky, 'The Internment of Ukrainians in Canada,' 12, 13, 22.

39 Canada, *Parliamentary Debates* (Commons), 134, 1 (1919): 757.

40 See Morton, *The Canadian General*, 362 and 'Otter and Internment Operations in Canada during the First World War,' *Canadian Historical Review* 55 (1974): 58.

41 See Avery, 'Ethnic and Class Tensions in Canada,' 85.

42 See Melnycky, 'Internment of Ukrainians in Canada,' 16, 80.

43 See ibid., 14, 65.

44 Interviews with N. Sakaliuk, Toronto, 14 February 1978 and 5 November 1980, catalogued as UKR-6283-SAK and UKR-8477-SAK (MHSO). Among the last known survivors of Canada's first national internment operations are two Canadian-born women, Mary Haskett (née Manko) and Stefania Pawliw (née Mielniczuk). Mrs Haskett was interned at age six, along with the rest of her family, at Spirit Lake, Quebec, where her younger sister, Nellie, perished. Mrs Pawliw was also interned at the Spirit Lake camp. Both women serve as honorary co-chairwomen of the National Redress Council,

Ukrainian Canadian Civil Liberties Association. More information on the Ukrainian Canadian community's ongoing campaign for an acknowledgment of this injustice, and for restitution, can be found on the WWW at the InfoUkes Home Page: see Internment of Ukrainians in Canada, 1914–1920, http://www.infoukes.com/history/internment/. Since 1994, trilingual plaques commemorating Canada's first national internment operations have been unveiled at a number of these concentration camp sites, largely through the efforts of the Ukrainian Canadian Civil Liberties Association, the Ukrainian Canadian Foundation of Taras Shevchenko, the Ukrainian Canadian Congress, and their supporters, as follows: Fort Henry, Kingston, Ontario, on 4 August 1994; Banff National Park (Castle Mountain and Cave and Basin), on 12 August 1995 and 1 June 1996; Kapuskasing, Ontario, on 14 October 1995; Jasper National Park, on 12 October 1996; Nanaimo, British Columbia, on 24 May 1997; Vernon, British Columbia, on 7 June 1997; Brandon, Manitoba, on 27 November 1997; Stanley Barracks, Toronto, on 2 October 1998; Winnipeg, on 11 October 1998; Victoria, British Columbia, on 20 June 1999; and Spirit Lake, Quebec, on 4 August 1999. Two statues depicting a Ukrainian internee by the sculptor John Boxtel, entitled *Why?* and *Never Forget*, were also unveiled at the Castle Mountain (Banff National Park) and Kapuskasing locations.

Educational materials dealing with the interment operations, intended primarily for high school use in Canada, are finally becoming available. One of Prentice-Hall Ginn Canada's four multimedia kits *Canadians in the Global Community* (Toronto, 1997), produced by the Social Program Evaluation Group of Queen's University for the CRB Foundation's Heritage Project, is entitled 'War, Peace, and Security.' It contains useful information on the internment operations and their impact on the Ukrainian community as well as more general information on the Ukrainian Canadian experience. Oxford University Press Canada's *World Affairs: Defining Canada's Role* (Toronto, 1998) contains a section entitled 'Enemy Aliens.' Regrettably, this section omits clear reference to the predominance of Ukrainian Canadians among the internees, an error that the series editor, Don Quinlan, has indicated will be corrected in future editions.

Canadian editorialists have been overwhelmingly supportive of the Ukrainian Canadian community's efforts to secure an acknowledgment of this injustice and the restitution of that portion of the internees' confiscated wealth that was never returned by the government. See the articles reproduced in *Righting an Injustice*, ed. Luciuk. But there have been some efforts to undermine this campaign, notably by Sol Littman, the Canadian representative of the Friends of the Simon Wiesenthal Center for Holocaust Studies. On 25 April 1989, Littman argued that a 'nationalist, right-wing segment of the Ukrainian-Canadian community seems to be suffering from what can best be described as a severe case of "issue envy" ... The most recent case of issue envy involves the effort by some Ukrainians, led by Kingston's own Lubomir [sic] Luciuk, to persuade Canadians that Ukrainians suffered a great injustice during World War I, equal in quality and extent to that suffered by Japanese Canadians during World War II.' More recently Littman was quoted in *Canadian Jewish News* ('Holocaust Museum May Be Derailed: Ukrainian-Led Effort Could Disrupt Plans,' by David Lazarus and Paul Lungen, 9 April 1999), as alleging that Ukrainian Canadians were guilty of 'issue envy' because they favoured the development of a federally funded Genocide Museum that would be *inclusive*, dealing with episodes of genocide not only in Europe but elsewhere in the world both during and before the twentieth century rather than with the Jewish *Shoah* alone. I am grateful to Mr Harvey Schachter, at the time the managing editor of the *Whig Standard*, for providing me with a copy of Littman's letter of 25 April 1989.

45 An estimate of the economic losses experienced by Ukrainian Canadians during these internment operations was prepared by Price Waterhouse in 1991. This report, 'Economic Losses of Ukrainian Canadians Resulting from Internment during World War I,' suggested that the pecuniary losses suffered by internees in terms of lost wages and confiscated cash would amount to nearly thirty-three million dollars.

46 For the remarks by H.A. Mackie, MP, to Prime Minister Borden, 16 October 1918, see Document #10 in *A Delicate and Difficult Question*, ed. Kordan and Luciuk, 38. After A.E. Kemp, Canada's minister of militia and defence, was given a memorandum on the issue of Ukrainian enlistment in Canada's armed forces, prepared by Ukrainian Canadians in Edmonton and submitted to Prime Minister Borden on 13 December 1916, he asked his personal secretary, Captain E. Bristol, to summarize its contents. Bristol's confidential memorandum indicated that over two thousand 'Ruthenians' had already enlisted; a large number of Ukrainian Canadian volunteers, organized into a Ruthenian Forestry Company, would sail for England with the Canadian Forestry Corps. Some later served in France. See V.J. Kaye's articles entitled 'Ruthenian Forestry Company' and 'Ukrainian Canadians Serving in the Canadian Forestry Corps' in *Ukrainian Canadians in Canada's Wars*, ed. Gregorovich, 35–42 and 43–54. The same volume contains the biography of Filip Konowal, Canada's only Ukrainian Victoria Cross winner, 57–8. Konowal was finally honoured by the Ukrainian Canadian community when arrangements were made for a marker acknowledging his Victoria Cross to be erected at his gravesite in the Notre Dame Cemetery in Ottawa. Plaques commemorating his wartime valour were erected at the

Cartier Square Drill Hall of the Governor General's Foot Guards in Ottawa (15 July 1996), at the Royal Canadian Legion Branch 360 (Konowal Branch) in Toronto (4 August 1996), and on the Armoury of the Royal Westminster Regiment, New Westminster, British Columbia (5 April 1997); the commemoration events were organized by the various veterans' groups concerned and the Ukrainian Canadian Civil Liberties Association. A fourth plaque was unveiled at the cenotaph dedicated to the Unknown Ukrainian Soldier, located near Dauphin, Manitoba, on 31 July 1998, and a statue and plaque in his village of Kutkiw, Ukraine, on 21 August 2000; see L.Y. Luciuk, 'Remembering Filip Konowal: A Visit to His Village in Ukraine,' *Ukrainian Weekly,* 16 April 2000, 9, and 'Victoria Cross Winner No Longer an Unsung Hero,' *National Post,* 21 August 2000, A14. See L.Y. Luciuk and R. Sorobey, *Konowal* (Kingston, 1996), and 'Konowal to Be Honoured at Selo Ukraina,' *Dauphin Herald,* 23 September 1997, B14.

47 See H.A. Mackie, Document #10 in *A Delicate and Difficult Question,* ed. Kordan and Luciuk, 36.

48 See the minutes on a file entitled 'Treatment of Austro-Hungarian Friends in Canada,' 20 January 1915, FO 383/1. The point is repeated in a file 'Austro-Hungarian Subjects Hostile to Austro-Hungarian Rule,' by A. Bonar Law, 8 February 1915, FO 383/1, and in several letters found in 'Preferential Treatment of Friendly Aliens,' February 1915, FO 383/1.

49 As cited by Swyripa, 'The Ukrainian Image: Loyal Citizen or Disloyal Alien,' in *Loyalties in Conflict,* ed. Swyripa and Thompson, 52, 66.

50 As cited by Thompson, 'The Enemy Alien and the Canadian General Election of 1917,' 40, 45.

51 *Edmonton Bulletin,* 6 October 1914.

52 A student of the Ukrainian Canadian experience concluded, 'The event leaving the deepest scars on the Ukrainian Canadian psyche was treatment as enemy aliens during World War I.' See F. Swyripa, 'Ukrainians,' in *Encyclopedia of Canada's Peoples,* ed. P.R. Magocsi (Toronto, 1999), 1309.

53 As cited by D. Avery, *Dangerous Foreigners: European Immigrant Workers and Labour Radicalism in Canada, 1896–1932* (Toronto, 1979), 81 n14.

Chapter 3: 'The Man Who Knew'

1 On the Ukrainian liberation struggle during the First World War, see J. Borys, *The Sovietization of Ukraine, 1917–1923: The Communist Doctrine and Practice of National Self Determination* (Edmonton, 1980); *The Ukraine, 1917–1921: A Study in Revolution,* ed. T. Hunczak (Cambridge, 1977); J.S. Reshetar, *The Ukrainian Revolution, 1917–1920* (Princeton, 1952); and S.O. Pidhainy, *The Formation of the Ukrainian Republic* (Toronto, 1966). See also R. Sullivant,

'The Problem of Eastern Galicia,' M.A. thesis, University of California at Los Angeles, 1948.

2 The Ukrainian War Veterans' Association (Ukrainska striletska hromada, or UWVA) was founded in 1928 by former members of the Ukrainian Sich Riflemen and the Ukrainian Galician Army. On the eve of the Second World War the UWVA had almost seven hundred members in Canada, organized into twenty branches. See O. Woycenko, 'Community Organizations,' in *A Heritage in Transition*, ed. Lupul, 183.

3 See P. Krawchuk, *The Ukrainian Socialist Movement in Canada, 1907–1918* (Toronto, 1979).

4 A document entitled 'An Appeal to Ukrainian Teachers in Manitoba,' dated 1915, signed by I. Rudachek and W. Mihaychuk, the president and secretary of The Ukrainian Teachers' Association, proclaimed: 'Are we to be or not to be – this is the big question. This means, are we to be Ukrainians, live the life we know best and naturally which suits us best, or are we to be unworthy of a man's name – the hewers of wood and drawers of water for the ruling elements? Two pathways lie open before us. We stand at the very crossroads of these pathways. One of these leads towards the natural growth of the people, the other to assimilation. It is impossible to put our foot forward without stepping upon one of the roads. The road leading towards the growth of our people is a thorny one, but it opens the vista into a bright future. We must have a strong belief in a bright future. In order to attain this bright future we must resolutely proceed along this true road.' Cited by Marunchak, *The Ukrainian Canadians*, 340–1.

5 See the confidential 'U.S.S.R. Memoranda' prepared by the British Foreign Office Research Department, 15 September 1943, FO 371/36974. These memoranda contained information on Canadian Ukrainians under headings such as 'Ecclesiastical Affiliations,' 'Political Alignments,' 'Censure from Moscow,' and 'The Winnipeg Congress.'

6 *Canadian Ruthenian*, 25 October 1916. Aware of the growth of national Ukrainian consciousness among this population, the newspaper's owners renamed it the *Kanadyiskyi ukrainets* (*Canadian Ukrainian*) in 1919.

7 *Ukrainian Voice*, 1 November 1916. In his preliminary lecture to the students at the Mohyla Institute, which opened its doors in mid-September 1916 in a building at 716 Lansdowne Avenue in Saskatoon, the Institute's first rector, Wasyl Swystun, told his thirty-five students, 'It is necessary for us to destroy all artificial borders created in the old country among us by our enemies, and the best possible way to do that is through the Peter Mohyla Institute, and similar educational institutions, where children of Greek Catholic and Orthodox families can live together and get acquainted with each other as children of one Ukrainian nation.' Cited by H. Udod, *Julian W.*

Stechishin: His Life and Work (Saskatoon, 1978), 21. For more on the Institute, see *Twenty Five Years of the P. Mohyla Institute in Saskatoon* (Winnipeg, 1945). Religious factionalism plagued Ukrainian Canadian life in this period. See, for example, the description of a 3 July 1915 vote on whether the Kotsko *bursa* in Winnipeg should be national, Ukrainian Catholic, or Catholic in orientation, published in *Twenty Five Years*, 39. The vote resulted in an 82-68-2 split. It also caused considerable acrimony among the delegates. The Mohyla Institute's alumni included a large number who would later distinguish themselves in Ukrainian Canadian life, including Orest Zerebko, the first Ukrainian Canadian student to receive a B.A., Jaroslav Arsenych, Canada's first Ukrainian lawyer, and Ukrainian Orthodox community activists like Wasyl Swystun, Myroslav and Julian Stechishin, and Bohdan Panchuk.

8 On the church's early history, see P. Yuzyk, *The Ukrainian Greek Orthodox Church of Canada, 1918–1951* (Ottawa, 1981). A translation of the letter of 27 May 1918, calling for delegates to attend a conference to set up this church, is found in Document #8 in *A Delicate and Difficult Question*, ed. Kordan and Luciuk, 32–4. The resolutions adopted at a national church meeting, held in July 1918, are reprinted in Document #9, 34–6.

9 These figures are taken from P. Krawchuk's *Na noviy zemli (On New Soil)*, (Toronto, 1958), 303.

10 On the WBA, see the partisan account *Friends in Need: The WBA Story: A Canadian Epic in Fraternalism*, ed. A. Bilecki, W. Repka, and M. Sago (Winnipeg, 1972). Bilecki was interviewed in Winnipeg, 3 December 1982 (CIUS).

11 For the circulation figures of these newspapers, see Table 1, 'Circulation of the Ukrainian Pro-Communist Press for the Years 1925, 1927, and 1929,' in Kolasky, *The Shattered Illusion*, 6.

12 See Document #17, 26 March 1929, in *A Delicate and Difficult Question*, ed. Kordan and Luciuk, 52. En route home after leading a delegation to the USSR in April 1931, John Navis, the ULFTA's secretary in Winnipeg, stopped off in Toronto to attend a July CPC executive meeting. He expressed himself candidly, if unwittingly, to Toronto police chief Denis Draper's 'inside man' in the Party about conditions in the Soviet Union. There was starvation, Navis admitted, the Five Year Plan was collapsing, and the Kremlin even feared a counter-revolution. The Soviets felt their only hope for survival lay in the strength they could develop among the workers of Poland, Germany, China, the United States, and Canada. Navis also told his questioner that one of his delegation's members, John Boychuk, was under instructions to keep the Soviets informed about conditions in Canada. Navis claimed Moscow planned to spend seventy-five thousand dollars in Canada that year to promote its cause and five hundred thousand

dollars for the same purpose in the United States. Boychuk was also identified as the paymaster for Canada. When the undercover police officer inquired about the possibility of Canadian workers rising in revolt against the government, Navis replied that this was impractical, since the workers had no trained forces or ammunition. Yet in these Depression years there were occasional scares about armed insurrection breaking out in Canada and fears about the malignant role of foreign-born agitators. Stern measures were called for. For example, Prime Minister R.B. Bennett fulminated in the House of Commons on 29 July 1931 about Canada's communists and spoke up openly about taking action against any persons who, 'in our judgement ... have not proved themselves worthy of Canadian citizenship.' Winnipeg's mayor, Colonel Ralph Webb, called publicly for emergency measures to deal with Bolshevik agents in Canada, telling the Montreal *Gazette* that the Dominion 'ought to maintain a secret service expressly for combatting the Bolshevik menace.' He advised that 'the ring-leaders, instead of being hauled up in the ordinary law courts and allowed to hire high-priced counsel, ought to be just spirited out of the country and back to where they came from.' According to L.-R. Betcherman, *The Little Band: The Clashes between the Communists and the Political and Legal Establishment in Canada, 1928–1932* (Ottawa, 1983), 96, the outspoken Mayor Webb is still remembered in Winnipeg for his statement that all Reds should be dumped in the Red River. See Betcherman, 168 and 232 nn 43, 45. The RCMP commissioner Starnes took a more realistic view. On whether it would be possible to deal with the Bolsheviks by deporting them, as was recommended by Brother Stanislav of Yorkton's St Joseph's College in the wake of the troubles in that community in July 1928, Starnes drafted a memorandum in which he considered whether the deportation of a few Ukrainians would have any significant impact on the communist movement. He noted that much of the agitation was being carried out by English-speaking provacateurs. They had made 'little impression' upon the English-speaking public. What did exist, and was troubling, was how the communists had organized themselves, for their structures were 'expressly designed to enable them to "go underground" in the event of the attack which they fully expect.' Starnes noted that the Communist party proper was covered by the ULFTA, which was itself covered by the WBA, which would serve as a 'legal' body if the parent societies were proscribed. Holding companies owned the four revolutionary Ukrainian newspapers, and other subsidiary societies existed, making it legally difficult and tedious to attempt any suppression. Possibly the most useful route to take would be to deport a few individual agitators and trust that some examples of that sort would 'cow the mass of the extremist element.' Promising as a method perhaps, but, as Starnes saw it, not as simple as was suggested. Some of the agitators were naturalized subjects, like Matthew Popowich, 'probably the brains of the entire movement.' If non-naturalized members were deported, 'the action might leave a sense of unfairness prejudicial to future relations between the mass of our Ukrainians and their fellow-Canadians.' Starnes opined that the best method would be the prosecution of agitators for sedition and their conviction under the Criminal Code, because convictions in open court, under all the safeguards of the criminal system, would be 'far more satisfactory and convincing to public opinion than purely administrative action' and would be followed by automatic deportation. But even here there was a problem, for that would entail getting at least four provincial attorneys general (in Ontario, Manitoba, Alberta, and British Columbia) to act. It would be justified in order to make the 'considerable effort' required, however, because, Starnes noted, of the 'existence of the numerous revolutionary schools which are poisoning too large a proportion of the foreign-born youth.' About three thousand Ukrainian children alone were under 'tuition of the most mischievous kind.' They were being taught to grow up in the most anti-social spirit imaginable, as were Finns and, 'probably in a lesser degree,' the 'foreign-born Jews.' While Starnes found the actual agitation of adults to be 'annoying rather than dangerous,' this 'pollution of the children promises ill for the future.'

13 This figure is taken from Kolasky, *The Shattered Illusion*, 13, 17. In Document #19 of *A Delicate and Difficult Question*, ed. Kordan and Luciuk, 56, a CPC functionary reported that in 1929 'of more than 5,000 workers organized around the U.L.F.T.A. only 400 are members' of the Party. In *The Little Band*, 164, Betcherman claims that a contemporary RCMP estimate of 5000 CPC members, composed of 3000 Finns, 800 Ukrainians, 400 Jews, and 200 Anglo-Canadians, was ill informed. She cites a letter sent by Sam Carr to Moscow, 25 March 1931, in which he noted that the party had only 1300 dues-paying members, even if it had reported 4000 paid-up members, along with 25,000 sympathizers.

14 Kolasky, *The Shattered Illusion*, 17.

15 Ibid., 13–14.

16 Ibid., 17, 21. Evidence about Stalinist repression in Ukraine, including news about the liquidation of the kulaks, forced collectivization, the politically engineered Great Famine of 1932–3, and the suicides of the commissar of education for Soviet Ukraine, Mykola Skrypnyk, and the prominent writer Mykola Khvylovy, provoked a split within the ULFTA, climaxing on 10 March 1935, when Danylo Lobay openly questioned Soviet policies at a communist fraction meeting gathered in preparation for the fifteenth ULFTA convention. Lobay subsequently relinquished his post as editor of

Ukrainian Labour News. With the aid of John Hladun and Toma Kobzey, who resigned from his post as the ULFTA's national secretary, Lobay formed the Workers and Farmers Educational Association, based in Winnipeg. Eventually they began publishing a weekly newspaper, *Pravda* (*Truth*). When the UCC was created, his group, by then known as the Ukrainian Workers' League, joined. See N. Wiseman, 'The Politics of Manitoba's Ukrainians between the Wars,' *Prairie Forum* 12:1 (1987).

17 See Document #19 in *A Delicate and Difficult Question*, ed. Kordan and Luciuk, 55.

18 See Document #20, 13 February 1930, ibid., 58.

19 See Kolasky, *The Shattered Illusion*, 51.

20 For additional information on Myroslav Stechishin, see Petryshyn, *Peasants in the Promised Land*, 163–9, 178, 204–6. On Julian Stechishin, see Udod, *Julian W. Stechishin: His Life and Work*. Stechishin's 'enemy alien' certificate is reproduced in this book. His wife, Savella Stechishin, was interviewed in Saskatoon, 16 August 1983 (CIUS). Not all outside observers found the three Stetchishin brothers agreeable. At least one RCMP investigator did not have a high opinion of Michael Stechishin. After meeting with him on 16 July 1928, RCMP sergeant George Clifford wrote, 'I am informed that this Stechinhin [*sic*], Slipchenko and Slipchenko's brother, and one Walter Semec are the advocates of cheap labor around Yorkton and that they get hold of all the foreigners possible, take a sum of money from them on promise of a job and when they get the money they send the men out into the country but in many cases there is no job when the men arrive out in the country and also that this man Semec has only been in this country about one year and was supposed to come to this country for farming but has never been out of Yorkton and assists in the work amongst themselves of getting all the money easy out of the foreigners.'

21 For a favourable exposition of the USRL's ideology, see W. Burianyk, *S.U.S. – Its Meaning and Significance* (Toronto, 1967). Burianyk stressed that the USRL, as a 'non-political' group, had adopted a 'Canadian outlook,' had never been a part of any political party or organization in Europe, and 'takes no orders from abroad.' The USRL was formed from the fusion of five groups, who supported the Mohyla and Hrushevsky students' institutes established in Saskatoon in 1916 and in Edmonton in 1918; the Union of Ukrainian Community Centres; the Ukrainian Women's Association of Canada; the Ukrainian Canadian Youth Association; and the Ukrainian Students' Circles. For more on the USRL; see interviews with W. Burianyk, Winnipeg, 30 May 1982 (MHSO) and 28 November 1982 (CIUS). The USRL program of December 1927 is reproduced in Document #15 in *A Delicate and Difficult Question*, ed. Kordan and Luciuk, 48–50, and summarized by O.

Woycenko in 'Community Organizations,' in *A Heritage in Transition*, ed. Lupul, 181. An RCMP report recently declassified under the Access to Information Act reveals that the RCMP's commissioner S.T. Wood reported favourably on the USRL. On 2 June 1938 he wrote to the under-secretary of state for Canada, in Ottawa, to note that this group, 'although confessing loyalty to the European home of these people,' appears to be 'mainly concerned with the promotion of Ukrainian culture in Canada within the framework of Canadian law and institutions. It is generally conceded that their activities have been a great factor in counteracting Communist influence among the Ukrainians in Canada.'

22 See the 2 October 1928 editorial from *Ukrainian Voice*, reprinted as Document #16 in *A Delicate and Difficult Question*, ed. Kordan and Luciuk, 51. The two letters, of 27 July and 6 August 1914, written by Bishop Nykyta Budka, are reproduced as Documents #6 and #7, 28–32. For a sympathetic treatment of the bishop, see S. Hryniuk, 'The Bishop Budka Controversy: A New Perspective,' *Canadian Slavonic Papers* 23:2 (1981): 154–65.

23 Document #15 in *A Delicate and Difficult Question*, ed. Kordan and Luciuk, 49. This description of the USRL's founders as a 'nationalist intelligentsia' is taken from Petryshyn, *Peasants in the Promised Land*. See also Document #15 in *A Delicate and Difficult Question*, 49. There is fragmentary evidence to suggest that, despite their public stand on non-involvement in 'European' problems, at least one of the USRL's founders, Wasyl Swystun, was in direct and secret communication with members of the OUN, including that group's leader, Colonel E. Konovalets, during the mid-1930s. See 'Anti-Polish Activities of Ukrainian Nationalists Abroad,' 9 March 1936, FO 371/ 19962. For a description of what transpired during a more public meeting between USRL and OUN representatives, see the articles by Reverend S. Sawchuk entitled 'A Talk with Colonel Evhen Konovalets,' *Ukrainian Voice*, 7 June 1939; 21 June 1939; and 28 June 1939; and Myroslav Stechishin's article of 5 July 1939, which reproduces a letter sent to the OUN from the USRL's W. Swystun and M. Stechishin, on 18 January 1931. In it these USRL leaders pointed out that 'in Canada the work of nationalists is done by the USRL.' Marunchak, in *The Ukrainian Canadians*, 397, concluded that the USRL was a nationalistic group, a view shared by some Canadian officials. For example, in a memorandum sent to L.D. Wilgress, Canadian ambassador to the USSR during the Second World War, Norman Robertson of External Affairs considered that the word 'self-reliance' in the organization's name suggested 'independence' and described the essentially nationalistic outlook of the USRL's members. See Document #34, 28 May 1943, in *A Delicate and Difficult Question*, 96–7. On 6 September 1940, Skelton of External Affairs wrote to RCMP commissioner S.T. Wood to say that he had had a

number of fairly lengthy conversations with Swystun over the past year and had formed a 'frankly favourable' impression of him. 'Whether his first loyalty is to Canada or to the idea of a united Ukraine,' Skelton continued, 'I should not like to say,' but Skelton was not willing to accept, uncritically, Polish evidence against the leaders or policies of the Ukrainian national movement. True, developments in Europe would have to be 'watched carefully' for their impact on the loyalty of Canada's Ukrainian population, but any 'precipitate action' to proscribe Canadian Ukrainian organizations was unnecessary at that time. See Skelton to Wood, 6 September 1940, DEA 165–39C. On Norman Robertson's career, see J.L. Granatstein, *A Man of Influence: Norman A. Robertson and Canadian Statecraft, 1929–68* (Ottawa, 1981).

24 Document #21, 30 October 1930, in *A Delicate and Difficult Question*, ed. Kordan and Luciuk, 60.

25 Ibid.

26 On the UVO, see chapter 9 in A.J. Motyl, *The Turn to the Right: The Ideological Origins and Development of Ukrainian Nationalism, 1919–1929* (Boulder, Colo., 1980).

27 Those papers of the UNF which are preserved at the Archives of Ontario do not contain much evidence regarding fund-raising in Canada on behalf of the nationalist underground in eastern Europe, but oral history interviews with UNF members confirm that this became one of the principal functions of the Federation. For a discussion of the UNF, its ideological orientation, and the difficulties encountered by it before and during the war, see T. Prymak, *Maple Leaf and Trident: The Ukrainian Canadians during the Second World War* (Toronto, 1988). I am also indebted to Mr W. Voynarowsky of Toronto for a copy of his notes dealing with the UNF and his own involvement in its activities, beginning in 1931.

28 See Marunchak, *The Ukrainian Canadians*, 400–1.

29 Tape-recorded interviews with A. Bilecki, 3 December 1982 (CIUS), and W. Kardash, Winnipeg, 30 November 1982 (CIUS). W. Repka and K.M. Repka, *Dangerous Patriots: Canada's Unknown Prisoners of War* (Vancouver, 1982), try to make a case for injustice being done to anti-fascist Ukrainian Canadians interned in Canada during the Second World War, as does P. Krawchuk, *Interned without Cause: The Internment of Canadian Antifascists during World War Two* (Toronto, 1985). Commenting on similar claims made at the time, Pearson of External Affairs noted that 'the point is stressed, *ad nauseam*, that these men should be freed so that they can fight the Nazis. Naturally, no mention is made of the fact that they were interned because they refused to fight those same Nazis.' See Pearson's 'Memorandum for Under-Secretary of State,' 12 October 1941, DEA 2118-S-40. Pearson, known as 'Mike,' was

born in Newtonbrook, Ontario, in 1897, and went on to become one of Canada's foremost diplomats during the post–Second World War period. Before that he served as first secretary in the Canadian High Commission in London (1935), as second in command at the Canadian Legation in Washington (1942), and as Canadian ambassador to the United States in 1945, in which capacity he attended the founding conference of the United Nations at San Francisco. Later, Prime Minister King appointed Pearson his deputy minister of the Department of External Affairs (September 1946) and minister of external affairs (1948–57). Representing Algoma East, Pearson entered the House of Commons in September 1948 as an MP for the Liberal Party of Canada. He was elected prime minister in April 1963.

30 See Kolasky, *The Shattered Illusion*, 38.

31 The 1941 constitution of the Association to Aid the Fatherland is reproduced as Document #29 in *A Delicate and Difficult Question*, ed. Kordan and Luciuk, 77. E.W. Stapleford, director of voluntary services, Department of National War Services, wrote to Hugh Keenleyside of External Affairs seeking advice about whether to grant the Association's request for registration under the War Charities Act. He received a reply marked 'secret' from R. Tait, assistant commissioner to the director of criminal investigations, which alerted him to details about the applicants. Michael Mutzak, the Association's president, was a CPC member and former provincial organizer of the youth section of the ULFTA. Members and former sympathizers of the ULFTA, as well as CPC members, were reportedly joining this new association, a pattern which suggested that it was 'Communist-inspired and its activities subject to the policy of the Communist Party of Canada.' For Stapleford's letter to Keenleyside, 23 September 1941, and Tait's reply, 2 October 1941, see DEA 2514–40. Keenleyside, born in Toronto in 1898, joined External Affairs in 1928 but left in 1947, after becoming disillusioned with diplomatic life. Subsequently, he was deputy minister of mines and resources and commissioner of the Northwest Territories in 1947–50.

In the same file there is a 'Note for Mr. Robertson Re "Medical Aid Fund to Soviet Union War Victims,"' 10 October 1941, which, after mentioning the 'sudden shift' of communist policy in support of Canada's war effort, argued that it would be 'extremely shortsighted' to underestimate the importance of using the assistance which the Ukrainian Canadian Left now seemed 'eager to give.' Likewise, Pearson of External Affairs noted that 'whatever the reasons may be, the Russians are fighting on our side and the communists have become ardent protagonists for an all-out war effort,' and that meant the treatment of the Ukrainian Canadian Left must be re-evaluated. See Pearson's memorandum to J. Pickersgill, 13 October 1941,

DEA 2118–S-40. Secret investigations carried out in Fort William, Winnipeg, Saskatoon, and Vancouver during 1941, by Special Constable Michael Petrowsky, resulted in a lengthy report called 'Communist Party (Amongst Ukrainians), Canada Generally,' dated 29 October 1941, circulated to the 'A,' 'C,' 'D,' 'E,' 'F,' 'H,' 'J,' 'K,' and 'O' divisions of the RCMP. Recently declassified under the Access to Information Act, this document describes RCMP concerns about the 'Communist element,' which was described as displaying such 'real animation' that it was 'considered [to be] the most active Ukrainian group in Canada.' Its membership was motivated by 'the peril to the Soviet Union, their avowed "Fatherland."' According to informants questioned by the RCMP, all communist declarations of loyalty should be dismissed as 'slogans ... as false as the communists themselves.' It was noted that these communists were 'in fact, the people who would betray Canada.' Certain elements among the British Canadian population were giving their moral support to the Ukrainian communists, and there was some concern that a well-organized underground communist movement was 'methodically organizing for a bloody upheaval probably at the end of this war.' Apparently in speaking with Wasyl Swystun the RCMP learned that, in his view, the communists were guided by a spirit of expediency of a kind similar to that 'which had guided Stalin in accepting the Nazi–Soviet pact from Hitler.' Communists might manifest patriotism with respect to Canada, but at the same time 'they are disposed to betray, to stab the country in the back whenever an opportunity should offer itself.' In Vancouver, Petrowsky learned that the local communists were untroubled by the RCMP. 'Unaware of my official connections,' one of his informants told him that the local RCMP force lacked 'alertness and proper understanding as far as the Communist activities are concerned.' In the end, however, it was decided that the Association's application should be supported, 'on the grounds that the cause is a worthy one,' but with the caveat that it would be necessary to keep 'close checks on the manner in which any funds collected will be spent.' That such monitoring took place and continued even after the war is revealed by correspondence preserved in DEA 282-Z (s), which discusses the travel of two AUUC officials, William Teresio and Peter Krawchuk, to Soviet Ukraine in May 1948, 'ostensibly in connection with the dispatch of foodstuffs, medical supplies and clothing.' These goods were purchased using the $250,000 in contributions collected in 1947 by the AUUC- and WBA-sponsored 'Ukrainian War Orphan Fund.' Professor George Simpson, chairman of the Committee on Co-operation in Canadian Citizenship of the Department of National War Services, wrote to Robertson on 4 April 1942 to tell him about the recently announced plan of the Association to change its name to the 'Association of Ukrainian Canadians.' This was obviously intended to 'confuse the public and appropriate the place now held by the Ukrainian Canadian Committee.'

The newspaper *Ukrainian Life* began appearing in Toronto in August 1941. *Ukrainian Word* was published in Winnipeg from 20 January 1943 until November 1965. The two merged and became *Zhyttia i Slovo* (*Life and Word*), published in Toronto, with a reported circulation in 1946 of twenty-five thousand copies. Kolasky asserted in *The Shattered Illusion*, 186, that the paper's circulation had fallen to forty-five hundred by 1973.

32 See Document #38, 4 July 1944, in *A Delicate and Difficult Question*, ed. Kordan and Luciuk, 78.

33 For a ULFTA cartoonist's interpretation of how his group regained confiscated labour temples in Toronto and St Catharines, see Kolasky, *The Shattered Illusion*, 43, which reproduces a drawing from the 3 February 1944 issue of *Ukrainian Life*. It depicts two Ukrainian nationalist 'rats' being booted out of these halls, and is captioned 'The Rightful Owners Have Begun a Cleanup of Their Homes.'

34 Interview with Raymond A. Davies, Montreal, 6 June 1983 (CIUS). Davies, whose real name was Rudolph Shohan, was an able polemicist whose allegations about connections between Ukrainian nationalists and the Nazis caused considerable worry to supporters of the UCC throughout the war years, and inspired subsequent disinformation efforts along the same lines. See his 'Ukrainian-Canadians and the War's New Phase,' in *Saturday Night*, 12 July 1941, which elicited a quick reply from W. Swystun, 'The Ukrainian Canadians and the Russo-German War,' *Saturday Night*, 31 July 1941. Swystun had left the USRL by then and joined the UNF. He was, at just about the same time, attempting to buoy Tracy Philipps's spirits. See nn 59 and 60, below. Philipps had written, on 22 July 1941, 'If experience of the past offers any criterion for the future, any man who tries conscientiously to be of service to the Ukrainians will have to be prepared to suffer misrepresentation from within and stabs in the back from Ukrainians themselves [and] that is a position which, so far as I am concerned, any man who likes that kind of thing can have. He will have to be prepared to emerge from it with his public and private life beset with lies. Like Nansen under whom I had the honour to work in East Europe, Lawrence of Arabia made clear ... the bitter lot and final disillusionment of those of us who give our lives to work for men of other blood ... I have almost had enough. I have been both humiliated and disillusioned, I have suffered both the technique of the kindly public kiss of Judas and the private betrayal of Delilah.' Swystun replied, on 24 July, trying to reassure Philipps that at least a 'limited number' of Ukrainians deeply appreciated what he had done and that they

expected he would continue to do more, notwithstanding his present feelings, 'for our cause.' See NAC MG30 E350. As for Davies, his most widely read statement on Ukrainian Canadian attitudes and the war effort was entitled *This Is Our Land: Ukrainian Canadians against Hitler* (Toronto, 1943). Wilgress discussed it in a memorandum sent to Glazebrook on 18 June 1943, DEA 165-39C. He remarked that by 'excluding the element of time and by making a careful selection of newspaper clippings' Davies had built up a 'pretty impressive picture of a sinister conspiracy against Canada's allies, — The U.S.S.R., Poland and Czechoslovakia.' The book had as its threefold purpose the discrediting of the 'ultra-nationalist leadership' of the Ukrainian Canadians, meaning Kossar, Hethman, Swystun, and Hlynka; the strengthening of the case for the return of ULFTA properties; and the opening of the way for 'further collaboration' between the Ukrainian Canadian Association and the moderate elements represented by the USRL, which Davies had been 'careful to exclude ... from charges of pro-Nazi activity.' Wilgress concluded by observing that he hated to think what impression the book would produce on Ukrainian specialists in the USSR's Commissariat of Foreign Affairs. In 1943, while considering Davies's proposed visit as a CBC correspondent to the Soviet Union, External Affairs officials noted that he was of Jewish origin, even though he 'claims to be a Ukrainian.' It was also pointed out that he had been a member of the Young Communist League (see also Kolasky, *The Shattered Illusion*, 37). Writing from Moscow, Wilgress observed, on 8 May 1944, that 'assertions of objectivity' by Davies were doubtful. Nevertheless, External Affairs observers apparently found Davies no less objectionable than the UCC's booster, Professor Watson Kirkconnell. A memorandum presented to Mr Rae of External Affairs pointed out that while Davies was 'intellectually dishonest' and had made 'a highly partisan speech at a meeting of the Ukrainian Association in Winnipeg,' Professor Kirkconnell's address before the UCC congress could be ranked as equal in all respects. See 'Visit to Soviet Union of Raymond Arthur Davies,' 15 September 1943, DEA 5616-40. Interestingly enough, Kirkconnell's two-hour speech denouncing both fascism and communism was not printed in the official proceedings of the conference. Similarly, General Vladimir Sikevich's reportedly 'violent, anti-Russian' banquet speech, in which he exclaimed that the UCC was the only real representative of the Ukrainian people, that its congress was a 'Ukrainian parliament,' and that 'the UCC is our ambassador!' was likewise omitted. Even Hlynka's heated denunciation of Canada's Ukrainian communists as 'blind puppets of the enemy of the Ukrainian people in the homeland' was edited before being printed in the form of a much abbreviated summary describing the congress banquet. But loudspeakers carried both General Sikevich's speech and Hlynka's anti-communist message throughout the Royal Alexandra Hotel, where the congress was held, and, probably not coincidentally, where two delegates of the Soviet legation, Tounkin and Volenko, were staying. The latter were in Winnipeg to take part in a rival demonstration being held that weekend by Ukrainian, Russian, Lithuanian, and Carpatho-Russian Leftists. For a fascinating description of a conversation held between Philipps and Davies at the Canadian Institute of International Affairs in Toronto on 10 November 1942, see Philipps's secret report submitted to the Department of National War Services in NAC MG30 E350.

35 See Document #29, 26 July 1941, in *A Delicate and Difficult Question*, ed. Kordan and Luciuk, 77.

36 See Document #31, 30 September 1941, ibid., 81–90.

37 See Document #32, 6 March 1942, ibid., 80.

38 See Document #31, 30 September 1941, ibid., 87. That members of the UNF remained committed to the idea of Ukrainian national independence is indisputable. For example, Swystun threatened to resign from the UCC's executive after an October 1942 meeting decided the 'Ukrainian Question' in Europe would not be placed on the agenda of the coming national congress. Kaye played a role in convincing Swystun to drop his protest. As Tony Yaremovich wrote to Kossar, on 20 October 1942, 'Dr. Kaye certainly influenced Mr. Swystun to change his mind. Just the day before the meeting he threatened me that if we are going to insist upon holding the congress on a Canadian basis he is going to resign. Dr. Kaye came around and "Lo and Behold" Mr. Swystun sees the possibility of holding the congress on a purely Canadian basis. You should have seen the grin on everybody's face.' Cited by Prymak, *Maple Leaf and Trident*, 167 n30. Kossar's speech to this congress, 'Ukrainian Canadians in Canada's War Effort,' ended with a reminder to his audience that 'the contribution of the Ukrainians to the War Effort will assure their future in Canada.' Nevertheless, and rather oddly, Swystun, whom 'some Canadian officials described as 'possibly the most influential leader ever produced by the Ukrainians in Canada,' resigned from the UNF and the UCC just prior to this congress, taking the position that 'untimely issues [that is, Ukrainian independence] were certain to be brought up' and that this would 'do more harm than good.' See British Security Co-ordination report #426, 12 October 1943. The congress was also boycotted by the League of Ukrainian Organizations (also known as the Lobay group, or LUO), at the last minute. In total, 501 official delegates, representing the UCC (155), BUC (112), UNF (103), USRL (100), UHO (27), and LUO (4), as well as another 287 guests, participated.

39 See Document #31, 30 September 1941, in *A Delicate and Difficult Question*,
   ed. Kordan and Luciuk, 90. As evidence of Canadian and British cooperation in exchanging intelligence on Ukrainian issues, see Robertson of External Affairs to RCMP Commissioner Wood, 1 October 1941. Robertson noted
   that because 'Special Constable Petrowsky's report seems to me to be a
   quite first-rate job, which describes the dilemma in which the Ukrainian
   nationalists now find themselves very clearly and objectively,' he had
   decided 'to send a copy of it to the UK authorities who are wrestling
   with the problems of postwar frontiers and the organization of eastern
   Europe ...' See NAC RG25, vol. 1896, file 165A. Petrowsky, skilled at 'dis-
   creetly' obtaining information from 'several authoritative Ukrainian leaders in Winnipeg,' continued to work for the RCMP after the war,
   monitoring the activity of the UCRF. For example, on 9 November 1947,
   after visiting the Petrowsky home for supper, Yaremovich recorded in his
   diary that his host had asked quite a few questions about CURB, about life
   among the DPs, and about the distribution of relief supplies – how it was
   carried out and whether the refugee intelligentsia was favoured. Petrowsky
   also inquired about the refugees' political parties and their activities. Yaremovich noted that he had 'spared no words' in answering questions and
   had 'described all as is & not as often presented by the people.' I am
   indebted to the late Mr Yaremovich for making a copy of his diary available. The original document remains with his family in Winnipeg.
40 Document #32, 6 March 1942, in *A Delicate and Difficult Question*, ed. Kordan
   and Luciuk, 91.
41 See Document #32, ibid. Accusations about 'divided loyalties' continued to
   enjoy widespread currency in Canada until the end of the war, and even
   beyond. See, for example, Harold L. Weir's letter, published in the 29 March
   1945 issue of the *Edmonton Bulletin*, entitled 'Canadians Can Speak for Canada and Only Canada: Too Many Instances of Dual Loyalty in This Country.' Weir criticized parliamentarian Hlynka's 26 March 1945 address in the
   House of Commons, during which the Social Credit MP for Vegreville said
   the UCC and the Ukrainian Congress Committee of America (Ukrainskyi
   kongresovyi komitet Ameryky) should be given the right to speak at the
   forthcoming San Francisco conference of the United Nations on behalf of
   Ukraine, which Hlynka also described as one of the 'submerged nations'
   within the Russian Empire. Weir wrote, 'If Canadian Ukrainian societies
   should go to San Francisco to present the claims of the Ukraine, what is the
   matter with some fanatic group of Petainist sympathizers going to San
   Francisco to present the views of Vichy or with some isolationist Irish society in this country (if one could be found) going to San Francisco to present

the views of De Valera?' Weir probably echoed the feelings of more than a
few Canadians when he reprimanded those who thought like Hlynka, by
asserting that 'This is Canada – no hyphens!'

42 Lazarowich to the *Edmonton Bulletin*, 9 March 1942.

43 FO 371/24473 contains several letters by Frank Savery, then with the British
embassy to Poland in Angers, on Ukrainian–Polish relations; a file entitled
'Unofficial Conversation about the Ukraine,' 1 March 1940, which reports
on Danylo Skoropadsky's interpretation of contemporary events; another
file entitled 'Ukrainian Problem,' which contains letters between various
Foreign Office specialists and diplomats on Ukrainian–Polish relations during January–February 1940; and a lengthy memorandum, prepared by S.E.
Carlton, a surveyor and underwriter who had lived in Poland for ten years,
entitled 'The Ukraine, with Particular Reference to the Polish Ukrainian
Problem,' 5 March 1940.

44 See 'Anti-Polish activities of Ukrainian Nationalists Abroad,' 9 March 1936,
FO 371/19962.

45 See 'Pro-Ally Ukrainians in France,' 9 July 1941, FO 371/29532, in which
the main points of a conversation between M. Wszelaki, of the Polish Ministry for Foreign Affairs, and L. Collier, of the British Northern Department,
on the subject of utilizing 'Petliurist' exiles among the large Ukrainian populations of Canada and the United States, are recorded. During the spring
1941 visit of the Polish premier, General Wladyslaw Sikorski, to Canada,
Robertson of External Affairs told the Polish consul general in Montreal
that Canadian Ukrainians were becoming 'very troublesome' and urged the
Polish government to make a declaration that would 'keep them on the
right lines.' Apparently, Robertson repeated this request on 30 June 1941.
Meanwhile, Sikorski spoke publicly about the need for setting up a strong
postwar Polish–Czechoslovak federation of fifty million, probably including the Western Ukrainian regions of Subcarpathia, Galicia, and western
Volhynia. The Ukrainian Canadian public was outraged and expressed its
anger through a memorandum to Prime Minister Mackenzie King, presented on 23 May by a delegation of MPs which included Hlynka, Joseph
Thorson, Walter Tucker, and Robert Fair, all of whom had large numbers
of Ukrainian voters in their ridings. See also the file entitled 'Western
Ukrainian Nationalist organization,' 6 October 1941, FO 371/29532, which
contains a copy of a Canadian postal intercept of the Ukrainian American
newspaper *Liberty* reporting on the OUN's declaration of the renewal of an
independent Ukrainian state in Lviv, 30 June 1941. A member of the Northern Department minuted, 'This shows that the Ukrainian Separatists have
little to hope from Germany.'

46 Document #33, 6 May 1943, in *A Delicate and Difficult Question*, ed. Kordan and Luciuk, 93.

47 Document #34, 28 May 1943, ibid., 100.

48 A number of the leading Ukrainian Canadian newspapers and groups quickly reaffirmed their unconditional loyalty and allegiance to Canada upon the outbreak of the war. For example, on 6 September 1939, Winnipeg's *Ukrainian Voice* declared that the USRL's members had never wavered in their loyalty to Canada, the British Crown, or democratic institutions. That same day *Canadian Farmer*, also published in Winnipeg, counselled readers to give their unreserved support to the Canadian war effort. The day before, Edmonton's Ukrainian Catholic newspaper, *Ukrainski visti* (*Ukrainian News*), noted that 'Canadian Ukrainians, as loyal subjects of Canada, await the command of our government.' The UNF's organ, *New Pathway*, also affirmed Ukrainian Canadian loyalty in a carefully written editorial, 'What Will Happen to Ukraine?' published on 30 June 1941. While underscoring that 'Canadian Ukrainians are primarily interested in seeing that the armed conflict between Nazism and Bolshevism will bring the greatest benefit to the military cause of Canada and Britain, because we all hope for a quick and complete victory for our adopted homeland and the British Commonwealth of Nations,' it also wondered 'what will happen to Ukraine?' in the aftermath of an Allied victory. On 17 July 1941 another *New Pathway* editorial entitled 'Please Do Not Worry ...' offered a rebuttal to the Davies article which had just been published in *Saturday Night*. It made clear that the Federation, within a few days of the declaration of the war, had, like all the other member groups of the UCC, ranged itself on the side of Canada and Britain, 'without any qualifications and irrespective of any possible "phases of war."' The UNF's members had thereby proved their loyalty by their actions and had done so 'at the very beginning of the war[;] they are doing it now and will be doing it in the future.' Nationally minded Ukrainians, the editorial continued, had not carried out any propaganda against Canada's war effort as the communists had done, both openly and secretly, for as long as Stalin and Hitler had been partners. Always contrasting themselves to their pro-Soviet antagonists, the UCC's supporters insisted on their personal and collective commitment and loyalty to Canada. They said they believed that one of the principles for which Canada and Britain had gone to war, namely, the right of all peoples to live in freedom, gave them hope that after an Allied victory Ukrainians in Europe would have a chance to live as freely as Ukrainians did in Canada. But Ottawa apparently felt otherwise. When *New Pathway* editorials continued intertwining Canada's war aims with the idea of postwar Ukrainian

national independence, the publisher received a firm warning from the official press censor. Any criticism of the Soviet Union, implicit or explicit, would not be permitted. See the letter from F. Charpenter to M. Pohorecky, 6 August 1941, W. Kossar Collection, NAC MG30, vol. 4, file 36. For a prewar commentary on Kossar by Skelton of External Affairs, see DEA 165-39C, 15 June 1939. Observing that the endeavours made by Germany to weaken Poland and the Soviet Union by supporting the Ukrainian national movement 'had some repercussions in Canada,' Skelton nevertheless insisted that the Ukrainian representatives with whom he had been in contact had 'on all occasions emphasized their desire to put Canada and the British Commonwealth first,' even if they were 'equally strong in believing that an independent or autonomous Ukraine would be in the interests of the United Kingdom and indirectly of the other members of the British Commonwealth.' After meeting, that very week, with Kossar, who was then en route to London and Europe, Skelton noted that while he appreciated the strength of Kossar's convictions he assumed that 'like other Canadians, [Kossar] would be primarily concerned in the interests of Canada, not in the interests of any part of the European Continent.' He further told Kossar, before passing him along to Robertson, who also had been dealing with 'alien questions,' that while he would communicate Kossar's points to the Canadian government, the government would not, of course, 'give any endorsement to these proposals.' Quite simply, it would not 'be appropriate [for Canada] to put forward the representations of a group which, so far at least as many of its members are concerned, is more European than Canadian in its interests.'

49 Kaye to Philipps, 14 September 1940, NAC MG30 E350 v2. Kaye noted that the minister for agriculture, James Gardiner, had recently 'had a long talk with some of our Ukr. politicals in Saskatchewan (which is his home) and expressed the opinion that the Government should have one or two reliable Ukrainian Canadians in Ottawa,' whose purpose would be 'to inform the Government on everything what is going on etc.' In Kaye's words, 'it sounds like a superior "operative," but, he quickly added, I have no blessed idea what is going on in Ottawa and what the Government intends to do.' He also mentioned that one of the persons being considered for the job was Wasyl Burianyk, 'a man of confidence of the Liberal Party in Saskatchewan' over the previous twenty years. Burianyk certainly enjoyed the sympathy of the Liberal MP of Rosthern, Saskatchewan, Walter Tucker. See Tucker's letter about Burianyk to Skelton, received in Ottawa on 3 August 1939.

50 Ibid.

51 On these two committees, see Marunchak, *The Ukrainian Canadians*, 549–50.

While the RCUC tended to be Catholic and inclined to the political Right, the CCUC was more closely identified with the Orthodox church and politically was of the Centre to moderate Left. A 12 June 1940 editorial in the Orthodox newspaper *Ukrainian Voice* argued that because four out of six pro-independence newspapers supported the CCUC this group could count on the support of some thirty thousand subscribers. In contrast, the combined circulation of the two newspapers connected with the RCUC, a 'reactionary group,' totalled only thirteen thousand, which made the latter a minority. Of course, supporters of the RCUC were quick to point out that they enjoyed the support of the Ukrainian Catholic Church, with which some 80 per cent of Ukrainian Canadian believers were affiliated at this time, and that that made their alliance the numerically superior one, and certainly possessed of a much larger financial base. Writing about the CCUC, Kossar – an RCUC man – expressed the view that this 'conglomeration of republicans, Hetmanites, Communists, Trotskyists, and other kinds of socialists won't stick together for long,' if only because one could be sure that the Stechishins would soon 'botch things up.' Cited in Prymak, *Maple Leaf and Trident*, 45 and n26, 158.

52 See Kaye to Philipps, 11 August 1940, NAC MG30 E350 v2. See also Kaye's enclosure entitled 'The Ukrainian Canadian Committee,' in which he pointed out that during his national lecture tour (12 July–11 August 1940) he had come to believe that there could not be a 'complete and efficient utilization of all available forces in connection with the present war efforts' in so far as Ukrainian Canadians were concerned, unless a common committee were set up. Although the RCUC and CCUC had identical aims, they were, Kaye observed, hostile to each other, partly on ideological grounds but 'to a great extent' simply because of personal differences among the leaders of the groups, as he proceeded to detail. Community factionalism naturally did not abate, or at least not entirely so, after the UCC's formation. And the government was well aware of that fact. For example, see the 'Review of the Canadian Foreign-Language Press,' prepared by the Office of Examiner of Publications, Department of National Revenue, 11 May 1943, a copy of which went to External Affairs. This report indicated that in the 1, 8, and 15 April 1943 issues of Toronto's *Ukrainian Life* there was an 'interesting discussion' on a joint communiqué issued by the Ukrainian Catholic Mission Society of St Josaphat and the St Methodius Priests Association. Certain Ukrainian Catholic clergymen apparently deplored the fact that Ukrainian Catholic organizations in Canada had joined the UCC, thus conceding 'parity to their most bitter enemies, the Orthodox Ukrainians.' Cooperation with 'schismatics' was described as a 'terrible sin,' and, for

that reason the UCC should be fought as an organization 'detrimental to the Ukrainian Catholic Church.' See DEA 3846-A-40-C. In British Security Co-ordination report #426, 12 October 1943, this Ukrainian Catholic opposition was described as the 'ultra-Catholic faction' of the Ukrainian clergy, headed by Reverend M. Krywitsky. Apparently Bishop Ladyka of Winnipeg, 'who belongs to this group,' had refused to attend any meeting graced by the presence of Orthodox archbishop Theodorovich, and had 'virtually fled to Toronto in order to be absent from the city during the Congress.' The USRL's Jaroslav Arsenych wrote to Michael Stechishin, on 16 November 1940, that while the UCC's executive had a 'pretty well balanced appearance' many key positions were held by USRL and Ukrainian Greek Orthodox Church supporters. I am indebted to the late Reverend S. Sawchuk for a copy of this letter.

53 Ibid. Regrettably, no history of the UHO, the Hetmantsi, exists. However, there are indications that its activities were monitored in Canada. For example, as RCMP documents recently declassified under the Access to Information Act show, official surveillance of the Ukrainian Sitch Organization began in the 1920s. The interest of the Department of National Defence in the 'Sitch' was certainly sparked by 'a collision' between individual members of the militia and the Ukrainian organization known as 'Sitch' at a militia camp near Yorkton, Saskatchewan, in mid-July 1928. Superintendent W.P. Lindsay, commanding the RCMP's Southern Saskatchewan District, wrote to Ottawa on 20 July that Detective-Sergeant G. Clifford and Corporal Kelleher had been sent into the field earlier that month to investigate. He attached their reports. Despite the apparent reluctance of Colonel Jenkins, the commanding officer, to have his men testify about this incident, Clifford was able to interview several eyewitnesses. Apparently several members of the 'Sitch,' attending a convention of that organization in Yorkton, visited the army camp afterwards on the invitation of Colonel Jenkins. Then troubles began, apparently over arguments having to do with the loyalty of 'Sitch' members – would they fight for the pope or for the king? Sergeant J.L. Ford told the investigators that on the evening of Saturday, 7 July and again on the next day, at the militia camp, he saw a man agitating among the troops, 'running down the Sitch movement,' saying that the 'Sitch' should be 'run out of the country.' Ford asked the man whether he was 'in favour of the K.K.K.' (Ku Klux Klan), to which he replied, 'Most decidedly.' Other witnesses described the agitator as a Mr Donald MacDonald, a blacksmith from Yorkton, whose rhetoric about how 'Sitch was a body of Foreigners that was endeavouring to get control of Canada and should not be allowed to wear uniforms and side-arms' so inflamed some

of the militia that some seventy-five of them had marched to the vicinity of St Joseph's College 'to clear the town of the Sitch bohunks.' They had to be dispersed by local police and, eventually, their officers. Clifford later interviewed MacDonald himself. MacDonald stated that he had observed flags flying at St Joseph's College on Saturday, 7 July, specifically the 'Sitch' flag but no Union Jack, which action he protested; he claimed, however, not to be a member of the KKK and stated that he had refrained from causing any trouble. See also 'Troops Resent Big Ukrainian Uniform Show,' *Edmonton Bulletin*, 10 July 1928; 'Parade in Yorkton by Ukrainian Sitch Threatens Trouble,' *Manitoba Free Press*, 10 July 1928; and 'Says Yorkton Demonstration Was Instigated by Radicals,' ibid., 11 July 1928, in which the 'Sitch' leader, W. Bossy, was said to have observed that he organized the 'Sitch' because of the general belief in Canada that Ukrainians are not loyal to Canadian ideals and aspirations, which he intended to counter by organizing Ukrainian units that would eventually be added to the Canadian regular militia. On 11 August 1928 the Department of National Defence's Colonel H.H. Matthews, the director of military operations and intelligence, wrote to Colonel Cortlandt Starnes, commissioner of the RCMP, to request, 'for General Thacker's information,' a resumé of the Sitch movement's aims and activities, particularly because, he noted, he had been informed that Sitch detachments 'frequently parade armed and in uniform.' On 13 August the commissioner replied, noting first that the RCMP had been 'aware of the activities of "Sitch" for about four years.' Starnes then went on to quote at length from a memorandum he had on file from the previous year describing the work of Mr Bossy, the organizer of the 'Sitch.' It stated that Bossy was 'a Ukrainian Nationalist,' and that the 'tendency of his agitation' was to promote among 'residents in Canada of Ukrainian race adhesion to the Ukrainian language and nationality, loyalty to the separate Ukrainian Republic which it is desired to establish, opposition to Bolshevism, and adherence to the Greek Catholic form of religious faith.' Bossy had come under RCMP scrutiny on several occasions, all connected with his 'antagonism to Bolshevism' and 'support of the church over which Bishop Budka presides in Canada.' Described by an anonymous informant as a well-educated man with a military background, (General) Bossy was said to be 'very bitter against the red element,' who, in their turn, were highly antagonistic towards his movement, to the extent that he had received 'several letters threatening his life.' Undeterred, Bossy apparently continued to 'bring to the notice of the authorities any information that he obtained that could be used in suppressing communism.' Starnes remarked on this favourably: 'I attach importance to the opposition Mr.

Bosy [*sic*] and his adherents offer to Bolshevism. Although not the only means of combatting this social disease, they constitute an important one. Even if I entertained a worse opinion of his movement than I do, I should regard it as of service as a counter-irritant.' Bossy's followers were also subjected to a certain amount of persecution, as the RCMP noted. At least two of their recent meetings had 'been invaded and broken up,' the one in Calgary, and another in February 1925 at Espanola, Ontario. During that fray between 'Sitch' supporters and 'Bolshevistic Ukrainians,' two police officers ('one a member of this Force') were assaulted.

54 Document #27, 18 February 1940, in *A Delicate and Difficult Question*, ed. Kordan and Luciuk, 71–3.
55 For another view on the UCC's formation see S.W. Frolick, *The Ukrainian Canadian Committee: A History* (Toronto, 1978). Frolick contended that, because Ukrainians in Canada suffer from a 'siege mentality,' feeling 'insecure, inferior, and threatened, individually and collectively,' they have tried to conceal the community's 'mistakes and shortcomings *even from ourselves*,' particularly with respect to the UCC's history. From his perspective, 'it was the federal government of Canada that stepped in to bring the warring Ukrainian churches and organizations together.' He based his interpretation on conversations he had with Tracy Philipps in London in 1945. Philipps apparently told Frolick that Professors Kirkconnell and Simpson and he were tasked with creating the UCC, mainly because the British and Canadian governments felt the half million Ukrainians in Canada might pose an internal security threat if Nazi Germany embraced a pro-Ukrainian policy in Europe. This problem could not be contained through internment operations like those utilized against Japanese Canadians after 1941 because there were simply too many Ukrainians in Canada for such measures to be practical. For Philipps's own view of the role he played in creating the UCC, see his remarks of 8 January 1941, reproduced in Document #28, in *A Delicate and Difficult Question*, ed. Kordan and Luciuk, 74–6. Of course, the UCC did enjoy a measure of popular support among Ukrainian Canadians. In a report prepared for the Citizenship Division of the Department of National War Services, entitled 'Canadians of Recent European Origin: A Survey' (Ottawa, 1945), Kaye cited remarks made at the first UCC congress by Reverend Sawchuk to the effect that the UCC had the support of 149 Ukrainian Greek Catholic and Ukrainian Greek Orthodox priests, who ministered to 656 congregations, along with that of 700 to 800 Ukrainian schoolteachers and a large number of local community leaders. In all, Sawchuk claimed, the UCC had the backing of 1429 centres, which meant it enjoyed the endorsement of the 'preponderant majority of the Ukrainian

Canadians.' By 1950 there were a reported 168 UCC branches across the country. But whatever moral support the UCC might have, this never fully translated into financial backing. The group's first treasurer, Teodor Datzkiw, reminded delegates attending its first congress that the UCC was basically a 'purely public institution dependent upon the voluntary work of such persons as compose the Executive and Praesidium.' It was his 'unpleasant duty' to announce publicly that 'our people have not yet risen to the heights expected of a nation striving for independent sovereignty,' for only 52 per cent of the projected $38,755 budget fixed for 1945 had been collected. Was it, Datzkiw wondered, impossible to collect $37,500 in 1946 from 350,000 Ukrainian Canadians, especially when the need for funds to be used for helping the Ukrainian DPs, of whom 'there are as many ... over there as there are Ukrainians in Canada,' was so obvious? Certainly, in the past, almost everyone had complained of the 'disunity that cursed our social relations in Canada.' But now there was an 'all-national union' in existence, where representatives of various religious and political groups sat around one table deliberating harmoniously on matters pertaining to the welfare of the Ukrainian people as a whole. Simply stated, the UCC needed funds with which to do its work. With that plea Datzkiw ended his remarks. See *Second All-Canadian Congress of Ukrainians in Canada* (Winnipeg, 1946), 26, 29. Deficits have plagued the UCC ever since. An undated sheet entitled simply 'Ukrainian Canadian Committee, Winnipeg Branch Budget 1946' gives a detailed break-down of how fund-raising was conducted in that city. Various parishes and organizations were called upon to levy specific sums of money. The document records the successes, but mostly there were failures. Six parishes asked to raise $1050 managed to collect only $210. Secular groups like the USRL, UHO, UNF, the Ukrainian Peoples' Home, and Ukrainian Institute 'Prosvita,' given the task of raising $800, managed to gather only $200, and all of that from supporters of the Ukrainian Peoples' Home. Of a total projected budget of $2250 for 1946, only $575.10 was gathered, a shortfall of $1674.90. Such limited financial support has seriously undercut the feasibility of many worthwhile UCC projects, then and since.

56 This point is made by O. Gerus, 'The Ukrainian Canadian Committee,' in *A Heritage in Transition*, ed. Lupul, 198–9. Even after the UCC's formation there were those in Canadian government circles who wondered whether it would not be preferable to bring Petliurist exiles, like Myroslav Prokopovych and Oleksander Shulhyn, to Canada from France and use them to set up 'some kind of centre of [pro-Allied] information' to serve as a counterfoil to any puppet Ukrainian regime the Germans might set up. See 'Sug-

gested creation in Canada of a Ukrainian Political Centre,' 9 January 1941, FO 371/26721. The idea of making use of the indigenous Ukrainian Canadian leadership was rejected by British analysts, who deemed most of them to be 'second class people.'

57 See the RCMP's 'Report re: 8th National Convention of Ukrainian National Federation of Canada and the Affiliated Sections,' held in Winnipeg from 25 to 31 August 1941, an abridged version of which is reproduced as Document #31, in *A Delicate and Difficult Question*, ed. Kordan and Luciuk, 80–90. On government plans for interning Ukrainian Canadian nationalists, see the confidential memorandum from the RCMP's commissioner to the Minister of Justice, 25 August 1939, in the E. Lapointe Papers, NAC MG27 III B10, vol. 50.

58 See the front-page story in the *Winnipeg Free Press*, 'All for One – One for All,' 27 November 1940, and J.C. Royle's article, 'Unity among Ukrainian-Canadians,' *Winnipeg Tribune*, 25 November 1940. For a detailed description of Ukrainians (and other 'European racial groups') in Canada in 1945 published by the Citizenship Division of the Department of National War Services, see V.J. Kaye, *Canadians of Recent European Origin: A Survey* (Ottawa, 1945).

59 See Philipps's confidential 'Brief Report, As Asked, for the Personal Information of General LaFleche, Minister for National War Services, (a) On the Origin, (b) Aim and (c) Functions of the Nationalities Branch,' 26 December 1942, NAC MG30 E350. Philipps wrote, in November 1940, that he was in Canada 'on Canadian invitation and British selection' on a temporary 'dollar-a-year mission' – this, when he was asked by the associate deputy minister of war services, Mr Justice T.C. Davis, if he would use his 'specialized experience of Eastcentral European Minorities, including Ukrainians,' to 'induce Canadians of Ukrainian stock to suspend their European political vendettas (which ever since Ukrainians came to Canada they have never been prevailed on to compose) in order to co-ordinate their conflicting Committees "for warwork for the duration."' As documents released under the Access to Information Act underscore, the RCMP was briefed in detail about the organizational activities of the Ukrainian Canadian community. The RCMP's Intelligence Section filed a lengthy memorandum, dated 29 June 1943, on the UCC congress held in Winnipeg between 22 and 24 June. Appended to that report, among other documents, was the complete text of Professor Watson Kirkconnell's address, 'In Defence of New Canadians.' In it, Kirkconnell shed additional light on how the UCC originated and on the services performed by Tracy Philipps in that regard.

Given the importance which the UCC was to assume in Ukrainian Canadian society and the continuing debate over Philipps's role in its formation, this document bears citing at some length: 'The final stage in the co-ordination of Ukrainian organizations came in the autumn of 1940. In this case the initiative came from the federal Department of National War Services, after consultation with the Department of External Affairs. Lack of unity among the Ukrainians was regarded as inimical to the war effort, and the Government wanted action. The man chosen to act as official peace-maker was Mr. Tracy Philipps, recently appointed European adviser to the Canadian government. Inasmuch as much vile abuse has been hurled at Mr. Philipps by the Communists for the past three years, it will be in order to explain something as to his background. Mr. Philipps was born in 1890, the son of a distinguished old English family, with Canadian affiliations. (One ancestor, Sir Edward Philipps, was Governor of Nova Scotia from 1717 to 1749 and is buried in Westminster Abbey). Mr. Tracy Philipps was educated at Marlborough College, Oxford University and Durham University (President of the Union, Master of Arts, Bachelor of Literature). He entered the Government service in 1912, and gave the next twenty years of his life to his country, finally retiring with the rank of the governor of a province. In the last war he was already in hand-to-hand fighting in the field (Africa) during the first week of the war. He was three times wounded, mentioned in despatches, and awarded the Military Cross. He was subsequently attached to the British Embassy in Rome and to the British Legation in Athens. He worked with Lawrence of Arabia. He is a distinguished scientist, Fellow of the Royal Geographical Society and Fellow of the Royal Anthropological Institute, and is the author of sixteen books in the fields of geography and anthropology. He holds decorations for distinguished service conferred on him by the Egyptian, Turkish, Belgian and Hellenic governments. His alma mater, Durham University, conferred on him the degree of Doctor of Civil Laws (honoris causa) in recognition of his eminence as a colonial administrator and public servant. His presence in Canada came as the result of official invitation from this side. He had never had any association with any individual Ukrainian organization, and his work as a negotiator in Winnipeg was undertaken in general terms for the good of Canada.'

After dismissing Canadian communist attacks on Philipps, specifically those reproduced in an 'occasional mimeographed news-sheet in New York, called *The Hour* and edited by Albert Kahn and Michael Sayre,' Kirkconnell continued: 'Let us return to October 1940, when Mr. Philipps arrived in Winnipeg, commissioned by the government to try to find a means and a formula by which the Canadians of Ukrainian stock could be co-ordinated for war services. (There was no more question of uniting or

fusing the parties than there is any question, in a democracy, of fusing all
parliamentary parties into one because of a state of war). After considerable difficulty, the parties agreed to have delegates in Winnipeg to discuss
the proposal. Then after protracted discussions of the formula submitted
by Mr. Philipps at a meeting at which he preferred not to be present, an
agreement was finally reached. The various leaders agreed, for the first
time, to sit at the same table, for the duration. When the consequent question of representation, which was also a matter of personalities, had to be
settled, Mr. Philipps consulted Mr. Victor Sifton and Mr. Edgar Tarr, and
asked Professor Simpson if he could come from Saskatoon. A formula of
representation was then also found. The leaders agreed in the interests of
Canada to relegate their burning differences to a secondary place for the
period of the war.' Kirkconnell then went on to savage the 'fantastic [anti-
UCC] arguments being brought forward in 1943 by Communist apologists'
like Raymond Arthur Davies, whose book, *This Is Our Land*, dishonestly
tried to blacken the good name of the UCC. Kirkconnell argued that the
real purpose of the communists was to try to make the Ukrainian Canadian community a 'political closed shop' of which they would be 'the sole
bargaining agents.' For him, such a situation would be the equivalent of
'Judas, instead of committing suicide, [wanting] to be made sole spokesman for the Apostles.' Although the Soviet Union might indeed now be an
Allied power, Kirkconnell still held that it was the UCC alone which
deserved Ottawa's support, despite the communists' propagandistic
efforts to the contrary: 'Their campaign is an insult even to the hard-boiled
Ottawa politician; for why any serious campaigner would want to rely on
20,000 yelping members of a seditious organization rather than on 300,000
loyal citizens (all bitter enemies of the aforesaid 20,000) is a problem in
psychiatry. But the question is not merely one for the electioneer. It is a
matter of the common decencies of political life. For to have politicians
or civil servants dream of smiling on the sons of sedition while cold-
shouldering the overwhelming majority of a loyal community would be
a disgrace to any nation.'

60 For Philipps's 'Personal Dossier,' see NAC MG30 E350, vols 1 and 2. Philipps apparently had a rather colourful career, serving as an officer on the
Western Front in the First World War, later with Lawrence of Arabia, then in
the Caucasus and Ukraine during 1920–3 and again during the 'second
great (artificial) famine in Ukraine 1932/33.' He also worked in Italy, Africa,
Palestine, Greece, Bulgaria, Turkey, and Russia. Allegedly he was a skilled
linguist, fluent in several European languages and at least thirteen African
ones. The character 'Philip Tracy' in F.A.M. Webster's book *The Man Who*

Knew (1927) is loosely modelled on Philipps. File 2 preserves a letter, dated 15 August 1942, from Philipps to Senator A. Knatchbull-Hugessen at Dalhousie, New Brunswick. In it he confided that he had been asked by Lord Halifax to go to Canada 'on special duty' and noted that the position he had been asked to play was 'a particularly delicate one and full of pitfalls with lots of people waiting to push me in. By the grace of God and by working more carefully and harder than I ever worked before, I am out of the wood and in a position to render real service and to pull my full weight, both for Canada and for the wider Allied world. My mind and my energies have, as you can imagine, been stretched and strained to the utmost.' However, in a file entitled 'Mr. Tracy Philipps: Mission Dealing with Ukraine Problem,' FO 371/26721, there is a letter dated 29 January 1941 from R.M. Makins, addressed to Volodymyr Korostovets (also known as Vladimir de Korostovetz). After thanking him for his letter of 8 January 1941 on the Ukrainian problem, Makins asserted that 'Mr. Tracy Phillips has no connexion with the FO and the press reports to which you refer are therefore quite unfounded.' The original draft of this letter contained an even more direct denial. It said that Philipps, 'in spite of anything he may say to the contrary [had not been] charged with any ... mission by the Foreign Office.' On 12 February 1941, Makins again wrote to Korostovets to let him know that Philipps also had no connection with the British Ministry of Information. Danylo Skoropadsky communicated these facts to the UCC's Datzkiw, who represented the UHO in the UCC, on 4 February 1941, as the British press censors watching their correspondence duly recorded. Even earlier, Whitehall had denied knowing who Philipps might be. After G.O. Wiskemann of the Ministry of Information forwarded a copy of a report by Philipps entitled 'Russia Is Not an Enigma' (1 November 1939), Laurence Collier replied to say not only that he did not know who Philipps was but that he had not found the report very interesting. Many observations Philipps made, Collier noted, hardly bore out his claim to have been a 'close student of Russian affairs since 1921.' For example, when Philipps wrote that Stalin and Hitler both feared and loathed the Jews because of a genuine conviction that 'the Democracies are both exploited and inspired by the Jews,' he was obviously wrong. Evidence the British possessed clearly contradicted any assertion about Stalin hating Jews, the most obvious proof of which was that Stalin had married Lazar Kaganovich's sister, Maria. See FO 371/23698, 16 November 1939. In contrast, L. Rapoport, in *Stalin's War against the Jews: The Doctors' Plot and the Soviet Solution* (New York, 1990), argues that – despite the scores of Jews who played prominent and often quite despicable roles in the Soviet state, party, and secret police apparatuses – Stalin intended to launch an anti-Semitic purge in the early 1950s, and was prevented only by his own death in March 1953.

Whether the UHO informed other Ukrainian Canadian groups of the British government's denial of any responsibility for Philipps is not known. Certainly, for his part, Philipps took a highly critical stance towards the Hetmantsi; on 30 June 1941 he wrote that the UHO was, 'to put it mildly, very unCanadian,' and that 'the most suitable place for Korostovets ... to exercise his talents would be in internment.' See Philipps's 'strictly confidential' notes, 'The Immediate Problem of the Foreign-Born and Canadian Unity,' 30 June 1941, in NAC MG30 E350. Philipps's role and the identity of those who authorized it remain enigmatic. In the personal and confidential 'Report to You of the 13th January and Subsequent Memoranda,' sent to Judge Davis, 25 February 1941, Philipps pointed out that twenty years of British government service, largely among east-central European peoples as a soldier, as an adviser to 'the Genevan League for Relief around Russia,' as an ethnologist, and most recently as a diplomatic correspondent covering these same peoples, had made him 'into something of a Specialist in the racial mentality and the political affairs of the peoples who have the misfortune to exist between the Russian and the Prussian empires.' Other contemporary observers certainly assigned a pivotal role to Phillips. Thus, in *The Ukrainian Canadian Committee: A History*, Frolick described him as 'an emissary of the British Government, linked with the British Secret Service.' The question remains why Philipps, if he was not working for the British government, was allowed such latitude for several years within the Canadian bureaucracy. On the activities of the Skoropadsky-Korostovets party, Collier noted that they were 'variously judged,' which meant that, 'just like some hotels in Baedeker,' they were given mostly unfavourable judgments. Collier minuted that he had met Korostovets personally several times but had 'never been able to decide whether he is honest or using the Ukrainian movement to get himself a livelihood.' At any rate, His Majesty's Government did not favour the movement, for it was clearly 'aimed at the disruption of a State with which we are in normal relations.' See Collier's minutes addressed to Sir L. Oliphant, 26 October 1933, FO 371/17247. Collier was the same Foreign Office official who, in reference to the Great Famine of 1932–3 in Ukraine, would write, 'The truth of the matter is, of course, that we have a certain amount of information about famine conditions ... and that there is no obligation on us not to make it public. We do not want to make it public, however, because the Soviet Government would resent it and our relations with them would be prejudiced' (see Collier's notes in a file entitled 'Famine Conditions in the Soviet Union,' 30 June 1934, FO 371/

18320). He, and many other British officials, knew quite well that 'the Soviet Government's policy of ruthless agricultural collectivisation created famine conditions in many parts of the Soviet Union, particularly in the Ukraine' (see Collier's memorandum in 'Famine Relief in the Soviet Union,' 24 June 1935, FO 371/19467). In *Hitler and Stalin: Parallel Lives*, Bullock observes that there 'was no part of Russia where dekulakization and collectivization bore more harshly on the peasantry than the Ukraine ... The Ukraine ... was the first East European country to experience, from 1918–1920, the forcible suppression of its independence by Russia ... It has remained the largest national group in Europe not to have achieved independence in the twentieth century ... [Collectivization] ruthlessly enforced cost the lives of as many as five million Ukrainian peasants, out of a farm population of twenty to twenty-five million ... Like the Jews under the Nazis, the kulaks ... were pushed out of human society and declared to be subhuman. In both cases what counted was not what a kulak or a Jew had done, but the simple fact of what they were, which condemned them, members of an outlawed class or race denied all human rights' (269, 273, 277).

61 Philipps to Sir Gerald Campbell, 14 March 1941, NAC MG30 E350, file 18.
62 See Philipps's confidential 'Memorandum to the Commissioner on Organization and Personnel,' 28 May 1941, NAC MG30 E350, file 6.
63 See Philipps's confidential 'Reports, Dated Chicago, 1st and 7th May by H.B.M. Consul General on Ukrainian Organizations in the United States, with Their Links throughout the Americas (in Hemisphere Defence,) and with Russia Opposite Canada,' 4 June 1941, NAC MG30 E350.
64 Philipps to Judge Davis, 28 June 1941, NAC MG30 E350. In it he pointed out that there were no foreign-born communities in Canada that were disloyal or even 'disquietingly discontented *as Canadians*,' although the state of international affairs was exciting many of these ethnic communities. Until External Affairs provided a clear interpretation of what Canadian policy might be on the 'Ukrainian Question,' he declared, he was unwilling to speak to this subject, and he added that any statements made had better take into consideration the likely reactions of the 'million Ukrainians in the vital defence industries' of North America, for that is where the 'main danger' lay. In his confidential 'Reports, Dated Chicago ...,' 4 June 1941, NAC MG30 E350, Philipps asked rhetorically, 'What then, after a year and a half of war, are the Allies proposing to offer Ukrainians on the day of victory, if Ukrainians agree to refuse what the enemy offers?' He answered by pointing out that the Allies claimed to be engaged in a 'crusade for Christian civilization,' and that they said they were 'fighting for the right of peoples to organize themselves as independent national units.'

If this was true, then 'no new promise is necessary for Ukrainians,' since they too were 'actively resisting the imposition of Militant Godlessness' and wanted only to achieve independence. Philipps reminded his readers in government circles that they 'could not now honestly (or safely) pretend that our declarations mean that we are out to help only our nearest and strategically useful neighbours, and ... God help the rest.' In the last war, in Philipps's view, the lack of clarity and sincerity in Allied declarations had done 'our reputation ... deadly damage' among the peoples of the Near East, such as Jews and Arabs, Bulgars and Turks. In this war, if the Allies had the courage to be clear and to dissipate doubts about the principles for which they had gone to war, they would be able to 'harmonize [the Ukrainians'] Cause with ours and canalize it to help generate more power for the Cause of the English-speaking peoples, of whom a million and a half Ukrainians of North America are now a part.' Otherwise, he presciently observed, the Anglo-American powers would be forced to keep compiling 'voluminous reports about Ukrainians as potential enemies or at least as rather doubtful friends.'

65 See Philipps, 'Memorandum for the Deputy Minister and for the Committee,' 25 September 1942, NAC MG30 E350 v2. Philipps compared the official administrative machinery put in place in Canada and the United States to cope with 'foreign-born communities' and 'war services,' and pointed out that the American OSS Foreign Nationalities Branch enjoyed far greater support.

66 Ibid.

67 Ibid.

68 On Philipps's views on 'Canadianism,' see Document #28, 8 January 1941, in *A Delicate and Difficult Question*, ed. Kordan and Luciuk, 74–6. For him, the Nationalities Branch had a higher mandate than simply mobilizing ethnic groups to help 'win the war.' Its purpose was also to 'consolidate the nation.' Such a blending together would come naturally enough, but only if the feeling on the part of many of the foreign-born that they been neglected was countered. And that would require the promulgation of a 'dynamic and cohesive national mysticism for Canadianism and for Canada.'

69 See Philipps's confidential 'Reports, Dated Chicago ...,' 4 June 1941, NAC MG30 E350.

70 See Philipps, 'Memorandum for the Deputy Minister ...,' 25 September 1942, NAC MG30 E350 v2.

71 See Document #28, 8 January 1941, in *A Delicate and Difficult Question*, ed. Kordan and Luciuk, 74–6. To corroborate the view that Philipps played a decisive role in setting up the UCC, see Office of the Deputy Minister to

Philipps, 15 April 1941, and Kaye to Philipps, 1 June 1941, in files 16 and 21, NAC MG30 E350.

72 See Philipps, 'Memorandum for the Deputy Minister ...,' 25 September 1942, NAC MG30 E350 v2.

73 See *Ukrainian Life*, December 1940, 3,5. This editorial chided that the 'unity' suddenly achieved through the UCC's formation had appeared despite the trend towards disunity which had, only recently, been so characteristic of Ukrainian Canadian organizational life. By way of example it noted that in the 6 November 1940 issue of *Ukrainian Voice* there was a lengthy column attacking the UNF, described as an organization 'executing the will of Berlin.' Yet, ironically, two days later the USRL joined the UNF in forming the UCC.

74 See 'Philipps's 'Report Part II Dated Ottawa 13 January 1941: Subsequent Observations,' NAC MG30 E350, vol. 2. In Phillips to Judge Davis, 9 November 1942, NAC MG30 E350, vol. 2, the former expressed the opinion that 'we have so far done little positively to reinforce the liberal-minded, Canadian-minded centre of the foreign-born.' The term 'foreign-born' included anyone born in Canada one or both of whose parents had been born outside the country.

Some officials, like the deputy minister of the Department of National War Services, congratulated Philipps on his work with the UCC, writing on 15 April 1941: 'You did a very excellent job for us ... and you were largely instrumental in having a Canadian Ukrainian Committee created in Winnipeg. The committee is representative of every element in the Ukrainian population in Canada. I believe this is the first time in the history of this country when they all got together in one organization.' But there were also attacks on Philipps and other UCC-boosters like Kaye, which had their negative consequences. For example, see Philipps's 1 October 1943 letter in reference to Kaye's breakdown and withdrawal from public service, and the unflattering description of Philipps's work circulated by John Grierson of the Wartime Information Board on 23 October 1943, both found in NAC MG 30 E350.

For a good example of the kind of defamation Phillips was subjected to, see 'Mr Phillips Goes to Washington,' *The Hour*, 26 September 1942. Describing him as a 'dapper gentleman' who had been in touch with the 'appeasement circles' in England before the war, the article went on to record that shortly after his arrival in Canada on 10 June 1940 Philipps had been contacted by Luke Myshuha, the editor of the 'pro-Nazi Ukrainian American newspapers, *Svoboda*.' Philips had also been welcomed by another 'fascist-Ukrainian,' W. Kissilevsky (*sic*), who had apparently spread the word that Philipps was coming to Canada as a 'special emissary of Lord Halifax.' That ensured that Philipps was hailed enthusiastically by fascist-Ukrainian organizations 'set up by representatives of the German Intelligence Service.' This was not surprising, said *The Hour*, because both Kissilevsky and Philipps were also connected with 'Nazi-Ukrainian agents from all parts of the world,' including one Jacob Macohin, whom Philipps had visited in Alassio, Italy, in the summer of 1939. Macohin had reportedly been quoted in the London *Daily Express* of 5 December 1938 as saying that he intended to lead a 'fascist-Ukrainian army of 600,000 men, trained and equipped by Nazi Germany, against Soviet Russia.' How could a man with such 'strange connections and expressed opinion' as Tracy Philipps organize effective support for the war effort at the Canadian Department of War Services or give advice to the United States State Department? wondered *The Hour*.

The editor of *The Hour* was Albert E. Kahn, a Stalinist. See *Sabotage! The Secret War against America* by M. Sayers and A.E. Kahn (New York, 1942). The United States Senate Internal Security subcommittee concluded, in 1955, that Kahn had belonged at one time or another to some twenty-five communist front organizations and had 'cooperated in the effort of the Soviet Government to discredit anti-Soviet Russians abroad through his magazine *The Hour* and through his book *The Great Conspiracy*.' For more on how the American Ukrainian community suffered because of its anti-communist militancy, see M.B. Kuropas, *The Ukrainian Americans: Roots and Aspirations, 1884–1954* (Toronto, 1991), 220–9, and his discussion in chapter 7, 'Nationalist Aspirations,' of the work of the House Un-American Activities Committee (formed 6 June 1938, under the chairmanship of Congressman Martin Dies). Some say the disreputable tradition of misinformation by the likes of Kahn and Sayer was continued in the writings of J. Loftus, *The Belarus Secret* (New York, 1982); A.A. Ryan, *Quiet Neighbors: Prosecuting Nazi War Criminals in America* (New York, 1984); R.G. Saidel, *The Outraged Conscience: Seekers of Justice for Nazi War Criminals in America* (Albany, 1984); and C. Higham, *American Swastika* (New York, 1985), and through the labours of their Canadian counterpart, Sol Littman. In 1986 the Honourable Mr Justice Jules Deschênes concluded, in *Commission of Inquiry on War Criminals: Report, Part 1: Public* (Ottawa, 1986), 245–9 and 260–1, that Mr Littman was one of those who, between 1971 and 1986, made public statements that 'spread increasingly large and grossly exaggerated figures' about the number of alleged Nazi war criminals hiding in Canada. The Commission found that 'even leaving aside the figure of 6,000 ventured in 1986 by Mr. Simon Wiesenthal ... this list already shows no less than a 400 per cent over-estimate by the proponents of those figures.' It bears repeating that the Commission found that the Ukrainian Division 'Galicia' should 'not be indicted as a group,' that 'members of the Galicia Division were individually screened for security purposes before admission to Canada,' that charges of war crimes against members of the Galicia Division 'have never been substantiated, either in 1950 when they were first preferred, or in 1984 when they were renewed,' or before the Commission, and that 'in the absence of evidence of participation in or knowledge of specific war crimes, mere membership in the Galicia Division is insufficient to justify prosecution.' These findings have not troubled those for whom they were inconvenient, not to say embarrassing. Littman, for example, did not even mention his public drubbing in *War Criminal on Trial*, 2d ed. (Toronto, 1998), other than to level some rather contemptuous allegations about the objectivity of Justice Deschênes – 'one often wonders which side Deschênes is on' (p. 210) – suggesting a deficient understanding of the principles of judicial independence. Nor are J.E. McKenzie's *War Criminals in Canada* (Calgary, 1995) and Howard Margolian's *Unauthorized Entry: The Truth about Nazi War Criminals in Canada* (Toronto, 2000) much more credible, although the latter offers a useful corrective to the 'cast of mind argument' that infuses so much of this literature, and it does conclude that at most only a tiny fraction of the nearly 1.5 million people who emigrated to Canada in the first decade after the Second World War, perhaps one-eighth of one per cent of the total, might have been collaborators.

75 Philipps, 'Report Part II Dated Ottawa 13 January 1941 ...,' NAC MG30 E350.

76 Kaye to Philipps, 7 April 1941, NAC MG30 E350.

77 See Philipps's secret letter 'Finnish, Ukrainian, Italian etc. Halls Closed and Confiscated to the Custodian,' 22 May 1943, NAC MG30 E350 v2, file 12. He added a footnote to the effect that for members of the Association to Aid the Fatherland the 'Fatherland is not Canada.' In a secret letter from Assistant Commissioner R.R. Tait, director of criminal investigation, to E.W. Stapleford, director of voluntary services for the Department of National War Services, dated 2 October 1941, Tait noted that almost every former ULFTA member, and many members of the CPC, were joining the Association, which led him to conclude that it was 'Communist-inspired and its activities subject to the policy of the Communist Party of Canada.' See also Stapleford's 3 October letter to Keenleyside of External Affairs, DEA 2514-40C.

78 See the articles in *Ukrainian Life*, 22 January 1942 and 26 May 1943. The Ukrainian Canadian Left kept up its attack on the UCC, news of which occasionally spilled over into the mainstream press. See, for example, a report on an anti-UCC protest staged by the Ukrainian Canadian Associa-

tion, the ULFTA, and the WBA, under the title 'Deny Winnipeg Group Speaks for Ukrainian Canadians,' *Edmonton Journal*, 7 February 1945, 2.

79 See Philipps to Robertson, 17 July 1942, NAC MG30 E350 v2, file 10, and his letter of 14 May 1943, in which he presents a tabular summary of the attacks against UCC supporters allegedly made by the Ukrainian Canadian Left, NAC MG30 E350 v2, file 10.

80 UNF to the Minister of Justice, 19 October 1942, NAC MG30 E350 v2, file 10, and G.W. Simpson's letter to Philipps regarding these 'incidents,' 23 October 1942, NAC MG30 E350 v2, file 10. The UCC was directly and specifically denounced by the Soviet Union. See 'Ukrainian Canadian Committee Has Not Learnt from History,' 15 May 1943, in *Soviet Monitor: Radio Bulletins from the U.S.S.R.*, a copy of which is in FO 371/36974. A Soviet poet, P. Tychina, described the Committee as a 'Quisling clique' and warned these 'Fascists' to 'take their dirty hands off Ukraine.' The 20 May issue of Toronto's *Ukrainian Life* carried an editorial entitled 'Is This a Reward for Ukraine?' which further chastised the 'handful of traitors' who made up the UCC, labelling them 'Ukrainian-German nationalists' trying to hamper the struggle for Ukraine's freedom and harming not only Ukraine but also Canada and the Soviet Union. The editorial insisted that Ottawa give back the confiscated ULFTA labour temples and, it was implied, shut down its creation, the UCC. See the special report submitted to Robertson of External Affairs, 23 June 1943, by the Office of Examiner of Publications, Department of National Revenue, DEA 3846-A-40-C. That Ottawa's observers were aware of Moscow's interest in Ukrainian Canadian affairs is confirmed by comments included in a report entitled 'Restoration of Property of Ukrainian Farmer Labour Temples: Basic Considerations Which Should Determine Government Policy,' 7 June 1943, which pointed out that, 'although before June, 1941, the Left Wing Ukrainians were undoubtedly a drag on the Canadian war effort insofar as they followed the communist party line, it is not unreasonable to expect that the Nationalist elements among the Right Wing Ukrainians will become a greater source of embarrassment to the Canadian government insofar as their aspirations center in the creation of an independent Ukraine; we know that this irredentism among Canadian Ukrainians is being closely followed in Moscow and is resented.' See the W.L.M. King Papers, NAC, vol. 336, file entitled 'Ukrainian Canadians.' Professor Simpson of the Committee on Co-operation in Canadian Citizenship earlier informed External Affairs that members of the UCC 'resent fiercely the charge that they are fascists.' He added that it was false to picture the Ukrainian national movement as simply a German intrigue, 'a charge which is the stock-in-trade charge of all anti-Ukrainians.'

See Simpson to Robertson, 'Re: Mr. Hlynka's Speech on Ukrainian Question,' 4 April 1942, DEA 165–39C.

81 W. Burianyk to G.W. Simpson, 3 June 1942, NAC MG30 E350.

82 See 'Collection of Relief Funds in Canada by Canadian Ukrainians,' particularly the 'Note for Mr Robertson,' of 10 October 1941 in DEA 2514-40C. The need for 'close checks' on the manner in which funds were spent was stressed.

83 See Document #35, 4 June 1943, in *A Delicate and Difficult Question*, ed. Kordan and Luciuk, 100–3.

84 See Document #37, July 1943 [?], ibid., 111–13, for an abridged version of the secret RCMP report on the first UCC congress. Part of Monsignor Kushnir's address is reprinted in Document #36, 22–4 June 1943, 104–10. R.G. Riddell of External Affairs' European and Commonwealth Division noted in his summary of the secret RCMP report that 'the conference leaders were concerned to avoid statements or discussions of a kind which would cause embarrassment to the Government,' 111. As documents recently declassified under the Access to Information Act demonstrate, RCMP surveillance of the Ukrainian Canadian community was extensive and systematic, and did not neglect even some of the smallest communities, such as that in Kingston, Ontario. On 19 February 1942 the RCMP detachment in Kingston noted that a branch of the UCC had been active in that city 'for the past three weeks' and had a membership of approximately twenty-five people, who held teas at private homes, usually on Sundays, the residences of Michael Biss and John Wityk being two such known meeting places. Working with the City Police of Kingston, Constable H.F. McEwen of the RCMP's Kingston detachment wrote seeking information on whether there was any reason to suspect this group of being 'subversively inclined.' On 13 March a reply marked 'secret' came from Inspector C. Batch, in Ottawa, informing Kingston's RCMP that the UCC was 'an Organization which has the unofficial sanction of the Canadian Government. It was organized with a view to co-ordinating Canada's war effort generally, among the Ukrainians in this Country ... According to all reports at hand, the Committee is doing good work in the interest of Canada's war effort.' Correspondence about the Ukrainian community in Kingston continued until at least 17 June 1942, when it was noted that there was nothing more of importance to report about the UCC branch there, which had not increased in size, since there were 'no more than 50 Ukrainians in this city and 40 of this number belong to the C.U.C.' It was concluded that there was little chance of any Ukrainian communist element being organized in the city.

85 T.C. Davis's memorandum 'Re Committee on Co-operation in Canadian

Citizenship,' to Major-General L.R. LaFleche, minister of National War Services' 13 November 1942, NAC MG30 E350. Judge Davis observed that the 'different groups of persons who have their origin in Europe,' excluding the French, included a large number of first-generation Canadians who were still influenced by their origin.' Unfortunately, he wrote, these groups 'bring to Canada a lot of illwill and hatreds which have been the fruit of European development of many centuries, and this creates a problem in Canada of trying to weave them all into the fabric of Canada and to make them Canadians.' Davis argued that because Philipps and Kysilewsky (Kaye) had recently been publicly attacked in the press and the attack had sparked controversy, their usefulness to the government had been reduced significantly. Part of the controversy was engendered by *The Hour*, published in New York; see n74 above. The Wartime Information Board and External Affairs, Davis wrote, would be better able to carry on with the work which Philipps and Kysilewsky had concerned themselves. Their services should be dispensed with. Philipps eventually resigned, on 12 May 1944.

86 John W. Dafoe to Philipps, 8 July 1943, in NAC MG30 E350. Dafoe, a liberal reformer and man of the political Centre, editor and president of the Winnipeg Free Press Company Limited, was one of Canada's most influential journalists. He informed Philipps that the question of Ukrainian independence had been 'fought shy of' at the recent UCC congress in Winnipeg. While he recognized that those attacking the UCC through the pages of the *Canadian Tribune* and otherwise were 'outright Communists and therefore to be treated with the reserve which is very necessary in accepting any statement which they make,' he added, 'We have rather been taking the line that the sensible thing for the Ukrainians to do is to forget about their European hopes and ambitions and concentrate upon taking full advantage of their Canadian citizenship.' He also wrote, 'I hear that a good number of the leading Ukrainians agree that this is the wise course to follow.'

87 For Governor-General Lord Tweedsmuir's remarks of 21 September 1936, see Document #24 in *A Delicate and Difficult Question*, ed. Kordan and Luciuk, 63–4. Suggestive of how the governor-general's comments were interpreted by leading Ukrainians are G.R.B. Panchuk's remarks in *Heroes of Their Day: The Reminiscences of Bohhan Panchuk* (Toronto, 1983), 34. When he and other Ukrainian Canadians established their UCSA 'London Club,' they printed letterhead which listed Lady Susan Tweedsmuir as their 'honorary patron,' hoping to preserve the idea that what they were doing was quite in keeping with the acceptable formula of ethnic self-identification the governor-general had provided. Ukrainian Canadians did not forget Tweedsmuir. When he died, Reverend Sawchuk cabled condolences on behalf of the Ukrainian Greek Orthodox Church of Canada and reminded

Tweedsmuir's widow about what a positive impact her late husband had made on the Ukrainian Canadians when he visited them in Winnipeg, Selkirk, and Fraserwood in 1936. Sawchuk notified the *Winnipeg Free Press* on 16 February that he had asked Ukrainian priests throughout Canada to pray for the late Lord Tweedsmuir. See his diary entries for 13 and 16 February 1940, found in a manuscript entitled 'The History of the Formation of the Ukrainian Canadian Committee (Excerpts from the Diary of Reverend S. Sawchuk).' The late Reverend Sawchuk kindly allowed me to review this document, the original of which remains with his archives in Winnipeg.

Chapter 4: 'Saskatchewan's Son'

1 Gordon Richard Bohdan Panchuk, personal diary entry, 3 September 1944. Hereafter 'Diary.' This diary remains in the possession of Mrs Anne Panchuk (née Cherniawsky) in Montreal.
2 Panchuk, *Heroes of Their Day*, 26.
3 Ibid., 32.
4 Ibid., 34, 40–1.
5 Ibid., 34.
6 Ibid., 41. The pivotal role Panchuk played in creating UCSA was attested by William ('Bill') Kereliuk, in an article entitled 'Looking Back,' *UCSA News Letter* 1:3 (November–December 1943). Kereliuk wrote that 'it is not often that so much depends on one individual,' but 'take away our President Bohdan Panchuk and you've taken away most of our Association.' Kereliuk, an UCSA activist, served in the Mediterranean theatre during the war, having entered Rome in the early summer of 1944. There he established contact with a leading Ukrainian Greek Catholic prelate, Bishop Ivan Buchko. Although the bishop was under surveillance by Allied intelligence organs suspicious of his contacts with the Ukrainian nationalist movement, these organs did not interfere with UCSA, although some of Kereliuk's letters were opened and examined. During the summer of 1944, Ukrainian Canadians also began meeting fellow Ukrainians serving with the Polish army, many of whom served with distinction in the fierce fighting around Monte Cassino. A marker remains to record their sacrifices.
7 Ibid.
8 For a sociological analysis, see W.R. Petryshyn, 'Britain's Ukrainian Community: A Study of the Political Dimension in Ethnic Community Development,' Ph.D. thesis, University of Bristol, 1980.
9 Panchuk, 'Diary,' 14 December 1942.
10 Panchuk, *Heroes of their Day*, 47. See also *Addresses at a Religious and Social Gathering*, ed. G.R.B. Panchuk (Manchester, 1943), which reproduces

speeches from the second 'Get-Together,' held in the St Chad's Church School hall, Cheetham Hill Road, Manchester, on 2 May 1943. A Ukrainian Social Club had been organized in Manchester prior to the arrival of Ukrainian Canadian troops and UCSA's formation. The Manchester club's chairman was Peter Tarnawski.

11 In an unpublished report prepared for the Citizenship Division of the Department of National War Services, 'Canadians of Recent European Origin' (Ottawa, 1945), 70–1, Kaye noted that UCSA had social, historical, and humanitarian functions. It provided social contacts for Ukrainian Canadians on active service overseas; represented these Ukrainian Canadian servicemen's interests; arranged periodic 'Get-Togethers' and religious events; compiled lists of Ukrainian Canadians on active service overseas; drew up brief historical and biographical accounts of these Ukrainian Canadian soldiers' service records; tried to compile as complete a 'casualty list' of Ukrainian Canadians as possible; looked after the graves of the Ukrainian Canadian dead; ensured that next-of-kin were kept informed about the conditions of these graves; prepared lists of Ukrainian Canadian POWs; and laid the foundation for a group that would minister to the wants and needs of wounded or disabled Ukrainian Canadian veterans after the war. The first UCSA executive included Flight Officer Panchuk as president; Lieutenant J.P. Nikiforuk and Flight Officer A. Podoreski as vice-presidents; Calgary's Sergeant Helen C. Kozicky as secretary; Winnipeg's Lieutenant Ann Crapleve as treasurer; and Vegreville's Corporal Anne Cherniawsky as club director and records keeper. Corporal Steve Kalin of Hafford, Saskatchewan, was to be UCSA's historian. UCSA committees were also set up in Italy and Canada; Flight Lieutenant W. Kereliuk, Gunner A. Nykoluk, Gunner A.E. Kowal, and Captain Stephen Worobetz were in charge of the 'Central Mediterranean Branch,' started with the aid of Bishop Ivan Buchko after a commemorative Ukrainian Christmas 'Get-Together' was held in Rome on 6–7 January 1945. Flight Lieutenant J. Kohut, Captain John Karasevich, Flight Officer 'Tommy' Hewus, and Flight Officer D.A. Zuck ran the latter. The padres of UCSA were Honorary Captain S.W. Sawchuk, representing the Ukrainian Greek Orthodox Church of Canada, and Honorary Captain Michael Horoshko, of the Ukrainian Greek Catholic Church. From the start, UCSA was described as having 'no religious or political character.' Members were free to 'adhere to any religious or political group' in their 'own personal life,' but 'no influences or controversy' would be 'allowed or tolerated at any time' in the Association. Anyone 'inclined' to introduce such 'influences' might lose the privilege of being an UCSA member. See *Memorial Souvenir Book 1 (UCAS–UCVA)*, ed. G.R.B. Panchuk

(Montreal, 1986), 15–16. Panchuk had begun publicizing the Ukrainian Canadian contribution to the war effort even before he went overseas. See his article 'Ukrainian Boys – The Canadian Army,' written while he was at RCAF Wireless School in Montreal and published in *Ukrainian Voice*, 3 December 1941. Panchuk wrote that Ukrainian Canadians would do well to follow the lead of the Jewish-Canadian community, which he felt was doing a good job of pointing out its service to the country. No history of UCSA or of its successor, UCVA, has been written, although Panchuk's *Heroes of their Day* and Prymak's *Maple Leaf and Trident* provide partial accounts. For a commentary on the Ukrainian Canadian Left and Canada's war effort, see P. Krawchuk, *Our Contribution to Victory* (Toronto, 1985). The work of UCSA and CURB and the establishment of the AUGB were commemorated in London, England, on 19 September 1995, when a bilingual bronze plaque was installed on the façade of the building at 218 Sussex Gardens, Paddington, where UCSA, CURB, and the AUGB were headquartered. See Lubomyr Luciuk, 'Ottawa Snubs Ukrainian-Canadian Vets,' *Globe and Mail*, 19 September 1995, and 'Honoring a Champion of Liberty,' *The Whig Standard*, 21 September 1995.

12 J. Yuzyk to Panchuk, 29 January 1945, Panchuk Collection. The 'London Club' (see the text below) attracted soldiers from other Allied armies, including Ukrainians serving in the Polish and Czechoslovakian armed forces. This caused some concern in Canada in both official and Ukrainian Canadian circles. For example, Canadian Forces Headquarters, after being approached for official recognition of UCSA, replied on 12 October 1943 that 'any official action supporting the idea that Canadian Forces be broken up into groups would not be in the best interests of the Services or of the members themselves.' Cited by T. Prymak, 'UCSA Overseas: A Chapter in the History of the Ukrainian Canadians during World War II,' *Forum* (Scranton, Pennsylvania, 1984). Similarly, various Ukrainian Canadian organizations expressed reservations about UCSA's purpose. The UNF's dominion executive wrote to Sergeant Stephen (Stefan) Davidovich asking him to visit the Club and report about what was going on there, while the USRL activist John Solomon cautioned Panchuk on 22 July 1943 about the dangers that might arise if UCSA 'drifts away from its original purpose.' Solomon was evidently worried that because UCSA represented an 'organized body,' some 'agencies that have ulterior motives' might attempt to involve it in matters that would bring Ukrainian Canadians into difficulty. While, he wrote, he was not suggesting that 'other boys from different countries' associating with the Club were not sincere, he did want Panchuk to know that 'their conception of what is right and what is wrong is natu-

rally based on their bringing-up and, consequently, they would have a different slant on affairs.' Since Panchuk was, in Solomon's view, 'one of our most promising boys,' he wanted to warn him in advance about getting involved in matters that might later hurt his career. I am indebted to the late J.R. Solomon for a copy of this letter. On the UNF's concerns see postal intercept, 4 January 1943, NAC RG25, vol. 1896, file 165. Government censors closely monitored correspondence between various Ukrainian Canadians serving overseas and their North American friends. See also postal intercept, NAC RG25, vol. 1896, file 165–39c, in which Kereliuk's correspondence about Bishop Buchko is found.

13 Panchuk acknowledged this financial and moral support in a letter sent to the UCC's national executive secretary, Andrew Zaharychuk, on 28 February 1945, but added, 'The Club as well as the Servicemen's Association were the spontaneous effort of the men themselves.' If there had been no financial assistance, he maintained, there would still have been a Club, although, admittedly, one which would not have reached 'the standard or proportions' that it had with UCC assistance. As early as September 1943 the UCC was cabling funds to UCSA. See the telegram from Anthony ('Tony') J. Yaremovich, the UCC's correspondence secretary, to UCSA, on the occasion of its third 'Get-Together,' held in London 31 July–1 August 1943. It is reproduced in *Memorial Souvenir Book 1*, ed. Panchuk, 48. The Club was also mentioned in the Canadian press. See, for example, 'A Homey Overseas Meeting Place: Ukrainian-Canadians Have Club in London,' *Winnipeg Free Press*, 19 April 1944, in which Corporal Ann Crapleve is quoted as saying: 'The club means more to us than other Canadians. Now we have a place where we can drop in, make a cup of tea as we do at home and chat with our own people.' Many attracted to the Club were reportedly not averse also to spending a little time at a nearby pub, the 'Whole in the Ground.' UCC boosters used their support of UCSA as evidence of their loyalty to Canada. For example, a photograph of the UCSA Club was published in the UCC publication *First All-Canadian Congress of Ukrainians in Canada* (Winnipeg, 1943), 148. Photographs of many of UCSA's key personnel are reproduced in an article by Steve Kalin, 'From UCSA Overseas to UCVA in Canada,' *UCVA News Letter: Convention issue*, 2:11–12 (Toronto, 1954): 31–63.

14 In January 1945, Philipps characterized Ukrainian Canadians as follows: '90 percent are decent, hard-working, liberal-minded strongly religious people devoted to their Canadian churches ... The greater part are now Canadian-born ... so loyal that between 30–40,000 of their boys and girls went from the outset into the Armed Forces and are mostly already overseas.'

15 See the transcript of Father Michael Horoshko's remarks during 'Padre's Hour,' 25 November 1945, Panchuk Collection.

16 *First All-Canadian Congress of Ukrainians in Canada*. Solomon, writing to Panchuk on 22 July 1943, proclaimed that this first UCC congress had been 'a huge success' which 'demonstrated effectively that the Canadians of Ukrainian origin are united behind [the] Canadian war effort and that they are willing to bury their differences, if not forever, then at least for the duration.' He continued that the problems facing Ukrainian Canadians as an ethnic group in Canada could be solved, 'providing that we tackle the matter properly, calmly and without causing any commotion.' External Affairs officials had been very nervous about the prospect of this congress, fearing it might be critical of Canada's Soviet ally. And so, when Professor George Simpson first let the under-secretary of state for external affairs, Norman A. Robertson, know the congress had been postponed, Robertson expressed relief. See Robertson to Judge Davis, 7 October 1942, NAC RG44, vol. 25, filed under 'Bureau of Public Information.' When the congress was finally held, the UCC's request for the presence of a senior minister was denied. This refusal was made all the more galling by the fact that official greetings, including those of the prime minister, had been sent to a pro-Soviet Ukrainian Canadian Association rally staged at the Royal Alexandra Hotel in Winnipeg at the very same time as, and obviously in direct competition with, the UCC's national meeting. Behind the scenes, Philipps's attempts to get 'at least one publishable message of encouragement from the Federal Government' failed. See an undated letter from Philipps to Simpson in the George Simpson Collection, Saskatchewan Provincial Archives, Saskatoon, 'Ukrainian file.' That other Canadian political figures were reluctant to participate in UCC events without prior guarantees as to their disposition is evident from the letter sent by the lieutenant-governor of Manitoba, the Honourable R.F. McWilliams, to the UCC's secretary, J. Arsenych, 12 June 1943. Noting that he had spoken with Dr. Kushner (*sic*) and Mr Solomon about participating in a Victory Rally, to be held at the Playhouse Theatre on 22 June, the lieutenant-governor indicated that he would be pleased to attend. But he immediately qualified his acceptance by noting that he was 'taking it for granted that this meeting is wholly a meeting for the support of the war effort by the Ukrainian people.' He indicated his awareness of the 'sharp differences amongst the Ukrainians in Canada,' particularly with regard to the future of Western Ukraine in relation to Poland and to Russia, and that 'these differences had to be taken into account by the Government of Canada in their dealings with our allies.' He concluded that it would be 'impossible' for him to take any

action, such as attending or speaking at a meeting, 'in which one or other view is being put forward by the speakers.'

17 See Document #37, July 1943 [?], in *A Delicate and Difficult Question*, ed. Kordan and Luciuk, 111. For Canadian press coverage see 'Communists Flayed at Ukrainian Parley,' *Winnipeg Tribune*, 23 June 1943; 'Discontented Ukraine Given as War Cause,' ibid., 24 June; and 'Ukrainians to Place Canada's Interests First,' ibid., 25 June.

18 See Document #39, 8 August 1944, in *A Delicate and Difficult Question*, ed. Kordan and Luciuk, 128.

19 Ibid. The Ukrainian American press was apparently dissatisfied with the UCC's congress. On 10 July 1943 an article in Jersey City's *Svoboda* pointed out that nowhere in the congress resolutions was there even 'the slightest direct mention of the fact that democratically-minded Ukrainians in their native land Ukraine and their kinsmen in Canada as well as here in America and elsewhere desire to see established after this war a free and independent state of Ukraine.'

20 Panchuk to Messrs Kohut, Wojcichowski, and Hewus, 29 July 1944, Panchuk Collection. Canada's security services moved quickly to investigate who was organizing a Ukrainian Canadian Servicemen's Club in Manchester, as documents obtained under the Access to Information Act confirm. For example, on 29 May 1943, Group Captain M.M. Sisley, the director of provost and security services for the Air Service of the Department of National Defence, addressed a secret letter to RCMP inspector E.H. Perlson asking whether the names of Alec William Kreptul, Stephen Kalin, and Gordon Richard Panchuk could be found in RCMP records, and if any of them 'have come to your attention at any time in the past as the result of being been a supporter or member of any subversive or illegal organization.' Official interest in the activities of UCSA (also described in RCMP documents as the 'League of Ukrainian-Canadian Soldiers, Overseas,') continued throughout the war years, growing generally more favourable. On 28 March 1944, for example, Superintendent F.W. Schutz, commanding the RCMP's 'O' Division, forwarded the commissioner a translated article which had been published in the 5 November 1943 issue of the *Ukrainian Toiler*. It provided the names of most of UCSA's organizers, and information about parcels they were receiving from supporters in Canada, such as Miss Mona Volk of Sioux Lookout, Ontario, and Mrs K. Vypruk of Montreal. Just over a year later, Senior Inspector J. Leopold wrote to the director of military intelligence in Ottawa, confirming that UCSA was 'giving complete free service to any Ukrainian-Canadian Soldier, regardless of his political or religious connection. The only requirement for entry to this Servicemen's

Association is that the entrant must be of Ukrainian blood and in Canadian uniform.' He added that both Lady Tweedsmuir and Viscount Bennett were included among UCSA's patrons, and that there [was] no doubt of the loyalty of this organization,' a point reiterated in another confidential RCMP memorandum, signed by Commissioner S.T. Wood on 24 April 1945. Canada's Department of National Defence was also worried about the reliability of soldiers of Ukrainian origin who acknowledged membership in Ukrainian Canadian organizations. As recently declassified documents released under the Access to Information Act prove, for example, the army contacted the RCMP on 21 April 1944 and asked for a list of Ukrainian organizations in Canada in three categories: 'Communist inspired,' 'Fascist inspired,' and 'Organizations considered loyal to Canada.' The reply listed the ULFTA and its youth wing, the Canadian Ukrainian Youth Federation, the WBA, the Workers and Farmers Publishing Association, the People's Cooperative Association (Winnipeg), and the Society for the Liberation of Western Ukraine in the first category; described the USRL, UNF, UHO, and Ukrainian Mutual Benefit Society as loyal; and noted, 'There are actually no Ukrainian organizations within this ['fascist-inspired'] category, but the Communist Ukrainian organizations always claim and describe non-communist Ukrainian organizations as 'fascist.'

21 Panchuk, 'Diary,' 27 August 1942. For more on Panchuk's activities in the RCAF, see M. Berger and B.J. Street, *Invasion Without Tears: The Story of Canada's Top-Scoring Spitfire Wing in Europe during the Second World War* (Toronto, 1994).

22 Panchuk, *Heroes of their Day*, 61. Another Ukrainian Canadian soldier on the Normandy beaches was Captain John Karasevich. Badly wounded, he was repatriated to Canada, where he nevertheless continued to be active in the Ukrainian Canadian community, by corresponding regularly with Panchuk and helping to organize UCSA and later the first branch of UCVA.

23 'Resumé of Bureau Meetings held April 13th, 14th [1946] – London,' Panchuk Collection. Among those present were Monsignor Kushnir, B. Panchuk, Captain Peter Smylski, Flight Lieutenant Joe Romanow, D. Andrievsky, S.W. Frolick, D. Skoropadsky, and G. Kluchevsky.

24 Panchuk, *Heroes of Their Day*, 62. D-Day was 6 June 1944. Ukrainians in North America became aware of the Ukrainian DP problem in Europe only afterwards; this issue, along with that of how the 'Ukrainian Question' should be represented in international forums, was discussed on 23–4 September 1944 by delegates at a joint UCC and Ukrainian Congress Committee of America meeting, held in New York. See the 'Joint Communiqué of the Ukrainian Congress Committee of America and the Ukrainian Cana-

dian Committee,' *Ukrainian Quarterly* 1:1 (New York, 1944): 82–4. An article about this gathering, written by M. Chubaty, was published in the 13 October 1944 issue of *Svoboda*.

25 Interview with M. Lucyk, Toronto, 15 April 1982 (MHSO). On Captain Lucyk's role in lobbying on behalf of Ukrainian DP immigration to Canada, see 'Haven in Canada for Kin Fearing Moscow Tyranny Ukrainians' Humble Plea,' *Telegram* (Toronto), 1 April 1946, which described a pro-refugee immigration rally held in Massey Hall the day before. Born in Toronto, Michael Lucyk graduated from the University of Toronto and served overseas with the Canadian Dental Corps, also becoming an active UCSA member. For another Ukrainian Canadian soldier's account of conditions in a Ukrainian-populated DP camp near Kiel, in the British Zone of Germany, see Major M. Syrotiuk's letter to Reverend Sawchuk, 11 January 1946, Panchuk Collection.

26 Panchuk, 'Diary,' 12 June 1945.
27 Ibid., 8 July 1945.
28 Panchuk, *Heroes of Their Day*, 63.
29 Panchuk, 'Diary,' 15 April 1945.
30 Panchuk, *Heroes of Their Day*, 64.
31 Panchuk, 'The Situation with Regard to Ukrainian Refugees,' sent to the UUARC's Dr Walter Gallan, 10 June 1945, from Hamburg, Germany, in NAC MG28 v9, vol. 15. This memorandum was widely distributed, as evidenced by the fact that it can also be found in DEA 2514-40C and several British Foreign Office files. For more on Gallan and the UUARC, see Myron B. Kuropas, *Ukrainian-American Citadel: The First One Hundred Years of the Ukrainian National Association* (Boulder, Colorado, 1996), especially 358–67.
32 For a more recent estimate regarding the number of Ukrainian political refugees and DPs in the post–Second World War period, see I. Stebelsky, 'Ukrainians in the Displaced Persons Camps of Austria and Germany after World War II,' *Ukrainian Historian* 23:1–2 (1986) and 'Ukrainian Population Migration after World War II,' in *The Refugee Experience: Ukrainian Displaced Persons after World War II*, ed. W.W. Isajiw, Y. Boshyk, and R. Senkus (Edmonton, 1992), 21–68.
33 Panchuk, 'The Situation with Regard to Ukrainian Refugees,' 10 June 1945, NAC MG28 v9, vol. 15.
34 Ibid.
35 Ibid.
36 Ibid.
37 P. Worobetz to Panchuk, 11 April 1945, Panchuk Collection. Worobetz was

interviewed in Saskatoon, 21 August 1983 (CIUS). A schoolteacher, Worobetz arrived in England in November 1943, where he joined UCSA and
became its vice-president.

38 Ibid. Panchuk's pique is captured in this excerpt from his letter of 27 February 1945 to Worobetz (Panchuk Collection): 'to come straight out of the
blue sky with a statement that "you are taking part in activities and associations beyond the purpose of this organization," as if I didn't know why we
organized or what we have continuously strived for, and making it appear
as if *all* my activities and associations are detrimental to the organization –
after electing me unanimously for the third term, after sending me off as
you did when I visited last ... I am forced to realize that either the outfit I
have been working with is a bunch of hypocrites or else ... they are being
made a catspaw for ulterior purposes by some other influence. Whatever
the true reason is, I feel that I am not willing to be part and parcel of any
organization like that, and that is *not* the code and principle that urged us
to form the association ... I will be only too glad to take a back seat for a
change.'

39 Worobetz to Panchuk, 11 April 1945, Panchuk Collection.

40 J. Yuzyk to Panchuk, 10 March 1945, Panchuk Collection. 'Johnnie' Yuzyk
was interviewed in Winnipeg, 28 November 1982 (CIUS). See also Yuzyk's
letter to Panchuk, 13 April 1945, which describes the participation of 'Bill'
Kereliuk, 'the big Boss,' and Bill Burianyk in the UCSA Club's London
activities.

41 Panchuk to Worobetz, 27 February 1945, Panchuk Collection.

42 *Edmonton Journal*, 12 February 1945. The pro-Soviet Ukrainian Canadian
press carried on an active anti-DP immigration campaign. For example, a
cartoon in *Ukrainian Life*, 10 February 1944, captioned 'How the UCC Is
"Defending" Ukraine,' portrayed the Ukrainian political refugees as war
criminals and collaborators – a recurrent theme in the left-wing press of
that day and one resurrected periodically by similarly minded groups and
individuals up to the present. See Ukrainian Canadian Committee, Civil
Liberties Commission, *On the Record: The Debate over Alleged War Criminals
in Canada* (Toronto, 1987).

More recently, additional information has begun to surface in connection
with the controversial issue of bringing Soviet war criminals and collaborators, some of whom are Jewish, to justice, possibly even with the help of the
Israeli judicial system. According to an editorial, 'Compromising Positions,' in the *Globe and Mail*, 20 April 1999, Israel has recently passed a law
that should make it easier to extradite Israeli citizens for crimes committed
abroad. Previously Israeli law in this area had been based on the principle

that 'only Jews could fairly judge Jews.' This resulted in Israel's becoming a safe haven for some rather notorious communist collaborators, among them Shlomo (Solomon) Morel. He is wanted by Poland for murderous actions while serving as the comandant of the notorious Swietochlowice and Jaworzno concentration camps (see A. LeBor, 'Israel Protects Concentration Camp Boss,' *The Independent*, 29 December 1998; 'Israel Refuses to Hand Over War Crimes Suspect,' *Calgary Herald*, 8 December 1998; and the letter to the editor, 'Challenge Israel's Refusal,' by B. Sydoruk, ibid., 10 December 1998). Another alleged Soviet collaborator is Nachmanas Dusanskis, wanted by Lithuania for his role in the deportation of Lithuanian Jews and others to the Siberian gulag in 1941. See L. Luciuk, 'A Man-Made Hell Preserved for All to See,' *National Post*, 15 April 1999. The willing collaboration of *some* Jews with the Soviets and other communist regimes in eastern Europe, although still a theme requiring more intensive scrutiny and elaboration, is documented by J.T. Gross in *Revolution from Abroad: The Soviet Conquest of Poland's Western Ukraine and Western Belorussia* (Princeton, 1988), especially 29, 32–3. See also his epilogue, 'The Spoiler State,' 225–40, for its insightful comparison of the Nazi and Soviet occupations. Others providing evidence on this issue include Rapoport, *Stalin's War against the Jews*, and A. Vaksberg, *Stalin against the Jews* (New York, 1994).

In commenting on some of the more controversial aspects of Jewish–Ukrainian relations, the historian Robert Conquest, in 'Stalin and the Jews,' *New York Review of Books*, 11 July 1996, 46–9, describes how some authors have crudely indicted the entire Ukrainian nation in their discussions of the Holocaust. Conquest notes that 'Ukrainian nationalists were able to organize a major partisan army which, as Khruschev complained, fought first against the Germans and then against the Soviets. As in every country occupied by the Nazis, there were also active collaborators in Ukraine, and some were directly involved in the murders of the Jews ... But the numbers of Ukrainian war criminals seem similar to those of other occupied territories – though there were, of course (as in all other territories), collaborators who cannot be accused of taking part in killing. In any case, the world "collaborator" should remind us of those with whom they collaborated – the principals of whom they were the accomplices. The Holocaust was, after all, a German operation.' Citing Raul Hilberg, who was himself excerpting captured German documents, Conquest also reminds his readers that in wartime Ukraine the Germans found that 'almost nowhere can the population be persuaded to take active steps against the Jews ... that the inhabitants were not betraying the movements of hidden Jews,' and that 'only the ethnic Germans in the area were busily working with the *Einsatzgruppe*.'

Hilberg likewise recorded that, according to these documents, 'truly spontaneous pogroms, free from *Einsatzgruppen* influence, did not take place. All outbreaks were either organized or inspired by the *Einsatzgruppe*. Second, all pogroms were implemented within a short time after the arrival of the killing units. They were not self-perpetuating, nor could new ones be started after things had settled down.' Emphasizing the links between Nazism and Stalinism, Conquest quotes the novelist Vasily Grossman, who stressed that a Manichean division of humanity into categories formed the common bond between the two totalitarian ideologies: 'Just as the Germans proclaimed the Jews are not human beings thus did Lenin and Stalin proclaim *Kulaks* are not human beings.'

According to D. Volkogonov, *Lenin: A New Biography* (New York, 1994), 350, on 27 December 1929, Stalin announced, 'We have moved from a policy of *limiting* the *kulaks'* exploitative tendencies to a policy of *liquidating* the *kulaks* as a class.' A Politburo directive developed at this time affected at least two million men, women, and children, although Volkogonov estimates that the number was closer to a figure between eight and nine and a half million people, about a quarter of whom died within a few months, and another quarter within a year. On the issue of Lenin's genealogy and the troubling issues it raises over the role of some Jews in the 1917 Bolshevik *coup d'état* and the Soviet state apparatus, Volkogonov correctly points out (p. 9) that Lenin was of mixed Russian, Kalmyk, Jewish, German, and Swedish descent. According to Volkogonov's research, the Party commissioned Lenin's elder sister, Anna Yelizarova, to collect the necessary materials for writing a definitive account of the Ulyanov family shortly after Lenin's death. In 1932 she provided Stalin with her report. Her covering letter included a rather un-Marxist assessment of Lenin's ancestry: 'It's probably no secret for you that the research on our grandfather shows that he came from a poor Jewish family, that he was, as his baptismal certificate says, the son of Zhitomir *meshchanin* Moishe Blank.' Yelizarova, however, felt that Lenin's Jewish roots could be used to help combat anti-Semitism, and claimed his part-Jewish origins were a 'further confirmation of the exceptional abilities of the Semitic tribe, [confirmation] always shared by Ilyich [Lenin] ... Ilyich always valued the Jews highly.' Stalin suppressed her letter, but just over a year later she approached him again, asserting that 'in the Lenin Institute, as well as in the Institute of the Brain ... they have long recognized the great gifts of this nation and the extremely beneficial effects of its blood on the progeny of mixed marriages. Ilyich himself rated their revolutionary qualities highly, their "tenacity" in the struggle, as he put it, contrasting it with the more sluggish and unstable character of the Russians. He often pointed out that the great [attributes of] organization and the strength of the revolutionary bodies in the south and west [of Russia] arose precisely from the fact that 50 per cent of their members were of that nationality.' Stalin's prohibition on the publication of the Yelizarova report nevertheless remained in force until the disintegration of the Soviet state.

43 See Document #40, 15 November 1944, in *A Delicate and Difficult Question*, ed. Kordan and Luciuk, 131–3.

44 See Wilgress to Robertson, 25 January 1945, DEA 2514-40C, in which he expressed his agreement with George Pifher's reservations about Canadian government approval for a Ukrainian Canadian refugee relief fund. Earlier, Leo Malania of External Affairs had cautioned F. Foulds of the Citizenship Division, Department of National War Services, about allowing the UCRF to be registered. Malania wrote that he felt the UCC project had 'very dangerous international implications,' for it 'quite frankly' proposed to render assistance to political refugees who would not be able to return to their homeland after the war. Although Malania claimed that he was not 'passing any judgement on the merits or otherwise of this proposal on humanitarian grounds,' he was doing exactly that, for his confidential notes made it clear that he did not favour this initiative because the 'activities of the Fund would have a direct bearing upon our diplomatic relations with the Soviet and the Polish Governments.' Maintaining cordial relations with these regimes, Malania insisted, must take priority over saving refugees. Paradoxically, while it has been suggested that Tracy Philipps's marriage to the noted Ukrainian concert pianist Lubka Kolessa inclined him towards a pro-Ukrainian stance (see Gerus, 'The Ukrainian Canadian Committee,' in *A Heritage in Transition*, ed. Lupul, 212), no similar suggestion has been tendered about the effect of marriage on Wilgress. Presuming that a spouse can indeed exert influence over a partner's role as a foreign policy-maker, it remains to be determined to what extent Wilgress was influenced by his half-Russian wife, Olga Buergin. Certainly, he seems always to have been more sympathetić to the Soviet Russian point of view than to concerns expressed by Ukrainians in Canada, or even by the Polish 'London Government.' For example, on 17 May 1943, Wilgress advised Ottawa that, in his view, it was 'essential that Tracy Philipps should cease to have any official connection with the Canadian government, and in this connection, it is important that he should be sent back to the U.K. where he can do less harm.' Philipps was apparently regarded with some distaste by the Soviets and obviously by some Canadian officials. See Wilgress to the Department of External Affairs, NAC RG25, vol. 1896, file 165. A few months later (12 October 1943) others concurred. In Report #426, entitled 'Canada:

Ukrainian Groups and Mr. Tracy Philipps,' drafted by British Security Co-
ordination, criticisms were made about the 'strange position [Philipps held]
vis-à-vis the Government of Canada.' It was noted that, despite the fact that
External Affairs officials would 'be very pleased if Philipps would go
home,' they were, 'for some reason which remains unexplained,' unable to
do anything about him. Philipps, it was noted, had been the 'leading
mover' behind the first UCC congress. Despite the 'potential dangers'
involved, which External Affairs 'fully realized,' no action had been taken
to block the gathering. Even earlier Wilgress had taken umbrage over the
UCC's position on Ukrainian independence. When, on 30 March 1943, the
Committee submitted a very moderately worded memorandum to the
prime minister on the 'Ukrainian Question,' couched in the language of the
Atlantic Charter, Wilgress reacted vehemently. He informed Ottawa of the
uproar engendered in the Soviet press by the publication of this memorandum and went so far as to urge the Canadian government to reconsider its
commitment to the Charter's principles: 'It is my hope that the peaceful
atmosphere of Ottawa [where the Allied leaders are shortly to meet] may
permit the drafting of a statement of war aims less likely to be used to promote disunity than the document drafted on the stormy waters of the
Atlantic.' See Wilgress to the Department of External Affairs, 17 May and 19
May 1943, NAC RG25, vol. 1896, file 165. Not surprisingly, the Ukrainian
Canadian intelligentsia's opinion of the Charter was very different from
that embraced by Wilgress. See, for example, M. Stechishin's address at the
UCC congress, 'The Ukrainian Problem in the Present International Situation,' in which he said straightforwardly: 'We do know why we are
engaged in the present conflict. We are fighting this war to achieve the principles of the Atlantic Charter.' Yet, despite his leanings, Wilgress's reports
from Moscow, according to J.L. Granatstein, *The Ottawa Men: The Civil Service Mandarins 1935–1957* (Toronto, 1982), 229, 232–4, were treated seriously
by government officials in London, Washington and Ottawa. The Soviet
Union, as D. Smith notes, *Diplomacy of Fear: Canada and the Cold War, 1941–
1948* (Toronto, 1988), 29 – which had violated Charter principles in Poland,
in the Baltic countries, and in Finland in 1939–40 – was unhappy that it had
not been consulted in the drafting of the document, and let the British government know of its dissatisfaction. While the Soviet ambassador to the
United Kingdom, Ivan Maisky, endorsed the Charter at the inter-Allied
conference in London in September 1941, he added the reservation that the
Charter would have to be adapted to 'the circumstances, needs and historic
peculiarities of particular countries.' When Stalin met with the British foreign secretary, Anthony Eden, in Moscow, at midnight on 17 December

1941, he expressed his surprise over the Atlantic Charter, saying he had thought it was directed against 'those people who were trying to establish world dominion,' but that it 'now looks as if the Charter was directed against the USSR.' Eden denied that it did. During the same conversation Stalin raised the question of the postwar Soviet–Polish boundary and the 'Ukrainian Question,' suggesting slyly that the British 'might well say tomorrow' that they 'do not recognize the Ukraine as forming part of the USSR.' Not revealing a very deep appreciation of the geopolitical situation of eastern Europe, Eden replied that 'only changes from the prewar frontiers' were not recognized. 'The only change in the Ukraine,' he continued, was 'its occupation by Germany, so, of course, we accept the Ukraine as being part of the USSR.' See Document #23 in *Anglo-American Perspectives on the Ukrainian Question, 1938–1951: A Documentary Collection*, ed. L.Y. Luciuk and B.S. Kordan (Kingston and Vestal, 1987), 132–2. This document was incorrectly dated 17 December 1942; the meeting actually took place on 17 December 1941.

45 See J.E. Riddell's confidential 'Memorandum for Mr. Robertson,' 15 May 1945, DEA 2514-40C.

46 See Mrs A. Mandryka's address to the second UCC congress, 'Report and Outline of Achievements of the Ukrainian Canadian Relief Fund, Covering the period from February 15, 1945 to June 1, 1946,' in the *Second All-Canadian Congress of Ukrainians in Canada*, 33–9. Mrs Mandryka reported that the UCRF's work had been made possible in large measure by 150 mainly Canadian-born 'volunteer workers, women and girls, who gave much of their time in the evenings ... eagerly, happily and ungrudgingly.' In the future 'more energetic efforts' had to be made to raise a million dollars, which the Fund's executive would use to continue with its 'informational activity in all matters which are of interest to the displaced persons and in the things which interest the Ukrainians about the displaced persons.' The UCRF would also make information about DPs available to the North American press, search for relatives of the refugees in Canada, make arrangements for prospective immigrants, help with the special and immediate needs of some refugees, and keep in contact with CURB, the UUARC, and other institutions and groups involved in refugee aid and resettlement. At the third national UCC congress, held in Winnipeg, 7–9 February 1950, the executive director, V. Kochan (Kokhan), indicated that between 15 November 1940 and 31 December 1949, 28.34 per cent of the UCC's budget had been spent on CURB, a total amounting to $23,950. By way of comparison, $11,816.11 had been assigned to the UCSA Club in London during its years of operation. See *Third All-Canadian Congress of Ukrainians in Canada* (Winnipeg, 1950), 15.

47 A. Mandryka, 'Report and Outline ...,' 36, 37.
48 Ibid., 34, 35, 37.
49 Ibid.
50 Ibid. The author of the report, Mrs A. Mandryka, also wrote about saving
    those 'who wish to walk in dignity and enjoy the rights of human beings,
    for those who prefer exile, yea, even death, rather than bow down before
    the Moloch of autocracy' (ibid., 39).
51 'Minute of an interview with the Soviet Ambassador, April 30, 1945,'
    DEA 2514-40C. Both the 'Canadian Ukrainian Refugee Fund' and
    'Anti-Soviet Statements in the Press and on the C.B.C.' were discussed.
    The ambassador was accompanied by another Soviet official, V.
    Pavlov.
52 See Riddell's 'Memorandum for Mr. Robertson,' 15 May 1945, DEA 2514-
    40C.
53 See Document #41, 25 August 1945, in *A Delicate and Difficult Question*, ed.
    Kordan and Luciuk, 133–4.
54 'Statement Submitted by B. Panchuk in Connection with Administra-
    tive and Financial Statement of CURB,' [undated], Panchuk Collec-
    tion.
55 Ibid.
56 The AUGB was formally constituted on 19 January 1946. See Panchuk,
    Heroes of Their Day, 77. Earlier a Relief Committee for the United Kingdom
    had been set up in Manchester, 28 July 1945. See Corporal W.D. Usick,
    'Organisational Meeting of the Ukrainian United Kingdom Relief Commit-
    tee,' Panchuk Collection.
57 A reconstruction of what took place between late 1945 and early 1946 is
    made somewhat difficult by the loss of many relevant files during the Win-
    nipeg Flood of 1950 and a subsequent fire in the AUGB offices. Several of
    the principal actors in CURB attempted to locate and preserve parts of the
    Bureau's archives in later years, with varying degrees of success. See
    Frolick's correspondence with M.R. Lupul on this question, 29 December
    1977, found in the personal papers of S.W. Frolick, hereafter referred to as
    the Frolick Collection, NAC. For another description of CURB's sponsors
    and aims and the support it received from North America's Ukrainian com-
    munities, see the letter describing these arrangements, 24 September 1945,
    in Panchuk Collection.
58 Panchuk to Karasevich and others in UCVA, 7 November 1945. Panchuk
    wrote that he had no interest in creating another Ukrainian political party
    in Canada, but that a 'Central Veterans Executive of our own' was needed
    because of the difference of 'interests and problems' between Ukrainian
    Canadian and other veterans. This caveat echoed his earlier statements to

Karasevich, Wojcichowski, and Kereliuk. Panchuk wrote again on 1 August 1945 agreeing that while 'very close affiliation may have many indisputable merits, *it is also bound to have restrictions* which may be regrettable and undesirable.' Both letters are in the Panchuk Collection. On Karasevich's wartime record and postwar efforts, refer to the interview with Mrs Marie Karasevich, Winnipeg, 7 October 1983 (CIUS). On discrimination in the Canadian armed forces during the war, see Wojcichowski's correspondence with Professor Simpson, Appendix B in Prymak's *Trident and Maple Leaf*, and the interview with Ludwig Kaye (Wojcichowski) in Saskatoon, 16 August 1983 (CIUS).

59 See Karasevich to Panchuk, 28 March 1947, Panchuk Collection. Karasevich pointed out that 'all Organizations of K.U.K. are strongly on guard against the U.C.V.A. taking the credit for the solution of the refugee problem.' He added that 'rumours are floating already that U.C.V.A. with Karasevich and Panchuk, along with others, will become just another political group in Canada and this is certainly not desired by the already existing groups.' If the Ukrainian Canadian team on the Continent was sufficient to take care of the DPs, he advised Panchuk to 'come home,' for it was 'high time' that a 'Brain Trust' be established within the Ukrainian Canadian community to cope with the problems which needed to be addressed in Canada. 'As a further tip,' he urged Panchuk 'most confidentially,' 'Never let it appear that preference is given to the Orthodoz [sic] refugees,' for that would result in a 'kick back' against UCVA.

60 See Zaharychuk to Panchuk, 16 November 1945, and the telegram from Kushnir to Panchuk, 17 November 1945, Panchuk Collection. See also Panchuk's letter to the UCC, 19 November 1945, in NAC MG28 v9, vol. 14. The spelling of Frolack's surname was changed to Frolick after the war; the latter will be used hereafter.

61 Western Union cablegram from the UCC to S.W. Frolack [Frolick], 6 February 1946. Frolick's account of CURB and his experiences overseas is recounted in *Between Two Worlds: The Memoirs of Stanley Frolick* (Toronto, 1990). Frolick began working with CURB towards the latter part of 1945. As Panchuk noted in a letter to the UCC, 20 September 1945, he and the Bureau were being 'assisted considerably by Captain Frolack,' Panchuk Collection. According to Panchuk's 'Diary,' Frolick had arrived in London, England, by 25 May 1945. Frolick's CCG document, no. 3455, stamped 29 June 1945, designated his role as an interpreter, with the rank of Captain. Frolick joined UCSA, becoming member no. 1406, on 29 July 1945. Both documents are preserved in the Frolick Collection.

62 Panchuk to the UCC, 19 November 1945, NAC MG28 v9, vol. 14.

63 See Zaharychuk to Panchuk, 8 February 1946, Panchuk Collection. CURB's annual budget was fixed at $16,000; Panchuk, as president, and Frolick, as general secretary, were to be paid $250 each per month. CURB was to be supported financially on a '50–50' basis between the UCC and the Ukrain-ian Congress Committee of America, the UUARC's parent organization.

64 Panchuk to the UCC, 19 November 1945, NAC MG28 v9, vol. 14.

65 Panchuk to Air Officer Commanding-in-Chief, RCAF Overseas Headquar-ters, London, re 'Leave Of Absence – Without Pay, Application For,' 19 November 1945, Panchuk Collection.

66 UCSA formally concluded activities on 10 November 1945 with a 'Get-Together' in London. See the *UCSA News Letter Supplement – Souvenir Issue*, reproduced in *Memorial Souvenir Book 1*, ed. Panchuk, 151–63. The first UCSA News Letter appeared in September 1943. The eleventh and final 'Get-Together' was held in London on Ukrainian Christmas, 5–6 January 1946. The twelfth and last issue of the *UCSA News Letter* (vol. 1, no. 12) was published in January 1946.

67 See Reverend B. Kusznir [*sic*], 'Application for Permission to Travel to Con-tinental Europe,' 1 November 1945, DEA 6980–GR-40.

68 See Robertson to Turgeon, 2 January 1946, DEA 6980–GR-40. Robertson made the point that the UCC was 'well known' to the Soviet authorities, who had often objected to the activities of these Ukrainian nationalists in Canada. Turgeon was appointed as Canadian ambassador to Belgium and minister to Luxembourg in the fall of 1944. Prior to that he served as Cana-dian ambassador to Mexico and as chief justice and attorney general of Saskatchewan.

69 Notes about the WBA's protest cable are found in Panchuk Collection, 5 January 1946. Its signatories were obviously confused about CURB. Since the Bureau did not come into being until the war's very end, it could not have been involved in any 'anti-Ukrainian and Fascist' efforts during the war, as alleged. And, presumably, the cable's signatories were not referring to the UCSA 'London Club,' for that institution was occasionally fre-quented by ULFTA members serving with the Canadian armed forces.

70 See 'Complaint of Ukrainian Delegation at UNO against Activities of Ukrainians Abroad,' 12 February 1946, FO 371/56791. This file contains correspondence between John W. Holmes, of the Office of the High Com-missioner for Canada in London, and the Foreign Office's Thomas Brimelow, as well as Robertson's letter to the UCC's secretary, Arsenych, dealing with the forcible repatriation of refugees to the USSR. At least until the end of 1945, Brimelow was not particularly sympathetic to the plight of

these refugees. For example, on 13 December 1945 he sent a letter marked 'confidential and immediate' to Lieutenant Colonel V.M. Hammer at the War Office, commenting on the 'unsatisfactory progress' of measures being taken to repatriate Soviet nationals, including those who did not want to return to the USSR. 'We are unaware,' he noted, 'of any reasons why our policy regarding the use of force to effect repatriation should not be applied in the British Zone of Austria, as in all theatres where no account has to be taken of American views.' He went on to urge that 'suitable instructions' be issued to the military authorities in Austria with regard to the nature of British obligations as a result of the Yalta Agreement, concluding that this was 'a matter ... of the utmost urgency.' See Brimelow to V.M. Hammer, FO 945/598.

71 See Robertson, Office of the High Commissioner for Canada, to Pearson, 7 January 1946, DEA 6980-GR-40.

72 Cypher telegram from the High Commissioner of Canada to the Secretary of State for External Affairs, 14 February 1946, DEA 6980–GR-40.

73 See Robertson, Office of the High Commissioner for Canada, to Pearson, 7 January 1946, DEA 6980-GR-40.

74 See Brimelow's minutes on the file entitled 'Request from Central Ukrainian Relief Bureau for Personal Interview,' 25 February 1946, FO 371/56791.

75 A Mr Williamson noted on a file labelled 'Arrival in United Kingdom of Ukrainians from Italy': 'We take quite a good view of CURB, which has very influential friends in Canada and elsewhere. Although it is anti-Soviet, it is not blatantly so, and so far as we are aware, it confines its activities to relief and resettlement.' See FO 371/66355, 5 May 1947.

76 See Robertson, Office of the High Commissioner for Canada, to Pearson, 7 January 1946, DEA 6980-GR-40.

77 Ibid.

Chapter 5: 'A Subject Which We Cannot Ignore'

1 See, for example, Panchuk to Rhys J. Davies, MP, House of Commons, London, 17 September 1945, NAC MG28 v9, vol. 15.

2 See Philipps's personal and confidential note regarding forcible repatriation to W.J. Hasler, 5 October 1945, NAC MG30 E350 v2. He enclosed a document from Evhen De Batchinsky, director of the Ukrainian Red Cross in Geneva, describing the distress of Ukrainian refugees at the Landeck DP Camp. Philipps, given to both insight and hyperbole, observed that the 'matter, you will see, is of the stuff of which the solidarity of empires is

made, or marred.' He also warned that Canadians of Ukrainian origin had '14 newspapers in which to air this kind of thing.' Batchinsky, born in Katerynoslav in 1885, was a civic and religious leader, journalist, and editor, imprisoned for revolutionary activities in St Petersburg in 1908. He escaped to western Europe and was active in the Paris Ukrainian *Hromada* from 1909 to 1912. In 1914 he moved to Geneva and founded a Ukrainian community there. During the First World War Batchinsky was the representative of the 'Union for the Liberation of Ukraine,' editor of its newspaper, *La revue ukrainienne*, and, in 1918, consul for the Ukrainian National Republic. From 1922 he also represented the Ukrainian Autocephalous Orthodox church in western Europe. He was consecrated a bishop in 1955. His work for the Ukrainian Red Cross began in 1939 and continued until 1950. He died in Bulle, Switzerland, in 1978.

3 See Philipps, 'For Refugees What Refuge?' published in *Free Europe*, April 1946, a copy of which is found in NAC MG28 v9, vol. 17.

4 See Robertson's letter to the UCC's secretary, Arsenych, 1 February 1946, FO 371/56791.

5 See Professor W. Kirkconnell, chairman of the Social Service Committee of the Baptist Federation of Canada, to Prime Minister MacKenzie King, 28 January 1946, DEA 82-96-40. Kirkconnell referred to forcible repatriation as a 'crime against humanity.' For a contemptuous view of his role, see 'The Two-Faced Kirkconnell,' an editorial in the 1 July 1943 issue of *Ukrainian Life*. Labelling him the 'old chameleon,' the writer reminded readers that Kirkconnell had first become an 'expert' on Canada's 'foreign-language groups' while serving as 'a clerk at a concentration camp during the last war.' Having started out as a staunch magyarophile, he had evolved into a polonophile and, more lately, had given up his condemnation of the 'Ukrainian-German nationalists' to become a Ukrainian patriot. Now he was helping Ottawa as an 'expert,' but one whose behaviour was so confusing that undoubtedly he was 'drifting in that direction as do all people with pro-fascist mentality' – towards mental abnormality. His participation at the first UCC congress was derided as being nothing more than an 'address against the Ukrainian people at an anti-Soviet mob meeting.' This anti-Kirkconnell article was reported to Robertson of External Affairs. See Office of Examiner of Publications, Department of National Revenue, 5 July 1943, DEA 3846-A-40-C. Kirkconnell was not, of course, alone in criticizing Canadian complicity in the forcible repatriation of refugees or in speaking out in favour of Ukrainian refugee immigration. For example, Pastor Jacob Janzen of the Mennonite Church of Waterloo-Kitchener also addressed a letter on these issues to Prime Minister King. In it he pointed out that the Ukrainian

DPs would be 'a real asset to any country that would give them recourse and shelter, and an opportunity to start life anew' (ibid.).

6 See the petition addressed to Lord Noel Baker from Ukrainian refugees in the Regensburg DP camp, 12 November 1945, FO 371/47908. The petitioners noted that Lord Noel had spoken favourably to the third conference of the head council of UNRRA in London, on 18 August 1945, favouring the rights of those displaced persons who did not want to return to their countries of origin. They reminded him that, as Ukrainians, they could not return to Ukraine 'as long as there exists an autocratic Soviet rule of Moscow.'

7 See Bishop Ivan Buchko's letter to British foreign secretary Ernest Bevin, 5 January 1946, in 'Forcible Repatriation of Ukrainians to the Soviet Union,' FO 371/56791. The bishop wrote that, rather than return to the Soviet Union, a number of Ukrainian DPs were 'preparing themselves for a Christian death.' On 28 July 1945, Pope Pius XII personally appointed Ivan Buchko, the auxiliary bishop of Lviv, to minister to all Ukrainian (Ruthenian) Catholics in Italy. Buchko established a Ukrainian Relief Committee in Rome and worked intensively on behalf of his flock. On 21 November 1946 he was appointed General Apostolic Visitator of all Ukrainian Catholics in western Europe. Buchko's first pastoral letter to the Ukrainian refugees, published on 30 November 1948, called upon the Ukrainian Catholic faithful to remain true to the Roman Apostolic See because it had protected them against forcible repatriation and was helping all Ukrainian DPs without regard to religious confession. For more on Buchko's work, see A. Baran, 'The Ukranian Catholic Church,' in *The Refugee Experience: Ukrainian Displaced Persons after World War II*, ed. Isajiw, Boshyk, and Senkus, 147–57. On the roles of Pope Pius XII, Cardinal E. Tisserant, and Bishop Buchko in protecting Ukrainians and other DPs against forcible repatriation, see W. Dushnyck, 'Archbishop Buchko – Arch-Shepherd of Ukrainian Refugees,' *Ukrainian Quarterly* 31:1. For a biography of Bevin, see A. Bullock, *Ernest Bevin: Foreign Secretary, 1945–1951* (London, 1983).

8 See Frolick to Davies, MP, House of Commons, London, 25 February 1946, and Frolick to Sir Waldron Smithers, MP, House of Commons, London, 8 March 1946, in 'Forcible Repatriation of Ukrainians,' FO 371/56791. In the latter, Frolick made it 'emphatically clear' that CURB, which 'is sponsored by, and has the active support not only of non-political organizations in Canada and the U.S.A. but also of all our churches in both countries,' was 'not concerned with matters other than those responsible for, or arising directly from, relief.' He emphasized that 'there could be no pretension' of CURB's representing any movements other than the relief organizations

enumerated on its letterhead and those 'important elements of British subjects and American citizens who are deeply and not improperly concerned
with the essential humanitarian and social issues which are now being
rightly emphasized by Christian civilization and by the churches of the
world.' Sir Orme Sargent raised doubts about CURB's allegedly apolitical
character when he wrote to Sir Waldron later that month, observing that
when Messrs Frolick and Andrievsky asked for an interview in February
they had submitted 'various papers which they wished to discuss.' Those
documents all 'raised political questions, which we could not recognise the
competence of the Central Ukrainian Relief Bureau to discuss.' See Sir O.
Sargent to Sir W. Smithers, 22 March 1946, FO 371/56791.

 9 The translation of the letter from Metropolitan Polikarp of the Ukrainian
Autocephalous Orthodox Church and Archbishop of Volhynia and Luck to
His Grace to the Lord Archbishop of Canterbury, 3 April 1946, is found in
NAC MG28 v9, vol. 15. The metropolitan wrote to the archbishop after
receiving a letter from four DPs representing the 354 Ukrainians living in
the Ukrainian camp 'Kreigschule,' located near Hersfeld in the American
Zone of Occupation. These Ukrainians protested that, on 25 March 1946, an
American officer and soldiers, accompanied by UNRRA director Colonel
Scharthose, had forcibly evicted a number of Ukrainians from the camp.
The unfortunate refugees were beaten with rifle butts, some to the point of
unconsciousness, and then dragged onto waiting Soviet lorries. The peti-
tioners begged the metropolitan to raise his voice in their defence against
'the satanical Soviet attempts at our lives and souls.' Violent resistance to
forcible repatriation is also reported by Y. Boshyk, 'Repatriation: Ukrainian
DPs and Political Regugees in Germany and Austria, 1945–8,' in *The Refugee
Experience*, ed. Isajiw, Boshyk, and Senkus, 360–82. In August 1945, at
Kempten, Germany, 'the soldiers entered and began to drag people out
forcibly. They dragged the women by their hair and twisted the men's arms
up their back, beating them with the butts of their rifles. One soldier took
the cross from the priest and hit him with the butt of his rifle. Pandemonium broke loose. The people in a panic threw themselves from the second
floor, for the church was in the second storey of the building, and they fell
to their death or were crippled for life. In the church were also suicide
attempts.'

10 See S. Thorne, Central Offices of the Religious Society of Friends, London,
to the Right Honourable Clement R. Attlee, Prime Minister, 8 March 1946,
in the file entitled 'Forcible Repatriation of Ukrainians,' FO 371/56791.

11 Extract from 'Letter from a Responsible Allied Officer En Route in Austria,'
9 January 1946, Panchuk Collection. Stencils were made of this extract on

19 January and widely distributed. The original is marked 'Material Received from T. Philipps' and initialled by 'SWF' (S.W. Frolick). It may have been penned by Panchuk.

12 These remarks are recorded on a table labelled 'Repatriation of Agreed Soviet Nationals from Zone under British Control,' in the 'Weekly Report,' October 1945, found in FO 371/47907. See also the 'Weekly Report' covering the period up to 14 August 1945, found in FO 371/46811.

13 The submission by Yvonne Marrack, Friends Relief Service, 'Statement on Repatriation of Ukrainians from Goslar, Germany,' 2 February 1946, is found in FO 371/56791. This information was sent to Prime Minister Attlee by the Quakers. Marrack wrote that Britain had once stood 'for freedom' in the eyes of the people of the Continent. The relief team, Marrack went on, had found the Ukrainian and White Ruthenian refugees 'intelligent, skilful and industrious.' In comparison with other nationalities the Ukrainians had also shown 'a far greater readiness for hard work and a better capacity to adapt themselves to the exigencies of displacement.' Most had been brought out of Ukraine for forced labour in Germany between 1941 and 1943. The brutal behaviour of the German occupation forces in Ukraine, where Ukrainians had been treated as an inferior people fit only to be slaves, had produced among them a feeling that they could look to the British for their liberation. They were being bluntly disabused of this notion by British participation in their forcible repatriation to the Soviet Union.

14 See the file entitled 'The Position with Regard to the Repatriation of Soviet Citizens,' 7 September 1945, FO 371/47906. On the Soviet Union's efforts to persuade Ukrainian and other DPs to return voluntarily to their homes, M. Elliott, 'The Soviet Repatriation Campaign,' in *The Refugee Experience*, ed. Isajiw, Boshyk, and Senkus, 342–59, concludes: 'In the Kremlin's campaign for total repatriation, results based on the Soviet missions in the West were modest, but results based on Moscow's litany of promises and direct appeals fell between negligible and nonexistent. Its monumental dimensions notwithstanding, the Soviet campaign for total repatriation failed. The USSR did retrieve 3 million of its nationals from Eastern Europe and 2 million from Western occupation zones, but the remaining DPs, roughly 500,000 persons, could not be moved by any persuasion short of force. The Soviet government distrusted persons captured alive by the enemy and declared them traitors, prepared a hostile reception for all repatriates, and construed a refusal or even a reluctance to return home as most unpatriotic. Refugees with time to ponder sensed these attitudes through the veil of promises and solicitious attention. Although concern for effect more than accuracy determined what went into Soviet appeals to refugees abroad, few

returned home as a result of Soviet propaganda. In the final analysis, the Soviet Union's campaign to regain custody of every one of its displaced citizens failed because refugees with a choice detected the insincerity of Moscow's appeals. Half-hearted promises of a happy homecoming did not successfully disguise the regime's vindictive spirit.'

15 See the report by Yvonne Marrack of the Friends Relief Service, 'Statement on Repatriation of Ukrainians from Goslar, Germany,' 2 February 1946, FO 371/56791.

16 For firsthand reports on the situation in the Soviet Ukrainian port city of Odessa, see WO 32/1119, June 1945. For an account of the fate of some Soviet citizens repatriated to Murmansk, see the letter of Lieutenant Colonel P. Lloyd Williams, of the Hospital Ship *Aba*, to Colonel T.L. Thompson of the British War Office, 7 August 1945, FO 371/47904.

17 The British war cabinet discussed the question of what to do with Soviet citizens on 17 July 1944, at which time the matter was referred to the Soviet government for comment. A reply written on 23 August 1944 asked that all such Soviet citizens be repatriated 'at the earliest opportunity.' Concerned, the secretary of state for war requested a cabinet ruling 'in view of the probability that if we do as the Soviet Government wants and return all these prisoners to the Soviet Union, whether they are willing to return to the Soviet Union or no, we shall be sending some of them to their death.' The British cabinet decided that if the Soviet government wanted these persons 'it can come and fetch them,' for no British transport was available to return them. This delaying tactic also avoided any chance of German reprisals against Allied POWs still interned inside the Third Reich. Recently, J.D. Saunders, M.A. Sauter, and R.C. Kirkwood have argued in *Soldiers of Misfortune: Washington's Secret Betrayal of American POWs in the Soviet Union* (Washington, 1992) that Stalin deliberately held back American, British, and other Commonwealth POWs liberated by the Red Army from the Germans against the return by the Allies of all 'Soviet citizens.' Allegedly, the Anglo-American powers realized this but did nothing in protest, preferring instead to sift the DP camps for human assets they could use against the Soviets in any future conflict, thus consigning their own POWs to the Soviet gulag.

18 See the secret letter from R.G. Riddell of External Affairs' European and Commonwealth Division to H.H. Wrong, Associate Under-Secretary of State for External Affairs, 28 November 1945, on the issue of Ukrainian Canadian protests against the forcible repatriation of Ukrainian refugees to the USSR, in DEA 82-96-40. Previously, Wrong had been head of External Affairs' European and Commonwealth Division.

19 See Holmes, Office of the High Commissioner for Canada, to Brimelow, 5 November 1945, with respect to a telegram sent to Prime Minister Mackenzie King by 24 Canadian parliamentarians protesting against the forcible repatriation of Ukrainian refugees, in FO 371/47909. Gosuev arrived in Ottawa on 12 October 1942. Shortly afterwards, Dana Wilgress, then deputy minister of trade and commerce, was named Canadian representative to the Soviet Union. Wilgress had served previously as a Canadian trade commissioner in Omsk, Siberia, in 1916. During the civil war he stayed in Vladivostok, as a member of the Canadian Economic Commission to Siberia. He returned to Ottawa in 1919 after the collapse of the Allied intervention, his career subsequently taking him to postings in Bucharest, Milan, London, and Hamburg. In 1931 he was back in Ottawa, where he rose to be deputy minister by October 1940. During the interwar period he visited the USSR with Canadian trade delegations in 1921 and 1936. In *Diplomacy of Fear*, 41, 42, 196–7, Smith points out that Wilgress 'showed a marked preference for the company and views of those diplomats who were sympathetic towards the Soviet Union,' and that 'for as long as they could conscientiously do so, the Canadian mission would put the best face on the Soviet regime.' Writing in response to a March 1947 invitation by Pearson to comment on the implications of the Truman Doctrine on Canadian foreign policy, Wilgress urged the Western powers not to use eastern Europe as a testing ground for the clash between their policies and those of the USSR, arguing that Soviet rule was so secure there that any Western attempts to challenge it would fail and only end up fuelling Soviet suspicions. Instead of supporting anti-Soviet politicians in eastern Europe (and presumably among the émigré communities), Western powers should employ a policy of 'mild tolerance' towards communist-dominated governments. This noninterference should be tied to a clearly articulated acceptance by both sides of their delineated spheres of influence.

20 See 'Note for Mr. Riddell,' 21 December 1945, DEA 82-96-40, with respect to Prime Minister Mackenzie King's reply in the House of Commons to a question about the repatriation of Ukrainians posed by A. Hlynka, MP, on 18 December 1945. See also Canada, House of Commons, *Debates*, 18 December 1945, p. 3789, 'Repatriation of Ukrainians: Protection of Interests of Ukrainians in Military Occupation Zones.'

21 See Document #42, 5 December 1945, in *A Delicate and Difficult Question*, ed. Kordan and Luciuk, 135–8.

22 See Document #43, 22 December 1945, ibid., 139–42. Malania, a University of Toronto graduate in history and political science, was recruited into External Affairs as a temporary assistant in April 1943, along with H.G.

Skilling and Professor F.H. Soward. Until 28 September 1945, Malania consistently argued for an accommodation with the Soviet Union. On that date, Emma Woikin, a clerk working for External Affairs, was transferred from the department's Cipher Division after the defector Igor Gouzenko implicated her in the passing of information to the Soviets. Woikin had lived with the Malanias in their house at 357 Chapel Street in Ottawa, a neighbourhood sprinkled with families from the Soviet embassy and other Slavic immigrants. Although no evidence linking Malania to Woikin's treachery was ever brought to light, he was compromised and had to resign from External Affairs by mid-August 1946. Subsequently, Malania was posted as secretary of the Canadian delegation to the Preparatory Commission of the United Nations in London, and made secretary-general of the Canadian delegation to the first General Assembly of the United Nations. With Hume Wrong's help, Malania secured a position in the office of the UN secretary-general in the late winter of 1946, a job he retained into the 1950s. He became an Episcopalian priest with a New York City parish and reportedly committed suicide.

23 See Document #42, 5 December 1945, in *A Delicate and Difficult Question*, ed. Kordan and Luciuk, 138.

24 See Stanley Knowles's remarks in Document #43, 15 December 1945, ibid., 141.

25 See Malania's postscriptive remarks, 22 December 1945, in Document #43, ibid., 140. Malania had even earlier been involved in monitoring Ukrainian Canadian activities. See the 'personal and confidential' letter sent 'by safe hand' on 10 May [1944?] to Herbert M. Sichel of the British Security Co-ordination in New York, concerning Wasyl Swystun, 'the former Nationalist leader' who had by then begun waging 'a one-man campaign among Ukrainian Nationalists to convince them that this war has settled the Ukrainian question ... and [that] Ukrainian Canadians [should] accept [this] verdict, forget their nationalist dreams and concentrate on purely Canadian affairs.' Swystun visited Soviet Ukraine in 1954. For his impressions of the grave conditions there as related to the Canadian ambassador in Moscow, see the dispatch of 7 June 1954 in DEA 50166-40.

26 Granatstein in *The Ottawa Men* presents a useful discussion of the personalities and careers of many of Canada's leading civil servants during this period.

27 See H. Thomas, *Armed Truce: The Beginnings of the Cold War, 1945–1946* (London, 1986).

28 Indicative of a growing disenchantment with the Soviet Union at this time were analyses like that presented by the American *chargé d'affaires* in Mos-

cow, George Kennan. On 22 February 1946 he sent out the now famous 'long telegram' which argued that the Soviet regime saw the world as being divided into two conflicting realms, socialist and capitalist, between which there could be 'no permanent peaceful coexistence.' Kennan questioned the accuracy of Moscow's 'neurotic view of world affairs' but nevertheless recommended that in dealings with the Soviet Union a steady display of firmness backed by 'sufficient force' was essential. Later, under the pseudonym 'Mr X,' Kennan would publish a paper entitled 'The Sources of Soviet Conduct,' *Foreign Affairs* 25 (July 1947): 566–82, which would promote a strategy of 'containment' in Western dealings with the USSR. Shortly after Kennan's 'long telegram' was sent out of Moscow, Prime Minister Winston Churchill delivered a speech at Westminster College, in Fulton, Missouri,   5 March 1946, with a similar message. Churchill foresaw disaster unless the Anglo-American powers worked together in the postwar world. Deploring the spread of Soviet-dominated 'police governments' throughout eastern Europe, the great statesman lamented that 'from Stettin in the Baltic to Trieste in the Adriatic, an iron curtain has descended across the Continent.' While Canadian diplomats like Wilgress had recognized, probably by April 1945, that their interpretations of the moderate postwar intentions of the Soviets had misguided the Canadian government, he did not accept the Kennan line. He even formally challenged the proposed policy of Western 'toughness' towards the Soviet Union in a dispatch dated 14 November 1945. For his part, Malania expended considerable energy in deprecating four memoranda regarding Soviet intentions which a Canadian third secretary attached to Canada's Moscow embassy, Arnold C. Smith, had drafted in April 1945. Smith offered a startlingly different and sombre interpretation of Soviet behaviour and suggested various tactics for coping with the Soviet regime's plans, among which he included the creation of a Western bloc. He had also argued that the USSR was intent on carving out its own relatively exclusive spheres of influence in eastern Europe and elsewhere. Malania, who seems to have wanted to discredit Smith's credibility as an authority on Soviet affairs, argued for a more conciliatory, diplomatic approach to the Soviets, one intended to allay their suspicions of the West and leave them to, and with, what he regarded as their proper sphere of influence. See Smith, *Diplomacy of Fear*, 75–85, 116, 142–4. The four Smith memoranda are found in DEA 7-H (s), along with a covering letter from Leon Maynard to the Secretary of State for External Affairs, dated 16 April 1945.

29 See H. Wrong's secret letter to the High Commissioner for Canada, 20 March 1946, DEA 82-96-40.

30 H. Wrong to G. Riddell, Canadian consulate general in New York, 13 June

1946, DEA 82-96-40. See also P.T. Molson's notes 'Displaced Persons in Europe: The Yalta Agreement,' 20 February 1946, in the same file. Panchuk would later assist Molson and the Canadian delegation at the PCIRO meetings in Geneva, 1947. See the photograph of Panchuk with Dr Waddams and Mr Molson reproduced in *Heroes of Their Day.*

31 See Granatstein, *The Ottawa Men,* 17.

32 A copy of the orders of the HQ 30 Corps District, 29 December 1945, which state that His Majesty's Government 'do not recognize *Ukrainian* as a nationality' and call for the immediate disbanding of Ukrainian organizations is found in the Panchuk Collection. Attached to it is a document, dated 27 November 1945 and signed by Captain R. Wallach on behalf of a Lieutenant Colonel Newman, both of whom were attached to the military government in Gross-Hassen. It is entitled 'Release of Soviet citizens, Subject to Repatriation in Accordance with the Yalta Agreement from Labour for the Germans in the American Zone.' German employers were forbidden to employ any 'Soviet citizen' who might be subject to repatriation in accordance with the Yalta Agreement. 'Soviet citizens' were defined as all those who were 'physically present in the USSR, and who were citizens of the USSR on the 17 September 1939, and who were removed from the USSR or left the USSR beginning the 22 June 1941.' All such persons were to be collected and transferred to the Soviet-administered Neukirchen camp. While the use of troops for gathering 'Soviet citizens' was expressly forbidden, it was pointed out that anyone falling into this category would not, after 8 December 1945, be able to benefit from the assistance and support provided in any DP camp under British control. This document was included in an appendix to a 1946 CURB memorandum addressed to the United Nations on the theme of Ukrainian refugees, co-signed by Reverend Dr V. Kushnir and S.W. Frolick. For British reaction to Ukrainian Canadian protests over these orders, see Brimelow's minutes, 12 February 1946, in 'Treatment of Ukrainians in British Zone of Germany,' FO 371/56791. Additional information on the HQ 30 Corps District orders, and their interpretation, is found in FO 945/598. See, in particular, the letter of 4 August 1945 from John Gray of the Friends Relief Service to Foreign Secretary Bevin. It pointed out that it would be 'contrary to the liberal English tradition towards refugees to forcibly transfer [them] to Russia.' Similar orders were still being circulated as late as 9 July 1946. See the memorandum circulated from UNRRA headquarters in Klagenfurt, Austria, to all UNRRA camps, on that date, a copy of which is found in Box 6, A. Brownlee Collection, Hoover Institution on War, Revolution and Peace.

33 See Brimelow's 18 January 1946 minutes to a file entitled 'Ruthenian Dis-

placed Persons,' FO 371/57813. Brimelow was responding to a personal and confidential note by Philipps, 'Need & Advisability of Aided Education for D.P. Ukrainians Whose Ancestors (& Selves) Have Never been Russian or Soviet Subjects.' Apparently, Philipps enjoyed no greater confidence among British officials than he had among their Canadian counterparts. Brimelow dismissed his account, noting that it 'contains many inaccuracies.' Another colleague commented that he did not think Philipps 'a very good authority' on the subject of Ukrainians; a third opined that the document 'has unmistakable signs of having been written by Mr. Tracy Philipps.' which meant 'we must be prepared for some exaggeration.'

34 A copy of a Ukrainian Red Cross identification card is reproduced in Panchuk, *Heroes of Their Day*. He was aided in distributing these cards by Flight Lieutenant Burianyk, although the occupation authorities eventually caught on, after which they were both forced to desist.

35 See 'Confidential Minutes of the First Day of the Conference Held in London, 7–8 February 1946 of C.U.R.B. and Representatives of Ukrainian Relief Committees,' Frolick Collection.

36 Panchuk's reports to CURB about visits to these refugee camps are dated 20 February 1946 (Report #1), 28 February–1 March 1946 (Report #2), 12 March 1946 (Report #3), and 18 March 1946 (Report #4), Panchuk Collection.

37 See Panchuk's report to the UCC, 30 January 1946, January 1946, NAC MG28 v9, vol. 17.

38 Ibid.

39 Ibid.

40 See 'Confidential minutes ...,' Frolick Collection. According to Frolick, 'A Lost Page of History,' 4–6, CURB served as 'a joint European outpost' for the UCC and its Ukrainian American equivalent, the Ukrainian American Congress Committee, and their refugee relief organs, the UCRF and UUARC. Refugee relief committees were also organized by the DPs themselves. For example, there was a Central Relief Committee for Austria, run by Dr Roslak and Mr Y. Spolsky, and another operating in the American and British zones of Germany, which counted among its members Mr W. Mudryj, Professor Vietuchiw, Mr Milanych, Dr Wojewidka, and Dr Borys Andrievsky (one of the organizers of the Ukrainian Red Cross in Germany). There were other committees in France (Reverend Perridon, Dr N. Procyk, Mr Popovitch), Belgium (Messrs Hrab, Mulkewytsch, and Pryschlak), and Switzerland (Messrs Batchinsky and Barran), and smaller groups in Italy, Turkey, various South American countries, and elsewhere. CURB attempted to coordinate the work of these various committees and, sporadically, organized conferences in Paris, Brussels, and London to which their

representatives were invited. Contact was maintained among them by a network of men and women serving in the Canadian and American armed forces. Stationed in various posts around the Continent, and themselves served by a reasonably efficient military postal service which represented the only reliable mail service available at that time, they willingly passed mail among the various refugee communities. While working with CURB, Joe Romanow developed an elaborate cross-indexed filing system which allowed the Bureau to maintain contact with DPs, service personnel, and civilians throughout Europe.

41 D. Andrievsky is listed as being on the payroll of CURB, with a salary of 3 pounds sterling per week as of 9 February 1946, the day after the London conference concluded. In a circular letter to CURB's staff, Panchuk stated that Frolick's salary would be 10 pounds sterling a week, while Monsignor Kushnir was to be given 'expenses unlimited,' with 200 pounds sterling apportioned for his use on the Continent and another 100 pounds sterling while he visited the United Kingston. See Panchuk to 'Dear Fellow Workers,' 9 February 1946, Panchuk Collection.

42 See 'Confidential minutes ...,' Frolick Collection.

43 See ibid.

44 Interviews with Frolick in Toronto, 1 July 1981; 16–24 December 1983; 4–6 January 1984 (MHSO); and 10 January 1983 (CIUS). The UHVR was established after a gathering of representatives from the various regions of Ukraine was held in the Carpathian Mountains, 11–15 July 1944. This Council was intended to be Ukraine's provisional parliament. It was mandated to direct the Ukrainian revolutionary struggle and represent the nation internationally. The Council issued a *universal*, or Appeal, to the Ukrainian people which explained that the UHVR was 'the largest and sole guiding body of the Ukrainian nation for the duration of the revolutionary struggle, until the creation of the government of the independent and Sovereign Ukrainian State.' The UPA immediately recognized the UHVR as a legitimate revolutionary government, to which its members swore an oath of allegiance. UPA Headquarters also published an article in its underground press about the UHVR, entitled 'The Sole Political Leadership of United Ukraine.' See *Litopys UPA: The UPA in Light of German Documents: Book 1* (Toronto, 1983), 26–7. The same volume also reproduces lists of Ukrainians executed by the Nazis for being members of the OUNb and UPA and for sheltering Jews. In *Litopys UPA: The UPA in Light of German Documents: Book 2* (Toronto, 1983), 44–9, there are German-language translations of two UHVR documents, 'The Fundamental Principles of the UHVR' and 'General Proclamation of the UHVR,' which present the political plat-

form of the movement. Several documents in this collection underscore that the Ukrainian national liberation movement was continuing to fight against all forces of occupation in Ukraine, including the German, the Soviet, Vlasov's Russian, and the Polish. See Documents #31, 32, 36, and 53. The insurgency's strength was variously estimated at between 80,000 and 100,000 soldiers, although two *Abwehr* documents (#23, #24) record that some Ukrainian sources put the strength of regular UPA units at between 400,000 and 2 million. Volumes 8, 9, and 10 of the *Litopys UPA* series reproduce other UHVR documents and official publications. The documentary collection compiled by P.J. Potichnyj and E. Shtendera, eds, *The Political Thought of the Ukrainian Underground, 1943–1951* (Edmonton, 1986), presents a useful selection of the same, in English translation.

45 See 'Confidential minutes ...,' Frolick Collection.

46 See ibid.

47 Panchuk's Report #1 to CURB, 20 February 1946, mentioned that he left London on 11 February 1946 and that Kushnir was already in western Europe by that date; Panchuk Collection.

48 'Résumé of Bureau Meetings ...,' Panchuk Collection.

49 Panchuk to Kaye, 3 May 1946. Panchuk informed Kaye that he and his wife expected to leave England on 7 May 1946 aboard the *Isle de France*, to arrive in Canada on 13 May 1946. In *Heroes of Their Day*, 89, Panchuk recalled that they departed aboard the *Queen Elizabeth*. Once in Canada, the Panchuks and Yaremovich went as UCVA delegates to the second national UCC congress, held in Toronto, 4–6 June, where they joined 395 other delegates (UCC, 111; USRL, 96; UNF, 90; BUC, 37; UHO, 31; and UCVA, 30) in resolving that it 'was necessary that the Ukrainian Canadian Committee ... continue to function ... for the good of Canada, of its people, and of the Ukrainians.' After reiterating that Ukrainian Canadians had, under the UCC's leadership, proved their loyalty to Canada during the war, they passed a resolution establishing a special committee to confer with the Dominion government 'in the matter of settling political refugees on the land in Canada.' Significantly, given the manner in which the 'Ukrainian Question' had essentially been avoided at the first UCC congress, at this second meeting the delegates openly noted that the UCC had been organized not only to aid Canada in the prosecution of the war but also 'to interpret to the Canadian Government the wishes and thoughts of the Ukrainian people in Canada and Europe.' Since the 'Ukrainian matter' had not been 'executed in a positive fashion,' the 'voice of the Ukrainian Emigration' had become 'more important and necessary.' The delegates collectively voiced their 'dissatisfaction because the principles of the Atlantic

Charter and the Four Freedoms were not utilized for the good of the nations which were freed from the yoke of foreign occupants and the majority of which have fallen, without their consent, into the hands of the Soviet Union under a different form of oppression and enslavement.' While the delegates were satisfied that Ukrainian lands in Europe had finally been united, and that Ukraine had been recognized by being given a seat in the United Nations, the 'original desires of the Ukrainian people' had not been fulfilled, for Ukraine was neither sovereign nor independent. The delegates condemned the policy of Canada's Ukrainian communists toward the DPs, especially because these communists were attempting to denounce the Ukrainian refugees as 'war criminals' and protesting against their admission to Canada. They also voiced complete satisfaction with the work, of the UCRF, authorized its continuing work, and formally thanked Panchuk and UCSA for their efforts on behalf of the refugees. At the concluding congress banquet, held in the Crystal Ball Room of the King Edward Hotel on Thursday evening, 6 June 1946, the 550 guests and delegates heard John Solomon, MLA, speak about his experiences as a member of the delegation which addressed the Senate Standing Committee on Immigration and Labour (29 May 1946) on the issue of refugee immigration. Solomon emphasized that the 'hideous manner' in which the communist delegation had attacked this proposed immigration of 'Ukrainian exiles' into Canada had convinced him 'that there can never be any bond of interest between the Ukrainian Nationalists and Ukrainian Communists.' See *Second All-Canadian Congress of Ukrainians in Canada.*

50 Panchuk, *Heroes of Their Day,* 130.
51 Panchuk to CURB, Report #1, 20 February 1946, Panchuk Collection.
52 Panchuk to CURB, Report #2, 28 February–1 March 1946, Panchuk Collection.
53 Panchuk to CURB, Report #3, 12 March 1946, Panchuk Collection.
54 Panchuk to CURB, Report #2, 28 February–1 March 1946.
55 Panchuk to CURB, Report #3, 12 March 1946.
56 Panchuk to CURB, Report #4, 18 March 1946, Panchuk Collection. Religious feuding, he claimed, had subsided: 'One of the outstanding features of Ukrainian camp life is the religious tolerance and broadminded understanding that exists.'
57 Panchuk to CURB, Report #1, 20 February 1946.
58 Panchuk to CURB, Report #2, 28 February–1 March 1946.
59 Panchuk to CURB, Report #4, 18 March 1946.
60 Panchuk to CURB, Report #2, 28 February–1 March 1946.
61 Panchuk to CURB, Report #3, 12 March 1946. In his next report, Report #4,

18 March 1946, Panchuk suggested setting up a CURB branch office in Hamburg. Eventually, one was established in Bielefeld/Lemgo, near the centre of operations for the BAOR.

62 Panchuk to 'Dear Fellow Workers' from Utersen, near Hamburg, 15 March 1946, Panchuk Collection. By February–March 1946 the Panchuks were both fatigued by their exertions on behalf of the refugees and had personal reasons for thinking seriously about returning home. See Panchuk, 'Diary,' 19 February, 27 February, and 6 March 1946.

63 Panchuk to Kaye, 3 May 1946, Panchuk Collection.

64 In WO 208/1734, 21 August 1940, British military intelligence described Stephen Davidovich as the London-based publisher of the *Ukrainian Bulletin* and 'a representative of the Ukrainian nationalistic circles in London and particularly those in Canada' and as a man who 'has OUN connections.' Davidovich, interviewed in Toronto, 8 March 1982 (MHSO), was reluctant to discuss his prewar ties to the nationalists, although it is indisputable that he was sent to London in 1938 to run a Ukrainian Information Bureau on behalf of the OUN. Formally, he was paid by an American-Ukrainian group known as the Organization for the Rebirth of Ukraine (ODVU, Orhanizatsiia derzhavnoho vidrodzhennia ukrainy). He served as a publicist and lobbyist for the Ukrainian nationalist movement until 1941, when the British authorities told him to shut down this bureau. He subsequently joined the Canadian army overseas.

65 'Resumé of Bureau Meetings ...,' Panchuk Collection.

66 Frolick recalled that Davidovich had dissociated himself from the OUN by this time. Davidovich subsequently became an ardent UCC supporter. Being of Ukrainian Orthodox faith (his father came from eastern Ukraine), he enjoyed the support of his co-religionist Panchuk, which might explain why he rather than Frolick was recommended for the post of CURB's director. British military intelligence analysts recorded, on 21 August 1940, that Davidovich's negative attitude towards Poland 'has passed lately a certain evolution and he is persuaded that Poland can be the only Ukrainian ally in the East.' See WO 208/1734.

67 Panchuk, 'Diary,' 19 February 1946.

68 Panchuk, 'Diary,' 19 March 1946.

69 Interviews with Frolick (n44 above).

70 See Ukrainian Youth Federation, *Seven Presidents in Uniform* (Winnipeg, 1945).

71 According to Frolick's testimony, all speeches presented at the first All-Canadian Congress of Ukrainians were, by joint agreement, subject to censorship by the participating groups. His address, on behalf of the Young

Ukrainian Nationalists, was so heavily censored by USRL representatives that at first he refused to deliver it. In 'The Ukrainian Canadian Committee: A History,' 17–18, Frolick wrote: 'The original draft of my speech was rejected as being too nationalistically Ukrainian, i.e. was not servile enough and did not sufficiently stress our loyalty to Canada. The final version delivered by me bore only a slight resemblance to my original paper and contained very little of my true feelings and ideas which I thought were important to convey to my peer group, those, as I, born in this country, but nevertheless feeling a strong sense of obligation to our kinfolk in Ukraine.'

72 See Kossar's photograph with one of the prewar leaders of the UVO, O. Senyk-Hrybiwsky, reproduced in Marunchak, *The Ukrainian Canadians*, 509.

73 As related by Frolick in Toronto, 28 September 1987. Kossar's note of 10 March 1945, testifying to Frolick's trustworthiness, is preserved in the Frolick Collection.

74 Dontsov was, as late as 26 June 1946, still staying at CURB, or so Private J. Ratushniak wrote to Panchuk. Despite appealing for Professor Kirkconnell's intervention so that he could emigrate to Canada (see Dontsov to Kirkconnell, 31 July 1946, NAC MG28 v9, vol. 1) it would be some time before Dontsov rather surreptitiously managed to leave London. Dontsov first came to the Bureau in February 1946, where he became something of a house guest. This happened, according to Panchuk, even though it was generally agreed that Dontsov should seek private quarters elsewhere so as to avoid any political repercussions. See 'Meeting of the Relief Team,' 18 October 1946, Panchuk Collection. On 24 October the UCC's secretary, A. Zaharychuk, responding to Panchuk's letter of 17 October, advised him that Winnipeg's view was that Dontsov should leave 218 Sussex Gardens forthwith, for CURB's work might be complicated by his presence there. The UIS, whose bulletin Frolick edited, should not be confused with the Ukrainian Press Service (UPS), edited by Roman Rakhmanny. The UPS began publishing a Ukrainian-language newsletter on 1 February 1946. An English-language version of the UPS newsletter made its first appearance on 25 March 1946. CURB also briefly published its own English-language periodical, *The Refugee* (London). An example – volume 1, nos 1–2 (January 1947) is in the Panchuk Collection. For evidence of how news concerning the Ukrainian liberation movement got through to the Western press and even back into Ukraine, where it was reprinted in the underground press, see *Litopys UPA: Underground Journals from Ukraine beyond the Curzon Line, 1945–1947* (Toronto, 1987).

75 See S.W. Frolick, 'Saving the DPs: The Central Ukrainian Relief Bureau,'

unpublished manuscript of a lecture delivered in the Canadian Institute of Ukrainian Studies lecture series, Toronto, 13 November 1978, 23–4, Frolick Collection.

76 Frolick to the UUARC's Gallan, 22 May 1946, Frolick Collection.

77 Ibid.

78 In 'Saving the DPs ...,' 23, Frolick emphasized that if news about the Banderivtsi happened to take up much of the space in UIS newsletters, that was only because this particular movement predominated as a political force in the emigration, and not proof of any personal bias or selectivity on his part.

79 Ibid., 25.

80 Ibid., 26. This telegram must have been sent from Toronto, where Monsignor Kushnir and Dr Gallan were participating in the second national UCC congress (4–6 June 1946).

81 On the UIS, see Frolick to the UUARC, 22 May 1946. Examples of UIS literature can be found in the Panchuk Collection. For instance, see the mimeographed information sheets of late January 1946, 2 February 1946, and 9 February 1946, which list 218 Sussex Gardens in London – the address of CURB – as the UIS mailing address. This material, at least in hindsight, appears unobjectionable. The first, entitled 'Life in the Lager,' was a reprint of an editorial first appearing in a British army newspaper, the *Sphinx Gazette*, published in Kiel, Germany, on 26 January 1946. The next UIS press release was nothing more than a reprint of a Reuters report, written by S. Relleur, which dealt with a CURB memorandum submitted to the United Nations secretariat on behalf of the Ukrainian DPs. The last, entitled 'Ukrainians Are Still Being Forcibly Repatriated,' made reference to an article which appeared in the *Catholic Herald* of 9 February 1946 and cited eyewitness accounts of the brutality of these deportations.

82 See correspondence between the Political Division of the Main Headquarters for the CCG to the Northern Department, 17 May 1946, in 'Forcible Repatriation of Ukrainians,' FO 371/56791. Additional material on forcible repatriation can be found in FO 945/598.

83 M. Howson of the Canadian Red Cross, BAOR, to Philipps, 24 May 1946, NAC MG30 E350.

84 Philipps to '[Kirkconnell] and Watson,' 25 May 1946, NAC MG30 E350.

85 Ibid.

86 Panchuk from Saskatoon to Lieutenant Colonel Frost, Commissioner of the Canadian Red Cross Overseas Headquarters, London, 26 May 1946, Panchuk Collection.

87 Panchuk to Kaye, 3 May 1946, Panchuk Collection.

88 V.J. Kaye to Gracie Kaye, 29 May 1946, NAC MG30 E350. The UCC delega-

tion which went to Ottawa consisted of Messrs Panchuk, Kushnir, Hlynka, Solomon, Sawchuk, and E. Dowhan of Montreal. They were publicly thanked for 'so manfully and eloquently' presenting the case for Ukrainian refugee immigration by Father M. Horoshko when the latter commented on the speech of Dr Luka Mishuha, a Ukrainian Congress Committee of America delegate to the second UCC congress. See *Second All-Canadian Congress of Ukrainians in Canada*, 91.

89 See Senate of Canada, *Proceedings of the Senate Standing Committee on Immigration and Labour* (Ottawa, 1946). On 5 June 1947 the Ukrainian Canadian Left submitted another brief to the Senate committee. Signed by Messrs Teresio, Prokop, Korl, Bilecki, Philipowich, Boychuk, Krentz, and Macievich and Mrs E. Pashkowska, this document argued in favour of increasing immigration opportunities for workers and farmers in preference to white collar workers, and criticized the 'tendency' to allow for an immigration of people 'of a particular religious or political background.' The existing policy, which they derided as 'selective immigration,' was nothing more than a 'mask to cover the bringing over to Canada of pro-Nazi remnants in Europe.' Aside from Jews and Spanish anti-fascists, no 'so-called displaced persons' should be admitted, because the DPs in Germany, Austria, and Italy, both inside and outside the refugee camps, 'are either war criminals and Nazi collaborators who are wanted by the governments of their countries to stand trial or persons free to return to their homelands.' Canada must not, the AUUC's interveners concluded, become a 'haven for war criminals and pro-Nazi politicians under the guise of immigration.' In response to surprisingly similar allegations raised publicly in 1984, the government of Canada established a commission to investigate the alleged presence in Canada of war criminals. After considerable research and much public debate, this Commission of Inquiry on War Criminals, headed by Mr Justice Jules Deschênes, concluded that there was no evidence confirming the presence of large numbers of Nazi war criminals in Canada and that the entire issue had been 'grossly exaggerated' by groups like the Los Angeles–based Simon Wiesenthal Center and its Canadian lobbyists. Apparently, no war criminals of Ukrainian origin were found. See Deschênes, *Commission of Inquiry on War Criminals, Report: Part 1, Public*.

90 Ibid.

91 Interview with J. Solomon, Winnipeg, 30 November 1982 (CIUS).

92 Canada, Order-in-Council no. 2071, 28 May 1946. See Marunchak, *The Ukrainian Canadians*, 563, fn6.

93 Identifying himself as CURB's director, Frolick co-signed this document

with the UUARC's Gallan, who gave his title as 'Chairman of the Board of Directors of the United Ukrainian American Relief Committee, and the Ukrainian Canadian Relief Fund.' Gallan did not protest Frolick's self-description as 'Director, Central Ukrainian Relief Bureau in London.' See W. Gallan and S.W. Frolick to the Honourable E. Bevin, Foreign Secretary, London, 10 August 1945, FO 945/722. Another copy is found in FO 371/58H 70, under the same date. Gallan and Frolick forwarded a second memorandum to Bevin, dated 12 August 1946, which pointed out that Ukrainian refugees were not suffering as much from a want of material aid – such as food, shelter, or clothing – as from 'uncertainty of their true future, constant fear of forcible repatriation and lack of true information about the external world, discussions and decisions of various bodies such as U.N.R.R.A., United Nations, etc., pertaining to and affecting the lives of the refugees and stating the possibilities of resettlement and emigration.' They petitioned Bevin to grant them the permission and resources required to organize the publication of a 'non-political' Ukrainian-language daily newspaper in the British Zone of Germany, with a projected circulation of fifty thousand copies. The paper, they promised, would be under British control. They also asked for the privilege of having Ukrainian advisers attached to UNRRA headquarters and other bodies charged with looking after the DPs, arguing that Jews and members of the Baltic nationalities already had such representatives, whereas Ukrainian refugees, 'the largest racial group amongst the refugees ... who are in the worst position in many respects,' had none. Finally, they asked Bevin to facilitate the placement of UUARC and UCRF field representatives in the British zones of Germany and Austria. This memorandum was also signed jointly by Gallan and Frolick, with the latter again using the title of CURB director. A copy is found in FO 945/385. Frolick was also working the British lecture circuit at this time. See, for example, the notes for a speech he delivered on the 'Ukrainian Question' on 11 February 1946, to a meeting of the League for the Freedom of Europe, in Conway Hall, chaired by the Duchess of Atholl, in the Panchuk Collection.

94 Escott Reid, Acting Under-Secretary of State for External Affairs, to F. Foulds, Canadian Citizenship Branch of the Department of the Secretary of State, Ottawa, 26 August 1946, DEA 82-96-40.

95 Acting High Commissioner for Canada, London, to the Department of External Affairs, 9 August 1946, DEA 82-96-40.

96 Ibid.

97 Panchuk to Philipps, 17 August 1946 and 28 September 1946; Panchuk to Kirkconnell, 17 August 1946; Panchuk to Kaye, 21 September; and Panchuk to Kaye and Davidovich, 27 September 1946, all in the Panchuk Collection.

98 Panchuk to Frolick, 4 September 1946, Panchuk Collection.

99 Ibid.

100 Ibid.

101 Panchuk to the UCC, 17 August 1946, NAC MG28 v9, vol. 15.

102 Ibid.

103 Letter from Panchuk, in Saskatoon, to Kaye, at the Canadian Citizenship Branch, Ottawa, 21 September 1946, Panchuk Collection.

104 See Panchuk's letter from Saskatoon to the 'Diplomatic Division' of the Canadian Department of External Affairs, 1 October 1946, DEA 6980-GR-40.

105 See Panchuk's letter from Saskatoon to A. Hlynka, MP, House of Commons, Ottawa, 28 September 1946, Panchuk Collection.

106 Panchuk to Kaye, 21 September 1946, and Panchuk to Kaye and Davidovich, 27 September 1946, Panchuk Collection. Despite the UCC's promises, by 9 December 1946, Karasevich was reporting that UCVA was 'experiencing a tough battle' with the UCC, much of which was centred on the Team's overseas efforts. As Karasevich recorded: 'The ultimatum presented to KYK by UCVA ... and the Renaissance Plan, has certainly more than doubled our opposition from East to West. All organizations of KYK have placed themselves on guard against UCVA Plans ... Was it a mistake to submit the memorandum on unity? ... Maybe our tactics should have been to lead rather than to tell them that they cannot see nor can they walk.' A copy of the 'Renaissance Plans (Rebirth and Relief to Victims of War),' an original of which was recently located in the 'Oseredok' Ukrainian Archives and Museum of Winnipeg, has now been placed in the Panchuk Collection at the Archives of Ontario. It had been presumed lost. The Plans called for an English-language journal aimed at Ukrainian Canadian youth, with a distribution of seventy-five thousand copies; the creation of memorial homes (United Ukrainian Cultural Centres) coinciding with a moratorium on the building of any competitive '2×4' halls; the acceptance of common community schools and educational programs; and the provision of resources for a relief team for work overseas among the refugees. The document was signed by Panchuk, on behalf of UCVA, on 11 September 1946.

107 See Panchuk's letter from Saskatoon to the 'Diplomatic Division' of External Affairs, 1 October 1946, DEA 6980-GR-40.

108 A photograph of the distinctive, if unofficial, cloth shoulder flash worn by Team members is reproduced in Panchuk, *Heroes of Their Day*. The CRM had its own letterhead, which identified G.R.B. Panchuk, M.B.E., as director; A.J. Yaremovich as assistant director and field representative; Miss

Ann Crapleve, B.E.M., as secretary-treasurer; and Mrs Anne Panchuk as welfare officer. For an example of this letterhead, see Panchuk's letter to Mr Moore of the German Refugee Department, 18 April 1947, FO 945/722.

109 Zaharychuk to Frolick, 20 September 1946, Frolick Collection.

110 Panchuk to the UCC and UCRF, 'Report #2 – Covering Period October 13 (Arrival in England) until the End of November,' 30 November 1946, Panchuk Collection.

111 See Panchuk's Canadian Pacific telegraph to the UCC, 14 October 1946, Panchuk Collection.

112 See Reverend Kushnir by Canadian National telegraph to Frolick, 15 October 1946, Frolick Collection. Panchuk was informed of the message to Frolick from Kushnir, also by Canadian National telegraph, the same day.

113 See Panchuk's notes, 'Meeting of the Relief Team,' 18 October 1946, and his telegram to the UCC, 19 October 1946. He cabled, 'Everything settled satisfactorily,' yet noted that the Bureau had only fifteen dollars on account and would require an immediate advance of three thousand dollars, Panchuk Collection.

114 Ibid.

115 Frolick to the UCRF and UUARC, 17 October 1946, Frolick Collection.

116 Ibid.

117 Ibid.

118 'Minutes of the Third Conference of Representatives of Ukrainian Relief Committees of Europe and North America, Held 30 October–3 November 1946 in Paris,' Frolick Collection.

119 Interviews with Frolick (n44 above). Frolick's anger is well captured in this excerpt from the letter dated 30 December 1946 (Frolick Collection), which he sent to Panchuk after returning to Canada: 'So that is how you keep your part of ... a gentleman's agreement? Just before I departed from London you thought of a way of gagging me and preventing me from telling the people over here a few facts which would serve as eye-openers, by making out that you have never done any wrong to me and do not intend to, that we should let by-gones be by-gones, bury the hatchet and be friends "for the good of the cause." What perfidity! [sic] No sooner did I return than you start your poisoned-dart-shooting, driving a knife into my back, in the form of your famous auditing report! A masterful bit of intrigue executed by an expert! You do not openly accuse anyone of embezzling Bureau funds, for you might get into trouble doing that, but make sure that the artfully concealed accusation sinks into every readers' mind, by the cunning use of the phrases such as "discrepancies," etc. Although, as you admit, the auditing is not complete; you cannot wait to

thrust home the dagger! You do all this well knowing that not a penny of the Bureau's money, to the best of our knowledge, was appropriated by either Kluchevsky, myself or any other of my assistants. On the contrary if not all then certainly most of my own money was spent in or for the Bureau, a fact of which I have no doubt you are well aware of.

'I just wanted to let you know two things. Firstly, that I am fully aware of your manipulations and reason behind it, and secondly, that although I haven't said anything yet, I might lose self-control and let out a few truthful facts – not fabricated lies and unsavory insinuations, but facts. I'm just bidding my time, waiting for your next move, probably your "final" report on the "auditing," and if it is the same mud-slinging device as the letter already received I shall have no alternative but to forget the gentleman's agreement of a truce broken by you already and tell the public what I know. Let there be no doubt – I know plenty and can reach the ear of the public.'

120 Zaharychuk to Panchuk, 18 October 1946, Panchuk Collection. The British were also aware of the UHVR's activities in England. See, for example, the letter of 16 October 1946 from 'Sviatoslav Boyarich,' whose letterhead identified him as a representative of the Secretariat-General for Foreign Affairs of the 'Supreme Ukrainian Liberation Council,' to British foreign secretary Bevin, and the enclosure, dated at Paris, 3 October 1946, from Mykola Lebed, the UHVR's secretary general of foreign affairs. 'Boyarich' listed his return address as the Royal Automobile Club in Pall Mall, which, perhaps coincidentally, seems to have been one of the preferred London clubs frequented by both Korostovets and Tracy Philipps. In forwarding the UHVR's communiqués on to Whitehall's J.P. Henniker, John Addis of the Prime Minister's Office indicated, 'I have not, of course, sent any acknowledgement.' See FO 371/56973.

121 UCC to Frolick, 18 October 1946, Frolick Collection.

122 See Panchuk's handwritten note, 23 November 1946, on the UCC's letter of dismissal to Frolick, dated 18 October 1946, in the Frolick Collection. Frolick, who had been away in Germany 'on vacation,' seems to have been unaware of his formal release from CURB's service for several weeks, even though Panchuk knew of the UCC's decision before he attended the Paris conference, on 30 October–3 November.

123 See Panchuk to the UCC, 20 October 1946, Panchuk Collection, in which he forwarded the purloined samples of UHVR letterhead. Panchuk recorded that there were a few hundred sheets of UHVR letterhead in Frolick's locked desk.

124 Writing to the UCC on 20 October 1946, Panchuk reminded Winnipeg that

on 19 October he had mailed them copies of three political tracts printed in the United Kingdom and mailed from the Bureau's address, which constituted further proof of Frolick's undercover activities; Panchuk Collection.

125 Panchuk to the UCC, 7 December 1946, Panchuk Collection. The enclosures were correspondence on 31 October 1946 between individuals with the code names 'Vil' (Ox) and 'Bureviy' (Stormbird) – Panchuk thought the latter was Petro Pihichyn, an AUGB member and editor of its newspaper *Nash klych* (*Our Watchword*); an undated letter from 'Ivan Bulka' (possibly, according to Panchuk's interpretation, a Ukrainian in the Polish armed forces); an undated letter to 'Petrus' concerning UPA war bonds Frolick was selling; the 2 October letter from 'Yuri' to an unidentified comrade, which discussed Panchuk's imminent return to England and his political views; another letter from 'Ivan Bulka,' dated 17 July 1946, to an unidentified comrade concerning the distribution of UPA war bonds (a reference in this letter to a 'Boris' suggested to Panchuk that a former CURB employee who had been responsible for the mail room, Boris Melnychuk, had been recruited by the Banderivtsi); another letter from 'Yuri' to his comrade, 2 October 1946, which enclosed two secret codes, a handwritten one to be used for correspondence between members of the Organization in England and a second, typewritten code, to be used exclusively by 'Yuri,' his comrade, and 'Vlodko' (Savinsky, whom Panchuk also identified as Shevchuk, a member of the Polish armed forces) when they corresponded with the OUNb's leadership on the Continent – this letter also identified Frolick's code name as 'Ulas'; and a letter from I. Kryvyj, editor of *Our Watchword* in Buenos Aires to Frolick, 15 November 1946, which criticized the schism in the OUN and blamed Bandera and his youthful followers for it; a letter from A. Holowaty of the Ukrainian Committee for Aid to Victims of War, an auxiliary of the Argentinean Red Cross, to Frolick in his capacity as general secretary for the UHVR, 18 November 1946 (Panchuk observed that Holowaty had infiltrated the Argentinean Red Cross and was using it for political purposes much like Frolick had used CURB. He also fulminated over the fact that Holowaty had addressed the envelope not to Frolick personally but to the Bureau, which suggested that Holowaty perceived CURB to be nothing more than a front for the OUNb). Panchuk sent another lengthy letter to Winnipeg, 17 December 1946, which he noted should be considered an addition to his letter of 7 December. In it he enclosed instructions sent out to members of the OUNb on 10 April 1946; a 4 April 1946 memorandum cautioning OUNb propagandists in the emigration about the need for protecting their

sources; a 10 September 1946 advisory about what items should be dealt with in reports prepared by the OUNb network for their leadership; directions about the objectives and content of propaganda work which must be carried out in April–May 1946; coding information; Report #1, 17 October 1946, by 'Bureviy,' which dealt with propaganda work, finances, external affairs, what was happening in London, and Panchuk's return from 'Zoya,' the code name for Canada. In this instruction Panchuk was characterized as being the representative of the *zoyivsko-malynovyj ostriv* (from 'Zoya's raspberry island'), the code name given to the Ukrainian Canadian community, and as a man who was 'unusually zealous' in his dedication to the Canadian government. As such Panchuk could also be described as a *chort* (devil), apparently the OUNb codeword for 'democrat.' Frolick was described as being subordinate to Panchuk, although it was suggested that he would not likely accept that status and would either return to Canada soon or else be sent to Turkey. It was also noted that the AUGB's executive had recently been asked by the British authorities whether they had contacts with Ukrainian revolutionary forces in the homeland or were sending literature into the DP camps. Subsequent enclosures contained correspondence between Roman Rakhmanny, director of the Ukrainian Press Service, and Pihychyn; additional correspondence between 'Vil' and 'Bureviy,' which tied them in with Frolick; more correspondence between 'Ivan Bulka' (whom Panchuk described as the courier among 'Vil,' 'Bureviy,' and Frolick); general correspondence between various individuals and Pihychyn, including letters from 'Yuri' and 'Hryc' (identified by Panchuk as Mr Hryhorii Drabat of the Polish armed forces); and an envelope of financial records and invoices which, Panchuk insisted, demonstrated how moneys supposedly gathered for the UPA were 'disappearing into the hands of the activists.'

126 See Datzkiw to Panchuk, 28 October 1946, Panchuk Collection.

127 In his 28 October letter to Panchuk, Datzkiw stated that the Fund's national executive was not pleased with Frolick's financial statement or with his letter of 17 October 1946. They had resolved that they would consider paying for his return to Canada, but only if he first satisfied them as to the Bureau's expenses during his tenure.

128 Datzkiw to Panchuk, 28 October 1946, Panchuk Collection.

129 See Panchuk's confidential letter to Kaye, 28 November 1946, Panchuk Collection.

130 Ibid.

131 Ibid.

132 Ibid. On the same day Kaye sent Panchuk a letter advising him to 'stress'

to the various refugee committees that they must concentrate attention on relief work and on resettlement and avoid 'the luxury of politics,' for 'everything they do is watched with a telescopic magnifying glass and is used against them.' See Kaye's letter to Panchuk, 28 November 1946, Panchuk Collection.

133 See 'Communiqué #1,' Co-ordinating Ukrainian Committee, 11 September 1946, Frolick Collection. M. Yurkevich, 'Ukrainian Nationalists and DP Politics,' in *The Refugee Experience*, ed. Isajiw, Boshyk, and Senkus, 125–43, provides a useful overview of the formation of the Co-ordinating Ukrainian Committee on 14 July 1946, and of its subsequent fragmentation, starting with the withdrawal of the Banderivtsi on 4 September 1946.

134 See Panchuk's confidential 'Report on Conference with British Foreign Office,' 18 November 1946, Panchuk Collection.

135 See Panchuk's confidential 'Report on Visit to War Office,' 22 November 1946, Panchuk Collection.

136 See Panchuk's confidential reports entitled 'Meeting with USA Embassy in London' and 'Report on Meeting with Mr. S.L. Ackard, American Red Cross Area Executive (UK),' both dated 18 November 1946, and his confidential 'Report on Meeting with the Friends Relief Service (Quakers) Great Britain,' 20 November 1946, Panchuk Collection.

137 See Panchuk's letter of 11 December 1946 and his report to the UCRF and UUARC regarding the meeting with Sir Herbert Emerson, 12 December 1946, Panchuk Collection. The former was marked 'No Part of the Information Given in This Letter Should Be Publicized or Used in the Press.'

138 Ibid.

139 Ibid.

140 See Panchuk's confidential 'Report on an Interview with Sir George Rendell, Deputy to Mr. Hector McNeil Who Handles Refugee Problems As Far As the British Government Is Concerned,' held at Canada House, London, 13 December 1946, Panchuk Collection. There is also Panchuk's letter to Sir George, 2 January 1947, in which he included a memorandum (dated 22 December 1946), 'The Work Lying before the Joint Canadian and American Relief Mission to Ukrainian Refugees, Displaced Persons and Victims of War in Western Europe' (FO 945/722). Panchuk noted that the Ukrainian relief organizations of North America had already bought two homes to be used as orphanages for Ukrainian children; had shipped 227 bales of used clothing and 3000 yards of new flannel cloth for newborn babies and small children on board the S.S. *Beaconsfield* (Cunard White Star Line) via Antwerp to Frankfurt, where the contents would be distributed in both the American and British zones, *'where the need is greatest'*; and had pur-

chased educational supplies for Ukrainian universities set up in Augsburg and Regensburg. He also noted that the UUARC intended to spend about $50,000 on 'Care' parcels for special cases; that the Ukrainian Relief Committee of Brazil had sent 54 cases of clothing aboard the S.S. *Stamford*, which were unloaded in London; that the UCRF had sent 9 large crates of school supplies for Ukrainian camp schools and universities in Germany; and that both the UCRF and UUARC had purchased over $20,000 worth of medical supplies through the International Red Cross at Geneva, intended for the Ukrainian refugee camps in Germany and Austria. Finally, Panchuk added that relief supplies were being sent through the 'Save the Children Fund' organization in London; that educational materials were being shipped to the Ukrainian SEP in Rimini via a Ukrainian Relief Committee in Vatican City; and the arrangements were being made through the British Red Cross to help a Ukrainian refugee camp in Northern Rhodesia, where an epidemic of malaria had broken out. Over and above the 'immediate problems of *concrete relief*,' however, Panchuk declared that the primary purpose 'of all of us' and 'the best solution of the entire problem of Refugees,' was '*immigration and resettlement*.'

141 Panchuk, 'Report on an Interview with Sir George Rendell, Deputy to Mr. Hector McNeil ...,' 13 December 1946, Panchuk Collection.

142 See L.Y. Luciuk and B.S. Kordan, 'The Anglo-American Powers and the Ukrainian National Question,' in *Anglo-American Perspectives on the Ukrainian Question*, ed. Luciuk and Kordan, 1–12, for an interpretation of the attitudes taken by these governments towards the Ukrainian independence movement. The text of the Atlantic Charter is reproduced in B.S. Kordan, 'Ethnicity, the State, and War: Canada and the Ukrainian Problem, 1939–1945: A Study in Statecraft,' Ph.D. thesis, Arizona State University, 1988, 287.

143 See Holmes's report 'Ukrainian Refugees in Europe,' 13 December 1946, DEA 6980-GR-40. Panchuk expressed the opinion that Robertson, then acting as high commissioner for Canada in London, had 'warmed considerably' to the principle of helping refugees, and particularly Ukrainians, largely as a result of his conversations with Sir George Rendel. Supposedly, Rendel had earlier taken a positive attitude towards the Ukrainian Canadian relief mission. See Panchuk's confidential 'Report on Meeting with Mr. Norman Robertson, High Commissioner of Canada, Canada House' to the UCRF, 4 December 1946, Panchuk Collection.

144 Panchuk to Mr Moore, DP/PW Section of the Allied Control Commission for Germany (British Element), London, 6 December 1946, Panchuk Collection.

145 For example, Panchuk reported that on 27 November 1946 he had a meeting with a Mr Gurton, who represented the Canadian National Railways
Company, in London. Gurton explained that the CNR was 'vitally interested' in colonization and an immigration of DPs, and that it was 'only
waiting for the Government (of Canada) to open the gates.' See Panchuk's
'Report on Interview with Mr. Gurton, European Commissioner, Department of Colonization and Agriculture, Canadian National Railways (London),' to the UCRF, 27 November 1946, Panchuk Collection. The Dome
mining company of Canada was similarly interested in an immigration of
semi-skilled labourers. See George Lambert's letter to H. McNeil, 5 December 1946, FO 371/56572. As well, the Canadian Metal Mining Association
felt that '2,300 men could be absorbed at once' since they would not be taking jobs wanted by Canadian workers.

Chapter 6: 'The Least Inspiring of Postwar Problems'

1 See, by way of example, Documents #37 (July 1943?) and #39 (8 August
1944) in *A Delicate and Difficult Question*, ed. Kordan and Luciuk, 111–13 and
116–31, in which, respectively, the RCMP and the OSS, the forerunner of the
CIA, report on the first UCC congress and Ukrainian Canadian affairs in
general. For a finding aid to the British materials, see J.V. Koshiw, *British
Foreign Office Files on Ukraine and Ukrainians, 1917–1948* (Edmonton, 1997).
2 See the minutes to the file 'Ukrainian Troubles in Poland,' 21 November
1930, FO 371/14827.
3 See Sir W. Erskine to Mr A. Henderson, 'Ukrainian Troubles in Poland,'
24 November 1930, FO 371/14827.
4 See Mr Voight's 26 November 1930 letter to Commander Kenworthy in
'Polish Atrocities in Eastern Galicia,' FO 371/14828.
5 Frank Savery's minutes to the file 'Polish Atrocities in Eastern Galicia,'
29 November 1930, FO 371/14828. See also a minute penned on 3 December 1930 in 'Affairs in Eastern Galicia,' initialled 'HAD,' which notes, 'I am
rather sorry that Mr. Savery practically expressed applause of the 'pacifica-
tory action' to a Polish official. I fear that his bias is growing rather danger-
ously.'
6 A copy of V.J. Kushnir's *Polish Atrocities in the West Ukraine: An Appeal to the
League for the Rights of Man and the Citizen* (Vienna, 1931) is found in FO
371/21807, 1931. Ukrainian Canadian protests against 'Polish terrorism' in
Eastern Galicia, and appeals for British intervention, were received frequently in Whitehall. See, for example, the file entitled 'Ukrainian Troubles
in Poland,' which includes a telegram to the prime minister from the

Ukrainian People's Home of Fort William and a protest resolution from the USRL, in Winnipeg, 27 October 1930. That they were addressed to the British prime minister caused consternation within the British bureaucracy as the Foreign and Dominion offices tried to sort out who should reply to 'communications regarding foreign affairs from British subjects in any part of the Empire.' The matter was resolved, at least in so far as replying was concerned, on 3 November 1930, when Laurence Collier decided: 'These are Canadians, but I suppose we should ignore them, like [we ignored] the American Ukrainians.' See 'Ukrainian Troubles in Poland,' FO 371/14827. This is not to say that the British ignored developments in Western Ukraine. For evidence of British appreciation of the strength of the nationalist movement there, see the dispatches of 8 and 15 September 1930 from P.M. Broadmead to A. Henderson at the Foreign Office, found in 'Political Arrests of Ukrainians,' FO 317/14827. In the first, Broadmead reported that the activities of the 'Ukrainian terrorist organization had reached such a pitch that drastic action had to be taken by the authorities responsible for the peace and protection of the country.' In the second, he estimated that sabotage and arson had caused about 150,000 pounds sterling worth of damages. See also 'Ukrainian Unrest in Poland,' 6 October 1930, FO 371/14827. By the end of the decade British frustration with Ukrainian protests had reached the breaking point. As R.L. Speaight minuted, 'Ukrainian propaganda would be more effective if less long winded.' See 'Ukrainians in Poland,' 17 May 1938, FO 371/23138.

7 See the report by E. Lachowitch entitled 'Political Differentiation in Ukraine,' 6 July 1934, FO 371/18321. In his narrative, Lachowitch provided the British with a statement of the principles of the OUN and correctly located its core in Galicia, the 'Piedmont' of Ukrainian nationalism.

8 See FO 371/17793 for two dispatches from Sir W. Erskine of the British embassy in Warsaw, one of them dealing with UNDO's condemnation of the OUN (31 July 1934), the other with conciliatory attempts made by the Polish authorities with respect to creating a Ukrainian agricultural college (17 October 1934).

9 See 'Anti-Polish Activities of Ukrainian Nationalists Abroad,' 9 March 1936, FO 371/19962.

10 Ibid.

11 See 'Position of the Ukraine in the International Situation,' 17 November 1938, FO 371/22295.

12 Ibid.

13 Ibid.

14 See 'German Aspirations in the Ukraine,' for the remarks of the Central

Department to the British embassy in Warsaw, 8 December 1938, in FO 371/
21676. Sir G. Ogilvie-Forbes wrote to Lord Halifax on 23 November that the
British military attaché at the Berlin embassy, a Colonel MacFarlane, had
told him that his Polish counterparts were very worried about a German
drive towards the Dnieper River. As for Carpatho-Ukraine, that was not an
issue, the Poles felt, given their assessment that the population there were
little better than 'ignorant Indians.' Still, he wrote, the question of Ukraine's
status 'is being much canvassed in Nazi circles at the moment and it is even
said that the problem will have to be tackled next year.' Understandably,
that worried both the British and the Poles.

15 See the letter from W. Reiss to Chamberlain, 7 December 1938, FO 371/
21676.

16 See General Mannerheim's remarks, as reported by Collier of the Northern
Department, 15 December 1938, FO 371/21676.

17 See Sullivant, 'The Problem of Eastern Galicia.' For a Polish view, see M.
Felinski, *The Ukrainians in Poland* (London, 1931). A contrary Ukrainian
interpretation is provided by S. Horak, *Poland and Her National Minorities,
1919–1939* (New York, 1961). When Rhys Davis, MP, rose in the British Parliament on 14 June 1939 to ask the prime minister whether, 'in view of the
need for a settlement of the Ukrainian question in Poland,' His Majesty's
Government still regarded itself as committed to the principle laid down at
the Council of Ambassadors in 1923, namely, that the ethnographic conditions of Eastern Galicia necessitated an autonomous regime, he set off a
flurry of inter- and intra-departmental minutes in the Foreign Office. R.L.
Speaight minuted, on 14 June, that 'the best line' in answering Davis would
be to say that 'we regard the present moment inopportune for raising the
Ukrainian question.' His first version of that sentence, crossed out, read 'we
regard the question as one which is primarily for the Poles themselves to
settle.' A Mr I. Kirkpatrick commented, on 16 June, that 'Mr. Rhys Davis is
forcing us to tell the truth – unpalatable to Poland and worse still of use to
the Germans engaged in trying to disrupt Poland and force the Ukrainians
under the Nazi jackboot. If it were pointed out to Mr. Davis that he is asking us to abet German aims – without in any way doing a service to his
Ukrainian friends – perhaps he would allow his question to lapse.' A Mr
Channon did speak to Davis, who then did let the matter drop. 'Well done,'
minuted a colleague.

18 See 'Situation in Ukrainian Provinces of Poland,' 17 December 1938, FO
371/21810. The Poles also protested against Carpatho-Ukrainian agitation
to the Czech government, although the British doubted whether the government in Prague had much effective control over its Carpatho-Ruthenian

lands. Poland's foreign minister Beck specifically charged that Ukrainian 'terrorists' were occupying important official posts in Ruthenia (see FO 371/21810, 23 December 1938). A British officer, Major M. Moss, subsequently spent two months in the area and concluded that reports of German activity were 'greatly exaggerated.' He added that while the government of Father Voloshyn, 'an elderly pedant,' might be interested in the idea of a 'Greater Ukraine,' the 'mostly illiterate' peasant population had 'not the slightest interest' in this issue (FO 371/22893, 30 January 1939). After German forces occupied Prague and dismembered Czechoslovakia, in March 1939, Hungarian troops occupied Carpatho-Ukraine. Armed opposition to the Hungarian invaders broke out, with indigenous resistance forces strengthened by OUN members who had earlier slipped into the Carpatho-Ukrainian republic from Galicia. Their defeat, and Hitler's acquiescence to the Hungarian invasion, paid dividends for the Germans, since Poland, the Soviet Union, and Hungary were all against the existence of even a tiny independent Ukrainian state. At the same time, however, many Ukrainian nationalists learned a rough lesson about German duplicity. They were fated to learn even more of the same kind of lesson, although the British consul in Lviv reported that despite 'being bitterly disappointed' many Western Ukrainians remained convinced that 'Hitler will yet prove to be their liberator.' The Ukrainians were further encouraged in this hope by daily Ukrainian-language wireless broadcasts transmitted from Vienna. For their part, the Polish authorities were responding with 'active measures of repression.' See the report of the British vice consul in Lviv, 'Ukrainians in Poland,' 13 April 1939, FO 371/23138. In the weeks immediately after the end of the Second World War, Carpatho-Ukraine was plunged into 'chaos and terror.' The territory was made 'part of Ukraine' by an agreement signed between the governments of Czechoslovakia and the USSR, in Moscow on 29 June 1945. With respect to this agreement, His Magesty's Government 'has not expressed either approval or disapproval of its terms.' NKVD massacres of the population of Carpatho-Ukraine are described in this same file. See the letter from the British embassy in Prague to W.D. Allen, 27 September 1946, FO 371/56738. The letter appealed to the British to uphold their commitment to the Atlantic Charter and to undo the wrongs being done to the Ruthenian people by the Soviet annexation of their lands. For a study of prewar Polish activities in this region, see R.A. Woytak, *On the Border of War and Peace: Polish Intelligence and Diplomacy in 1937–1939 and the Origins of the Ultra Secret* (New York, 1979). A Ukrainian perspective is presented by P.G. Stercho, *Diplomacy of Double Morality: Europe's Crossroads in Carpatho-Ukraine, 1919–1939* (New York, 1971), while a more general and balanced account is found in P.R. Magocsi, *The Shaping of a National Identity: Subcarpathian Rus,' 1848–1948* (Cambridge, 1978).

19 See Sir H. Kennard's letter from the British embassy in Warsaw to Lord Halifax, 'Situation in the Ukrainian Provinces of Poland,' 14 December 1938, FO 371/21810.

20 Ibid.

21 See the minutes on 'Situation in the Ukrainian Provinces of Poland,' FO 371/21810.

22 See Mr Watson's 'Report on Tour of Non-Soviet Ukraine Made in June and July, 1939,' FO 371/23056.

23 Ibid.

24 Extracts from a report on the 'Ukrainian problem,' 6 July 1939, FO 371/23138. This British observer had 'only 3 days ago' been in the 'Polish Ukraine.'

25 Ibid.

26 See Collier's 19 January 1939 minutes on the file entitled 'Ukrainian Question,' FO 371/22461. The 'vacuum' Eastern Ukrainians had lived in under Soviet rule was actually terror-filled. Some of the mass graves of Stalin's victims began to be uncovered in Ukraine in the late 1980s and early 1990s. See, for example, 'Pit Grave Unearthed in Ukraine,' *Winnipeg Free Press*, 2 March 1989, 1, 4, which reports on the presence of between two and three hundred thousand bodies in a mass grave near Bykivnia, Ukraine. Three earlier Soviet commissions of inquiry attempted to describe this killing field as a Nazi atrocity, despite eyewitnesses who testified that all the bodies were buried between 1936 and the week prior to the 22 June 1941 invasion of the Soviet Union by Nazi Germany. Finally, on 24 March 1989, a fourth commission concluded that the victims were murdered in the time of Stalin. See 'Stalin Cited for Killing Thousands,' *Globe and Mail*, 25 March 1989, 1, 2. The revival of historical memory in Ukraine did much to propel the emergence of the broadly based national movement known as the Rukh (Movement) and of the Ukrainian Voluntary Historical and Educational Society, known as *Memorial*, which dedicated itself to uncovering Soviet crimes against humanity and war crimes. For documentary information on these groups, see *Memorial*, comp. L.Y. Luciuk and A. Chyczij (Kingston, 1989). See also Scott Shane, *Dismantling Utopia: How Information Ended the Soviet Union* (Chicago, 1994), and Adam Hochschild, *The Unquiet Ghost: Russians Remember Stalin* (New York, 1994).

27 See the 10 January 1939 letter from the British embassy in Warsaw to the Right Honourable Viscount Halifax in a file labelled 'Ukrainian Question,' FO 371/22461.

28 See the 'most secret' comments, dated 14 January 1939, 'Ukrainian Question,' FO 371/22461. At this time, the British still felt that if a German attack against the Soviet Union was launched from Rumanian territory, the Poles would probably remain neutral, although if sufficient inducements or pressure was exerted, the Poles might even join in.

29 This view was commonly held by many displaced persons. For example, in *The Free Press of the Suppressed Nations* (Augsburg, 1950), 14, R. Ilnytskyj wrote: 'The goals of World War II were not realized. Only the brown half of totalitarianism had been defeated, whereas the red half remains even more triumphant than ever.' Earlier, Lev Orlyhora, in a pamphlet entitled *Pro bolshevystskyi fashyzm* [On Bolshevik Fascism] (Nuremberg, 1946), argued that the Soviet system represented a 'new fascism.' It was the particular historical mission of the Ukrainian nation, he argued, to issue in a 'new era' by hastening the downfall of the Soviet system. See *Political Writings of Post–World War Two Ukrainian Emigrés: Annotated Bibliography and Guide to Research*, ed. W.R. Petryshyn and N. Chomiak (Edmonton, 1984), 251.

30 See the letter from G. Vereker of the British embassy in Moscow to Collier of the Northern Department in 'Situation in the Ukraine,' 24 December 1938, FO 371/23677. This letter has been reproduced as Document #4 in *Anglo-American Perspectives on the Ukrainian Question*, ed. Luciuk and Kordan, 32–3.

31 Ibid. According to Rapoport, *Stalin's War against the Jews*, 17, Litvinov was once described by Lenin as possessing the 'virtues of a clever and adroit Jew.'

32 Ibid.

33 See Document #5, 10 January 1939, in *Anglo-American Perspectives on the Ukrainian Question*, ed. Luciuk and Kordan, 34–42.

34 See Document #7, 2 February 1939, ibid., 45–50.

35 According to FO 371/56889, dated 29 October 1945, a postwar British analysis of captured German documents revealed that the first steps toward the negotiation of a non-aggression pact between Nazi Germany and the Soviet Union came from the Soviet side. The UIS referred to this pact in its postwar bulletins, implying that if Nazi foreign minister Ribbentrop had to stand before the Nuremberg court and face judgment, so too should Soviet foreign minister Molotov. See the (undated) UIS bulletin 'The Ribbentrop-Molotov Partnership,' Panchuk Collection.

36 On population transfers and movements during the Second World War, see E.M. Kulischer, *Europe on the Move: War and Population Changes, 1917–1947* (New York, 1948), and his *Displacement of Population in Europe* (Montreal, 1943). Good overviews of refugee problems in this century are provided by

M.J. Proudfoot, *European Refugees, 1939–1952: A Study in Forced Population Movement* (London, 1957), and M.R. Marrus, *The Unwanted: European Refugees in the Twentieth Century* (New York, 1985). See also 'The Political Aspects of the Soviet Occupation of Poland,' published by the Polish Ministry of Information, London, 1 February 1941, a copy of which is in DEA 266-40. In DEA 266-40-C there is a confidential memorandum, dated December 1943, entitled 'Soviet Deportation of the Inhabitants of Eastern Poland in 1939–1945.' The report did not aim 'to contribute to any further dispute in the camps of the United Nations,' since 'it is in the interest both of Poland and the Soviet Union to re-establish friendly relations.' Nevertheless, its author felt that it was 'advisable that a few persons, especially selected for this purpose,' be informed of the fate of Polish citizens under Soviet rule, in order to ensure that no 'misunderstandings' arise in the future and perhaps to prevent a repetition of the 'regrettable events' which took place in Eastern Poland in 1939–45. This report detailed conditions of life in this occupied territory and described at length the 'four great waves' of deportations which took place in February, April, and June 1940 and in June 1941. Over a million people were involved, about half of whom were women and children. By nationality, approximately 52 per cent were Poles, 30 per cent Jews, and between 18 and 20 per cent Ukrainians and Belarussians (Byelorussians or White Ruthenians). These deportees were sent to Soviet concentration camps, resettled in empty villages throughout Central Russia, or sent to Kazakhstan, the Yakutsk region, and elsewhere, mainly to work on collective farms. After 30 June 1941, when an agreement was signed between the Polish and the Soviet governments in London, a 'great south-bound trek' took place as this 'mass of Polish citizens' sought out Polish government representatives and helped organize a new Polish army. When the trek ended, it became clear that only about half of those originally deported could be accounted for. Of the remainder, an estimated two hundred thousand men, women, and children had perished.

37 See the 'most immediate' telegram, #286, from Sir W. Seeds, 17 September 1939, FO 371/23103. It contained a translation of a note by Molotov which, Seeds noted, had 'just [been] delivered at the Embassy.' Sent at 12:40 p.m., Seeds's telegram was received in London at 2:00 p.m.

38 See telegram #289, 17 September 1939, FO 371/23107. It was received in Whitehall at 11:50 p.m.

39 See War Cabinet, 'Conclusions,' 18 September 1939, FO 371/23107.

40 See Collier's minutes on FO 371/23138, 20 October 1939, reproduced as Document #9 in *Anglo-American Perspectives on the Ukrainian Question*, ed. Luciuk and Kordan, 66–7.

41 See R.K. Leeper's letter to Mr Makins in a file entitled 'Ukrainian Problem,' 20 October 1939, FO 371/23138, reproduced as Document #9 in *Anglo-American Perspectives,* ed. Luciuk and Kordan, 64–5.

42 See the memorandum regarding a conversation between J.H. Watson and E.S. Carlton, 22 January 1940, FO 371/24473, reproduced as Document #11 in *Anglo-American Perspectives,* ed. Luciuk and Kordan, 70–2.

43 Ibid.

44 Ibid., See R.M.A. Hankey's minutes on this file, reproduced in *Anglo-American Perspectives on the Ukrainian Question,* ed. Luciuk and Kordan, 72–3.

45 Ibid.

46 Ibid. See Mr Watson's comment, reproduced as Document #11 in *Anglo-American Perspectives on the Ukrainian Question,* ed. Luciuk and Kordan, 71.

47 These statistics are taken from an UNRRA European Regional Office paper, 'Economic Rehabilitation of Ukraine,' dated April 1947, preserved at the Hoover Institution on War, Revolution and Peace archives. Edgar Snow, in 'The Ukraine Pays the Bill,' *Saturday Evening Post* (27 January 1945), concluded that the Second World War had 'in all truth and in many costly ways, been first of all a Ukrainian war ... No single European country suffered deeper wounds to its cities, its industries, its farmlands and its humanity.' I am grateful to Professor Norman A. Davies for providing me with a manuscript copy of his booklet *Cataclysm: The Second World War in Eastern Europe, 1939–1945,* which also deals with this issue.

48 For a recent estimate of Ukraine's population losses, see Taras Hunczak, 'The Ukrainian Losses during World War II,' in *A Mosaic of Victims: Non-Jews Persecuted and Murdered by the Nazis,* ed. Michael Berenbaum (New York, 1990), 116–27, and Luciuk, 'Ukraine,' in *The Oxford Companion,* ed. Dear and Foot, 1159–65. Nazi designs for eastern Europe are exposed in a secret memorandum 'Considerations Regarding the Treatment of Foreign Ethnical Groups in the East,' signed by Heinrich Himmler on 15 May 1940 and forwarded to Hitler. In part it reads: 'In handling the foreign ethnical groups in the East we must pay heed to recognize and to show attention to as many searate peoples as possible. Thus, next to the Poles and Jews, the Ukrainians, the White Russians, the Gorelians, Lemkians and Kashubians should be considered. If any other fragmentary national group can be found, we must recognize it as well. I want to state thereby that we must have great concern not to unite the people of the East, but to dissect them into as many parts and splinters as possible. Also within the ethnical groups, it is not our endeavor to lead them to unity and to greatness, perhaps even to instil national consciousness into them, and a national culture. We must dissolve them into innumerable small fragments and atoms ... Only by dissolving

this whole stew of people in the Government General, numbering some 15 million inhabitants, and likewise the 8 million of the Eastern provinces, will we succeed in carrying through the racial selection, which must remain the foundation for our plans. We will shift the racially valuable elements out of this stew and send them to Germany, there to assimilate them ... In 4 to 5 years I believe the notion of the Kashubians must have become unknown. There will be no more Kashubian people (this also applies to the West Prussians). The notion of there being a Jewry, I hope to see disappear, by virtue of a mass emigration of all Jews to Africa or into some colony. It must also be possible within a somewhat longer stretch of time, to bring about the disappearance of the ethnical concepts of the Ukrainians, Gorelians, and Lemkians ... The non-German population of the East will have no higher education beyond the four years of grade school. The aim of this grade school will be: Simple calculus up to 500, writing of the name, the knowledge that is a divine commandment to show obedience to the German, honesty, hard work and good behaviour. Reading I consider superfluous. Outside of this school there will be no other schools in the East. Parents who plan on giving their children a better schooling ... must make an application ... [It] will mainly be judged on the grounds of the racial purity of the child, and its measuring up to our standard. If we recognize such a child as being of our blood, the parents will be told that the child is sent to school in Germany, and will remain there for the duration. Cruel and tragic as such cases may be, this method will prove the mildest and the best, if our innermost belief rejects as un-Germanic and impossible the Bolshevist method of physically exterminating a nation ... I esteem it as an obvious necessity (logically as well as emotionally) that the children and their parents should not be treated as lepers, in the schools or in public life, when they move to Germany. After having changed their name, they should be fitted organically into Germany society ... Swear words such as "Polacke" or "Ukrainer" or the like must disappear ... By firmly applying these measures during the coming 10 years, the population of the Government General will be composed only of the remaining second-rate population ... available as leaderless labour'; excerpted from the U.S. 3d Army IPW Reports, August 1944–May 1945, U.S. National Archives. I am grateful to Dr Leonard Leshuk for calling this document to my attention.

49 See FO 371/66354, 4 January 1947.
50 P. Wright, author of *Spycatcher: The Candid Autobiography of a Senior Intelligence Officer* (Toronto, 1987), discovered two microphones concealed in the plaster of the ceiling in the cipher room of the British embassy in Moscow. Since there were two clerks handling embassy one-time pad communica-

tions, one reading the clear text while the other enciphered messages, the Soviets were likely privy to British thinking on issues like the 'Ukrainian Question' throughout the war and afterwards, or at least from 1942 on, when the embassy staff who had temporarily been relocated to Kuibyshev were returned to Moscow. See also FO 371/43315, 12 May 1944. British officials in Moscow let Whitehall know that any telegrams concerning the Ukrainian separatist movement had better be sent in cypher 'lest our interest is misunderstood.' They also pointed out that the delicacy of the issues involved made raising questions with their Soviet counterparts about Ukrainian irredentism difficult, which further circumscribed what little they could find out.

51 See Document #10, 6 November 1939, in *Anglo-American Perspectives on the Ukrainian Question*, ed. Luciuk and Kordan, 68–9. For other opinions about Savery, see Collier's remarks in Document #9, 20 October 1939, 67.

52 See Savery, British embassy to Poland at Angers, to Hankey of the British legation in Bucharest, 25 April 1940, FO 371/24473.

53 This document, 'The Polish Territory Occupied by the Soviets,' published by the Information Department of the Polish Government (Angers–Paris) is found in the Hoover Institution on War, Revolution and Peace archives.

54 Ibid., 12.

55 See 'The Ukraine, with Particular Reference to the Polish Ukrainian Problem,' by S.E. Carlton, 5 March 1940, and Savery's comments addressed to Hankey, 8 April 1940, FO 371/24473.

56 See the file entitled 'German Occupied Poland,' particularly the notes dealing with the Ukrainian movement, 22 July 1940, WO 208/1734. See also WO 208/1734, 24 July 1940, which suggests that the Polish government might have been willing to seek an accommodation with the Soviets by renouncing Polish interests in Ukrainian territories and agreeing that those lands would thereafter fall into the Russian sphere of interest.

57 See B.H. Sumner to Major E.R. Sword at the War Office, 30 July 1940, FO 371/24473.

58 FO 371/24473, 10 October 1940. See also the 13 October 1940 issue of *Narodne slovo* (*National Word*), published in Pittsburgh, Pennsylvania.

59 See secret 'Notes on German Support of Ukrainian Nationalists,' 5 August 1940, WO 308/1734.

60 Hankey of the British legation in Bucharest to Viscount Halifax, 5 August 1940, FO 371/24473.

61 'The Polish Territory Occupied by the Soviets' (see n53 above).

62 Ibid.

63 Ibid.

64 See the covering letter from Savery in London to F.K. Roberts, 6 May 1941, FO 371/29480.

65 See the secret report prepared by the British representative with the provisional Czechoslovak government to Sir Orme Sargent, 8 May 1941, FO 371/29532.

66 See FO 371/29840, 6 May 1941. The British Foreign Office had earlier indications of a split within the OUN. In FO 371/24473 there is a copy of an article published on 26 September 1940 in the Left-wing Ukrainian-language newspaper *Narodna volia* (*National Will*) of Scranton, Pennsylvania, entitled 'Revolution in a Dirty Puddle,' which explained the factionalism of the nationalist movement as a struggle between the 'young leaders' and the 'Old Guard' headed by Colonel A. Melnyk. Despite the partial tone of this newspaper, there were some within Whitehall who felt no hesitation about using this opportunity to comment on Ukrainian nationalism, referring to an alleged 'gradual Nazification of the OUN.' The *National Will* article was based on a story which appeared originally in *Ukrainian Voice*, from Winnipeg, 18 September 1940.

67 The best general study of the Ukrainian nationalist movement during the Second World War period remains J.A. Armstrong, *Ukrainian Nationalism*, 3d rev. ed (Englewood, Colorado, 1990).

68 On the Ukrainian experience during the war, see *Ukraine during World War II: History and Its Aftermath*, ed. Y. Boshyk.

69 On the OUN/UPA/UHVR, see chapter 4 in Y. Bilinsky, *The Second Soviet Republic: The Ukraine after World War II* (New Brunswick, N.J., 1964), and Y.T. Krohmaliuk, *UPA Warfare in Ukraine* (New York, 1972). A declaration entitled 'What Is the UPA Fighting For?' briefly explains the UPA's program. The establishment of an independent Ukrainian state with a just social system, free of Bolshevik commissars and capitalists, was stated as being the movement's principal goal. The UPA also proclaimed that it was fighting for the right of all nations to have their own independent states. More specifically, the Ukrainian insurgents said they were engaged in an armed struggle with Russian and German imperialism on behalf of the occupied Ukrainian nation. Their manifesto reaffirmed the cardinal tenet of the OUN as being the struggle for a sovereign and independent Ukrainian state, a position forcefully restated at the Third Extraordinary Congress of the OUN, held 21–5 August 1943. This declaration is reproduced in *Litopys UPA: Volyn' and Polissya: German Occupation: Book 2* (Toronto, 1978), 83–4. Significantly, the political and military wings of the Ukrainian revolutionary liberation movement were merged into one at this Extraordinary Congress, when Roman Shukhevych succeeded Mykola Lebed, becoming

commander-in-chief of the UPA (*nom de guerre*, 'Taras Chuprynka'). For the reminiscences of a female member of the OUNb, arrested by the Nazis on 11 December 1943 and sent to the Ravensbrück concentration camp, see the interview with O. Eliashevsky, the aunt of S.W. Frolick (28 April 1982, MHSO). Mrs Eliashevsky was arrested because she 'belonged to an Organization which is trying to undermine the German Reich,' that is, the OUN. Several of her friends killed themselves rather than fall into the hands of the Gestapo. As for conditions in Ravensbrück, where women were made the subjects of Nazi medical experiments, Eliashevksy recalled that 'one of the most horrible things was waking up in the morning and seeing the bodies of people who had flung themselves onto the electrified barbed wire fence surrounding the camps – people who just gave up and killed themselves, burned themselves to death to escape the camp ... You weren't a person there, you were a number. I wore a red triangle, the mark of a political prisoner, and a number.' Another account by a Ukrainian woman political prisoner is provided by S. Stepaniuk, arrested on 16 July 1943 by the Gestapo. Interned in Rivno prison, in cell #45, she and 49 other women (approximately 30 Ukrainians, 17 Jews, and several Poles) were systematically brutalized. She details the torture and execution of Dr Kharytia Kononenko, an activist with the Ukrainian Red Cross, on 15 October 1943, and the murder of most of her cellmates. See her account, in *Litopys UPA: Volyn' and Polissya: German Occupation: Book 3* (Toronto, 1984), 223–52. For another Ukrainian concentration camp survivor's testimony on Buchenwald, see the interview with M. Gawa (Toronto, 10 February 1982, MHSO). Some idea of the numbers of Ukrainians involved in this anti-Nazi and anti-Soviet resistance movement are suggested in R. Conquest's *The Harvest of Sorrow: Soviet Collectivization and the Terror-Famine* (London, 1986), 334, where remarks made by Kutsevol, a Communist Party of the Soviet Union first secretary in Lviv, are noted. Kutsevol reported that since 1956, fifty-five thousand members of the OUN had returned to Lviv province alone, having survived the sentences imposed on them. Then too Nikita Khrushchev, remarking on Stalin's deportation of the Crimean Tatars and other smaller nationalities during 1943–5, said that Stalin had wanted to do the same to the Ukrainians, 'but there were too many of them.' Michael Scammell's *Solzhenitsyn: A Biography* (London, 1984) contains several references to the postwar fate of these Ukrainian nationalists in the Gulag Archipelago. According to Solzhenitsyn, the disciplined Banderivtsi not only protected their fellow political prisoners against the depredations of criminal elements in the camps and against their Soviet jailers, but also played a significant role in various uprisings within the gulag, like that at Norilsk in

1953. On this revolt, see D. Shumuk, *Life Sentence: Memoirs of a Ukrainian Political Prisoner* (Edmonton, 1984).

70 See D.V. Kelly to W. Strang, 22 October 1941, in 'Suggested Creation in Canada of Ukrainian Political Centre,' FO 371/26721. Some British observers had a different and more sympathetic view. For his part, Philipps recognized that for Ukrainians throughout the world, this was 'the most momentous moment of their history,' although he also believed that Hitler was now in a position to offer the Ukrainian nation 'the dearest object of a peoples' mystic dreams,' namely, a state of their own. See Philipps to Judge Davis, 28 June 1941, in NAC MG30 E350.

71 For examples of Koch's policies and attitudes towards the Ukrainians, see 'Erich Koch on the Economic Exploitation of Ukraine,' 26–8 August 1942, and 'Memorandum from Erich Koch to Alfred Rosenberg on Harsh Measures Adopted in Ukraine by the German Administration,' 16 March 1943, 180–2, reprinted in *Ukraine during World War II*, ed. Boshyk, and D. Marples, 'The Ukraine in World War II,' *Radio Liberty Research Bulletin*, RL Supplement 1/85 (Munich, 1985). Koch was never brought to trial for war crimes committed in Ukraine. He died in Polish custody in 1987.

72 See the confidential report 'The German Administrative Organization in the Ukraine,' prepared by the Ministry of Economic Warfare (Russian Section), August 1943, FO 371/36974, and the Research Department's 'The Dismemberment of Poland: German Intentions,' 4 October 1943, FO 181/978. Commenting on why Western Ukraine (Eastern Galicia) had not been incorporated into the Reichskommissariat Ukraine, the British observed: 'It might have seemed more logical for the Germans to incorporate the southeastern Vovoidships of Tarnopol, Stanislawow and Lwow east of the San, which have a considerable Ukrainian majority in the New Reich Commissariat for the Ukraine, rather than to attach them ... to the General Government. The considerations prompting this choice were probably the wish to avoid any possibility of a strong Pan-Ukrainian Nationalist movement, the advantage of having a large and relatively friendly Ukrainian minority in the General Government as a counterpoise to the hostile Poles, the economic importance of the Galician oil fields and finally, regard for the historical fact that these provinces had before 1914 formed part of the Austro-Hungarian Empire.'

73 Cited by Krawchenko, *Social Change and National Consciousness in Twentieth Century Ukraine*, 162, 167.

74 See Reitlinger, *The House Built on Sand*, 183.

75 See Dallin, *German Rule in Russia*, 426–7.

76 See Krawchenko, *Social Change and National Consciousness in Twentieth Cen-*

tury Ukraine, 166. For a contemporary statement on Nazi occupation policies in Ukraine, see Joachim Joesten, 'Hitler's Fiasco in the Ukraine,' *Foreign Affairs* 21:2 (1943). Joesten noted that 'whole generations of Germans' had been 'brought up to think of conquest of the Ukraine as offering the surest road to a more abundant German life.' After describing the economic exploitation, colonization policies, and political subjugation which the Nazi regime had imposed on the Ukrainians, Joesten concluded that it was 'small wonder that the Ukrainian nation, even that part of it which has the bitter taste of the Bolshevik regime still in its mouth, shows little eagerness to co-operate with Herr Koch. One need not be a prophet to forecast that the kind of slave state which Hitler has set up in the Ukraine will never work.'

77 On the *Ostarbeiter,* see U. Herbert, *Hitler's Foreign Workers: Enforced Foreign Labour in Germany under the Third Reich* (Cambridge, 1997). The postwar repatriation experience suffered by many Ukrainian, Russian, and other east European slave labourers is treated in F.N. Smith, 'The American Role in the Repatriation of Certain Soviet Citizens, Forcible and Otherwise, to the USSR Following World War II,' Ph.D. thesis, Georgetown University, 1970; P.J. Huxley-Blythe, *The East Came West* (Caldwell, Idaho, 1968); N. Bethell, *The Last Secret: Forcible Repatriation to Russia, 1944–47* (London, 1974); and N. Tolstoy, *Victims of Yalta* (Toronto, 1977).

78 Reitlinger, *The House Built on Sand,* 273.

79 Ibid., 271.

80 See Kamenetsky, *Hitler's Occupation of Ukraine,* and B. Wytwycky, *The Other Holocaust.*

81 See the secret, interim report of the Political Warfare Executive, 'Propaganda Bearing on Germany's Manpower Crisis,' 1942, FO 898/3HO. The British knew that as many as 2.5 million slave and foreign labourers had been brought into the Third Reich. According to a report in this same file, between 15,000 to 20,000 were being brought in from Ukraine on a daily basis. The author's mother was one of them.

82 See J.W. Rusell to the Northern Department, 11 August 1943, FO 181/979. On the Vlasov movement, see W. Strik-Strikfeldt, *Against Stalin and Hitler: Memoir of the Russian Liberation Movement, 1941–1945* (London, 1970), and C. Andreyev, *Vlasov and the Russian Liberation Army: Soviet Reality and Emigré Theories* (Cambridge, 1987).

83 See the 'most secret' report entitled 'Employment of Russian Nationals in France,' 21 February 1944, FO 371/43382. Further evidence about Soviet POWs used by the Germans in France in anti-resistance units is found in a top secret file, 'Employment of Russian Prisoners in France by German Armed Forces,' 7 July 1944, FO 371/43382.

84 'Personal and most secret' letter from Sir Archibald Clark Kerr, of the British embassy in Moscow, to Soviet foreign minister V.M. Molotov, 28 May 1944, in 'Ukrainian and White Russian Troops Fighting for the Germans under General Vlasov,' FO 371/43387. A delightful description of this British ambassador was penned by an admiring Dana Wilgress a year earlier. Kerr, wrote the Canadian representative, was a lesson in diplomatic style, for 'he poses as a Scottish squire, fond of the great outdoors and disdainful of the less robust pleasures of mankind. He dislikes diplomatic dinners, hardly ever goes to the theatre and loves to poke fun at his generals, admirals and members of his chancery staff about their enthusiasm for the ballet. He usually regales Mr. Stalin with an account of the latest foibles of these Britishers in their admiration of ballerinas. The remarkable thing is that Mr. Stalin seems to love this banter in spite of the almost sacred regard in which the ballet is held by Russians. Like Mr. Stalin Sir Archibald is a pipe smoker and he always takes along a few pipes which he presents to Mr. Stalin. The latter in return gives him some of his tobacco which the Ambassador smokes when he is with Mr. Stalin but never elsewhere. Sir Archibald's technique is to stay a long time, usually two hours, when he sees either Mr. Stalin or Mr. Molotov. He never allows the conversation to descend to the formal plane. He endeavours to chat informally, brighten up the conversation with touches of humour and intersperse questions on the points he has come to discuss. These tactics are proving admirably successful in gaining the confidence of the two most important Soviet statesmen. Even the most delicate questions are discussed in a frank and friendly manner without tempers ever being ruffled on either side. This is being achieved by an Ambassador who is devoid of any interest in communist ideology.' Cited by Smith, *Diplomacy of Fear*, 47–8.
85 See Molotov's 'personal and most secret' reply to Kerr, 31 May 1944, FO 371/43387.
86 See 'Soviet Prisoners of War: Memo by Secretary of State for Foreign Affairs,' 3 September 1944, in War Cabinet minutes (44) 492. Even so, some eleven thousand Soviet nationals and sixty-seven civilians had been prepared for repatriation by mid-October 1944. See 'Repatriation of Soviet Nationals,' 17 October 1944, WO 32/11137.
87 See War Cabinet minutes (44) 492, 3 September 1944.
88 See R.A. Sykes's minutes on a file entitled 'Tour of DP Camps in Br. Zone of Germany by a Member of PW/DP Division,' 8 October 1947, FO 371/67435.
89 'The Extent and Directions of Unauthorized Mass Trekking,' 28 June 1944, FO 371/42829.
90 Top secret memorandum #14, 'Control of Displaced Persons,' 16 August

1944, WO 219/3806. As later became obvious, Field Marshall Montgomery was not very sympathetic to the 'former slaves of the Nazis,' apparently because of the lawlessness of some Russian and Polish DPs. In Argus Telegram no. 18 it was recorded that the German population was 'losing its respect for the British government,' with people commonly saying that at least the 'old Nazi regime was ... able to keep order.' Coal production was suffering because many miners refused to go to work, fearful that in their absence their wives might be attacked by 'unruly mobs.' Some Germans were forming vigilante groups. Montgomery ordered 'drastic measures against offenders,' and Whitehall was asked to comment on his order. Sir Orme Sargent said he hoped it would be possible to 'restrain the Field Marshall from treating these wretched displaced persons as vermin.' The remedy he suggested was that all DPs be collected together in camps, where they could be properly fed and housed and 'kept out of mischief.' If necessary, he added, the Germans were to be turned out of their homes to make way for these 'wretched people.' After all, the refugees had become what they were as a result of German aggression. Eventually, the secretary of state discussed the matter with the prime minister, and they agreed the field marshall should be advised to notify the refugees, using all possible means of publicity, of a time and place by which they should report. Once at these appointed places they should be maintained and fed until ready for repatriation. Those caught committing excesses after this notification would be subject to 'drastic action.' Montgomery was also told to discuss this proposal with his Soviet counterpart to ensure that 'he carries Marshal Zhukov with him.' See minutes of 8 August 1945 on FO 371/46811.

91 'The Employment of Displaced Persons: Its Development in Austria,' Allied Commission for Austria (British Element), 10 December 1947, FO 371/63899.
92 C. Heathcote-Smith, 'The Irrepatriates of Europe,' October 1945, FO 371/57700.
93 Ibid.
94 See Lieutenant Colonel R. Morris Wilson, UNRRA HQ (Team 318) in Vienna, to A.L. Smith, MP (Calgary West), 16 March 1946, NAC MG30 E350.
95 Ibid.
96 Alexander Glazer to K. Gregory, MP, 18 December 1946, FO 371/56495. Gregory forwarded a copy to the Foreign Office's G.P. Mayhew.
97 Ibid.
98 'The Position with Regard to the Repatriation of Soviet Citizens,' 7 September 1945, FO 371/47906.

99 See the 'Weekly Report to 14 August 1945,' FO 371/46811.
100 Panchuk to Mr Malin of the IGCR, August 1945, NAC 2MG28 v9, Vol. 14.
101 See notes by Mr D. Allen, 18 June 1945, FO 371/47718.
102 For a description of how 'summary justice' was meted out to repatriates at the Ukrainian port city of Odessa, see the June 1945 reports found in WO 32/1119. In the 23 September 1983 issue of the *Wall Street Journal*, R.A. Davison, of Texas A&M University, provided another personal account of how forcible repatriation was carried out by American forces. In August 1945 he was a nineteen-year-old rifleman serving in Company G, 318th Infantry, stationed in Kempten, Germany. On a Sunday morning the soldiers were ordered into formation, issued ammunition, and told that the American government had promised to return 'all the Russians' who had entered Germany. Professor Davison continues: 'These Russians were refusing to go. Some had committed suicide and others had taken refuge in an Orthodox church, claiming they would die there rather than return to Russia. Our orders were to load them on trucks for deportation even if we had to kill them. Then the C.O. added that Stalin had promised that they wouldn't be harmed. A low laugh rippled through the formation, and to me that laugh is more significant than the brutality that followed. We were battle-hardened veterans but most of us were in our late teens and twenties; yet we knew, even in 1945, that Stalin would probably kill these people. How then could our leaders, including Truman, not have known, or worse not have cared, especially in view of the trials that were about to begin at Nuremberg. We marched down to the church and the people were inside. Another rifleman and I were left to guard a gate. All the courtyard gates were guarded and then a few score men went inside to clear the church. A wild battle ensued, including the Orthodox priest wielding his cross, but rifle butts won and soon the battered people were driven from the church. An old woman sprawled at the door apparently suffering a heart attack. Some of the people rushed for the gates and about ten headed toward my buddy and me. We threw our rifles to our shoulders and screamed halt. A shot rang from the courtyard and I was within a second of firing point blank into those people when they stopped. A little woman with tears running down her face and my rifle pointing at her head said in broken English, "I thought Americans were good."'
103 See Panchuk to Rhys Davis, MP, 17 September 1945, NAC MG28 v9, vol. 15.
104 See 'Conditions in Konigsberg after Soviet Occupation,' 2 May 1946, FO 371/56889. Herman Matzkowski wrote to the Service Council of the Society of Friends to say that he had been a communist but that his experi-

ences under Soviet occupation had quickly disabused him of those earlier political sympathies. His disaffection began after he was forced, on 20 June, to witness a public mass execution by guillotine of more than a thousand political prisoners. On 6–7 November, Red Army Day, soldiers were granted the right to complete licence. As a result many Germans were beaten, and most women in his community were raped, including, Matzkowski wrote, 'my old mother of 71, who died at Christmas.' Reports penned by British officials observed that 'it would be unreasonable to expect Anglo-Saxon standards of behaviour from a primitive and largely Asiatic race' like the Soviets. Yet, even 'making every allowance for semi-Orientals in a generally lower state of social and intellectual development than our own,' the British military attaché from Warsaw wrote, the type of behaviour he witnessed convinced him that 'all is not well with the Russian army.' See the top secret memorandum entitled 'Discipline of Russian Troops in Poland,' 1 October 1945, FO 371/47594. On Soviet war crimes, see N. Tolstoy, *Stalin's Secret War* (New York, 1982). On the depredations of Jewish members of the Office of State Security in postwar Poland, see J. Sack, *An Eye for an Eye: The Untold Story of Jewish Revenge against Germans in 1945* (New York, 1993).

105 Soviet representative Ratov to General Sir A. Thorne, 6 September 1945, FO 371/47906.

106 See Allied Forces HQ to the War Office, August 1945, regarding General Basilov's activities and attitudes, WO 32/11119.

107 C.F.A Warner to Sir Alexander Cadogen, 18 August 1945, FO 371/47903. However, differences in interpretation between officials of the Foreign and War offices emerged during a meeting held at the War Office on 31 July 1945. For an interpretation of the legal issues involved, see chapter 18, 'Legal Factors and Reasons of State,' in Tolstoy, *Victims of Yalta*, 410–30.

108 See Warner to Cadogen, 18 August 1945, FO 371/47903.

109 See the 'particularly secret' telegram from the Foreign Office to Washington, 15 October 1945, FO 371/47907.

110 See FO 371/47907.

111 'Memo: On Conditions of Compulsory Repatriation of Displaced Persons in Europe to Their Places of Origin,' 27 August 1946, DEA 8296-40. Canada's S.M. Scott commented that his reading of the Yalta Agreement did not suggest there was any call for the enforced return of anyone. He therefore counselled Canadian agreement with the American interpretation. He also pointed out that the British seem to have yielded to the Soviets on this issue 'because they did not care much, partly because their camps were overcrowded and chiefly because the Russians will not

help our boys until theirs were on the boats.' He added, however, that 'Yalta is a long way off,' and that 'maybe the Foreign Office did not tell me all they were thinking.'

112 'Policy for the Repatriation of Soviet Citizens in British Zones of Germany and Austria,' 1 July 1946, FO 371/56717, and DEA 8296-40, 27 August 1946.

113 See the secret 'Repatriation of Soviet Citizens: Memo by the Secretary of State for Foreign Affairs,' 29 May 1946, FO 371/56716.

114 The most damning assessment of British policy concerning these refugees is provided by Tolstoy, *Victims of Yalta*. An equally condemnatory assessment of American complicity is M.R. Elliott, *Pawns of Yalta: Soviet Refugees and America's Role in Their Repatriation* (Urbana, 1982). See also Y. Boshyk, 'Repatriation and Resistance: Ukrainian Refugees and Displaced Persons in Occupied Germany and Austria, 1945–1948,' in *Refugees In the Age of Total War*, ed. A.C. Bramwell (London, 1988). For an account which suggests why some return migration took place, see the correspondence between the British embassy in Oslo and A.E. Lambert, especially the letter of 4 December 1945, in FO 371/56489. Life in the refugee camps had become so 'boring' that many were returning home voluntarily.

115 See L. Dudin to Foreign Secretary Bevin, 20 February 1946, FO 371/56832.

116 The Foreign Office reported that the United Nations War Crimes Commission (UNWCC) 'have no Ukrainians on their lists of war criminals, nor have the names of any Ukrainians been submitted to them for consideration.' See FO 371/56791, 19 March 1946. The Ukrainian-American newspaper *Svoboda* (*Liberty*), decried the campaign aimed at blocking Ukrainian refugee immigration in an editorial published in its January–February 1946 issue. The editor claimed that the pro-Soviet press was trying to 'discredit the struggle of the Ukrainian people for freedom. And the sad part of it is that an effort is being made to identify the movement with anti-semitism, Jewish pogroms and robberies with the intention of convincing Anglo-Saxon public opinion that Ukrainian refugees must be turned over to the Soviets.' An article by the Prague correspondent of *The Times*, reporting on the well-trained army of Ukrainian insurgents headed by the 'Banderovcii,' reported that 'the only Jew questioned by the writer expressed no apprehension of the Banderovcii.' A copy is found in NAC MG28 v9, vol. 17, 9 May 1946.

117 Repatriation, whether forcible or persuaded, was, as Lieutenant General Sir Frederick Morgan observed in a letter to Foreign Secretary Bevin, the 'cold-blooded' solution to what should be done about the postwar DP situation. His stricture 'I cannot think that this solution would be one in keeping with

our professed ethical outlook' seems to have been ignored. See FO 371/
57703, 10 March 1946. Perhaps Morgan was troubled by incidents like the
one which took place at the 'Weser-Flug' refugee camp near Delmenhorst
on the evening of 2 February 1946. A group composed of one inebriated
British lieutenant, a Russian officer, fifteen French-Canadian soldiers, and
eight German policemen entered the camp in the early morning hours and
threatened its Ukrainian inhabitants with fixed bayonets, pistols, and rifle
fire, while shouting, 'Go home.' Later a soldier explained that, prior to the
raid, the British and Soviet officers had been 'drinking a good deal' and that
the Soviet officer had offered large quantities of cognac and whisky to anyone who would help them seize refugees and throw the captives into a
waiting vehicle. See 'A Translated Copy of a Description of Events Which
Took Place at a D.P. Camp at 'Waser-Flug,' Delmenhorst, on the Night of
Saturday, February 2nd 1946,' Panchuk Collection.

118 See the notes detailing Philipps's BBC broadcast about his participation in
the UN Special Committee on Refugees, June 1946, found in NAC MG30
350. Philipps explained to his listeners that, as of 31 March 1946, there
were still 1,675,000 UN nationals in refugee camps in Europe and the Middle East, at least half a million of whom he considered irrepatriable.

119 Ibid.

120 Secret 'Repatriation of Soviet Citizens: Memo by the Secretary of State for
Foreign Affairs,' 29 May 1946, FO 371/56716. An earlier statement suggested there would be some 750,00 non-repatriables whom UNRRA officials would have to urge home. See DEA 2295-AE-3-40, 1 August 1945. On
the particular plight of Ukrainian women refugees, see A. Crapleve and A.
Panchuk to the UCRF, 17 November 1946, Panchuk Collection. Philipps
had become involved in protesting against forcible repatriation upon the
urging of Ukrainian Canadian friends. Writing to Whitehall's W.J. Hasler,
Philipps observed that the manner in which the issue of forcible repatriation was handled by the British authorities was 'the stuff of which the solidarity of empires is made, or marred.' See NAC MG30 E350, 5 October
1945. Certainly the Ukrainian Canadians in London took a similar view.
For example, Frolick and Panchuk, corresponding with the UUARC's Gallan on 19 October 1945, insisted that the critical issue for Ukrainians was
not immigration but 'security and asylum.' See NAC MG28 v9, vol. 5.
Their protests and lobbying had some impact on Canadian officials. For
example, R.G. Riddell, writing to his colleague at External Affairs, H.
Wrong, noted that the department had been 'receiving a large number of
representations from Ukrainian organizations and their sympathizers protesting against the forcible repatriation of Ukrainian refugees to the Soviet

Union.' See DEA 82-96-40, 28 November 1945. Holmes, at the Office of the
High Commissioner for Canada in London, corresponding with the Foreign Office's Brimelow, apologized for bothering the latter about this issue
but pointed out that 'it is a subject which we cannot ignore in Canada,'
given the size of the Ukrainian Canadian constituency. See Holmes to
Brimelow, 5 November 1945, FO 371/47909. For an example of a CURB
protest against forcible repatriation sent to British foreign secretary Bevin,
see the letter signed by Panchuk, Frolick, and Kluchevsky, 16 December
1945, FO 371/47957. They reported that the proposed repatriation of several thousand Ukrainians in the American Zone had already resulted in
'eight self murders' in Mannheim, and a request on the part of the DPs for
a two-week delay so that they could prepare themselves to die like Christians. C.F. Warner of the Northern Department acknowledged the letter
and replied on 9 January 1946 to the effect that since the refugees which
CURB's memo referred to were not in the British Zone of Germany, Mr
Bevin would be unable to intervene on their behalf.
121 See FO 371/56718, 19 September 1946.
122 Ibid.
123 Ibid.
124 Ibid. Earlier, Soviet officials complained that 'Soviet citizens,' after their
    liberation by British forces, had been left in miserable conditions, with
    insufficient rations and medical aid, a situation which resulted in 'numer-
    ous deaths.' They also protested against the activities of a 'Ukrainian Red
    Cross' and a 'Ukrainian Central Committee.' See FO 371/47906, 19 July
    1945, and FO 371/47903, 29 July 1945. For the complaints of a Soviet liai-
    son officer who, while visiting a refugee camp near Kassel, claimed to be
    been 'handled roughly and threatened' as a result of the anti-Soviet propa-
    ganda of a 'Ukrainian Relief Organization,' see FO 371/47901, 2 July 1946.
    After investigations by the G-5 Division of SHAEF it was concluded that
    these complaints had been 'well founded.' Oral history accounts confirm
    that the DPs organized self-defence units within their camps and
    attempted to undermine Soviet efforts to visit the camps or conduct
    repatriation campaigns.
125 See FO 371/56718, 19 September 1946.
126 'UNRRA Relations with Ukrainian Nationalist Movement in the West,' 24
    October 1946, FO 371/56793. Major-General G.W.R. Templer, chief of staff
    in the British Zone of Occupation in Germany, wrote to the War Office
    on 6 September 1945 to complain that the 'continuous, vague and largely
    unfounded series or alleged series of allegations made by various Soviet
    authorities can but produce one impression on the many officers and men

who must devote time and labour to their investigation – namely, that their intention is mischievous.' See Templer's letter to the Under-Secretary of State for Foreign Affairs, 6 September 1945, FO 371/47906.

127 R. Hankey to Sir M. Peterson in Moscow, 28 November 1946, FO 371/56718.

128 Ibid.

129 Ibid.

130 Secret correspondence entitled 'Repatriation of Displaced Persons in Europe' between the Secretary of State for Dominion Affairs and Canada's Secretary of State for External Affairs, 14 November 1945, DEA 58-H(s). See also R. Crawford of the Control Office for Germany and Austria, in London, to C.J. Edmonds at the Refugee Department, 1 October 1946, FO 371/57905. Western Ukrainians, sometimes referred to in the official records as 'Polish Ukrainians' to distinguish them from 'Russian Ukrainians,' that is, those who lived in the Soviet Union prior to the outbreak of the war, were not subject to forcible repatriation because, legally, they had been Polish citizens. However, the Polish government made no attempt to secure their return, being determined not to have a sizeable Ukrainian minority reconstituted within postwar Poland's boundaries. Indeed, to the fullest extent possible the Polish authorities forcibly deported many Ukrainians remaining inside Poland to the adjacent Soviet Ukraine. I. Stebelksy has also noted that while the Polish government desired the return of all Polish DPs, including Polish Jews, Warsaw was opposed to accepting any Ukrainians, regardless of their prewar citizenship. On 6 July 1946 an agreement concluded with the Soviet government provided for the exchange of Ukrainians in Poland for Poles from the Soviet Union, setting the stage for the final elimination of the Ukrainian minority in Poland. See I. Stebelsky, 'Ukrainian Population Migration after World War II,' in *The Refugee Experience*, ed. Isajiw, Boshyk, and Senkus, 21–6. Intriguingly, however, there is some evidence to suggest that Ukrainian infants were taken to Poland from the refugee camps. On 19 July 1946, for example, a UNRAA repatriation officer, Dr Bedo, wrote to Martin Sherry, a child welfare supervisor, stating that 'Ukrainian children that the Poles reject may be turned over to the Soviet Mission if acceptable to them'; A. Brownlee Collection, Hoover Institution on War, Revolution and Peace.

131 See Mr MacKillop's remarks of 21 June 1946, FO 371/56539.

132 Ibid.

133 Ibid.

134 Ibid.

135 Ibid.

136 Edmonds, of the Refugee Department, had a similar point of view. He
   minuted a file on 23 September 1946: 'The truth is that the whole problem
   of refugees and displaced persons has reached unmanageable proportions. Large overseas resettlement schemes are likely to be very slow in
   getting going. The best hope for anybody who does not want to die of old
   age in a camp is to go home, however uncomfortable it may be.'
137 See Mr MacKillop's remarks of 21 June 1946, FO 371/56539.
138 Ibid. See also Panchuk's 'Report #3 – End of November–End of January,
   1946–47' to the UCC and UCRF executives, 30 January 1947, Panchuk Collection. He refers to the 'rather negative approach of many officials and
   particularly UNRRA who are definitely most interested in repatriation
   rather than immigration.' In his 'Report on Refugees and Displaced Persons in Germany and Austria: Visit of Representative to Germany and
   Austria,' 20 August 1947, Panchuk wrote that an UNRRA representative he
   met held 'strong pro-Communist views and was able to influence policy to
   the detriment of the displaced persons and refugees.' Referring to the repatriation drives in the American zones, he added that UNRRA had
   appointed persons 'who were notorious for their pro-Communist views
   and others who readily followed the philo-Communist lead.' Some DPs
   shared this critical view of UNRRA. See, for example, the testimony of
   N. Serjij and J. Kacmarskyj in a letter dated 2 February 1947 sent to the
   'Regional Representative of Ukrainian Emigration for Svabia in Augsburg.' They testified that UNRRA Team 1062 had used 'persuasive force' at
   the 'Somme Kaserne' camp to get people to return to the Soviet Union (see
   NAC MG28 v9, vol. 15). M.B. Kuropas, 'Ukrainian-American Resettlement
   Efforts, 1944–54,' in *The Refugee Experience*, ed. Isajiw, Boshyk, and Senkus,
   391, also reports that some UNRAA officials were pro-Soviet and unsympathetic to refugees who refused to return to the USSR. In the spring of
   1947, for example, Meyer Cohen, acting chief of UNRAA's DP operations,
   was still urging the DPs to 'go home this spring ... Go home to help your
   countrymen rebuild and to share the fruits of that rebuilding ... Do not be
   misled by false rumors. Seize this opportunity now. Your relatives, your
   friends, your country await you.' Canadian officials were well aware, by
   this time, of the annoyance felt by many of their American counterparts
   towards UNRRA. An officer from External Affairs, writing on 17 October
   1946, pointed out, 'in retrospect,' that UNRRA had been founded on a
   'false concept,' for its basic principle was supposed to have been taking
   politics out of international relief operations. The Anglo-American powers
   had been willing to lend UNRRA their full support 'in the expectation of
   Soviet postwar political cooperation with the democracies.' This had

proved to be a vain hope. Furthermore, it had become apparent that the distribution of UNRRA supplies was, in effect, resulting in North American surpluses being used to 'finance the Soviet rearmament program, Soviet occupation policies [and the] consolidation of totalitarian regimes in Eastern Europe.' It was suggested that if no UNRRA food supplies were sent into Ukraine, the Soviet government would presumably have to demobilize the Red Army rapidly and send its soldiers to work on the collective farms. This Canadian official, L.B. Pearson, ended by observing that the five hundred thousand tons of wheat recently shipped to France from the Soviet Union, 'for political propaganda purposes' had come from Ukraine – 'we replace this wheat with Spam.' See the note in DEA 9255-40C, 'US Relief Policy at the Forthcoming Assembly,' 24 October 1946.

139 See 'UNRRA Relations with Ukrainian Nationalist Movement in the West,' 24 October 1946, FO 371/56793.

140 See Lieutenant General Sir F. Morgan's letter to Foreign Secretary Bevin, 10 March 1946, FO 371/57703.

141 Warner's request for more information on Major Cregeen, 4 December 1944, is in FO 371/43381. This was not the only such incident. For example, after a tour of a Yugoslavian refugee camp housing Serbian Chetniks, a British officer complained of the way Britain was treating these 'peasant peoples of simplicity and courage' who were 'placing their trust in us.' He wondered 'what does Britain stand for,' and why British policy was so apparently intent on placating 'our foes.' For his part, he wished these DPs 'good luck.' The Whitehall officials reading this report wanted to know who the officer was. See FO 371/67435, 8 October 1947.

142 Social Administration Division, 'The Employment of Displaced Persons: Its Development in Austria,' 10 December 1947, FO 371/63989.

143 For Moscow's protests about the alleged decision to resettle Western Ukrainian refugees in Canada, see the letter dated 16 May 1946, FO 371/56715. By 25 May it had been determined that this was a false rumour. The high commissioner for Canada added his formal denial on 10 July 1946.

144 See the telegram 'Disposal of Unrepatriable Soviet Citizens in the British Zone of Germany,' 24 August 1946, FO 374/56718. Even rumours about emigration brought forth 'immediate protests' from Moscow. On 27 August 1946, the Foreign Office declared that as long as Soviet Repatriation Missions were active in the British Zone, there was no possibility of removing any people considered 'Soviet citizens.' Once the missions were withdrawn, however, it was decided that anyone left over, and not in a category subject to compulsory repatriation, should be resettled. Of course, 'no publicity' could be given to this finding 'at the moment.'

145 This petition is found in FO 945/722. This file contains a second similar petition, also penned in refugee camp #751.

146 See A.W. Wilkinson's comments, 'Soviet Press Campaign on the Treatment of Displaced Persons,' 11 June 1947, FO 371/31590.

147 See 'Psychological Problems of Displaced Persons,' June 1945, in the A. Brownlee Collection, Hoover Institute on War, Revolution and Peace. A Ukrainian Canadian interpretation of the mental state of the Ukrainian refugees was also drafted at this time. See 'Psychological Appreciation of Ukrainian Displaced Persons as Aid in Administration of Their Camps,' [undated], Panchuk Collection. Its author suggested that because there had been no independent Ukrainian state for the last three hundred years, entire generations of Ukrainians had lived under various forms of government. Ethnically 'all these Ukrainians [might] come from the same stock,' but, the Ukrainian nation having been subdivided politically, Ukrainians had developed 'as varied an outlook upon life as the forms of government under which they lived.' This meant the occupation authorities would be faced 'with problems peculiar to the state from which they come,' which had nothing to do with the DPs' Ukrainian nationality. Some camps were well run and disciplined and a few 'in constant turmoil' as the direct result of differences between the political systems under which the Western, as opposed to the Eastern, Ukrainians had lived during the prewar period. Oral history accounts confirm that the world-view, expectations, and concerns of Western and Eastern Ukrainian DPs were indeed often markedly different.

148 See the report submitted to SHAEF, Psychological Warfare Division, Intelligence Section, 'Verdun Refugee Camp,' Special Report (France), no. 8, 29 September 1944, WO 219/3807.

149 Ibid.

150 Ibid.

151 Ibid.

152 Interview in Paris between Lady Monkswell and Monsignor Perridon, 29 September 1945, NAC MG28 v9, vol. 17.

153 Ibid. See Yaremovich, 'Report on a Tour of American and French Zones of Germany, French Zone of Austria, and Brief Visit to British and American Zones of Austria, 1–25 June 1947,' 30 June 1947, Panchuk Collection. Yaremovich confirmed that in those DP camps like 'Freiman Kasserne' near Munich, where refugees of various nationalities were 'mixed up instead of being grouped by ethnic origin,' intermingling exacerbated 'uneasiness and tension.' Camps with large Ukrainian populations included Haffkrug, Flensburg, Schleswig, Kiel, Lübeck, Celle, Hamburg, Lüneburg, Soltau,

Munster, and Unterlüss in the Kiel-Hamburg area; Wilhelmshaven, Old-
enburg, Papenburg, Delmenhorst, Bremen, Heidenau, Diepholz, Lingen,
Meppen, Quakenbrück, and Bramsche in the Bremen area; Minden,
Rheine, Osnabrück, Heroford, Bielefeld, Münster, Detmold, Paderborn,
Hoxter, Hannover, Brunswick, Bad Nenndorf, Goslar, Göttingen, Münden,
Kassel, Augustdort, Burgdorf, Hallendorf, Hildesheim, Karlsfeld, and
Salzgitter in the Münster-Hannover area; Adenau, Wittlich, Trier, Bad
Kissingen, Stuttgart, Kaiserslautern, Ludwigshafen, Frankfurt, Bayreuth,
and Nürnberg in the Mannheim-Frankfurt-Weimar area; Spandau in the
Berlin area; St Veit, Kempten, Schwarzach, Kufstein, Landeck, Ingolstadt,
Augsburg, Munich, Ulm, Innsbruck, Feldkirch, and Kaufbeuren in the
Innsbruck-Munich area; and Pilsen in Czechoslovakia. See the list found
in NAC MG28 v9, vol. 17, and the detailed tables compiled by Stebelsky,
'Ukrainian Population Migration after World War II,' in *The Refugee Experi-
ence*, ed. Isajiw, Boshyk, and Senkus, 21–66.

154 On violent DP crimes committed between 1 January and 31 July 1946, see
FO 371/56540, 30 August 1946. W. Strang informed V.W. Cavendish-
Bentinck, at the British embassy in Warsaw, that in response to Polish complaints about the British military authorities being 'unduly severe' in the
sentences imposed on Polish DPs, Cavendish-Bentinck should point out
that in the aforementioned period Poles had been responsible for 'no less
than 146 cases of murder, 58 of attempted murder, and over 1,300 cases of
robbery with violence.' Strang added, 'Against these figures the misdeeds
of the other D.P.'s appear relatively insignificant.' In fact 'other DPs' were
responsible for 22 murders, 15 attempted murders, and 278 incidents of
robbery with violence. The total of all crimes of violence in the British
Zone of Germany during 1 January to 31 July 1946 was 3703.

155 Letter from the CCG to O.C. Harvey, Assistant Under-Secretary of State
for Foreign Affairs, 16 August 1945, FO 371/46811. It noted that German
complaints about DP crime could not be dismissed simply by saying that
the Germans had brought these people into the country and must now
take the consequences, any more than the problem of providing food and
shelter for the German population could, 'to our way of thinking,' be disposed of as suggested by a Red Army officer, who said, 'Those Germans in
the Soviet Zone who did not die of cold next winter would die of starvation next spring, so why worry?'

156 See Lieutenant General F. Morgan to Foreign Secretary Bevin, 10 March
1946, FO 371/57703.

157 Ibid.

158 Soviet commentator Vittorov's address 'Anti-Soviet Organizations under

the Auspices of the Anglo-American Authorities,' published in *Pravda* and aired on Moscow radio, in July 1946, is found in FO 371/55616.

159 Ibid.

160 See FO 371/67435, 15 July 1947.

161 'Unauthorized Penetration of British Zone and Introduction of Political Literature from East of the Anglo-Russian Demarcation Line, ' 21 August 1946, FO 371/55618.

162 See 'Psychological Problems of Displaced Persons,' a report prepared for the Welfare Division of the European Regional Office of UNRRA by an Inter-Allied Psychological Study Group (London: June 1945), a copy of which is found in the A. Brownlee Collection, Box 8, Hoover Institution on War, Revolution and Peace. Another contemporary, if partial, description of how the DP camp experience affected camp inhabitants was provided by Lawrence Frenkel, appointed as UNRRA's chief public health officer for Austria at the end of the war. See his memorandum 'Displaced Person's Camps' in the Hoover Institution Archives. Frenkel insisted, unconvincingly, that with 'the exception of a fraction of one percent,' the DPs 'all immediately wanted to be repatriated to their home country,' which explained why '80%' had left the camps by the end of December 1945. The remaining refugees had come under the sway of leaders in whose interest it was to retain as many of them as possible, to increase their own security and stature and 'to create a permanent group of Displaced Persons for their own purposes.'

163 See 'Psychological Problems of Displaced Persons.'

164 Ibid.

165 Ibid.

166 Ibid.

167 Major Tufton Beamish and Mr C.R. Hobson, MP, 'Report by Parliamentary Special Committee of Investigation into the Implementation of His Majesty's Government's Policy in Connection with Displaced Persons in the British Zones of Germany and Austria,' March 1947, FO 371/66658. A third member, Mr F. Beswick, MP, did not sign this report. The Parliamentary Special Committee recognized that among the 'Polish Ukrainians' there were a 'considerable number of suitable men to help in our own agricultural industries.' On 24 July 1946, Lieutenant Colonel Arthur Hicks described the Ukrainian DPs to the Senate Committee on Immigration and Labour as 'predominantly farmers and their families ... a sturdy lot.' His personal view was that they, along with the Baltic peoples, most of the Poles, and many of the Yugoslavs, would make 'excellent settlers, and ultimately good citizens in Canada.' See Senate of Canada, *Proceedings of the Senate Standing Committee on Immigration and Labour*, 192–3.

168 Ukrainian Canadian observers familiar with the refugee situation came to the same conclusion. For example, Yaremovich wrote that the divisive political behaviour of the DPs, considered so irksome by the British, American, and Canadian governments, could be countered by the establishment of 'a sound Press and recognized Ethnic Organizations' in each occupation zone. See Yaremovich, 'Report on a Tour ...' 30 June 1947, Panchuk Collection.

The Ukrainian press published by political parties active in the DP camps was dominated by the Banderivtsi. The produced 5 periodicals for internal consumption and 6 weeklies distributed throughout western Europe. The Melnykivtsi produced 2 internal periodicals, 2 weeklies, and 2 monthlies. The OUN Abroad (OUNz), a breakaway faction of the OUNb, published 3 newspapers and 2 montlies. The URDP produced 2 journals and an important semi-weekly for mass distribution. In total, in 1945–55 there were about twenty partly influenced newspapers circulating among the DPs, along with a dozen monthly or quarterly periodicals. See V. Markus, 'Political Parties in the DP Camps,' 111–24, and R. Ilnytzkyj, 'A Survey of Ukrainian Camp Periodicals, 1945–50,' 271–91, in *The Refugee Experience*, ed. Isajiw, Boshyk, and Senkus.

169 On the Ukrainian émigré press, see *Political Writings of Post–World War Two Ukrainian Emigrés*, ed. Petryshyn and Chomiak. On the emergence of 'little Ukraines' in the refugee camps, see E. Wasylyshen to the UCRF, 'Report #5,' 20 June 1949, Wasylyshen Collection. This private collection remains in the care of Mrs A. Wasylyshen, in Winnipeg. She was interviewed in Winnipeg on 30 May 1982 (MHSO) and 30 November 1982 (CIUS). The author is grateful to Mrs Wasylyshen for allowing him to make copies of some of these materials.

170 See R. Ilnytzkyj, *The Free Press of the Suppressed Nations* (Augsburg, 1950), 24, 40.

171 For some people, the shared experience of refugee camp life had an undeniably positive effect. Several clubs exist which sporadically bring together former inhabitants of various refugee camps. For an example of the commemorative activities of one such group, see *Regensburg: Articles and Documents on the History of Ukrainian Emigration in Germany after World War II*, ed. O. Kushnir (New York, 1985). The English-language abstract introducing this volume states, 'Regensburg was for Ukrainians not only a haven from persecution, hunger, solitude, but a *community*, culturally rich and vibrant, politically an experiment in democratic government.' In 'The DP Camp as a Social System,' in *The Refugee Experience*, ed. Isajiw, Boshyk, and Senkus, 461–70, I.V. Zielyk reachs many of the same conclusions

found in this book. For example, Zielyk insightfully observes that 'because many things happened during this period ... which helped modify the perceptions, habits, and relationships of the camp residents ... the immigrants who entered the United States, Canada, and other Western countries in the late forties and early fifties were often not the "same" people who had left Ukraine prior to 1945 ... Life in the DP camp attained an unprecedented level of politicization, both in terms of the degree to which situations and problems were ideologically defined or endowed with political salience and in terms of the prevalence and intensity of involvement by individuals ... The DP experience also helped to carry on, even to strengthen, the tradition of Ukrainian patriotism, particularly in its irredentist form. The recency of exile, the events in Ukraine during and after the end of World War II, the erection of the Iron Curtain, the formation of a central body (CPUE) to represent the interests of all Ukrainian emigrants, and simple nostalgia all combined to create, within the camp, a heightened sense of national identity and unit. Ukrainians of diverse social backgrounds, from various regions and professing different religious faiths, were thrown together on a large scale ... As time passed [they] became more and more impressed that they shared the same basic language, intense (and, for some, new found) pride in their cultural heritage; and all the hopes, problems and frustrations of collectively seeking self-determination ... This whole process of social and attitudinal integration which unfolded in the camp constituted a perpetuation, dissemination, and probably intensification of the irredentist value system which had developed and matured on Ukrainian soil, and which the Ukrainian DPs subsequently carried to their new destinations ... It is still going strong, functioning simultaneously on a number of levels as a motivating force, as perhaps the only reliable cement that can unite all those who share Ukrainian ancestry, and as the prime guarantee of the maintenance of Ukrainian ethnic identity. Viewed from this standpoint, the DP camp, with all its ephemeral little drama, with all its sociological anomalies, may still one day be vindicated by historians as a crucial stage in the building and continuity of a genuinely free and self-aware Ukrainian society.'

172 See 'Psychological Problems of Displaced Persons.'

173 Both OUN factions tried to dominate organized life in the Ukrainian DP camps. Most accounts agree that the Banderivtsi were particularly successful. Other refugee camps came under the influence of competing political factions, like the Ukrainian Revolutionary Democratic Party (URDP), which drew its largest following from among the Eastern Ukrainians. Persons who joined the nationalist movement only after they came to be in a

refugee camp were sometimes derisively referred to as 'camp Banderivtsi' or 'camp Melnykivtsi' by long-standing members of these organizations. See, for example, the interview with I. Firman, Toronto, 30 May 1982 (MHSO). Students of the Ukrainian refugee experience are essentially agreed that the Banderivtsi came to dominate political life within this postwar emigration. In 'Common Organizational Efforts, 1945–52: Structure and People,' 90–108, T. Ciuciura reports that, for example, the 'Ukrainian Central Relief Committee – the Central Representation of the Ukrainian Emigration in Germany,' headed by Vasyl Mudry, former vice-marshal of the Polish parliament, was dominated by adherents of the OUNb. Markus, 'Political Parties in the DP Camps,' 111–24, notes that the nationalists of the OUN were the 'one political force that dominated the rest of the political groupings in the Ukrainian exile community,' and that the OUNb 'came to exercise a good deal of influence, since it was able to attract large numbers of voters and gain control of many camp administrations and social organizations.' He estimates that the OUNb had more than 5000 members in western Europe by the end of 1948, of whom 70 per cent were in the DP camps, as compared to 1200–1500 Melnykivtsi (OUNm), who were matched in number by the supporters of the Ukrainian Revolutionary Democratic Party. Several mini-parties, like the Alliance of Hetmanites (SHD), had 150–200 members. In total, Markus estimates, 8000 to 10,000 people were involved in Ukrainian party politics in the DP camps, along with over 15,000 sympathizers, financial contributors, and party press readers. He asserts that 'a relatively high proportion of people, some 12–15 per cent of the entire emigre population ... were politically active.' Both papers are found in The Refugee Experience, ed. Isajiw, Boshyk, and Senkus.

Chapter 7: Ironing Out the Differences

1 Panchuk to the UCRF, 'Report #4,' 18 March 1946, Panchuk Collection. A Ukrainian serving with the Polish forces in postwar Germany, and probably a sympathizer with or member of the Ukrainian nationalist movement, who signed himself with the pseudonym 'Ivan Bulka,' reported that there was 'nothing particularly new' with respect to the 'entire Ukrainian situation,' which continued to be 'most pathetic.' He reported that, at a large Ukrainian DP camp near Oldenburg, armed NKVD men had forcibly removed every Ukrainian refugee they could catch, regardless of whether the refugees had previously resided in the USSR or Poland. He went on to note that 'later some members of the N.K.V.D. also arrived dressed in

English Service uniforms.' These men were 'scouring the countryside searching for people who were in hiding.' Understandably, many Ukrainian refugees were 'panic-stricken.'

2 Panchuk to the UCRF, 'Report #2,' 28 February–1 March 1946, Panchuk Collection. What this forcible repatriation also accomplished – and possibly this was one of the reasons why the Soviets were so insistent upon trying to round up all 'Soviet citizens' – was the removal of many surviving witnesses to the politically engineered Great Famine of 1932–3. On the nature, course, and consequences of the famine in Ukraine, see Conquest, *The Harvest of Sorrow; Famine in Ukraine, 1932–1933*, ed. R. Serbyn and B. Krawchenko (Edmonton, 1986); *The Foreign Office and the Famine: British Documents on Ukraine and Great Famine of 1932–1933*, ed. M. Carynnyk, L.Y. Luciuk, and B.S. Kordan (Kingston and Vestal, 1988); Investigation of the Ukrainian Famine, 1932–1933, *First Interim Report of Meetings and Hearings of and before the Commission on the Ukraine Famine* (Washington, 1987), *Second Interim Report of Meetings and Hearings of and before the Commission on the Ukraine Famine* (Washington, 1988), and *Report to Congress: Commission on the Ukraine Famine* (Washington, 1988); and International Commission of Inquiry into the 1932–33 Famine in Ukraine, *The Final Report* (Toronto, 1990). A Polish researcher concluded that there was a demographic loss of 9,263,000 people in Ukraine between 1926 and 1939. See J. Radziejowski, 'Collectivization in Ukraine in Light of Soviet Historiography,' *Journal of Ukrainian Studies* 5:2 (1980): 3–17. For eyewitness accounts, see *The Black Deeds of the Kremlin: A White Book, vol. 2, The Great Famine in Ukraine*, ed. S. Pidhainy (Detroit, 1955); W. Hryshko, *The Ukrainian Holocaust of 1933*, ed. and trans. M. Carynnyk (Toronto, 1983); M. Dolot, *Execution by Hunger: The Hidden Holocaust* (New York, 1985); E. Ammende, *Human Life in Russia* (London, 1936), repr., with a historical introduction by J.E. Mace (Cleveland, 1984); O. Woropay, *The Ninth Circle: In Commemoration of the Victims of the Famine of 1933* (Cambridge, Mass., 1983); and *Days of Famine, Nights of Terror: Firsthand Accounts of Soviet Collectivization, 1928–1934*, ed. L. Leshuk (Kingston, Washington, Kyiv, 1995). The journalist Anna Reid, in her book *Borderland: A Journey through the History of Ukraine* (London, 1997), 132, has written: 'Killing more people than the First World War on all sides put together, the famine of 1932–33 was, and still is, one of the most under-reported atrocities of human history, a fact that contributes powerfully to Ukraine's persistent sense of victimisation.' For a telling indictment of communism, see F. Furet, *The Passing of an Illusion: The Idea of Communism in the Twentieth Century*, trans. D. Furet (Chicago, 1999). Grotesquely, given Ukraine's losses during the man-made famine, every morning at six o'clock

loudspeakers rigged up on lamp posts and walls throughout the centre of Kyiv would play what John Fischer, a UNRRA worker who spent some two months in Ukraine during the spring of 1946, described as a sort of municipal reveille, consisting of the first nine notes of the 'Internationale' repeated over and over, the accompanying words being 'Arise, ye prisoners of starvation.' See J. Fischer, *Why They Behave Like Russians* (New York, 1946), 35. Some of Fischer's observations would find censure today, for example his statement that the 'mammalian equipment' of Ukrainian mothers 'could only be described as magnificent,' so much so that 'Lana Turner wouldn't get a second glance in Kiev' (p. 31).

Questions regarding the nature, and particularly the intentionality of this famine, have become the focus of considerable inquiry in recent years, especially with the creation, by the World Congress of Free Ukrainians, of an independent international commission of inquiry in 1987. See N. Ashford, 'Time to Understand What Happened in the Ukraine,' *The Independent*, 1 July 1988. Throughout 1988–9 articles and letters to the editor describing this famine began appearing in the Soviet press, apparently as a consequence of the policy of *glasnost*, or 'openness,' instituted by M. Gorbachev. See 'Stalin's Grim Harvest,' *Pravda International* 2:11–12 (1989): 12–16, and Wasyl Pacharenko, 'Genocide: A White Book: The Truth about the Famine in Ukraine, 1933,' *October* (Lviv, Ukrainian SSR) 1 (531) (January 1989): 76–81 and 2 (532) (February 1989): 86–90 [in Ukrainian]. For Canadian press reaction, see P. Gombu, 'Policy Errors Caused Ukrainian Famine, Soviets Say,' *The Whig Standard*, 3 March 1989, 19; V. Malarek, 'Famine in Ukraine Stalin's Worst Crime, Soviet Experts Say,' *Globe and Mail*, 7 March 1989, 8; and the editorial by N. Reynolds, 'Ukraine Nationalism Will Grow from Memory of Terror Famine,' *Whig Standard*, 11 March 1989, 8. See also E. Margolis, 'Remembering Ukraine's Unknown Holocaust,' *Toronto Sun*, 13 December 1998. A rather cogent forecast about the likelihood of famine conditions in the Soviet Union was penned on 18 August 1922 by a Foreign Office official, who noted that 'the fundamental ill is communism, not the weather; & famine will be more or less chronic in Russia until either communism goes or the population is greatly reduced by nature's cruel & drastic methods' (see 'Famine in Russia,' FO 371/8150). For a particularly base example of famine-denial literature, see D. Tottle, *Fraud, Famine and Fascism: The Ukrainian Genocide Myth from Hitler to Harvard* (Toronto, 1987).

Ukraine's president Leonid Kuchma issued a presidential decree on 26 November 1998 proclaiming the fourth Saturday of each November as a National Day of Rememberance of the Famine Victims. Speaking at an official commemorative service in Kyiv on 28 November, Ukraine's deputy prime minister, Valerii Smolii, said, 'That the famine was artificially induced is a historical fact,' one of the 'deliberate criminal policies of the Communist regime.' The deputy prime minister also thanked the Ukrainian diaspora for keeping alive the memory of what happened: 'Ukrainians abroad consistently ... felt it a matter of honour and national dignity to let the world community know the truth about the unparalleled Stalinist crime. They put together titanic efforts so that all would realize: the Ukrainian Famine of 1933 stands on the level of the Armenian Genocide of 1915 and the Jewish Holocaust.' On 27 January 1999, Canada's prime minister, the Right Honourable Jean Chrétien, became the first Western leader to visit and lay a wreath at Ukraine's National Famine Monument in Kyiv. See 'UCC Welcomes Chrétien's Visit to Kyiv,' *Ukrainian Weekly,* 7 February 1999, 3.

3 'Memorandum on Ukrainian Refugees in Austria,' 1 February 1947, Panchuk Collection.

4 Panchuk to the UCRF, 'Report #2,' 28 February–1 March 1946, Panchuk Collection.

5 Ibid., and Panchuk to the UCRF, 'Report #4,' 18 March 1946, Panchuk Collection.

6 Panchuk, 'Memorandum on Ukrainian Refugees in Austria,' 1 February 1947, Panchuk Collection.

7 Panchuk to Joseph Choma, 21 May 1948, Panchuk Collection.

8 Panchuk to Karasevich, 21 December 1946, Panchuk Collection.

9 Ibid.

10 Ibid.

11 Ibid.

12 Ibid.

13 Ibid.

14 'Notes on Immigration of Ukrainian Refugees and Displaced Persons to Canada,' 8 October 1946, Panchuk Collection.

15 Ibid.

16 Panchuk to Karasevich, 21 December 1946, Panchuk Collection.

17 Ibid.

18 Panchuk to Mr Moore, Allied Control Commission for Germany (British Element) DP/PW Section, Norfolk House, St James Square, London, 6 December 1946, Panchuk Collection.

19 Ibid.

20 Panchuk to 'Dear Fellow Workers,' 12 February 1947, Panchuk Collection. Also entitled 'Report from the Continent, No. 1.' Reverend Sawchuk addressed a letter to Mr Moore of the DP/PW Section of the Allied Control

Commission for Germany (British Element) on 7 December 1946, explaining that the object of his visit was not to get into the DP camps but rather to undertake a 'religious mission,' which could be effective only if he made personal contact with bishops of the Ukrainian Orthodox church. He provided a list of the prelates he wished to meet, including Metropolitan Polikarp and seven other Ukrainian Orthodox bishops and archbishops then living in the British and American zones of occupation. Sawchuk was more explicit about his purposes when he wrote to Major T. Workman of the British Section Permit Office for Germany, in London, on 21 November 1946. He told Workman his visit was decided upon and approved by the Ninth General Council of the Ukrainian Greek Orthodox Church of Canada, which gave him three tasks to fulfil, namely, to study religious and church conditions among the refugees in order to ascertain how the Canadian church might be able to help; to contact Metropolitan Polikarp and other bishops for the purpose of exploring the possibility of getting one or two of them to serve as bishops for the Ukrainian Greek Orthodox Church in Canada; and to determine the possibility of bringing a number of younger priests and theological students and at least one or two professors 'of high standing' to Canada to lecture in theology at St Andrew's College in Winnipeg. Sawchuk's application was originally turned down by the Control Commission in Berlin, which cabled its London office on 6 December that the 'number of visitors from *Canada* on *Ukrainian* Affairs is very embarrassing, especially in view of difficulties we have with *Soviet* authorities on *Ukrainian* affairs.' That decision was reviewed and, by 2 January 1947, permission had been granted for Sawchuk to spend 14 days in the British Zone. Possibly the earlier, negative decision was reversed because Sawchuk had been able to present letters of reference supporting his application from the high commissioner for Canada and from the general secretary of the Church of England's Council on Foreign Relations, Reverend H.M. Waddams. See FO 945/722 for copies of this correspondence. Similarly, but even earlier (in January 1946), the French Canadian ukrainophile and Basilian father Reverend Josaphat Jean had gone overseas to rescue Catholic priests. He remained in Europe until August 1949, also setting up the St Theodore of Canterbury Ukrainian Catholic parish in London in May 1947. Panchuk's way was cleared by 8 January 1947, when a cipher telegram was sent from the Control Commission for Germany and Austria noting that both the Foreign Office and Canada House felt his application for a permit to visit the British Zone in Austria should be 'favourably received.' It was agreed that Panchuk's 'Canadian Ukrainian Mission' would be able 'to make real contribution to welfare of Ukrainian DPs and whose plans for resettlement might ease general problem.' Panchuk left London on 11 February and headed directly to Geneva, to take part in the PCIRO conference being held there. Afterward he went to Austria. Yaremovich planned to leave the United Kingdom on 15 February, and to establish a base in Lemgo, Germany. See the unclassified telegram from the Control Office in London to Lemgo, 13 February 1947, copies of which were sent to Brimelow and to Mr Edmonds in the Refugee Department. Ann Crapleve was apparently already in Lemgo by mid-December 1947. The entire team reassembled in Frankfurt in mid-April 1947 to 'compare notes on what has been done to date and to plan our further work,' as Panchuk duly informed Mr Moore, on 18 April 1947 (FO 945/722).

21 Karasevich to Panchuk, 28 March 1947, Panchuk Collection. Karasevich observed that UCVA was experiencing 'tough slugging' in its relations with the UCC's constituent groups, all of whom had 'placed themselves on guard' against the veterans' group, mainly because of the 'Renaissance Plans' UCVA had presented to the UCC's national executive. The latter's acceptance of that proposal had been made the condition for the dispatch of UCVA's Canadian Relief Mission overseas. The UCC did not, however, honour its obligation.

22 Panchuk to 'Dear Fellow Workers,' 12 February 1947. See also his notes about the CRM, 9 October 1947, Panchuk Collection.

23 Panchuk to Mrs Anna Mandryka of the UCRF, 30 May 1947, Panchuk Collection.

24 'Arrival in UK of Ukrainians from Italy,' 5 May 1947, FO 371/66355, particularly the minute penned by Mr Williamson on 14 May 1947.

25 Philipps from the Travellers Club in London to His Excellency Victor Dire, Canadian embassy in Brussels, 6 March 1947. See also NAC MG30 E350, 8 June 1947, where Philipps offered the opinion that it was sometimes an advantage '*not* to know too much about Ukrainian politics,' for, as in Panchuk's case, this enabled a person 'to see (and be) objective and never to be suspected of any political intrigue.' For these reasons Panchuk had, or so Philipps claimed, 'gained the confidence of UK and US officials whom he needed.' It was not until December 1947 that the high commissioner for Canada informed the British government with regard to Canada's position on the relationship that should exist between voluntary Canadian welfare organizations engaged in refugee work in Germany and other European countries and the Canadian government. While Ottawa, working through its Department of Mines and Resources, was prepared to accept certain offers of cooperation and assistance from such voluntary groups for the purpose of 'seeking out and assembling for inspection' prospective emi-

grants, the government would not formally sponsor any such group, for doing so would 'naturally involve the Government in some responsibility for the activities of these groups.' That was unacceptable. But even if it was not prepared to guarantee any group support, the Canadian government did want the PCIRO and the relevant control authorities to know that it had designated two voluntary Canadian organizations to which assistance and cooperation should be extended. These two groups were the 'Canadian Christian Council for the Resettlement of Refugees' and the 'Canadian-Ukrainian Committee.' See the letter from the Official Secretary of the High Commission for Canada to the Under-Secretary of State at the Foreign Office, 10 December 1947, FO 945/722.

26 See Panchuk's letter to Fort William's Dr P. Wenger, 8 September 1947, for information about the departure of Yaremovich and Crapleve, and with respect to the agreement he had made about staying overseas until 1 April 1948. Yaremovich arrived in Canada on Tuesday, 9 September, and was checked into Winnipeg's Hotel Corona by 12 September 1947. He wrote that day: 'Glad to be back in the city – so far no one officially knows of my presence in Winnipeg – will take a rest and look after personal things.' By 15 September, Crapleve had also returned to Winnipeg. That evening, Yaremovich and Crapleve went with W. Kossar to Reverend Kushnir's home for 'a real conference.' They told him about conditions on the Continent, 'the squabbling between groups, political intrigues, people anxious to cut one another's throats, [and the] constant reporting to authorities.' They also told Kushnir that their relations with Panchuk were not good, and that henceforth 'personal arrangements' would have to be made between them and the UCRF if the latter expected them to return to Europe. See Yaremovich, 'Diary,' 15 September 1947. As for Panchuk, he went to Geneva in early February 1947 to attend the PCIRO meetings, and from there he moved into northeastern Italy, where members of the Ukrainian Division 'Galicia' were interned, near Rimini. During April he assisted an American, Georgetown University's Professor M.W. Royse, and the British authorities, in their screening of these and other SEP. When the CRM formally ended its work, on 31 July 1947, the Panchuks, Yaremovich, and Crapleve signed individual contracts with the Fund. During the time they worked on the Continent, Bill Byblow served as CURB's acting director.

27 Panchuk to A. Mandryka, 5 September 1947, Panchuk Collection. On 24 June 1944 the Ukrainian Congress Committee of America (UCCA) established the Ukrainian American Relief Committee, headed by Dr Walter Gallan. At about the same time, a second committee, the Ukrainian War Relief, was set up in Michigan under the chairmanship of John Panchuk.

In October the two groups merged and created the United Ukrainian American Relief Committee (UUARC), with Gallan as chairman and Panchuk as co-chair. Reportedly, more than 35,000 Ukrainian DPs were resettled in the United States as a result of the UUARC's efforts. For a more detailed commentary on Ukrainian American activities on behalf of the DPs, see Kuropas, 'Ukrainian-American Resettlement Efforts, 1944–54,' in *The Refugee Experience*, ed. Isajiw, Boshyk, and Senkus, 385–401.

28 Ibid.
29 Panchuk to the UUARC's John Panchuk, [undated], Panchuk Collection.
30 Ibid.
31 Panchuk to the UUARC, 14 April 1947, Panchuk Collection.
32 Ibid.
33 Ibid.
34 Ibid.
35 Gallan to Panchuk in Geneva, 25 April 1947, Panchuk Collection.
36 Panchuk to the UCC, 2 May 1947, Panchuk Collection.
37 Panchuk to the UUARC, 10 May 1947, Panchuk Collection.
38 See Panchuk's personal letter from Geneva to Gallan, 12 May 1947, Panchuk Collection.
39 Ibid. Gallan visited Europe on behalf of the UUARC on three separate occasions. The first trip lasted from 21 June to 31 July 1946, the second from 29 October 1946 to 4 February 1947, and the third took place in November 1950. The UUARC was formally incorporated in Philadelphia on 24 June 1944. It maintained a branch office at 13, rue Taine, in Paris, France. For a Ukrainian Canadian perspective on how the UUARC managed that property, see Yaremovich's letter to the UCC, 26 July 1948, Yaremovich Collection. The Basilian order's Father Jean made use of this building for the temporary housing of several monks and sisters, while also serving as the UUARC's general manager and secretary in the French capital. See Z. Keywan, *A Turbulent Life: Biography of Josaphat Jean, O.S.B.M. (1885–1972)* (Verdun, Que., 1990), 132.
40 See Panchuk's personal letter from Geneva to Gallan, 12 May 1947, Panchuk Collection.
41 See Gallan's letter from Philadelphia to Panchuk, 23 June 1947, Panchuk Collection. See also interviews with G.R.B. Panchuk in Montreal, 5 May 1981 (MHSO), 24 July 1981 (MHSO), 4 April 1982 (MHSO), and 4 January 1983 (CIUS); and with Reverend S. Sawchuk, Winnipeg, 5 December 1982 (CIUS). Apparently there were Ukrainian Canadian groups which did try to exploit the issue of refugee relief for their own purposes. For example, E. Dudra, of Toronto, wrote to Panchuk on 30 January 1947, describing how,

after the previous October's clothes collection campaign, which involved all the major Ukrainian Canadian groups and churches, one package was reopened. Inside it, and in all the others, a 'misterious slip' [sic] was found, 'Gift of the Ukrainian Orthodox community.' Everyone reportedly was 'sore' about this, and the relief campaign had suffered accordingly. Karasevich, writing to Panchuk on 28 March 1947, pointed out that all the UCC's constituent organizations were trying to take credit for solving the refugee problem, while at the same time denouncing UCVA by claiming that he and Panchuk were trying to turn the veterans' group into just another political Ukrainian Canadian group. Most confidentially, 'as a further tip,' he advised Panchuk 'never [to] let it appear that preference is given to the Orthodoz [sic] refugees.' Any such rumour would seriously harm UCVA.

42 Panchuk to Gallan, 24 July 1947, Panchuk Collection. See also Panchuk to Kushnir and John Panchuk, 24 July 1947. Panchuk denied having sent a copy of his letter of 17 May to Kushnir. Yet Kushnir apparently told Gallan, during their meeting in Ottawa on 11 June, that he had seen a copy.

43 Zaharychuk to Panchuk, 4 July 1947, Panchuk Collection. Just before the end of July, Panchuk received a letter from another UCVA comrade, J. Yuzyk, who warned him: 'I am getting the impression that some of our well meaning people are going to keep you in Europe indefinitely (sort of in storage) because they are afraid of Youthful Leadership ... They feel that the best move is to keep you in Europe (sort of out of the way) ... The older leaders hate to see you getting so popular and also powerful ... You are my friend and I'd hate to see you get the old run around by some of our scheming friends.' See Yuzyk to Panchuk, 16 July 1947, Panchuk Collection. John ('Johnnie') Yuzyk was interviewed by the author in Winnipeg, 28 November 1982 (CIUS).

44 See Panchuk to Simpson, 26 June 1947, Panchuk Collection, where he mentioned his plans for returning to take part in the UCC congress. Panchuk returned alone, leaving his family in London.

45 Panchuk to P. Smylski, then in Burlington, 25 May 1947, Panchuk Collection. In November, the Ukrainian Canadians and their American counterparts held a Pan-American Ukrainian Conference (PAUC), attended among others by the Reverends Kushnir and Sawchuk, the UNF's Kossar, and the UHO's Datzkiw. The UCC also subsidized Dmytro Andrievsky's participation. Eventually, this body gave rise to the World Congress of Free Ukrainians, with Kushnir serving as its first chairman, a post he occupied from 1947 to 1967. See Karasevich to Panchuk, 3 November 1947,

Panchuk Collection. P. Smylski was interviewed in Toronto, 25 March 1982 (MHSO).

46 Panchuk to G. Luckyj, then in Saskatoon, 2 November 1947, Panchuk Collection. Panchuk's attitude with respect to the international importance of Great Britain changed. Whereas on 21 December 1946 he wrote that 'London is the place where the fate of our people will be solved and decided [more so than on the Continent],' in late February 1947 he observed that London's pride of place had 'just about passed,' although he still believed it should remain one of the focal points of the Ukrainian diaspora. See Panchuk to John Panchuk, [undated], Panchuk Collection.

47 Panchuk to Smylski, 25 May 1947, Panchuk Collection.

48 Panchuk to the UCC and UUARC executives, 6 February 1948, Panchuk Collection.

49 For Panchuk the fate of the Ukrainian SEP at Rimini was a *'first and prime* responsibility.' See Panchuk to 'Ann, Tony and all members of the team,' 17 July 1947, NAC MG28 v9, vol. 15. Getting the AUGB set up also occupied much of his time, even before this organization was formally incorporated, on 20 December 1947. See Panchuk to Smylski, 25 May 1947, Panchuk Collection. On the difficulties experienced by some Ukrainians who had served in the Polish armed forces, see the 'Memorandum of Rev. F.W. Wicenik, ex-Orthodox Chaplain-in-Chief, Polish Forces in Great Britain,' to the Polish War Ministry in London, undated, and Panchuk's 'Moral and Psychological Persecution of Minority National Groups in the Polish Armed Forces and the Polish Resettlement Corps,' 16 July 1947, Panchuk Collection.

50 Panchuk to Roman Smook, 17 October 1947, Panchuk Collection. Smook was the UUARC's first accredited representative overseas, granted a permit to operate in the American Zone of Germany on 29 July 1947. The UUARC opened an office in Munich on 1 December 1947. Permission to work in Austria was granted on 22 December, and the UUARC established an office in Salzburg on 15 February 1948. There was also a UUARC office in the French Zone of Germany, at Baden-Baden. By the end of September 1951, Gallan would report that the UUARC's efforts had helped bring 26,793 Ukrainian DPs into the United States.

51 Panchuk to Smook, 23 October 1947, Panchuk Collection. Panchuk returned to Montreal on 23 September and went from there to Winnipeg to take part in joint executive meetings of the UCRF and UUARC, 29 September to 3 October 1947. On 2 October it was decided that Panchuk, Crapleve, and Yaremovich, accompanied by Reverend Sawchuk representing both sponsoring groups, should travel to Ottawa to make their observations and rec-

ommendations about the Ukrainian refugee situation known to members of the government. The delegation's members were later joined by the UNF's Wasyl Hultay, from Toronto. They met on Wednesday morning, 8 October, at the Château Laurier, where they restructured a memorandum that had been prepared earlier, subdividing it into more specific sections, which were then redrafted and submitted to different government officials, including Colonel Colin Gibson, the secretary of state; Dr H. Keenleyside, deputy minister of mines and resources; A.L. Jolliffe, director of the Immigration Branch of the Department of Mines and Resources; Mr Chance, director of the Immigration Division of the Department of External Affairs; Mr Dawson, deputy to Mr McNamara, the deputy minister of labour; and others. See the 'Report of the Delegation Representing the Ukrainian Canadian Committee and the Ukrainian Canadian Relief Fund Attending Government Departments in Ottawa in Connection with Immigration of Refugees and Displaced Persons in Europe,' 10 October 1947, Panchuk Collection.

52 See Panchuk's 'Agenda for Meeting – Panchuk and Smook, Frankfurt, 7–8 November 1947,' Panchuk Collection.

53 Ibid.

54 See Panchuk's letter from Frankfurt to John Panchuk, 10 November 1947, Panchuk Collection.

55 See Yaremovich's letter from Toronto to Panchuk, 15 October 1947, Panchuk Collection. Yaremovich also complained about the 'very poor organization' of the relief campaign back in Canada, noting that 'the fault lies with the people in Winnipeg.' Yaremovich was interviewed in Winnipeg, 1 December 1982 (CIUS).

56 See Panchuk's letter from Geneva to Yaremovich, 29 October 1947, Panchuk Collection.

57 See Karasevich's letter from Winnipeg to Panchuk, 3 November 1947, Panchuk Collection.

58 Ibid.

59 See the UCRF's Arsenych and A. Mandryka to Panchuk, 18 November 1947, Panchuk Collection. Yaremovich left Canada for the United Kingdom aboard the *Queen Mary* on 13 November 1947. He and Crapleve entrained for Brussels on Sunday, 7 December 1947. Yaremovich noted in his diary that day, 'Glad to be on the way to something constructive.' He was particularly glad to be leaving London because he and Panchuk, who was 'very determined in his ways,' had quarrelled on the first day Yaremovich arrived at the Bureau, 18 November. Subsequently, Panchuk had become 'rather moody about Ann and me being away' and had 'insisted that things

remain unchanged.' On 19 November, Yaremovich recorded that he could not agree with 'Gordon' about how the Team should work. He summarized that day's events: 'not much team spirit exhibited among the members of the mission.' Yet Yaremovich remained confident of his own status and that of his colleague, Crapleve. Both had finalized their terms of employment directly with the UCC, at a meeting held in Winnipeg on Friday, 24 October 1947. There they had signed a contract (hand-dated 'Winnipeg, Man. October 31st 1947') which provided them with 'freedom of action,' specific work to do, and definite financial arrangements. And so Yaremovich could afford to challenge Panchuk's ideas on what needed to be done and how, and with Crapleve's agreement he did so. See Yaremovich, 'Diary,' 24 October, 18 November, 19 November, and 5 December 1947. (This October meeting seems to have been more or less a formality: a few days earlier, on 21 October, Yaremovich had met Karasevich on a Winnipeg street and been told that the terms he and Crapleve had proposed were going to be accepted).

60 Ibid.

61 Ibid.

62 Ibid. On his copy of this letter Panchuk underlined '*They arrived at a satisfactory agreement with KYK, but you will note that in a lot of ways they will be directly responsible to KYK.*'

63 Arsenych and A. Mandryka to Panchuk, 18 November 1947, Panchuk Collection. On 25 and 26 November 1947, Yaremovich recorded that the 'atmosphere' in the Bureau was 'quite frigid,' and further detailed his disappointment with Panchuk's behaviour. See Yaremovich, 'Diary.'

64 See Panchuk's telegram to Karasevich, 2 December 1947, Panchuk Collection.

65 Panchuk's letter from London to the board of directors of the UCC and UCRF, 27 November 1947, and Panchuk to Karasevich, 2 December 1947, Panchuk Collection.

66 Kushnir to Panchuk, 5 December 1947, Panchuk Collection.

67 Ibid.

68 Kushnir's cable to Yaremovich, 5 December 1947. A month later Yaremovich noted that Panchuk was still trying to get Ukrainian Canadian funds to help the SEP at Rimini. Worse, his financial accounts were 'not in order.' See Yaremovich, 'Diary,' 5 January 1948. Ironically, Panchuk left the UCRF's employ with a hint of financial scandal hanging over his administration, just as Frolick had before him. In neither case is there any supporting evidence of personal misappropriation of funds. Obviously, with incessant calls for aid being made upon CURB's personnel, and later those of the Mission, moneys were given out to various Continental refugee committees

and individual DPs, not all of which could be precisely accounted for. For those in Winnipeg, geographically far removed and working under normal civilian conditions, the situation in Europe was not readily understandable, so they almost incessantly questioned what their workers were doing overseas, especially when it came to spending money. Then too it must be recalled that neither the UCC nor UCRF executive had any prior experience of the sort which might have guided it in setting down realizable directives and policies. All this meant that, in the end, those in the field acted spontaneously, generously, and as they saw best, a state of affairs that could not but result in misunderstandings and difficulties with their overseers in Canada. For Frolick's views on Panchuk's charges about CURB's finances, see his vitriolic letter to Panchuk, 30 December 1946, Frolick Collection, and his more measured account in *Between Two Worlds*.

69 Panchuk to Philipps, 11 December 1947, Panchuk Collection. Panchuk kept in close touch with Philipps. For example, they cooperated in trying to expedite the emigration of the Kisilewsky family to Canada (see Philipps to Panchuk, 18 January 1948) and in protesting against the deportation from England to Germany of invalid or sick Ukrainian POWs, in December 1948. Philipps was certainly full of praise for the 'far-reaching, intelligent and common-sense scope of the wonderful work' which Panchuk had managed to do, 'so to speak, in your spare time' (Philipps to Panchuk, 22 November 1946). He also assisted Panchuk in the preparation of various memoranda, including one of 31 May 1948, which lobbied on behalf of fair treatment for members of the Ukrainian Division 'Galicia.' Philipps counselled Panchuk that, since this memo was 'presumably destined for Englishmen,' few 'if any' of whom had 'any background and knowledge of geography, history, ethnics, or recent events,' he would have to explain various terms and events carefully. Above all, Panchuk should keep in mind that for Englishmen 'Ukrainians are a troublesome kind of Russian, if not a recently discovered sub-species of natural history specimens, deriving from migrating cranes!' (Philipps to Panchuk, 20 June 1948). A few years later Philipps repeated his caveat, remarking that 'No average Englishman understands Volhynias or Podolias, which he probably thinks are exotic garden-flowers or tropical diseases!' One must therefore write memoranda in a way that was 'geographically understanded-of-the-peepul.' See Philipps to Panchuk, 5 November 1950. These letters, and additional Panchuk-Philipps correspondence, are found in the Panchuk Collection.

70 Panchuk to Kaye, 19 December 1947. As noted above, Panchuk had taken an early interest in the fate of the Ukrainian SEP interned near Rimini, Italy. He assisted Professor Royse in screening them and other SEP on behalf of a

British screening commission headed by Brigadier Maclean. He also paid
regular visits to these Ukrainian POWs once they were relocated to the
United Kingdom, a process more or less completed by the early fall of 1947.
Panchuk circulated several memoranda on the Ukrainian Division 'Galicia'
and assisted with their eventual 'civilianization.' See, for example, his
memoranda entitled 'Divisia Halychyna: A Total of about 9,000 Surrendered Enemy Personnel Now in Rimini, Italy' (17 December 1946); 'Release
and Resettlement of Rimini Group' (8 April 1948); and 'Ukrainian 'Divisia
Halychyna' (Ukrainian P.O.W. in Great Britain), Previously 'Surrendered
Enemy Personnel' in Rimini, Italy,' 31 May 1948, Panchuk Collection. Sporadic allegations have been made since the end of the war about Ukrainian
war criminals, many such stories originating from Soviet-inspired sources.
At the time, the British knew better than to accept these accusations. L.
Scopes, of the Foreign Office, wrote that while 'Communist propaganda'
had constantly attempted to depict these and other refugees as 'quislings
and war criminals,' it was 'interesting to note that no specific charges of
war crimes had been made by the Soviet or any other Government against
any member of this group.' See Document #51, 4 September 1950, in *Anglo-
American Perspectives on the Ukrainian Question*, ed. Luciuk and Kordan,
233–4. Panchuk himself observed that the principal reason he was selected
to aid Royse and the British was that the two governments had deliberately
'decided that they do not want a Pole or a Russian or a Jew who claims that
he knows the Ukrainian question, they want a Canadian or American of
Ukrainian origin who really does know the question, and who would not
be biased in any shape or form.' See Panchuk to the UCC, 8 May 1947, Panchuk Collection. Typical examples of Soviet or Soviet-inspired propaganda
aimed at portraying Ukrainian nationalists as 'war criminals,' 'fascists,' and
'Nazi collaborators,' include A. Bogomolets, *Soviet Ukraine and Ukrainian-
German Nationalists in Canada* (Toronto, 1943); V. Styrkul, *The SS Werewolves*
(Lviv, 1982) and *ABN: Backstage Exposé* (Lviv, 1983); M. Terlytsia, *Here Is the
Evidence* (Toronto, 1984); A. Sidyak, *The Bankrupts* (Lviv, 1984); Y. Korolevich, *The Emigré Inn* (Kiev, 1985); O.M. Butsko, *Never to Be Forgotten* ...
(Kiev, 1986). For a response, see L. Luciuk, 'Ukraine's Wartime Unit Never
Linked to War Crime,' *Globe and Mail*, 28 March 1985, 7. This propaganda
largely ceased with the disintegration of the USSR in 1991, although it continues to echo within certain North American Jewish circles and among
their supporters. This is odd given that the question of 'war criminality' on
the part of members of the Ukrainian Division 'Galicia' was explored thoroughly by Mr Justice Jules Deschênes, whose final public report noted that
members of the Division had been 'individually screened' before their

admission to Canada, that 'charges of war crimes against members of the
Galicia Division have never been substantiated,' that 'mere membership in
the Galicia Division is insufficient to justify prosecution,' and that, therefore, 'The Galicia Division ... should not be indicted as a group,' *Commission
of Inquiry on War Criminals, Report: Part 1, Public*, 261. Deschênes also criticized the 'loose language and somewhat careless public statements' of
some Jewish-Canadian activists, such as Sol Littman, a self-styled 'Nazi
hunter.' The Commission found that 'between 1971 and 1986, public statements by outside interveners concerning alleged war criminals residing in
Canada have spread increasingly large and grossly exaggerated figures as
to their estimated number.' A detailed examination of these various claims
suggested that there had been 'no less than a 400 per cent over-estimate by
the proponents of those figures,' 246, 249.

71 Writing to Kaye, 11 January 1949, Panchuk observed: 'You will also be
pleased to know that the last Ukrainian Prisoner of War has now been civil-
ianized and that the problem of the Ukrainian Division has finally been settled most happily. I humbly feel that it was one job of work which is
concrete and even if I had not done anything more throughout my period
overseas, that job alone makes me feel that my humble efforts were not in
vain.' In Yaremovich's view, the SEP, once in the United Kingdom, were in a
much better position than the DPs still in western Europe, for not only were
the former better fed, clothed, and housed, but they also faced 'no Red
Menace from the East.' And so, Yaremovich concluded, the UCRF would
have to put its limited relief dollars into helping refugees rather than SEP.
All the latter should get thereafter would be moral rather than material
help. See Yaremovich, 'Diary,' 6 January 1948. Similarly, P. Wenger wrote to
Panchuk on 14 March 1949 to say that he thought it was *'wrong'* to push
Ottawa about letting down its immigration barriers with respect to members of the Division, not only because the timing was politically inopportune in Canada but because 'they are needed in Britain as labourers.' If that
was so, they should stay there for as long as needed. Saying that they
wanted to leave the United Kingdom was foolish, for it made them appear
to be 'expressing their ingratitude.' Besides which, if they wanted to move
to Canada, that was *'not a Ukrainian problem* [but] a personal one,' so there
was no reason for Ukrainian Canadians to do anything to facilitate it: 'Have
they not a living the same as the English labourer? Have they not security
from the Russians?' Wenger asked. 'If they want anything more it is up to
themselves to get it. Our attitude in Canada is that they are fortunate to be
where they are and let us do what we can for those still in Germany and
Austria.' Panchuk disagreed, and that, he claimed, was one of the principal

reasons for his decision to leave CURB. Later he played a major role in helping the SEP in the United Kingdom. For example, he orchestrated a national protest against the deportation of sick and invalid Ukrainian POWs from the United Kingdom to Germany over Christmastime, 1948. See his memorandum on this issue dated 28 December 1948 in the Panchuk Collection. On the Ukrainian Division 'Galicia' and its screening, see 'Refugee Screening Commission: Report on Ukrainians in SEP Camp No. 574 Italy,' written by D.H. Porter, reproduced in Panchuk, *Heroes of Their Day*, 140–8; Brigadier Maclean's report in the Panchuk Collection; FO 371/71636, 23 January 1948; W.-D. Heike, *The Ukrainian Division 'Galicia,' 1943–45: A Memoir* (Toronto, 1988); and R. Landwehr, *Fighting for Freedom: The Ukrainian Volunteer Division of the Waffen SS* (Silver Spring, Md., 1985); and M.O. Logusz, *Galicia Division: The Waffen-SS 14th Grenadier Division, 1943–1945* (Atglen, Pa., 1997). See also M. Momryk, 'Ukrainian DP Immigration and Government Policy in Canada, 1946–52,' in *The Refugee Experience*, ed. Isajiw, Boshyk, and Senkus, 413–34, particularly his description of the Galicia Division's situation, found on 421–5. As noted in n70 above, Mr Justice Jules Deschênes concluded that there were no factual bases for accusing the Ukrainian Division 'Galicia' of participation in war crimes or crimes against humanity. And Canada's minister of justice, the Honourable Anne McLellan, MP, confirmed even more recently that 'over a number of years the War Crimes and Crimes Against Humanity Section of the Department of Justice has, in conjunction with the Royal Canadian Mounted Police, investigated allegations against individual members of the Division ... The evidence we have been able to uncover is insufficient to merit the commencement of court proceedings against any members of the Division.' Commenting, the chairman of the Ukrainian Canadian Civil Liberties Association, John B. Gregorovich, said: 'We trust this will bring to a close media reports about the alleged presence of thousands of Nazi war criminals hiding in Canada. These unfounded allegations were made before the Deschênes Commisssion and were found to be "grossly exaggerated." Ever since, however, the persons who originally made those claims have been molly-coddled by the media, which has continued to report the same old allegations as if they were proven fact, instead of fantasy. The Minister's letter confirms that no member of the Ukrainian Division "Galicia" can be prosecuted for a war crime or crime against humanity since no evidence of any such crime exists, as we have said all along. If Ottawa has compelling evidence that proves that a person is guilty of a war crime or crime against humanity let them make their case in a Canadian criminal court. We support that. We do not support trial by media or the less rigorous denaturalization and deportation procedures that the government retreated to after discovering that there is no hard evidence confirming the existence of any Nazi war criminals in Canada.' See 'McLellan Clears Division Members,' *Ukrainian News* (Edmonton), 2–15 December 1998, 3. Nevertheless, some Jewish-Canadian circles continue to raise this canard.

72 'Soviet Protest against Anti-Soviet Propaganda among Soviet Citizens in D.P. camps in the U.K.,' 10 June 1947, FO 371/31590. This same file contains the Soviet protest telegram, dated 4 June 1947.

73 Ibid. See also 'Ukrainian Displaced Persons in the U.K.,' 11 August 1948, FO 371/66713. Brimelow agreed that some Soviet complaints about the AUGB were justified, for Panchuk had been trying to give shelter to individuals about whom the Russians were anxious. Brimelow agreed, 'We should only deal with Mr Panchuk,' but insisted Panchuk would have to be 'warned not to drag in people about whom we have had complaints from the Russians.'

74 Panchuk to Yaremovich, 10 July 1947, Panchuk Collection. At a meeting in London on 30 November 1947, Panchuk made it clear that he was volunteering his services to the AUGB, and that CURB would be shutting down. See Yaremovich, 'Diary,' 30 November 1947. That very same day Yaremovich expressed further anxieties over 'Gordon's behaviour.' On what he described as a foggy Monday, 1 December 1947, Yaremovich recorded that there was still 'great tension in the Bureau – no outlook for the better.'

75 On N. Bura, who arrived in the United Kingdom in August 1943 with the Polish armed forces being relocated there from the Middle East ('the Anders Army'), see 'Soviet Protest against Anti-Soviet Propaganda among Soviet citizens in D.P. Camps in the U.K.,' 7 June 1947, FO 371/66451. Bura, of Volhynian origin, had served in the Polish *Sejm* (parliament). In October 1943 the British Home Office approved his employment with the Polish government in London. That he later became the first president of the AUGB may have been intended to foster a Polish–Ukrainian rapprochement. In response to the Soviet protest regarding Bura's activities as head of the AUGB, His Majesty's principal secretary of state for foreign affairs replied, on 30 July 1947, that while 'it is impossible to interfere with the complete freedom of speech of the press and of association enjoyed by inhabitants of this country,' the 'competent authorities' had been asked to 'endeavour to discourage the conduct of anti-Soviet propaganda amongst groups of Ukrainians living in camps' in the United Kingdom.

76 Kaye to Philipps, 7 March 1948, NAC MG30 E350.

77 Ibid.

78 Ibid. Panchuk wrote to Kaye on 10 June 1948, Panchuk Collection, asking

him to intervene with the Department of Veterans Affairs so that he could remain in the United Kingdom for 'at least another few years,' to supervise the work of the AUGB, while continuing with course work at the University of London. Kaye went to the Department of Veterans Affairs in Ottawa on 12 August and wrote to Panchuk about that meeting the next day, letting him know that his plans were approved and that he would suffer no loss of the benefits owed him as a veteran by staying in England. He added, 'We hope we shall be able to utilize your knowledge for the benefit of Canada when you return with the diploma.'

79 Not everyone was pleased with the UCRF's appointment of Yaremovich as CURB's new director. Korostovets, Danylo Skoropadsky's aide-de-camp, wrote privately to Kushnir from the Royal Automobile Club, in Pall Mall, to remind him that Panchuk had 'acquired a unique place of authority and excellent reputation' in Britain, and that, while he liked Yaremovich personally, substituting the latter for Panchuk 'is equal to a catastrophe,' [undated, likely late 1948], Panchuk Collection. Korostovets declared: 'Compare the position a year ago with what is now. The many thousand DPs including the Divisia Galicia are here and actually saved from the threat of being delivered to death into the hands of the Bolshis [sic]. This without Panchuk would be never achieved. I know enough the position here to vouch the truth of what I say here. Now that London becomes the centre of European Activities in the Anglo-American cooperation of saving the continent from Bolshevism, our work acquired here special importance, and nobody better than Panchuk can carry out the uphill complicated work, which is needed for our cause!' Korostovets added that Bishop Ivan Buchko, with whom he had spoken the day before, concurred.

80 See Yaremovich to the UCC, 26 July 1948, Panchuk Collection, for complaints regarding the UUARC and its activities with the Ukrainian refugee community in France, particularly with regard to the UUARC-purchased property in Paris.

81 See A. Mandryka to B. Byblow, 3 November 1948. The amount cited by Yaremovich in a letter to Panchuk, 6 July 1948, was 639 pounds sterling, 19 shillings, and 3 pence. By way of comparison, when Panchuk wrote to G. Kluchevsky, the treasurer of CURB during Frolick's tenure as director, he noted that there was a difference of 223 pounds sterling, 14 shillings and 8 pence between the financial statement co-signed by Frolick and Kluchevsky and what CURB's record books showed. See Panchuk to Kluchevsky, 3 December 1946, Panchuk Collection. Kluchevsky replied on 9 March 1947, and Frolick offered his own opinion on these allegations on 17 October 1946, Frolick Collection.

82 See Panchuk's letter on behalf of the AUGB to Yaremovich, the director of CURB, 9 July 1948, Panchuk Collection.
83 Byblow to the AUGB's Panchuk, 8 November 1948, Panchuk Collection.
84 See the AUGB's executive director, George Salsky, to CURB, 10 November 1948, and Panchuk to Salsky, 16 November 1948, Panchuk Collection. Salsky was interviewed in Aylmer, Québec, 16 September 1981 (MHSO).
85 Panchuk, 'Memorandum re: Liquidation of CURB, 48 Seymour Street, London,' 9 November 1948, Panchuk Collection.
86 Meetings were held on 23, 26, and 28 November 1948, at CURB's Seymour Street address. All CURB operations, it was agreed, would cease as of 11 December 1948, after which the UCRF relief and welfare activities would be devoted entirely to the British Zone of Germany, with headquarters in Bielefeld. Since only about one pound sterling was left in CURB's bank account, staff wages and other expenses had to be paid for with a thousand dollar grant cabled to London from the UCRF headquarters in Winnipeg.
87 Yaremovich to Panchuk, 26 August 1948, NAC MG28 v9, vol. 15, and Karasevich to Panchuk, 18 September 1948, Panchuk Collection. Despite these disagreements, Yaremovich and Panchuk would remain friendly in Canada, working together within the framework of UCVA to promote that organization's interests within Ukrainian Canadian society. Another possible reason for their ongoing commitment to UCVA was their shared belief in the role the veterans' group could play in dealing with the DPs in Canada. See Yaremovich's 'Diary,' 24 October 1947, where he expressed the view that the veterans were the 'most qualified' to 'do the job' of integrating the refugees into Ukrainian Canadian society.
88 See J. Yuzyk to Panchuk, 22 August 1948; Karasevich's telegram to Panchuk, 18 September 1948; and Panchuk's reply, 20 September 1948, all in the Panchuk Collection.
89 Panchuk to Smylski, then in Edmonton, 18 August 1948, Panchuk Collection.
90 Ibid.
91 See CURB's Byblow to the AUGB, 9 December 1948, Panchuk Collection. Although Panchuk wrote a congratulatory letter to Crapleve on 1 February 1949, complimenting her on how much UCRF operations had improved after she took over, he had not always been so generous. On 22 August 1948 he sent a long letter to Crapleve and Yaremovich in which, after reviewing the history of the CRM, and their various independent efforts in the fall of 1948, he bemoaned the way in which the UCC, which 'never had any plan and made no endeavour to prepare one,' had left everything up to the

Team, more specifically up to him as its director, a situation which ultimately resulted in some ill will among the three of them. See Panchuk to 'Dear Ann and Tony,' 22 August 1948, Panchuk Collection. J. Yuzyk wrote to Panchuk on 22 August 1948 pointing out that unless Yaremovich and Panchuk developed the 'most friendly relations,' the future would be 'as bright as the inside of a stove pipe,' for without their cooperation the entire structure of overseas work would become 'a complete wash out.' He urged them to meet 'as two old veterans should.' Pessimistically, but realistically, he added, 'Dreaming of raising millions in Canada for the cause can only be a dream'; Panchuk Collection.

92 See Panchuk's letter from London to the UCC and UCRF, 6 February 1948, Panchuk Collection, for a remarkably sensible memorandum on how the UCRF should be organizing its overseas operations.

93 E. Wasylyshen to J.H. Patterson, 28 April 1949, and A. Crapleve to the UCRF, 16 December 1948, Wasylyshen Collection. Mrs Wasylyshen (née Burianyk) was equally pleased that they had Crapleve, an 'old timer on the job,' to help them adjust to their new duties. Certainly life in the British Zone of Germany 'is anything but simple.' See A. Wasylyshen to Vera ?, 30 October 1949, Wasylyshen Collection.

94 On 16 February 1949, Panchuk wrote to Dmytro Gerych, a leading UWVA/UNF member from Winnipeg, who had served as one of the secretaries of the first UCC congress, to record that he had been interested to learn that 'somebody and his wife' were expecting to come over as a Ukrainian Canadian 'diplomatic mission.' He added that he would be grateful if Gerych could be more specific about who these people were. Unless those selected to come overseas were 'exceptionally capable, young and modern,' all qualities Panchuk felt were essential for working with the British authorities, there was no point to sending them. Besides which, Panchuk added, any 'diplomatic work' which needed to be done was being taken care of by those already in England. Panchuk did promise to help the Wasylyshens after he was informed of their departure. See Panchuk to the UCRF's Mandryka, 21 February 1949, Panchuk Collection. In his 'Report #2,' 28 March 1949, E. Wasylyshen noted that he and his wife left Winnipeg on 10 March 1949 and arrived at the port of Southampton on 15 March 1949, Wasylyshen Collection.

95 Interviews with Mrs Anne Wasylyshen, Winnipeg, 30 May 1982 (MHSO) and 30 November 1982 (CIUS). See also the interview with V. Maruniak (12 July, 1982 [MHSO]), who confirmed that E. Wasylyshen was a leading member of the OUNm.

96 See the photograph of Eustace Wasylyshen with Colonel Evhen Konova-

lets, leader of the UVO, and, until his assassination in 1938, of the OUN, reproduced in Marunchak, *The Ukrainian Canadians*, 509. W. Kossar, the long-term leader of the Ukrainian National Federation, and P. Shteppa, who will figure in the next chapter, both prominent members of the UWVA/UNF, were also members of PUN.

97 That Andrievsky was a member of PUN is confirmed by Motyl, *The Turn to the Right*, 45. Andrievsky accompanied Panchuk and Wasylyshen when they visited the Foreign Office, as noted in 'Meeting with Mr. Panchuk of the Association of Ukrainians in Great Britain, Mr. Andrievsky, a member of the Ukrainian National Council, and Mr. and Mrs. Eustace Wasylyshen,' 21 March 1949, FO 371/77586. On that occasion they were told by R.M.A. Hankey that it was essential that the displaced persons and political refugees be kept away from any political activities which might prove damaging to Anglo-Soviet relations. Andrievsky visited UCRF headquarters at Bielefeld on 24 May 1949, remaining there for two days before moving to the American Zone of Germany. In E. Wasylyshen's 'Report #4,' 25 May 1949, Wasylyshen Collection, there is a cryptic note to the effect that Andrievsky was 'officially' brought into the British Zone by the UCRF. He was 'temporarily on our establishment.' Crapleve expressed personal reservations about the kind of political work Wasylyshen and Andrievsky might have been doing alongside their UCRF responsibilities. Interviews with Ann Smith (née Crapleve) in Winnipeg, 20 May 1982 (MHSO) and 29 November 1982 (CIUS).

98 The Wasylyshens to Dallas ?, 16 March 1949, and E. Wasylyshen to J.H. Paterson, 28 April 1949, Wasylyshen Collection.

99 A. Wasylyshen to ?, 10 April 1949, Wasylyshen Collection. In a letter sent to Mrs D.E. Yanda, of Edmonton, 4 February 1950, Mrs Wasylyshen replied to a request for details about the composition of the Ukrainian refugee population. Some 60 per cent were Ukrainian Catholics. The remainder were of the Ukrainian Orthodox faith. In 'Report #6,' 5 August 1949, E. Wasylyshen described the 'Lysenko' DP camp near Hannover as containing 2203 Ukrainian inhabitants out of a total of 2787 refugees. Of the Ukrainian group a total of 1172 were males, and 1031 were females; there were 588 families present, along with 270 single males, 58 single females, and 720 children aged between 1 and 20 years old; Wasylyshen Collection.

100 E. Wasylyshen, 'Report #4,' 25 May 1949, Wasylyshen Collection.

101 Ibid.

102 E. Wasylyshen, 'Report #8,' 12 October 1949, Wasylyshen Collection. In 'Report #9,' dated 21 October 1949, Wasylyshen advised the UCRF that, at a meeting held in Bremen, involving Smook, Rodyk, and himself, he had

been told that while the UUARC had three thousand Assurances to dispose of they would not commit any to Ukrainian DPs in the British Zone, where Ukrainian Canadians did most of their work.

103 A. Wasylyshen to Stephie ?, 29 February 1950, Wasylyshen Collection. In the Wasylyshens' co-authored 'Final Report,' 2 October 1950, they expressed their regret that UUARC personnel 'persisted in considering the UCRF Mission a branch office or subsidiary of UUARC.' While cooperation between the two groups 'on the whole' had been friendly and cordial, 'we wish UUARC had been just as ready to grant the same credit to UCRF for their work in Europe, which, after all, began long before UUARC came on the scene.'

104 A. Wasylyshen to Donna ?, 18 April 1950, and E. Wasylyshen to Yaremovich, 24 August 1949, Wasylyshen Collection.

105 A. Wasylyshen to Donna ?, 19 April 1950, and A. Wasylyshen to Vera ?, 30 October 1949, Wasylyshen Collection.

106 A. Wasylyshen to Ann and Emil ?, 11 January 1950, Wasylyshen Collection.

107 A. Wasylyshen to Vera ?, 30 October 1949, Wasylyshen Collection.

108 A. Wasylyshen to Vera ?, 30 October 1949, and A. Wasylyshen to Ann and Emil ?, 11 January 1950, Wasylyshen Collection. In the latter, Mrs Wasylyshen expressed surprise at the attitude taken by some refugees to their prospects for emigration, and characterized some refugees' expectations as follows: 'It would really amaze you, to see how people feel they can pick and choose where they will go. America is their goal – Canadian immigration laws are too strict – Australia is too far, and too hot, and any other country is out of the question. Mothers of grown up daughters are insulted to the core if you suggest that their daughters could accept domestic work and then make arrangements to bring their parents – the students want information on scholarships, never about work, and are quite convinced that having finished "Gymnasium" in a DP camp they are ready for Canadian Universities.' 'After all,' as Mrs Wasylyshen parodied some of refugees' comments, 'the standard of education is so low in America.'

109 E. Wasylyshen, 'Report #5,' 20 June 1949, and A. Wasylyshen to Ann and Emil ?, Wasylyshen Collection. In a letter to friends in Canada, 10 April 1950, Wasylyshen Collection, Mrs Wasylyshen made a similar point: 'Otherwise we had nothing from Winnipeg until we received one or two short letters from a certain man which cast quite a shadow over our work for a couple of months. He gave us the first inkling of something rotten in the state of Denmark – about all kinds of intrigue and baseless gossip. It is very unfair to find out that all sorts of talk about us is going on, started by

goodness knows who and based on heaven only knows what rumour, and not have a chance to reply to it.'

110 For example, Panchuk, writing to J. Choma of Fort William, Ontario, commented that while he was grateful for the news Choma had provided, because it 'helped to bring us a little closer to Canada,' there 'are so few people writing anything about the activities there that we are almost completely lost now and it will not be long before we feel worse than the DPs themselves.' See Panchuk to Choma, 18 June 1948, Panchuk Collection.

111 See M.I. Mandryka, *Ukrainian Refugees* (Winnipeg, 1946). On Mandryka, see *A Heritage in Transition*, ed. Lupul, 183, 198, 296, 300, and 301; Marunchak, *The Ukrainian Canadians*, 409–10, 445, 475, 477–8, 481, 490, 525, 530–3, 457, 551, 596–7, and 606; A. Gospodin's article 'Dr. M.I. Mandryka – A Tireless Worker,' in *Ukrainian Voice*, September 1971; and the interviews with A. Gospodin, Winnipeg, 1 December 1982 and 21 January 1983 (CIUS).

112 The personal papers of the late Monsignor V. Kushnir and of Mr Volodymyr Kochan remain closed. However, in a letter Kochan wrote on 3 March 1955 to Dr V. KubijovyŠ, who had headed the Ukrainian Central Committee in the Generalgouvernement, he did note that when he first came to Canada there had been serious talk about liquidating the UCC, by persons who argued that the Committee had been formed only to last for the duration of the war. Kochan claimed that he had prevented this by talking privately with this dissident group's members, and, by making using of his status as UNRada's representative in Canada, convincing all concerned that they should let the UCC carry on. The third UCC congress formally acknowledged that the Committee had become a permanent fixture on the Ukrainian Canadian scene. Kochan also pointed out that some 80 per cent of the 'newcomers' had not joined any of the UCC's constituent organizations. At the third UCC congress there were a total of 406 delegates and 241 guests. The official delegates represented the USRL (114), BUC (106), UNF (95), UHO (35), UCC (28), UCVA (15), and Ukrainian Workers League (13). See *Third All-Canadian Congress of Ukrainians in Canada*, 82.

113 M. Mandryka to E. Wasylyshen, 14 November 1949, Wasylyshen Collection.

114 Ibid. Mandryka also claimed that the 'Catholic wing' was siding with the Hetmanite-Banderite bloc. Although this alleged alliance between the Hetmantsi and the Banderivtsi may on the surface seem unlikely, both groups were united in their opposition to the Ukrainian National Council and counted among their members immigrants from western Ukraine, generally persons of Ukrainian Catholic faith.

115 See E. Wasylyshen to Kochan, undated, in which the former noted that
since he kept his own files 'under lock and key,' as did Panchuk, there had
to have been 'a leak in Winnipeg,' which had resulted in the publication of
Panchuk's confidential letter. Certain 'elements' there, charged Wasylyshen, were exploiting the UCC's private correspondence files for their own
political purposes, a situation which could result in great 'damage to the
humanitarian effort' which the UCRF's officers were accomplishing overseas. Wasylyshen had indeed written to Kushnir about Panchuk's problems inside the AUGB, in March 1949, in order to ensure that Winnipeg
was fully informed. Now, however, Wasylyshen claimed, certain people
'willing to do harm to KYK' had infiltrated the UCC's offices in Winnipeg
and were launching 'provocations' which he believed were intended 'to
throw a shadow on the Fund.' Wasylyshen copied this letter to Kochan,
Kushnir, Kossar, the UCRF's national executive, and Panchuk. On 5 January 1950 he also wrote directly to Panchuk, apologizing for what had
happened. He also made note of the fact that Dr Mandryka's letter had
provided him with the 'first news' he had had of 'what's going on in Winnipeg.' Earlier, Wasylyshen had written to Panchuk making it clear that the
'leak' was on the Winnipeg end. See E. Wasylyshen to Panchuk, 28 October
1949, Wasylyshen Collection. Angered by these intrigues, Panchuk entered
the fray, aligning himself even more thoroughly with those ranged up
against the Banderivtsi and Hetmantsi, as he made clear in a letter to his
friend Karasevich, on 16 December 1949, Panchuk Collection. Panchuk
later vented some of his growing annoyance with the way in which 'Zaharychuk and an office full of DPs' were mismanaging the UCC in a letter to
the Wasylyshens and Crapleve, sent from London just after his brief return
to Canada, where he had participated in the third UCC congress. See Panchuk to the Wasylyshens and Crapleve, 3 March 1950, Panchuk Collection.
116 In 'Report #6,' 5 August 1949, Wasylyshen Collection, E. Wasylyshen
described Mr and Mrs Yanda's visit in passing. His wife, writing to their
personal friends, Ann and Emil ?, on 10 April 1950, dealt with the Yandas'
visit more forcefully. They had come 'looking for homage' but had left
annoyed at not receiving any, she claimed.
117 M. Mandryka to E. Wasylyshen, 14 November 1949, Wasylyshen Collection.
118 Ibid.
119 Ibid. Mandryka's social-democratic ideological orientation did place him
in the ranks of those opposed to the Hetmantsi as well as to Ukrainian
nationalists of both OUN factions, which possibly helps explain the motivations behind his allegations.

120 E. Wasylyshen to the UCRF, 30 January 1950, Wasylyshen Collection. For another report on the UCRF, see Yaremovich's address to delegates attending the third UCC congress. In the published proceedings, *Third All-Canadian Congress of Ukrainians in Canada*, 116, there is a financial statement on the UCRF's operations from 1945 to 31 December 1949. Officially, $222,653.79 had been collected and $203,342.78 spent. Of the latter amount, $50,000 had been forwarded to the Canadian Red Cross, just over $54,000 had been given as aid through the UCRF missions overseas, and nearly another $49,000 had been expended on direct relief. The sum of $12,253.90 was spent on resettlement costs. Only $18,203.72 went for salaries. This left nearly $21,000 in the UCRF's account in early 1950.

121 E. Wasylyshen to the UCRF, 30 January 1950, Wasylyshen Collection.

122 Ibid.

123 E. Wasylyshen to V. Kushnir, 24 March 1950, Wasylyshen Collection.

124 A. Wasylyshen to Donna ?, 18 April 1950, Wasylyshen Collection.

125 A. and E. Wasylyshen to the UCRF, 'Final Report,' 2 October 1950, and A. Wasylyshen to Donna ?, 18 April 1950, Wasylyshen Collection.

126 UCRF to E. Wasylyshen, 27 April 1950, Wasylyshen Collection.

127 E. Wasylyshen to the UCRF, 27 April 1950, Wasylyshen Collection.

128 See A. and E. Wasylyshen's 'Final Report' to the UCRF, 2 October 1950. Indicative of what they had accomplished in 1950, the Wasylyshens' report noted that a total of 6428 Ukrainian DPs had been resettled that year, the largest numbers emigrating to the United States (3050), Australia (2340) and Canada (918). Crapleve returned to Canada on 28 February 1952, having closed down the UCRF office in Bielefeld on 21 December 1951.

129 See 'Report of Work of the Ukrainian Canadian Relief Fund in Europe, 1945–51,' NAC MG28 v9, vol. 17, 1951.

130 Panchuk to Crapleve, 28 February 1951, Panchuk Collection. He estimated that as many as 50,000 Ukrainian DPs had gone to Canada. Of these, 80 per cent were 'official refugees' (by which he meant sponsored by UNRRA, the IGCR, or IRO); 10 per cent were members of the Polish and other allied forces; 7 per cent were old émigrés who had come from western European countries; and 3 per cent were veterans of the Ukrainian Division 'Galicia.' V.J. Kaye calculated that 33,667 Ukrainian refugees immigrated to Canada between 1946 and 1952. See NAC MG31 D69, vol. 26, [undated]. As an example of the composition of a typical boatload of DPs to Canada, see NAC RG2, series 18, vol. 83, file I-50-2, which describes the refugees sailing on the S.S. *General Stewart* from Bremerhaven, Germany, with an expected arrival date of 9 October 1947. Of the

775 people aboard, 675 were destined to work in lumber camps. Of these
the majority were Poles, followed by Lithuanians, Ukrainians, and Yugoslavs. By religious affiliation 541 were Catholic, 58 were Orthodox, 43
were Protestant, 29 were Jewish, 1 was a Muslim, 1 was a Mennonite, and
2 were listed as 'stateless.' One hundred of those on board were coming to
work as domestics. Eighty-two of the latter were Poles, Lithuanians, and
Ukrainians. The same file noted that, on 6 June 1947, Order-in-Council P.C.
2180 had provided for the admission of 5000 DPs from Europe; this number had been increased to 10,000 by P.C. 2856, 18 July 1947. By 18 September, 9619 had been selected for transportation to Canada, among them
4500 'woods-workers,' 1000 domestics, 1000 special cases, 2119 garment
workers, and 1000 labourers for the Hydro Electric Power Commission of
Ontario. The acting minister of mines and resources, C.D. Howe, proposed that another 10,000 DPs should be admitted to Canada, for use in
heavy industrial work, primary steel plants, metal manufacturing plants,
foundries, stone quarries, and brickyards, for construction work on power
plants and transmission lines; for railway construction; for track maintenance work; and for lumber camps. Two thousand women refugees would
also be admitted to serve as domestic workers. For another statistical
breakdown of refugees aboard the S.S. *General Stewart*, see R. Innes, Director of Resettlement, PCIRO, to J.P. Sigvaldason, Office of the High Commissioner for Canada, Canada House, London, 4 September 1947, NAC
RG25, series 12, vol. 2113, file 408/4 #2. In the first movement of 'woods-
workers' for Canada (24 July 1947), the average age of the 725 men on
board (all except 2 of whom were single, both of the non-single men being
listed as divorced) was 27.19 years old. Nearly 61 per cent of the men were
29 years of age or younger.

131 M. Mandryka to E. Wasylyshen, 7 December 1949, Wasylyshen Collection.
132 This report worried Wasylyshen, who, writing to Panchuk on 5 January
1950, observed that 'as long as Mrs Mandryka was in charge, we felt
assured of support'; Wasylyshen Collection.
133 M. Mandryka to E. Wasylyshen, 30 December 1949, Wasylyshen Collection.
134 Ibid.
135 M. Mandryka to E. Wasylyshen, 29 January 1950, Wasylyshen Collection.
136 A. Wasylyshen to Crapleve, 23 October 1950, Wasylyshen Collection. An
unidentified individual wrote to the Wasylyshens, on 11 September 1949,
to report that 'both KYK and Fund are passing through financial crisis.'
This was a result partially of the lack of a thought-out budget and an
effective fund-raising campaign but also of the fact that 'the organizers

were all DPs,' who 'meet with quite a bit of hostility from the Ukrainian Canadians.'

137 Ibid.

138 Panchuk had circulated memoranda such as 'The Welfare of Ukrainian European Voluntary Workers in the United Kingdom' (July 1947) and 'Moral and Psychological Persecution of Minority National Groups in the Polish Armed Forces and the Polish Resettlement Corps' (16 July 1947) even before he became the AUGB's second president. Visits by CURB-sponsored personnel, such as S.J. Jaworsky, were arranged to various hostels and camps where former Ukrainian SEP were housed, and a considerable amount of correspondence between CURB and the British authorities with respect to these immigrants' needs and expectations was generated. Jaworsky himself, before leaving for Canada in the summer of 1948, wrote nineteen reports concerning the status and treatment accorded to Ukrainian EVWs and POWs in various communities around Great Britain. Over Christmastime 1948, Panchuk helped orchestrate an effective protest on the part of Ukrainians throughout Great Britain against the proposed deportation of a number of sick or disabled Ukrainian POWs to Germany. For a copy of the mimeographed petition, which was widely distributed among Ukrainians in the United Kingdom, signed by them, and then sent to Prime Minister C.R. Attlee, see 'Resolution on Deportation of Ukrainian Prisoners of War to Germany,' 28 December 1948, Panchuk Collection. Even after he left the AUGB, Panchuk kept up this kind of work. See, for example, his letter to a Mr Blow of the Agriculture Executive Committee, County of Lincoln, 4 October 1950, Panchuk Collection. Part of this correspondence has been preserved on microfiche at the Rutherford Library of the University of Alberta, Edmonton. It is described in L.Y. Luciuk, 'An Annotated Guide to Certain Microfiched Archives of the Association of Ukrainians in Great Britain,' *Journal of Ukrainian Studies* 11:2 (1986): 77–91.

139 Interviews with O. Fundak and T. Danyliw, London, England, 4 August 1982 and 17 June 1982 (MHSO).

140 Panchuk to Crapleve, 15 March 1949, and Panchuk to the legal firm of Messrs Frere, Chomeley, and Nicholson, 16 March 1949, Panchuk Collection.

141 Panchuk to Crapleve, 15 March 1949, Panchuk Collection.

142 Ibid.

143 Panchuk to Messrs Frere, Chomeley, and Nicholson, 16 March 1949, and Panchuk to the AUGB, 1 April 1949, Panchuk Collection.

144 E. Wasylyshen to the UCC and UCRF, 23 March 1949, Wasylyshen Collection. It was likely this letter, along with another Panchuk had sent to the

Wasylyshens, which was subsequently 'leaked' by unknown persons in Winnipeg to the Ukrainian press. The culprit(s) possibly expected that the publication of these two letters would discredit Panchuk and the Wasylyshens, provoke dissent within the UCRF, and perhaps result in the recall of the UCRF mission.

145 Ibid.

146 E. Wasylyshen to the UCC and UCRF, 23 March 1949, and E. Wasylyshen to the UCRF, 'Report #3,' 10 April 1949, Wasylyshen Collection. At a meeting involving Wasylyshen, Fundak, Moncibovich, Danyliw, and Korostovets, held at 2:30 p.m. on 27 March, Wasylyshen listened to a series of grievances on the subject of Panchuk's administration of the AUGB. This session lasted until 11:00 p.m. On 28 June 1949 the new AUGB executive issued a news release in which it specified charges of financial mismanagement against Panchuk and most members of the former executive. Moncibovich and Danyliw, who co-signed this statement, observed that the AUGB's 1948 financial records were unsatisfactory, for approximately three thousand pounds sterling had been switched from various other accounts to the AUGB's central fund, ostensibly in order to hide a deficit. They claimed that when asked about this bookkeeping Panchuk had 'climbed onto a table,' given a speech insinuating that those challenging him were dishonest, and ended his harangue with the cry that whoever 'loved the AUGB' should follow him out of the room. Moncibovich and Danyliw countered Panchuk's allegations about political intrigues being responsible for the fracturing of the AUGB by turning the tables and blaming Panchuk's antics for the AUGB's internal troubles. They also claimed that his newly formed 'Ukrainian Bureau' was wasteful, for it only duplicated existing AUGB efforts. An 'Extraordinary General Meeting' of the AUGB, held on 29 October 1949, in London, failed to resolve these differences of interpretation and opinion; Panchuk and a small group of supporters ended up permanently outside the AUGB. For a recent, if incorrectly captioned, retrospective on Danyliw, see T. Leliw, 'Profile: The Founding Father of Association of Ukrainians in Great Britain,' *Ukrainian Weekly*, 12 February 1995, 8,12,

147 E. Wasylyshen, 'Report #3,' 10 April 1949, Wasylyshen Collection.

148 See J. Stewart to Panchuk, 10 April 1949, the latter's reply on 14 April 1949, and Stewart's letter to Panchuk, 16 April 1949, all in the Panchuk Collection. Stewart wrote again, on 26 October 1950, to defend the AUGB and the ABN, with which it had become identified. He observed: 'I know what these people *do*, but I do not know anything at all that the National Council [UNRada] *does* except talk. I cannot see why they were even formed at all

and can only think that it was out of personal jealousy to the other leaders of the Ukrainians and for reasons of personal aggrandizement. I think that the result is perfectly disastrous and I hope that if you have any power you will use it to the end of a united body.' Panchuk, writing to UNRada's Dr S. Wytwytsky, then in Augsburg in the American Zone of Germany, observed that while Stewart was 'sincerely devoted to the cause of liberating enslaved peoples,' he was 'obviously completely enslaved by a single group [the Banderivtsi] who are exploiting his naiveness to the maximum.' See Panchuk to Wytwytsky, 27 October 1950, Panchuk Collection.

149 Panchuk to Stewart, 14 April 1949, Panchuk Collection. Panchuk insisted that because he was 'Canadian born and bred,' and had no party affiliation, he could 'treat all of them objectively and as a realist.'

150 Ibid.

151 On UNRada, see 'An All-Ukrainian Council Formed in Exile,' *Ukrainian Bulletin* (New York), 15 August 1948, and D. Andrievsky, 'Outline of the Functions of the Ukrainian National Council,' 27 March 1949, FO 371/ 77586. On 21 March 1947, during the course of a personal interview, Hankey made it clear to Panchuk, Andrievsky, and the Wasylyshens that 'His Majesty's Government could not of course recognize the National Committee as having any sort of governmental status.' The Council's composition was again described in a memorandum sent to Hankey by Panchuk, dated 9 February 1951. Mr A.K.F. Uffen minuted (30 March 1951) this Ukrainian Bureau note to the effect that its 'question and answer' format 'bears all the marks of having been as spontaneously asked and answered as those in a Stalin interview with *Pravda*.' Panchuk's memorandum denounced the OUNb as a 'purely totalitarian group' and the Hetmantsi as non-democratic.

152 Panchuk to Stewart, 14 April 1949, Panchuk Collection.

153 Ibid.

154 Ibid.

155 Kaye to Panchuk, 12 April 1949, Panchuk Collection. Kaye told Panchuk that he had read a newspaper article about 'the whole revolution' in the AUGB, and that it all came as no surprise, since he had anticipated exactly these kinds of problems 'long ago.' Unfortunately, Kaye did not explain why he had not chosen to share his prescience with his friend Panchuk. Others in England also let colleagues in Canada know what was happening in the AUGB. For example, George Salsky, one of those who had joined Panchuk in leaving the meeting hall, wrote to his friend George Luckyj reporting on the motives and mechanics of the takeover. See G. Salsky to G. Luckyj, 15 March 1949, Panchuk Collection.

156 Panchuk to Kaye, 16 April 1949, Panchuk Collection. In a private letter to
Yaremovich, he claimed that the AUGB's membership was 'down from
22,000 in March to 7,200, of which only 3,000 pay fees,' further proof, he
asserted, of the harm brought about by the split within the AUGB. Panchuk's data seem to have been wildly inaccurate, in the AUGB's favour.
See Panchuk to Yaremovich, 21 November 1949, Panchuk Collection.

157 'Cessation by Mr. Panchuk of Membership and All Official Connections
with the Association of Ukrainians in Great Britain,' 15 April 1949, FO
371/77586.

158 Ibid., and Panchuk to Philipps, 3 June 1949, Panchuk Collection. Panchuk
did record that at least some of those who had voted against him had justified their action 'by saying that I am a "Britano-phil," in fact an "agent for
the British, Canadian and American authorities," "a member of the British
Intelligence Service" and such rot. It's pitiful ... but true.' See FO 371/
77586, 15 April 1949. In FO 371/94811, 16 October 1951, a Mrs Miller of the
Research Department observed that since his break with the AUGB Panchuk's attitude had become 'one of (doubtless reciprocal) hostility' to it.
She commented that he had fallen into disfavour 'because of his Liberal
views (he's strongly opposed to extremists such as Stetzko and B[andera],
because he consistently put the interests of Britain and the British Commonwealth before his allegiance to Ukrainian nationalists.'

159 Ibid. As documents released through the Access to Information Act show,
the RCMP were quite interested in the activities of the Ukrainian nationalist movement in Canada and abroad. For example, on 6 July 1951 a 'Memorandum for File' entitled 'Ukrainian Nationalist Movement' summed up
what the RCMP then knew about the competing factions of the Organization of Ukrainian Nationalists. It also noted that the Ukrainian National
Council formed in western Europe after the war's end was recognized by
the UCC 'as the sole legitimate spokesman for the Ukrainians,' while the
OUNb 'continued its insurrection even against this body, and is still maintaining the same hostile attitude.' The RCMP were also aware of the fact
that the OUNb had 'recently' allied itself with the Hetmanite supporters
within the Ukrainian emigration, and that, acting in concert, the two
groups had defeated Captain Panchuk in his bid to retain the presidency
of the London-based AUGB. In Canada, 'the insurrectionist policy of the
Bandera group' was being directed at the UCC, primarily in the pages of
the Ukrainian-language newspaper *Homin Ukrainy.*

160 See Panchuk's 'The Story of the Ukrainian Bureau in London, England,'
October 1949, Panchuk Collection, and 'Memorandum and Articles of
Association of the Ukrainian Bureau,' 16 April 1949, Panchuk Collection.

The Bureau was described as 'first and foremost a *representative, advice and information centre*' which 'would cater to no political parties, sects or creeds.' Ukrainians registered with the Bureau were to be organized into branches of a 'Ukrainian Self-Reliance Group,' while groups of Ukrainians and other British citizens would set up 'Anglo-Ukrainian Clubs,' whose activities were to be coordinated by the Bureau and the Central Office of Anglo-Ukrainian Clubs in Great Britain. The Bureau had its office at 64 Ridgmount Gardens, Chenies Street, London. The Central Office was at 122 Wardour Street, off Oxford Street, also in London. By 1951, the Bureau had also become identified as the European Office of the UCC. See Panchuk's confidential 'Summary Report: Contacts, Political and Public Relations Activities for the Period September 1st 1950 to March 31st 1951,' Panchuk Collection.

161 Panchuk, 'Memorandum and Articles ...,' 16 April 1949.
162 Philipps to Panchuk, 13 May 1949, Panchuk Collection.
163 Panchuk to Gallan, 1 September 1950, and Panchuk to Kaye, 18 April 1950, Panchuk Collection. Panchuk implored Kaye to intervene with the UCC and get it to provide adequate financial support for his Bureau. On his relations with Gallan, see Panchuk to Gallan, 20 September and 23 October 1950; Gallan to Panchuk, 17 October 1950; Panchuk to Gallan, 16 November and 6 December 1950; Gallan to Panchuk, 18 November 1950; and Panchuk to Gallan, 27 February 1951, all in the Panchuk Collection. Panchuk asserted that the Ukrainian Bureau, 're-organized and re-shaped' as of 1 September 1950, was 'in many ways' a continuation of CURB. He added that this European Office had been called into being at the third UCC congress. Its chief aim and purpose was 'to support the Ukrainian Liberation Movement insofar as this is possible in Great Britain and in the whole of western Europe.' Following the UCC's instructions, and his own predilections, Panchuk made sure the UCC's 'European Office' accorded complete and unequivocal political support to UNRada.
164 The AUGB seems to have grown despite its internal problems and Panchuk's prognosis. See 'Report on the Activities of the Association of Ukrainians in Great Britain, Limited, for the Period 1st January 1950 to 31st December 1950,' 2 April 1951, DEA 10268-40, vol. 1. The Association's secretary, T. Danyliw, reported that as of 31 December 1950 there were 19,443 active, registered AUGB members.
165 On the Federation of Ukrainians in Great Britain, see Panchuk to Byblow, 4 October 1950, Panchuk Collection.
166 See Panchuk to F. Hassan, 3 June 1949. With regard to relations between the new Bureau and the AUGB, see Panchuk to the AUGB, 24 October

1949, and Panchuk to Danyliw, 12 March 1951, Panchuk Collection. Panchuk also sent critical letters about the AUGB to various Ukrainian Canadian friends. For example, see his letter to Steve Kalin, October 1949, Panchuk Collection.

167 Panchuk later worked for the Ukrainian section of the CBC's International Services in Montreal. After leaving that position he taught high school, maintaining an active involvement in Ukrainian Canadian affairs. Resuscitating their earlier rivalry, Panchuk and Frolick ran against each other for the position of UCC president at the thirteenth UCC congress, held in Winnipeg 10–13 October 1980. Neither was successful.

168 E. Dudra to Panchuk, 30 January 1947, Panchuk Collection.

169 E. Wasylyshen to Yaremovich, 24 August 1949, Wasylyshen Collection.

170 Panchuk to D. Gerych, 10 September 1948, Panchuk Collection.

171 Panchuk, writing in July 1949 to several Ukrainian Canadian friends, commented that there was 'much to make [him] unhappy' about the impact the DPs were having on Ukrainian Canadian society. He added that there was a definite pattern to this entire process, 'as it appears in Canada so it is here in England, and so it has proved to be in France and on the Continent.' See Panchuk's letters to P. Wenger and Karasevich, 6 July 1949, and to Choma, 20 July 1949, Panchuk Collection. After his own visit to Canada a year later, he would write that his hopes for getting more DPs into Canada were 'not too bright,' since the people at home had grown 'increasingly indifferent' to or even 'annoyed' with the refugee issue and the DPs themselves. See Panchuk to E. Wasylyshen and Crapleve, 3 March 1950, Panchuk Collection.

172 G. Roussow to Shteppa, February 1949, Frolick Collection.

173 P. Wenger to Panchuk, 20 April 1949, Panchuk Collection. Panchuk certainly did not discourage the circulation of his interpretation of these events. For example, in a letter to Crapleve about his problems within the AUGB, he specifically asked her to 'pass this information along.' See Panchuk to Crapleve, 15 March 1949, Panchuk Collection.

174 ? to the Wasylyshens, 11 September 1949, Wasylyshen Collection.

175 Ibid.

176 Yaremovich to E. Wasylyshen, 2 July 1949, Wasylyshen Collection.

177 On Dmytro Dontsov's career, see chapter 6 in Motyl, *The Turn to the Right*. For correspondence about Dontsov's activities in Canada, see Choma to Panchuk, 18 July 1948, and Wenger to Panchuk, September 1948, Panchuk Collection. Dontsov's lecture tour in Canada was probably undertaken in direct response to a tour made by Andrievsky in the spring of 1948. Choma reported that Andrievsky had gone around the country giving

'fatherly advice' to the newly resettled DPs, particularly to the Banderivtsi among them, telling them they would do best to join existing Ukrainian Canadian groups rather than form any of their own. See Choma to Panchuk, 9 March 1948, Panchuk Collection. Dontsov seems to have been helped in getting to Canada by disaffected UNF supporters, like P. Shteppa (a former member of PUN and, in Canada, a once-prominent member of the UWVA and UNF) and Frolick. See Shteppa to Frolick, 9 December 1947; 5 January 1948; and, for references to Dontsov, 15 February 1948, all in the Frolick Collection.

178 Yaremovich to E. Wasylyshen, 2 July 1949, Wasylyshen Collection.
179 Kaye to Panchuk, 30 January 1949, and Karasevich to Panchuk, 1 May 1949, Panchuk Collection. Kaye had also suggested to Panchuk that his work with the AUGB had created one of the best-organized and best-disciplined Ukrainian groups in existence, a feat which was 'bordering on the impossible.' He had then observed that Panchuk had become an expert in Ukrainian matters, so much so that when he returned to Canada, 'nobody will be able to match you.' Was Panchuk interested in joining the federal civil service, perhaps working with Kaye in Ottawa or as a specialist for External Affairs, Kaye wondered? After all, the Canadian Citizenship Branch was 'constantly expanding' and needed dependable people. If Panchuk was interested, Kaye advised, he should keep in constant touch with the director of the Branch, 'giving him your observations on immigration, voluntary workers, on their integration in British way of life, etc.' The Department of External Affairs, Kaye reported, already had 'a high opinion of you and they know your abilities.' If Panchuk also added a degree from the University of London, that would give him the academic standing essential for further promotion. It would also be useful to 'make friends with Norman Robertson to put a good word for you [sic].' Of course, Kaye also promised, 'I shall do the rest what is necessary [sic].'
180 Panchuk to Karasevich, 6 July 1949, Panchuk Collection.
181 Yaremovich to E. Wasylyshen, 2 July 1949, Wasylyshen Collection.
182 Ibid.
183 Ibid.
184 Panchuk to Philipps, 18 February 1950, Panchuk Collection.
185 Ibid.

Chapter 8: 'Locking Horns on Canadian Soil'

1 See Panchuk's 'Notes on Immigration of Ukrainian Refugees and Displaced Persons to Canada,' 8 October 1946, Panchuk Collection. Britain's secretary

of state, E. Bevin, described the majority of the DPs in Europe in August 1947 as being 'of Slav origin,' but added that the refugee camps also included a considerable proportion of peoples from the Baltic countries, 'who have been universally recognized as excellent material for settlement in new countries.' He characterized these DPs as 'clean, industrious, law abiding, and well educated people, [who] include amongst their number a considerable sprinkling of men and women of the professional classes.' See Bevin to Viscount Addison, Secretary of State for Commonwealth Relations, 30 August 1947, FO 945/493.

2 Yaremovich to Premier C. Manning, 21 June 1948; Yaremovich to Premier George A. Drew, 14 June 1948; and Yaremovich to Walter Tucker, 15 June 1948, NAC MG28 v9, vol. 15. Tucker, Liberal MP for Rosthern, Saskatchewan, had long been sympathetic to Ukrainian Canadians. See, for example, the excerpts from an article by Tucker published in *UCSA News Letter* 1:8 (June 1945), in which he reviewed the Ukrainian Canadian community's 'splendid record' of commitment to the war effort, noting that 'over 10%' of the Ukrainians in Canada had enlisted, 'which is of course proportionately better than the population of Canada as a whole.' Tucker went on to state that the Ukrainians of Canada had such an 'inspiring' record because they were 'genuinely loyal to Canada which they feel with all their heart to be their own beloved country, their homeland, the land of their children for generations to come.' They were also 'deeply appreciative' of Canada's democratic and tolerant institutions and were united in these sentiments under the banner of the UCC. Tucker was also helpful with respect to the Ukrainian DPs. See his address in the House of Commons on 26 September 1945, which complemented Anthony Hlynka's (MP, Vegreville) similar speech of 24 September 1945. Premier Drew, as an ardent anti-communist, was likewise sympathetic to the Ukrainian Canadian community. Speaking in Toronto's Massey Hall to delegates attending the second UCC congress, Premier Drew vigorously attacked communism and, at the same time, praised the contributions of Ukrainians to Canadian life. Reportedly greeted by 'a terrific ovation,' he said, 'I have never been able to see the difference between the black fascism in Italy, the brown in Germany and the red of communism.' He went on to urge Ukrainian Canadians to 'keep alive in the minds of your children who were born in Canada a love of the country and traditions from which you yourselves came ... Not only should you think of the country in which you live. You will be better Canadians if you keep in your hearts all those things your parents loved before you.' His address to the second national UCC congress is abstracted in *Second All-Canadian Congress of Ukrainians in Canada*, 22–3. See also 'Asserts

Reds Determined to Lure Canadian Youth,' in the *Telegram*, 5 June 1946. A
7 June editorial in the same newspaper, 'All-Canada Ukrainian Congress an
Eye-Opener,' described the congress and Ukrainian contributions to Canada in positive terms rarely seen in the media: 'Canada needs more groups
inspired by the moderation, fairness and commonsense shown by the All-
Canada Ukrainian Canadian Congress in session in Toronto this week. The
Congress has been falsely denounced as fascist because it does not take
orders from Moscow. It can easily refute the allegation by pointing to its
loyal service to Canada when Stalin was acting as Hitler's other office boy.'
The editorial went on about the merits of the meeting. The delegates had
come 'without any wheedling for municipal or provincial grants.' Instead
of 'poulticing an inferiority complex by wailing for legislation against racial
discrimination, or braying for bi-lingualism, these Ukrainians' were willing
to 'settle with satisfaction in to the duties of full Canadian citizenship.'
They 'know they are good Canadians and know others must eventually
know it.' The editorial continued: 'They came to Canada with college diplo-
mas or calloused hands, their only capital brawn and brains ... They took
the first job offered. For many it was dish washing. None washed dishes
long. No race has made better progress in Canada in one generation than
the Ukrainians ... Canada has no more industrious citizens than her Ukrainians.' These same Ukrainian Canadians 'sent 40,000 men and women to
the fighting services ... without waiting to question whether this was a
"phoney," "imperialistic," "capitalistic" or "democratic war," or whether
Yadko Jo, as they call Marshall Stalin, wanted them to.' They were now, naturally enough, endorsing a broad immigration policy for the DPs – a 'nightmare phrase of a nightmare peace in Europe' – for many of the displaced
are 'their own fathers, mothers, aunts, uncles, nieces and nephews, chained
for seven years now behind the spreading iron curtain and menaced with
slavery.' The editorial commended the congress for having 'no patience
with the palaver that the first requirement regarding immigration must be
that it shall not affect the stranglehold of Quebec on Canada and its government and the second that it must not affect the security of entrenched organizations that will not work or let others work.' As for the UCC, it
continued lobbying Ottawa for a favourable immigration policy and in tandem campaigned within the Ukrainian Canadian community to mobilize
support for the Ukrainian refugees. See, for example, the leaflets *On the
Issue of Ukrainian Refugee Immigration to Canada* and *Save Our Brothers!*, published in Winnipeg on 1 October 1949. Copies of the latter, which appealed
directly to Ukrainian Canadian farmers by asking them to help sponsor the
immigration of Ukrainian DP families to Canada, were stamped 'From

House to House, From Hand to Hand!' in an effort to encourage their wide circulation within the community.

3 Ukrainian Canadians were, of course, not alone in their lobbying efforts. See, for example, the letter sent to Constance Hayward, of the Canadian National Committee on Refugees, by Mr T.G.M. Davidson, then with UNRRA Area Team 1068. On 26 November 1946 he wrote: 'It is my opinion that if Canada is to have a selection of qualified craftsmen and agricultural-ists [...] no time should be lost ... Those chosen would become permanent residents and good citizens eternally grateful for the opportunity given them.' See NAC MG28 v9, vol. 6.

4 See Stephen L. Holmes to C.W. Dixon in 'Ukrainian Problem,' 13 July 1939, FO 371/23138.

5 See Mr Makin's remarks of 21 July 1939, FO 371/23056. Foreign Office offi-cials were, of course, also interested in learning what Kossar had observed personally while visiting Carpatho-Ukraine.

6 'Report on Meeting with Mr. Norman Robertson, High Commissioner of Canada, Canada House,' 4 December 1946, Panchuk Collection. Canadian officials were not always so sympathetic. For example, in a 'Memorandum for Mr. Robertson,' dated 25 May 1945, which referred to telegrams and other representations made by the UCC and Kushnir on behalf of 'promi-nent Ukrainians who are likely to fall into the hands of the Soviet authori-ties,' an External Affairs official wrote that he did not think it advisable for the Canadian government to intervene on behalf of the Ukrainian political refugees. Doing so, he reasoned, would be 'prejudicial to our relations with the Soviet Union,' even if all the UCC had asked External Affairs to do was secure British help in saving these refugees. The Canadian bureaucrat went on to note that because the Soviets regarded the DPs as 'Fascists,' Canadian interest in their fate would be 'understood as an unfriendly act towards the Soviet Union.' He concluded that, 'from a purely strict legal point of view,' it was also 'no business of ours' what might happen to these Ukrainian nationalists, 'although this could not be very well used in reply to represen-tations submitted to us by the Ukrainian Canadian Committee.' See NAC RG25-F6, vol. 1022, file 134. I am indebted to the late John Kolasky for a photocopy of this memorandum.

7 See Panchuk's highly confidential 'Report on a Conference with Sir Herbert Emerson, Director of the Intergovernmental Committee,' to the UCRF, 11 December 1946, Panchuk Collection.

8 Ibid.

9 Ibid.

10 Confidential 'Report on an Interview with Sir George Rendel, Deputy to Mr

Hector McNeil Who Handles Refugee Problems As Far as the British Government Is Concerned,' 13 December 1946, Panchuk Collection.

11 Zinaidi Timofeichuk's (undated) letter is found in DEA 228-2 (s). In DEA 8296-40 there is a partial translation of the Russian-language booklet, *Answers to Disquieting Questions of Soviet Citizens Abroad as Displaced Persons* (Moscow, 1949). The booklet starts by noting that during the Second World War 'the German Fascist usurpers' drove millions of Soviet people into foreign countries. Only the great victory of the Soviet Union over 'Hitler-Germany' had saved their lives and given them an opportunity to return to their native country. The motherland 'had never, even for a minute, forgotten its sons and daughters in distress.' Thanks to 'the constant care' of the Soviet government, approximately 5.5 million Soviet people had already returned and become 'full-fledged citizens of the Great Soviet Union and active participants in the ... life of the country.' But not everyone had returned to 'share such lucky lots.' After more than four years, approximately 400,000 'Soviet citizens' were still living abroad as DPs. The reason for this was that 'different reactionary organizations and persons hostile to the Soviet Union' were obstructing the return of people to their native land, frightening them with various 'fictitious tales, disseminated lies ... and slander.' These enemies wanted to detach these 400,000 citizens and disperse them over the entire world 'like homeless vagrants,' which would 'condemn them to a miserable, lawless and hungry existence.' The booklet's purpose was given as representing the 'truth about life in their native country' to the DPs, whom the 'Mother country' would greet with 'attention and care.' Its 'question and answer' format informed readers about the full rights enjoyed by all 'Soviet citizens' who had returned home, promised that no one would be held responsible for not immediately returning after the war's end, related several instances of repatriated Soviet citizens who had been reinstated to their prewar positions or offered even better work, and claimed that returnees were trusted – they could even find work in the Soviet government, enlist in the armed forces, or enrol in universities. And, of course, the Soviet government would pay all the returnees' transportation costs and medical expenses and even help individuals settle into their new homes. As for those who had served during the war in German military formations, whether as soldiers and officers, they were reminded that, in November 1944, a Soviet spokesman, Colonel General Golikov, had told the press that even those who had acted against Soviet interests would not be held responsible. That promise had been repeated by the Supreme Soviet of the Ukrainian SSR in November 1948. All anyone wanting to return to the Soviet Union had to do was make contact with a Soviet Repa-

triation Mission. After that they would be sent to Brandenburg, an assembly point for repatriates. They would spend a few days there, 'with their own people,' enjoying three meals a day and any required medical treatment, after which they would be transported to Soviet Russia on a special train, equipped with a dining car.

For two more accurate accounts of postwar life under Soviet rule, in Western Ukraine, by women who risked travelling to the Canadian embassy in Moscow seeking assistance for emigration, see R.A.J. Phillips's secret 'Conversations with Mrs. A.' (24 June 1947) and 'Conversations with Mrs. B.' (18 July 1947). Both women stated their opposition to collectivization and were mistrustful of the Soviet regime. Mrs A. had lived in Western Ukraine during the first Soviet occupation (1939–41), survived German rule, and witnessed the Soviet reoccupation in 1944. Phillips observed that 'she had nothing to say about the Germans which could be described as complimentary in the absolute sense but she said that German administration was more just than the Soviet, either before or since.' Phillips concluded his June report by stating that he had 'the impression that as [Mrs A.] spoke, she was talking not only for herself and her neighbours but, to some extent, for nearly all those people in the Soviet Union whose names fill our immigration files.' See DEA 50166-40, vol 1.

12 Panchuk to CURB, 'Memo on Camp "Afbau," Pfarkirchen, in the U.S. Zone,' 8 October 1946, Panchuk Collection.

13 For Miss Claire V. Tait's letter of 21 November 1945, see DEA 8116-40. For Canadian government thinking on the question of what should be done with the Ukrainian refugees, see DEA 82-96-40, which contains a 'Memorandum re Ukrainian Refugees,' penned by P.J. Molson, 10 December 1945. R.G. Riddell of External Affairs wrote to H.H. Wrong that same day, enclosing the draft of a 'Note to the Prime Minister' in which he pointed out that during the past few months the government had been receiving 'numerous representations' from Ukrainian groups and other interested parties on the question of Ukrainian DPs and their forcible repatriation. These submissions were of two kinds: about fifty had been received from Ukrainian nationalist groups protesting against the return of Ukrainians to Soviet territory, whereas approximately a dozen had been received from pro-Soviet groups claiming that the nationalists' appeals were inspired by a desire to find refuge in Canada for pro-German Ukrainians. Although, as Molson noted, this issue was continuing 'to arouse considerable feeling among Canadian citizens of Ukrainian origin,' Riddell recommended that no reply be made to any such correspondence received, since the whole question of the DPs was 'one of great difficulty at the moment.'

14 Senate of Canada, *Proceedings of the Senate Standing Committee on Immigration and Labour.* That the AUUC made concerted efforts to influence public
attitudes against the Ukrainian DPs, while also trying to recruit some of
them into its own ranks, is underscored by several documents recently
declassified under the Access to Information Act. For example, on 24
December 1947, Sub/Inspector R.J. Belec, commanding the Quebec Sub/
Division of the RCMP, wrote that 'the Communist element in Noranda is
attempting to spread their ideologies to newly arrived Immigrants from
D.P. Camps, with very little success.' When, on 4 December 1948, the
AUUC's national executive committee circulated a press release regarding
what it described as the 'anti-democratic activities of fascist elements
among the Ukrainian displaced persons,' the RCMP also took note. The
AUUC statement argued that 'punishment, including deportation, of DP's
who engage in terrorist activities in Canada' was essential. Its authors then
listed several such instances, including a 29 October attack against a ULFTA
hall in Saskatoon; a 7 November raid of a public meeting in Edmonton's
Gem Theatre, during which a 'bomb was exploded near the platform'; and
a 10 November attack against a newspaperman, Mr W. Hluchaniuk, in
Spedden, Alberta. Commenting in a letter to Mr A. MacNamara, deputy
minister of labour, dated 27 December, the RCMP's commissioner S.T.
Wood observed that 'the greatest stumbling block the A.U.U.C. have
encountered in recent years is the voice of the Displaced Persons in Canada
who have actually lived under the Soviet Regime and can give personal
accounts of existing conditions. The Communists realize this and fear possible repercussions in their organization. Consequently, since D.P.'s have
begun arriving in Canada, the Ukrainian Communists, openly, have done
everything in their power to discredit these people in an effort to nullify
their accusations against the Communist Regime. Through the pages of the
Ukrainian Communist Press, on the platform, through letters to newspapers, the D.P.'s are branded as Fascists and traitors, awaiting only the
opportunity of turning Canada into a Fascist state. Surreptitiously, however, the Communists endeavour to inveigle D.P.'s into their organization
for the obvious purpose of having them refute accusations made by other
D.P.'s. They are experiencing practically no success whatsoever in this
endeavour and consequently are stepping up their output of propaganda
against the D.P.'s.' Commenting on the specifics of the allegations made in
the AUUC press release, Commissioner Wood noted that the incident was
being exaggerated, 'the usual Communist manoeuvre of building a minor
incident into a catastrophe to serve their purpose.' The bomb referred to
was only a tear gas device, manufactured by the T.W. Hand Fireworks

Company Limited, of Toronto, which went off and discomforted only those within about a five-foot radius, without doing any injury. Indeed, the speaker 'picked the bomb up from the floor, placed it on a table on the stage and advised the audience that the matter would be drawn to the attention of the local police. The meeting then continued as usual.' The commissioner also noted that investigations had not even proved that the bombing was the work of one of the DPs, of whom there were from 35 to 50 in an audience of about 300 people. He concluded by noting that the 'incident in the Gem Theatre is not an isolated case of Ukrainian Communists attempting to vindicate their own actions by publishing allegations against the D.P.'s with absolutely no substantiating evidence.' Another RCMP report, dated 15 April 1948 and entitled 'Communist Activities amongst Immigrants from D.P. Camps – Rouyn-Noranda, P.Q.,' obtained under the Access to Information Act, documented that 'discreet enquiries' had been made at the Noranda mine about the DPs employed there. Although 'strong pressure' was being exerted on these men to join 'different subversive organizations,' it was found that 'the D.P.'s are all entirely against Communism' and 'will not stand any propaganda.' The Labour Progessive party and what were referred to as other subversive organizations 'have tried hard to have these D.P.'s join them but they were unable to do so up to the present time. They have started a campaign against them, the Union accusing them of replacing the Canadians in their jobs and the subversive organizations calling them Fascist and murderers.' Another RCMP officer observed that 'conditions among the D.P.'s in the District are satisfactory. No communist sympathizers have been found amongst them to-date, and their behaviour is normal. Considerable pressure has been used in an effort to win D.P.'s to the Communist movement but with negative results.'

15 Document #46, 7 June 1947, in *A Delicate and Difficult Question*, ed. Kordan and Luciuk, 149–51.
16 For Brand's letter of 22 June 1948 to Glen, see NAC MG26, vol. 116.
17 For Hay's letter of 13 August 1948 to the prime minister, see NAC RG26, vol. 116. For a sympathetic account of the DPs, addressed to Prime Minister Mackenzie King and copied to Ontario's premier, G. Drew, and Quebec's premier, M. Duplessis, see the letter found in recently declassified RCMP files released under the Access to Information Act, dated 2 March 1948, sent from Kirkland Lake, Ontario (name of author deleted). The writer noted that he had been working on behalf of Polish, Lithuanian, Latvian, Estonian, and Ukrainian DPs in the lumber and mining industries of northern Ontario and Quebec since November 1947. 'I am fully convinced,' he

added, 'that they are all fully qualified as very promising future Canadian citizens. They are deeply religious, and industrious and they definitely despise fascism, Nazism, and Communism ... All these Canadians like Canada and its Democratic Institutions. They are most grateful to you, Sir, and Your Government for giving them the opportunity to come to Canada, and re-establish themselves, and live as human beings.' Describing 'a very malicious and dangerous' campaign on the part of 'Communistic agencies' in this area, the writer advised the prime minister as to how certain union leaders and agitators were trying to convince the DPs that they might not find work if they did not join the Communist party, all of which was quite disturbing. Therefore, he strongly urged the prime minister to 'devise some means to prevent mental and possible physical torture to those who suffered most under Nazi and Soviet regimes,' of which he knew something since he had visited DP camps in Europe, 'during my service in the Canadian army.'

18 'Record of a Meeting between the Secretary of State for Dominion Affairs and the High Commissioner, re: Plight of Polish Refugees,' 12 April 1946, Dominion Office 121/14. When he served as Canada's high commissioner in London, Vincent Massey was aware of the activities of UCSA and somewhat more subtle in expressing his sentiments when communicating with members of that group. For example, on the occasion of the UCSA Club's official opening, 15 April 1944, he sent greetings, expressing his conviction that the Club was 'a symbol of the enterprise of loyal Canadians of Ukrainian descent' which would provide 'pleasant comradeship in time of war,' and, in the end, 'promote also happy and enduring associations in due course in our Canadian home country.' See UCSA News Letter 1:5 (August 1944).

19 For example, see Datzkiw's reply on behalf of the UCC to a refugee, Wasyl Didiuk, 2 November 1946, in NAC MG28 v9, vol. 1, 'File: Refugee Requests for Immigration Aid, 1946–1947.' The same file contains Didiuk's letter from Goslar, 29 July 1946, in which he requests help in getting to Canada. Didiuk, a supporter of the Banderivtsi, emigrated to Canada a few years later, and became a prominent member of the CLLU, where he served for many years as national executive secretary. He also became a leading member of the Ontario Council of the Ukrainian Canadian Congress and godfather to the author's sister.

20 Hlynka would write to the UCRF's Mandryka, on 26 September 1947, claiming that there were already some people in his Vegreville riding who were spreading rumours to the effect that he was too involved with the DPs to be doing a good job at home for his constituents. When Hlynka eventu-

ally lost his seat, in 1949, to another Ukrainian Canadian, Liberal candidate John Decore (Dikur), he was certain that his efforts on behalf of the refugees had harmed his electoral chances. For Hlynka's views on postwar immigration and the DPs, see his address to the second UCC national congress, Toronto, 5 June 1946, published in the proceedings, *Second All-Canadian Congress of Ukrainians in Canada*, 113–21. For more on Hlynka's career, see *Antin Hlynka: Posol federalnoho parliamentu Kanady, 1940–1949* (*Anthony Hlynka: Member of the Federal Parliament of Canada, 1940–1949*), ed. S. Hlynka (Toronto, 1982).

21 Philipps to Panchuk, 18 January 1948, Panchuk Collection. Others also commented on the anti-DP campaign. For example, an editorial in *The Star*, published in Val D'Or, observed that 'Communists, fellow travellers and thoughtless persons who pass along every rumour they hear' were engaged in an 'organized whispering campaign' against 'new Canadians.' Charging that the latter were 'all Fascists' and implicating them in 'every local criminal activity in which the perpetrator has been actually identified and apprehended' was deceitful, the editorialist observed. Furthermore, 'any Canadian who bears such tales should check the source before accepting them as facts and should remember that if he passes them along he is acting as a tool for the far left wingers.' The writer went on to state, 'We ... have discovered that most if not all of them are better Canadians than many born in this country.' See 'The Anti-Immigrant,' *The Star* (Val D'Or, Quebec), 18 March 1949, 4, which was itself a commentary on a similarly pro-DP immigration speech given by Andrew Robertson, manager of Golden Manitou Mines Limited, to a meeting of the Kiwanis Club in Val D'Or, reported in the 11 March 1949 issue of this newspaper. Robertson not only criticized those who were against the immigration of DP miners – 'When I hear anyone running down the immigrant miners without just cause, I am forced to assume that they are either Communist Party members, fellow travellers, or thoughtless persons who repeat propaganda that is passed along to them' – but also pointed to the economic benefits of this immigration. Before any immigrants had arrived at Golden Manitou in November 1947, he reported, the company's payroll was $54,000. By November 1948, with the advent of some 'New Canadians,' the payroll had increased to $67,000. This additional money, Robertson stated, 'is going almost completely into the community for various services.' And the immigrant miners were not taking anyone's job, which meant that they were, 'in fact, benefitting the whole community and increasing the job potential.'

22 Shteppa to Hlynka, MP, 19 April 1948, and Shteppa to Frolick, 8 April 1948, Frolick Collection.

23 Panchuk to Wenger, 3 September 1948, Panchuk Collection.

24 Panchuk from Geneva to F. Zaplitny, MP, in Ottawa, 17 May 1947, Panchuk Collection.

25 Ibid.

26 Panchuk would estimate that some fifty thousand Ukrainian DPs had been admitted to Canada. See Panchuk to Crapleve, 28 February 1951, Panchuk Collection.

27 'Report of the Delegation Representing the Ukrainian Canadian Committee and the Ukrainian Canadian Relief Fund Attending Government Departments in Ottawa in Connection with Immigration of Refugees and Displaced Persons in Europe,' 10 October 1947, Panchuk Collection. Earlier that fall, Britain's secretary of state, E. Bevin, had written to Viscount Addison, the secretary of state for Commonwealth relations, expressing concern about 'the many thousands of displaced persons who are still housed in camps in the British zones of Germany and Austria and for whom there seems little immediate prospect of resettlement.' Bevin inquired whether anything could be done to persuade the Commonwealth countries to increase their contribution towards a solution of this refugee problem, particularly since, in the case of Canada, the total number emigrating seemed likely to be only 'a very small proportion of what the country should be capable of taking.' W. Henderson, of the Commonwealth Relations Office, replied, on 19 September 1947, with a memorandum entitled 'Settlement of Displaced Persons.' It noted that Canada had recently announced it would accept between 30,000 and 35,000 DPs if the United States agreed to admit 400,000 refugee immigrants. Canada, Henderson reported, was giving priority to 'persons likely to be capable of absorption in industries where there is a reasonable guarantee of steady employment, and, in view of the housing shortage, to single persons.' Those selected need not be relatives of anyone already resident in Canada. He concluded that the whole question of immigration policy in Canada was controversial. A section of public opinion, headed by Colonel Drew, the Conservative premier of Ontario, favoured a 'maximum immigration of British subjects from the United Kingdom,' whereas French Canada, 'on which the present Canadian Government largely depends for support,' is equally strongly opposed to such a policy. See Henderson to Bevin, 19 September 1947, FO 945/493. Subsequently, Mary Appleby confidentially informed Mr Dov, of the PCIRO, that the British government was 'trying to launch a drive in London to encourage countries of the British Commonwealth to do rather more by way of offering resettlement possibilities to D.P.'s.' See her letter of 25 September 1947, FO 945/493.

28 Kaye to Philipps, 7 March 1948, NAC MG30 E350. The Ontario government even arranged Ukrainian language broadcasts for the new immigrants thirteen times weekly, the program being organized by Stephen Davidovich, former director of the Ukrainian National Information Service, which both the Organization for the Rebirth of Ukraine and the UNF had sponsored in prewar London.

29 See Yaremovich's report of 1 July–31 August 1947 to the UCRF, Panchuk Collection.

30 Lieutenant Colonel R.L. Telfer of the War Office to P.F. Hancock, 20 October 1947, FO 371/66271.

31 Panchuk to Kaye, 3 June 1947, Panchuk Collection. On the 'Close Relatives Scheme,' see M. Danys, *DP: Lithuanian Immigration to Canada after the Second World War* (Toronto, 1986), 77, 217–18, 220–1. An order-in-council (PC 1734) allowed for the admission to Canada of 'The husband or wife; the son, daughter, brother or sister, together with husband or wife and unmarried children, if any; the father or mother; the orphan nephew or niece under twenty-one years of age; of any person legally resident in Canada who is in a position to receive and care for such relatives ... as well as a person entering Canada for the purpose of marriage to a legal resident thereof; provided the prospective husband is able to maintain his intended wife.' At the same time another order-in-council (PC 2180) approved the immigration of five thousand DPs on labour contracts for specific jobs. For a description of the immigration experience of another eastern European group, see Karl Aun, *The Political Refugees: A History of the Estonians in Canada*, (Toronto, 1985). Panchuk observed that veterans of the Ukrainian Division 'Galicia' might be able to get to Canada under the terms of this scheme, in a CURB memorandum entitled 'Ukrainian Prisoners of War in Great Britain (Formerly Ukrainian S.E.P. in Rimini, Italy)' 14 June 1947. This memo was addressed to the War and Foreign offices. Some of the men listed in appendix 'A' eventually emigrated to Canada. See NAC MG28 v9, vol. 15.

32 Wasylyshen to the UCRF, 'Report #5,' 20 June 1949, Wasylyshen Collection.

33 For example, see the 107 advertisements placed in the 15 February 1946 issue of *Visti* (*News*), 5–6, published in Belgium.

34 See 'Minutes of the 8th Meeting of the Polish Land Forces Disposal Committee,' 21 June 1946, FO 371/56566. In the letter from the Home Office (Aliens Department) to P.F. Hancock, 20 June 1946, FO 371/56565, a British official described Canadian recruiting efforts as a 'creaming proposition' intended to remove to Canada's benefit only the best workers, leaving behind the sick, invalids, and less qualified workers for the British to take care of. Some British officers working with the DPs had other thoughts on

this subject. For example, a Major Strachan, whom Yaremovich met near Hannover, told him the British should have 'first choice' from the refugee population since Britain had 'sacrificed enough to justify her getting the pick of DPs.' In the Major's view the Balts ranked first, the Poles last. See Yaremovich's 'Diary,' 11 March 1947. A few years later, Panchuk, writing to P.R. Rhodes, of Montreal, on 9 March 1949, alleged that there was some kind of 'understanding' between Canadian and British authorities which amounted to an 'economic exploitation' of the Ukrainians who had been resettled in the United Kingdom, particularly ex-members of the Ukrainian Division 'Galicia.' According to him, many of these veterans were being held in the United Kingdom even though they wanted to relocate to Canada; Panchuk Collection.

35 'Memorandum of Interview with Minister of Mines, Ottawa,' 1 November 1946, FO 371/56572. Present were the minister, J.A. Glen, the acting deputy minister, C.W. Jackson, J.G. McCrea of the Canadian Metal Association, and Mr V.C. Wansbrough. See also N. Robertson's remarks, 'Draft Proposal for Immediate Measures to Regulate Immigration into Canada,' 12 February 1947, DEA 939-40C.

36 See the memorandum by H.H. Carter, 'International Obligations Arising from the Refugee Situation,' 12 February 1947, DEA 939-40C. On the other side of the Atlantic, A.W.H. Wilkinson of the Foreign Office was suggesting that the provision of extra shipping 'for *British* emigrants' would benefit the refugee problem by removing 'non-producers' and those not essential to the British economy, leaving more accommodation free for EVWs, who could then be brought in to do essential work. He also felt that the Dominions would be more willing to take refugees 'if they could be assured of enough British immigrants to make assimilation of foreigners easier and to preserve the British characteristics of the Dominions concerned.' See Wilkinson's memorandum in FO 945/493, 24 September 1947, written in response to a note sent from Secretary of State Bevin to Viscount Addison, Secretary of State for Commonwealth Relations, on 30 August 1947.

37 'International Obligations Arising from the Refugee Situation,' 12 February 1947, DEA 939-40C. Colonel S.M. Scott, attached to a Canadian military mission in Berlin headed by Maurice Pope, prepared a memorandum entitled 'Displaced Persons in Germany' (4 November 1946), which suggested a different rank-ordering of DPs by nationality. Scott wrote that in the British Zone the most popular were the Balts, among whom the Estonians had a slight edge over the Latvians, with the Lithuanians a clear third. In general, Balts were considered well behaved, well educated, industrious, and clean. Next in terms of an 'all-round scale of virtue' were the Ukrainians. By

way of comparison the Ukrainians were ranked at the top of the general scale, 'especially for ingenuity,' in the American Zone, with the Mennonites at the same level or higher. The Americans, Scott reported, also placed the Balts 'very close to the Ukrainians.' Poles came well below these other groups. As for the Jews, Scott admitted, 'I hardly know what to say.' They were 'not popular,' but he was unable to determine whether this was a consequence of anti-Semitism or the fruit of the authorities' 'practical experience' with this group. It was 'universally stated' that the Jews were 'physically lazy,' and (though not so universally) that 'they will not even do their own camp work.' In Scott's assessment, the DPs could be ranked in terms of their desirability as immigrants as follows: 'émigré Russians, Mennonites, Ukrainians, Balts, Poles and Jews, the last two about equal.' He added that it was not so much their characteristics as DPs which mattered as 'their potentialities as future citizens.' Accordingly, docility, 'so much praised among the Balts,' should not be regarded as 'the highest attribute of a citizen of a democracy.' Commenting on Scott's memorandum, Wing Commander J.W.P. Thompson agreed with most of the observations, but suggested a different 'order of preference,' as follows: 'Balts, Yugoslavs, Czechs, Ukrainians equal with Poles, Russians, Jews.' Although any such listing, Thompson wrote, was, 'as you will probably agree, problematic ... and anything but exact,' he explained that he placed the Balts first because of their 'cleanliness and the remarkable order which they are able to establish in a camp,' and the Yugoslavs next in line because of their 'general courteous demeanour, verging on a native sort of elegance.' The Poles were placed 'rather far down' because it was 'difficult to ignore prevailing opinion.' Jews fell to the bottom of Thompson's list because 'on the whole they demonstrate less charity to others not members of their own group.' For Scott's memorandum of 4 November 1946 and Thompson's letter of 18 November 1946, see NAC RG25, series 1712, vol. 2113, file 408/5.

38 See also Pearson's 17 January 1948 letter to Robertson, NAC RG26, vol. 105. When Canada's parliament debated immigration policy in the spring of 1947, Prime Minister Mackenzie King frankly observed: 'With regard to the selection of immigrants much has been said about discrimination. I wish to make it clear that Canada is perfectly within her rights in selecting persons whom we regard as desirable future citizens. It is not a "fundamental human right" of any alien to enter Canada. It is a privilege. It is a matter of domestic policy. Immigration is subject to the control of the parliament of Canada ... There will, I am sure, be general agreement with the view that the people of Canada do not wish, as a result of mass immigration, to make a fundamental alteration in the character of the population.' See Canada,

House of Commons, *Debates*, 1 May 1947, 2644–7. Canada's gatekeepers have long since abandoned this judicious perspective, as the author learned during his tenure as a member of the Immigration and Refugee Board.

39 See the letter from the UCC to Prime Minister W.L. Mackenzie King, 30 August 1947, DEA 10268-40, vol. 1.

40 'Comments with Respect to Immigration and Resettlement of Refugees and Displaced Persons and Selection by Immigration Missions,' 6 November 1947, Panchuk Collection.

41 E. Wasylyshen to the UCRF, 'Report #1,' 7 March 1949, Wasylyshen Collection. This meeting was held in Ottawa on 24 February 1949.

42 For a Ukrainian Canadian critique of Canadian government immigration policy at the time, see the editorial 'Trickeries of the Immigration Commissions,' *New Pathway*, 2 October 1948.

43 See Yaremovich's letter of 24 June 1948 to H.W. Herridge, MP, regarding Herridge's remarks as reported in *Hansard*, 31 May 1948, NAC MG28 v9, vol. 15.

44 See Panchuk's letter of 30 April 1948 to Yaremovich, NAC MG31 D69.

45 See the letter from 'R.M.W.' of the Department of Mines and Resources to Mr Jolliffe, 3 November 1949, NAC RG26, vol. 121.

46 See Panchuk's letter of 28 February 1951 to Crapleve in Bielefeld, NAC MG28 v9, vol. 15.

47 Ibid.

48 Kaye estimated that 23,411 Ukrainian DPs had arrived in Canada between 1946 and 1951, a figure which rose to 34,238 if the period is extended from 1946 to the end of the first seven months of 1953, when he made his estimate. See NAC MG31 D69, vol. 26, [undated].

49 See D. Gerych of the Canadian European Bureau, in Winnipeg, to Panchuk, 4 September 1948, Panchuk Collection.

50 G. Roussow to Shteppa, February 1949, Frolick Collection, and Panchuk to the Wasylyshens et al., 3 March 1950, Panchuk Collection.

51 See Panchuk's report to CURB, 30 January 1946, NAC28 v9, vol. 17. In the spring of 1947, Yaremovich visited the Latzen refugee camp, located some five kilometres from the border with the Soviet Zone. He recorded that for its inhabitants the camp was 'a village of their own.' See Yaremovich, 'Diary,' 22 March 1947.

52 See Crapleve's 'Report on the U.S. Area of Control, Germany, from April to 31 July 1947,' 29 September 1947, Panchuk Collection.

53 See Panchuk's report to CURB, 30 January 1946, NAC28 v9, vol. 17.

54 See Panchuk's 'Report #3,' 12 March 1946, Panchuk Collection.

55 See Yaremovich's 'Report on a Tour of American and French Zones of Ger-

many, French Zone of Austria, and a Brief Visit to the British and American
Zones of Austria, between 1 and 25 June 1947,' 30 June 1947, Panchuk
Collection. On 27 February 1947, Yaremovich noted in his diary that at a
Ukrainian-populated camp near Mannheim/Rhur the Poles were in charge,
which was a 'cause of friction.'

56 Major Tufton Beamish and Mr C.E. Hobson, MP, 'Report by Parliamentary
Special Committee of Investigations into the Implementation of His Majesty Government's Policy in Connection with Displaced Persons in the British Zones of Germany and Austria,' March 1947, FO 371/66658.

57 See Yaremovich's 'Report on a Tour ...,' 30 June 1947, Panchuk Collection. A
few weeks earlier, after visiting with a Ukrainian refugee by the name of
Pelensky, Yaremovich noted that this refugee was 'convinced about the
impending war with the Soviets – the sooner the better.' Admitting that he
was a supporter of the UHVR and the Banderivtsi, Pelensky nevertheless
added that 'should there be no war – within the next year or so,' then the
nationalist movement, being 'fundamentally a revolutionary' force 'interested in tearing down things' but having 'no policy for the future,' would
get 'completely lost.' The Ukrainian nationalist organizations, he said, had
been built 'upon force and discipline rather than anything else,' and he
wondered how much further they could get with such 'methods of behaviour.' In Pelensky's view what they must do was ally themselves with some
other group, for otherwise they would 'disappear.' He also pointed out that
the Banderivtsi wanted to set up a newspaper in the British Zone and had
the financial capital to do so. See Yaremovich, 'Diary,' 6 April 1947. Craplève
reported to the UCRF on 9 January 1948 that she had arrived in the British
Zone of Germany to find that the 'Bandurivits group' had blocked the
previous arrangements which had been made for setting up a neutral
Ukrainian press. They were also trying to start up their own printing plant
in Hannover, without the knowledge of the occupation authorities. She
added, 'For your information Lysenko camp in Hannover is still the leading
Ukrainian camp for political disturbances and now a hot bed for religious
strife.' See Craplève to the UCRF, 'Field Representative's Report Ending
31 December 1947 on the British Zone of Germany,' Panchuk Collection.

58 As an example of how disciplined members of the nationalist underground
were, see the letter from 'Sviatoslav,' a military affairs specialist with the
Melnykivtsi in region 'A,' to the national command of the OUNm, 28 June
1948. In this letter 'Sviatoslav' formally requested permission to emigrate to
Canada, on the ground that his elderly father there needed his help. He
pledged that if he did not receive permission to leave he would not emigrate, although he added that if his Organization granted his request he

would remain loyal and obedient to it, even in Canada. Pointing out that he needed an early reply, since the boat that would transport him to Canada was leaving within the week, he awaited the executive's decision. It was negative. True to his oath, he remained in Europe for several more months. 'Sviatoslav' was interviewed in 1982. A number of other nationalists, from both factions of the OUN, confirmed that they had deliberately delayed their departures from Europe at the express command of their leaders. For example, I. Firman (Toronto, 30 May 1982, MHSO), who joined the OUN in 1938 and served in an OUNb 'task group' sent into Soviet Ukraine (only three of its fifteen members survived), described how he quarrelled with his superiors over this issue in March 1949: 'I told the Organization that I was leaving Europe. They said no. I said yes. In England the same thing happened when I reported how I was planning to move to Canada. They forbade me to do so. They didn't even give me the passwords for Canada. Eventually, they did bring these around to my home but I said no thanks, you wouldn't provide them when I asked, I don't want them now. Why didn't they want me to leave, you ask? Simple. They wanted to send me back to Warsaw to work in our underground there. Or else we were to go off for training somewhere in Spain, after which we would be sent into Ukraine.'

For a general and apparently non-partisan description of what were described as the responsibilities facing Ukrainians in the emigration, see *Pamyatka ukrayinskoho emigranta (Memoir of a Ukrainian Emigré)* published in Aschaffenburg in 1948 by the printers of the newspaper *Nedilya (Sunday)*. This booklet's anonymous author insisted that the cardinal rules for the postwar Ukrainian diaspora were, most important, not to forget the fatherland; then, to defend the good name of the Ukrainian people; to remember that one must place the national good above party politics; to love all one's countrymen as one would a brother; to further Ukrainian national culture; to remember to give aid and comfort to those who are old and infirm or otherwise disadvantaged; and to treasure the country that gives you shelter. Above all, the emigrants were reminded that they should never forget how they and their resources were still needed by their native land. G.R.B. Panchuk provided me with a xerox copy of this booklet.

59 See Crapleve's 'Report on the US Area of Control ...,' 29 September 1947, Panchuk Collection. For a similar comment, see also Crapleve's 'Field Representative's Report of Work Done in the British Zone, Ending 31 January 1948,' 31 January 1948, Panchuk Collection. Crapleve observed that even though the Ukrainian Council in the 'Fallingbostel' transit camp had official approval, there was 'an undercover fight by certain members for relief

supplies to be allotted to their favoured political parties for distribution,' and 'pilferage was rather high.' A meeting was called to explain to the camp's inhabitants that the relief supplies they were receiving came from the UCRF and were not 'gifts from DP political parties.' For another, more satirical look at the 'pecking order' which developed within many refugee camps, see the cartoon in the émigré newspaper *Sunday*, 7 January 1947, 7, which portrays a rank-ordering of privilege and power in a Ukrainian DP camp near Aschaffenburg. The cartoon shows the camp commandant receiving 7 packages of Chesterfield cigarettes, the regional leader getting 5 packages, the assistant commandant 4, and the block leader two and a half, while a non-aligned refugee gets only a half-smoked butt.

60 See Crapleve's 'Field Representative's Report Ending 31 December 1947 on the British Zone of Germany,' 9 January 1948, Panchuk Collection. On 31 January 1948 she reported that religious tensions had become so severe, particularly between the competing Orthodox factions of Metropolitan Polikarp and Bishop Gregory, that 'riots' had broken out, intense enough to warrant calling in the German and military police.

61 See Crapleve's 'Report on US Area of Control ...,' 29 September 1947, Panchuk Collection. For one description of strife in a DP camp, between supporters of the OUNb and the URDP, see 'H.Q. European Command Monthly Intelligence Summary,' June 1949, FO 371/77585.

62 Panchuk to CURB, 30 January 1946, NAC28 v9, vol. 17, and Panchuk to Sir George Rendel, 30 December 1946, FO 371/66689.

63 See Panchuk's letter of 30 December 1946 to Sir George Rendel for his comments on the Hannover refugee camp, FO 371/66689.

64 Ibid.

65 See Panchuk's letter from Brussels to Yaremovich, 10 March 1947, Panchuk Collection.

66 Ibid.

67 Panchuk to Philipps, 19 November 1947, Panchuk Collection.

68 Ibid. See also Panchuk to Philipps, 3 June 1949, Panchuk Collection, in which he complained that some of those who had ousted him from the AUGB's presidency were persons who claimed they had done so because he was a 'Britano-phil.'

69 Wenger to Panchuk, 21 October 1948, and Panchuk's reply, 22 November 1948, Panchuk Collection.

70 Wenger to Panchuk, 20 April 1949, Panchuk Collection. On 20 April 1949, Wenger wrote to Panchuk (Panchuk Collection) after getting the latter's report on the fracas at the AUGB: 'We in Canada feel bitterly about it. It is a kick in the pants not only for you, but also indirectly at us.' He added that

Panchuk's caution against the activities of the 'fake Ukrainian patriots' was welcome since the latter would not now get away with any similar attempt to take over organized Ukrainian Canadian life. Wenger then lamented: 'How immature our people are politically, what a small percentage of them are really patriotic as we understand it! We Canadians would like to see an independent Ukraine for the sake of the principle itself. The majority of the DPs here seem to have different ideas – they think of an independent Ukraine only in terms of what they might profit personally by it. One sometimes wonders whether our ideas are just a waste of time and whether they are worth bothering about. I suppose though that we will stay and plug away like fools just because of the "principle."'

71 Panchuk to Wenger, 6 July 1949, and Panchuk to Choma, 22 July 1949, Panchuk Collection. Choma was an interwar immigrant from Peremyshyl who enlisted in the Canadian army in 1940. He served as an UCSA executive member in 1943.

72 Panchuk to Karasevich, 16 December 1949, Panchuk Collection.

73 Panchuk to Philipps, 17 April 1950, and Panchuk to the British Home Office, 7 May 1950, Panchuk Collection.

74 Panchuk to Miss Hanson of the British Ministry of Labour, in London, 30 April 1949, Panchuk Collection. Panchuk's assessment of what took place in the Ukrainian DP camps is corroborated by responses given by a representative sample of postwar Ukrainian immigrants to Canada when they were asked whether the camp phase of the Ukrainian refugee experience had strengthened their nationalist convictions. Fifty-nine per cent reported that it had. This survey, distributed in 1981 to a cross-section of postwar Ukrainian immigrants to Canada, is found in L.Y. Luciuk, 'Searching for Place: Ukrainian Refugee Migration to Canada after World War II,' Ph.D. thesis, University of Alberta, 1984, in its original Ukrainian-language form and in an English-language translation, appendix 2, 532–55.

75 Ibid. There is a considerable range of opinion even among the Ukrainian nationalists as to what constitutes a 'political emigration' and who can claim rightfully to be a member of such a movement. V. Makar (Toronto, 23 March 1982, MHSO) offered an opinion: 'Yes, you can call us a political emigration because all those who fled the Bolsheviks, willingly or otherwise, who knew that the greatest enemy of Ukraine was approaching, did so knowing that only death was coming our way, and in the hope that elsewhere we would survive and still be able to do something for Ukraine.' A different interpretation is suggested by O. Eliashevsky (Toronto, 28 April 1982, MHSO), who commented: 'Not everyone can claim to be a political emigrant ... Eighty to 90 per cent fled because they were afraid of the Bol-

sheviks ... Only those who were involved in political activity and knew what would greet them should they return home – a bullet in the head – can claim that description ... I had sat in a Nazi concentration camp yet I believed that if I went back home the Soviets would twist that fact around and label me a fascist. Who knows if I would have survived under Soviet rule? Likely not.' In I. Firman's view (Toronto, 30 May 1982, MHSO): 'No, this was not entirely a political emigration, for many of these emigrants didn't have any political understanding. True, they were nationally conscious, they are Ukrainians, but even among this immigration there were more than a few who didn't even have that much sense ... Some of them, from Odessa, Kharkiv, and other cities in Eastern Ukraine, were supposedly Ukrainian, but spiritually, in their hearts, they were often closer to being Russian than Ukrainian. No, not everyone is a political emigrant ... What is truly important is that you feel being a Ukrainian is the most important thing in your life.'

76 Kaye to Panchuk, 22 January 1949, Panchuk Collection.
77 Kaye to Panchuk, 30 January 1949, Panchuk Collection.
78 Before departing for Europe aboard the *Queen Elizabeth*, the Wasylyshens spent several days in southwestern Ontario. In Hamilton, on 25 February 1949, the issue of how the local UCC branch should react to a forthcoming public lecture by the editor of *Ukrainian Echo* was raised. Their concern was over what to do if this speaker criticized the UCC. See A. and E. Wasylyshen to the UCRF, 'Report #2,' 28 March 1949, Wasylyshen Collection. For another critical view of the appearance of *Ukrainian Echo*, see John Hladun to Panchuk, 22 July 1949, Panchuk Collection. Hladun wrote: 'Our right wing totalitarians are publishing their paper here and are using that boy Froliak [*sic*] as their front ... I have made a few moves that will compel them to either toe the line or go out of business. What makes me mad is that a group of irresponsible youngsters feel that they can make a living by exploiting the patriotic feelings of our people.' Hladun, formerly a member of the Ukrainian Canadian Left, was the editor and publisher of *The Worker* and *Our Age*.
79 Panchuk to Gerych, 16 February 1949, Panchuk Collection.
80 Ibid.
81 Karasevich to Panchuk, 1 May 1949, Panchuk Collection.
82 Panchuk to Karasevich, 6 July 1949, Panchuk Collection.
83 The Melnykivtsi, and their sympathizers among the DPs, helped form fourteen new branches of the Ukrainian National Federation, nine of these in Ontario. However, their growing domination of this Ukrainian Canadian group provoked dissent within the UNF. This erupted publicly on

21 August 1960, when a two-page mimeographed letter was sent to all UNF branches. It started off with a rhetorical question, 'What has happened to the UNF in Canada?' and went on to list a series of Ukrainian Canadian grievances against the 'newcomers' who had so thoroughly penetrated the Federation. The chief problem, this letter proclaimed, was that the 'first loyalty' of the postwar immigrants was to 'their former European organizations' and not to Canada. A second bulletin of this self-styled 'Defence Committee of the UNF' (also known as the 'Committee for the Rejuvenation of the UNF') alleged that a 'secret network of OUN' had infiltrated the Federation and was manipulating the organization's conventions, the editorial offices of the UNF newspaper, *New Pathway*, and several UNF branch executives, all in an anti-democratic fashion. This development, it was protested, had to be reversed, for the UNF had always been a Canadian organization and must never let itself 'come under the domination of political parties or organizations outside Canada.' The Federation, while admittedly supportive of the Ukrainian liberation struggle, would offer the nationalist movement aid, but only if they could do so 'strictly within Canadian law' and never under 'any external compulsion.' Every member of the Defence Committee ended up being suspended from the UNF's membership by a national executive which was in fact dominated by Melnykivtsi. Among those expelled were Paul Yuzyk, Michael Pohorecky, W. Klymkiw, W. Topolnycky, and I. Hewryk. Although these men insisted they would never compromise with the 'unscrupulous individuals' who had taken over the UNF, their protest faded. See the two bulletins of the 'Defence Committee of the UNF,' 21 August 1960 and 20 February 1961; the counter-condemnation issued by the UNF's national executive, from Toronto, on 12 February 1960; and the commentary made in a UWVA circular letter dated 19 February 1961. Lending credence to the idea that the Melnykivtsi infiltrated and came to dominate the UNF is an interview held with V. Maruniak, in Munich, on 12 July 1982 (MHSO). Maruniak confirmed that the OUNm had deliberately sent its own people into the emigration, with the specific purpose of rallying support behind the Melnykivtsi and contesting the influence of the Banderivtsi in the postwar diaspora. The recapture of the UNF's national executive from the Melnykivtsi, by a slate consisting of some of the children and grandchildren of the Federation's original founders, was reported on page 1 of *Ukrainian News* (Edmonton), 17–30 June 1998, and editorialized about on page 6 of the same issue, 'Ukrainian Canadian Community Needs Development,' by M. Levytsky. See also the commentary by M.B. Kuropas, 'Return of the Natives,' *Ukrainian Weekly*, 24 January 1999, 7.

84 Nearly 77 per cent of the Ukrainian DPs resettled in Canada surveyed by

the author (see n74 above) agreed that their arrival had precipitated friction in Ukrainian Canadian society.

85 Yaremovich to E. Wasylyshen, 2 July 1949, Panchuk Collection.
86 Ibid.
87 Smylski to Panchuk, 24 July 1949, Panchuk Collection.
88 Yaremovich to Panchuk, 6 November 1949, Panchuk Collection.
89 Ibid. They were, of course, being watched. According to documents obtained under the Access to Information Act, Michael Petrowsky, continuing to serve as a special constable on behalf of the RCMP, attended, for example, the third UCC congress in Winnipeg, after Mr M. Black, the chief translator, wrote to the RCMP's special branch on 1 February observing that it appeared as if 'the disintegration of the Ukrainian Canadian Committee may well take place at the forthcoming congress' because of the 'tensions existing between the various groups which compose that Committee.' Commenting on why the third UCC congress would be relevant, Petrowsky wrote, on 31 January 1950, that this would likely be 'the most critical congress of the entire, ten-year existence of the U.C.C. and it may well end in the collapse of the whole organization under the persistent assaults of hostile groups from within and from without.' If that happened, the Ukrainian organizations 'would simply revert to pre-war factional strife, both political and religious,' which would be 'to the joy of the Communists who, together with the Ukrainian nationalist extremists, will benefit most from such a condition.' In Petrowsky's view such a state of affairs would be 'harmful both to the country and to the Ukrainians themselves, especially in the event of another war.' He categorized the problems within by observing that the UCC faced the opposition of 'the uncompromising Catholics,' of the 'nationalist extremists organized within the League for the Liberation of Ukraine,' of the Hetmanites (who, he noted, 'work hand-in-hand with the above-mentioned League'), of the Ukrainian communists, and of Wasyl Swystun and his group, known as the Association for Cultural Relations with Soviet Ukraine. Petrowsky observed that the Catholics, banded together into the BUC, were averse to fraternizing with 'their old enemies,' meaning socialists, agnostics, and members of the Ukrainian Orthodox faith. To that end they saw the UCC's president, Monsignor Kushnir, as nothing more than a figurehead, a man 'without real backing from the hierarchy, church organizations and their press organs.' They were therefore allying with the nationalists, 'fostering an ideology that strikes at the very root of the Canadian conception of national unity.' According to Petrowsky, the Catholics and nationalists were promoters of a 'French-Canadian conception of minority rights; also, on the Swiss canton system.' Ignoring, he claimed, 'the general

trends of national unity,' the Catholic and nationalist press were urging
Ukrainians in Canada to preserve 'Ukrainian unity' and to build up a
'Ukrainian minority,' which 'some day would form a co-partnership with
the Anglo-Saxon and French-speaking Canadians, which would operate on
the pattern of German, French and Italian cantons in Switzerland.' They also
supported 'the line of the ultra-nationalist groups in according all-out support to the 'fighting Ukraine,' meaning the Ukrainian Insurgent Army,
thereby subordinating all their activities to that end.' Although the League
was not a member of the UCC, it had its allies there, not only among the
Ukrainian Catholics guided by Reverend Semen Izyk, but in the UHO,
which marched together with the nationalists in joint opposition to the
Ukrainian National Council in Europe. The Hetmanite group in Canada,
Petrowsky claimed, had been taken over in the past three years 'by educated
DP's of all sorts.' As for the Ukrainian communists, the constable reminded
his readers that the AUUC had 'been trying to destroy the U.C.C. for the past
ten years in an obvious effort to impose the Communist leadership upon the
disunited people.' Then, finally, 'like his bedfellows, the Communists,' there
was Wasyl Swystun, who had 'old scores to settle with leaders of the U.C.C.'
and who seemed willing to act in concert with the AUUC to do just that.

90 Panchuk to Philipps, 18 February 1950, Panchuk Collection.
91 Panchuk to A. and E. Wasylyshen, 3 March 1950, Panchuk Collection. See
    also M. Mandryka to A. and E. Wasylyshen, 14 November 1949, 7 Decem-
    ber 1949, and 29 January 1950, Wasylyshen Collection.
92 Panchuk to A. and E. Wasylyshen et al., 3 March 1950, Panchuk Collection.
93 Ibid.
94 Smylski to Panchuk, 14 February 1947, Panchuk Collection.
95 Shteppa was, by his own admission, a member of the OUN's PUN. See his
    letter of 18 March 1949 to Frolick, Frolick Collection.
96 Shteppa to Frolick, 12 December 1946, Frolick Collection.
97 Shteppa to Frolick, 9 March 1947 and 14 March 1947, Frolick Collection.
98 Shteppa to Frolick, 18 March 1947. See also Shteppa to Frolick, 5 February
    1948 and 28 October 1948, Frolick Collection.
99 Frolick to Shteppa, 5 January 1948, Frolick Collection. J. Humeniuk, a vet-
    eran of the UPA, born in 1918, confirms that upon his arrival in Sault Ste
    Marie in December 1948, where he went to work for Algoma Steel, he
    quickly got in touch with members of the Ukrainian nationalist movement
    by reading *Ukrainian Echo*. On 4 February 1954 he and his colleagues orga-
    nized a League branch in Sault Ste Marie. The vice-president of the branch
    was an interwar immigrant by the name of Bardiniuk. Interview with J.
    Humeniuk, Sault Ste Marie, 15 May 1982 (MHSO).

100 Frolick to Shteppa, 15 February 1948, Frolick Collection.

101 Shteppa to Frolick, 28 October 1948, Frolick Collection.

102 Shteppa to Frolick, 8 April 1948, 3 May 1948, and 28 October 1948, Frolick Collection.

103 Frolick to Shteppa, 5 January 1948, Frolick Collection.

104 Frolick to Shteppa, 22 April 1948, Frolick Collection.

105 Shteppa to Frolick, 8 April 1948, Frolick Collection. Shteppa died in Toronto in March 1980.

106 Shteppa to Frolick, 5 February 1948, Frolick Collection. Shteppa urged that 'our people' be sent into the cities, where they could join existing Ukrainian Canadian groups and, working from within, take them over. This would eliminate any need for building up new organizations, which was unnecessary and much harder than just taking over existing organizations. P. Boyko, born in 1920, became a member of the OUN in 1937 and later joined the UPA. Captured by the Nazis in 1944, he was press-ganged into an auxiliary military unit sent to France, from which he defected to the French resistance. He confirms that his emigration was handled by the Organization, through its Paris cell. 'I was told who to register with when I came to Canada.' Interview with P. Boyko, Sault Ste Marie, 15 May 1982 (MHSO). Similarly, V. Makar (Toronto, 23 March 1982, MHSO) recalled: 'You just didn't emigrate when and where you wanted to. You asked for permission and you moved from contact to contact, all under the Organization's discipline, just like a soldier ... Of course, there was no punishment for those who dropped out, and there were people who did, people who joined us probably only out of self-interest ... [Certainly] I had a contact in Canada. The Organization had a network that extended right into Canada by the time I got here.'

107 Frolick to Shteppa, 15 February 1948, Frolick Collection.

108 S. Kulyk to Frolick, 3 August 1947, Frolick Collection.

109 Ibid.

110 Ibid. Attempts to suborn the 'newcomers' were recorded from across Canada. For example, as noted in recently declassified RCMP documents released under the Access to Information Act, the RCMP detachment in Fort William reported on 9 December 1947 that around Beardmore, Ontario, 'small groups of 'Reds' had been approaching the D.P's, and advising them that they 'shouldn't have come here, that they are fascists and are not wanted.' On another occasion, in August of that year, it was reported that two members of the Lumber & Sawmill Workers' Union, from Toronto, had visited camps #115 and #126 at Savanne and told the DPs that they were 'not wanted, that they had made a great mistake in

coming here and that they should have gone back to Russia.' Angered, the DPs apparently advised the two men that 'if they liked it so much why did they not go to Russia,' at which point the two 'were forced to leave the camp before a fight took place.' D/Constable D.J. McMahon further noted that none of the 'Communistic influence directed at the D.P's has had any effect whatsoever. Many of these D.P's are brilliant men, some being Doctors, Professors, engineers, teachers, etc., and having had to live underneath communist reign in Europe don't want any more of it. They are very thankful to be in Canada enjoying our way of life and as the result of their experiences can spot the red element at once.'

111 Kulyk to Frolick, 19 August 1947, Frolick Collection.

112 Myron ? to Frolick, 21 December 1948, Frolick Collection.

113 Minutes of the second national congress of the Canadian League for the Liberation of Ukraine, Toronto, 24 December 1950. I am grateful to the late Andrij Bandera and the late Mykola Bartkiw, formerly the executive secretary of the League, for making various documents available for my inspection. The originals remain in the League's archives in Toronto. For a sympathetic account of the history of the League, see O. Romanyshyn, 'The Canadian League for the Liberation of Ukraine,' *Polyphony* 10 (1988): 153–66, and *A Historical Outline of the Canadian League for the Liberation of Ukraine*, ed. W. Solonynka, Romanyshyn stresses the importance which a document entitled *An Appeal from Embattled Ukraine to All Ukrainians Abroad*, issued in October 1949 by the Ukrainian nationalist forces in Ukraine, had in motivating Ukrainians in Canada to set up the League. The decision to set up the League was actually made on 1 May 1949, at a public meeting in Toronto called by Frolick. On 4 May a Central Organizing Bureau was set up, and on 9 May 1949 a declaration of principles was adopted, being published in *Ukrainian Echo* on 14 May. The first League branch was organized in Toronto in July 1949, and the first conference of the organization held in that same city on 25 December 1949. By then, branches of the League existed in Toronto, Hamilton, Oshawa, and St Thomas. Between 1949 and 1989 a total of fifty-seven League branches were organized across Canada, the majority (thirty-eight) in Ontario, with a total membership officially given as ten to twelve thousand, which probably included both formal members and sympathizers.

114 Minutes of meetings of the national executive of the Canadian League for the Liberation of Ukraine, Toronto, 15 April 1951 and 3 June 1951.

115 Minutes of the third national congress of the Canadian League for the Liberation of Ukraine, Toronto, 22–3 December 1951.

116 Minutes of meetings of the national executive of the Canadian League

for the Liberation of Ukraine, Toronto, 14 March 1952 and 6 November 1952.
117 Minutes of a meeting of the national executive of the Canadian League for the Liberation of Ukraine, Toronto, 24 December 1952.
118 Interview with V. Makar (Toronto, 23 March 1982, MHSO).
119 Minutes of the fourth national congress of the Canadian League for the Liberation of Ukraine, Toronto, 18–19 July 1953. The fourth national UCC congress was held in Winnipeg on 8–10 July. It was attended by 377 official delegates, representing the USRL (100), UNF (100), UCC (84), BUC (81), UCVA (9), and Ukrainian Workers League (3). Small numbers of postwar immigrants, representing groups like Suzero (7), the Carpatho-Ukrainian War Veterans' Association (5), and ODUM (3), had also begun to take part in these Ukrainian Canadian gatherings. Judging from the debate that took place during a pre-congress meeting, held in Winnipeg on 5–6 December, the minutes of which were published as part of the official congress proceedings, sharp differences of opinion over the respective merits of UNRada and the UHVR continued to split the organized Ukrainian Canadian community. See *Fourth All-Canadian Congress of Ukrainians in Canada* (Winnipeg, 1953), 106–15. Canada's prime minister, the Right Honourable Louis St Laurent, addressed this congress, making comments about Ukrainian contributions to Canada of the sort which had by then (and have ever since then) become a staple of most 'official' speeches. The prime minister not only attacked 'alien communism' but went on to claim that there was 'no chapter more glorious than that of the Ukrainian people' in the struggle against communist and alien control. Even so, St Laurent allowed himself the opportunity presented by this meeting to notify his listeners that it was 'easier for those not charged with the responsibility of government' to make promises of liberation to those who were suffering than it was 'for us in office.' Whatever the personal sympathies of those in government might be, the governments in Washington, London, and Ottawa had to be careful, for 'the words one uses have to be related to the possibility and desirability of following them up by action,' and 'the interpretations that may be given them by friend and foe' had to be kept in mind. Ukrainian Canadians were in effect told that while they might enjoy the sympathy of the government, they should expect nothing more than sympathy – words aplenty, deeds none.
120 Minutes of the fifth national congress of the Canadian League for the Liberation of Ukraine, Toronto, 17–18 July 1954.
121 Minutes of a meeting of the national executive of the Canadian League for the Liberation of Ukraine, Toronto, 23 April 1959.

122 See V.J Kaye, NAC MG31 D69, vol. 26, 19, [1953?].
123 Kaye to Kirkconnell, 4 January 1951, NAC MG31 D69.
124 See the UCC's letter to Pearson, 11 September 1950, DEA 6980-GR-40. The UCC formally committed itself to supporting UNRada at its third national congress, held in Winnipeg, 7–9 February 1950.
125 See DEA 10919-40 for the *Winnipeg Free Press* article, dated 26 February 1951.

Chapter 9: 'The Vexed Ukrainian Question'

1 See FO 181/980, 20 August 1943, and 'Transfer of Minorities,' 20 January 1944, FO 371/39012. Sir Owen O'Malley, of the British embassy in Warsaw, wrote to Mr Eden to point out that even the use of a word like 'minority' was 'in its application to foreign affairs ... not a term of art: it has no precise meaning.' Nevertheless, he suggested a definition: a minority was 'a group of citizens cherishing national aspirations which conflict with the national aspirations of the majority of the citizens of the State in which they live.' Basic texts on interwar eastern Europe's national minorities include C.A. Macarthy, *National States and National Minorities* (London, 1934); R. Pearson, *National Minorities in Eastern Europe, 1848–1945* (London, 1983); and H. Seton-Watson, *Eastern Europe between the Wars, 1918–1941* (Cambridge, 1946). An account intended for 'the important but elusive ... Man-in-the-Street' is presented by B. Newman, *Danger Spots of Europe* (London, 1938). For an excellent overview of the historical geography of east-central Europe, see P.R. Magocsi, *Historical Atlas of East Central Europe* (Seattle, 1993).
2 'Transfer of Minorities,' 20 January 1944, FO 371/39012.
3 The British recognized that the various prewar minority treaties had not worked. That meant, as Sir Owen O'Malley put it, that 'a fresh series of Minority Treaties cannot be regarded with any enthusiasm.' See FO 371/39012, 24 January 1944.
4 See Nichols's statement of 20 August 1943, FO 181/980.
5 For Frank Savery's analysis, see enclosure #1 in 'Transfer of Minorities,' 24 January 1944, FO 371/39012.
6 Ibid.
7 Ibid. On 3 April 1944 the Research Department sent a note to F. Roberts of the Central Department critiquing Savery's interpretation of Polish behaviour towards Ukrainians. It expressed exasperation with Savery's attempt to credit the Polish authorities with 'moral principles like our own.' It was suggested that the last sentence of Savery's 'moving passage' would not

have been much differently phrased if it had been written by the Nazi propaganda chief, Dr Goebbels.

8 British embassy in Warsaw to E. Bevin, 27 May 1947, FO 371/66355. In DEA 58-H(s), 29 September–6 October 1945, Canadian officials noted that the British ambassador to Warsaw had recorded that some two million Poles had moved into eastern Poland from the Soviet side of the frontier, in accordance with the Soviet–Polish agreement on population transfers. While many Ukrainians west of the Curzon line wished to remain in Poland, Warsaw seemed determined 'to get them out,' and appropriate measures were being taken to remove them. For a recent study see Kordan, 'Making Borders Stick,' *International Migration Review* 31:3 (1997). For a very partial account of Polish–Ukrainian relations in the area, see M. Terles, *Ethnic Cleansing of Poles in Volhynia and Eastern Galicia, 1942–1946* (Toronto, 1993). W. Wolski, general plenipotentiary of the Polish government for repatriation, informed UNRRA's Austrian Mission, on 1 November 1946, that 'citizens of Ukrainian nationality who were living in areas ceded to Ukrainia by Poland and having the Polish citizenship to 1939, had this citizenship because they lived in former Polish areas. After these areas were included in the Ukrainian territories they lost their Polish citizenship and were not eligible for repatriation. This matter was settled by an agreement; even those Ukrainians, who are living in the present Polish boundaries are subject to repatriation to Ukrainia.' See the A. Brownlee Collection, Box 6, Hoover Institution on War, Revolution and Peace.

9 Ibid. Adding to the terror of those being forcibly relocated was their exposure to the depredations of the Polish Office of State Security, whose officials, mostly Jews, rounded up thousands of innocent civilians and ran hundreds of concentration camps, the inhabitants of which were often tortured and murdered. For a description of these relatively unknown events, see J. Sack, *An Eye for an Eye: The Untold Story of Jewish Revenge against Germans in 1945* (New York, 1993), and the references in T. Piotrowski, *Poland's Holocaust: Ethnic Strife, Collaboration with Occupying Forces, and Genocide in the Second Republic, 1918–1947* (Jefferson, N.C., 1998). One of the most notorious of these mass murderers, Shlomo Morel, currently lives in Israel, which has refused to extradite him to Poland to stand trial for his crimes reportedly because the statute of limitations has run out on the case. See 'Extradition of Jew Refused,' *Toronto Star*, 8 December 1998; 'Israel Refuses to Hand Over War Crimes Suspect,' *Calgary Herald*, 8 December 1998; and 'Israel Protects Concentration Camp Boss,' *The Independent*, 29 December 1998, by A. LeBor. For a comment on this issue, see the letter to the editor 'Israel's Hypocrisy Indefensible,' by L. Luciuk, 16 December 1998, in the

Toronto Star. The government has ignored repeated appeals made by the Ukrainian Canadian Civil Liberties Association for an investigation into the presence of alleged communist war criminals in Canada.

10 'Polish Ukrainian Refugees in the British Zone of Austria,' 1 October 1946, FO 371/57905. Mr Crawford also noted that the effect of this Polish decision was that the Ukrainian community could not be repatriated. That fact had to be kept in mind when a resettlement scheme was decided, particularly one which justified the British practice of 'distinguishing Ukrainians from other sorts of Poles.'

11 'Annual Report on Poland, 1946,' 5 March 1947, FO 371/66236.

12 See British embassy in Warsaw to Bevin, 27 May 1947, FO 371/66355. It was observed that the Polish government and the 'itinerant' Soviet Repatriation Commissions 'showed a keen desire to remove all Ukrainians from Poland.'

13 See British embassy in Prague, 9 February 1949, FO 371/77584, which noted evidence of Slovak collaboration with the Ukrainian insurgents.

14 See FO 371/66355, 27 May 1947. For a British report on the Soviet view of Ukrainian nationalism, and particularly for their critique of the works of the Ukrainian statesman and historian Mykhailo Hrushevsky, see the report from the British embassy in Moscow, 27 February 1947, FO 371/66354.

15 See Document #29, 12 May 1944, in *Anglo-American Perspectives on the Ukrainian Question*, ed. Luciuk and Kordan, 151.

16 See Documents #36, 13 December 1945, and #42, 29 January 1948, ibid., 167–83 and 199–201.

17 See Document #44, 17 March 1948, ibid., 204–8. On the OSS and United States policy towards the Soviet Union in the Cold War period in general, see B.F. Smith, *The Shadow Warriors: O.S.S. and the Origins of the C.I.A.* (New York, 1983); A.C. Brown, *The Last Hero: Wild Bill Donovan* (New York, 1982); Ranelagh, *The Agency: The Rise and Decline of the CIA*; M. McClintock, *Instruments of Statecraft: U.S. Guerrilla Warfare, Counter-Insurgency, and Counter-Terrorism, 1940–1990* (New York, 1992); and M.P. Leffler, *A Preponderance of Power: National Security, the Truman Administration, and the Cold War* (Stanford, Calif., 1992), and P. Grose, *Operation Rollback: America's Secret War behind the Iron Curtain* (Boston, 2000).

18 Document #44, 17 March 1948, in *Anglo-American Perspectives on the Ukrainian Question*, ed. Luciuk and Kordan, 208.

19 Document #45, 18 August 1948, ibid., 209–12.

20 Documents #47, 27 October 1948, and #49, March 1949, ibid., 215 and 218–30.

21 Document #49, March 1949, ibid., 230.
22 Document #51, 4 September 1950, ibid., 233–4.
23 'Memorandum on the Recent Political Situation in the Ukraine,' 22 April 1949, FO 371/77586.
24 'Information about Forced Labour Camps in the USSR,' 13 August 1949, FO 371/77585. A letter on this subject was submitted to the Foreign Office by Y. Stetsko on 7 August 1949. The ABN was founded after the First Conference of the Captive Nations of Eastern Europe and Asia, held near Zhytomyr, Ukraine, on 21–2 November 1943. Organized by Ukrainian nationalists, the conference was attended by thirty-nine delegates representing thirteen of the nationalities found in the USSR. A series of resolutions were adopted which characterized the war between the Soviet Union and Nazi Germany as a 'typical' imperialistic struggle, draining the strength of both belligerents. In these circumstances there was an opportunity for the 'captive nations' to free themselves. Coordination of their simultaneous military struggles was therefore called for, and the importance of developing contacts with anti-German forces in the West noted. An organizational structure was given to the ABN in Munich, in 1946, after which it extended its scope to include representatives of various other eastern European diaspora communities. The principal ABN goal remained revolutionary struggle leading to the dismemberment of the Soviet Union into national states. The ABN continues to exist as an international anti-communist organization even if its original purposes have largely been met. Documents released by the Ukrainian liberation movement after the Zhytomer conference are reproduced in *Litopys UPA: Volyn' and Polissya: German Occupation: Book 1* (Toronto, 1978), 226–36. A similar theme – the growing wartime exhaustion of the Nazi and Bolshevik regimes – was presented in an editorial entitled 'In The Whirlwind of War,' first published in the bulletin of the UIS, 1:1 (1 April 1944). It was argued that, given the inherently expansionist tendencies of 'Russian Bolshevism,' tensions between the Soviets and the West would develop in the wake of the war. That would inevitably lead to a clash between those countries which stood for freedom and Russia with its totalitarian system. This editorial is reproduced in *Litopys UPA: Volyn' and Polissya: German Occupation: Book 2* (Toronto, 1977), 77–82.

The notion that war would break out between the Western Allies and the Soviet Union was not restricted to émigré circles. For example, even Canada's ambassador to Moscow, Dana Wilgress, wrote at the end of August 1943 about 'an increasing rift' in the relations between the Soviet Union and the Western Allies. It was 'sufficiently critical to warrant the exercise of the most prudent statesmanship ... On the handling of the present situation depends the chances of future co-operation of the Soviet Union in the tasks of organizing a peaceful and stable world and I doubt if this fundamental truth is fully appreciated in the western capitals. One can understand the impatience with Soviet attempts to dictate Allied strategy by means of press campaigns and with the need of always having to consider the "touchiness" of a government which itself has consistently followed an arbitrary and chauvinistic foreign policy. We have also to be careful not to fall again into the discredited attitude of appeasement. But in the relations with the Soviet Union a large measure of appeasement can be shown to be justified. Here we have a country wavering between a policy of close co-operation with other countries in maintaining a peaceful and stable world and a policy of isolationism backed up by armed strength. All signs have hitherto pointed to the rulers of the Soviet Union favouring the former policy and they are likely only to adopt the latter policy through mistrust and suspicion of the intentions of other countries. It is surely the duty of statesmanship to attempt to remove all cause for such mistrust and suspicion.' Detecting signs that the Soviet Union was preparing for the possibility of another major conflict, Wilgress admitted, 'This comes as somewhat of a shock to one who has firmly believed that Stalin's chief aim is to secure a prolonged period of external peace.' Prime Minister Mackenzie King also seems to have been overtaken by fears about the imminent likelihood of another world war after speaking with Winston Churchill in London, during the autumn of 1947. See Smith, *Diplomacy of Fear*, 49, 212–16.

25 See FO 371/77585 for Hankey's remarks on Y. Stetsko's letter of 7 August 1949.

26 An 'Englishman's Englishman,' the late Kim Philby, one-time head of the British Secret Intelligence Service's (MI6) anti-Soviet section, mentions the fate of some of the 1949–51 border penetration missions in *My Silent War*, 163–5. While serving in Washington as a liaison with the CIA and FBI, Philby, a traitor and Soviet spy, was positioned to derail various Anglo-American efforts aimed at working with the Ukrainian resistance. He did exactly that. The British and Americans, he later recalled, had exchanged precise information about the timing and geographical coordinates of their operations into Ukraine. This information he passed to the Soviets, who were therefore able to ambush most of the Ukrainian teams. As Philby cynically put it: 'I do not know what happened to the parties concerned. But I can make an informed guess.' In Ranelagh's *The Agency*, 137, the role of the American Office of Policy Coordination and of the CIA's Office of Special Operations is described as follows: 'Agents were briefed and given false papers and sent on missions throughout the Eastern bloc, including into the

USSR itself, where for several years after the war a Ukrainian resistance movement continued to fight the Red Army. This was a major and fascinating undertaking. The Ukraine was an acknowledged part of the USSR, so the operations were tantamount to war. It demonstrated the determination with which the United States entered the cold war. It also demonstrated a cold ruthlessness: the Ukrainian resistance had no hope of winning unless America was prepared to go to war on its behalf. Since America was not prepared to go to war, America was in effect encouraging Ukrainians to go to their deaths.' In *Philby: K.G.B. Masterspy* (London, 1988), P. Knightley maintains that Philby did not have details of every covert action attempted by the Anglo-Americans and so cannot be held responsible for all the resulting betrayals. He also claims that many of the resistance movements in eastern Europe were already thoroughly penetrated by the Soviets. Rather unconvincingly, however, he adds that 'all these penetrations were doomed from the start' because such missions can be effective only when the 'internal forces of a country were already moving in the direction the CIA wished to push them.' Knightley also repeats the canard that many of the émigrés recruited by the Americans were 'former nazi collaborators,' later smuggled into the United States with the connivance of the CIA. No evidence for that conclusion is given, other than a reference to a not particularly credible source, N. Yakovlev's booklet *CIA Target: The USSR* (Moscow, 1982).

27 See R.A. Faber's minutes, 16 January 1951, FO 371/94964. His colleague, J.H. Peck, noted on 12 February 1951 that Stewart's 'obstinate insistence' on the value of the 'near-apocryphal resistance movements behind the Iron Curtain' made his practical recommendations 'not merely foolish but dangerous.' He went on to reiterate that plans for dividing up the USSR were, as the Foreign Office's Research Department had concluded, nothing more than attempts to 'put the clock back 400 years.'

28 See Faber's minutes of 21 March 1951 on the file 'Requests Approval of a Memorandum by the Anti-Bolshevik Bloc of Nations,' FO 371/94445.

29 So did many Ukrainian Canadians. Walter Skorochid, writing to the *Globe and Mail* (8 July 1949), noted, 'Since the DPs began streaming into Canada, many communists and sympathizers have forsaken the ... movement because they have heard first hand information about what communism ... is really like.' The letter was not published. Personal papers of W. Skorochid, interviewed in Hamilton, 21 March 1982 (MHSO).

30 *Globe and Mail*, 8 July 1949. A particularly astute contemporary account of the tensions between DPs and communists in Canada, written by Ralph Hyman, was published in two instalments in the *Globe and Mail*, 14 and

15 July 1949, 'They Don't Scare Easily: DP's Greatest Menace to Communists Here, Know Reds' Strategy' and 'DP's Surprised to Find Communists
in Canada; Lead Fight against Reds.' Hyman first observed that 'Canadian
Communists are fighting a vicious, desperate and losing battle against an
enemy who presents the greatest menace to the future of communism in
this country – the displaced person.' In completing a survey of DPs in
Toronto, Hyman found that they had not lost their hatred of communism
and had already, in the short time they had been in Canada, succeeded 'in
weakening the hold of Communists on the foreign-born population.' What
was happening in Toronto was also 'happening right across the Dominion,
in every city and town where DP's and Communists meet.' This 'warfare'
might have been kept under the surface until recently, Hyman observed,
but it was now breaking out into the open, 'with the Communists resorting
to violence in an effort to intimidate these newcomers.' In interviewing
Walter Skorochid, Dmytro Hunkivich, and Reverend Peter Sametz, Hyman
learned that the DPS 'don't scare easily,' and, from Reverend Sametz, that
'there isn't a better agitator against communism than a DP.' What particularly worried the Canadian Left was the impact these DPs were having on
Canadian political life. Thus, when the Canadian communist leader Tim
Buck ran a poor third in the 27 June election in Trinity riding, 'despite lav-
ish spending of money by the Reds,' the results were interpreted as due in
large degree to the anti-communist activities of the DPs in Toronto. Michael
Zaverucha, secretary of Branch 360 of the Royal Canadian Legion, was
quoted as saying: 'Canadian Communists strongly opposed the entry of
DP's into Canada ... They are well aware of the fact that DP's are living witnesses of what is happening in the terror behind the Iron Curtain.' Another
person interviewed, described only as a 'well educated DP, master of half a
dozen languages, including English,' speaking about the positive effect of
the DPs on the foreign-born population, said: 'They are suspicious of what
they read in the press and hear over the air ... But they believe the DP's.
That is why the Communists hate and fear the DP's.' As recently declassified RCMP documents released under the Access to Information Act show,
many of the articles and editorials published in the newspapers of the
Ukrainian Canadian Left distorted actual events. For example, the 4 March
1948 issue of Ukrainian Life carried an article written by W. Clobber (said to
be the pen-name of a communist writer from Atikokan, Ontario) which
made reference to a brutal attack on an unnamed Ukrainian professor who
had lectured at Fort William, Ontario, the previous winter. On 20 May 1948
the commissioner of the RCMP was informed that the story of an attack
was 'entirely false.' Excerpts of the article, in translation, are found in an

RCMP file dated 21 April and give evidence of how vicious 'Clawbar' was in his denunciations of the speakers at an event held in the Ukrainian Greek Orthodox Church hall in West Fort William: 'The professor from Kiev was spewing with the stinking German goulash. The parishioners had to hold their noses in order not to smell this drivel ... On the following day, on Monday, November 24, this Kiev professor was given "thanks" for his fairy story of the previous day – someone has beaten him in the head and broke two or three ribs. Seriously injured he wound up in a hospital in Fort William ...' Disparaging the DPs, 'Clawbar' went on to write: 'You, gents, are not crying for the Ukrainian people but because the Ukrainian people are not going to work for you any more, therefore you must shift for yourself. We realize that the Canadian stews in the sawmill, or in the bush camps at Kapuskasing, is not to your taste. It is all over. You will not get any more from the Ukrainian people, neither the roast goose, chicken, nor cheese dumplings fried in butter. Here you must toil to earn your living by the sweat of your brow and sometimes even to get a beating with the two-by-four across your ribs.' The official translator underscored what he took to be the most important passages which, in his view, showed that 'Communist "Clawbars" ... are quite openly [telling the DPs in Canada] that if they continue to expose the Soviet conditions in their homeland, they will wind up in hospital with fractured skulls, and broken ribs, in the same manner as that D.P. professor.' He added, somewhat maliciously in his own right, that 'one would not be surprised if the writer himself did not use the clobber to beat up the above mentioned D.P. speaker, since he knows so much about it and has chosen that particular tool for his pen-name.' A report by the Special Branch of the RCMP detachment in Prince Albert, Saskatchewan, dated 10 March 1948, describing the activities of the AUUC branch in Wakaw, recently declassified under the Access to Information Act, reported that a UCC meeting held in the Ukrainian Greek Orthodox hall on 25 February, attended by some hundred people, was interrupted by a few communists, one of whom accused the speaker of being a former agent of the Polish police, and added that the crowd should refuse to give any money for the benefit of the Ukrainian refugees because he had sent money to a relative in a DP camp who later wrote to say that she never received it. A/Cpl. J.D. Lewak further recorded: 'It is very likely that the local Communists went to this meeting for the express purpose of disrupting it, and they succeeded to a certain extent. There is a strong suspicion that it was arranged before[hand] to "smear" the character of the speaker, with a personal attack ... My informants advise that the C.U.C. will continue to hold meetings and invite speakers who will [give] anti-Communist addresses. It is anticipated that the local Communist[s] will attend these for the purpose of disrupting the meetings.'

31 Skorochid to the *Globe and Mail*, 8 July 1949. In his view the political refugees were 'doing a splendid job of cleansing our city of the communist bacteria.' As for the ULFTA temple at 300 Bathurst Street, it was nothing more than 'the Communist Schoolhouse.' Another Ukrainian Canadian, the veteran M. Zaverucha, a member of the Royal Canadian Legion Branch 360 in Toronto, wrote to the *Globe and Mail* explaining that 'local communists' were responsible for provoking the DPs into fighting, their purpose being to arouse Canadian public opinion against the refugee immigrants. See Zaverucha to the *Globe and Mail*, 9 July 1949, unpublished, found in the personal papers of the late Stephen Pawluk, Toronto.

32 See William A. Kardash, *Winnipeg Free Press*, 22 October 1949, and the author's interview with Kardash, Winnipeg, 30 November 1982 (CIUS). For published reports on protests against communist harassment of European refugees, see, for example, 'Communists Harass D.P.'s – Bishop Ladyka,' *Toronto Star*, 23 December 1947. The bishop charged that a 'large-scale, Moscow-directed campaign by Canadian communists to spread disloyalty and treason among immigrants to Canada' was afoot, that some of the orders emanated from Winnipeg, and that communists were telling recently arrived immigrants that they had been exported to Canada to become slave labourers, who could be rescued only if they joined the ranks of the Communist party, which would ransom them. Communist sympathizers in Canada apparently continued with their attempts to sway the hearts and minds of DPS. See 'Calgarians Boost Russia to D.P.'s,' 21 August 1948, *Calgary Herald*. A reporter, accompanied by an interpreter, overheard three Calgary women conversing with a group of Polish, Yugoslavian, Ukrainian, and other DPS who were heading east by train to join relatives or farm in western Canada. The three women, described as 'middle-aged and well dressed,' talked to the DPS as they wandered along the station platform, 'speaking mainly to the Ukrainians.' They told them that 'they had made a mistake in coming to Canada because they would be better off in Russia. In Russia, they said, there were not rich people and no poor.' Responding, a Ukrainian girl, 'dressed in shabby clothes,' pointed to the tailored suit and fur stole which one of the Calgary women wore and told her that no one in Russia would be dressed that well. The Calgary women refused to tell the reporter their names.

33 See S. Skoblak to the *Winnipeg Free Press*, 25 October 1949, NAC MG28 v9, vol. 7. For a government opinion on the political positions of the AUUC and its affiliate, the WBA, see DEA 4174-40, 24 July 1950. According to a

secret RCMP report sent to T.L. Carter of External Affairs, the WBA was nothing more than a 'Communist front organization originally designed in 1922, to act as the fiscal agent of the Ukrainian Communist mass language organization, then known as the UFLTA ... now known as the ... AUUC.' It would be 'hardly credible' for someone belonging to the WBA not to know this, added the RCMP writer, for Ukrainians are 'particularly politically conscious.'

34 Kolasky, *The Shattered Illusion*, 103–7. Incidents of violence directed against the Ukrainian Left by the DPs are confirmed in some RCMP documents recently declassified under the Access to Information Act. On 27 November 1947 the RCMP took note of an article in *Ukrainian Life*, 'Displaced Persons in Canadian Bushes Are Contemplating a War.' Written by G. Lukan, a bush worker, this letter, marked 'Mile 133–3, A/C/R, Ontario,' read, in part: 'There are a great many enemies here ... enemies of all the Canadian progressive citizens. These are human beings in appearance, but beastly in their nature ... Anyone can see by their behaviour that these are the displaced persons, and some of them even war criminals. A great many of the latter have soaked their hands in a brotherly blood ... I want to shout at the top of my voice in order that all the Canadians even in the remotest part of our country should hear: *Beware*. For we have here, in the bush, real Fascists imported from Europe, who from morning till night, talk of war, and desire for war against you! ... The Canadian government ... informed the people saying that only selected persons are being admitted to Canada, that they would make "Good Canadians." Indeed, everything shows that they were selected, only those who made the selection, probably had Fascist preferences and tastes themselves.' Certainly, there were clashes between the newly arrived DP immigrants and the Left. For example, on 11 December 1948, S/Inspector K. Shakespeare, in charge of an RCMP Special Section in Toronto, wrote regarding an altercation that took place in Timmins, Ontario, on 14 November. Apparently a group of forty to fifty DPs marched to the AUUC hall in that city when they discovered that the organization was holding a concert on the very same night that the Ukrainian nationalists were 'honoring some Ukrainian liberty day.' The DPs 'lined up outside their hall (50 men in all), formed fours and marched off in a very business like manner. This formidable group must have really worried the small group of Communists at the A.U.U.C. hall. Probably it was fortunate that very few were left there as there may have been a small riot. As it was they all dispersed quietly and when the City Police arrived there was only 1 DP still loudly and profanely advising the AUUC members of their pedegree [*sic*].' For an article which suggests that the DPs kept members of their own

immigration from joining the Left, see *Ukrainian Life*, 22 April 1948, 'Displaced Persons Manifest Their Beastly Instincts.' Written by an anonymous writer from Timmins, this report tells of a beating administered by DPs to a recent immigrant who, allegedly, had communist sympathies, and condemns the treatment accorded to those who want to subscribe to a 'progressive way of thinking.' Certainly tensions between the DP newcomers and the Ukrainian Canadian Left did not dissipate for several years. See, for example, an article in the Toronto *Telegram*, 26 February 1951, 'Communist Gang Blamed As Oshawa DPS Beaten.'

35 Unpublished letter in the personal papers of W. Skorochid, 10 October 1950, Hamilton. I am grateful to Mr Skorochid for making a copy of this letter and other related materials available.

36 Unpublished letter in the personal papers of S. Pawluk, 13 October 1950, Toronto.

37 For the perspective of the Ukrainian Canadian Left on this incident, see 'Nazis Bomb AUUC Hall,' 15 October 1950, and 'Hunt Nazis Who Bombed AUUC Hall,' 1 November 1950, *Ukrainian Canadian* (Toronto); and 'At Murder-Bomb Protest Rally Name 5 Top SS Men in Canada As DP'S,' *Canadian Tribune* 23 October 1950. AUUC spokesman John Weir claimed the 'Banderists DP's' had created the League for the Liberation of Ukraine because they had found the UCC too moderate, and that these nationalists were responsible for terrorism in Canada. All his organization wanted was for 'our mothers to be able to gather together without fear of exploding bombs. We want our children to study music and dancing with carefree hearts. We want to be able to argue any question without knives and bullets.' The aforementioned issue of *Ukrainian Canadian* also carried the article 'I Was Bombed,' by D. Kostyniuk, and the editorial 'A Word to the DP's,' which cautioned them, in a surprisingly mild-mannered tone given the subject and the source, to behave like human beings. By the time this December issue made its appearance, some AUUC members had become very frustrated that no arrests had been made. An article headlined 'Why Are They Free?' questioned whether the perpetrators of the 'death bomb' attack on the temple were even being hunted by the police. Of course, AUUC writers and editorialists were ill disposed to the DPs even before the 'bombing' of the Toronto labour temple. On 15 January 1949 the *Ukrainian Canadian* reported that refugees were being 'groomed to attack' members of the AUUC, and alleged that the government had 'screened' these immigrants 'to allow into this country the very type of people who should have been kept away from our shores.' A similar charge was made in the 15 May 1949 editorial, 'What's Doing among DP's,' which claimed that 'the care-

fully "screened" DP's provided good material for union-busting – the RCMP "screeners" saw to that.' On 1 November 1949 there was an editorial entitled 'Deport D.P. Thugs!' and, on 15 November 1949, one entitled 'D.P. Gangsterism,' which chastised those responsible for a 16 October attack on Winnipeg's labour temple. On 1 March 1950 the magazine also claimed that established Ukrainian Canadian nationalist groups were being infiltrated by refugees who were planning even more future terrorist actions. In the same issue of *Ukrainian Canadian*, Weir charged not only that the UCC had been 'formed on the initiative of the Canadian government,' but that the DPs had been brought into Canada 'to be stormtroopers in a future war.' Echoing an attitude shared by many Canadian government officials, he went on to suggest that if Canadians of Ukrainian descent were to be 'worthy of Canadian citizenship' they must 'stop bickering about the Ukraine,' for 'so long as they are devoting themselves to the remote affairs of the Ukraine we cannot see that they are of any use to Canada.' Doubtless he did not appreciate that many government officials would have regarded him with no less apprehension and disdain than they did his nationalist competitors. See 'This Is Our Stand,' *Ukrainian Canadian*, 1 March 1950.

Certainly, the Ukrainian Canadian Left was determined to promote itself as the only truly representative and legitimate Ukrainian Canadian group, exactly parallel to what the UCC was attempting. See, for example, the editorial 'Roots of the AUUC' published in the *Ukrainian Canadian*, 15 January 1950. The AUUC described itself as '*The* organization' of Ukrainian Canadians because it was 'the largest' group and the one which best expressed their 'deepest interests.' Unlike other Ukrainian Canadian organizations, the AUUC was also the 'only truly Canadian' group since its chief purpose, which was to link 'our people with Canadian working people,' placed AUUC members 'foursquare in the camp of Canadian democracy' and made them 'partners in shaping the destiny of Canada.' It was also the 'only truly Ukrainian' group because it linked Ukrainian Canadians with the people of Ukraine, their history, and their culture. From an AUUC perspective none of the other Ukrainian Canadian groups met these criteria.

38 Unpublished letter in the personal papers of W. Skorochid, 10 October 1950, Hamilton.

39 Document #54, 4 May 1951, in *Anglo-American Perspectives on the Ukrainian Question*, ed. Luciuk and Kordan, 239. Of course, attempts were made by the left-wing Ukrainian Canadian organizations to entice recently arrived Ukrainian refugee immigrants into their organizations, usually without success. An article in the *Toronto Star* described one such incident. Fifty-nine Ukrainians who arrived in Timmins, October, on 15 December 1947 to

begin work at the Hollinger Consolidated Gold Mines described how they had been approached 'at every station stop on their trip north by men bearing Communist pamphlets and other literature.' These DPs, 'who sang Christmas carols throughout the 500-mile train trip from Toronto,' were so annoyed by the agitators sent among them that they reportedly seized two of them, 'beat them and tossed them off the train.' A Hollinger official intervened during this incident, which took place at North Bay, breaking it up before anyone was seriously injured. Asked to explain themselves, a spokesman for the DPs, Mike Mosal, aged twenty-two, put it bluntly: 'Was no good, we didn't like.'

Commenting on this incident in the letters section of *The Gazette* (Montreal) on 24 December, Robert Wickham, from St Lambert, wrote approvingly of the DPs: 'We read recently that Red propagandists were beaten up and thrown off a train by Ukrainian immigrants. The latter were headed for work in Ontario gold mines. Can anyone surpass the effrontery of the Communists? They send their agitators among men who know only too well the meaning of Communism. These Ukrainians (more power to them) were in no mood to be fooled by lies or threats. They sang because they were happy to be in this free land of ours. They had left behind them, perhaps, bitter memories of a homeland enslaved. And now, breathing the air of freedom, they in the sheer exuberance of it, kicked out the freedom-hating wretches. And so, let us guard our precious institutions. Send the malcontents to the land and system they so admire! Let us welcome in their stead all the freedom-loving peoples. I am sure the exchange will benefit Canada immensely.' For a response on the part of the Ukrainian Left, see the editorial in *Ukrainian Life* 'It Is Starting,' published on 25 December 1947. In part, it reads: 'All that against which the progressive Ukrainians have been warning the government of Canada if it decides to open the door of the country to Fascist elements, is happening now. The Fascist nurslings imported to Canada against the will of her democratic people, are getting down to their business – the cracking of heads of Canadian workers. After this we can expect from them strike-breaking, informing, and smashing of trade unions ... But the displaced Fascists who escaped from justice ... must be shown that Canada is not a Hitlerite Germany. They came here as undesired intruders at the expense and to the detriment of the Canadian people. Obviously, the government is not concerned with the type these people are ... We Ukrainians know best the nature of these degenerates. But this is not enough. It is necessary to have the entire working population ... learn of this. The displaced Fascists must be isolated, like a contagion ...' The same edition also carried a column on page 5 entitled 'Canada Is Not a D.P. Zone in Germany.'

40 Kaye to Kirkconnell, 25 October 1950, NAC MG31 D69.
41 Defence Liaison to the European Division, 18 April 1951, DEA 10919-40.
    Indicative of earlier British thinking on the subject of the best means for
    dealing with émigré groups are notes made by Hankey shortly after he had
    finished meeting with Panchuk, Andrievsky, and the Wasylyshens. Hankey
    recorded that he had explained how His Majesty's Government sympa-
    thized with the desire of émigré groups not to be divided because, in gen-
    eral, 'our view was that it was better both for the émigré communities and
    for the countries where they had to settle if they could avoid political divi-
    sions among themselves, whether they achieved this by the formation of
    national councils or in any other way. The existence of such political diver-
    sities led the world to think less well of the community concerned and was
    therefore damaging to the refugees themselves.' Groups like the Ukrainian
    National Council would render the best possible service to their compatri-
    ots, he said, if they concentrated on 'welfare work.' He promised they
    would eventually discover that 'when the Ukrainian community was pros-
    perous and flourishing they would be readily listened to and would also be
    able to exercise [political] influence which would be quite impossible if
    they were poor, unsettled and divided.' He added, with respect to Ukraini-
    ans in Britain, that it would be better not to arouse them to 'any great polit-
    ical activity,' for that would lead almost inevitably to competitive political
    activity on the part of other communities (e.g., Poles, Lithuanians, Latvi-
    ans), and 'the result would be liable to bewilder and disturb British opin-
    ion.' His listeners, Hankey observed, 'seemed [thoroughly] to understand
    this point of view' and 'hastened to say that they hoped to avoid any
    unpleasant incidents of the sort I had hinted at.' See Hankey's notes,
    21 March 1949, FO 371/77586.
42 Defence Liaison to the European Division, 18 April 1951, DEA 10919-40.
    By 1947 it had become apparent to Ottawa that British power was in
    decline nearly everywhere, while America's role in world affairs was
    increasingly influential and that Canada fell within the American sphere
    of interest. After the Truman Doctrine was articulated – J. Balfour of the
    British embassy in Washington described its main purpose as the preven-
    tion 'of the imposition of Communist regimes in countries into which
    they have not yet crept' – and an announcement made about the Mar-
    shall Plan for Europe, it became obvious that a worldwide competition
    existed between Washington and Moscow. Influenced by Winston
    Churchill, Canada's Mackenzie King authorized modest cooperation in
    American plans aimed at recruiting intelligence agents and various opera-
    tives from the postwar exile communities for use against the Soviet Union

and other eastern European countries. Ukrainians in Canada were among them.

43 Ibid.
44 Ibid.
45 Ibid.
46 Ibid.
47 Ibid.
48 Document #54, 4 May 1951, in *Anglo-American Perspectives on the Ukrainian Question*, ed. Luciuk and Kordan, 239–40.
49 See the comments regarding the UCC's memorandum to Pearson, 11 September 1950, DEA 6980-GR-40. The UCC executive had been advised by Professor George Simpson, in the spring of 1945, not to try to represent itself as speaking for Europe's Ukrainians, a claim which A. Hlynka had advanced even before the war's end, in a House of Commons speech, 26 March 1945. The UCC accepted this advice in drawing up its own 'Memorandum to the Canadian Delegation at the San Francisco United Nations Conference on International Organization,' reprinted in the 26 May 1945 edition of *New Pathway*. This document claimed that the UCC represented only Ukrainians in Canada. It went on, rather weakly, however, to make the point that Ukrainians in Europe lacked the freedom to express their own preferences and needed a 'free and independent state within Ukrainian ethnographic boundaries.' After nationalistic DPs began arriving and establishing groups in Canada which openly claimed to represent 'embattled Ukraine,' the UCC partially revived the Hlynka argument, at least to the extent that it publicly disputed the legitimacy of organizations like the ABN. See, for example, the *Winnipeg Free Press*, 26 February 1951, for an article on this very subject, which caught the attention of Canadian officials and was preserved in DEA 10919-40. Not surprisingly, the Ukrainian Canadian Left attacked Hlynka's remarks, taking the line that his speech was an unjustifiable intervention in the internal affairs of the USSR, and an irritation to an ally of Canada in the war effort. Harold Weir argued in the *Edmonton Bulletin* ('Canadians Can Speak for Canada and Only Canada: Too Many Instances of Dual Loyalty in this Country'), on 29 March 1945, that Hlynka's remarks came 'perilously close to disloyalty' and concluded with an admonition that, ironically, was one which many of the government's men were quite comfortable with: 'This is Canada – No hyphens!' Of course, the government, although mindful of these squabbles within the Ukrainian Canadian fold, had no intention whatsoever of acquiescing to Hlynka's suggestion or according any formal recognition to the UCC, the ABN, or any other Ukrainian organization, in Canada or overseas.

50 Notes entitled 'Meeting on Ukrainian Labour Farmer Temples,' 28 February
   1951, DEA 10268-40, vol. 1. Present were the RCMP's Commissioner Wood,
   Norman Robertson, E.H. Coleman, P.M. Anderson, and G.P. de T. Glazebrook. In Coleman's view, and contrary to the AUUC's claims about the
   economic losses suffered as a result of these confiscations, the seized
   ULFTA properties were found 'in better financial shape now than when
   they had been taken over.'
51 Comments on 'Invitation Extended to the Secretary of State for the Commonwealth to Attend 60th Anniversary Celebrations of Arrival in Canada
   of Ukrainian Pioneers,' 18 September 1951, FO 371/94938.
52 Ibid.
53 Ibid.
54 Secret report 'Ukrainian Nationalism and the Ukrainian Canadian Committee,' September 1952, DEA 10268-40.
55 Ibid.
56 Ibid.
57 Confidential memorandum 'The Ukraine,' by Jules Léger, Under-Secretary
   of State for External Affairs, to the Canadian ambassador to the USSR,
   18 July 1956, DEA 10268-40, reproduced as Document #51 in *A Delicate and
   Difficult Question*, ed. Kordan and Luciuk, 161–6.
58 Ibid.
59 Ibid. A negative attitude towards the question of Ukrainian independence
   was not new among Canadian officials. This unsympathetic orientation
   probably had a lot to do with the annoyance Ottawa's men felt over the
   difficulties arising from the presence of an active, nationally conscious
   Ukrainian ethnic group in Canada, an organized community which had
   often introduced complications into their conduct of foreign and domestic
   affairs. For example, during the war years, the Anglo-American powers
   consulted among themselves with respect to granting legal recognition to
   the Soviet republics, including Ukraine, and then entering into diplomatic
   relations with them. See Documents #31, #38, #40, and #41 in *Anglo-
   American Perspectives on the Ukrainian Question*, ed. Luciuk and Kordan. In
   response to a British note on the possibility of recognizing the international
   status of the Ukrainian Soviet Socialist Republic, External Affairs officials
   informed the prime minister that they supported such a move. But this
   seemingly contradictory and positive finding was predicated not so much
   on the fact that Ukraine was the second-largest Slavic state and important to
   the world economy, as on their hope that by recognizing the legitimacy of
   Soviet Ukraine the federal government would, with a single stroke, 'drive
   from the nationalists' minds the mirage of absolute Ukrainian indepen-

dence and in this way hasten the process of their assimilation.' See 'Secret
Memo for the Prime Minister,' 4 July 1944, NAC RG25, vol. 1896, file 165-A.
60 DEA 10919-40, 4 February 1955.
61 For a description of the meeting between Yaroslav Stetsko and Messrs Watkins, McCordick, and Crowe, see a report dated 25 April 1952, DEA 10919-
40. On 13 April, Stetsko spoke at a rally held in Toronto's Massey Hall. The
resolutions accepted there were forwarded to Canada's secretary of state
for external affairs, L.B. Pearson, on 14 April 1952, by W. Lyzaniwsky of
the ABN's Information Section (Canada), a document preserved in DEA
10919-40. A similar statement was submitted to Pearson by Stetsko on
21 April 1952. Apparently some meetings between members of External
Affairs, such as Léger of the European Division, and members of the
Ukrainian liberation movement were facilitated by John Decore (Dikur), a
Liberal MP who represented Vegreville in the House of Commons from
1949 to 1957. See Léger's 'Memorandum for File,' 7 March 1951, regarding
a meeting he had with M. Lebed, the UHVR's secretary general for foreign
affairs, and Reverend Dr Hrynioch, a member of the UHVR's presidium
and chairman of its Foreign Affairs Committee. The UHVR, Léger was
told, was in close contact with the Ukrainian underground and had as its
ultimate aim the dismemberment of Soviet Russia and independence for
Ukraine. These delegates showed Léger a few documents, 'the most interesting of which' was a decree of the Supreme Presidium of the USSR,
dated 1949, offering amnesty to the partisans if they renounced their
underground activities. The main criticism Lebed and Hrynioch made of
Western policy towards Soviet Russia was that it was too inclined to 'combat Communism and to forget that the real enemy is not Communism but
Russian imperialism.'
62 'Re: Admission of Stetsko to Canada,' 21 February 1951, DEA 10919-40.
McCordick had been a third secretary attached to the Canadian embassy
established in Moscow in March 1943. At the time, Wilgress headed the
Canadian mission.
63 Document #53, 21 February 1951, in *Anglo-American Perspectives on the
Ukrainian Question*, in Luciuk and Kordan, 237–328.
64 DEA 10919-40, 25 April 1952. Stetsko's tour was more successful. According to Kaye, who cited an article published in the *Sudbury Daily Star*, a city
Stetsko visited on 11 June 1952, the speaker drew 'five times as many listeners as did Tim Buck,' the leader of the CPC. The second ABN congress was
held shortly afterwards in Toronto, 21–2 March 1952. For more on Kaye's
views regarding the ABN, see 'Factual Statements on the Situation Respecting Governments-in-Exile,' December 1957, DEA 10919-40.

65 DEA 10268-40, 6 November 1957, reproduced as Document #52 in *A Delicate and Difficult Question*, ed. Kordan and Luciuk, 166–7.
66 Robertson to the Secretary of State for External Affairs, 'Canadian Attitude to Ukrainian Nationalism,' 15 January 1962, DEA 10268-40, reproduced as Document #55 in *A Delicate and Difficult Question*, ed. Kordan and Luciuk, 171–3.
67 On 20 December 1961, in response to a letter from His Excellency D.O. Hay, Australia's high commissioner to Canada, Jean Fournier of External Affairs noted that Canada's attitude to the recognition of Belarussia and Ukraine had been defined in the House of Commons on 17 May 1954. At the time the parliamentary assistant to the secretary of state for external affairs made it clear that 'Canada does not recognize Byelorussia and Ukraine as separate and sovereign states, but regards them as constituent parts of the USSR.' See Fournier's confidential letter to Hay, DEA 6126-40. Worries about the possible negative consequences of any public participation in Ukrainian Canadian affairs continued to trouble Canadian political leaders well into the 1980s, as documents recently declassified under the Access to Information Act reveal. For example, when Professor Bohdan Krawchenko wrote, on 13 July 1993, to the Honourable Bob Kaplan, the solicitor-general of Canada, inviting him to speak on the occasion of the unveiling of a monument in Edmonton commemorating the man-made famine of 1932–3 in Ukraine, the security services were consulted to determine what the minister's response should be. On 22 August a secret memorandum was delivered, by hand, from Mr J. Giroux, director general of the Security Service, to Mr J.M. Shoemaker, QC, senior assistant to the Police and Security Branch of the ministry. That document noted that the UCC, on whose behalf Dr Krawchenko had extended the invitation, was 'a legitimate and prominent organization in Edmonton which represents the anti-Soviet Ukrainian groups in the city,' adding that 'it is felt that the Minister would not be placed in an embarrassing position should he attend.' Despite Professor Krawchenko's appeal, which concluded, 'In view of the public stance you have taken on the Holocaust we thought it most appropriate to invite you to participate with us in marking the Ukrainian tragedy,' the minister did not attend.

These attitudes persisted. For example, on 23 October 1986 the Right Honourable Joe Clark, MP, secretary of state for external affairs, wrote to Mr M. Wawryshyn of Toronto, in response to Wawryshyn's question as to why, during an Argentinean tour by the Ukrainian Canadian choral group Vesnivka, the Canadian embassy had not officially endorsed or attended its Buenos Aires concert. Clark replied that there were 'foreign policy' implications involved. Since the folk group had, alongside a Canadian flag, 'prominently displayed' the 'flag of the wartime Republic of the Ukraine and [sung] the national anthem of that Republic,' the attendance of Canadian diplomatic personnel at such a concert might have been 'subject to possible misinterpretation regarding Canadian policy towards the Ukraine.' Following a public outcry (see Canada, House of Commons, *Debates*, 4 December 1986, 'Canadian Policy tooward Ukraine–Buenos Aires Concert Incident,' and the editorial 'Time for Clarification,' *Ukrainian Echo* [Toronto], 26 November 1986), Mr Clark offered an apology of sorts on 14 November 1986. In this letter Clark confused the issues involved by noting that 'it has never been the policy or intention of this Government to discourage the promotion of multiculturalism in Canada.' He went on that the Canadian government recognized 'a distinct Ukrainian culture and community' and would do all it could to 'assist the Ukrainian community in Canada to promote and preserve its culture.' He concluded that the 'displaying of the Ukrainian national flag and the singing of the Ukrainian national anthem were not in any way the reason for the absence of Embassy representatives,' and that such items on a concert agenda would not lead to such absences in future. However, Clark avoided making any statement with regard to the issue of the Ukrainian nation's right to independence, which was the core reason for the protests raised over his first letter. See Claire Hoy, 'Hard Insult, Soft Excuse,' *Toronto Sun*, 5 December 1986. The subsequent testimony of the associate under-secretary of state for external affairs, Mr Stanford, further clarified government thinking on the issue of Ukrainian independence. Responding to a question from E. Epp, MP for Thunder Bay–Nipigon, Stanford said: 'I cannot assure you that the policy is going to be changed. I think it is worth while identifying the policy, and it is that when the Canadian government extended formal recognition to the U.S.S.R. in 1924 it accepted that the territory of the Soviet Union included the Ukraine. All successive Canadian governments have recognized the Ukraine as an integral part of the U.S.S.R.' Canada, House of Commons, *Minutes of Proceedings and Evidence of the Standing Committee on Multiculturalism*, #22, Ottawa, 29 June 1988. Of course, the disintegration of the Soviet Union and Ukraine's 1991 proclamation of independence forced External Affair's mandarins to review their prescription. The Supreme Rada of Ukraine formally announced the country's independence on 24 August 1991, a status confirmed overwhelmingly by a national referendum held on 1 December. Canada formally recognized Ukraine on 2 December 1991. The United States of America did so on 25 December 1991. On contemporary Ukraine's situation, see J.A. Motyl, *Dilemmas of Independence: Ukraine after*

Totalitarianism (New York, 1993); T. Kuzio and A. Wilson, *Ukraine: Perestroika to Independence* (Edmonton, 1994); Mroz and Pavliuk, 'Ukraine: Europe's Linchpin,' *Foreign Affairs* 75:3 (May–June 1996): 52–6; and A. Wilson, *Ukrainian Nationalism in the 1990s: A Minority Faith*. Most Western governments have remained curiously indisposed to the viability of the new Ukrainian state. See the articles of Lubomyr Luciuk as reprinted in L.Y. Luciuk, *Welcome to Absurdistan: Ukraine, the Soviet Disunion, and the West* (Kingston, 1995).

Chapter 10: 'A Good Canadian'

1 On Canadian immigration policy, see G.E. Dirks, *Canada's Refugee Policy: Indifference or Opportunism?* (Montreal, 1977) and his more recent statement 'World Refugees: The Canadian Response,' *Behind the Headlines* (Toronto: Canadian Institute of International Relations) 45:5 (May–June 1988). Another, although rather unevenly researched interpretation, is provided by R. Whitaker, *Double Standard: The Secret History of Canadian Immigration* (Toronto, 1987). See also D.A. Avery, *Reluctant Host: Canada's Response to Immigrant Workers, 1896–1994* (Toronto, 1995), and N. Kelley and M. Trebilcock, *The Making of the Mosaic: A History of Canadian Immigration Policy* (Toronto, 1999).

2 Philipps to Panchuk, 5 November 1950. This comment is reminiscent of Philipps's earlier remark to Panchuk, 20 June 1948, when he noted that for Englishmen Ukrainians were nothing more than 'a troublesome kind of Russian'; Panchuk Collection. For another example of stilted British thinking on the question of Ukrainian nationality, see the footnote to Document #7, 2 February 1939, in *Anglo-American Perspectives on the Ukrainian Question*, ed. Luciuk and Kordan, 45. An analyst with the Department of Overseas Trade advised, on 2 February 1939: 'Some authorities assert that Ukrainians are of artificial origin without any real claim to race distinction and are in fact a collection of magnificent crossbred scallywags. There seems as least a case that their origin and development has been more due to political than ethnological causes.'

3 Dennis Stairs makes a similar point in 'The Political Culture of Canadian Foreign Policy,' *Canadian Journal of Political Science* 15:4 (1982) 667–90, describing the bureaucrats in Canada's Department of External Affairs as lacking 'breadth of vision and integrity of purpose.' At their worst, Stairs writes, 'when they are old and steeped too long in the practice of barter, they appear jaded and corrupt ... when they are young and governed too much by the lusts of ambition, they display the crude cynicisms of back-

room fixers, their identities defined by experience of the joys of manipulation, and by their proximity to power.' Stairs concludes that 'in none of this is there much to attract the admiration of those who believe in the primacy of the political profession and in the importance of ideas to its honourable conduct.'

4 See P. Dean's 15 January 1945 minutes on the file 'Soviet Prisoners of War in the United Kingdom,' FO 371/50606. For an example of persons claiming Ukrainian nationality, see the list attached to a letter from Captain W.L. Roots of the War Office to Dean at the Foreign Office, 11 January 1945, FO 371/50606. The list presents cases like that of POW Nicolas Leshczyszyn, captured in Normandy on 1 August 1944 while serving with the SS Division 'Hohenstauffen.' Born in Ternopil province in 1920, Leshczyszyn asserted that his citizenship at birth, and on 1 September 1939, was legally Polish but that his nationality was Ukrainian, not that of 'whoever occupies the country.' Substantiating his claim to Ukrainian nationality was his religious affiliation, listed as 'R.C. rite Orientale.' He had been drafted into the German army on 9 May 1944. Another POW claiming to be Ukrainian said that, since he now lived in England, he 'considers himself British,' while a third, also describing himself as Ukrainian, insisted that he now wanted 'to become a Pole,' even if his Polish-language skills were limited. 'In view of this Ukrainian difficulty,' minuted G. Wilson, 'I would prefer to omit this column altogether. "Nationality" to the Russians means "citizenship," and the equivalent of our "nationality" is "race".' The possibilities of misunderstanding – or worse – are thus quite endless if we start referring to Ukrainian nationality. The only thing is to base ourselves on the fact that, whatever these people may in fact be, under British law they are not Soviet citizens.' However convoluted, this ruling probably saved more than a few Ukrainians from forcible repatriation.

5 Brimelow's minutes on 'Ruthenian Displaced Persons,' 18 January 1946, FO 371/57813.

6 Instructions signed by Major General C.L. Adcock of the Office of Military Government, United States Forces HQ, European Theatre, 'Determination and Reporting of Nationalities,' 16 November 1945, FO 371/55782.

7 See a copy of the order of the Brigadier of 30 Corps District, 29 December 1945, Panchuk Collection. It noted that 'H.M.G. do not recognize *Ukrainian* as a nationality, and persons coming from the *Ukraine* are classed as citizens of the country in which they had their residence on 1 September 1939. No recognition can be given to any Ukrainian organizations or representatives as such.' All persons calling themselves Ukrainians and who had lived in Soviet territory on or before the above date were to be 'compulsorily

returned to the USSR.' Over half a year later, the same kind of document
was still circulating in European UNRRA circles. The Control Office for
Germany and Austria informed the Office of the Deputy Military Governor
CCG (British Element) in Berlin, on 27 May 1946, that 'H.M.G. do no recognize the Ukrainians as belonging to a separate nationality: their nationality
is Russian, Pole, or Czech, according to their place of residence on 1st Sept
1939, or they may be stateless. It is not therefore possible to provide a precise definition of who are Ukrainians.' This document is found in the A.
Brownlee Collection, Box 6, Hoover Institution on War, Revolution and
Peace.

8 A.E. Lambert to R.S. Crawford, 10 May 1946, FO 371/56791. Later that
month it was noted that it was His Majesty's Government's policy that
'Ukrainians are not considered to possess a separate nationality as such.'
However, since the definition of Ukrainian nationality could not be based
on a legal concept, a language criterion or a person's expressed desire not to
be treated as a Pole, Russian, or Czech had to be used. Even so, 'it must ...
be established definitely that any definition accepted by H.M.G. is not to be
regarded as acceptance by H.M.G. of the word 'Ukrainian,' as denoting a
nationality.' See FO 945/385, 22 May 1946. Other groups fared no better. For
example, in 'Treatment of Ukrainians in British Zone of Germany' (FO 371/
56791) there is a note from the Refugee Department, dated 13 February
1946, which points out that 'there is no Jewish nationality.' As for whether
or not Ukrainians in Germany should be allowed to create organizations,
'the primary consideration is of course the effect of whatever is decided on
relations with the Soviet Union and that is a matter for Northern Department.' Brimelow advised Miss B.M. Crosoer of the office of the Chancellor
of the Duchy of Lancaster, on 12 March 1946, that the British did not 'exercise ... discrimination between Ukrainians and Jews as regards repatriation
to the Soviet Union.' This policy was based on the Yalta Agreement, which
made 'no provision for racial discrimination,' which meant the British
authorities had 'carried out this agreement without regard to the race of the
persons affected by it.' An account dealing with forcible repatriation and its
impact on Jewish DPs remains to be written. Jews were listed as a distinct
category in military government reports when it came to detailing the
nationality of refugees in the British Zone of Germany, but none seem to
have been repatriated, if these British statistical materials are accurate. See,
for example, the table 'Displaced Persons Fortnightly Situation Report:
Position in British Zone As of 1 July 1947,' FO 371/66667.

9 See the orders signed by Lieutenant Colonel A.C. Chubb of the 3 Canadian
Infantry Division, 'Disposal of Ukrainians,' 26 July 1945, a copy of which is

found in the Department of National Defence War Diaries, 3 Division
CADF Files, 581.009 (D87) Instruction and Policy Rulings.

10 'Memorandum to PCIRO (Geneva, Switzerland), Subject: Ukrainian Refugees and Displaced Persons, Relief, Social Welfare, Immigration and Resettlement,' 12 September 1947, Panchuk Collection.

11 See the report by Bishop Buxton and Reverend John Findlow of the Church
of England's Council on Foreign Relations, 'Displaced Persons Camps in
British Zone in Germany,' 13 July 1947, FO 371/66667. They toured DP
camps between 2 and 15 June 1947 and noted that there were still some one
hundred thousand Ukrainians in the British Zone, thirty thousand of
whom lived privately.

12 See C.R.A. Rae's minutes of 19 August 1948 on Panchuk's 'Memorandum
on Ukraine and the Ukrainians,' FO 371/71636.

13 'Home Office Circular no. 5/1949. "A." Entries to be made concerning
Nationality in Registration Certificates of Aliens Claiming to Be of Ukrainian Origin,' signed by J.B. Howard (Home Office/Aliens Department),
12 January 1949, FO 371/77586.

14 See Mrs A. Freeman, Department of Citizenship and Immigration, to Mrs
A. Goralezuk of Welland, 16 March 1955, NAC MG28 v9, vol. 1.

15 Senator R.B. Horner, 20 March 1950, Senate of Canada, *Official Report of
Debates*, Ottawa, with respect to the incorporation of the Ukrainian
National Federation.

16 Director of the Citizenship Branch to Deputy Minister of Citizenship and
Immigration, May 1958, reproduced as Document #53 in *A Delicate and Difficult Question*, ed. Kordan and Luciuk, 168–9.

17 Lord Tweedsmuir's remarks in Fraserwood, Manitoba, on 21 September
1936 are reproduced as Document #24 in *A Delicate and Difficult Question*,
ed. Kordan and Luciuk, 63–4.

18 For example, Panchuk repeated the governor-general's remarks during a
talk on BBC radio, 8 July 1947, in the 'London Calling Europe' series. Panchuk claimed Canada was proud of Canadians of Ukrainian origin. All the
British need do was look to Canada for 'evidence and proof' of the qualities
of these Ukrainian settlers, who, he assured his listeners, would contribute
to national prosperity after they took 'the oath of loyalty to a king and to a
country of their own choice.' The revised text of his remarks is reprinted in
Memorial Souvenir Book 1, ed. Panchuk (Montreal, 1986), 184–5. This theme
was also frequently picked up by Canadian politicians. Ontario's Premier
George Drew, addressing the second national UCC congress, appealed to
the assembled delegates 'to foster in the minds of your children who were
born in Canada, love for the traditions of their forebears, and love for the

country from which their parents spring.' He went on: 'You should think not only of the country in which you now live, but of the land in which your parents once lived. You will become all the better Canadians if you cherish the things which were once dear to the ancestors who preceded you. Canadians would gain much by their co-habitation with Ukrainians.' See *Second All-Canadian Congress of Ukrainians in Canada*, 23.

19 'An Immigration Lesson,' *Globe* (Toronto), 8 February 1929, 4. The story which provoked this stinging editorial response was published on 7 February, under the title 'Ukrainian Petition Said to Hold Threat of Political Union,' 2. For a police perspective on this issue, we have the recently declassified remarks of the RCMP commissioner C. Starnes. Commenting on how groups like the 'Sitch' were regarded in terms of their impact on Canadian society, Starnes perceptively observed, on 13 August 1928, that 'Mr. Bosy's [*sic*] propaganda does not make for Canadianization, at all events immediately; it is instead designed to promote loyalty to the European home of these people. Speaking for myself I see no great evil in this; Canadianization has not been hindered by the devotion of French, English, Scottish or Irish Canadians to the lands of their origin, and I conceive that Ukrainians in the end might be better Canadians if convinced that they have an honourable national tradition to contribute to our common civilisation in Canada.'

20 *Windsor Daily Star*, 20 April 1948.

21 For this characterization of Kaye, see M. Petrowsky's comments in NAC MG30 E350, 29 July 1941. Earlier that month Kaye had written from his Mary Lake Farm, near King, Ontario, that his 'preference [was] to stay where I am ... you know how I love my farming and how I fear intrigues and mistrust politics.' See Kaye to Philipps, 1 June 1941, NAC MG30 E350. About how Ukrainian Canadians should start thinking 'Canadian,' see File 6, May 1941. For Judge T.C. Davis's remarks to Major-General L.R. LaFleche regarding the Committee on Co-operation in Canadian Citizenship, see the letter of 13 November 1942 in NAC MG30 E350, and also Philipps's correspondence with J.W. DaFoe, editor of the *Winnipeg Free Press*, especially the letter dated 8 July 1943, found in this same NAC manuscript group. The late S.W. Frolick left an equally critical portrayal of Kaye in his autobiographical account *Between Two Worlds*.

Sources

I. Unpublished Materials

Archival and Private Collections

Association of Ukrainians in Great Britain (AUGB) archives, London, England.

A. Brownlee Collection, Hoover Institution on War, Revolution and Peace, Stanford, California.

League of Ukrainian Canadians archives, Toronto.

Department of External Affairs (Canada) Archives, Ottawa.

Department of National Defence (Canada) Archives, Directorate of History, Ottawa.

Foreign Office (Britain) Archives, Public Record Office, London, England.

S.W. Frolick Collection, National Archives of Canada, Ottawa.

J. and M. Karasevich Papers, private, Winnipeg.

V.J. Kaye-Kysilewsky Papers, National Archives of Canada, Ottawa.

W.L.M. King Papers, National Archives of Canada, Ottawa.

W. Kossar Collection, National Archives of Canada, Ottawa.

E. Lapointe Papers, National Archives of Canada, Ottawa.

Multicultural History Society of Ontario, Toronto.

G.R.B. Panchuk Collection, Archives of Ontario, Toronto.

G.R.B. Panchuk Collection, National Archives of Canada, Ottawa.

S. Pawluk private papers, Toronto.

T. Philipps Collection, National Archives of Canada, Ottawa.

S. Sawchuk private papers, Winnipeg.

G. Simpson Papers, University of Saskatchewan Archives, Saskatoon.

W. Skorochid private papers, Hamilton.

A. Smith (Crapleve) private papers, Winnipeg.

Ukrainian Canadian Committee (UCC) Collection, National Archives of Canada, Ottawa.
Ukrainian Cultural and Educational Centre 'Oseredok,' Winnipeg.
Ukrainian National Federation (UNF) Collection, Archives of Ontario, Toronto.
E. and A. Wasylyshen private papers, Winnipeg.
A.J. Yaremovich private papers, Winnipeg.

Theses and Lectures

Avery, D. 'Canadian Immigration Policy and the Alien Question, 1896–1919: The Anglo-Canadian Perspective.' Ph.D. diss., University of Western Ontario, 1973.
Boudreau, J. 'The Enemy Alien Problem in Canada, 1914–1920.' Ph.D. diss., University of California at Los Angeles, 1965.
Deverell, J. 'The Ukrainian Teacher as an Agent of Cultural Assimilation.' M.A. thesis, University of Toronto, 1941.
Frolick, S.W. 'Saving the Displaced Persons: The Central Ukrainian Relief Bureau.' Mimeographed. Lecture presented at CIUS Lecture Series, Toronto, 13 November 1978. S.W. Frolick Papers, National Archives of Canada, Ottawa.
Gulka-Tiechko, M. 'Inter-War Ukrainian Immigration to Canada, 1919–1939.' M.A. thesis, University of Manitoba, 1983.
Kordan, B.S. 'Disunity and Duality: Ukrainian Canadians and the Second World War.' M.A. thesis, Carleton University, 1981.
– 'Ethnicity, the State, and War: Canada and the Ukrainian Problem, 1939–1945: A Study in Statecraft.' Ph.D. diss., Arizona State University, 1988.
Lehr, J. 'The Process and Pattern of Ukrainian Rural Settlement in Western Canada, 1891–1914.' Ph.D. diss., University of Manitoba, 1978.
Luciuk, L.Y. 'Searching for Place: Ukrainian Refugee Migration to Canada after World War II.' Ph.D. diss., University of Alberta, 1984.
Melnycky, P. 'A Political History of the Ukrainian Community in Manitoba, 1899–1962.' M.A. thesis, University of Manitoba, 1979.
Petryshyn, R. 'Britain's Ukrainian Community: A Study of the Political Dimension in Ethnic Community Development.' Ph.D. diss., University of Bristol, 1980.
Smith, F.N. 'The American Role in the Repatriation of Certain Soviet Citizens, Forcible and Otherwise, to the USSR Following World War II.' Ph.D. diss., Georgetown University, 1970.
Sullivant, R. 'The Problem of Eastern Galicia.' M.A. thesis, University of California at Los Angeles, 1948.

Veryha, W. 'The Ukrainian Canadian Committee: Its Origins and War Activity.'
   M.A. thesis, University of Ottawa, 1967.
Wilfong, R. 'The United Nations Relief and Rehabilitation Administration and
   the Displaced Persons.' Ph.D. diss., Harvard University, 1966.

II. Selected Oral History Interviews

The following are tape-recorded interviews held by the author with a large
number of Ukrainians who found themselves in the DP camps of Europe after
the Second World War. They are stored at the Multicultural History Society of
Ontario (MHSO) and at the Canadian Institute of Ukrainian Studies (CIUS) at
the University of Alberta, Edmonton. The MHSO is located at 43 Queen's Park
Crescent East, Toronto. Different access restrictions apply. For a brief description of some of the MHSO's holdings, see *A Guide to the Collections of the Multicultural History Society of Ontario*, ed. N.G. Forte and G. Scardellato (Toronto,
1992).

Alexewich, N. Edmonton, 18 November 1982. CIUS.
Andruschak, F. Saskatoon, 20 August 1983. CIUS.
Babenko, L. Toronto, 21 April 1982. MHSO.
Babiak, S., Toronto, 22 April 1982. MHSO.
Babiuk, J., Regina, 6 October 1983. CIUS.
Banach, R. Toronto, 2 April 1982. MHSO.
Baryckyj, R. Sudbury, 14 May 1982. MHSO.
Bashuk, P. Winnipeg, 24 January 1983. CIUS.
Bayrack, M. Edmonton, 10 November 1982. CIUS.
Bezchlibnyk, W. Toronto, 30 June 1981 and 1 July 1981. MHSO.
Bilecki, A. Winnipeg, 3 December 1982. CIUS.
Bogdan, F. Vancouver, 28 March 1984. MHSO.
Bojcun, R. Toronto, 24 March 1982. MHSO.
Borowyk, M. Ottawa, 14 September 1981. MHSO.
Boyko, P. Sault Ste Marie, 15 May 1982. MHSO.
Boykowich, M. Saskatoon, 17 August 1983. CIUS.
Bratko, D. Toronto, 8 April 1982. CIUS.
Bukowsky, N. Saskatoon, 17 August, 1983. CIUS.
Bulat, Y. Toronto, 8 April 1982. MHSO.
Burianyk, W. Winnipeg, 30 May 1982. MHSO, and 28 November 1982, CIUS.
Cap, W. Winnipeg, 28 November 1982. CIUS.
Charchalis, M. Toronto, 29 April 1982. MHSO.
Cymbalisty, P. London, England, 15 June 1982. CIUS.

Cymbaliuk, F. Toronto, 9 April 1982. MHSO.

Czich, M. Ottawa, 18 September, 1981. MHSO.

Danyliw, T. London, England, 17 June 1982. MHSO.

Danyliuk, P. Winnipeg, 29 January 1983. CIUS.

Davidovich, S. Toronto, 8 March 1982. MHSO.

Davies, R. Montreal, 6 June 1983. CIUS.

Dawydiak, W. Sudbury, 14 May 1982. MHSO.

Didowycz, W. Munich, West Germany, 22 July 1982. MHSO.

Dmytriw, I. London, England, 16 June 1982. MHSO.

Dobriansky, M. London, England, 21 June 1982. MHSO.

Duvalko, I. Toronto, 20 April 1982. MHSO.

Eliashevsky, I. Toronto, 11 February 1982. MHSO.

Eliashevsky, O. Toronto, 28 April 1982. MHSO.

Fedak, M. Toronto, 9 April 1982. MHSO.

Fedorowich, R. Regina, 2 October 1983. CIUS.

Fedorowycz, W. Toronto, 6 April 1982. MHSO.

Firman, I. Toronto, 30 May 1982. MHSO.

Frolick, S.W. Toronto, 1 July 1981, 16–24 December 1983, and 4–6 January 1984,
    MHSO, and 10 January 1983, CIUS.

Fundak, O. London, England, 4 August 1982. MHSO.

Fyshkevytch, J. Toronto, 9 April 1982. MHSO.

Gawa, M. Toronto, 10 February 1982. MHSO.

Gayowsky, I. Winnipeg, 26 January 1983. CIUS.

Gembatiuk, Y. Toronto, 5 April 1982. MHSO.

Gospodin, A. Winnipeg, 1 December 1982 and 21 January 1983. CIUS.

Haskett, M. Toronto, 19 February 1989. MHSO.

Hawrysch, M. Toronto, 5 April 1982. MHSO.

Hawrysh, N. Saskatoon, 17 August 1982, CIUS.

Horishnyj, I. Toronto, 31 March and 7 April 1982. MHSO.

Horlatsch, S. Toronto, 1 May 1982. MHSO.

Hrabusevich, J. Thunder Bay, 16 May 1982. MHSO.

Hryn, M. Toronto, 19 April 1982. MHSO.

Humeniuk, J. Sault Ste Marie, 15 May 1982. MHSO.

Iwaskiw, L. Thunder Bay, 17 May 1982. MHSO.

Izyk, S. Winnipeg, 21 May 1982. CIUS.

Jaworskyj, V. Toronto, 13 February 1982. MHSO.

Kachynycz, W. Thunder Bay, 16 May 1982. MHSO.

Kapusta, M. Toronto, 10 May 1982. MHSO.

Karasevich, M. Winnipeg, 7 October 1983. CIUS.

Kardash, W. Winnipeg, 30 November 1982. CIUS.

Kaye, L. Saskatoon, 16 August 1983. CIUS.

Kindrachuk, F. Saskatoon, 25 November 1982. CIUS.

Kis, H. Ottawa, 18 September 1981. MHSO.

Kis, T. Ottawa, 18 September 1981. MHSO.

Klish, W. Toronto, 21 June 1983. CIUS.

Knehinicki, J. Winnipeg, 29 November 1982. CIUS.

Knysh, Z. Toronto, 10 March 1982. MHSO.

Kocijowsky, M. Sudbury, 14 May 1982. MHSO.

Kolasky, J. Edmonton, 8 May 1983. CIUS.

Kolos, T. Toronto, 3 May 1982. MHSO.

Kolysher, P. Saskatoon, 19 August 1983. CIUS.

Konopka, O. Saskatoon, 18 August 1983. CIUS.

Konopka, W. Saskatoon, 18 August 1983. CIUS.

Korchinski, B. Regina, 3 October 1983. CIUS.

Korda, I. Thunder Bay, 18 May 1982. MHSO.

Korda, W. Saskatoon, 17 August 1983. CIUS.

Kordiuk, B. Munich, West Germany, 13 July 1982. MHSO.

Kosak, J. Munich, West Germany, 13 July 1982. MHSO.

Kostiuk, A. London, England, 19 June 1982. MHSO.

Kostiuk, R. Toronto, 27 April 1982. MHSO.

Kowalsky, A. Toronto, 22 April 1982. MSHO.

Kozicky, H. Calgary, 5 July 1983. CIUS.

Kozyra, I. Thunder Bay, 18 May 1982. MHSO.

Kril, M. Toronto, 12 February 1982. MHSO.

Kruzelecky, J. Toronto, 24 April 1982. MHSO.

Krynycky, B. Ottawa, 6 September 1981. MHSO.

Krysak, W. Toronto, 21 April 1982. MHSO.

Kryvoruchko, A. Ottawa, 17 September 1981. MHSO.

Kryzanowska, M. Toronto, 26 April 1982. MHSO.

Kupchak, A. Victoria, 1 April 1984. CIUS.

Kurdydyk, A. Winnipeg, 20 January 1983. CIUS.

Kuryliw, W. Sudbury, 15 May 1982. MHSO.

Kushmelyn, W. Toronto, 7 April 1982. MHSO.

Kushnir, O. Toronto, 5 April 1982. MHSO.

Kuzma, S. Saskatoon, 23 August 1983. CIUS.

Lapchuk, A. Regina, 6 October 1983. CIUS.

Lashin, S. Vancouver, 4 April 1984. CIUS.

Lenyk, V. Munich, West Germany, 9 July 1982. MHSO.

Lisczynski, W. Victoria, 2 April 1984. CIUS.

Lobay, S. Vancouver. 3 April 1984. CIUS.

Majstrenko, I. Barrie, Ontario, 9 July 1982. MHSO.

Makar, V. Toronto, 23 March 1982. MHSO.

Makohon, P. Toronto, 24 April 1982. MHSO.

Makoweckyj, J. Munich, West Germany, 12 July 1982. MHSO.

Maksymluk, A. Barrie, Ontario, 12 May 1982. MHSO.

Malaschuk, R. Toronto, 25 March 1982. MHSO.

Maleckyj, M. Toronto, 9 March 1982. MHSO.

Marunchak, M. Winnipeg, 31 May 1982. MHSO.

Maruniak, V. Munich, West Germany, 12 July 1982. MHSO.

Maryglad, T. Toronto, 1 April 1982. MHSO.

Maryglad, V. Toronto, 1 April 1982. MHSO.

Matla, A. Toronto, 24 March 1982. MHSO.

Melnyk, P. Victoria, 30 March 1984. CIUS.

Melnyk, P. Toronto, 23 April 1984. MHSO.

Melnyk-Kaluzynska, H. London, England, 6 August 1982. MHSO.

Migus, M. Toronto, 2 April 1982. MHSO.

Mykytiuk, D. Winnipeg. 4 December 1982 and 18 January 1983. CIUS.

Moros, H. Toronto, 27 March 1982. MHSO.

Mucha, M. Toronto, 26 March 1982. MHSO.

Mudryk, S. Munich, West Germany, 13 July 1982. MHSO.

Mychalchuk, I. Ottawa, 19 September 1982. MHSO.

Myhal, B. Ottawa, 7 September 1981. MHSO.

Mykytczuk, K. Toronto, 15 and 23 April 1982. MHSO.

Naklowycz, S. Vienna, Austria, 6 July 1982. MHSO.

Nebeluk, M. Toronto, 9 March 1982. MHSO.

Nemilowich, M. Winnipeg, 29 November 1982. CIUS.

Olah, W. Toronto, 3 May 1982. MHSO.

Olynyk, R. Montreal, 14 July 1983. CIUS.

Oranski, B. Toronto, 7 April 1982. MHSO.

Paladiychuk, R. Toronto, 22 March and 4 April 1982. MHSO.

Panchuk, G.R.B. Montreal, 5 May 1981, 24 July 1981, 4 April 1982, MHSO, and
    4 January 1983. CIUS.

Pankiw, J. Winnipeg, 22 January 1983. CIUS.

Pawlik, A. Winnipeg, 1 December 1982. CIUS.

Pawluk, S. Toronto, 25 November 1981. MHSO.

Petrash, K. Oshawa, 29 January 1978. MHSO.

Petryshyn, A. Thunder Bay, 17 May 1982. MHSO.

Petryshyn, M. Saskatoon, 16 August 1983. CIUS.

Pidlisny, M. Toronto, 25 April 1982. MHSO.

Piniuta, H. Fort Frances, Ontario, 5 May 1984. CIUS.

Pisocky, S. Thunder Bay, 18 May 1982. MHSO.

Pizag, P. Victoria, 30 March 1984. CIUS.

Primak, W. Vancouver, 31 March 1984. CIUS.

Prozak, M. Sault Ste Marie, 15 May 1982. MHSO.

Rawluk, I. London, England, 16 June 1982. MHSO.

Romaniw, S. Winnipeg, 27 January 1983. CIUS.

Romanow, J. Ottawa, 20 September 1982. MHSO.

Romanow, M. Saskatoon, 17 and 23 August 1983. CIUS.

Rosocha, S. Toronto, 4 May 1982. MHSO.

Rutich, K. Victoria, 31 March 1984. CIUS.

Sagacz, W. Regina, 5 October 1983. CIUS.

Salsky, G. Aylmer, Québec, 16 September 1981. MHSO.

Samchuk, U. Toronto, 23 April 1982. MHSO.

Sawchuk, S. Winnipeg, 5 December 1982. CIUS.

Semchuk, S. Winnipeg, 3 December 1982. CIUS.

Serbyn, Y. Toronto, 30 June 1981. MHSO.

Shankowsky, L. Philadelphia, 3 September 1981. MHSO.

Shatulsky, M. Toronto, 5 April 1984. MHSO.

Shebech, M. Toronto, 23 March 1982. MHSO.

Shiposh. M. Sudbury, 13 May 1982. MHSO.

Shtendera, E. Ottawa, 7 September 1982. MHSO.

Skorochid, W. Hamilton, 21 March 1982. MHSO.

Skoropad, W. Sudbury, 17 May 1982. MHSO.

Smith (née Crapleve), A. Winnipeg, 20 May 1982 MHSO, and 29 November 1982. CIUS.

Smylski, P. Toronto, 25 March 1982. MHSO.

Sokolsky, O. Toronto, 3 December 1981. MHSO.

Solomon, J. Winnipeg, 30 November 1982. CIUS.

Solonynka, W. Toronto, 23 March 1982. MHSO.

Sosna, A. Oshawa, 16 April 1982. MHSO.

Stanko, Y. Toronto, 14 April 1982. MHSO.

Stasiuk, S. Sudbury, 14 May 1982. MHSO.

Stebelsky, B. Toronto, 17 March 1982. MHSO.

Stechishin, S. Saskatoon, 16 August 1983. CIUS.

Stepaniuk, A. Toronto, 3 May 1982. MHSO.

Stetsko, S. Munich, West Germany, 9 July 1982. MHSO.

Stetsko, Y. Munich, West Germany, 14 July 1982. MHSO.

Stratichuk, J. Sault Ste Marie, 15 May 1982. MHSO.

Stratychuk, R. Saskatoon, 16 August 1983. CIUS.

Supynyk, G. Regina, 4 October 1983. CIUS.

Swyrydenko, D. Thunder Bay, 17 May 1982. MHSO.
Tesla, I. Ottawa, 7 September 1982. MHSO.
Tkachuk, M. Saskatoon, 25 November 1982. CIUS.
Waler, M. Toronto, 27 April 1982. MHSO.
Wasylenko, R. Ottawa, 9 September 1981. MHSO.
Wasylyshen, A. Winnipeg, 30 May 1982 (MHSO) and 30 November 1982 (CIUS).
Worobetz, P. Saskatoon, 21 August 1983. CIUS.
Wowk, L. Saskatoon, 21 August 1983. CIUS.
Yaremovich, A. Winnipeg, 1 December 1982. CIUS.
Yuzwa, P. Saskatoon, 25 November 1982. CIUS.
Yuzyk, J. Winnipeg, 28 November 1982. CIUS.
Zenchyshyn, J. Regina, 1 October 1983. CIUS.
Zvarych, N. Kenora, Ontario, 3 May 1984. CIUS.

III. Selected Published Sources

Atlases, Bibliographies, Documentary Collections, Encyclopaedias, Guides, Pamphlets, Reports, and Aids to Research

Birch, J. *The Ukrainian Nationalist Movement in the U.S.S.R. since 1956*. London: Ukrainian Information Service, 1971.
Bogomolets, A. *Soviet Ukraine and Ukrainian-German Nationalists in Canada*. Toronto: Ukrainian Canadian Association, 1943.
Butsko, O.M. *Never to Be Forgotten* ... Kyiv: Ukraina Society, 1986.
Boshyk, Y., and B. Balan, eds. *Political Refugees and 'Displaced Persons,' 1945–1954: A Select Bibliography and Guide to Research, with Special Reference to the Ukrainians*. Research Report no. 2. Edmonton: Canadian Institute of Ukrainian Studies, 1982.
Bramwell, A.C., ed. *Refugees in the Age of Total War*. London: Unwin Hyman, 1988.
Carynnyk, M. 'The Killing Fields of Kiev.' *Commentary* 90:4 (1990): 19–25.
Carynnyk, M., L.Y. Luciuk, and B.S. Kordan, eds. *The Foreign Office and the Famine: British Documents on Ukraine and the Great Famine of 1932–1933*. Kingston and Vestal: Limestone, 1988.
Cohen, R., ed. *The Cambridge Survey of World Migration*. Cambridge: Cambridge University Press, 1995.
Darcovich, W., and P. Yuzyk, eds. *A Statistical Compendium on the Ukrainians of Canada, 1891–1976*. Ottawa: University of Ottawa Press, 1980.
Dear, I.C.B., and M.R.D. Foot, eds. *The Oxford Companion to the Second World War*. Oxford: Oxford University Press, 1995.

Deschênes, J. *Commission of Inquiry on War Criminals: Report, Part 1: Public.* Ottawa: Canadian Government Publishing Centre, 1986.

Forte, N.G., and G. Scardellato, eds. *A Guide to the Collections of the Multicultural History Society of Ontario.* Toronto: Multicultural History Society of Ontario, 1992.

Friends of Ukraine. *The Jewish Pogroms in Ukraine: Authoritative Statements on the Question of Responsibility for Recent Outbreaks against the Jews in Ukraine.* Washington, 1919.

Gregorovich, J.B., ed. *Ukrainian Canadians in Canada's Wars: Materials for Ukrainian Canadian History.* Vol. 1. Toronto: Ukrainian Canadian Research Foundation, 1983.

Hilliker, J.F., ed. *Documents on Canadian External Relations, 1944–1945.* Vol. 10, part 1. Ottawa: Department of External Affairs, 1987.

Hoover Institution on War, Revolution and Peace. *List of Periodical Publications Published by Byelorussian, Russian, and Ukrainian DP's, 1945–1951: Holdings of the Hoover Library.* Stanford, Calif.: Stanford University, n.d.

International Commission of Inquiry into the 1932–33 Famine in Ukraine. *The Final Report.* Toronto, 1990.

Investigation of the Ukrainian Famine, 1932–1933. *First Interim Report of Meetings and Hearings of and before the Commission on the Ukraine Famine.* Washington: United States Government Printing Office, 1987.

– *Second Interim Report of Meetings and Hearings of and before the Commission on the Ukraine Famine.* Washington: United States Printing Office, 1988.

– *Report to Congress: Commission on the Ukraine Famine.* Washington: United States Government Printing Office, 1988.

Kalbach, W.E. *The Impact of Post–World War II Immigration on the Canadian Population.* Census monograph. Ottawa: Dominion Bureau of Statistics, 1969.

Knysh, Z., ed. *For Honour, Glory, and the Nation: A Collection of Articles for the Golden Jubilee of the Ukrainian War Veterans' Association in Canada, 1928–1978.* [In Ukrainian]. Toronto: New Pathway, 1978.

Kolasky, J., ed. *Prophets and Proletarians: Documents on the History of the Rise and Decline of Ukrainian Communism in Canada.* Edmonton: Canadian Institute of Ukrainian Studies, 1990.

Kordan, B.S. *Ukrainians and the 1981 Canada Census: A Data Handbook.* Research Report no. 9. Edmonton: Canadian Institute of Ukrainian Studies, 1985.

Kordan, B.S., and L.Y. Luciuk, eds. *A Delicate and Difficult Question: Documents in the History of Ukrainians in Canada, 1899–1962.* Kingston: Limestone, 1986.

Korolevich, Y. *The Emigré Inn.* Kyiv: Dnipro, 1985.

Koshiw, J.V. *British Foreign Office Files on Ukraine and Ukrainians, 1917–1948.*

Research Report no. 60. Edmonton: Canadian Institute of Ukrainian Studies, 1997.

KubijovyŜ, V., ed. *Encyclopedia of Ukraine*. 2 vols. Toronto: University of Toronto Press, 1984–8.

Leshuk, L., ed. *Days of Famine, Nights of Terror: Firsthand Accounts of Soviet Collectivization, 1928–1934*. Kingston, Washington, Kyiv: Kashtan, 1995.

Litopys UPA. *Litopys Ukrainskoi povstanskoi armii*. Toronto, 1978– .

Luciuk, L.Y. 'An Annotated Guide to Certain Microfiched Archives of the Association of Ukrainians in Great Britain.' *Journal of Ukrainian Studies* 11:2 (1986): 77–91.

– , ed. *Righting an Injustice: The Debate over Redress for Canada's First National Internment Operations*. Toronto: Justinian, 1994.

Luciuk, L.Y., and A. Chyczij, comps. *Memorial*. Trans. M. Carynnyk. Kingston: Kashtan, 1989.

Luciuk, L.Y., and B.S. Kordan, eds. *Anglo-American Perspectives on the Ukrainian Question 1938–1951: A Documentary Collection*. Kingston and Vestal: Limestone, 1987.

– , eds. *Creating a Landscape: A Geography of Ukrainians in Canada*. Toronto: University of Toronto Press, 1989.

Luciuk, L.Y., and Z. Zwarycz. 'The G.R.B. Panchuk Collection.' *Journal of Ukrainian Studies* 7:1 (1982): 79–81.

Magocsi, P.R. *Galicia: A Historical Survey and Bibliographical Guide*. Toronto: University of Toronto Press in association with the Canadian Institute of Ukrainian Studies and the Harvard Ukrainian Research Institute, 1983.

– *Historical Atlas of East Central Europe*. Seattle: University of Washington Press, 1993.

– *Ukraine: A Historical Atlas*. Toronto: University of Toronto Press, 1985.

Marsh, J.H., ed. *The Canadian Encyclopedia*. 2d ed. 4 vols. Edmonton: Hurtig, 1988.

P. Mohyla Institute. *Twenty Five Years of the P. Mohyla Institute in Saskatoon*. [In Ukrainian]. Winnipeg: Ukrainian Publishing Company of Canada, 1945.

Panchuk, G.R.B., ed. *Addresses at a Religious and Social Gathering Attended by Canadians of Ukrainian Descent Serving with the Canadian Forces (Overseas), and Other Members of the Ukrainian Community in England*. Manchester: Ukrainian Canadian Servicemen's Association (Active Service – Overseas) and the Ukrainian Social Club, 1943.

– ed. *Memorial Souvenir Book 1 (UCSA–UCVA): Ukrainian Branches of the Royal Canadian Legion*. Montreal: Ukrainian Canadian Veterans' Association, 1986.

– ed. *UCVA News Letter: Convention Issue* 2:11–12 (Toronto, 1954).

Petryshyn, W.R., and N. Chomiak, eds. *Political Writings of Post–World War Two*

Ukrainian Emigrés: Annotated Bibliography and Guide to Research. Research Report no. 4. Edmonton: Canadian Institute of Ukrainian Studies, 1984.

Polonsky, A., ed. *The Great Powers and the Polish Question, 1941–1945: A Documentary Study in Cold War Origins*. London: London School of Economics, 1976.

Potichnyj, P.J., and E. Shtendera, eds. *The Political Thought of the Ukrainian Underground, 1943–1951*. Edmonton: Canadian Institute of Ukrainian Studies, 1986.

Sidyak, A. *The Bankrupts*. Lviv: Kamenyar, 1984.

Smith, H.S. *Is It Nothing to You? The Refugee Problem in Europe*. London: Refugees Defence Committee, 1949.

Sopinka, J. *Ukrainian Canadian Committee Submission to the Commission of Inquiry on War Criminals*. Toronto: Justinian, 1986.

Styrkul, V. *ABN: Backstage Exposé*. Lviv: Kamenyar, 1983.

– *The SS Werewolves*. Lviv: Kamenyar, 1992.

Swyripa, F. *Oral Sources for Researching Ukrainian Canadians: A Survey of Interviews, Lectures, and Programmes Recorded to December 1980*. Research Report no. 11, Edmonton: Canadian Institute of Ukrainian Studies, 1985.

Terlytsia, M. *Here Is the Evidence*. Toronto: Kobzar, 1984.

Ukrainian Canadian Committee. *First All-Canadian Congress of Ukrainians in Canada*. Winnipeg, 1943.

– *Second All-Canadian Congress of Ukrainians in Canada*. Winnipeg, 1946.

– *Third All-Canadian Congress of Ukrainians in Canada*. Winnipeg, 1950.

– *Fourth All-Canadian Congress of Ukrainians in Canada*. Winnipeg, 1953.

– *Resettlement of Displaced Persons: Memorandum by the Ukrainian Canadian Committee, Representing Canadian Citizens of Ukrainian Origin, to the Economic and Social Council and the General Assembly of the United Nations*. Winnipeg, 1946.

Ukrainian Canadian Committee, Civil Liberties Commission. *On the Record: The Debate over Alleged War Criminals in Canada*. Toronto: Justinian, 1987.

– *War Crimes: A Submission to the Government of Ukraine on Crimes against Humanity and War Crimes*. Toronto and Kyiv: Justinian, 1992.

Ukrainian National Council. *The Reign of Terror in Poland: Three Documents*. Geneva, 1925.

Ukrainian National Federation of Canada. *Na shliakhu do natsiionalnoi yednosty.* [Towards National Unity: Fifty Years of Service by the Ukrainian National Federation, 1932–1982]. 2 vols. Toronto: Ukrainian National Federation, National Executive, 1982.

United Hetman Organization. *Za Ukrainy.* [For Ukraine: The Tour of the Honourable Mr Danylo Skoropadsky in the United States of America and

Canada, Autumn 1937–Spring 1938]. Edmonton: Ukrainian News Publishers, 1938.

Zumbakis, S.P. *Soviet Evidence in North American Courts*. Chicago: Americans for Due Process, 1988.

Monographs and Articles

Adams, A.E. *Bolsheviks in the Ukraine, 1918–1919*. New Haven: Yale University Press, 1963.

Aldrich, R.J., ed. *British Intelligence, Strategy, and the Cold War, 1945–1951*. London: Routledge, 1992.

Ammende, E. *Human Life in Russia*. London: George Allen and Unwin, 1936. Repr. with a historical introduction by J.E. Mace. Cleveland: John T. Zubal, 1984.

Anders, W. *An Army in Exile: The Story of the Second Polish Corps*. New York: Macmillan, 1949.

Andrew, C. *Secret Service: The Making of the British Intelligence Community*. London: Heinemann, 1985.

Andreyev, C. *Vlasov and the Russian Liberation Army: Soviet Reality and Emigré Theories*. Soviet and East European Studies Series. Cambridge: Cambridge University Press, 1987.

Angus, I. *Canadian Bolsheviks: The Early Years of the Communist Party of Canada*. Montreal: Vanguard, 1981.

Armstrong, J.A. *Ukrainian Nationalism*. 3rd rev. ed. Englewood, Colo.: Ukrainian Academic Press, 1990.

– , ed. *Soviet Partisans in World War II*. Madison: University of Wisconsin Press, 1964.

Aster, H., and P.J. Potichnyj, eds. *Jewish-Ukrainian Relations: Two Solitudes*. Rev. ed. Oakville, Ont.: Mosaic, 1987.

Aun, K. *The Political Refugees: A History of the Estonians in Canada*. Toronto: McClelland and Stewart, in association with the Multiculturalism Directorate, Department of the Secretary of State, Canada, 1985.

Avakumovic, I. *The Communist Party in Canada: A History*. Toronto: McClelland and Stewart, 1975.

Avery, D. 'Canadian Immigration Policy and the Foreign Navvy, 1896–1914.' Canadian Historical Association. *Historical Papers* (1972).

– 'Continental European Immigrant Workers in Canada, 1896–1919: From "Stalwart Peasant to Radical Proletariat,"' *Canadian Review of Sociology and Anthropology*, 12:1 (1975).

- 'Dangerous Foreigners': European Immigrant Workers and Labour Radicalism in Canada, 1896–1932. Toronto: McClelland and Stewart, 1979.
- 'Divided Loyalties: The Ukrainian Left and the Canadian State,' in L.Y. Luciuk and S. Hryniuk, eds. Canada's Ukrainians, 271–87.
- 'Ethnic and Class Tensions in Canada, 1918–20: Anglo-Canadians and the Alien Worker,' in F. Swyripa and J.H. Thompson, eds. Loyalties in Conflict, 79–98.
- Reluctant Host: Canada's Response to Immigrant Workers, 1896–1994. Toronto: McClelland and Stewart, 1995.
Bahryany, I. 'Why I Do Not Want to Go Home,' reprinted from Ukrainian Quarterly 2:3 (1946).
Balawyder, A. The Maple Leaf and the White Eagle: Canadian–Polish Relations, 1918–1978. Boulder, Colo.: East European Monographs, 1980.
- , ed. Canadian–Soviet Relations, 1939–1980. Oakville, Ont.: Mosaic, 1981.
Balfour, M., and J. Mair. Four Power Control in Germany and Austria, 1945–1946. New York: Oxford University Press, 1956.
Barth, F. Ethnic Groups and Boundaries: The Social Organization of Culture. Boston: Little, Brown, 1969.
Beeching, W.C. Canadian Volunteers in Spain, 1936–1939. Regina: Canadian Plains Research Center, 1989.
Bender, R.J., and H.P. Taylor. Uniforms, Organization, and History of the Waffen-SS. San José, Calif.: R. James Bender, 1975.
Bercuson, D.J. Confrontation at Winnipeg: Labour, Industrial Relations, and the General Strike. Montreal: McGill-Queen's University Press, 1974.
- Fools and Wise Men: The Rise and Fall of the One Big Union. Toronto: McGraw-Hill Ryerson, 1976.
- 'Labour Radicalism and the Western Industrial Frontier, 1897–1919.' Canadian Historical Review 58:2 (1977).
Bercuson, D.J., and H. Palmer. Settling the Canadian West. Toronto: Grolier, 1984.
Berenbaum, M., ed. A Mosaic of Victims: Non-Jews Persecuted and Murdered by the Nazis. New York: New York University Press, 1990.
Berger, C., and R. Cook, eds. The West and the Nation: Essays in Honour of W.L. Morton. Toronto: McClelland and Stewart, 1976.
Berger, M., and B.J. Street. Invasion without Tears: The Story of Canada's Top-Scoring Spitfire Wing in Europe during the Second World War. Toronto: Random House, 1994.
Berton, P. The Promised Land: Settling the West, 1896–1914. Toronto: McClelland and Stewart, 1984.

– Betcherman, L.-R. *The Little Band: The Clashes between the Communists and the Political and Legal Establishment in Canada, 1928–1932*. Ottawa: Deneau, 1983.

– *The Swastika and the Maple Leaf: Fascist Movements in Canada in the Thirties*. Toronto: Fitzhenry and Whiteside, 1975.

Bethell, N. *The Last Secret: Forcible Repatriation to Russia, 1944–1947*. London: Andre Deutsch, 1974.

Biega, A., and M. Diakowsky, eds. *The Ukrainian Experience in Quebec*. Toronto: Basilian, 1994.

Bilecki, A., W. Repka, and M. Sago, eds. *Friends in Need: The WBA Story. A Canadian Epic in Fraternalism*. Winnipeg: Workers Benevolent Association, 1972.

Bilinsky, Y. *The Second Soviet Republic: The Ukraine after World War II*. New Brunswick, N.J.: Rutgers University Press, 1964.

Bodnar, J. 'Immigration and Modernization: The Case of Slavic Peasants in Industrial America.' *Journal of Social History* 10 (1976).

Bodrug, J. *Independent Orthodox Church: Memoirs Pertaining to the History of a Ukrainian Canadian Church in the Years 1903–1913*. Toronto: Ukrainian Canadian Research Foundation, 1982.

Borys, J. *The Sovietization of Ukraine, 1917–1923: The Communist Doctrine and Practice of National Determination*. Edmonton: Canadian Institute of Ukrainian Studies, 1980.

Boshyk, Y., ed. *Ukraine during World War II: History and Its Aftermath*. Edmonton: Canadian Institute of Ukrainian Studies, 1986.

Bossy, W. *A Call to Socially Minded Christians*. Montreal: League of Canadian Classocrats, 1934.

Bothwell, R., and J.L. Granatstein, eds. *The Gouzenko Transcripts: The Evidence Presented to the Kellock-Taschereau Royal Commission of 1946*. Ottawa: Deneau, 1982.

Bradwin, E. *The Bunkhouse Man: A Study of Work and Pay in the Camps of Canada, 1903–1914*. Toronto: University of Toronto Press, 1972.

Bregy, P., and S. Obolensky. *The Ukraine – A Russian Land*. London: Selwyn and Blount, 1940.

Brown, A.C. *The Last Hero: Wild Bill Donovan*. New York: Vintage, 1984.

Brown, A.C., and C.B. MacDonald. *On a Field of Red: The Communist International and the Coming of World War II*. New York: Putnam, 1981.

Brzezinski, Z. *The Grand Failure: The Birth and Death of Communism in the Twentieth Century*. New York: Scribner's, 1989.

Buck, T. *Yours in the Struggle: Reminiscences of Tim Buck*. Toronto: New Canada, 1977.

Budurowycz, B., 'Poland and the Ukrainian Problem, 1921–1939.' *Canadian Slavonic Papers* 25:4 (1983).

Bullock, A. *Ernest Bevin: Foreign Secretary, 1945–1951*. London: Heinemann, 1983.

– *Hitler and Stalin: Parallel Lives*. New York: Knopf, 1992.

– *Hitler: A Study in Tyranny*. New York: Harper and Row, 1964.

Burianyk, W. *S.U.S. – Its Meaning and Significance*. Toronto: Ukrainian Self-Reliance League, 1967.

Burleigh, M. *Germany Turns Eastward: A Study of Ostforschung in the Third Reich*. Cambridge: Cambridge University Press, 1988.

Buzan, B. *People, States, and Fear: The National Security Problem in International Relations*. Chapel Hill: University of North Carolina Press, 1983.

Carter, D. *Behind Canadian Barbed Wire: Alien, Refugee, and Prisoner of War Camps in Canada, 1914–1946*. Calgary: Tumbleweed, 1980. 2d rev. ed. Elkwater, Alberta: Eagle Butte, 1998.

Carynnyk, M. 'Swallowing Stalinism: Pro-Communist Ukrainian Canadians and Soviet Ukraine in the 1930s,' in L.Y. Luciuk and S. Hryniuk, eds. *Canada's Ukrainians*, 187–205.

Caute, D. *The Fellow-Travellers: Intellectual Friends of Communism*. Rev ed. New Haven: Yale University Press, 1988.

Chalk, F., and K. Jonassohn, eds. *The History and Sociology of Genocide: Analyses and Case Studies*. New Haven: Yale University Press, 1990.

Chamberlain, W.H. *The Ukraine: A Submerged Nation*. New York: Macmillan, 1944.

Cirtautas, K.C. *The Refugee: A Psychological Study*. Boston: Meador, 1957.

Clemens, D.S. *Yalta: A Study in Soviet–American Relations*. New York: Oxford University Press, 1970.

Conquest, R. *The Great Terror: A Reassessment*. New York: Oxford University Press, 1990.

– *The Harvest of Sorrow: Soviet Collectivization and the Terror-Famine*. London: Century Hutchinson, 1986.

– *Stalin: Breaker of Nations*. London: Weidenfeld and Nicolson, 1991.

Dallin, A. *German Rule in Russia, 1941–1945: A Study of Occupation Policies*. 1957. 2d rev. ed. Boulder, Colo: Westview, 1981.

– *The Kaminsky Brigade, 1941–1944: A Case Study of German Military Exploitation of Soviet Dissatisfaction*. Cambridge, Mass.: Russian Research Center, Harvard University, 1956.

– *Odessa, 1941–1944: A Case Study of Soviet Territory under Foreign Rule*. Santa Monica, Calif.: Rand, 1957.

Danys, M. *DP: Lithuanian Immigration to Canada after the Second World War*. Studies in Ethnic and Immigration History. Toronto: Multicultural History Society of Ontario, 1986.

Darcovich, W. *Ukrainians in Canada: The Struggle to Retain Their Identity.* Ottawa: Ukrainian Self-Reliance League, 1967.

David, H. 'Involuntary International Migration: Adaptation of Refugees.' *International Migration Review* 7 (1969).

Davies, N. *God's Playground: A History of Poland: 1795 to the Present.* New York: Columbia University Press, 1982.

Davies, R.A. *This Is Our Land: Ukrainian Canadians against Hitler!* Toronto: Progress, 1943.

– 'Ukrainian Canadians and the War's New Phase.' *Saturday Night,* 12 July 1941.

d'Encausse, H.C. *Decline of an Empire: The Soviet Socialist Republics in Revolt.* New York: Harper Colophon, 1978.

– *The Great Challenge: Nationalities and the Bolshevik State, 1917–1930.* New York: Holmes and Meir, 1992.

De Santis, H. *The Diplomacy of Silence: The American Foreign Service, the Soviet Union, and the Cold War, 1933–1947.* Chicago: University of Chicago Press, 1980.

Dirks, G.E. *Canada's Refugee Policy: Indifference or Opportunism?* Montreal: McGill-Queen's University Press, 1977.

Dmytryshyn, B. 'The Nazis and the SS Volunteer Division "Galicia."' *American Slavic and East European Review* 15:1 (1956).

Dolot, M. *Execution by Hunger: The Hidden Holocaust.* New York: Norton, 1985.

Dreisziger, N.F. 'Tracy Philipps and the Achievement of Ukrainian-Canadian Unity,' in L.Y. Luciuk and S. Hryniuk, eds. *Canada's Ukrainians,* 326–41.

Driedger, L. 'Impelled Group Migration: Minority Struggle to Maintain Institutional Completeness.' *International Migration Review* 7:3 (1973).

Eichenbaum, J. 'A Matrix of Human Movement.' *International Migration* 13:1–2 (1975).

Eisenstadt, S.N. *The Absorption of Immigrants.* London: Routledge and Kegan, 1954.

Elliott, M.R. *Pawns of Yalta: Soviet Refugees and America's Role in Their Repatriation.* Urbana: University of Illinois Press, 1982.

– 'The Soviet Repatriation Campaign,' in W.W. Isajiw, Y. Boshyk, and R. Senkus, eds, *The Refugee Experience,* 341–59.

Engel, D. *In the Shadow of Auschwitz: The Polish Government-in-Exile and the Jews, 1939–1942.* Chapel Hill: University of North Carolina Press, 1987.

England, R. *The Central European Immigrant in Canada.* Toronto: Macmillan, 1929.

Enloe, C. *Ethnic Soldiers: State Security in a Divided Society.* New York: Penguin, 1980.

Epstein, J. *Operation Keelhaul: The Story of Forced Repatriation from 1944 to the Present*. Old Greenwich, Conn. Devin-Adair, 1973.

Ewanchuk, M. *Spruce, Swamp, and Stone: A History of the Pioneer Ukrainian Settlements in the Gimli Area*. Winnipeg, 1977.

Fedyshyn, O.S. *Germany's Drive to the East and the Ukrainian Revolution, 1917–1918*. New Brunswick, N.J.: Rutgers University Press, 1971.

Felinski, M. *The Ukrainians in Poland*. Published by the author, London, 1931.

Ferguson, B. 'British-Canadian Intellectuals, Ukrainian Immigrants, and Canadian National Identity,' in L.Y. Luciuk and S. Hryniuk, eds. *Canada's Ukrainians*, 304–25.

Fireside, H. *Icon and Swastika: The Russian Orthodox Church under Nazi and Soviet Control*. Cambridge, Mass.: Harvard University Press, 1979.

Fischer, G. *Soviet Defection in World War II*. Cambridge, Mass.: Harvard University Press, 1950.

– *Soviet Opposition to Stalin: A Case Study in World War II*. Cambridge, Mass.: Harvard University Press, 1952.

Fischer, L. *The Road to Yalta: Soviet Foreign Relations, 1941–1945*. New York: Harper, 1972.

Fishman, J.A., et al. *Language Loyalty in the United States: The Maintenance and Perpetuation of Non-English Mother Tongues by American Ethnic and Religious Groups*. The Hague: Mouton, 1966.

Freisen, G. *The Canadian Prairies: A History*. Toronto: University of Toronto Press, 1984.

Frolick, S.W. *Between Two Worlds: The Memoirs of Stanley Frolick*. Ed. with an introduction by L.Y. Luciuk and M. Carynnyk. Toronto: Multicultural History Society of Ontario, 1990.

Furet, F. *The Passing of an Illusion: The Idea of Communism in the Twentieth Century*. Trans. D. Furet. Chicago: University of Chicago Press, 1999.

Gambal, M.S. *Our Ukrainian Background*. Scranton, Pa.: Ukrainian Workingmen's Association, 1936.

Garnett, S.W. *Keystone in the Arch: Ukraine in the Emerging Security Environment of Central and Eastern Europe*. Carnegie Endowmnent for International Peace, 1999.

Gerus, O. 'Consolidating the Community: The Ukrainian Self-Reliance League,' in L.Y. Luciuk and S. Hryniuk, eds. *Canada's Ukrainians*, 157–86.

– 'The Ukrainian Canadian Committee,' in M. Lupul, ed. *A Heritage in Transition*, 195–214.

Getty, J.S., and R.T. Manning, eds. *Stalinist Terror: New Perspectives*. Cambridge: Cambridge University Press, 1992.

Glazer, N., and D.P. Moynihan, eds. *Ethnicity: Theory and Experience*. Cambridge, Mass.: Harvard University Press, 1975.

Goa, D.J., ed. *The Ukrainian Religious Experience: Tradition and the Canadian Cultural Context*. Edmonton: Canadian Institute of Ukrainian Studies, 1989.

Granatstein, J.L. *A Man of Influence: Norman A. Robertson and Canadian Statecraft, 1929–1968*. Ottawa: Deneau, 1981.

– *The Ottawa Men: The Civil Service Mandarins, 1935–1957*. Toronto: Oxford University Press, 1982.

Grigorenko, P.G. *Memoirs*. Trans. T.P. Whitney. New York: Norton, 1982.

Grose, P. *Operation Rollback: America's Secret War behind the Iron Curtain*. Boston: Houghton Mifflin, 2000.

Gross, J.T. *Polish Society under German Occupation: The Generalgouvernement, 1939–1944*. Princeton, N.J.: Princeton University Press, 1979.

– *Revolution from Abroad: The Soviet Conquest of Poland's Western Ukraine and Western Byelorussia*. Princeton, N.J.: Princeton University Press, 1988.

Haigh, R.H., D.S. Morris, and A.R. Peters, The *Years of Triumph? German Diplomatic and Military Policy, 1933–1941*. Aldershot, England: Gower, 1986.

Hall, D.J. *Clifford Sifton: The Young Napoleon*. Vancouver: University of British Columbia Press, 1981.

Handlin, O. *The Uprooted: The Epic Story of the Great Migrations That Made the American People*. New York: Grosset and Dunlap, 1951.

Hannant, L. *The Infernal Machine: Investigating the Loyalty of Canada's Citizens*. Toronto: University of Toronto Press, 1995.

Hansen, A., and A. Oliver-Smith, eds. *Involuntary Migration and Resettlement: The Problems and Responses of Dislocated People*. Boulder, Colo.: Westview, 1982.

Heike, W.-D. *The Ukrainian Division 'Galicia,' 1943–45: A Memoir*. Trans. A. Wynnyckyj. Ed. Y. Boshyk. Toronto, Paris, Munich: Shevchenko Scientific Society, 1988.

Herbert, U. *Hitler's Foreign Workers: Enforced Foreign Labour in Germany under the Third Reich*. Cambridge: Cambridge University Press, 1997.

Heron, C., ed. *The Workers' Revolt in Canada, 1917–1925*. Toronto: University of Toronto Press, 1998.

Hillmer, N.J., B.S. Kordan, and L.Y. Luciuk, eds. *On Guard for Thee: War, Ethnicity, and the Canadian State, 1939–1945*. Ottawa: Canadian Committee for the Study of the History of the Second World War, 1989.

Himka, J.-P. *Galician Villagers and the Ukrainian National Movement in the Nineteenth Century*. Edmonton: Canadian Institute of Ukrainian Studies in association with Macmillan Press, 1988.

Hirschfeld, G., ed. *The Policies of Genocide: Jews and Soviet Prisoners of War in Nazi Germany*. London: Allen and Unwin, 1986.

Hlynka, S., ed. *Anthony Hlynka: Member of the Federal Parliament of Canada, 1940–1949*. Toronto: Kiev Printers, 1982.

Holborn, L.W. *The International Refugee Organization – A Specialized Agency of the United Nations: Its History and Work, 1946–1952*. London: Geoffrey Cumberlege, 1956.

– *Refugees: A Problem of Our Time: The Work of the United Nations High Commission for Refugees, 1951–1972*. 2 vols. Metuchen, N.J.: Scarecrow, 1975.

Homze, E.L. *Foreign Labor in Nazi Germany*. Princeton, N.J.: Princeton University Press, 1967.

Hooson, D.J.M. 'The Distribution of Population as the Essential Geographical Expression.' *Canadian Geographer* 17:10 (1960).

Horak, S. *Poland and Her National Minorities, 1919–1939*. New York: Vantage, 1961.

Hryniuk, S. 'The Bishop Budka Controversy: A New Perspective.' *Canadian Slavonic Papers* 23:2 (1981): 154–65.

– *Peasants with Promise: Ukrainians in Southeastern Galicia, 1880–1900*. Edmonton: Canadian Institute of Ukrainian Studies, 1991.

Hryshko, W. *The Ukrainian Holocaust of 1933*. Ed. and trans. M. Carynnyk. Toronto: Bahriany Foundation, Suzhero, Dobrus, 1983.

Hulme, K. *The Wild Place*. Boston: Little, Brown, 1953.

Hunczak, T., ed. *The Ukraine, 1917–1921: A Study in Revolution*. Cambridge, Mass.: Harvard Ukrainian Research Institute, 1977.

Hunter, I.A. 'Putting History on Trial: The Ukrainian Famine of 1932–33.' *Gazette* (Law Society of Upper Canada, Toronto) 26:2 (June 1992): 138–62.

Huxley-Blythe, P.J. *The East Came West*. Caldwell, Idaho: Caxton, 1968.

Ilyniak, M. 'Still Coming to Terms: Ukrainians, Jews, and the Deschênes Commission,' in L.Y. Luciuk and S. Hryniuk, eds. *Canada's Ukrainians*, 377–90.

Inkeles, A., and R.A. Bauer. *The Soviet Citizen: Daily Life in a Totalitarian Society*. Cambridge, Mass.: Harvard University Press, 1959.

Irving, D. *Hitler's War*. New York: Viking, 1977.

Isajiw, W.W., Y. Boshyk, and R. Senkus, eds. *The Refugee Experience: Ukrainian Displaced Persons after World War II*. Edmonton: Canadian Institute of Ukrainian Studies, 1992.

Izyk, S. *The Bitter Laughter: Memoirs from the Second World War, 1939–1947*. Winnipeg: Progress, 1961.

Jackson, J.A., ed. *Migration*. Cambridge: Cambridge University Press, 1969.

Johnston, R.H. *New Mecca, New Babylon: Paris and the Russian Exiles, 1920–1945*. Kingston: McGill-Queen's University Press, 1988.

Kalin, S. 'From UCSA Overseas to UCVA in Canada,' *UCVA News Letter: Convention Issue* 2:11–12 (Toronto, 1954): 31–63.

Kamenetsky, I. *Hitler's Occupation of Ukraine, 1941–1944: A Study of Totalitarian Imperialism*. Milwaukee: Marquette University Press, 1956.

– *Secret Nazi Plans for Eastern Europe: A Study of Lebensraum Policies*. New York: Bookman, 1961.

Kardash, W.A. *Hitler's Agents in Canada: A Revealing Story of Potentially Dangerous Fifth Column Activities in Canada among Ukrainian Canadians*. Toronto, 1942.

Kay, D., and R. Miles. 'Refugees or Migrant Workers? The Case of European Volunteer Workers in Britain (1946–1951).' *Journal of Refugee Studies* 1:3–4 (1988).

Kaye, V.J. *Early Ukrainian Settlements in Canada, 1895–1900: Dr Josef Oleskow's Role in the Settlement of the Canadian Northwest*. Toronto: University of Toronto Press, 1964.

Keenleyside, H. *On the Bridge of Time: Memoirs*. Vol. 2. Toronto: McClelland and Stewart, 1982.

Keller, S.L. *Uprooting and Social Change: The Role of Refugees in Development*. Delhi, India: Manohar, 1975.

Kelley, N., and M. Trebilcock. *The Making of the Mosaic: A History of Canadian Immigration Policy*. Toronto: University of Toronto Press, 1999.

Keywan, Z. *A Turbulent Life: Biography of Josaphat Jean, O.S.B.M. (1885–1972)*. Verdun, Que.: Clio, 1990.

Kirkconnell, W. *Canada, Europe, and Hitler*. Toronto: Oxford University Press, 1939.

– *Canadians All: A Primer of Canadian National Unity*. Ottawa, 1941.

– *European Elements in Canadian Life*. Toronto: Canadian Club, 1940.

– 'Kapuskasing – An Historical Sketch.' *Bulletin of the Departments of History and Political Economic Science in Queen's University* 38 (January 1921): 1–15.

– *Our Communists and the New Canadians*. Toronto: Southam, 1943.

– *Our Ukrainian Loyalists: The Ukrainian Canadian Committee*. Winnipeg: Ukrainian Canadian Committee, 1943.

– *Seven Pillars of Freedom*. Toronto: Oxford University Press, 1944.

– *A Slice of Canada: Memoirs*. Toronto: University of Toronto Press, 1967.

– *The Ukrainian Canadians and the War*. Toronto: Oxford University Press, 1940.

– 'When We Locked Up Fritz: The First Authentic Story of Our Internment Camps.' *Maclean's*, 1 September 1920, 20–1, 58–63.

Klemme, M. *The Inside Story of UNRRA: An Experience in Internationalism*. New York: Lifetime, 1949.

Knightley, P. *Philby: K.G.B. Masterspy*. London: Andre Deutsch, 1988.

– *The Second Oldest Profession: Spies and Spying in the Twentieth Century*. New York: Norton, 1986.

Koel, R.L. *The Black Corps: The Structure and Power Struggles of the Nazi SS*. Madison: University of Wisconsin Press, 1983.

– *RKFDV: German Resettlement and Population Policy, 1939–1945: A History of the Reich Commission for the Strengthening of Germandom*. Cambridge, Mass.: Harvard University Press, 1957.

Kolasky, J. *Partners in Tyranny: The Nazi–Soviet Non-Aggression Pact, August 23, 1939*. Toronto: Mackenzie Institute, 1990.

– *The Shattered Illusion: The History of Ukrainian Pro-Communist Organizations in Canada*. Toronto: Peter Martin, 1979.

Kordan, B.S. 'Making Borders Stick: Population Transfer and Resettlement in the Trans-Curzon Territories, 1944–1949.' *International Migration Review* 3 (1997): 704–20.

– 'Soviet-Canadian Relations and the Ukrainian Ethnic Problem.' *Journal of Ethnic Studies* 13:2 (1985).

Kordan, B.S., and P. Melnycky, eds. *In the Shadow of the Rockies: Diary of the Castle Mountain Internment Camp, 1915–1917*. Edmonton: Canadian Institute of Ukrainian Studies, 1991.

Kostash, M. *All of Baba's Children*. Edmonton: Hurtig, 1977.

Kostiuk, H. *Stalinist Rule in the Ukraine: A Study of the Decade of Mass Terror (1929–1939)*. New York: Praeger, 1960.

Kosyk, W. 'Ukraine's Losses during the Second World War.' *Ukrainian Review* 33:2 (1985).

Krausnick, H., and M. Broszat. *Anatomy of the SS State*. London: Paladin, 1973.

Krawchenko, B. *Social Change and National Consciousness in Twentieth Century Ukraine*. London: Macmillan, 1985.

Krawchuk, P. *For Your Freedom and Ours*. Toronto: Kobzar, 1976.

– *Interned without Cause: The Internment of Canadian Antifascists during World War Two*. Trans. P. Prokop. Toronto: Kobzar, 1985.

– *Our Contribution to Victory*. Trans. M. Skrypnyk. Toronto: Kobzar, 1985.

– *The Ukrainian Socialist Movement in Canada, 1907–1918*. Toronto: Progress, 1979.

Kulischer, E.M. *Displacement of Population in Europe*. Montreal: International Labour Office, 1943.

– *Europe on the Move: War and Population Changes, 1917–1947*. New York: Columbia University Press, 1948.

Kunz, E.F. 'Exile and Resettlement: Refugee Theory.' *International Migration Review* 15:53–4 (1981).

– 'The Refugee in Flight: Kinetic Models and Forms of Displacement.' *International Migration Review* 7:2 (1973).

Kuropas, M.B. *Scourging of a Nation: CBS and the Defamation of Ukraine.* Kingston and Kyiv: Kashtan, 1995.

– *Ukrainian-American Citadel: The First One Hundred Years of the Ukrainian National Association.* Boulder, Colo.: East European Monographs, 1996.

– 'Ukrainian-American Resettlement Efforts, 1944–1954,' in W.W. Isajiw, Y. Boshyk, and R. Senkus, eds, *The Refugee Experience*, 385–401.

– *The Ukrainian Americans: Roots and Aspirations, 1884–1954.* Toronto: University of Toronto Press, 1991.

Kushnir, O., ed. *Regensburg: Articles and Documents on the History of Ukrainian Emigration in Germany after World War II.* New York: Shevchenko Scientific Society, 1985.

Kushnir, V.J. *Polish Atrocities in the West Ukraine: An Appeal to the League for the Rights of Man and the Citizen.* Vienna: Gerald, 1931.

Landwehr, R. *Fighting for Freedom: The Ukrainian Volunteer Division of the Waffen-SS.* Silver Spring, Md.: Bibliophile Legion, 1985.

Lanphier, C.M. 'Canada's Response to Refugees.' *International Migration Review* 15:1–2 (1981).

Lawton, L. *Ukraine: Europe's Greatest Problem.* London, 1939.

– *The Ukrainian Question.* Address given by Mr Lancelot Lawton in a committee room of the House of Commons, 29 May 1935. Published for the Anglo-Ukrainian Committee. London: Serjeants, 1935.

Lee, E.S. 'A Theory of Migration.' *Demography* 3 (1966).

Lehr, J.C. 'The Government and the Immigrant: Perspectives on Ukrainian Bloc Settlement in the Canadian West.' *Canadian Ethnic Studies* 9:2 (1977).

– 'Peopling the Prairies with Ukrainians,' in L.Y. Luciuk and S. Hryniuk, eds. *Canada's Ukrainians*, 17–29.

Lehr, J.C., and D.W. Moodie. 'Government Coercion in the Settlement of Ukrainian Immigrants in Western Canada.' *Prairie Forum* 8:2 (1983).

– 'The Polemics of Pioneer Settlement: Ukrainian Immigration and the Winnipeg Press.' *Canadian Ethnic Studies* 12:2 (1980).

Littlejohn, D. *Foreign Legions of the Third Reich.* Vol 4. *Poland, the Ukraine, Bulgaria, Romania, Free India, Estonia, Latvia, Lithuania, Finland, and Russia.* San José, Calif.: Bender 1987.

– *The Patriotic Traitors: A History of Collaboration in German Occupied Europe, 1940–1945.* London: Heinemann, 1972.

Loescher, G., and J.A. Scanlan. *Calculated Kindness: Refugees and America's Half Open Door, 1945 to the Present.* New York: Free Press, 1986.

Logusz, M.O. *Galicia Division: The Waffen-SS 14th Grenadier Division, 1943–1945.* Atglen, Pa.: Schiffer Military History, 1997.

Lucas, J. *Last Days of the Reich: The Collapse of Nazi Germany, May 1945*. Toronto: Stoddart, 1986.

Luciuk, L.Y. 'A Continuing Presence: North America's Ukrainians,' in R. Cohen, ed. *The Cambridge Survey of World Migration*, 109–13.

– 'Internal Security and an Ethnic Minority: The Ukrainians and Internment Operations in Canada, 1914–1920.' *Signum* 4:2 (1980).

– '"This Should Never Be Spoken or Quoted Publicly": Canada's Ukrainians and Their Encounter with the DPs,' in L.Y. Luciuk and S. Hryniuk, eds. *Canada's Ukrainians*, 103–22.

– *A Time for Atonement: Canada's First National Internment Operations and the Ukrainian Canadians, 1914–1920*. Kingston: Limestone, 1988.

– '"Trouble All Around": Ukrainian Canadians and Their Encounter with the Ukrainian Refugees of Europe, 1943–1951.' *Canadian Ethnic Studies* 21:3 (1989): 37–54.

– 'A Troubled Venture: Ukrainian-Canadian Refugee Relief Efforts, 1945–51,' in W.W. Isajiw, Y. Boshyk, and R. Senkus, eds, *The Refugee Experience*, 435–60.

– 'Ukraine,' in I.C.B. Dear and M.R.D. Foot., eds. *The Oxford Companion to the Second World War*, 1159–65.

– *Ukrainians in the Making: Their Kingston Story*. Kingston: Limestone, 1980.

– 'Unintended Consequences in Refugee Resettlement: Post-War Ukrainian Refugee Immigration to Canada.' *International Migration Review* 20:2 (1986): 467–82.

– *Welcome to Absurdistan: Ukraine, the Soviet Disunion, and the West*. Kingston: Kashtan, 1995.

Luciuk, L.Y., and S. Hryniuk, eds. *Canada's Ukrainians: Negotiating an Identity*. Toronto: University of Toronto Press, 1991.

Luciuk, L.Y., and R. Sorobey. *Konowal*. Kingston: Kashtan, 1996.

Luciuk, L.Y., and B. Sydoruk. *In My Charge: The Canadian Internment Camp Photographs of Sergeant William Buck*. Kingston: Kashtan, 1997.

Luciuk, L.Y., and I. Wynnyckyj, eds. *Ukrainians in Ontario. Polyphony* 10. Toronto: Multicultural History Society of Ontario, 1988.

Luciuk, L.Y., N. Yurieva, and R. Zakaluzny, eds. *Roll Call: Lest We Forget*. Kingston: Kashtan, 1999.

Lukas, R.C. *Forgotten Holocaust: The Poles under German Occupation, 1939–1944*. Lexington: University Press of Kentucky, 1986.

Lupul, M., ed. *A Heritage in Transition: Essays in the History of Ukrainians in Canada*. Toronto: McClelland and Stewart in association with the Multiculturalism Directorate of the Department of the Secretary of State, Canada, 1982.

– *Multiculturalism, Separatism, and Ukrainian Canadians: An Assessment*. Edmonton: Canadian Institute of Ukrainian Studies, 1977.

Lysenko, V. *Men in Sheepskin Coats*. Toronto: Ryerson, 1949.

Macarthy, C.A. *National States and National Minorities*. London: Oxford University Press, 1934.

Mace, J.E. *Communism and the Dilemmas of National Liberation: National Communism in Soviet Ukraine, 1918–1937*. Cambridge, Mass.: Harvard University Press, 1983.

Magocsi, P.R. *A History of Ukraine*. Toronto: University of Toronto Press, 1996.

– *The Shaping of a National Identity: Subcarpathian Rus', 1848–1948*. Cambridge, Mass.: Harvard University Press, 1978.

– , ed. *Morality and Reality: The Life and Times of Andrei Sheptyts'kyi*. Edmonton: Canadian Institute of Ukrainian Studies, 1989.

Maksudov, S. 'The Geography of the Soviet Famine of 1933.' *Journal of Ukrainian Studies* 8:2 (1983).

Makuch, N. 'The Influence of the Ukrainian Revolution on Ukrainians in Canada, 1917–22.' *Journal of Ukrainian Graduate Studies* 4:1 (1979).

Malaschuk, R. *From the Book of My Life: Memoirs*. Toronto: Homin Ukrainy, 1987.

Mandryka, M.I. *The Ukrainian Question*. Winnipeg, 1940.

– *Ukrainian Refugees*. Winnipeg: Canadian Ukrainian Educational Association, 1946.

Manning, C.A. 'Significance of the Soviet Refugees.' *Ukrainian Quarterly* 2 (1945).

Margolian, H. *Unauthorized Entry: The Truth about Nazi War Criminals in Canada*, Toronto: University of Toronto Press, 2000.

Margolin, A.D. *From a Political Diary: Russia, the Ukraine, and America, 1905–1945*. New York: Columbia University Press, 1946.

Marples, D. 'Western Ukraine and Western Belorussia under Soviet Occupation: The Development of Socialist Farming, 1939–1941.' *Canadian Slavonic Papers* 27:2 (1985).

Marrus, M.R. *The Unwanted: European Refugees in the Twentieth Century*. New York: Oxford University Press, 1985.

Martynowych, O., *Ukrainians in Canada: The Formative Years, 1891–1924*. Edmonton: Canadian Institute of Ukrainian Studies, 1991.

– 'The Ukrainian Socialist Movement in Canada: 1900–1918.' *Journal of Ukrainian Graduate Studies* 1:1 (1976).

– 'The Ukrainian Socialist Movement in Canada: 1900–1918 (II).' *Journal of Ukrainian Graduate Studies* 2:1 (1977).

Marunchak, M.I. *The Ukrainian Canadians: A History*. Winnipeg: Ukrainian Academy of Arts and Sciences in Canada, 1970; 2d ed. 1982.

Mastny, V. *Russia's Road to the Cold War: Diplomacy, Warfare, and the Politics of Communism, 1941–1945*. New York: Columbia University Press, 1979.

McCartney, C.A., and A.W. Palmer. *Independent Eastern Europe: A History.* London: St Martin's, 1962.

McKenzie, K.E. *Comintern and World Revolution, 1928–1943: The Shaping of Doctrine*. New York: Columbia University Press, 1964.

McNeil, M. *By the Rivers of Babylon: A Story of Relief Work among the Displaced Persons of Europe*. London, 1956.

Medvedev, R.A. *Let History Judge: The Origins and Consequences of Stalinism*. Rev. ed., New York: Columbia University Press, 1989.

Medvedev, Z.A. *Soviet Agriculture*. New York: Norton, 1987.

Melnycky, P. 'The Internment of Ukrainians in Canada,' in F. Swyripa and J.H. Thompson, eds. *Loyalties in Conflict*, 1–24.

Minenko, M. 'Without Just Cause: Canada's First National Internment Operations,' in L.Y. Luciuk and S. Hryniuk, eds. *Canada's Ukrainians*, 288–303.

Mirchuk, P. *In the German Mills of Death*. New York: Vantage, 1976.

Morton, D. *The Canadian General: Sir William Otter*. Toronto: Hakkert, 1974.

– 'Sir William Otter and Internment Operations in Canada during the First World War.' *Canadian Historical Review* 55 (1974).

Morton, D., and J.L. Granatstein. *Marching to Armageddon: Canadians and the Great War, 1914–1919*. Toronto: Lester and Orpen Dennys, 1989.

Morton, D., and G. Wright. *Winning the Second Battle: Canadian Veterans and the Return to Civilian Life, 1915–1930*. Toronto: University of Toronto Press, 1987.

Motyl, A.J. *Dilemmas of Independence: Ukraine after Totalitarianism*. New York: Council on Foreign Relations Press, 1993.

– *The Turn to the Right: The Ideological Origins and Development of Ukrainian Nationalism, 1919–1929*. Boulder, Colo.: East European Monographs, 1980.

– 'Ukrainian Nationalist Political Violence in Inter-War Poland, 1921–1939.' *East European Quarterly* 19:1 (1985).

– *Will the Non-Russians Rebel? State, Ethnicity, and Stability in the USSR*. Ithaca: Cornell University Press, 1987.

Murphy, H.B.M., ed. *Flight and Resettlement*. Paris: UNESCO, 1955.

Nahaylo, B., and V. Swoboda. *Soviet Disunion: A History of the Nationalities Problem in the USSR*. London: Hamish Hamilton, 1990.

Nekrich, A.M. *The Punished Peoples: The Deportation and Fate of Soviet Minorities at the End of the Second World War*. New York: Norton, 1978.

Newman, B. *Danger Spots of Europe*. London: Robert Hale, 1938.

Nolte, E. *Three Faces of Fascism: Action Française, Italian Fascism, National Socialism*. New York: Mentor, 1969.

O'Neill, W.L. *A Better World: The Great Schism: Stalinism and the American Intellectuals*. New York: Simon and Schuster, 1982.

Osborne, B.S., '"Non-Preferred" People: Inter-war Ukrainian Immigration to Canada,' in L. Luciuk and S. Hryniuk, eds. *Canada's Ukrainians*, 81–102.

Ovendale, R. *The English-Speaking Alliance: Britain, the United States, the Dominions, and the Cold War, 1945–51*. London: Allen and Unwin, 1985.

Palij, M. *The Anarchism of Nestor Makhno, 1918–1921: An Aspect of the Ukrainian Revolution*. Seattle: University of Washington Press, 1976.

Palmer, H. 'Ethnic Relations in Wartime: Nationalism and European Minorities in Alberta during the Second World War.' *Canadian Ethnic Studies* 14:3 (1982).

– *Patterns of Prejudice: A History of Nativism in Alberta*. Toronto: McClelland and Stewart, 1982.

Paluk, W. *Canadian Cossacks: Essays, Articles, and Stories on Ukrainian-Canadian Life*. Winnipeg: Canadian Ukrainian Review, 1943.

Panchuk, G.R.B. *Heroes of Their Day: The Reminiscences of Bohdan Panchuk*. Ed. with an introduction by L.Y. Luciuk. Toronto: Multicultural History Society of Ontario, 1983.

Pearson, R. *National Minorities in Eastern Europe, 1848–1945*. London: Macmillan, 1983.

Petelycky, S. *Into Auschwitz, for Ukraine*. Kingston: Kashtan, 1999.

Petryshyn, J. *Peasants in the Promised Land: Canada and the Ukrainians, 1891–1914*. Toronto: James Lorimer, 1985.

Petryshyn, W.R., ed. *Changing Realities: Social Trends among Ukrainian Canadians*. Edmonton: Canadian Institute of Ukrainian Studies, 1980.

Philby, K. *My Silent War*. London: MacGibbon and Kee, 1968.

Pidhainy, S.O., ed. *The Black Deeds of the Kremlin: A White Book*. 2 vols. Toronto: Ukrainian Association of Victims of Russian Communist Terror, 1953 and Detroit: World Federation of Ukrainian Former Political Prisoners and Victims of the Soviet Regime, 1955.

Piniuta, H., ed. *Land of Pain, Land of Promise: First Person Accounts by Ukrainian Pioneers, 1891–1914*. Saskatoon: Western Producer Prairie Books, 1978.

Porter, J. *The Vertical Mosaic: An Analysis of Social Class and Power in Canada*. Toronto: University of Toronto Press, 1965.

Potichnyj, P.J., ed. *Poland and Ukraine: Past and Present*. Edmonton: Canadian Institute of Ukrainian Studies, 1980.

Potichnyj, P.J. and H. Aster, eds. *Ukrainian–Jewish Relations in Historical Perspective*. Edmonton: Canadian Institute of Ukrainian Studies, 1988.

Potrebenko, H. *No Streets of Gold: A Social History of Ukrainians in Alberta*. Vancouver: New Star, 1977.

Prados, J. *Presidents' Secret Wars: CIA and Pentagon Covert Operations from World War II through Iranscam*. New York: William Morrow, 1986.

Prazmowska, A. *Britain, Poland, and the Eastern Front, 1939.* Soviet and East European Studies. Cambridge: Cambridge University Press, 1987.

Prociuk, S.G. 'Human Losses in the Ukraine in World War I and II.' *Annals of the Ukrainian Academy of Arts and Sciences in the United States* 13:35–36 (1973).

Prokop, P. *Fifty Years, 1918–1968: Association of United Ukrainian Canadians.* Toronto: Association of United Ukrainian Canadians, 1968.

Proudfoot, M.J. *European Refugees, 1939–1952: A Study in Forced Population Movement.* London: Faber and Faber, 1957.

Radziejowski, J. *The Communist Party of Western Ukraine, 1919–1929.* Edmonton: Canadian Institute of Ukrainian Studies, 1983.

Rakhmanny, R. *In Defence of the Ukrainian Cause.* North Quincy, Mass.: Christopher, 1979.

Ranelagh, J., *The Agency: The Rise and Decline of the CIA from Wild Bill Donovan to William Casey.* New York: Simon and Schuster, 1986.

Rapoport, L. *Stalin's War against the Jews: The Doctors' Plot and the Soviet Solution.* New York: Free Press, 1990.

Read, A., and D. Fisher. *The Deadly Embrace: Hitler, Stalin, and the Nazi-Soviet Pact, 1939–1941.* New York: Norton, 1988.

Reid, A. *Borderland: A Journey through the History of Ukraine.* London: Phoenix, 1997.

Reid, E. *On Duty: A Canadian at the Making of the United Nations, 1945–1946.* Toronto: McClelland and Stewart, 1983.

– *Time of Fear and Hope: The Making of the North Atlantic Treaty, 1947–1949.* Toronto: McClelland and Stewart, 1977.

Reitlinger, G. *The House Built on Sand: The Conflicts of German Policy in Russia, 1939–1945.* New York: Viking, 1960.

Repka, W., and K.M. Repka. *Dangerous Patriots: Canada's Unknown Prisoners of War.* Vancouver: New Star, 1982.

Reshetar, J.S. *The Ukrainian Revolution, 1917–1920.* Princeton, N.J.: Princeton University Press, 1952.

Richmond, A.J. *Post-War Immigrants in Canada.* Toronto: University of Toronto Press, 1967.

Roberts, B. *Whence They Came: Deportation from Canada, 1900–1935.* Ottawa: University of Ottawa Press, 1988.

Ross, G., ed. *The Foreign Office and the Kremlin: British Documents on Anglo-Soviet Relations, 1941–45.* Cambridge: Cambridge University Press, 1984.

Rothschild, J. *East Central Europe between the Two World Wars.* Vol. 9 of *A History of East Central Europe.* Seattle: University of Washington Press, 1974.

Royick, A. 'Ukrainian Settlements in Alberta.' *Canadian Slavonic Papers* 10:3 (1968).

Rozumnyj, J., ed. *New Soil – Old Roots: The Ukrainian Experience in Canada.* Winnipeg: Ukrainian Academy of Arts and Sciences in Canada, 1983.

Rudnitsky, S. *Ukraine: The Land and Its People.* New York: Ukrainian Alliance of America, 1918.

Rudnytsky, I.L., ed. *Essays in Modern Ukrainian History.* Edmonton: Canadian Institute of Ukrainian Studies, 1987.

– *Rethinking Ukrainian History.* Edmonton: Canadian Institute of Ukrainian Studies, 1981.

Sack, J. *An Eye for an Eye: The Untold Story of Jewish Revenge against Germans in 1945.* New York: Basic, 1993.

Sands, B. *The Ukraine.* London: Ukraine Committee, 1914.

Saunders, J.D., M.A. Sauter, and R.C. Kirkwood. *Soldiers of Misfortune: Washington's Secret Betrayal of American POWs in the Soviet Union.* Washington: National Press, 1992.

Sawczuk, K. *The Ukraine in the United Nations Organization: A Study in Soviet Foreign Policy, 1944–1950.* Boulder, Colo. East European Quarterly, 1975.

Scammell, M. *Solzhenitsyn: A Biography.* London: Hutchinson, 1984.

Schechtman, J.B. *European Population Transfers, 1939–1945.* New York: Russell and Russell, 1946.

Schlichtmann, H. 'Ethnic Themes in Geographical Research on Western Canada.' *Canadian Ethnic Studies* 9:2 (1977).

Segev, T. *The Seventh Million: The Israelis and the Holocaust.* New York: Hill and Wang, 1993.

Serbyn, R., and B. Krawchenko, eds. *Famine in Ukraine, 1932–1933.* Edmonton: Canadian Institute of Ukrainian Studies, 1986.

Seton-Watson, H. *Eastern Europe between the Wars, 1918–1941.* Cambridge: Cambridge University Press, 1946.

– *The East European Revolution.* 3d ed. New York: Praeger, 1956.

– *Nations and States: An Enquiry into the Origins of the Nations and the Politics of Nationalism.* Repr. Boulder, Colo.: Westview, 1973.

Shandruk, P. *Arms of Valor.* Trans. by R. Olesnicki. New York: Robert Speller, 1959.

Shumuk, D. *Life Sentence: Memoirs of a Ukrainian Political Prisoner.* Ed. I. Jaworsky. Trans. I. Jaworsky and H. Kowalska. Edmonton: Canadian Institute of Ukrainian Studies, 1984.

Shykula, M., and B. Korchinski, eds. *Pioneer Bishop: The Story of Bishop Budka's Fifteen Years in Canada.* Regina: Bishop Budka Council #5914, Knights of Columbus, Regina, 1990.

Simpson, J.H. *The Refugee Problem: Report of a Survey.* New York: Oxford University Press, 1939.

− *Refugees: A Review of the Situation since September, 1938.* New York: Oxford University Press, 1939.

Smith, A.L. *Churchill's German Army: Wartime Strategy and Cold War Politics, 1943–1947.* vol. 54. Beverly Hills, Calif.: Sage Library of Social Research, 1977.

Smith, B.F. *The Shadow Warriors: O.S.S. and the Origins of the C.I.A.* New York: Basic, 1983.

Smith, D. *Diplomacy of Fear: Canada and the Cold War, 1941–1948.* Toronto: University of Toronto Press, 1988.

Smith, G., ed. *The Nationalities Question in the Soviet Union.* London: Longman, 1990.

Solonynka, W., ed. *A Historical Outline of the Canadian League for the Liberation of Ukraine.* [In Ukrainian]. Toronto: National Executive of the Canadian League for the Liberation of Ukraine, 1984.

Solzhenitsyn, A.I. *The Gulag Archipelago: An Experiment in Literary Investigation.* Trans. T.P. Whitney. 3 vols. New York: Harper and Row, 1973.

Stairs, D. 'The Political Culture of Canadian Foreign Policy.' *Canadian Journal of Political Science* 15:4 (1982): 667–90.

Stebelsky, I. 'The Resettlement of Ukrainian Refugees after the Second World War,' in L.Y. Luciuk and S. Hryniuk, eds. *Canada's Ukrainians,* 123–54.

− 'Ukrainian Population Migration after World War II,' in W.W. Isajiw, Y. Boshyk, and R. Senkus, eds. *The Refugee Experience,* 21–66.

Stein, B.N. 'The Refugee Experience: Defining the Parameters of a Field of Study.' *International Migration Review* 15:1–2 (1981).

Stephan, J.J. *The Russian Fascists: Tragedy and Farce in Exile, 1925–1945.* New York: Harper and Row, 1978.

Stercho, P.G. *Diplomacy of Double Morality: Europe's Crossroads in Carpatho-Ukraine 1919–1938.* New York: Carpathian Research Center, 1971.

Stern, F. *The Politics of Cultural Despair: A Study in the Rise of the Germanic Ideology.* Berkeley: University of California Press, 1961.

Stern, G. *The Rise and Decline of International Communism.* Aldershot, England: Edward Elger, 1990.

Stoakes, G. *Hitler and the Quest for World Dominion: Nazi Ideology and Foreign Policy in the 1920s.* New York: St Martin's, 1986.

Stafford, D. *Britain and European Resistance, 1940–1945: A Survey of the Special Operations Executive, with Documents.* Toronto: University of Toronto Press, 1983.

Strik-Strikfeldt, W. *Against Stalin and Hitler: Memoir of the Russian Liberation Movement, 1941–1945.* London: Macmillan, 1970.

Subtelny, O. *Ukraine: A History.* Toronto: University of Toronto Press in association with the Canadian Institute of Ukrainian Studies, 1988.

Sullivant, R.S. *Soviet Politics and the Ukraine, 1917–1957*. New York: Columbia University Press, 1962.
Swyripa, F. *Ukrainian Canadians: A Survey of Their Portrayal in English-Language Works*. Edmonton: Canadian Institute of Ukrainian Studies, 1978.
– *Wedded to the Cause: Ukrainian-Canadian Women and Ethnic Identity, 1891–1991*. Toronto: University of Toronto Press, 1993.
Swyripa, F., and J.H. Thompson, eds. *Loyalties in Conflict: Ukrainians in Canada during the Great War*. Edmonton: Canadian Institute of Ukrainian Studies, 1983.
Swystun, W. *Ukraine: The Sorest Spot in Europe*. Winnipeg: Ukrainian Information Bureau, 1931.
– 'The Ukrainian Canadians and the Russo-German War.' *Saturday Night*, 26 July 1941.
Tabori, P. *The Anatomy of Exile: A Semantic and Historical Study*. London: Harrap, 1972.
Talmon, J.L. *The Myth of the Nation and the Vision of Revolution: The Origins of Ideological Polarization in the Twentieth Century*. London: Secker and Warburg, 1986.
Tannahill, J.A. *European Voluntary Workers in Britain*. Manchester: Manchester University Press, 1958.
Tarnawsky, O. *Brat Bratovi / Brother's Helping Hand: History of the United Ukrainian American Relief Committee*. Philadelphia: United Ukrainian American Relief Committee, 1971.
Terles, M. *Ethnic Cleansing of Poles in Volhynia and Eastern Galicia, 1942–1946*. Toronto: Alliance of the Polish Eastern Provinces, 1993.
Thomas, H. *Armed Truce: The Beginnings of the Cold War, 1945–46*. London: Hamish Hamilton, 1986.
Thompson, J.H. 'The Enemy Alien and the Canadian General Election of 1917,' in F. Swyripa and J.H. Thompson, eds. *Loyalties in Conflict*, 25–45.
– *The Harvests of War: The Prairie West, 1914–1918*. Toronto: McClelland and Stewart, 1978.
Thorwald, J. *The Illusion: Soviet Soldiers in Hitler's Armies*. Trans. R. and C. Winston. New York and London: Harcourt Brace Jovanovich, 1975.
Tolstoy, N. *The Minister and the Massacres*. London: Century Hutchinson, 1986.
– *Stalin's Secret War*. New York: Holt, Rinehart and Winston, 1982.
– *Trial and Error: Canada's Commission of Inquiry on War Criminals and the Soviets*. Toronto: Justinian, 1986.
– *Victims of Yalta*. Toronto: Hodder and Stoughton, 1977.
Torke, H.-J., and J.-P. Himka, eds. *German–Ukrainian Relations in Historical Perspective*. Edmonton: Canadian Institute of Ukrainian Studies, 1994.
Tottle, D. *Fraud, Famine, and Fascism: The Ukrainian Genocide Myth from Hitler to Harvard*. Toronto: Progress, 1987.

Trewartha, G.T., 'A Case for Population Geography.' *Annals of the American Association of Geographers* 43:2 (1953).

Trosky, O.S. *The Ukrainian Greek Orthodox Church in Canada*. Winnipeg: Bulman, 1968.

Trunk, I. *Judenrat: The Jewish Councils in Eastern Europe under Nazi Occupation*. New York: Macmillan, 1972.

Tys-Krokhmaliuk, Y. *UPA Warfare in Ukraine: Strategical, Tactical, and Organizational Problems of Ukrainian Resistance in World War II*. Trans. W. Dushnyck. New York: Society of Veterans of the Ukrainian Insurgent Army, 1972.

Udod, H. *Julian W. Stechishin: His Life and Work*. Saskatoon: Mohyla Institute, 1978.

Ukrainian Youth Federation. *Seven Presidents in Uniform*. Winnipeg, 1945.

Vaksberg, Arkady. *Stalin against the Jews*. New York: Knopf, 1994.

Vernant, J. *The Refugee in the Post-War World*. New Haven, Conn.: Yale University Press, 1953.

Volkogonov, D. *Lenin: A New Biography*. New York: Free Press, 1994.

– *Stalin: Triumph and Tragedy*. New York: Grove Weidenfeld, 1988.

Waiser, B. *Park Prisoners: The Untold Story of Western Canada's National Parks, 1915–1946*. Saskatoon: Fifth House, 1995.

Weir, J. *Slavs*. Toronto: Canadian Slav Committee, 1949.

Werth, A. *Russia at War, 1941–1945*. New York: Carroll and Graf, 1984.

West, N. *A Matter of Trust: MI5, 1945–72*. London: Weidenfeld and Nicolson, 1982.

– *MI5: British Security Service Operations, 1909–1945*. Reading, England: Triad / Granada, 1983.

– *MI6: British Secret Intelligence Service Operations, 1909–45*. London: Panther, 1985.

Whitaker, R. *Double Standard: The Secret History of Canadian Immigration*. Toronto: Lester and Orpen Dennys, 1987.

White, P., and R. Woods, eds. *The Geographical Impact of Migration*. London: Longman, 1980.

White, S.E. 'A Philosophical Dichotomy in Migration Research.' *Professional Geographer* 32:1 (1980).

Wiesel, E. *The Jews of Silence: A Personal Report on Soviet Jewry*. New York: Holt, Rinehart and Winston, 1966.

Wilgress, L.D. *Memoirs*. Toronto: Ryerson, 1967.

Willis, F.R. *The French in Germany: 1945–1949*. Palo Alto, Calif.: Stanford University Press, 1962.

Wilson, A. *Ukrainian Nationalism in the 1990s: A Minority Faith*. Cambridge: Cambridge University Press, 1997.

Wiseman, N. 'The Politics of Manitoba's Ukrainians between the Wars.' *Prairie Forum* 12:1 (1987).

Wolkonsky, A. *The Ukraine Question: The Historic Truth versus the Separatist Propaganda*. Rome: Armani, 1920.

Wolpert, J., 'Behavioral Aspects of the Decision to Migrate.' *Papers and Proceedings, Regional Science Association* 15 (1965).

– 'Migration as an Adjustment to Environmental Stress.' *Journal of Social Issues* 22 (1966).

Woodbridge, G. *UNRRA: The History of the United Nations Relief and Rehabilitation Administration*. 3 vols. New York: Columbia University Press, 1950.

Woodsworth, J.S. *Strangers within Our Gates*. Toronto: University of Toronto Press, 1909.

Woropay, O. *The Ninth Circle: In Commemoration of the Victims of the Famine of 1933*. Cambridge, Mass.: Harvard University Ukrainian Studies Fund, 1983.

Woycenko, O. 'Community Organizations,' in M. Lupul, ed., *A Heritage in Transition*, 173–94.

– *The Ukrainians in Canada*. 2d rev. ed. Winnipeg: Trident, 1968.

Woytak, R.A. *On the Border of War and Peace: Polish Intelligence and Diplomacy in 1937–1939 and the Origins of the Ultra Secret*. New York: Columbia University Press, 1979.

Wright, P. *Spycatcher: The Candid Autobiography of a Senior Intelligence Officer*. Toronto: Stoddart, 1987.

Wytwycky, B. *The Other Holocaust: Many Circles of Hell*. Washington: Novak Report, 1980.

Yancey, W., E. Ericksen, and R. Juliani. 'Emergent Ethnicity: A Review and Reformulation.' *American Sociological Review* 41:3 (1976).

Yaremovich, A.J. 'Displaced Persons and Refugees,' *Opinion* (Ukrainian Canadian Veterans' Association) 4:5 (November 1948): 3–4, 13.

Young, C.H. *The Ukrainian Canadians: A Study in Assimilation*. Toronto: Nelson, 1931.

Yuzyk, P. *Ukrainian Canadians: Their Place and Role in Canadian Life*. Toronto: Ukrainian Canadian Business and Professional Federation, 1967.

– *The Ukrainian Greek Orthodox Church of Canada, 1918–1951*. Ottawa: University of Ottawa Press, 1981.

– *The Ukrainians in Manitoba: A Social History*. Toronto: University of Toronto Press, 1953.

Zielyk, I.V. 'The DP Camp as a Social System,' in W.W. Isajiw, Y. Boshyk, and R. Senkus, eds. *The Refugee Experience*, 461–70.

Zink, H. *The United States in Germany, 1944–1955*. Princeton, N.J.: Van Nostrand, 1957.

Index

alleged war criminals: Civil Liberties Commission (UCC) on, 290 n7, 347 n42; Commission of Inquiry re Ukrainian Division 'Galicia' and, 424–5 n70; communist propaganda re Ukrainian nationalists as, 153, 424 n70; debate over, 288 n7, 334–5 n74, 347 n42, 423–5 n70, 426–7 n71; and justice in Canadian criminal court, 287–9 n7, 426–7 n71; 'grossly exaggerated' allegations about, 426 n71; minuscule numbers of, 335 n74; Panchuk on, 153; Soviet crimes against humanity, 290 n7; Ukrainian Canadian position on, 290 n7, 426–7 n71; Ukrainian Canadian Left and, 373 n89

American Zone of Germany: Kushnir's visit to, 87; UUARC's Munich office, 420 n50

Andrievsky, Dmytro: advice to DPs in Canada, 442–3 n177; employee of CURB, 175, 367 n41; at first CURB conference, 86; and Frolick, 92; and Kushnir 86; member of OUNm, 86, 431 n97; member of UNRada, 431 n97; at Pan-American Ukrainian

conference, 419 n45; with Panchuk and Wasylyshens at Foreign Office, 431 n96; re politics fragmenting diaspora, 86; and Sir Orme Sargent, 359 n8; and UCRF establishment, 431 n97; and Wasylyshen, 175–6, 187

Anglo-American powers and Ukrainian independence: 'Allied Scheme of History', 284 n3; British and Ukrainian separatism, 114, 258, 268–9; British and support for UCC and ABN, 258; British on disintegration of USSR, 251; Canadian government and Ukrainian independence, 259–60, 260–7, 271–2, 486 n67; cautious Western thinking on, 261, 468 n119; diplomatic recognition of Soviet Ukraine, 484–5 n59; independence and US military assistance, 249–50; nationalists as intelligence assets, 218–19, 242, 248–51, 254, 256; powers never wanted nor felt they needed a free Ukraine, 263; preserving émigré resources, 254; in prewar period, 112–13; St Laurent at fourth UCC

kanadiiskykh voiakiv, UCSA): Central Mediterranean Branch of, 340 n11; commemorative plaque, 341 n11; as conduit of information about DPs, 63; CURB an extension of, 70; executive re Panchuk's work with DPs, 66–7; financial support from UCC, 60, 342 n13; final, 11th 'Get Together,' 355 n66; first 'Get Together,' 59; formal conclusion of activities, 10 November 1945, 355 n66; investigated by RCMP, 344–5 n20; Kaye on history of, 340 n11; Kereliuk in, 339 n6; 'London Club,' 60, 65, 71, 72, 98, 110, 157, 267, 338 n87, 341 n12, 352–3 n46, 355 n69; Massey on opening of, 451 n18; members in Canada, 340 n11; members of first executive, 340 n11; move to 218 Sussex Gardens, London, 60; no history of, 341 n11; no official recognition, 341 n12; nucleus of CURB, 59; official closing of 'London Club,' 72; *Padre's Hour*, 60–1; Renaissance Plans of, 375 n106, 416 n21; second 'Get Together,' 340 n10; under surveillance, 62; Lady Tweedsmuir honorary patron, 338–9 n87; *UCSA News Letter*, 60, 62, 444, 355 n66; ULFTA members at 'London Club,' 355 n69; wartime camaraderie, 60, 71, 340–1 n11, 341 n12
Ukrainian Canadian Veterans' Association (Soiuz ukrainskykh kanadiiskykh veteraniv, UCVA): cooperation of Yaremovich and Panchuk within, 429 n87; decline of, 71–2; delegates in fourth UCC congress, 468 n119; differences from UCSA and Royal Canadian Legion, 71, 353–4 n58; formation of, 70; Panchuk's attempt to mould from abroad, 71; Panchuk's promotion of, 97; and Relief Team, 98–9; and Renaissance Plans, 98–9; and UCC, 71–2; USRL and UNF attitude towards, 71; Yaremovich on its role re DPs, 429 n87
Ukrainian Canadian Youth Association (SUMK), 309 n21
Ukrainian (Greek) Catholic Church, 4, 28–9, 321–2 n52, 464–5 n89
Ukrainian Catholic Mission Society of St Josaphat, 321–2 n52
Ukrainian Central Committee for the Defence of the Bilingual School System, 300 n28
Ukrainian Central Relief Committee in Germany, 76
Ukrainian Congress Committee of America (Ukrainskyi kongresovyi komitet Ameryky): establishment of Ukrainian American Relief Committee, 417 n27; joint communiqué on DP problem, 345–6 n24; on right to speak for Ukraine at UN, 317 n41; on right to undertake political activity, 93; support of CURB, 355 n63
Ukrainian Division 'Galicia': as best material among postwar DP population, 170; Canada's minister of justice McLellan on, 426 n71; civilianization of, 174, 424 n70, 425 n71; Commission of Inquiry on charges of war crimes against, 335 n74; as core of AUGB, 162, 169; Kaye on, 170–1; Korostovets on Panchuk's role in saving, 428 n79;